A PRACTITIONER'S GUIDE TO PROBATE AND THE ADMINISTRATION OF ESTATES

FOURTH EDITION

A PRACTITIONER'S GUIDE TO PROBATE AND THE ADMINISTRATION OF ESTATES

FOURTH EDITION

Keith Biggs and Samantha Edward

WS &H

Wildy, Simmonds & Hill Publishing

ISBN: 9780854902361

British Library Cataloguing in Publication Data

A catalogue record for this book is available from the British Library

Third edition 2012

This edition published in 2018 by

Wildy, Simmonds & Hill Publishing
Wildy & Sons Ltd
Lincoln's Inn Archway
Carey Street
London WC2A 2JD
www.wildy.com

Typeset by Heather Jones, North Petherton, Somerset.
Printed by CPI Group (UK) Ltd, Croydon CR0 4YY

Preface

As in previous editions, we follow our aim to provide practitioners with an account of the law and practice relating to non-contentious probate and the administration of estates. To achieve our purpose, we have adopted a practical approach drawn from our experience in practice and in the registry.

We continue to be grateful to friends, colleagues and practitioners for their kind comments and constructive criticism, which we have taken on board in pursuit of our stated purpose and in our approach to this fourth edition.

Since the third edition, the consultation on the proposed revision of the Non-Contentious Probate Rules 1987 culminated in the publication of the draft Probate Rules 2013. Since then, it appears that little has happened, and the 1987 Rules remain in force to regulate the practice of non-contentious applications. There was a change to the 1987 Rules effective from 1 November 2016 to set up a pilot scheme to enable online personal applications. The Rules were further amended with effect from 20 November 2017 to make a similar provision for a pilot scheme for the delivery of solicitor applications online. As at the time of going to press, no Practice Directions to regulate the procedure have been issued.

There have also been several decisions by the Chancery judges which affect the practice of the probate registries. The Inheritance and Trustees' Powers Act 2014, *inter alia*, made changes to the distribution of estates on intestacy. The effects of these changes, the Finance Acts since 2012, and the procedural changes occasioned by the amendments to the Inheritance Tax (Delivery of Accounts) (Excepted Estates) Regulations 2004, are dealt with in this edition.

The specimen forms in Appendix C have been revised to reflect changes in the law and practice.

Emma Gaudern's family and professional commitments made it impossible for her to write for this edition, but she has kept a watchful eye on the revision and has been a very competent consultant.

We are grateful for the help and encouragement in the preparation of this edition provided by Andrew Riddoch of Wildy, Simmonds & Hill.

For brevity, the masculine pronoun has been used throughout to include the feminine.

Keith Biggs, Hampshire
Samantha Edward, Durham

Contents

Appendices

Table of Cases

References are to page numbers

Table of Statutes

References are to page numbers

Table of Statutory Instruments

References are to page numbers

Table of Conventions

References are to page numbers

Table of EU Material

References are to page numbers

Table of Non-statutory Material

References are to page numbers

Chapter 1

Making a Start

A legal adviser often first hears of a death in a telephone call from a member of the deceased's family. If the legal adviser is to act in relation to the estate, a first meeting should be arranged. The legal adviser should check whether the firm holds a will for the deceased. If so, it should be retrieved from storage before the meeting, together with any other deeds or documents held on behalf of the deceased. Old files of papers may also prove useful, particularly if they relate to trusts in which the deceased was in some way concerned, lifetime gifts made by the deceased, or property sales and purchases showing the deceased down-sizing their home.

1.1 FIRST MEETING

The initial meeting between client and legal adviser varies greatly from estate to estate. Much depends on who are to be the personal representatives: if the spouse, civil partner or children of the deceased are to be the personal representatives, the first meeting may well be emotionally charged, but this is less likely if the personal representatives are to be professional people.

1.1.1 Capacity of the client

Where a solicitor is acting in the administration of an estate, his clients are the personal representatives in their capacity as such. The expression 'personal representatives' (defined by section 55(i)(xi) of the Administration of Estates Act 1925) covers both executors and administrators – the people who will take out the grant of probate or letters of administration. Often, individuals may have a number of different capacities. Consider the situation where the deceased left a wife, whom he named to act as executrix of his estate, and they had a child, who received the entirety of his estate under the will. The client is the wife in her capacity as executrix, but she is also a grieving widow, a potential claimant against the estate (because of any lack of provision made for her), and a mother concerned to act in the best interests of her child. It is the solicitor's task to help her separate out those roles and ensure that her actions as personal representative are properly carried out in that capacity.

The first meeting may not always be with the client. If professionals are instructed to deal with the estate administration, it may be productive to arrange initial discussions with the family members of the deceased, who are likely to have more information about the conduct of the deceased's affairs and about his assets.

1.1.2 Collation of information

There is often much information to be garnered at the first meeting. It is suggested that the most effective method of ensuring that all necessary topics have been covered is to use a checklist. A sample checklist is included at Appendix A. There is a broad range of topics that must be discussed, but these can be broken down into four main categories.

Family

All possible details of the deceased's family, including any spouse, partner or civil partner, together with ex-spouses or partners, children (legitimate, illegitimate, legitimated and adopted), brothers and sisters, nieces and nephews, and parents, should be obtained. A useful summary of the list of people to be discussed may be taken from section 1(1) of the Inheritance (Provision for Family and Dependants) Act 1975. This lists the categories of people who may make a claim against the estate of a deceased. It is useful to establish who falls into these categories, and whether any of them may have any cause to make a claim against the estate.

All the children mentioned above – legitimate, illegitimate, legitimated and adopted – are treated as children of the deceased or of any beneficiary of his estate, under sections 1 and 19 of the Family Law Reform Act 1987, unless they are specifically excluded by the deceased's will. It must be remembered that under section 67 of the Adoption and Children Act 2002, adopted children become the children of their adopters and cease to be the children of their natural parents from the date of the adoption order. If a child is adopted, consider the country of adoption and whether this adoption equates to a legal adoption in England.

Assets

All assets which the deceased held in his name should be identified. The capacity in which he held them must also be established – for example, he may have held property as a trustee or it may have belonged to the deceased beneficially. Were assets held jointly with anyone else, and if so did the owners hold the assets as joint tenants or tenants in common? This establishes whether they pass under the will/intestacy or by survivorship. Was the deceased a beneficiary of any trust, and if so what was his entitlement under it? Are any other assets or payments to which the deceased was not entitled during his lifetime likely to fall into the estate as a result of his death (e.g. death benefit under a work-related life assurance scheme)? Did the deceased make any gifts over the annual exemption in the last 7 years of his life?

Will or intestacy

Did the deceased leave a will, and if so is it valid on the face of it? Can the personal representatives be sure they have the last will (see para 1.3 as to the checks that should be made)? Did the will appoint executors, and are they all still alive and willing and able to act as such? If none is willing or able to act, or if there is no will, who are to act as administrators? It is important to consider who is most suitable for this role. For example, suppose the deceased is intestate, with all his assets passing to his minor child, but he is also survived by a former spouse who is the mother of the child but receives nothing. Although the former spouse would be the first choice to act as administratrix, this could prejudice her relationship with the child as she is the person with parental responsibility for the minor and entitled to apply under rule 32 of the Non-Contentious Probate Rules 1987 (SI 1987/2024), with a nominated co-administrator. In such circumstances it may be wise to seek an alternative administrator. Application may be made to the probate registry for the appointment of alternative administrators under rule 32(4).

Other matters

There are often various miscellaneous issues, some of which can be disposed of quickly and some of which may require more thought. For example, are there any foreign issues? Was the deceased domiciled in any other country, or did he own assets abroad? For a more detailed discussion of such issues, see paras 4.4.1 and 4.4.17.

If the deceased and his spouse or civil partner died together, for example, in a car crash, it is important to establish the order in which they died. Section 184 of the Law of Property Act 1925 states that if two people die in circumstances in which the order of death cannot be ascertained, the younger is deemed to have survived the elder for the purposes of administering the estate. This is known as the principle of *commorientes*. The rule is modified in relation to inheritance tax, as sections 4(2) and 54(4) of the Inheritance Tax Act 1984 state that for inheritance tax purposes the couple are treated as though they died at the same instant. Also, section 1(1) of the Law Reform (Succession) Act 1995 states that for a surviving spouse or civil partner to take an interest under the estate of his deceased spouse or civil partner who dies intestate, that spouse or civil partner must survive the deceased by 28 days. The deceased's wills may also have made provision for what is to happen in the event of simultaneous deaths.

It is recommended for clients to be advised that, although it is recognised that they wish to obtain the grant to the estate as soon as possible, they must allow sufficient time to speak to the relevant people and organisations to obtain all of the necessary information to avoid errors and omissions down the line. Such errors and omissions can prolong matters unnecessarily and, where HM Revenue and Customs is concerned, provide circumstances whereby penalties may be imposed.

1.2 URGENT STEPS

Often, members of the deceased's family deal with many of the immediate issues that arise upon a person's death without professional help. Where the deceased had no family, however, these matters may have to be overseen by the personal representatives. It should be made clear to the beneficiaries of the estate, before a professional person is instructed to take on the tasks in question, that this may be time-consuming and will increase the cost of dealing with the estate.

1.2.1 Registration of the death

The requirements for registering a death are contained in the Births and Deaths Registration Act 1953 and the Registration of Births and Deaths Regulations 1987 (SI 1987/2088) as amended. A relative often registers the death with the Registrar of Births, Deaths and Marriages. The persons responsible for registering a death are:

- those present at the death;
- the occupier of the house where the death occurred;
- any person living in the house who was aware of the death; or
- the person arranging disposal of the body (not the funeral director).

For these purposes, a 'house' includes a prison, hospital and a nursing home, where the 'occupier' is the governor or matron.

The death must be registered within 5 days of the death or of the finding of the body. This may be extended to 14 days if the registrar, within 5 days, receives a written notice that a doctor has signed a certificate regarding the cause of death.

The relevant registrar is the registrar for the sub-district in which the death occurred or the body was found.

The information and papers required to register the death are:

- a certificate of death signed by a doctor;
- the deceased's medical card (where possible);
- the deceased's date and place of birth (obtained from his birth certificate);
- the deceased's full name, occupation, address and marital status; and
- the name and occupation of any widow(er).

On registration of the death, the registrar issues a certificate for burial or cremation (which will be required by the funeral director), and a Department for Work and Pensions certificate that can be used to claim any arrears of benefits to which the deceased was entitled.

The 'Tell Us Once' service allows the person registering a death to report it to most government organisations in one go. The service will notify HM Revenue and Customs, the Department for Work and Pensions, the Post Office, the DVLA, the local council and public sector/armed forces pension schemes. The registrar will let you know if the service is operating in your area.

If the service is available, the registrar will provide a unique reference number to use with both the online service and the telephone alternative. To use this service, the following information will be required:

- the deceased's date of birth;
- the deceased's National Insurance number;
- the deceased's driving licence number;
- the deceased's passport number;
- details of the deceased's entitlement to benefits and state pension;
- details of the deceased's public sector or armed forces pension schemes;
- details of any local council services the deceased benefited from, for example, Blue Badge;
- the name and address of the deceased's next of kin and any surviving spouse or civil partner; and
- the name, address and contact details of the person dealing with the administration of the estate.

The death certificate is also produced. The registrar retains the original, and certified copies can be obtained upon payment of, currently, £4 per copy. Certified copies are available directly from the registrar for a period of one year, to anyone who applies, upon payment of the correct amount, which is currently

£9.25. After the expiry of that year, application must be made to the Superintendent Registrar at the General Register Office (see Appendix B for the address). In both cases, the information required to obtain a copy death certificate is the deceased's name, and the place and date of death (see, now, the Registration of Births, Deaths and Marriages (Fees) Order 2010 (SI 2010/441)). It is possible to apply online for a certificate at www.gov.uk/order-copy-birth-death-marriage-certificate.

If the deceased died abroad and the death was registered with the British Consul or the High Commissioner to the country in question, a certified copy of the death certificate can be obtained from the Overseas Registration Service of the General Register Office.

If an inquest is being held, the issue of a death certificate is delayed until the coroner reaches a verdict. To allow the body to be disposed of before the inquest, the coroner can issue an interim certificate allowing burial, as an alternative to the burial or cremation certificate usually issued by the registrar.

If the deceased was in the armed forces, the Ministry of Defence issues a certificate of notification of death or of presumption of death, instead of a death certificate. If he was a merchant seaman, the Registrar General of Shipping and Seamen produces a certificate or evidence of death.

If there is no death certificate, or if there is doubt about the sufficiency of the certificate, or if there is no direct evidence of the death, but there is sufficient circumstantial evidence to lead to a presumption of death, a decree of presumption of death and dissolution of marriage or civil partnership may have been granted under section 19 of the Matrimonial Causes Act 1973. This is not enough in itself to obtain a death certificate; nor is it sufficient proof of death to obtain a grant of representation. In these circumstances, the person wishing to take out a grant must apply to a district judge or registrar for an order for leave to swear the death. The application is made on an *ex parte* basis to the probate registry (see para 10.5).

1.2.2 Funeral

Usually, the funeral has taken place by the time instructions are received, but if not, it must be arranged. A firm which has been appointed executor and holds the will must check the will to see whether the testator expressed any wish as to the disposal of his or her body, bearing in mind that any such directions are not enforceable at law (see *Williams v Williams* (1882) 20 Ch D 659). In common law it is the duty of the person under whose roof the deceased died to make arrangements for the disposal of the body.

Generally, an executor has the right to make arrangements for the disposal of the body. Provided there is no dispute about the appointment of the executor, the executor's right to dispose of the body would override that of a close relative (see *In Re Grandison* (1989) 4 BMLR 140). The executor's decision is one with which the court would not lightly interfere.

The question of the right to dispose of a body was considered in the case of *Lewisham Hospital NHS Trust v Hamuth and Others* [2006] EWHC 1609 (Ch), [2006] All ER (D) 145 (Jan). In this case the will was disputed, so the executor's appointment and standing were unclear. In his will, the testator had expressed a wish to be cremated, but several members of his family wished to bury him in a family plot. The court held that as the executor's appointment was in question, the NHS Trust, as the lawful possessor of the body, should make the decision. The Trust indicated it was minded to allow the family to bury the body.

In *Burrows v HM Coroner for Preston & Joan McManus* [2008] EWHC 1387 (Admin), [2008] 2 FLR 1225, there was a dispute between the deceased's uncle and his mother over funeral arrangements which came before the court on a judicial review. The deceased had been raised by his uncle as his parents (both drug addicts) had been incapable. The deceased who had a history of self-harm committed suicide aged 15. He had expressed a wish to be cremated. The court held the uncle should make the arrangements. Although, following *Williams*, it would be the mother who would be the personal representative, the court had power to pass over the person first entitled if it was necessary or expedient under the discretionary powers contained in section 116 of the Senior Courts Act 1981. The case law says that where there is a dispute the deceased's wishes should be taken into account and this was a 'special circumstance' under section 116. The uncle should be the replacement personal representative as he had been closer to the deceased and he should make the arrangements. Following from this, the court said that Article 8(1) of the European Convention for the Protection of Human Rights and Fundamental Freedoms 1950 has a bearing in this type of dispute. In *Hartshorne v Gardner* [2008] EWHC B3, [2008] 2 FLR 1681, the deceased's divorced parents could not agree on the place of burial. The usual rule, that determination rested with the person entitled to the grant of representation, could not be applied as both parents were equally entitled. The court held that in the absence of any known wish of the deceased the decision should reflect, firstly, the wishes of the majority of those he left behind and, secondly, where he had most recently lived. Where his father wished him buried was also closest for the deceased's brother and near where the deceased's fiancée lived. The father's wishes were to be followed.

In *Ibuna and another v Arroyo and another* [2012] EWHC 428 (Ch), [2012] All ER (D) 36 (Mar), the court ruled it was settled law that there was no right of ownership in a dead body. However, there was a duty at common law to arrange for its proper disposal, which fell primarily on the personal representatives of the deceased. If there was no executor or administrator, the duty to bury a body fell residually on the local authority for the area where the body was found. On settled law, where there was no executor, the question of the appointment of an administrator arose which concerned the power of the court to pass over prior claims to a grant of administration.

The deceased was a congressman in the Philippines and was resident in both the Philippines and California but he was domiciled in the Philippines. This therefore was a 'foreign domicile case'. The deceased had made a will in California and also an advanced healthcare directive which included directions 'to make anatomical gifts, authorise an autopsy and direct disposition of my remains'. The healthcare directive authorised his partner to make the decisions, not his estranged wife. In those circumstances, there were special circumstances enabling the court to exercise its powers under section 116 of the Senior Courts Act 1981 and to appoint the partner a joint administrator with the person entitled under rule 30(1)(a) of the Non-Contentious Probate Rules 1987. That would mean that the executrix under his will and the person recognised by him in the healthcare directive would jointly have the responsibility of taking possession of the body and disposing of it in accordance with the deceased's wishes.

Similarly, before the funeral is arranged, the will must be checked to ascertain whether the deceased had expressed any wishes as to the use of any of his body parts for transplant or for medical science.

In order for the body or parts of the body to be donated to science, the deceased must have given signed written consent to the donation. Such donation is governed by the Human Tissue Act 2004, which came into force on 1 September 2006. These wishes must be acted upon in a timely manner, especially if parts can be used for transplant purposes, due to the body's rapid deterioration. Doctors can accept and act upon the deceased's wishes despite there being family objections to such a donation, although they have the discretion not to. If no choice has been made by the deceased and, after reasonable enquiries have been made, there is no evidence of the deceased expressing his objection to this in his lifetime, or his family objecting, then donation of the deceased's body can be authorised by the person who has lawful possession of the body.

The deceased may have purchased a pre-payment plan to cover the costs of the funeral. Reasonable funeral expenses are payable out of the deceased's estate. The will may expressly authorise the costs of an elaborate funeral. If not, the personal representatives or other organiser of such a funeral may become personally liable for the cost unless the residuary beneficiaries of the estate specifically approve it.

If the personal representatives are in any doubt, they should ask the beneficiaries for specific authorisation before any costs are incurred or paid.

If the deceased was receiving state benefits at the time of his death, and the assets in his estate are not sufficient to cover the cost of a funeral, the Department for Work and Pensions may make a grant for or towards the cost of the funeral.

1.2.3 Insurance

The deceased's property and chattels must continue to be properly insured. The insurance company should be notified of the death so that it can update its records. Insurance documents should be checked for the date of expiry, which must not be overlooked. Sufficient funds may not be available at the date of renewal to meet the premiums, for example, because the grant of representation has not been received and the family is unwilling or unable to pay. It is suggested that a solicitor acting on behalf of the personal representatives should meet the premium out of office account and claim a reimbursement later, rather than leave the premium unpaid and risk a claim for negligence. Since the commencement of the Trustee Act 2000, personal representatives have been authorised under section 19 of the Trustee Act 1925 (as amended) to insure assets in an estate to their full value and against any risk. While the personal representatives (or the solicitor acting as their agent) should not have to carry out actions which it is unreasonable for them to undertake, if it is plain on the face of the insurance policy that assets are not insured to their full value, then, to avoid criticism, the personal representatives should discuss with the beneficiaries whether the insurance cover for those assets should be increased.

Particular care is needed in relation to chattels. The insurance policy may specify that certain chattels must be removed from the deceased's home if it is to remain empty. The insurance company must be notified if the property is to remain unoccupied as this may affect the cover provided; the cover may continue but the insurers may require an additional premium. In any event, the home should be secured and the fact that it is unoccupied should be made as inconspicuous as possible, by, for example, cancelling newspaper and milk deliveries. Regular visits may have to be made to the home to check on the chattels remaining there; if no one else is willing or able to attend to these matters, the personal representatives must oversee them. The personal representatives should also be careful to secure all relevant documents or books of title.

If an item is specifically bequeathed to a beneficiary under the will, the beneficiary must pay for storing and insuring that item. The personal representatives should liaise with him as to the best method of dealing with that asset as quickly as possible.

1.2.4 Duty to prevent loss

The personal representatives have a duty to ensure that no loss is caused to the estate. Thus, they must give notice of the death to any other party to a contract which the deceased made and which continues to exist, and arrange to terminate it. Examples of such contracts are tenancy agreements and contracts for digital television services. Any items rented by the deceased should be returned to the owners as soon as possible to stop rent accruing; hire purchase providers should be notified and any outstanding liability calculated. Banks and credit card companies should be made aware of the death and standing orders or direct debits should be cancelled. If the deceased was acting as guarantor in relation to another party's debt, the creditor must be informed as soon as possible; if not, the estate may be held responsible for any default by the borrower under the credit agreement.

1.2.5 Firearms

If the deceased was the owner of any firearms the police should be informed. They will decide how any firearm should be disposed of and set a time limit within which that must be done. Depending on the weapon, the time may be as short as 24 hours, so the personal representatives must be prepared to act swiftly. It may be appropriate for the personal representatives to contact the Firearms Licensing Department. A temporary permit can be issued under section 7 of the Firearms Act 1968, authorising the personal representatives to be in lawful possession of the gun. Such a permit is free of charge, but for a limited term. A 3-month period is a reasonable term to apply for. However, the police may ask for the gun's removal, as above, where there is a demonstrable risk to security,

1.2.6 Urgent grants

The personal representatives must consider whether there is any matter which can be dealt with only after the issue of a grant of representation, but which must be urgently attended to. For example, is the limitation period about to expire on any claim that could be brought by the estate, or did the deceased contract to buy or sell real property but die before completion of the transaction? The authority of an executor stems from the will, and therefore an executor is entitled to deal with the deceased's affairs from the date of death onwards. The grant of probate merely serves to confirm this authority. In some situations an executor may therefore be able to proceed and deal with some issues before a grant is issued. If the exchange of contracts for the sale of a property is urgently required the executor is able to sign the contract, but it is unlikely that the purchaser's solicitor will be willing to complete before a grant is issued. On first reading this appears to be an advantage, but executors must be wary of entering into a situation whereby they will be contractually bound to convey a property in respect of which they have no proof of title. It may be sensible to apply for a temporary grant of representation to deal with a particular matter. The personal representatives of the deceased have a duty to protect and preserve the deceased's estate during the administration period. Indeed, anyone who can demonstrate to the court there is a need for a grant to deal urgently with some part of the estate may apply for a temporary limited grant. This is covered in more detail at para 10.12. Alternatively, contracts for sale or purchase can be exchanged, but completion could be made conditional upon the issue of a grant. Such a contract usually provides a 'longstop' date after which the contract becomes void unless the parties agree otherwise.

If there is no will, or if the executor named does not have the power to take a grant of probate, or if he becomes unable to do so before taking the grant, the assets in the estate vest in the Public Trustee, under section 9 of the Administration of Estates Act 1925, until a grant issues. Afterwards, the authority is retrospective to the date of death, so that an administrator can confirm actions undertaken earlier.

1.2.7 Advertisements

The safeguarding of the personal representatives, and the advertisements they should place to protect themselves from personal liability to creditors, are discussed at para 24.6. Since 2 months must elapse between the advertisement and the distribution of the estate, the advertisements should be placed as soon as possible to allow the personal representatives to distribute the estate quickly.

1.3 TRACING THE LAST WILL

A key point to establish at the outset is whether the deceased left a will; and, if so, whether the will in the personal representatives' possession is the last one he made. If the solicitor acting in the administration also acted for the deceased in a personal capacity in the period ending with his death, this may be easily done. If not, the deceased's professional advisers and his bankers should be approached to find out what they know. A solicitor or other professional adviser has no right of lien over a will or codicil in respect of unpaid charges.

The deceased may have deposited his will with the Principal Registry of the Family Division, so a search should be made. The search may be made through any district probate registry on payment of a fee, currently £10. Advertisements for a will can also be placed in the *Law Society Gazette*.

If it is believed that a person has information regarding the existence of a will or codicil, which that person is refusing to impart, an order can be obtained under rule 50 of the Non-Contentious Probate Rules 1987 (by application under section 122 or section 123 of the Senior Courts Act 1981) for the person to be examined in court or subpoenaed to bring the will or codicil to court (see para 10.4).

Even if the personal representatives are reasonably sure that they have the final will, they must still consider the possibility that the testator may have executed a codicil or codicils, and ensure they are in possession of all such documents as have not been revoked.

1.4 NON-URGENT MATTERS

Often, the personal representatives are under pressure from the beneficiaries of the estate to distribute assets as soon as possible. While a personal representative has a duty to act swiftly and efficiently, he should also be mindful of his duties to creditors, and the obligation to distribute the estate properly. Bearing this in mind, a personal representative should not allow himself to be persuaded to make distributions prematurely, or which may leave him with insufficient assets to discharge debts, even if further assets may fall into the estate later. For example, the deceased leaves a sum of money, a portfolio of shares and a house; the beneficiaries may request that the cash is distributed to them immediately, and that the debts of the estate are discharged once the shares and the house are sold. The values of the house and the shares cannot, however, be certain, and it is suggested that nothing should be distributed until the quantum of debts has been finalised and the 2-month period for responses from creditors, mentioned above, has elapsed. In addition, some or all of the shares, and the house, should be sold to cover the debts in full, and the sale proceeds received, before the cash is distributed. While a distribution could be made if urgent, with the beneficiary giving an indemnity to repay the distribution if it later becomes evident that the estate requires it, the personal representative risks becoming personally liable if the beneficiary no longer has the funds with which to repay the distribution.

1.5 AVOIDING DELAY

One of the most frequent criticisms levelled at personal representatives when administering an estate is that they are too slow in dealing with matters. To some extent, delay is unavoidable – it is rare that beneficiaries appreciate the delays which can arise in liaising with HM Revenue and Customs, or that a distribution should not be made within 6 months of obtaining the grant if allowance is to be made for possible claims against the estate under the Inheritance (Provision for Family and Dependants) Act 1975. These are, however, all matters that can be explained to the beneficiaries and it is wise for personal representatives to do so, then the beneficiaries will have a realistic expectation of when distributions are likely to be made.

Another major cause of delay is that many personal representatives tend to be reactive rather than proactive. Some tips on how to avoid delay are set out below.

1.5.1 Valuations

When seeking to establish the value of the estate, the personal representatives write to various institutions about assets held by them on behalf of the deceased. Many of these institutions are large and it is inevitable that paperwork is sometimes mislaid. It is suggested that the personal representatives should review the letters they have written every 2 weeks. Any organisation which has not responded should be reminded, by another letter or a telephone call. Waiting for a response to a letter that did not reach the correct destination in the first place can waste much time.

1.5.2 Repaying an inheritance tax loan

Delay in repaying a commercial loan taken out to pay inheritance tax can be expensive. Such loans always carry interest, and the more time that elapses before the loan is repaid, the more interest becomes due. If such a loan is taken out, it is advisable for the personal representatives to prepare all the necessary forms to encash sufficient assets to repay the loan and interest in full, while the probate application is being processed. The forms should be signed by the personal representatives during that time, so that they can be sent off immediately upon receipt of the grant. In particular, if shares are to be encashed it is wise to check at the outset that all the share certificates are in the possession of the personal representatives. If any have been lost, an indemnity must be signed, and may need to be guaranteed by a bank; this should be prepared in advance where possible.

These days, however, the cases in which a loan is required are relatively few. For a discussion of the options available to personal representatives to meet a bill for inheritance tax, see para 4.4.22.

1.6 CHECKING THE ASSETS

In many first meetings reams of paper are produced – receipts, old building society passbooks, correspondence regarding life assurance policies – the list is endless. While the ideal situation would be that these papers all relate to easily identifiable, current assets, in reality this is unlikely to be the case. The personal representatives must read through all the details supplied and investigate anything that may indicate an asset exists. Particularly difficult can be old life assurance documents. Life assurance companies have merged and been taken over so many times that it may be difficult to trace whether old policies are still in force, or to identify the company with which they are now held. The Association of British Insurers (see Appendix B for the address) is usually very helpful and a call to its telephone helpline generally elicits the current identity of a company which appears no longer to exist, as well as contact details for that company.

1.7 SOME PITFALLS

It is all too easy, when presented with a grieving spouse and children, to make assumptions about the family situation and to feel uneasy about asking awkward questions; but, if the will of a deceased leaves a gift to 'my children', that includes illegitimate and adopted children, but not step-children (sections 1 and 19(1) of the Family Law Reform Act 1987) unless the will states to the contrary. It is important to establish the exact identity and relationship to the deceased of each beneficiary.

In relation to items specifically bequeathed, a will speaks from the date upon which it was written. If an asset is specifically gifted in a will, the solicitor must ensure that it is the same asset as that comprised in the deceased's estate upon his death. For example, if the deceased gifted 'my car' to his son, that gift is effective only if the car owned by the deceased at the time the will was made was still his car when he died. If the gift was of 'such car as I shall own at the date of my death', it takes effect as the car owned by the deceased when he died. The will should always be read carefully for traps such as these and unclear matters must be resolved. For more detail on these issues, see Chapter 18.

1.8 COMMUNICATING WITH BENEFICIARIES

The beneficiaries should be kept fully informed of the progress of the administration. It is far easier to send out a letter giving a summary of the up-to-date position than to receive an irate telephone call from a beneficiary who feels he is being kept in the dark.

In addition, the beneficiaries have to make decisions about the administration of the estate. If there is inheritance tax to be paid, the beneficiaries may wish to lend funds to the estate to pay it, rather than take out a commercial loan and incur interest charges. They should also be consulted as to whether assets should be sold or appropriated to the beneficiaries *in specie*.

By raising these issues early, and giving the beneficiaries time to consider them, the personal representatives are able to progress the administration of the estate as swiftly as possible.

1.9 ASSETS FOR WHICH A GRANT IS NOT REQUIRED

Some assets can be obtained before a grant is issued, either because they do not form part of the deceased's estate for the purposes of the grant and as such are not dealt with by the grant, or because it is possible to realise them without the production of a grant, notwithstanding that they do form part of his estate. These assets are described below.

1.9.1 Life assurance policies written into trust

Life assurance policies written into trust do not form part of the deceased's estate for the purposes of the grant and can be encashed by the surviving trustees. If the deceased was the sole surviving trustee, his personal representatives have power to appoint new trustees, but the life assurance company may allow them to encash the policy themselves without appointing new trustees.

1.9.2 Death benefit payable under a pension scheme

Trustees of company pension schemes often reserve to themselves the right to decide how the death benefit payable under the scheme should pass. If this is the case, the trustees generally pay it to the persons they select without sight of a grant.

If the pension scheme is personal, or a retirement annuity contract, the death benefit usually passes automatically to the deceased's estate if it was not written into trust. In that case, a grant must be obtained before the benefit can be paid. But if the death benefit was written into trust, it is transferred to the trustees once they have produced evidence of the death. Many personal pension providers now draw up policies which reserve to themselves the right to decide to whom the death benefit will be paid; if so, the death benefit should be paid without sight of a grant, and again does not form part of the estate for inheritance tax purposes.

1.9.3 Joint assets

If the deceased owned an asset in joint names with another person, the legal title to that asset always passes to the other person automatically, although if the asset is land, the co-owner needs to appoint at least one new trustee to act with him on any disposal of the land. How the beneficial ownership passes depends on how the asset was held. There are two methods of holding the beneficial interest in an asset jointly – as joint tenants, or as tenants in common. If an asset was held as joint tenants, the beneficial interest automatically passes by survivorship to the co-owner upon the deceased's death. Joint tenants do not own identifiable 'shares' in an asset and therefore cannot own that asset in any manner other than equally between them. Tenants in common can own an asset in varying proportions. The portion owned by the deceased passes under his will or intestacy, not to his surviving co-owner. For how to transfer the beneficial ownership in a jointly held asset, see para 15.11.

However, under section 5(2) of the Inheritance Tax Act 1984, where the deceased had the ability to control the use or determine the destination of some or all of the asset, it is to be treated as an estate asset for inheritance tax purposes. This is because the control that can be exercised over the asset equates to a general power of appointment. See the case of *Sillars v IRC* [2004] STC (SCD) 180, where it was determined that the whole value of a joint bank account held by the deceased and the two daughters was to be treated as an estate asset in accordance with section 5(2). It was also held that a further reason for including the full value of the bank account within the estate was that it was determined that the ownership of this account by the deceased was a gift with a reservation of benefit under section 102(1) of the Finance Act 1986.

1.9.4 Nominated assets

Some National Savings products and building society accounts can be dealt with by a nomination rather than under the deceased's will or intestacy. To do this, the deceased must have completed a form of nomination indicating how the asset should pass after his death. The deceased's personal papers need careful checking for such a nomination.

1.9.5 Assets held in bare trust

If a third party held assets as nominee for the deceased, the nominee is known as a bare trustee. The assets subject to the bare trust form part of the deceased's estate and are dealt with under the will or intestacy. As legal title to the asset was not vested in the deceased, a grant does not need to be produced for the asset to be realised.

1.9.6 Assets of low value

Under the Administration of Estates (Small Payments) Act 1965, any asset worth less than £5,000 *may*, at the discretion of the asset holder, be paid out without a grant. The Act, however, does not apply to banks, building societies and life assurance companies. Consequently, such organisations can exercise their own discretion. Many high street banks will, for instance, release assets that do not exceed £15,000. However, it is worth noting that each organisation will have its own criteria, but will certainly want sight of the original will or a certified copy of this and the death certificate, and will mostly likely ask the intended personal representative to swear a statutory declaration and/or sign an indemnity. It is to be noted that the Act allows the asset holder to pay out the fund; the provision is permissive, not mandatory.

Funds valued at less than £5,000 belonging to a deceased who died testate or intestate and which are held in court can now be paid out to anyone who appears to be entitled to them, under rule 24(4)–(6) of the Court Funds Rules 2011 (SI 2011/1734).

The outstanding salary of a public servant employed by a government department, a member of Her Majesty's Forces, a merchant seaman and a Member of Parliament can be paid without sight of a grant.

On the other hand, banks, and sometimes other institutions, may require the personal representatives to complete an undertaking, and possibly also to sign an indemnity, that the funds are properly payable. There is usually a charge for preparing the form of indemnity. In this case, it may be cheaper and quicker for a grant to be extracted, particularly if this would be necessary in any event.

1.9.7 Chattels

Documentation confirming the ownership of chattels rarely exists, and title to them can therefore pass by delivery. If the chattels are of low value and the personal representatives are satisfied that they will not need recourse to the proceeds of their sale to pay tax or debts, they can often be passed to the beneficiaries named in the will or entitled under the intestacy, or distributed in accordance with the wishes of the family, immediately. A practical approach is often the most sensible here – provided there appears to be no conflict, it is often wisest to allow assets not specifically bequeathed to be distributed by the deceased's family. The chattels should, though, always be valued for the purposes of the probate papers. In addition, it should be agreed with the residuary beneficiaries whether the chattels received by them are to be taken into account when calculating the share of the estate each beneficiary has taken *in specie*.

The definition of personal chattels under section 55(1)(x) of the Administration of Estates Act 1925 has been amended by section 3 of the Inheritance and Trustees' Powers Act 2014 for all wills and trusts created on or after 1 October

2014 if the statutory definition is referred to, unless there is contrary intention in the will or trust. The new definition extends to all tangible movable property other than property that consists of money or securities for money, property used at the death of an intestate solely or mainly for business purposes or owned by the intestate at death solely as an investment.

The definition raises two main practical considerations. The first is that a decision must now be made as to whether property is solely or mainly for business purposes, and the second is whether a high value personal chattel, for example, a work of art, should be included within a gift of personal chattels or whether it will pass into the residuary estate. It will be necessary to decide whether or not the deceased owned the work of art solely as an investment.

1.9.8 Partnership assets

If the deceased was a partner in a business, the partnership agreement usually specifies what happens on the death of a partner. Often, this is that the assets pass to the surviving partners, and a formula is provided for calculating the compensation to be paid to the deceased's estate. Section 33 of the Partnership Act 1890 states that if no agreement is in existence, the partnership is deemed to dissolve on the date of the partner's death, and the assets are to be divided among all the partners (including the deceased) in accordance with the ratio in which they shared the partnership profits.

1.9.9 *Donatio mortis causa*

Prior to his death, the deceased may have made a gift under the doctrine of *donatio mortis causa*. This provides that where a gift is made by the deceased in contemplation of death, which was conditional upon his death, and title to the property gifted was capable of being passed via a *donatio mortis causa*, the gift was properly made and accordingly passes to the recipient of the gift outside of the deceased's will.

1.10 FOREIGN ASSETS

Not all of the assets owned by a deceased but held in a foreign country necessarily pass under his UK will. Initially, the UK will should be checked to see whether it is capable of dealing with any foreign assets, or if it is limited to the testator's UK estate. If it does not cover the country in which the foreign assets are situated, enquiries should be made as to whether a will exists to deal with the assets in that country. In any event, the personal representatives should check whether a later will was made in the foreign country to deal specifically with the assets there. If there is no will disposing of those assets, the rules of intestacy may apply to them, and it is usually advisable to instruct a foreign agent to deal with them. Which rules of intestacy – those of the United Kingdom or those of the foreign country – apply depends on whether the property is movable or immovable; though a will may not specifically deal with foreign assets, it may be the law of the country concerned to accept the will as a proper document to pass title.

The meaning of the 'situation' of property – the *lex situs* – is important. Immovable property (such as land) is treated as situated in the country in which it is physically present. Movable property is treated as situated in the country in which it is registered. For the purposes of inheritance law, movable property generally passes in accordance with the law of the country of domicile (or, more likely in respect of EU countries except the Republic of Ireland, the law applicable in the country of habitual residence) of the deceased, whereas immovable property must pass in accordance with the law of the country in which it is situated. If a person dies domiciled in England, but with a house in France, the French will consider that the succession is governed by the law of habitual residence. However, English law would apply *lex situs* to the French property and send it back to France – called the *Renvoi* – so that the succession of the French property will be governed by French law. Therefore, even if the deceased's will purports to deal with his house in France, the French rules of heirship or reserved portions would override the will to the extent that they differ from it. This is significant in relation to European countries, in particular as many of them have rules of forced heirship that provide, *inter alia*, for the deceased's children to take a fixed share of his estate upon his death.

The European Union adopted the Succession Regulation (EU) No 650/2012 (known as Brussels IV) on 4 July 2012, which came into force on 17 August 2015. The UK government exercised its right not to opt in to Brussels IV; yet, despite this, and despite the United Kingdom's forthcoming exit from the European Union, the effect of Brussels IV may be extremely significant for people who own foreign property. Article 20 confirms that the law that applies, whether by choice or default, can be the law of a country which is not a member state. Article 21 sets out the general rule that the law applicable to succession is that of habitual residence at the time of death, unless the deceased was 'manifestly more closely connected with another state'. However, Article 22 allows any person to choose the law of his own nationality as the governing law to his succession, regardless as to where the asset is situated. The choice can be both explicit and implicit.

Making a choice of the law of nationality provides certainty. Without such a choice being made, doubt as to the deceased's habitual residence, or whether the deceased were manifestly more closely connected to another state, could hamper the estate administration. If the client who lived in England with French property made an election of the law of nationality in his will, then English law would govern the succession of the French property and France would accept this choice so that its forced heirship rules would not apply. If no such choice is made, France would accept the *Renvoi* and French law would still apply to the French property.

'Succession' for these purposes does not include property passing by survivorship, by *En Tontine* (a French mechanism similar to survivorship), by usufruct or under matrimonial regimes where the jurisdiction of the country in which the parties married may govern the passing of property. Succession also, and often most importantly, does not impact on the tax or administrative matters of a country. These matters are still governed by the applicable country's existing rules. Bearing this in mind, it is therefore still advisable for clients who own foreign property to make a separate will in the jurisdiction of their property so that they may obtain the relevant advice in respect of the tax and administrative consequences of electing the law of their nationality as the governing law for the devolution of their estate. For example, clients who have a vulnerable beneficiary and wish to include a discretionary trust of their residuary estate in their will may be subject to a 60 per cent tax charge in France for doing so. An additional benefit of a separate foreign will is the time it could save, as the estate can be administered in parallel rather than in series. Where an election has been made, it would be prudent to recite in the second will the election made in the earlier will, with confirmation that the election still applies.

Chapter 2

Assets and Liabilities: Initial Enquiries

2.1 INTRODUCTION

The first substantial task of the personal representatives is to ascertain and value the assets and liabilities of the estate. To do this, the personal representatives must provide the holder of each asset with an original certified copy death certificate. Certificates can be ordered online using the General Register Office online ordering service. A certificate may also be ordered by telephone, by post or from the local register office where the death was registered. Extra copies of the same certificate can be issued at the same time for all applications. There is currently a fee of £9.25 for standard service and £23.40 for priority service. Any death certificates (from 1837 onwards) can be ordered online using the General Register Office index reference. If you do not have the reference, a certificate can still be ordered as long as there is enough information to identify the birth, marriage or death.

The Law Society has produced a protocol containing a standard letter and form for use in lieu of a certified copy death certificate; copies of the protocol can be obtained from the Law Society. All asset holders, however, have the right to insist that an original certified copy of the death certificate is forwarded to them. In practice, very few institutions enforce this right, although life assurance companies generally do.

In view of the above, it is generally simpler to make the initial contact with the asset holders in writing, rather than by telephone, requesting a valuation of the asset as at the date of death, and enclosing the certified copy death certificate. An asset holder needs to be able to identify the deceased on its records and find the relevant information; details of the deceased's name, address (including the postcode) and account/reference number(s) are usually sufficient.

While the value of the asset as at the date of death is the main information required, certain other questions, raised at the outset, speed up matters later in the administration. Examples of queries which can usefully be raised in respect of each type of asset are given below.

Where it is clear that the value of the deceased's estate is below the inheritance tax nil rate band (£325,000 in respect of deaths on after 6 April 2009), or that it falls within the surviving spouse/civil partner or charity exemption from inheritance tax (see paras 3.10 and 3.17), it may be tempting for the personal representatives to 'guesstimate' the value of an asset, or to use an old valuation. For a number of reasons this should not be done:

(a) if it later becomes clear that the estate of the deceased is greater than originally thought and a full inheritance tax account must be filed, the personal representatives will have to go back and obtain proper values of assets. This will delay the administration and cost more than if the matter were dealt with properly in the first place;
(b) the personal representatives have a duty to produce proper and accurate estate accounts. This duty is not complied with if the original information is not correct;
(c) the base cost for capital gains tax purposes of the assets in the hands of the personal representatives, or any beneficiary to whom an asset is assented, is the value at the date of the deceased's death. That value must be accurate, to save time later when proving the base cost to HM Revenue and Customs after a sale of the asset in question.

2.2 TRACING ALL THE ASSETS

The personal representatives can never be sure that they have traced all the deceased's assets, but they must do everything they possibly can to do so. Generally, this means going through all the papers held by the deceased which may prove the existence of an asset. Every possibility, no matter how remote, must be followed through. The deceased's family and professional advisers (particularly accountants) should be helpful in this regard. It may also be useful, especially where the deceased lived alone, for a mail redirection to be placed on the address. Where the executors know little of the deceased's estate it may be advisable to search both the Unclaimed Assets Register (see para 2.19), and the 'mylostaccount' website, at www.mylostaccount.org.uk/.

2.3 BASIS OF VALUATION

As shown below, most assets of the deceased, such as bank accounts and shares in public limited companies, have a clearly ascertainable value. Some assets, such as land and chattels, however, can be valued only on the basis of a professional opinion that cannot be objectively verified unless the assets are sold. Where that is the case, the asset must be appraised at its 'open market value' (section 160 of the Inheritance Tax Act 1984). This cannot be reduced on the grounds that '… the property is to be placed on the market at one and the same time', but must instead be calculated on the assumption that a sale will be made between a willing buyer and a willing seller. It used to be the case that a 'probate value' could be obtained and submitted as the value at the date of death. 'Probate value' used to be understood to be the open market value less a discount of around 10 per cent or more. HM Revenue and Customs has become much stricter, insisting that an open market value is used. Any documents submitted to HM Revenue and Customs showing that a 'probate valuation' has been prepared will be queried, and if the value submitted is shown to be lower than the open market value, a penalty may be payable (see para 3.20). 'Probate value' in this book means full market value.

2.4 BANKS

Questions to be addressed to the bank(s) at which the deceased held an account include:

- How much was in the account at the date of death?
- How much interest had accrued on the account but was unpaid at the date of death? (This is an asset of the estate for inheritance tax purposes.)
- Does the bank hold any testamentary documents, deeds, documents or safety deposit boxes for the deceased? If so, who may have access to them, and how?
- What standing orders and direct debits are in place? (This information will help identify other potential assets and liabilities of the estate.)
- Did the deceased hold any other accounts, either in his sole name or with another person?
- How much interest was paid on the deceased's account(s) for the period from 6 April to the date of death, and how much income tax was deducted? (This information is required to complete the deceased's income tax return for the period from 6 April last to the date of death. In addition, if the deceased died shortly after 6 April, leaving his tax return for the previous year not completed and filed, the like details in respect of the previous tax year should be requested.) However, from 6 April 2016, banks and building societies will pay only gross interest. Whilst this is the case, a credit interest summary for the relevant periods should be requested.
- Is the bank willing to release funds held by it to pay inheritance tax and funeral expenses? (Banks are much more accommodating in this since the new system for paying inheritance tax (see para 4.4.22) was introduced.)

- What are the requirements to close the account and what are the necessary closure forms for completion?
- What formalities will be required for the personal representatives to open an account of their own for use during the administration of the estate?

The bank should be asked to transfer any credit balances to any accounts having a debit balance to stop interest accruing on them, and then to transfer any outstanding credit balances to an interest-bearing account if they are in an account that does not bear interest. This ensures that the personal representatives do all they can to maximise the value of the estate.

2.5 BUILDING SOCIETIES

The following questions may usefully be addressed to the appropriate building society/ies:

- How much was in the account at the date of death?
- How much interest had accrued on the account but was unpaid at the date of death?
- Did the deceased hold any other accounts, either in his sole name or with another person?
- Is the building society willing to release funds held by it to pay inheritance tax and funeral expenses? (For security purposes, the cheque is only ever drawn in favour of HM Revenue and Customs, or the funds are transferred pursuant to the new regime.)
- What are the requirements to close the account and what are the necessary closure forms?

The passbook, if there is one, should be sent to the building society with a request that it be brought up to date. An updated passbook usually shows the interest paid to the deceased from 6 April to the date of death, and the income tax deducted from it; if not, this information should be requested.

Any forms which the personal representatives must complete to close the account should be requested.

Building society 'windfalls' paid to account holders on the demutualisation of a society form part of the deceased's estate for inheritance tax if the building society formally announced its plans to demutualise, by issuing a transfer document or prospectus, before the date of death. It may, though, be possible to discount the value of the windfall if there is uncertainty over whether it will be paid (as, for instance, where the members may not approve the demutualisation), or if a substantial delay before payment is expected. If the death occurs before the demutualisation has been approved, the discount available will be in the region of 25 per cent to 35 per cent of the value of the windfall. If the approval has already been given, a discount of 10 per cent to 17.5 per cent may be allowed (*Inland Revenue Tax Bulletin*, April 1998, p. 520).

2.6 LIFE ASSURANCE COMPANIES

The following questions may be addressed to life assurance companies which issued relevant policies:

- What is the value of any policy where a lump sum is due to the estate as a result of the death? (Often, the value of a life assurance policy is based on the value of the units in the relevant fund that have been purchased with the premiums paid by the deceased, subject to a minimum amount assured. This is generally accepted by HM Revenue and Customs as the value of the policy as at the date of death. However, see the note below on the difference between the settlement or surrender value and the maturity value or open market value at the date of death.)
- How much will be paid out under the policy as at the date of death?
- What is the value of any policy that does not pay out as a result of the death, but from which the deceased has or may have the right to benefit when another person dies, such as a joint life and survivor policy or a second-hand policy?
- What is the value of any policy taken out on another person's life, but held on trust for the benefit of the deceased or for his benefit and the benefit of another person or other persons?
- What is the value of any policy in the name of the deceased that is nominated and what are the details of the person to whom it is nominated?
- Has the policy been written into trust and, if so, what is the value of the policy at the date it was written into trust? Copies of any relevant documents, such as the trust deed, and details of the trustees should be requested.
- Is there a gain arising on the policy that is chargeable to income tax? If so, a chargeable event certificate (see below) should be requested.

The forms required to claim the policy proceeds, together with any necessary indemnity if the original policy document cannot be located, should be requested.

Any lump sum payable under the policy is an asset in the estate since the deceased was entitled to it immediately before death. However, the value for inheritance tax purposes is the maturity value of the policy, which is often different to the value immediately before death, often known as the settlement or surrender value.

The maturity value is usually greater than the settlement/surrender value as a consequence of the deceased's death. Section 171 of the Inheritance Tax Act 1984 provides that where a death causes an asset to either increase or decrease in value, that change must be taken into account when valuing assets for inheritance tax purposes. It is therefore the maturity value or the open market value at the date of death that should be reported to HM Revenue and Customs.

Life assurance companies require a certified copy of the death certificate in order to set the maturity value of the policy and, consequently, it is important to ensure that the life assurance company is provided with a certified copy of the death certificate rather than a solicitor's death certificate verification form.

The death of a life assured is a chargeable event in relation to most 'non-qualifying' life assurance policies and to some 'qualifying' life assurance policies (Part 10 of the Corporation Tax Act 2009), but there are a number of factors that affect whether or not tax is payable. However, the death of the life assured is not a chargeable event for mortgage protection policies and certain other policies specified in that Act. The gain deemed to arise on the chargeable event is assessed to income tax on the person originally owning the policy (even if he has since assigned it to a trust) or on his personal representatives. The life assurance company should be asked to clarify whether the gain arising on the policy is chargeable to income tax, and if so a chargeable event certificate should be requested, showing the gain made. This can then be used when completing the estate's or the deceased's income tax return, as the case may be.

2.7 NATIONAL SAVINGS

There are many different types of National Savings investments, but one correspondence address, this is given in Appendix B. Very generally, each investment should be valued at the date of death, and the forms to encash the investments should be requested. A valuation of all the deceased's National Savings investments can be requested on form NS&I904 or it can be done online (www.nsandi.com) or free of charge by phone on 08085 007 007. Many National Savings investments can be transferred to the beneficiaries *in specie*, and the relevant forms should be requested if this is a possibility. In addition, National Savings may be willing to issue a cheque to HM Revenue and Customs, from the assets held by it, to pay any inheritance tax due (see, also, para 4.4.22). This should be investigated at the earliest opportunity.

Interest on National Savings certificates is free of income tax, but is still subject to inheritance tax within the deceased's estate. Details of interest which had accrued, but was unpaid, at the date of death must be requested in respect of all investments, for declaration regarding inheritance tax. In addition, confirmation of all income paid on the investment for the period from 6 April to the date of death should be sought, for declaration, if necessary, on the income tax return to the date of death.

Premium bonds may remain in the prize draw for up to a year from the date of death and the personal representatives should, in consultation with the beneficiaries of the estate, decide whether they wish this to happen, since it may delay the administration of the estate. It is a strange fact that the premium bonds of many a deceased holder appear to win more in the year after death than during the owner's lifetime. In any event, consent to leave the funds in the draw is not irrevocable – the personal representatives can ask for the bonds to be encashed at any time. If the holder's card cannot be located, National Savings will require a copy of the deceased's signature to verify that the holder was the same person as the deceased. A copy of the signature page of the will or codicil is generally sufficient.

2.8 PENSIONS AND ANNUITIES

The following information should be sought from relevant pension providers:

- Will any lump sum be payable as a result of the deceased's death? If the pension scheme is personal or a retirement annuity contract, was this lump sum written into trust, must it be paid to the estate, or is it payable at the discretion of the pension company? If so, such confirmation that it was paid at their discretion will be required as evidence for HM Revenue and Customs. If it was a company scheme, the death benefit will probably be paid at the discretion of the scheme trustees. In the case of a scheme which allows discretion as to who will be paid the lump sum, however, guidance as to the deceased's family situation and the beneficiaries of his will or intestacy may be needed.
- Is any pension to be paid to the deceased's spouse, civil partner, children or other dependants? If so, the forms to be completed to claim it should be requested.
- What pension was paid to the deceased from 6 April to the date of death and what income tax was deducted?
- Were there any changes to the deceased's pension rights or benefits?
- Were there any contributions made to the pension in the 2 years immediately before death?

2.9 STATE PENSION AND BENEFITS

The personal representatives should contact the Pensions Service, part of the Department for Work and Pensions (for the appropriate address, see www.dwp.gov.uk), for details of any state retirement pension the deceased was receiving, and whether any was unpaid at the date of death. If a pension book can be found, any unused counterfoils should be sent with the initial enquiry letter.

The Department for Work and Pensions should be approached in connection with attendance allowance and all other benefits. The deceased's National Insurance number will need to be given. Again, any benefits that were due to the deceased but unpaid at the date of death can be claimed by the personal representatives, but if the deceased was entitled to any benefits that he was not claiming, it is unlikely that the personal representatives will be able to submit a posthumous claim.

If any of the benefits the deceased was claiming were means-tested, the Department for Work and Pensions may check with the probate registry the value of the estate given in the application for the grant of representation. If not fully satisfied, the Department may investigate further, and request more information, including a summary of the estate, from the personal representatives. If this investigation shows that the deceased was over-claiming, or wrongly claiming, the estate will have to repay that which was over-claimed.

The Department for Work and Pensions is another institution which often has a large backlog of correspondence and it is generally wise for the personal representatives to keep in close contact to ensure that matters are being dealt with and that correspondence has not become mislaid.

The personal representatives also need to know what and how much pension and benefits were received by the deceased from 6 April to the date of death, as these may need to be declared on the deceased's final income tax return.

2.10 CHATTELS

Where the estate of the deceased is not subject to inheritance tax and the deceased did not own any chattels which are out of the ordinary or which appear to have any significant value, the personal representatives' estimate of the value of the chattels should be sufficient. If they are in any doubt about the value of the estate or the chattels, the personal representatives should obtain a professional valuation. This can also be useful where the entire estate falls within the surviving spouse/civil partner exemption (see para 3.10) but the deceased appeared to own chattels of significant value, as it will confirm the base cost at which the spouse/civil partner takes those chattels (that is, the value of the chattels at the deceased's death) for capital gains tax purposes should the spouse/civil partner later sell those assets and realise a gain.

If the deceased held a linked group of chattels, for example, a set of china, the group must be valued as a set rather than as individual pieces.

It is suggested that, when asking for a valuation, the personal representatives should request that any items worth more than £100 are shown individually, and a global value is inserted for all other chattels. The insurance value of an item is not the same as its open market value. An insurance value relates to how much it would cost to replace the asset, whereas the open market value is how much it would sell for. Often, the insurance value is greater than the open market value.

The amended definition of 'personal chattels' in section 3 of the Inheritance and Trustees' Powers Act 2014 detailed at para 1.9.7 should be borne in mind.

2.11 REAL PROPERTY

Any land and buildings held by the deceased must always be valued by a professional person. For assets of material value, it should be ensured that the professional instructed is a qualified independent valuer, and that the valuation meets the standards of the Royal Institution of Chartered Surveyors or an equivalent standard. Any instruction should ask for the open market value of the property at the date of the death of the deceased, for inheritance tax purposes.

HM Revenue and Customs advises in its online Inheritance Tax toolkit (www.gov.uk/government/publications/hmrc-inheritance-tax-toolkit) that any letter of instruction should explain the context of the valuation requested, and draws the valuer's attention to the definition in section 160 of the Inheritance Tax Act 1984 of 'market value':

> the value at any time of any property shall for the purposes of this Act be the price which the property might reasonably be expected to fetch if sold in the open market at that time; but that price shall not be assumed to be reduced on the ground that the whole property is to be placed on the market at one and the same time.

It may also be relevant to ask for a valuation of any development potential which the property may have. This is because development potential can increase the value of the property for inheritance tax purposes. Of course, a higher inheritance tax value will reduce any future capital gains tax liability which may arise when the property is later sold, as this value will become the base value of the asset when calculating any gain on a future sale.

The valuation instruction may also include confirmation of any discount to be given, where the property is owned jointly by the deceased and others. This is because the value of jointly owned property can sometimes be discounted to reflect the difficulty in selling a share in the property while others own a share in it (see *Wight and Moss v IRC* (1984) 24 RVR 163; (1982) 264 EG 935 (Lands Tribunal)). However, it should be noted that the discount may not be available if the related property rules apply. This will be the case where the deceased owned the property jointly with his spouse or civil partner, and where the only other joint owners are trustees of a trust in which the deceased (or his spouse or civil partner) had an interest in possession before 22 March 2006 and a qualifying interest in possession after that date.

Further, the letter of instruction should provide all relevant detail in relation to the property, including details of any tenancies or rights of occupancy. Copies of any written agreements should be provided or full details of any verbal agreement that exists and details of any rights and usage. Farm valuations should include a plan and photographs of the farmhouse, buildings and land.

2.12 SHARES, SECURITIES AND UNIT TRUSTS

Shares and securities tradable on the open market should be valued on the 'quarter up' basis. This is calculated by consulting a newspaper (the *Financial Times* is generally the most helpful) published on the day after the deceased died, for the prices at which the shares were selling on the day of death. If the deceased died on a day when the shares were not traded, the figures from the previous or the next day's trading can be used, whichever are the most favourable. The newspaper will show the highest and lowest prices at which the shares were traded. The lowest price should be deducted from the highest price. One-quarter of the difference should then be added to the lowest price, to find the 'quarter up' price.

If any share is marked 'XD' in the newspaper, it was 'ex-dividend' at the date of death. The register of shareholders of a company cannot be updated every day to include new owners of shares – it is always a few weeks out of date. As a result, the person registered as the owner of shares on the date a dividend is paid may have sold those shares and so is not entitled to that dividend. To counteract any unfairness, 4–6 weeks before a dividend is paid, a share is declared to be 'ex-dividend'. This means that a purchaser of the shares will not be entitled to receive the next dividend; it will instead pass to the seller of the shares. As a result, the price of the shares in the open market is reduced. Therefore, if a shareholding is declared to be 'ex-dividend' at the date of death, the value of the dividend should be included in the deceased's estate for inheritance tax purposes.

For example, Fred held 100 shares in Boots plc at the date of his death. The paper shows that the shares were marked 'XD' at the date of death, and that the dividend declared was 1p per share. The lowest trading price of the shares on the date of death was £1 per share, and the highest was £1.40. The value of the shares at the date of death is calculated as follows:

- £1.40 – £1 = 40p;
- one quarter of 40p = 10p;
- £1 + 10p = £1.10 per share x 100 shares = £110;
- the dividend on the shares is 1p per share x 100 shares = £1;
- the total value of the shares is £110 + £1 = £111.

Shareholders may be entitled to new shares, or to buy new shares, either now or in the future. If any of these rights had accrued to the deceased's shares at the date of death, the value of the new shares or the right to buy them must be included as part of the capital value of his estate.

Interest-bearing securities accrue interest at a daily rate. If sold, the sale may be with the benefit of the interest, or the seller of the securities may retain the interest. Securities marked 'IK' or 'IM' transfer to a purchaser with the benefit of the interest accrued during the seller's ownership – those marked 'IKX' or 'IMX' do not. The value of the interest should therefore be deducted from, or added to, the market value of the securities at the date of death, as appropriate.

In addition, the company in which the shares were held may have been going through a capitalisation or merger at the date of death. If the shares were marked as 'XC', 'XR' or 'XE', the deceased would also have been entitled to new shares or cash in lieu, and the value of those shares or that cash must be shown as part of the estate.

Unit trusts, investment trusts and interests in open ended investment companies are not valued on the quarter-up basis, but on the lowest of the prices shown per unit. The manager of the relevant fund must be approached about outstanding dividends and distributions, as these are not published in the press. In any event, the fund manager's valuation may well be the most accurate, and often no charge is made for this.

If there are a number of shareholdings, or the personal representatives are not confident about preparing an accurate valuation, any stockbroker will prepare a valuation on payment of a fee. Alternatively, the London Stock Exchange Historic Price Service (see Appendix B) provides valuations upon receipt of the details of the shares and securities held by the deceased, together with confirmation of the date of death. A charge is made for this service.

Unquoted shares and securities are more difficult to value. A good starting place is the accountants to the company in question, as they are generally in the best position to provide a realistic valuation. The memorandum and articles of association of the company should be considered carefully. They may restrict how the shares may pass after the death of a shareholder. While this cannot be used to depress artificially the value of the shares, it is permissible for the open market valuation to reflect that these conditions would be imposed on any purchaser of the shares and would thus affect his ability to sell them onwards. This may affect the number of purchasers, or the price they would be willing to pay.

2.13 PARTNERSHIP INTERESTS

The factors to be taken into account when valuing a partnership interest are similar to those which apply when valuing unquoted shares. Often the accountants or auditors are the best people to approach first. Any partnership agreement should be consulted as it may contain provisions applying on the death of a partner.

2.14 ASSETS AT LLOYD'S

A detailed discussion of the manner in which Lloyd's underwriting is conducted and the method of valuing Lloyd's assets is beyond the scope of this book. Personal representatives may, however, need some understanding of what it means to be a 'Lloyd's name' and the consequences for the estate. Very briefly, Lloyd's carries on the business of underwriting insurance, like any other insurance company. But the method of distributing the profits and funding the losses is unique. Lloyd's has various 'names', who effectively participate in the underwriting business. Each name has links with an agency company, and with one agent within that company. The agent liaises with the name regarding how much the name is willing to underwrite, and the type of underwriting business the name wishes to be involved in. The agent and the name decide which underwriting 'syndicates' the name is to participate in, and the extent of his participation, as a percentage share. Each syndicate covers one type of underwriting business in one year. Effectively, the name is agreeing to meet that percentage of losses of that syndicate for that year (should it make a loss), and establishing the percentage of profits he will receive if it makes a profit.

Once the extent of the name's total involvement at Lloyd's has been decided, the agent calculates the value of assets the name must deposit with Lloyd's to secure the position should the syndicates he participates in incur a loss and thus require him to make a payment to fund that loss. The name must then deposit assets (shares, land, cash or bank guarantees are good examples of suitable assets) with Lloyd's to secure his liability. Lloyd's can easily liquidate these assets to fund a loss should that be necessary.

The results of each Lloyd's syndicate are not quantified until 3 years after that syndicate has closed down (each syndicate runs for one calendar year). This means that there is always a delay between the year in which a profit or loss arises and when it is paid. If a name dies during a year, his last year of participation is deemed to have ended on 31 December prior to his death.

The assets of a Lloyd's name include the assets held by him at Lloyd's to secure his underwriting liability, and the profits and losses which arise from years that are 'open'; a valuation on death includes both elements. Generally, assets held at Lloyd's to secure the name's liability qualify for business property relief from inheritance tax, although this depends to some extent on whether the name retained at Lloyd's assets in excess of the underwriting requirement, in which case the relief may be limited.

The best method of valuing assets in connection with Lloyd's is to contact the agent for the name. The agent is often an invaluable source of information, and may deal directly with HM Revenue and Customs regarding any queries raised by HMRC.

Obviously, if the syndicates in which the deceased participated are not finalised at his death, the quantum of his likely profits or losses can only be estimated. If losses arise, they must be met by the estate, but this may greatly hinder the distribution. This may be offset somewhat if the name took out an estate protection plan. This is basically an insurance policy under which the insurer agrees to pay the losses of a Lloyd's name accruing after his death. Like many other insurance policies, there is usually an excess, which may run to several thousand pounds. This generally means that, providing the personal representatives allow sufficient assets to remain at Lloyd's to cover the payment of that excess, they can proceed to liquidate and distribute the deceased's remaining Lloyd's assets without fear that they will be called upon to meet future losses. For further commentary on this, see para 24.8. The insurer under the estate protection plan, however, has a lien over any future profits payable to the estate of the deceased, to the extent that it has funded his losses.

2.15 JOINT ASSETS

Assets held jointly with a third party must be valued as a whole, and the value of the deceased's share then calculated. If the asset can be easily separated into the shares held by the deceased and his co-owner (e.g. a bank account in the names of the deceased and his partner), the value of the deceased's share is the proportion of the asset owned by him. But where the assets cannot be readily split down (as in the case of land), a discount is permitted, for inheritance tax purposes, on the value of the share owned by the deceased. Generally, this discount is 10 per cent to 15 per cent of the value of the asset at the date of the deceased's death, based on the asset itself and the proportion owned by the deceased. With this in mind, it may be wise for the personal representatives to claim a 15 per cent discount; HM Revenue and Customs may seek to negotiate downwards, but the personal representatives are in a stronger position than if they are trying to negotiate the discount upwards.

The joint owner should be approached to discover whether the asset was held as joint tenants or tenants in common. For the differences between these two types of ownership, see para 1.9.3. It is usual for most assets, other than land and buildings, to be held as joint tenants, although this should never be assumed. In addition, where land was held as tenants in common and was rented out, any bank account holding the rental income is taken to be held in a tenancy in common, particularly if the co-owners held unequal proportions of the land.

Even if assets were originally held by persons as joint tenants, it is possible for the joint tenancy to be severed to create a tenancy in common. If land is held in a tenancy in common, this should be noted on the register at HM Land Registry, but the bundle of documents containing the title deeds should be checked in case severance has already taken place but has not been noted on the register. If the land is unregistered, the severance may be noted on the title document itself, or, again, may be a separate document held with it.

A severance does not have to be set out explicitly in writing, which can create difficulties for personal representatives who think severance may have taken place but cannot find definitive evidence. In *Re Woolnough, Perkins v Borden* [2002] WTLR 595, three siblings owned property as joint tenants. When the first sister died, her share in the property passed to her brother and sister as the surviving joint tenants. After that, the brother and sister both made wills at the same time, dealing with their half shares in the property. It was held that as they both acted in the belief that they could separately dispose of their own shares in the property, they had signified their intention to sever the joint tenancy and create a tenancy in common.

HM Revenue and Customs highlights a common misunderstanding of the meaning of 'joint property' in its online Inheritance Tax toolkit (www.gov.uk/government/publications/hmrc-inheritance-tax-toolkit), where it asserts that it is often interpreted as just houses and land, whereas its meaning is significantly wider and includes syndicates sharing race horses, jewellery and bank and building society accounts.

2.16 ASSETS SUBJECT TO AN OPTION TO PURCHASE

One or more of the deceased's assets may be subject to an option to purchase, an option having been granted before death, or arising under the deceased's will. If so, the assets must be valued on the open market and an appropriate deduction made in relation to the option. The deduction must relate to the position of the option at the date of death, and is not affected by events after death. For example, in *Re Bliss (deceased)* [2001] 1 WLR 1973 (ChD), the deceased left A an option to purchase her home subject to the right of her husband to live there for the rest of his life. Shortly after she died, the husband had to move into a nursing home and the home was sold pursuant to the option. It was held that the husband's timely move into the nursing home could not be taken into account when valuing the option, as this was an event subsequent to the deceased's death.

2.17 EMPLOYERS

The following questions may usefully be put to the deceased's employer:

- Was the deceased owed any outstanding salary or other payments at the date of death?
- Was the deceased a member of a group life assurance or pension scheme?

The employer should be asked to provide the personal representatives with a certificate showing the income and benefits received by the deceased for the period from 6 April last to the date of death. This will be required when completing the final income tax return for the deceased.

2.18 LIFE INTEREST TRUSTS

If the deceased was a beneficiary of a life interest trust, either as a life tenant or a remainderman entitled after the death of the life tenant, his interest must be valued. This applies to trusts created before 22 March 2006, and to trusts created after that date where the trust assets still form part of the life tenant's estate for inheritance tax purposes (that is, immediate post-death interests, disabled person's interests and transitional serial interests). The trustees of that trust should be contacted and asked for:

- their reference at HM Revenue and Customs;
- a copy of the will or other instrument which created the trust;
- details of the deceased's interest in the trust;

- the value of the trust at the date of death, together with the value of the deceased's interest in it;
- the value of any income or other sums due to the deceased from the trust at the date of death.

The trustees cannot be bound to supply the personal representatives with a copy of the trust document, as this is not strictly relevant to their needs, but they must supply all the information the personal representatives require to complete the inheritance tax forms.

Generally, a reversionary interest to which a remainderman is to become entitled in the future is 'excluded property' under section 48 of the Inheritance Tax Act 1984, unless it was purchased for value. The trustees of the life interest trust should notify HM Revenue and Customs if it is the life tenant who has died. This is done using form IHT100.

2.19 UNCLAIMED ASSETS REGISTER

If the executors are at all unsure whether they have traced all the deceased's assets, they would be well advised to check the Unclaimed Assets Register. It is a register that contains details of any investments, such as building society accounts or shareholdings, in respect of which the investment company believes that the owner of the asset may be untraceable. For details of how to contact Experian, the company controlling the register, see Appendix B. A search of the register costs £25.

2.20 CREDITORS

Evidence of debts offered by standing orders and direct debits paid from the deceased's bank account should all be followed up and the details ascertained. Any papers held by the deceased which indicated that he was a debtor should likewise be investigated.

The personal representatives should also place the advertisements and make the searches referred to in section 27 of the Trustee Act 1925 (see para 24.6) if they wish to be able to claim the exemption from personal liability offered by that section. This is also a matter of good practice, particularly if the personal representatives are unfamiliar with the deceased's personal affairs.

Most household bills are received monthly or quarterly and so these debts are notified (simply by being received in the post or by email) within 3 months of the deceased's death. In any event, it would be unusual to find a household that did not have most of the following utilities: gas, electricity, water and telephone; the personal representative should expect these bills and make appropriate enquiries if they are not received. Many people now receive bills online so a check of the deceased's personal computer may need to be done.

Any person who was a creditor of the deceased should be contacted and asked to confirm how much the deceased owed at the date of death, together with the rate at which interest is accruing on the debt. In relation to mortgages on properties of which the deceased was the landlord, a statement of the interest paid during the period from 6 April to the date of death should be requested, as this interest is deductible for the purposes of income tax.

It is vital that the personal representatives do not make any promise to pay any debt. If the estate is discovered to be insolvent and such a promise has been made, the personal representatives may become personally liable to pay the debt.

2.21 LIFETIME TRANSFERS

Any lifetime chargeable transfer (LCT) into a trust, gift, or the gift element of a transaction at an undervalue (the latter two being known as potentially exempt transfers or PETs) made within 7 years before the deceased's death may be brought back into the deceased's estate for inheritance tax purposes. In addition, LCTs made within 7 years of a PET are aggregated with that gift to determine the inheritance tax payable on it. A gift made under the doctrine of *donatio mortis causa* (see para 1.9.9) qualifies as a gift made prior to death for these purposes.

The deceased's family, the beneficiaries under his will and his professional advisers should be approached to discover whether any such gifts or transfers were made. Family members and associates of the deceased should be asked whether they have received anything from the deceased, including gifts for birthdays, Christmas or other relevant festivals, and also upon marriage. It should be highlighted that a gift includes the deceased paying for anything on their behalf, for example, holidays. The personal representatives should also point out that monies which were initially loaned, but subsequently waived will be classed as a gift for inheritance tax purposes. The value of the assets gifted should be ascertained, both at the date of the gift and at the date of death. If the value at death is less than the value at the time the gift was made, the personal representatives can elect to substitute the former for the latter for inheritance tax purposes. When considering the valuation of gifts, HM Revenue and Customs advises that personal representatives should use the *loss to the estate* principle.

HM Revenue and Customs strongly recommends that personal representatives should check all of the deceased's bank and building society account statements for the 7 years prior to the date of death to identify what transactions have taken place which may be regarded as gifting. HMRC advises that an initial check of the last 3 years should be undertaken in every estate, as this should provide a good indication of the deceased's gifting history. If this investigation identifies unusual withdrawals or transfers due to the amount or regularity, the personal representatives should consider a review of the statements for the full 7 years.

HM Revenue and Customs has given guidance as to how it will deal with undisclosed gifts and the penalties that may be incurred as a result. See para 3.20 for a more detailed analysis of this.

2.22 INCOME TAX AND CAPITAL GAINS TAX

If the deceased employed an accountant, the accountant should be approached for a copy of the last tax return filed or completed. This will provide much useful information as to the type and level of the deceased's assets at the date of death. If the deceased did not employ an accountant, HM Revenue and Customs should be asked for a copy of the last return filed. Either the accountant or HM Revenue and Customs should be able to confirm whether any further income tax or capital gains tax, or payments on account, are or will become due, and should know whether there is any dispute about the amount. HM Revenue and Customs normally postpones payments of outstanding amounts until 30 days after the issue of the grant of representation, after which time interest accrues.

As mentioned above, an income tax return or claim for repayment of tax must be completed for the deceased in respect of the period from 6 April to the date of death. In addition, if the death occurred before the return for the previous tax year had been filed, that return must also be completed. If the deceased did not employ an accountant, the personal representatives may decide to complete this return themselves. It is beyond the scope of this book to explain how an individual's tax return should be completed, but if the personal representatives are unsure how to proceed they should take professional advice. In any event, the personal representatives are responsible for ensuring that all the information contained in the return is correct.

2.23 MISCELLANEOUS MATTERS

2.23.1 Professional advisers

As outlined above, highly useful information regarding the deceased's estate can be obtained from the deceased's solicitor, accountant, stockbroker and any other professional agents employed by him during his lifetime.

2.23.2 Private health insurance

Inquiries should be made to ascertain whether the deceased held, or was entitled through his employment to, private health insurance; and, if so, whether any payments or reimbursements are due to the estate, or whether any other claim ought to be made.

2.23.3 Passport

The deceased's passport should be returned to the Passport Office for cancellation or destruction.

2.23.4 Court of Protection

If the deceased was a patient whose affairs were under the control of the Court of Protection, or if he was the donor of an enduring power of attorney or, after 1 October 2007, a lasting power of attorney which has been registered, the Office of the Public Guardian should be notified of the death.

2.24 CHECKLIST

At the commencement of the administration of an estate in particular, it can be very difficult to remember what assets are thought to be in the estate, who has been approached to provide a valuation and whether a response has been received. A good way to keep track of the assets in the estate is to prepare a table with seven headings as follows:

- description of asset/liability;
- date on which valuation requested;

- value obtained;
- date grant registered;
- date of sale or transfer to beneficiary;
- proceeds of sale or value at date transferred to beneficiary;
- date creditor paid.

This provides a quick guide to the progress of the estate administration and can be useful in keeping on top of matters that need to be chased up.

Chapter 3

Inheritance Tax Reliefs and Allowances

3.1 BASIS FOR THE CHARGE

Completing the inheritance tax forms for submission to HM Revenue and Customs is explained in Chapter 4, but it is important to understand how the inheritance tax regime operates.

Upon a person's death, he is deemed to make a 'transfer of value' of all the assets in his estate immediately before his death (section 4 of the Inheritance Tax Act 1984). A person's 'estate' is defined in section 5 as:

> … the aggregate of all the property to which he is beneficially entitled, except that … the estate of a person immediately before his death does not include … excluded property.

For the purposes of this section, property over which the deceased had a general power of appointment (i.e. he was able to control its destination by his will or codicil or other document executed by him during his lifetime) is treated as belonging to him beneficially.

Inheritance tax is charged at a rate of 40 per cent on the chargeable value of the estate. The chargeable value is calculated by deducting any allowable liabilities owed at the date of death, any available reliefs, any exemptions, and any available nil rate band, transferable nil rate band, residence nil rate band (RNRB) and transferable residence nil rate band (TRNRB) from the gross value of the assets at the date of the deceased's death.

3.2 EXCLUDED PROPERTY

'Excluded property' is referred to in various sections of the Inheritance Tax Act 1984. Section 6 defines 'excluded property' in a person's free estate (free estate being assets in the deceased's legal name and belonging to him beneficially) as:

- property situated outside the United Kingdom if the person to whom it beneficially belonged was not domiciled in the United Kingdom;
- UK government securities authorised as exempt, and owned by a person who was not resident or ordinarily resident in the United Kingdom when he died, and his death was after 6 April 1998;
- war savings certificates, National Savings certificates, premium bonds, deposits with the National Savings Bank and certain Save As You Earn (SAYE) schemes if they belonged to a person domiciled in the Channel Islands or the Isle of Man.

Foreign currency accounts held at some high street or foreign banks may qualify as excluded property if the deceased was non-domiciled and non-resident. Further, equities and bonds where the legal *situs* is offshore from the United Kingdom and, again, the deceased was non-domiciled and non-resident, may be excluded property. The legal *situs* is the country in which control can be exercised over an asset – an enquiry should be raised with HM Revenue and Customs if this may be the case.

Excluded property in relation to a trust is defined in section 48 of the Inheritance Tax Act 1984 as:

- a reversionary interest not acquired for money or money's worth; not belonging to the settlor or his spouse; and not arising under a lease upon which a full market rent is not payable;
- property in a trust held outside the United Kingdom where the settlor of the trust was not domiciled in the United Kingdom at the time he created the trust.

While property falling within the above definitions is not subject to inheritance tax at all, some assets may be partially or wholly relieved from the charge to inheritance tax. These reliefs and exemptions can operate in relation to property in the deceased's taxable estate (including any property forming part of his estate by virtue of his being entitled to it under a trust) or to gifts and transfers made by him prior to death but which are brought back into his taxable estate upon his death. There are several types of relief, explained below.

3.3 BUSINESS PROPERTY RELIEF

Business property relief is governed by sections 103–114 of the Inheritance Tax Act 1984. Section 104 provides for the relief. It applies to shares in companies, interests in businesses, and assets used by them both. Section 103(3) states that a business '... includes a business carried on in the exercise of a profession or vocation, but does not include a business carried on otherwise than for gain'. To be 'carried on for gain' does not mean that the business must be profitable, but it should be a '... serious undertaking earnestly pursued' (see *Rael Brook Limited v Minister of Housing and Local Government* [1967] 2 QB 65). The business must be more than a simple hobby or leisure pastime.

Before the relief is applied, the business interests or shares are valued. If the assets are shares in a company or an interest in a partnership, a discount may be applied to the value of the business because of the lack of realisability of the asset. Generally, if the deceased owned 75 per cent or more of the shares or business, the discount is limited. If he owned 50 per cent to 75 per cent of the business or shares, the discount is greater, the maximum applying if the deceased owned less than 50 per cent. The discount depends on the type of business or company, and how easy it would be to sell.

A separate decision is then taken as to how much of the business assets or shares qualify as 'relevant business property' (see para 3.3.2). The relief is applied to the relevant business property, to reduce its value. Inheritance tax is charged on the reduced value.

3.3.1 How much qualifies?

There is no limit to the amount of property that can qualify for business property relief, but the value of a business is its net value (including goodwill), after deducting any liabilities of the business, even if they are secured on non-business assets (section 110 of the Inheritance Tax Act 1984). While the value of an asset qualifying for business property relief should never be artificially inflated, there is nothing to be gained (and possibly much to be lost) by understating the value of assets qualifying for the relief. If the assets are relieved from tax in the deceased's estate, it makes no difference whether they are shown as worth £1 or £1 million, as long as the value is correct and can be substantiated. But there may be a substantial effect on future liability to capital gains tax. As the beneficiary taking the assets will have, as his capital gains tax base cost, the probate value of the assets in the deceased's estate, the beneficiary naturally wishes the probate value to be as high as possible.

In addition, even if an asset does not qualify for business property relief, if it can be shown that it is a business asset, the inheritance tax on it may be paid by instalments (see para 3.21.1). Thus it may be advisable for the personal representatives to seek to include as many assets as possible as business assets, even if they do not qualify for business property relief.

3.3.2 Relevant business property

To qualify, a business asset must be 'relevant business property', as defined in section 105 of the Inheritance Tax Act 1984. This is:

(a) a business or interest in a business – this includes a capital account held by a partner in a business. Once the partner retires from that business, however, he is treated as any other creditor and the account does not qualify as relevant business property (see *Beckman v IRC* [2000] STC (SCD) 59);

(b) unquoted securities in a company which, on their own or together with other unquoted shares and securities owned by the deceased, gave the deceased control of the company;

(c) any unquoted shares in a company (this includes companies listed on the Alternative Investment Market (AIM) as unquoted);

(d) quoted shares or securities in a company which, on their own or with other shares and securities owned by the deceased, gave him control of the company;

(e) any land or building, machinery or plant which was used wholly or mainly for the purposes of a business in which the deceased was a partner or a company that he controlled. If, though, this property was leased to the business or company by the deceased at a commercial rent, it may qualify as an investment property and as such fail to qualify for business property relief (see para 3.3.6);

(f) any land, building, machinery or plant which was used wholly or mainly for the purposes of a business carried on by the deceased and which was subject to a trust in which the deceased had an interest in possession.

The case of *Hardcastle v IRC* [2000] STC (SCD) 532 related to the estate of a Lloyd's name. It is of general application, however, in that it confirmed that ordinary commercial contracts, if they are not 'assets used in a business', even if they were incurred by the business or by a person acting on behalf of a business, are not to be taken into account in valuing the business for the purposes of business property relief. In the circumstances of the case, this decision was beneficial to the estate because it meant that losses arising on open accounts (that is, accounts under which the final profit/loss figures had not been announced before the deceased's death) that had not been declared by Lloyd's before the date of the deceased's death were not deductible when valuing the business assets for the purposes of business property relief. This meant that they could instead be deducted from the deceased's estate that would otherwise have been subject to inheritance tax. The decision would, however, have led to a greater inheritance tax bill in relation to the estate if the accounts in question had generated a profit.

The case of *IRC v Mallender* [2001] STC (SCD) 514 (ChD) also related to a Lloyd's name. The deceased's bank had guaranteed his Lloyd's liabilities in return for his giving the bank an indemnity. The indemnity was secured by a mortgage granted to the bank over commercial land owned by the deceased. Upon the deceased's death, the personal representatives submitted that the value of the land itself should be taken into account as an asset used for the purposes of a business because it was used as security. The Capital Taxes Office (forerunner of HM Revenue and Customs) argued that the land was not used in the business, but was only facilitating a guarantee. It agreed that the guarantee should be classed as a business asset. On appeal from the decision of the Special Commissioners, it was held that the Capital Taxes Office was correct. The land itself was not used for the purposes of the business – it merely supported other assets that were.

3.3.3 Period of ownership

An asset must have been held during the period of 2 years prior to the deceased's death if it is to qualify as relevant business property (section 106 of the Inheritance Tax Act 1984), although assets which have been held for less than 2 years may still qualify if they have replaced other relevant business property (section 107). If the deceased inherited the assets from a third party, he is treated as having owned them from the date of that party's death. If the third party was his spouse or civil partner, he is treated as having owned them throughout his spouse's or partner's period of ownership (section 108). These rules apply only to assets to which the deceased became entitled on someone else's death; if he purchased the assets from that person's estate, his ownership begins on the date of purchase.

3.3.4 Meaning of 'control'

As mentioned above, certain shares or securities qualify for business property relief only if they gave the deceased control of the company. 'Control' is defined in section 269(1) of the Inheritance Tax Act 1984 as:

> the control of powers of voting on all questions affecting the company as a whole which if exercised would yield a majority of the votes capable of being exercised on them.

The definition means that control can be beneficially held only by a person who holds more than 50 per cent of the shares in the company. In *Walkers Executors v IRC* [2001] STC (SCD) 86, however, the Special Commissioners held that owning 50 per cent of the voting shares, together with having a casting vote as chairman of the board of directors, meant that the shareholder had voting control of the company.

3.3.5 Rate of relief

The rate of relief depends on the date of death. For deaths after 6 April 1996, categories (a), (b) and (c) listed in para 3.3.2 qualify for relief at 100 per cent. Assets in categories (d), (e) and (f) qualify at 50 per cent. For deaths prior to that date, different rates applied in respect of unquoted shares in a company, depending on whether they gave a controlling holding, a substantial holding (more than 25 per cent of the voting rights), or less.

3.3.6 Assets which do not qualify

Assets used by a business or shares in a company do not qualify as relevant business property if the main or whole activity of the business or company is dealing in stocks, shares, land or buildings, or making or holding investments, unless the business or company is a market maker or discount house carrying on business in the United Kingdom, or is a holding company of a company whose business does not fall within one of those categories.

This means that even if the deceased owned unquoted shares in a trading company, the relief may be limited if the company held cash in excess of that which would be needed by the company either at the time the deceased died or in the foreseeable future.

Problems can arise where it is arguable whether an activity qualifies as a trade or an investment. A good example is the business of providing furnished holiday rentals. Properties that are rented out are investments, while the ownership and running of a hotel qualifies as a trade. Holiday lettings fall between these two categories. The HM Revenue and Customs *Inheritance Tax Manual* indicates, at IHTM 25278, that, in general, furnished holiday rentals will not qualify for business property relief as the income derived mostly consists of rent in return for the occupation of the holiday let. The guidance suggests there may be cases where the level of provided services is so extensive that the activity may be considered as non-investment, and that each case should be treated on its own facts. It is recommended, therefore, that such cases should be referred to the technical team for further consideration. However, the Upper Tribunal case of *Lockyer v Revenue and Customs Comrs* [2013] UKUT 050 (TCC) was an appeal by HMRC that the business of holiday lets undertaken by the late Mrs Pawson was, indeed, mainly one of holding an investment. In this case, the following activities were deemed investment: actively marketing and finding occupants for the holiday let, making the necessary arrangements with the occupants, collecting payment of the rent, spending on repairs, redecoration and improvement of the property, maintenance of the garden and grounds to keep them in a tidy condition, and keeping the property insured. It was confirmed that even services such as cleaning or providing a caretaker, the provision of heating and hot water, providing a TV and telephone, the provision of a welcome pack, and being on call to deal with queries and emergencies, were not sufficient to prevent the business from being mainly one of holding an investment. This approach was followed by *Green v Revenue and Customs Comrs* [2015] UKFTT 236 (TC) in the First-tier Tribunal. The *Pawson* case was also applied in *The Trustees of David Zetland Settlement v Revenue and Customs Comrs* [2013] UKFTT 284 (TC), where an actively managed commercial property was also deemed mainly an investment. Further, the case of *Re Ross* [2017] UKFTT 507 (TC) illustrates the difficulty of successfully arguing a holiday let business is not predominately an investment business.

The phrase 'wholly or mainly' in the definition of relevant business property means that where a business or company has both a trading and an investment operation, they may still qualify for business property relief. HM Revenue and Customs generally accepts that the 'wholly or mainly' criterion is satisfied if the trading operation is more than 50 per cent of the business. There are, however, many different methods of judging how much of the business is accounted for by trading activities. This has led to much case law, particularly in the field of the ownership of caravan parks, the nature of which typically includes both investment activities (the rental of caravans) and trading activities (the sale of goods to tenants, providing entertainment facilities). It was held in *Farmer and Another v IRC* [1999] STC (SCD) 321, that a global picture of the business should be examined and that regard should be had to five factors before a decision could be made. The five factors were: the overall context of the business, the net profits produced, the time spent on each activity, the capital employed in each activity and the level of turnover generated. That case highlighted that the presentation of the business accounts is also important. If they are presented as a single composite set, the business can be seen as one business consisting of different types of activity. This may mean that if the investment activities are too great given the context of the business, business property relief would not be available on the entire value of the business. If the accounts were separated out, however, this may mean that business property relief is available for one side of the business only, and not the other.

The approach of 'looking at things in the round' was also approved in the case of *IRC v George* [2003] EWCA Civ 1763, [2004] STC 147.

3.3.7 Contracts for sale

If the relevant business property is subject to a binding contract for sale at death, business property relief is refused under section 113 of the Inheritance Tax Act 1984. A binding contract for sale arises, not only if the deceased had made a contract to sell his shares but died before it could be completed, but also where a contract exists such that, upon the death of the deceased, his personal representatives must sell the assets to a third party. The personal representatives should examine any shareholders' agreement, the memorandum and articles of association, and any option agreement or partnership agreement, to check whether such a contract has been made. Generally, option agreements are 'safe' in that they do not impose on either party an obligation to buy or sell, but tightly structured 'put and call' agreements may come under scrutiny by HM Revenue and Customs.

Contracts for sale do, however, qualify if the sale is of a business or an interest in a business to a company which is to carry on the business, and the consideration for the sale is shares or securities in that company; or if the sale is of shares or securities in a company and the contract is made for the purposes of reconstruction or amalgamation.

3.3.8 Business and agricultural property

Section 114 of the Inheritance Tax Act 1984 provides that where an asset could qualify for both business property relief and agricultural property relief, agricultural property relief takes precedence.

3.4 AGRICULTURAL PROPERTY RELIEF

Sections 115–124 of the Inheritance Tax Act 1984 provide for agricultural property relief. It is awarded in respect of agricultural property and is dealt with in a manner similar to that relating to business property relief. The agricultural assets of the deceased are valued and the personal representatives then assess how much of that value is attributable to agricultural property. The relief appropriate is deducted from the value of the agricultural property to determine the value which is subject to the charge to inheritance tax.

3.4.1 Meaning of 'agricultural property'

Agricultural property is defined in section 115(2) of the Inheritance Tax Act 1984 as:

> … agricultural land or pasture and includes woodland and any building used in connection with the intensive rearing of livestock or fish if the woodland or building is occupied with agricultural land or pasture and the occupation is ancillary to that of the agricultural land or pasture; and also includes such cottages, farm buildings and farmhouses, together with the land occupied with them, as are of a character appropriate to the property.

Land only in the United Kingdom, Channel Islands or the Isle of Man qualifies.

Section 115(4) of the Inheritance Tax Act 1984 specifically states that the breeding, rearing and grazing of horses on a stud farm is agriculture and any buildings used in connection with that activity are farm buildings.

Only the agricultural value of agricultural property qualifies for relief from inheritance tax. The agricultural value is the value of the property as if it were subject to a perpetual covenant prohibiting its use otherwise than as agricultural property (section 115(3) of the Inheritance Tax Act 1984). Therefore, if land the deceased was farming at his death has an increased value because it has potential for development, only the value of the land attributable to the farming activities would qualify for relief; the increased development value would not, although it may be eligible for business property relief instead.

3.4.2 Meaning of 'agriculture'

The inheritance tax legislation does not itself define 'agriculture'. The most commonly used definition is contained in section 38(1) of the Agricultural Tenancies Act 1995, which provides that it includes:

> … horticulture, fruit growing, seed growing, dairy farming and livestock breeding and keeping, the use of land as grazing land, meadow land, osier land, market gardens and nursery grounds, and the use of land for woodlands where that use is ancillary to the farming of land for other agricultural purposes.

In addition, the HM Revenue and Customs *Inheritance Tax Manual* sets out the following, at IHTM 24061:

> The following land uses should be accepted as for the 'purposes of agriculture' within the meaning of IHTA84/S117:
>
> - cultivation to produce food for human consumption,
> - use to support livestock kept to produce food for human consumption, such as meat or milk or other products such as wool,
> - the keeping of such other animals as may be found on an ordinary farm, for example, horses kept for farm work,
> - the breeding and grazing of racehorses on a stud farm. This is not an agricultural purpose under general law, but is made one for the purposes of agricultural relief by IHTA84 S115(4),
> - land set aside for permanent or rotational fallow,
> - cultivation of short rotational coppice.

Land that is normally used for agricultural purposes may occasionally be used for other purposes. Provided those other purposes are not the primary reason for the occupation of the land, the land should be regarded as occupied 'for the purposes of agriculture' when considering a deduction for relief. One example is a normal working farm over which an annual point-to-point horse race is run.

Further, section 124C of the Inheritance Tax Act 1984 confirms that land used in certain habitat schemes (as specified in that section) is regarded as agriculture.

3.4.3 Period of occupation or ownership

The legislation allows agricultural property relief where:

- the deceased himself used the land for the purposes of agriculture; or
- the deceased owned the land and allowed it to be used by another for the purposes of agriculture.

In the first situation, to qualify for relief, the deceased must have occupied the land for a minimum of 2 years. In the second situation, the deceased must have owned the land for 7 years prior to his death and throughout that time it must have been occupied by a third party for the purposes of agriculture (section 117 of the Inheritance Tax Act 1984).

Section 118 of the Inheritance Tax Act 1984 provides for agricultural assets to qualify if, although they do not fulfil the above conditions, they were purchased as replacement assets for other agricultural assets, subject to certain conditions. Section 120 states that where the deceased inherited the land on the death of a third party, he is treated as having owned and occupied it (where relevant) from the date of the third party's death. As with business property relief, if the third party was his spouse, the deceased is deemed to have owned and occupied it throughout the time his spouse did so.

3.4.4 Meaning of 'occupation'

While ownership of land is largely a question of fact, occupation can be more difficult to define. The Special Commissioners, in *Harrold v IRC* [1996] STC (SCD) 195, concluded that the levels of activity required to qualify as occupation would vary significantly, depending on what agricultural activities were carried out on the land. For example, the cultivation of hay may require relatively minimal input, whereas the keeping of dairy cattle is labour-intensive.

Section 119 of the Inheritance Tax Act 1984 confirms that if a company occupies land for the purposes of agriculture, the land is deemed to be occupied by the person controlling that company.

3.4.5 Agricultural buildings

To satisfy the conditions for relief, a farm house or building must be of a 'character appropriate' to the agricultural property. This is a question of fact rather than law. The farm house should be the building from which the farm is run. In a letter to the magazine *Taxation* dated 15 June 2000, Peter Twiddy, the deputy director of HM Revenue and Customs, indicated that the district valuer would examine:

- whether the house is primarily a dwelling with land, or an agricultural unit incorporating an appropriate dwelling;
- local practice regarding what constitutes an appropriate farm house; and
- whether the land is capable of generating sufficient funds to maintain and run the house.

Farm buildings are generally easy to identify, but problems may be raised if farm cottages are rented, either to workers or as holiday cottages. Cottages rented to farm workers generally qualify for full relief, because they are occupied for the purposes of agriculture. If they do not qualify for 100 per cent relief, a reduced rate of 50 per cent may still be available. This is dealt with in the HM Revenue and Customs *Inheritance Tax Manual* and two extra-statutory concessions made in 1995. HM Revenue and Customs considers such matters on a case-by-case basis.

Holiday cottages on farms do not qualify for agricultural property relief at all, although they may qualify for business property relief.

3.4.6 Assets which do not qualify

While the farm land and buildings qualify for agricultural property relief, assets used on the farm, including machinery and animals, do not. They should instead qualify for business property relief.

Milk quotas are no longer treated as forming part of the land to which they relate. They are a separate asset and should qualify as relevant business property.

3.4.7 Rate of relief

The crucial date determining the rate at which agricultural property relief is given is 10 March 1992. If the deceased died before that date, and the land was in vacant possession, or the deceased had a right to obtain vacant possession within 12 months of his death, the rate of relief is 50 per cent. If vacant possession could not be obtained within that time, the rate is reduced to 30 per cent.

If the deceased died after 10 March 1992, the rates are 100 per cent and 50 per cent respectively. In addition, if the deceased could not obtain vacant possession within 12 months because the property was let on a tenancy beginning after 1 September 1995, the rate of relief remains at 100 per cent (section 116 of the Inheritance Tax Act 1984).

3.5 WOODLAND RELIEF

Generally, woodland qualifies for agricultural property relief if it is ancillary to farmland, or business property relief if it is commercial woodland, but sections 125–130 of the Inheritance Tax Act 1984 allow for 'woodland' relief in circumstances where woodland does not qualify for either relief. The deceased must have been entitled to the land during the 5 years prior to death, or become entitled to it without the payment of consideration. If either of those criteria is satisfied, and the person liable for the tax elects in writing within 2 years of death, the value of the underwood growing on the land (but not the land itself) can be deducted from the deceased's estate when calculating the liability to inheritance tax. This relief does not, however, operate to remove the liability to tax, only to defer it. When the underwood is later disposed of, inheritance tax must be paid on it at that time. In addition, the inheritance tax then charged is calculated on the value of the wood at the time of disposal, not at the time of the deceased's death. The difference in value of young woodland at the date of death and that of fully grown trees/timber at the date of sale should be borne in mind by personal representatives. From 6 April 2017, the Enactment of Extra-Statutory Concessions Order 2017 (SI 2017/495) confirms that transfers that include value attributable to woodlands that are subject to a deferred estate duty charge in circumstances where the transfer brings to an end the period during which estate duty is payable on the net sale proceeds of timber, will be potentially exempt from inheritance tax, except in relation to the value attributable to woodlands.

3.6 HERITAGE PROPERTY

Relief in respect of heritage property is highly complex and it is beyond the scope of this book to cover it in any great detail. It is, however, important to recognise when the heritage exemption may be available. It is granted by sections 30–35 of the Inheritance Tax Act 1984. Once again, this is a relief that allows deferral of the tax liability, but does not extinguish it altogether.

3.6.1 Eligible property

The exemption can apply to any real or personal property. HM Revenue and Customs must designate the property as:

- an object or collection of objects which are pre-eminent for their national, scientific, historic or artistic interest; or
- land which is of outstanding scenic, historic or scientific interest; or
- a building that should be preserved because of its historic or architectural interest and an area of land which is essential for its protection or an object which is historically associated with it (section 31 of the Inheritance Tax Act 1984).

Whether an asset qualifies for the exemption is usually determined by HM Revenue and Customs after taking advice from the appropriate body or council in relation to that asset, such as the National Trust. If an application for the exemption is to be made, it is often wise, before the papers are submitted, to discuss the position with the body that would be consulted by HM Revenue and Customs, so that the personal representatives can decide on the best approach.

3.6.2 Period of ownership

In relation to assets being transferred as a result of the deceased's death, there is no minimum period of ownership by the deceased. If the deceased made a gift of the asset during his lifetime, he must have owned it for a minimum period of 6 years unless he obtained it on the death of a third party (section 30(3) of the Inheritance Tax Act 1984).

3.6.3 Undertakings

To qualify for the exemption, the personal representatives in the first instance, and then the beneficiary entitled to the asset, must be willing to give undertakings to HM Revenue and Customs regarding the retention of the asset within the United Kingdom, preserving it, and allowing the general public access to it.

3.6.4 Crystallisation of tax burden

Inheritance tax becomes payable under section 32 of the Inheritance Tax Act 1984 if the undertakings are breached or the asset is sold. It also becomes chargeable if the new owner of the asset dies or gives it away, although in those circumstances a new exemption may be claimed.

The tax charge is calculated by reference to the value of the asset at the time of crystallisation, not the value at the date of death.

3.7 TAPER RELIEF

Taper relief is granted by section 7 of the Inheritance Tax Act 1984. It operates to reduce the inheritance tax payable on a PET or LCT that becomes chargeable on the subsequent death of the transferor. A popular misconception is that it reduces the value of the PET or LCT itself. This is not the case. Additionally, as a PET or LCT uses up the nil rate band of the deceased in priority to his chargeable estate (because it happened earlier in time than the deceased's death), it is often the case that the PET or LCT is not chargeable to tax at all, and so the relief is not available.

Taper relief becomes operative only if the deceased died more than 3 years after making the gift. If that is the case, the relief is as follows:

Number of whole calendar years between gift and death	*Percentage of tax payable*
3–4 years	80 per cent
4–5 years	60 per cent
5–6 years	40 per cent
6–7 years	20 per cent

3.8 QUICK SUCCESSION RELIEF

Where the deceased received assets from a third party, and those assets were subject to inheritance tax upon that party's death, and the assets are also subject to inheritance tax upon the deceased's death, quick succession relief is available to reduce the inheritance tax payable upon the deceased's death, provided the two deaths occurred within 5 years of each other. This relief is provided for by section 141 of the Inheritance Tax Act 1984. The rates are:

Periods of time between deaths in calendar years	*Percentage reduction in inheritance tax payable on second death*
less than 1 year	100 per cent
1–2 years	80 per cent
2–3 years	60 per cent
3–4 years	40 per cent
4–5 years	20 per cent

3.9 DOUBLE TAX RELIEF

As mentioned above, where the deceased held assets abroad, or if he could be held under the laws of two countries to be domiciled in each, it is possible that a double charge to inheritance tax could arise if his assets are taxed in both jurisdictions.

There are two systems in place to alleviate this burden. The first is the double tax treaty, which is dealt with by section 158 of the Inheritance Tax Act 1984. Where, under the rules of two countries, a person could be domiciled in both of them, the double tax treaty governs where the person is to be treated as domiciled, and which country has the right to tax his assets. Double tax treaties also generally provide for one country (usually the country of domicile) to allow a credit in respect of the inheritance tax already paid in the country of non-domicile so that assets are not subject to a double charge to tax. Double tax treaties currently now exist with many foreign countries. The countries are listed alphabetically on the HM Revenue and Customs website under 'double taxation treaties'.

Unilateral relief is also available under section 159 of the Inheritance Tax Act 1984. It applies where a tax (that is similar to inheritance tax) is chargeable in a foreign country on the deceased's assets, and those assets are also subject to inheritance tax in the United Kingdom. A credit is allowed in the United Kingdom in respect of the tax paid in the foreign jurisdiction, but only on the assets that are taxable in the United Kingdom. HM Revenue and Customs has published guidance at HS263 on calculating foreign tax credit relief.

In addition to the reliefs afforded in respect of the assets listed above, the identity of the beneficiary, or the value of a transfer, may also lead to an exemption from inheritance tax. The exemptions available are given below.

3.10 SPOUSE OR CIVIL PARTNER EXEMPTION

Section 18 of the Inheritance Tax Act 1984 provides that transfers to a spouse or civil partner are exempt from inheritance tax. If the gift to the spouse or civil partner takes effect only on the termination of any other interest in the asset (such as a life interest trust for the deceased's child with the interest in remainder passing to the spouse or civil partner), or if the transfer is dependent on a condition that is not satisfied within 12 months of the transfer, the exemption is not available.

Section 18(4) of the Inheritance Tax Act 1984 confirms that assets transferred to be held on trust for a spouse or civil partner qualify as assets passing to the spouse or civil partner. This means that the creation of a life interest trust for a spouse or civil partner would also be exempt if the spouse/partner is the life tenant and the interest qualifies as an immediate post-death interest under section 49A.

If the deceased was domiciled in the United Kingdom but the recipient spouse was not, the exemption is limited to assets to the value of £325,000.

If the deceased benefited under the will or intestacy of his spouse who died before 13 November 1974, the capital value of the assets he received may not be brought into account when valuing his estate if estate duty was paid or treated as paid when the spouse died and the deceased was not competent to dispose of those assets at his death (because, for example, they were held in trust for his benefit).

3.11 TRANSFERABLE NIL RATE BAND

The nil rate band is the sum that is chargeable to inheritance tax at a rate of 0 per cent. Each individual has a nil rate band, and at the time of writing the nil rate band is £325,000. HM Revenue and Customs sets out the various thresholds at www.gov.uk/government/uploads/system/uploads/attachment_data/file/588652/IHT400Rates_tables.pdf; however, the nil rate band will remain at this threshold until 5 April 2021. The nil rate band can be utilised in an individual's lifetime through making lifetime gifts within 7 years of his date of death, whether these be PETs or LCTs.

Section 10 of, and Schedule 4 to, the Finance Act 2008 inserted sections 8A–8C into the Inheritance Tax Act 1984, establishing what is known as a 'transferable nil rate band'. This legislation allows the personal representatives of the surviving spouse, where that person died on or after 9 October 2007, to claim any unused nil rate band of the first spouse to die and utilise this unused percentage on the surviving spouse's estate to reduce the liability to inheritance tax. The personal representatives must make such a claim within 24 months of the end of the month of death.

In order to claim successfully, the spouses must have been married at the date of the first death. It does not preclude a claim if the surviving spouse subsequently remarries. The date of the first death is only relevant in the case of a civil partner as the Civil Partnership Act 2004 did not come into force until 5 December 2005. Therefore, the transferable nil rate band will only apply to a civil partnership where the first civil partner died on or after 5 December 2005.

There is no such date for a spouse, even though inheritance tax was only introduced on 18 March 1986.

The personal representatives must calculate the percentage of unused nil rate band, and this percentage can then be used to uplift the applicable nil rate band at the date of the second death. If, therefore, the nil rate band had increased in value at the date of the second death, the surviving spouse's estate benefits from this additional uplift. However, the maximum that can be transferred is one additional nil rate band. This restriction provides for circumstances where a person has married more than once and survived more than one spouse. Whilst a claim can be made from each predeceasing spouse's estate, the maximum that can be claimed is one additional nil rate band.

It is therefore important when administering an estate of the first spouse to die to ensure that the evidence required to claim the transferable nil rate band (discussed at paras 4.2.2 and 4.4.2) is stored safely and is able to be found, in order to submit such a claim at the time of the surviving spouse's death. Evidence to be stored may be:

- grant of representation and any will and codicil;
- death certificate;
- marriage certificate;
- any deed of variation or deed of disclaimer;
- final estate accounts;
- final inheritance tax account and supporting schedules;
- stamped Schedule IHT421; and
- clearance certificate issued by HM Revenue and Customs.

3.12 RESIDENCE NIL RATE BAND

On 18 November 2015, section 9 of the Finance (No 2) Act 2015 inserted sections 8D–8H and 8J–8M into the Inheritance Tax Act 1984, thereby creating the RNRB. Section 93 of, and Schedule 15 to, the Finance Act 2016 also inserted section 8FA into the Inheritance Tax Act 1984 to allow for a 'down-sizing' adjustment to be taken into consideration.

The value of the RNRB or the 'residential enhancement' that can be claimed is dependent on the date of death, and the various bands are set out at para 4.4.25. However, such a claim will only be possible if certain criteria are met:

- The deceased must have died on or after 6 April 2017.
- The value of the net estate must be under the taper threshold which is currently set at £2 million. The benefits of the RNRB will be tapered away by a £1

reduction for every £2 of net estate over this threshold. Therefore, if the deceased died on or after 6 April 2017 and within the period up to 5 April 2018 with a net estate valued at £2,200,000, the RNRB will be tapered away to zero. For the purposes of the RNRB, an individual's estate includes all exempt gifts on death, assets that qualify for business property relief or agricultural property relief, assets in which the deceased had a qualifying interest in possession and gifts in which the deceased had a reservation of benefit. However, PETs, even failed PETs that are chargeable (whether or not subject to taper), will reduce the value of the deceased's estate in relation to the taper threshold.

- Section 8H of the Inheritance Tax Act 1984 provides that the RNRB will only be available if the estate includes a 'qualifying residential interest'. Within the deceased's estate immediately before death, there must be an interest in a dwelling house. Further, the deceased must have owned this property, or an interest in it, at a time that it was also his residence. It does not have to have been his main residence, only that he has lived in it at some stage or intended to live in it in due course, but was occupying other employment-related accommodation. If there are more than one potential qualifying residential interests within an estate, the personal representatives can nominate the property they wish HM Revenue and Customs to consider as the qualifying residential interest, as only one property can be designated as such. It is not possible to add together the values of two eligible properties. The sum of the RNRB allowed will be the lower of the value of the qualifying residential interest (therefore the value of the chosen property or the deceased's interest in it) and the applicable residential enhancement allowed.
- Section 8K of the Inheritance Tax Act 1984 confirms that the qualifying residential interest must be 'closely inherited'. This means it must be inherited by the deceased's 'lineal descendants' or the spouse or civil partner of such a lineal descendant who had not remarried at the date of the deceased's death. The definition of 'lineal descendants' includes children, step-children, adopted children, foster children, grandchildren, great-grandchildren and remoter descendants and a child that the deceased was appointed a guardian or special guardian for. An adopted child can be considered a lineal descendant of both the adoptive parents and the natural parents for qualification for the RNRB.
- In order to qualify for the RNRB, the qualifying residential interest must be closely inherited on death whether this is by way of the deceased's will, under the intestacy rules, by survivorship, or otherwise. It will only apply to the deceased's estate immediately before death. Consequently, any failed PETs or LCTs will not qualify. If the property passes into a settlement on the deceased's death, the lineal descendant must become beneficially entitled to an interest in possession. The qualifying trusts are therefore an immediate post-death interest under which the lineal descendant has an interest in possession, a disabled

person's interest under which the lineal descendant has an actual interest in possession or is treated as having such for inheritance tax purposes, a section 71D trust being an 18–25 trust for the benefit of a lineal descendant or a section 71A trust being a trust for a bereaved minor for the benefit of a lineal descendant. The lineal descendant must, therefore, inherit the property in one of the following ways:

- it was owned absolutely by the deceased and inherited by way of either absolute gift or into a qualifying trust on death;
- it is either an immediate post-death interest, a transitional serial interest or a disabled person's interest and is inherited as an absolute gift or a disabled person's interest on death. It is worth noting that where a deceased's qualifying residential interest is an interest in possession, the lineal descendant must inherit an absolute interest and not a successive interest in possession unless it is a disabled person's interest;
- it was given away in the deceased's lifetime to a lineal descendant absolutely but was subject to a reservation of benefit.

Unlike the basic nil rate band, the RNRB cannot be set off against lifetime gifts, whether these are chargeable transfers or PETs. This means the basic nil rate band could be completely utilised by lifetime gifts, but there would still be the RNRB to set off against the estate.

The RNRB may still be claimed if the qualifying residential interest was no longer owned at the deceased's death due to the down-sizing provisions. If, on or after 8 July 2015, the deceased had down-sized to a less valuable property or had ceased to own a property, for instance, if he had moved into residential care, and died on or after 6 April 2017, a claim can be made to utilise the proportion of the RNRB that would otherwise have been lost due to either the down-sizing or the disposal of the property.

To successfully claim the down-sizing addition, the property sold must have been owned by the deceased and would have qualified for the RNRB if it had still been in his estate at the date of death. The replacement property or other assets of equivalent value to the difference must be in the deceased's estate at date of death and this property or these assets must be closely inherited. The down-sizing addition is then combined with the primary RNRB; however, the RNRB claimed cannot be in excess of the applicable residential enhancement. The down-sizing addition is likewise subject to the tapering where the estate value exceeds the taper threshold. Only one move, sale or other disposition of a former home can be taken into account to calculate the down-sizing allowance. If there is more than one then the personal representative can choose which to use.

Similar to the transferable nil rate band, it is possible to claim any unused proportion of the first to die's RNRB to be utilised on the surviving spouse's estate. An unused RNRB will arise where the first to die did not have a qualifying residential interest or did own a qualifying residential interest and it was *not* closely inherited, for instance, it passed to the surviving spouse. A claim must be made by the surviving spouse's personal representatives within 2 years of the end of the month of death, and the surviving spouse must have died on or after 6 April 2017. Whilst a claim can be made on more than one predeceased spouses' estates, the total of the claims made cannot be more than a 100 per cent increase of the deceased's own RNRB.

3.13 ANNUAL EXEMPTION

The annual exemption allows each person to make gifts in any year to the value of £3,000, without inheritance tax becoming chargeable on them. In addition, if the deceased did not fully utilise his annual exemption in any one year, the unused part can be carried forward to the following year (but may only be carried forward for one year – not indefinitely). The annual exemption applies by reference to the date upon which the gift was made, so that if the deceased gave £3,000 to his daughter on day 1, and a further £3,000 to his son on day 2, the gift to the daughter would be entirely exempt, and the gift to the son would be taxable.

The exemption is permitted by section 19 of the Inheritance Tax Act 1984 and is allowed only in relation to gifts made during the deceased's lifetime; it does not apply to any dispositions made by will.

3.14 SMALL GIFTS

Section 20 of the Inheritance Tax Act 1984 allows the deceased to make gifts to as many individuals as he chooses in any year that do not exceed £250 in total per person. This exemption cannot be cumulated with the annual exemption in relation to any recipient, which means that either the recipient benefits from the £3,000 annual allowance (or part of it), or the gift made to him may fall within the small gifts exemption. The personal representatives must choose how to apply the exemptions in the most tax-efficient manner.

3.15 NORMAL EXPENDITURE OUT OF INCOME

Where a gift was made unconditionally by the deceased out of his income, as part of his normal expenditure, and after the gift was made he still had sufficient income to maintain his normal standard of living, that gift is exempt under section 21 of the Inheritance Tax Act 1984.

The most difficult aspect of claiming this exemption is proving that the gift was made out of income and not out of capital. Evidence of the deceased's annual income and outgoings is necessary (see schedule IHT403 for the level of information required). A client who kept accurate records of his income and expenditure in the years before his death simplifies this task greatly, although accountants can also be an invaluable source of information as to the amount of income received by the deceased. It is recommended that if a solicitor adviser knows that his client is making, or is planning to make, gifts out of his annual income, the client should be supplied with a copy of schedule IHT403 and be advised to keep sufficient records that this could be completed without great difficulty following his death.

The income gifted must also have formed part of the deceased's 'normal expenditure'. This is generally established by showing a regular pattern of payments. If the deceased dies after making only one or two payments, this does not necessarily preclude the exemption from applying, although it may make it more difficult to prove.

3.16 GIFTS IN CONSIDERATION OF MARRIAGE

A gift made on or shortly before a marriage, to either or both of the parties to that marriage (but so that only one exemption applies per marriage), may be exempt. If the deceased was a parent of one of the parties to the marriage, the amount exempt is £5,000. If either party was the grandchild or remoter issue of the deceased, the limit is £2,500; and if the party was any other person the amount allowed is £1,000 (section 22 of the Inheritance Tax Act 1984). The gift must be fully effective on the marriage taking place.

3.17 GIFTS TO CHARITIES

Section 23 of the Inheritance Tax Act 1984 states that a gift to a charity is exempt from inheritance tax provided the gift takes full effect within 12 months of the date of transfer and is not subject to any prior interest. The deceased cannot have reserved to himself, or anyone connected with him, the right to use or reside in the asset, unless he pays a full market rent for that use or residence.

The asset may be gifted into a trust for charity, providing it can be used for charitable purposes only. If the will is particularly restrictive of how the gifted asset may be used, this may disentitle the charity from the exemption.

For deaths on or after 6 April 2012, it is possible for a reduced rate of inheritance tax to apply where the 'charitable giving condition' set out in paragraph 2(2) of Schedule 1A to the Inheritance Tax Act 1984 is met. Section 209 of, and Schedule 33 to, the Finance Act 2012 inserted Schedule 1A to encourage charitable giving. This Schedule provides that where 10 per cent of the net estate is gifted to a charity which qualifies for charitable exemption under section 23 of the Inheritance Tax Act 1984, a 36 per cent rate of inheritance tax may apply. In the legislation, the word 'charity' has the normal meaning for inheritance tax purposes (HM Revenue and Customs *Inheritance Tax Manual*, at IHTM 11112), and includes registered community amateur sports clubs and organisations in the European Economic Area that meet the requirements for being a charity. The gift to charity may be by way of legacy, a share of residue or a quantifiable share of the estate. If the gift in the will is insufficient to meet the 10 per cent test then a deed of variation can also be made to rectify this (see para 25.2.11).

To determine what equates to 10 per cent, an estate for inheritance tax purposes is divided into three components, as the reduced rate may only apply to one such component. The components are:

- the survivorship component being the value of those assets that are held as joint tenants and pass by survivorship, Scottish assets that pass by special destination and overseas assets that pass by the law of the applicable country;
- the settled property component being the value of any settled property to which the deceased was beneficially entitled on death and in respect of which a charge arises under section 49(1) of the Inheritance Tax Act 1984 and therefore pre-March 2006 interests in possession, immediate post-death interests and interests in a disabled person's settlement if the deceased were treated as being entitled to the interest in possession together with property devolving under a settled land grant; and
- the general component being the value of the balance of the estate after the first two components have been deducted. The general component is equivalent to the free estate plus joint property held as tenants in common.

Any property where a reservation of benefit subsists is not included within any component as the rules governing reservation of benefit do not apply to gifts to charity. It is, however, possible to merge such property with another component. The option to merge components is discussed below.

The 36 per cent rate of tax applies where 10 per cent is given to charity from any component; this is called the 'donated amount'. In order to calculate this amount it is necessary to first calculate the 'baseline amount'. The baseline amount is the net value for inheritance tax purposes of the assets in the component in question after deducting all relevant exemptions and reliefs, and the appropriate proportion of the nil rate band and transferable nil rate band, and then adding back in the value of the assets in the component that charitable exemption will apply to. The steps to calculate the baseline amount are set out in Schedule 1A to the Inheritance Tax Act 1984; however, HM Revenue and Customs provides guidance in its *Inheritance Tax Manual* at IHTM 45009, and also a calculator at www.gov.uk/inheritance-tax-reduced-rate-calculator. HMRC encourages taxpayers to print out the results page from this calculator when lodging their application for the reduced rate of inheritance tax. Where the reduced rate of inheritance tax applies to an estate, Schedule IHT430 should be completed, see para 4.4.23.

It is also possible to make a merging election where an estate contains more than one component and the donated amount for one component is at least 10 per cent of its baseline amount. In these circumstances, an election can be made in writing to merge two or more components and apply the 10 per cent test as if they were a single component. If the donated amount is 10 per cent of the baseline for the newly merged single component then the 36 per cent rate of inheritance tax will apply to each of the components. Such an election must be made within 2 years of death and be submitted using Schedule IHT430.

The person able to make such an election is the 'appropriate person' and this is therefore the person liable for the tax for each component. The appropriate person, therefore, is the surviving joint tenant where the survivorship component is concerned, or the personal representatives where the surviving joint tenant has since also died; the trustees of the settled property where the settled property component is affected; and the personal representatives where the general component is involved. The appropriate person for property in which a reservation of benefit subsists is the person in whom the property is vested. The Schedule must be signed by the appropriate person and not by his agent. Such an election can also be withdrawn by the appropriate person within 2 years and 1 month of the date of death.

Within the 2-year timescale, it is also possible for an election to be made to opt out of the reduced rate of inheritance tax. HM Revenue and Customs gives the example where this may be appropriate where the administration costs of valuing assets and calculating the donated sum outweigh the benefits of the reduced rate of tax applying to the estate. Such an election can also be withdrawn within 2 years and 1 month of the date of death.

3.18 OTHER EXEMPTIONS

There are other exemptions in sections 24–28 of the Inheritance Tax Act 1984, which are not discussed in detail in this book. Very briefly, they relate to:

- gifts to political parties, if two members of the party were elected to the House of Commons at the most recent general election, or one member was elected but at least 150,000 votes were cast in favour of that party's candidates (section 24);
- gifts of land and buildings made to a registered housing association (section 24A);
- gifts made for 'national purposes' to various public bodies listed in Schedule 3 to the Act (sections 25 and 26A);
- gifts made into trust for the maintenance of certain heritage property (section 27);
- gifts made into trust for the benefit of employees of a certain company (section 28);
- ex gratia payments made to British prisoners of war held in Japan during the Second World War (extra-statutory concession F20).

3.19 HM REVENUE AND CUSTOMS REGISTER

HM Revenue and Customs has introduced a Trusts Registration Service (TRS) where trustees are required to update the online register every year that a trust generates a UK tax consequence. A trust should be registered by 5 October in the year it was set up or when it starts to make income or chargeable gains, if this is later. A UK tax consequence means income tax, capital gains tax, non-resident capital gains tax, inheritance tax, stamp duty land tax and stamp duty reserve tax. This means that even trusts that are resident outside the United Kingdom but have a UK tax liability must also be registered. This service replaces the paper form 41(g) (Trust) system to the extent that from the end of April 2017, HM Revenue and Customs no longer accepted these forms.

In subsequent years or where the trust is already registered for self-assessment, the trustees of a trust that incurs a UK tax liability are required to provide beneficial ownership information using the TRS by 31 January after the end of the tax year.

Agents are able to register on behalf of trustees from October 2017 and agents and lead trustees can enter updates for changes of circumstances from early 2018.

In order to register, the nominated lead trustee must provide the following:

- National Insurance number, passport or driving licence number;
- details of the trust assets put into trust including the date they were put in, such as the addresses of any property and their valuations; and

- details of the identity of the settlor, trustees, any protector, the beneficiaries or class of beneficiaries, such as the name, address, date of birth, National Insurance number or passport number.

Once registered, a unique taxpayer reference (UTR) will be provided via the post within 15 working days.

The trustees must provide an update each year that the trust generates a UK tax liability. All trusts must be registered including those already registered using form 41G (Trust). The trustees have a duty to ensure the TRS entry is accurate and up to date, guaranteeing that their obligations under the Fourth Money Laundering Directive (Directive (EU) 2015/849) are complied with.

Personal representatives are also required to register 'complex' estates on the TRS. HM Revenue and Customs defines a 'complex' estate as one where:

- the value of the estate exceeds £2,500,000;
- the tax due for the whole administration period exceeds £10,000; or
- the value of assets sold in any tax year for a date of death up to April 2016 exceeds £250,000 or £500,000 for a date of death after April 2016.

All complex estates are required to be registered, including those already registered with HM Revenue and Customs and still being administered. Once registered, a UTR will be allocated.

3.20 HM REVENUE AND CUSTOMS PENALTIES

In recent times, HM Revenue and Customs has become more ready to penalise personal representatives for submitting inaccurate values in form IHT400. There are three main reasons why inaccurate values are submitted:

- The personal representatives know they are submitting an incorrect figure but wish to mislead HM Revenue and Customs. Clearly this is fraud and attracts severe penalties.
- Knowingly submitting an estimated value that is later discovered to be wrong, generally with the intention of obtaining a grant as quickly as possible. If this is the case, for example, because an asset is difficult to value and it will take some time for a proper market appraisal to be produced, it is acceptable for an estimate to be shown on form IHT400, but it should be clearly identified as a provisional estimate in the box at the bottom left hand corner of page 12 of the form. The personal representatives must undertake to supply a proper valuation as soon as it is available (section 216(3A) of the Inheritance Tax Act

1984). Even so, HM Revenue and Customs may still seek to levy a penalty if it considers the estimate to have been unreasonable.

- Mistakenly submitting an incorrect valuation. HM Revenue and Customs may class this as a lack of reasonable care. 'Reasonable care' in these circumstances is subjective, and therefore differs depending on the person's knowledge and experience. Providing the personal representatives make their mistake known to HM Revenue and Customs as soon as possible and attempt to rectify it, they may escape without penalty.

These are rules of thumb and cannot be relied upon – every case is assessed on its merits. HM Revenue and Customs is permitted to penalise anyone liable to pay the tax in relation to an estate for:

- late delivery or non-delivery of an account (section 245);
- fraudulently or negligently delivering an incorrect account, supporting information or document (section 247); or
- failing within a reasonable time to rectify an error made in an account (section 248).

The level of the penalty is directly linked to the reason why the error occurred and the potential lost revenue, which is the additional tax due as a result of correcting the error. The more serious the reason, the higher the maximum penalty can be. HM Revenue and Customs can reduce the penalty if the personal representatives help HMRC to resolve the issue. HMRC gives the following examples of penalties charged in its guidance:

- if a penalty arises because of a lack of reasonable care, the penalty will be between 0 per cent and 30 per cent of the extra tax due;
- if the error is deliberate, the penalty will be between 20 and 70 per cent of the extra tax due;
- if the error is deliberate and concealed, the penalty will be between 30 and 100 per cent of the extra tax due.

HM Revenue and Customs further confirms that the penalty can be reduced if the personal representatives tell HMRC about the error, and it may make further reductions depending on the quality of the disclosure given.

As mentioned above, these sections are strictly interpreted by HM Revenue and Customs. The case of *Robertson v IRC (No 2)* [2002] STC (SCD) 242 demonstrates the harsh stance now being taken by HMRC, but offers some hope to the taxpayer that it may have to relax its attitude. In that case, the solicitor acting for the personal representatives submitted estimated values for various assets in the deceased's estate, but clearly marked them as estimates upon submission of form IHT200 (as it was at the time). When the proper market values for the assets were established, and were substantially higher than the estimated values which had been submitted, he notified HMRC immediately. HMRC sought to penalise him on the basis that he did not make 'the fullest enquiries reasonably practicable', as required by section 216(3A) of the Inheritance Tax Act 1984, and criticised the solicitor for his undue haste in submitting the form.

The Special Commissioners overruled the decision of HM Revenue and Customs. They said that the solicitor acted in accordance with good practice and made the fullest enquiries that were reasonably practicable in the circumstances. They also awarded the solicitor his costs of the matter – an award made only where the Special Commissioners consider HMRC to have acted unreasonably.

While this case is positive for the taxpayer, it is highly recommended that a proper valuation be obtained wherever possible before form IHT400 is completed. If such a valuation cannot be obtained, the estimate should be as accurate as possible and based upon a professional valuer's recommendations, so that the personal representatives can be seen to have acted properly.

HM Revenue and Customs has issued specific guidance in its December 2015 newsletter about the reporting of relevant gifts. Personal representatives are expected to ask family members, friends, associates, those named in any will and the deceased's solicitors, accountants or financial advisers whether they have received or whether they have any knowledge of any such gifts in this period. HMRC guides personal representatives to use its online Inheritance Tax toolkit (www.gov.uk/government/publications/hmrc-inheritance-tax-toolkit), which strongly recommends that personal representatives check 7 years of bank and building society statements to identify potential gift transactions as they can significantly impact on the amount of inheritance tax payable. HMRC highlights that it sometimes asks further questions, and if a gift has not been properly declared and there is additional inheritance tax payable, then there may also be interest and a penalty to pay. HMRC notes that the recipient of a gift also has a duty to report the gift under paragraph 1A of Schedule 24 of the Inheritance Tax Act 1984, and considers that a failure to advise the personal representatives of such a gift or a failure to report it to HMRC is deliberate behaviour, incurring a minimum penalty of 50 per cent of the tax undeclared. This penalty is payable by the recipient of the gift and not the personal representatives. This approach was upheld in *CRC v Hutchings* [2015] UKFTT 9 (TC), [2015] WTLR 1359. HMRC confirms that it will continue to take this line in similar cases, and therefore recommends that personal representatives may wish to refer to that decision when warning potential recipients of lifetime gifts of the potential consequences of failing to disclose them.

3.21 PROVIDING FOR INHERITANCE TAX

The inheritance tax payable on some assets must be paid immediately, and in respect of others it may be paid by instalments.

3.21.1 Instalment option property

Instalment option property is defined in sections 227–229 of the Inheritance Tax Act 1984 as 'qualifying property'. This is:

- land of any description, wherever situated;
- a business or an interest in a business;
- shares or securities in a company:
  - which gave the deceased control of the company (defined in section 269 as voting control, which is owning more than 50 per cent of the voting shares); or
  - which are unquoted, and 20 per cent or more of the total inheritance tax payable is attributable to them or to other property upon which the instalment option is available; or
  - which are unquoted and HM Revenue and Customs is satisfied that the inheritance tax payable on them cannot be paid in one lump sum without causing undue hardship;
- shares (not securities) in a company which are valued at more than £20,000 and either the nominal value of the shares is 10 per cent or more of the nominal value of all the shares in the company, or the shares are ordinary and their nominal value is not less than 10 per cent of the nominal value of all the ordinary shares in the company. Ordinary shares are defined in section 228(4) as shares carrying a right to dividends that are not restricted to a fixed rate, or to which are attached a right to be converted into shares of this type.

In addition, inheritance tax payable on the disposal of woodlands which previously qualified for relief under section 125 of the Inheritance Tax Act 1984 may be paid by instalments under section 229.

Inheritance tax due on a failed PET or LCT can be paid by instalments only if:

- the asset gifted continued to be held by the transferee at the date of the deceased's death; or

- if it did not continue to be so held, the property disposed of has been replaced by property which also qualified for business property relief or agricultural property relief within section 113B or section 124B; and
- in the case of unquoted shares, they remained unquoted at the date of death.

3.21.2 Interest

Although inheritance tax on qualifying property may be paid by instalments, interest is chargeable on those instalments from the date upon which the first instalment is due. Section 234 of the Inheritance Tax Act 1984, however, provides that interest on relevant business or agricultural property which has not qualified for relief from tax at 100 per cent will run only from the date upon which each instalment is due (that is, interest is payable only if the tax is paid late).

3.22 FUNDING THE PAYMENT

Any inheritance tax due must be paid on submission of form IHT400. Once the amount has been established, the personal representatives must decide how the liability is to be discharged. They have a number of options.

3.22.1 Using the assets in the estate

It may be possible to secure the release of funds from the deceased's bank or building society, if the relevant institution is willing to do so. For the procedure to enable a payment directly from the deceased's bank or building society, see para 4.4.22 – alternatively, the personal representatives may be willing to draw a cheque from the deceased's account made payable to 'HM Revenue and Customs' which can be sent in with form IHT400. It is recommended that the estate's inheritance tax reference is detailed on such a cheque.

Alternatively, National Savings investments or government stocks may be utilised. This can, though, be a lengthy process. For a full description, see para 4.4.22.

If the deceased owned shares that were held in the nominee name of a stockbroker, the shares can be sold by the nominee and the monies released by the stockbroker to fund the tax bill.

Lastly, if the deceased was a patient of the Court of Protection, the court may agree to pay the tax directly from funds held by it.

3.22.2 Life assurance policies

A life assurance policy on the deceased's life, which provides for payment on death, may have been taken out. If such a policy was taken out by the deceased and written into trust, the death benefit is automatically payable to the trustees upon proof of death. Equally, the owner of the policy may be a third party who took out a policy on the deceased's life. If this was the case and the beneficial owner of the proceeds of the policy (that is, the trust beneficiary or third party who owned the policy) is the same person as the residuary beneficiary of the estate, that person may be willing to allow the policy proceeds to be used to pay the inheritance tax bill.

If that person is not the residuary beneficiary, or if, for example, he is one of two residuary beneficiaries, he may be willing to lend the policy proceeds to the estate on terms more favourable than a commercial loan (see para 3.22.3).

3.22.3 Raising a loan

If the personal representatives are not able to raise sufficient funds to pay the inheritance tax bill in any other manner, they may have to take out a loan. This could be a loan from an estate beneficiary or someone who has benefited from a policy of assurance on the deceased's life. If so, it is to be hoped that the terms of the loan could be favourable to the estate, although the beneficiary may wish to charge some interest.

If no such loan is possible, the personal representatives may have to take out a commercial loan from a bank. This can be quite time-consuming as banks usually require a complete breakdown of the estate, and an undertaking from the personal representatives that they will treat the loan as a first charge on the estate when repaying the deceased's debts. A bank usually charges both an arrangement fee and interest on the loan. It may be worthwhile for the personal representatives to agree a higher rate of interest and a lower arrangement fee, as interest is deductible from the income of the estate for income tax purposes, but an arrangement fee is not.

3.22.4 Using trust funds

If the deceased was a beneficiary of a life interest trust, and the remaindermen of the trust are the same people as the residuary beneficiaries of the estate, the trustees may agree to utilise the trust fund to pay all the inheritance tax due, not just the part relating to the trust assets.

3.22.5 Transfer of assets in satisfaction

Under sections 230 and 231 of the Inheritance Tax Act 1984, HM Revenue and Customs may accept property transferred to it in lieu of the charge to inheritance tax and interest. The Secretary of State must agree to this. Any asset may be accepted, but in the case of chattels, they must be considered to be 'pre-eminent', for example, valuable works of art. The person making the offer can be anyone liable to pay the inheritance tax, and the asset offered does not have to be one upon which any of the inheritance tax is payable. So, for instance, a beneficiary of a person's estate can offer one of his own assets in satisfaction of the tax due in relation to the estate.

3.23 QUANTUM OF INHERITANCE TAX

When the personal representatives complete form IHT400, they calculate the inheritance tax liability as at the time of submitting the form. HM Revenue and Customs may, however, then raise queries with the personal representatives about the value of assets submitted, the level of reliefs claimed, or whether an asset forms part of the deceased's estate for inheritance tax purposes. The stance taken by HM Revenue and Customs in relation to any of these issues may be different from that of the personal representatives and it is always advisable for the personal representatives to try to reach negotiated agreement with HM Revenue and Customs. If agreement cannot be reached, the HM Revenue and Customs Inheritance Tax issues a notice of determination in relation to the disputed matter. The personal representatives have 30 days in which to appeal. Any appeal is heard by the Special Commissioners or the Lands Tribunal, depending on the nature of the dispute, although if the personal representatives disagree with HM Revenue and Customs on a point of law they can take the matter directly to the High Court (sections 222–225 of the Inheritance Tax Act 1984).

If an appeal is to be heard (whether by the Special Commissioners, the Lands Tribunal or the High Court), HM Revenue and Customs can in the meantime seek to recover only the inheritance tax agreed to be due. But if the taxpayer loses the appeal and wishes to appeal further, HM Revenue and Customs is entitled to be paid the inheritance tax in dispute while the second appeal is waiting to be heard (section 242 of the Inheritance Tax Act 1984).

3.24 LIABILITY FOR INHERITANCE TAX

Once the quantum of inheritance tax due has been established, it is important to consider who is liable to pay it. This is dealt with in sections 199 and 200 of the Inheritance Tax Act 1984.

The personal representatives are liable for all inheritance tax arising on the deceased's free estate (section 200(1)(a) of the Inheritance Tax Act 1984). If for some reason they do not pay the tax due, HM Revenue and Customs has a right of recourse against the beneficiaries of the estate or the trustees of any trust into which the deceased's assets pass. Significantly, a beneficiary entitled only to the income generated by an asset is treated for these purposes as though entitled to the entire asset (section 200(1) and (3)).

Any inheritance tax due on capital assets contained within a trust of which the deceased was life tenant is payable from that trust (section 201 of the Inheritance Tax Act 1984). Similarly, tax due on jointly held assets is payable by the person entitled to the asset after the deceased's death (section 200(1)(c)).

If inheritance tax is payable on a PET or LCT made by the deceased, the donee of the transfer is liable for it (sections 199(1) and 204(6) of the Inheritance Tax Act 1984). If that liability is not discharged within 12 months of the due date, or if the tax payable exceeds the value of the asset in the donee's hands, the personal representatives have a secondary liability to meet the tax payable (sections 199(1) and (2) and 204(8)). Unfortunately for the personal representatives, they do not have a statutory right of recovery against the donee in relation to any inheritance tax paid by them, unless the transfer was also a gift with reservation of benefit (not to a settlement) (section 211(3)).

Section 204 of the Inheritance Tax Act 1984 serves to limit the personal representatives' liability to inheritance tax, by providing that they are not liable for tax greater than the value of the assets passing into their hands, or the assets that would have passed into their hands but for their neglect or default (section 204(1)).

To secure the inheritance tax payable, HM Revenue and Customs automatically imposes a charge over any property that was transferred by a chargeable transfer, unless it was personal property beneficially owned by the deceased before his death, devolving on his personal representatives and situated in the United Kingdom (section 237 of the Inheritance Tax Act 1984). In most situations, HM Revenue and Customs does not seek to register this charge but that is of no effect – any disposition of the property in question is made subject to the charge, by virtue of section 237(6). The only exception is where the property is disposed of to a purchaser; here, if the charge is to continue to take effect after the purchase it must have been registered against the asset (in the case of land), or the purchaser must have had knowledge of the charge (in the case of personal property) (section 238).

Chapter 4

Inheritance Tax Accounts

4.1 CALCULATION OF THE ESTATE

There are two separate bases upon which the value of an estate is calculated. The first is the value of the estate in order to ascertain the inheritance tax payable. This takes into account all the assets deemed to form part of the deceased's estate for the purposes of inheritance tax, including assets held in the deceased's sole name or jointly with other persons otherwise than as trustee; foreign assets; assets held in a life interest trust for the deceased's benefit; and assets subject to a gift with reservation of benefit.

The second calculation is that of the deceased's estate that will pass under the grant of representation. This includes only assets held in the deceased's sole name, and may not include foreign assets if they fall to be dealt with under a foreign system of law.

In both situations the gross value is that of the assets only; the net value is the value remaining after any relevant liabilities have been deducted.

4.2 EXCEPTED ESTATES

Once the personal representatives have ascertained the value of the deceased's gross and net estates, they need to consider whether an inheritance tax account must be submitted to HM Revenue and Customs. A full account is not always necessary.

The requirements for an 'excepted estate' are prescribed by the Inheritance Tax (Delivery of Accounts) (Excepted Estates) Regulations 2004 (SI 2004/2543), as amended by the Inheritance Tax (Delivery of Accounts) (Excepted Estates) (Amendment) Regulations 2006 (SI 2006/2141) and the Inheritance Tax

(Delivery of Accounts) (Excepted Estates) (Amendment) Regulations 2011 (SI 2011/214) and the Inheritance Tax (Delivery of Accounts) (Excepted Estates) (Amendment) Regulations 2014 (SI 2014/488).

Since 6 April 2004, some type of inheritance tax return must be filled in for all estates, even those that qualify as excepted estates. The difference is that, if an estate is 'excepted', the return is not sent to HM Revenue and Customs, but delivered to the probate registry with the application for the grant.

For deaths on or after 1 March 2011, an estate is excepted if, immediately before his death:

(a) the deceased was domiciled in the United Kingdom (for a discussion of domicile, see para 4.4.1);
(b) the value of the deceased's estate is attributable wholly to property passing under his will or intestacy or under a nomination (see para 1.9.4) of an asset taking effect on death or under a single settlement in which he was entitled to an interest in possession in settled property or by survivorship in a beneficial joint tenancy;
(c) of that property:

    (i) not more than £150,000 represented value attributable to property which, immediately before the deceased's death, was settled property; and
    (ii) not more than £100,000 represented value attributable to property which, immediately before the deceased's death, was situated outside the United Kingdom;
    (iii) that person was not a person by reason of whose death one of the alternatively secured pension (ASP) fund provisions (being sections 151A–151C of the Inheritance Tax Act 1984) applies;

(d) the deceased died without having made any chargeable transfers during the period of 7 years ending with his death other than specified transfers (see below) where the aggregate value transferred did not exceed £150,000; and
(e) the aggregate of the gross value of the deceased's estate and of the value transferred by any specified transfers and specified exempt transfers made by the deceased did not exceed the nil rate band in place at his death (if he died after 6 August in any tax year), or the nil rate band applicable to the year before he died (if he died between 6 April and 5 August in any tax year).

An estate is also an excepted estate where:

(1) Conditions (a), (b), (c) and (d) above are satisfied (but note that in relation to (c) (i) settled property passing to a spouse, civil partner or charity is not included in the £150,000) and the aggregate of the gross value of the deceased's estate and of the value transferred by any specified transfers and specified exempt transfers made by the deceased did not exceed £1 million. In addition, the gross value of the deceased's estate, plus the value transferred by specified transfers and specified exempt transfers, less any transfers qualifying for the spouse, civil partner or charity exemptions, less the deceased's liabilities, must not exceed the nil rate band in place at his death (if he died after 6 August in any tax year), or the nil rate band applicable to the year before he died (if he died between 6 April and 5 August in any tax year).

(2)

- (a) the deceased was never domiciled in the United Kingdom or treated as domiciled ('deemed domiciled') in the United Kingdom by section 267 of the Inheritance Tax Act 1984; and
- (b) the value of that person's estate situated in the United Kingdom is wholly attributable to cash or quoted shares or securities passing under his will or intestacy or by survivorship in a beneficial joint tenancy, the gross value of which does not exceed £150,000; and
- (c) that person was not a person by reason of whose death one of the ASP fund provisions (being sections 151A–151C of the Inheritance Tax Act 1984) applies.

'Specified transfers' are chargeable transfers made during the period of 7 years ending with the deceased's death where the value transferred is attributable to:

- cash; or
- personal chattels or corporeal movable property; or
- quoted shares or securities; or
- an interest in or over land, save to the extent that:
  - sections 102 and 102A(2) of the Finance Act 1986 (gifts with reservation of benefit) apply to that transfer; or
  - the land became settled property on that transfer.

'Specified exempt transfers' are transfers of value made by a person during the 7 years ending with the deceased's death which are exempt only by reason of one of the following provisions of the Inheritance Tax Act 1984: section 18 (transfers between spouses or civil partners); section 23 (gifts to charities), section 24 (gifts to political parties); section 24A (gifts to housing associations); section 27 (maintenance funds for historic buildings); or section 28 (employee trusts).

Note that for the purposes of (e) and (1) above, under regulation 5A of the Inheritance Tax (Delivery of Accounts) (Excepted Estates) Regulations 2004 (as amended), the nil rate band referred to for the purposes of working out whether the estate is excepted may be increased by 100 per cent if:

(a) the person now deceased (the 'survivor') survived their spouse or civil partner (the 'first deceased person'); and
(b) either:

   (i) in a case where the first deceased person was the spouse of the survivor, the first deceased person died on or after 13 November 1974, or
   (ii) in a case where the first deceased person was the civil partner of the survivor, the first deceased person died on or after 5 December 2005; and

(c) a claim for the rollover of the inheritance tax nil rate band is made pursuant to section 8A of the Inheritance Tax Act 1984:

   (i) by virtue of which the nil rate band maximum at the time of the survivor's death is treated, for the purpose of the charge to tax on the death of the survivor, as increased by 100 per cent; and
   (ii) which is made in respect of not more than one first deceased person.

In addition there are the following requirements:

(a) the first deceased person died domiciled in the United Kingdom;
(b) the value of the first deceased person's estate is attributable wholly to property passing:

   (i) under the first deceased person's will or intestacy, or
   (ii) by survivorship in a beneficial joint tenancy;

(c) of that property, not more than £100,000 represented value attributable to property which immediately before the first deceased person's death was situated outside the United Kingdom;
(d) the first deceased person was not a person by reason of whose death one of the ASP fund provisions (being sections 151A–151C of the Inheritance Tax Act 1984) applies;
(e) the first deceased person died without having made any chargeable transfers during the period of 7 years ending with the first deceased person's death; and

(f) the value transferred by any chargeable transfer made on the death of the first deceased person was not reduced by virtue of section 104 (business property relief) or section 116 (agricultural property relief).

Note also the following points apply, which differ from the usual inheritance tax rules, when construing these regulations for the purposes of determining what an excepted estate is:

(a) When determining the value transferred by a chargeable transfer, the effects of business property relief (section 104 of the Inheritance Tax Act 1984) and agricultural property relief (section 116) are ignored (regulation 4(7) of the Inheritance Tax (Delivery of Accounts) (Excepted Estates) Regulations 2004 (as amended)).
(b) Chargeable transfers include transfers which are exempt by virtue of section 21 (regular gifts out of income) if they are made less than 7 years before the death of the deceased and total more than £3,000 in any one tax year (regulation 4(7A)).
(c) Transfers that would normally be exempt as transfers to a spouse or civil partner will not be treated as such if *at any time* prior to the transfer, the spouse or civil partner was not domiciled in the United Kingdom (regulation 5(2)).
(d) Transfers that would normally be exempt as transfers to a charity will not be so exempt if the property becomes comprised in a trust as a result of the transfer (regulation 5(3)).

Under section 176 of, and Schedule 36 to, the Finance Act 2013, rules have been introduced which impose restrictions on what is classed as a deductible liability for inheritance tax purposes. These rules apply to a certain extent when determining whether an estate qualifies as an exempted estate. The Inheritance Tax (Delivery of Accounts) (Excepted Estates) (Amendment) Regulations 2014 impact which liabilities can be taken into account when calculating the chargeable value of an exempt excepted estate.

These rules apply to a death on or after 1 April 2014 and serve to determine whether the existence and treatment of a liability affects whether an estate qualifies as an exempt excepted estate.

A liability will not be deductible if it is incurred by the deceased to acquire excluded property or property that has become excluded property. If the effect of disallowing such a deduction means that the net chargeable value is greater than the applicable nil rate band (but allowing for spouse or charity exemption) then the estate is not excepted and the personal representatives must lodge a full inheritance tax account IHT400. The personal representatives may still explain to HM Revenue and Customs why they believe the liability should be allowed.

A liability may only be deducted against the gross estate value to the extent that it is actually discharged out of the estate. Therefore, if a life policy pays into trust outside the estate and the monies are used to discharge a mortgage on an estate property, the mortgage will not be deductible from the gross estate value. If the personal representatives are aware that a particular liability will not be discharged from the estate, they must not deduct this liability to determine the net chargeable value. The personal representatives are given 6 months to lodge a full inheritance tax account on becoming aware that a liability deducted has not been discharged by the estate so that the net chargeable value is consequently greater than the available nil rate band.

4.2.1 Form IHT205 – Return of estate information

Procedure

If the estate qualifies as an excepted estate, form IHT205 (Return of estate information), is completed and forwarded, together with the application for the grant of representation, to the probate registry. All enquiries relating to tax must be made to HM Revenue and Customs; the probate registries are not involved.

When it issues the grant of representation, the registry forwards form IHT205 to HM Revenue and Customs. If HM Revenue and Customs does not call for an inheritance tax account to be completed within 35 days of the grant being issued, the personal representatives are deemed to have an automatic clearance from inheritance tax unless they failed to disclose all the facts at the time of their application to the probate registry; or property later becomes comprised in the estate, or property of which they were previously unaware comes to their attention, or a liability deducted was not discharged from estate monies rendering the estate 'unexcepted'. In that situation, the personal representatives have 6 months within which to file an account with HM Revenue and Customs.

Completing the form

Form IHT205 is the form used in the majority of estates, and the version to use depends on the date of death. The notes contained in form IHT206 are extremely useful when filling in the form.

The deceased's personal details are to be inserted in section 1. Boxes 1.1 to 1.3 are for details of the deceased's title and full name, and 1.4 is for the date of death. In box 1.5 a tick should be placed to indicate the deceased's marital status, and in box 1.6 the deceased's occupation. Box 1.7 is for the deceased's National Insurance number.

Questions 2 to 5 relate to the excepted estate rules. They act to confirm that form IHT205 is indeed the appropriate form, rather than the full IHT400. If the answer 'yes' is ticked to any box (and the relevant amounts are over the threshold listed on the form), the estate is not excepted and IHT400 must be filled in instead. Questions 2 and 3 relate to gifts made by the deceased. Question 4 relates to his interest in a trust, and question 5 to property held in a foreign country.

Question 6 deals with life insurance policies. In the following circumstances the answer to the question is 'no':

(a) if the policy was not held in trust, but the premiums were covered by the exemption for regular gifts out of income and an annuity was not purchased; or

(b) if the policy was held in trust, was put into trust more than 7 years ago, the premiums were covered by the regular gifts out of income exception and an annuity was not purchased.

If the above circumstances apply but the premium was not covered by the exemption, the answer must be 'yes' and the premiums must be treated as gifts and entered in the response to question 2.

If an annuity was purchased at any time, or the above circumstances do not apply, form IHT400 must be completed instead. The reason the purchase of an annuity is relevant, is to discover whether the deceased purchased a 'back to back' policy (see para 4.4.3).

Questions 7 and 8 relate to the deceased's pension arrangements. If the deceased only had a state pension answer 'no' to question 7 and ignore question 8.

Question 8 asks whether the deceased changed or disposed of any pension benefits in the last 2 years of life, bar any pensions paid to the spouse or civil partner. HMRC guidance confirms that you can answer 'no' to this questions if the deceased was drawing their retirement pension in full and had made no changes to their pension arrangements in the 2 years before death.

A person disposes of their pension benefits if they arrange to place their death benefits in trust or allocate all or a proportion of their benefits to another person. If a disposal is made outside the 2 year period but when the deceased had been diagnosed with a terminal illness or where they were deemed 'uninsurable' due to poor health, you must also answer 'yes' to question 8 and complete form IHT400 instead.

A person makes a change to their pension benefits if they make additional contributions to a pension scheme; transfer benefits from one pension scheme to another; fail to take their pension on attaining pension age; fail to request ill-health retirement where they meet the requirements; opting for income drawdown or changing such an arrangement; or opting for phased retirement or changing such an arrangement. Again, where the answer to question 8 is 'yes' stop filling in form IHT205 and complete IHT400 instead.

If pension payments continue after the deceased's death, as a result of a guarantee period, unless the payments are to be made to a surviving spouse or civil partner, the person completing the form must work out the value of those guaranteed payments for inheritance tax purposes. It is not a matter of straightforward addition. Firstly, the value of all the payments due to be received in the future must be calculated. The HM Revenue and Customs website contains a calculator at www.hmrc.gov.uk/cto/forms/g_annuity.pdf which allows the taxable value of the annuity to be worked out. Otherwise, guidance in IHT206 directs the personal representatives to calculate the value of the future payments and deduct 25 per cent; the value of the remaining lump sum is the figure to be entered in box 11.11.

Any lump sum payable to the deceased's estate, whether it arises:

- as of right;
- because no one else qualifies for the payment;
- because the deceased could have made a binding direction as to who the lump sum should be paid to, but failed to do so, or could create a situation (by revoking a nomination, for example) in which the benefits would be paid to the estate;
- because the lump sum is a refund of contributions,

will form part of the deceased's estate. The amount of the lump sum should be entered in box 11.11. Payments made at the discretion of trustees of the pension scheme, even if they are made to the estate, are not relevant to this question as they do not form part of the deceased's taxable estate. However, in this situation the name of the pension scheme and the reason why the personal representatives do not consider it to form part of the estate should be given in box 13.

Box 9.1 relates back to question 2 and asks for details of the gifts made by the deceased in the 7 years prior to death. In addition, the following information should be given:

- the date of the gift;
- the recipient;
- the nature of the asset gifted;
- its value;

- how any exemptions that have been deducted have been calculated. (The only exemptions that can be deducted in this box are the small gifts exemption, annual gifts exemption, exemption for gifts made on marriage or civil partnership and the exemption for gifts made out of income. However, remember that if the gifts out of income total more than £3,000 in any one year they will be treated as chargeable gifts and should be entered as such in box 9.1. If they exceed £3,000 and the personal representatives wish to claim the exemption for gifts out of income (presumably because, when aggregated with other gifts, they exceed the £150,000 excepted estates limit for gifts) the personal representatives will need to complete form IHT400.)

The spouse or charity exemption should not be claimed in this box, but instead in box 14.

Joint assets passing by survivorship should be inserted in box 9.2, with a description of the assets (including the address of any property) and their whole value, before the deceased's share is entered in the box for the value. Any spouse/civil partner exemption should again be claimed at box 14.

Box 9.3 relates back to the trust assets mentioned at question 4. Either the gross value of the trust, or its net value if there were debts to be deducted, can be entered. The name of the settlor and the date of the creation of the trust should also be inserted.

Box 9.4 is intended to cover nominated assets, such as National Savings investments and bank accounts (see para 1.9.4).

Box 9.5 relates to question 5 and any foreign assets held by the deceased. Values not in sterling must be calculated at an appropriate rate for the date of death, generally to be found in a newspaper. Assets in the Channel Islands or the Isle of Man qualify as foreign assets for these purposes.

The total of the answers to question 9 is inserted in box A.

Question 10 deals with any debts payable from the assets listed in question 9. Question 10.1 relates to jointly held mortgages over jointly owned assets (entered at box 9.2) and 10.2 relates to other debts over these assets, not secured by way of mortgage. A jointly owned mortgage protection policy is still an asset of the deceased, and his part share should be shown in box 9.2, before the debt is deducted in box 10.1.

Question 10.3 deals with debts payable from the assets of any trust that was declared at box 9.3. If the trustees of the trust have only supplied the personal representatives with a net value for the trust, they should leave box 10.3 blank and insert the net value in box 9.3.

Box 10.4 is intended to cover debts payable to creditors who are not in the United Kingdom. The total of boxes 10.1 to 10.4 is inserted in box B. Box B is then subtracted from box A and a net figure is inserted in box C.

Question 11 deals with listing the assets that were in the deceased's sole name, or held by him as tenant in common with a third party. If the assets were held as tenants in common, this must be specified in box 13. If a deed of variation has been executed so as to redirect assets away from the deceased's estate, this must be ignored and the value of those assets must still be included on form IHT205. The relevant figures must be included in boxes 11.1 to 11.11, and the figures totalled in box D.

Question 12 deals with all the different types of debt that the deceased could have left. Funeral expenses are included in box 12.1. Debts secured against assets in the deceased's sole name or those held as tenants in common are inserted in box 12.2. Unsecured debts are inserted in box 12.3. The debts are totalled in box E.

Box D, less box E, gives the net estate in the United Kingdom which passes under the grant and is inserted in box F.

Boxes C and F are added together to give the entire net estate (worldwide, whether passing under the grant or otherwise) and the total figure is inserted in box G. Boxes A and D are added together to give the gross value of the worldwide estate (whether a grant is required for those assets or not) and the total is inserted in box H.

Box 13 is left available to insert any further information that may be relevant, or as an 'overspill' box in relation to the answers to any of the previous questions.

Box 14 is used to describe any exemptions that have been deducted, such as the spouse, civil partner or charity exemptions. The different exemptions must be listed. Charitable legacies should be listed individually, but if there are several and there is not enough space in the box, smaller legacies can be sub-totalled, and only legacies over £25,000 specified. The total exemptions are inserted in box J. Box G (net estate), less box J (exemptions), gives the figure for box K, which is the net value of the estate. This must be a figure less than the nil rate band in force at the date of death (or two nil rate bands if the transfer of a previous nil rate band can be claimed, bearing in mind the restrictions discussed previously), or the estate is not excepted and a full form IHT400 must be completed.

The personal representatives must tick one of the three boxes to confirm why the estate is excepted then sign and enter their full names and addresses in the relevant boxes on the final page.

4.2.2 Form IHT217 – Claim to transfer unused nil rate band for excepted estates

This is the form that is used to 'roll over' the unused nil rate band of a previously deceased spouse/civil partner (the 'first deceased'), onto the surviving spouse/civil partner who is now deceased (the 'second deceased') and for whom the inheritance tax return is currently being completed. As will be seen below, this form can only be used in the simplest of situations in that 100 per cent of the unused nil rate band must be available to be transferred and where the estate of the second deceased falls within two nil rate bands. Other than that, forms IHT400 and IHT402 must be completed in order to claim the transfer of the first deceased's nil rate band to the second deceased's taxable estate.

The deceased's full name and date of death should be inserted in the top right hand corner of the form.

Questions 1 to 3 require the first deceased's personal details, being their name, address and date of death. Question 4 asks whether a grant was taken out to the estate of the first deceased, and if so the date upon which it was taken out and where it was extracted. This information should be available by undertaking a search at the Probate Registry if not already known. For the procedure, see para 27.1.

The date of the marriage or civil partnership is inserted at question 5, and the venue where it took place in box 6. These details should be available from the marriage certificate if not already known.

Questions 7 to 13 relate to the estate of the first deceased. Question 7 ascertains whether the first deceased was domiciled in the United Kingdom when he died. If he was not, the answer 'no' should be ticked but the form 217 cannot be completed in that instance. Instead, forms IHT400 and IHT402 must be completed.

Question 8 asks whether the estate of the first deceased was wholly exempt from the charge to inheritance tax. This would mean that the entire estate would have passed to a surviving spouse, civil partner or charity. If there was a legacy of even, say £1,000 which was left to a chargeable beneficiary, even if this was within the first deceased's nil rate band, the answer to this question must be 'no' and forms IHT400 and IHT402 must be completed.

Question 9 is based on the same theme but relates to jointly owned assets passing by survivorship on the death of the first deceased. Again, if jointly owned assets passed to anyone other than the second deceased, forms IHT400 and IHT402 must be completed.

Question 10 deals with gifts made by the first deceased in the 7 years before they died. If gifts were made which were not exempt from the charge to inheritance tax (in other words, they utilised part of the first deceased's available inheritance tax nil rate band), or even though they were exempt, they were made out of income and exceeded £3,000 in any one year, the answer 'yes' must be given and forms IHT400 and IHT402 must be completed.

Question 11 relates to business property relief and agricultural property relief. If this was deducted from any assets in the estate of the first deceased, or from any gifts made in the 7 years before he died, form IHT217 is not applicable and forms IHT400 and IHT402 must be completed instead.

Question 12 relates to gifts with reservation of benefit. If any were made by the first deceased to anyone other than his spouse or civil partner then, as previously, forms IHT400 and IHT402 should be completed instead of form IHT217.

Finally, question 13 asks whether the first deceased was a beneficiary of a trust during their lifetime. The question does not differentiate between the different types of trust available, so it could be assumed that if the first deceased was a beneficiary of any type of trust (including a discretionary trust), form IHT217 would no longer be applicable and, instead, forms IHT400 and IHT402 should be completed.

Box 14 asks for confirmation of the nil rate band in force at the date of death of the second deceased. This is then doubled and inserted in box 15. Lastly, the net values of the second deceased's taxable estate (to be taken from box K of form IHT205) is inserted in box 16. However, if this is greater than the value of the two nil rate bands combined together, again form IHT217 cannot be used to roll over the nil rate band and instead forms IHT400 and IHT402 must be completed in relation to the estate of the first deceased.

The personal representatives must then sign and date in the declaration section at the foot of page 3. The form IHT217 can then be submitted with form IHT205 in order to apply for a grant of representation.

4.3 INHERITANCE TAX FORMS

The inheritance tax forms comprise form IHT205 relating to excepted estates (see para 4.2.1), the main form – IHT400 – for estates liable to tax, in which all the figures in relation to the deceased's estate are inserted, and the schedules, in which are given details of how those figures are arrived at. There are 26 schedules in total. The forms are available from the HM Revenue and Customs stationery orderline, 0300 123 1074, and may be downloaded from the HM Revenue and Customs website, www.hmrc.gov.uk.

The manner of completing the forms may differ slightly if the deceased died domiciled in Scotland or Northern Ireland. The text below relates to persons dying domiciled in England and Wales only.

An inheritance tax form is completed to show all the assets that fall within a deceased's estate upon his death. If the assets are exempt (either automatically or because of the identity of the beneficiary to whom they will pass) or relieved from tax (see Chapter 3), they must still be shown on the form, but the exemption or relief can also be claimed. HM Revenue and Customs must be provided with the fullest information possible in order to approve or calculate the inheritance tax payable.

The full inheritance tax form should be filled in for all estates which do not fall within the criteria to complete IHT205. If in the first instance a limited grant is being applied for, in that it is intended to deal solely with certain assets, only those assets that will be subject to the grant need be shown on the form. The deceased's entire estate must, however, be taken into account when calculating the tax payable on the delivery of the form. As this requires the value of the entire estate to be ascertained, it is often simplest to complete one form covering all the assets, to avoid the risk of confusion or double counting, or of leaving assets out of the account completely.

If a deed of variation has been executed incorporating an inheritance tax election, or a deed of disclaimer executed (which requires no election) prior to completing the relevant inheritance tax form, it should be completed on the basis of the estate devolution following the deed.

This part of the chapter contains an explanation of how to fill in each element of IHT400 and the supporting schedules. As mentioned at para 2.3, the open market value must be entered on the form. Values given on the form should be rounded to the nearest pound.

4.3.1 Form IHT400 – Inheritance Tax Account

Whilst questions 1 to 6 are headed 'About the deceased', question 7 checks for Scottish domicile and question 8 to 16 are headed 'Deceased's details'; all of these questions can be completed by inserting the deceased's personal details. If inheritance tax is payable, it may be the case that the personal representatives have already obtained an inheritance tax reference (see para 4.5). If so, this should be inserted at question 3. Question 6 relates to the deceased's domicile and the relevant selection should be made between 'England & Wales', 'Northern Ireland' or 'Scotland'. If the deceased was UK domiciled at his death, form IHT400 should be completed to include details of his worldwide estate. If the deceased was not UK domiciled, the relevant country of domicile should be inserted in the final box for this question. On that basis, form IHT400 should be completed only in relation to his UK-based assets, but the value of his assets not situated in the United Kingdom must be entered at box 22 of schedule IHT401.

Question 7 relates only to a deceased domiciled in Scotland.

The deceased's marital status and date of marriage or civil partnership are dealt with in questions 8 and 9. Question 10 asks for details of all family members surviving the deceased. The number of children and grandchildren surviving should also be entered.

Question 11 asks for details of the final address that the deceased lived at. If the deceased lived in a nursing, or residential, home, at the time of his death, this is the address that should be inserted. This is so even if he continued to own his own home elsewhere. Question 12 asks for confirmation of the nature of this address. Question 13 asks for the deceased's occupation (or insert 'retired' followed by the previous occupation), question 14 for his National Insurance number and question 15 for his taxpayer reference number. Question 16 requires confirmation as to whether anyone acted on his behalf under any form of power of attorney. If one was granted, but not used, the answer to this question is 'no'. If the answer is 'yes', a copy of the power of attorney should be enclosed when submitting the return.

Questions 17 to 23 on page 3 ask for details of the personal representatives, or the solicitor acting on their behalf if appropriate. Note question 23, which deals with the question of to whom refunds for overpaid inheritance tax should be sent. Either a cheque would be made payable to the firm of solicitors dealing with the estate, or alternatively a name to put on the cheque should be stipulated.

Question 24 on page 3 asks whether the deceased made a will and codicils. If so, copies should be enclosed with the form, as should any instrument of variation that has been executed prior to completion of the form. Draft variations that have not yet been executed should not be attached as they are not enforceable at that point.

Question 25 on page 3 asks whether the address on the last will or codicil is the same as that given in box 11 as the deceased's final address. If not, question 26 on page 3 should be answered to confirm what happened to that property.

Questions 27 and 28 on page 4 seek to confirm whether any assets that the deceased owned when he made his will and codicils were still in his ownership at his death. It is a useful way for HM Revenue and Customs to establish whether the deceased made any gifts prior to his death. If any items that were specifically listed in the will or codicils will not be shown on the form because the deceased disposed of them, details of that disposal must be given at question 28.

Questions 29 to 48 on pages 5 and 6 are a series of questions offering 'yes' or 'no' answers. If the 'yes' box is ticked in reply to any question, the relevant schedule must be completed before the rest of form IHT400 is filled in.

Questions 49 and 50 on page 7 relate to jointly owned assets in the United Kingdom. If assets were jointly owned, they will be detailed on form IHT404 and the relevant figures carried forward to either box 49 (for joint tenants/tenants in common) or box 50 (for joint tenants/tenants in common).

Questions 51 to 76 on pages 7 and 8 relate to assets owned solely by the deceased. The form can be seen to split into two columns – A and B. Column A contains details of assets upon which the inheritance tax due may not be paid by instalments – column B has details of assets upon which it may. For a further discussion regarding instalment option property, see para 3.19.1. There is no choice as to which column to enter the figures in – each class of assets is listed only under one column or the other.

Box 51 (deceased's residence) should be completed to show the value of the deceased's home, even if he resided in a nursing home at the time of his death, unless the home falls within certain categories. Thus, if it was rented by the deceased to a third party, its value should be inserted in box 70 (other land, buildings and rights over land), together with any other property that was actually available to rent at the deceased's death. If the deceased owned any farm land, buildings or a farmhouse (including his home if it falls into this category), the value of that land and buildings should be given in box 68 (farms, farmhouses and farmland). Any timber or woodland not part of a farm should be given separately in box 69 (timber and woodland).

Generally, a professional valuation of any land or buildings should be prepared. If this is not possible or is deemed unnecessary (e.g. if the spouse exemption applies), a value can be ascertained by looking in local papers or visiting estate agents who have similar properties for sale. Factors that differentiate the deceased's land or buildings from any other, such as a particularly good or bad condition, or a better location, must be borne in mind. Since the value submitted becomes the beneficiary's base cost for capital gains tax purposes, it should be as accurate as possible.

All bank and building society accounts (including National Savings cash accounts) should be detailed on form IHT406 and totalled in box 52 (bank and building society accounts).

Box 53, 'cash', must show the total of:

- cash found on the deceased when the deceased died;
- cash held in safes and safety deposit boxes;
- cash held on account at a stockbroker;
- traveller's cheques; and
- uncashed cheques made out in favour of the deceased.

Cash held in a foreign currency (but which is not a foreign asset as it is not held abroad) should be converted to sterling using the 'pound spot forward against the pound' table published in the *Financial Times* the day after the date of death; this contains the figures relevant to the date of death. If the date of death was not a trading date, the table published the preceding or subsequent day, whichever is the more favourable, may be used. If the currency in question is not shown in that table, the figures from the *Financial Times Guide to World Currencies*, published every Monday, should be used.

All the deceased's National Savings investments (including premium bonds and cash accounts) must be listed on form IHT406 in box 5 and their total value inserted into box 54 (Premium Bonds & National Savings and Investment products).

The total value of the deceased's chattels as shown in box 6 of form IHT407 is carried to box 55 of the main form IHT400.

If payments under an annuity or a pension scheme continue to be made after the deceased's death, they should be shown in box 7 on form IHT409 if they are continuing income payments or box 15 on form IHT409 if it is a lump sum payment (see para 4.4.9). They should be totalled and transferred to box 56 (pensions) on IHT400, together with any arrears of pension due at the date of death.

If the deceased was either a life assured, or the owner of a life assurance policy on someone else's life, the value of the life assurance policy/ies should be stated in boxes 2 and 5 respectively on form IHT410 (see para 4.4.10). Monies due under mortgage protection policies should also be included here, even though they were linked to the deceased's interest in land. They are totalled in box 6 and that figure is transferred to box 57 (life assurance and mortgage protection policies).

If any payments under private medical insurance policies were due at the date of death but unpaid, the amount should also be inserted in box 57.

The figures in boxes 49 and 51 are totalled and carried forward to box 59, as they are the instalment option assets at that point. The figures in boxes 50 and 52 to 57 are totalled and carried forward to box 58 as they are non-instalment option assets. They are then carried forward to boxes 60 and 61 on page 8.

Box 62 (UK government and municipal securities) contains the total from box 1 on form IHT411 whilst box 63 (listed stocks, shares and investments that did not give the deceased control of the company) should show the total from box 2 on form IHT411 (see para 4.4.11). Box 65 (traded unlisted and unlisted shares except control holdings) is to be filled in to show the total value of shares shown in boxes 1 and 2 on form IHT412; and 67 (control holdings of unlisted, traded unlisted and listed shares), the total in boxes 3, 4 and 5 of that form. Outstanding dividends on all these assets are shown in box 64. There is also box 66 which can hold the value of traded unlisted and unlisted shares that were not a control holding in the company but where the personal representatives believe the value of the shares should qualify for the payment of inheritance tax by instalments in any event (as it would normally not qualify). The instalment option is only awarded in extreme circumstances where:

- payment of the tax in one lump sum would cause undue hardship; or
- at least 20 per cent of the tax upon which the same person, in the same capacity, is liable to pay, may be paid by instalments; or
- the value of the shares is at least £20,000 and represents at least 10 per cent of the company's nominal share capital or (if they are ordinary shares), the company's ordinary share capital.

The value of shares in a company quoted on the London Stock Exchange, which gave the deceased control of that company (more than 50 per cent of the shares), should be inserted in box 67, together with shares in companies that were unlisted or traded and unlisted but which gave the deceased control of the company. More detail in relation to these holdings must be given in form IHT412.

As mentioned above, the value of any farm, farmhouse or farmland should be inserted at box 68 after being detailed on forms IHT414 and IHT405. The value of the business itself, including any business assets and timber should be inserted at box 69. All other land, buildings and rights over land such as derelict buildings, lock-ups, redundant and unused land, quarries and mines, airfields and rights over land, such as mineral rights or fishing rights, should be listed on form IHT405 and inserted in box 70.

Box 69 is intended to cover the total value of all businesses in which the deceased had an interest as sole trader or partner and the assets used within them. If the deceased was a Lloyd's name, the value of his cash, shares and other assets used in his participation should be included here. Shares held as security by him at Lloyd's should be valued and entered on a form IHT411, separately from other shareholdings, but their total value should not be given in this schedule (to indicate that the total is not carried forward to boxes 62 to 67 of IHT400). If the deceased was party to more than one business, each should be described on a separate schedule IHT411, IHT412 or IHT413, as appropriate.

To ascertain the values required in relation to business assets, either the last set of accounts can be used (providing they are still accurate), or accounts should be prepared to the date of death.

If the deceased was a beneficiary under a third party's estate, any benefit he was due to receive from the estate, but had not received at the date of death, is to be shown in form IHT415 (see para 4.4.15) and carried to box 71 or box 72 (interest in another estate) as directed on that form.

A separate form IHT416 must be completed in respect of each debt due to the deceased. The total value of all loans made by the deceased should be inserted into box 73 (debts due to the estate). These include a director's loan account or other current account due to the deceased from any business or company in which he was concerned.

Any repayment of income tax or capital gains tax due from HM Revenue and Customs to the deceased should be included at box 74 (income tax or capital gains tax repayment).

Box 75 (trust income due to the deceased) which includes accrued and apportioned income relates to settled property of which the deceased was the life tenant. If income had been received by the trustees but not paid over to the deceased at the date of death (accrued income) or if it was due to the trustees (and therefore the deceased) at death, but not paid to them at that time (apportioned income) it should be inserted here.

Any other assets not falling within any of the above classes, but which were held in the deceased's sole name in the United Kingdom, should be detailed in the 'additional information' boxes on page 16 of the form and their value inserted in box 76 (other assets and income due to the deceased). If the deceased was landlord of any property, any rent outstanding and due to him at death must be inserted here.

All the figures are then added and inserted in boxes 77 and 78, depending on whether the assets are instalment or non-instalment option assets. These are then added together to give the gross value of the estate in box 79.

Questions 80 to 91 on pages 9 and 10 are concerned with the deceased's liabilities. Question 80 relates to mortgages and other debts secured on land or on the deceased's business – basically, any asset that he had in his sole name and which is instalment option property. The name of the creditor, description of the debt together with the property upon which it is secured and its value are given in the box. If the mortgage was secured on a property which was used partly for business and partly not, it should be apportioned in the same proportions as the division of the value between the non-business and business property. The debts are then totalled at the bottom of the box.

Question 81 asks for details of the funeral and reasonable mourning expenses of the close family and the cost of a headstone or tombstone. Again, the box is totalled at the bottom.

Question 82 then requires details of all the other liabilities of the deceased. These must be the liabilities which had been incurred by the deceased at the date of death, not those arising as a result of the death. For example, the date of a fee note for work carried out does not matter – as long as the work was undertaken prior to death and the fee is unpaid, the liability should be included in the total at this point. Thus, an accountant's outstanding charges for completing a tax return are deductible if the accountant completed the work before death. Fees for completing the final tax return to the date of death are not deductible if there is an income tax or capital gains tax bill to pay, but if the return results in a repayment of tax, the fees are a deductible debt but the repayment must of course be shown as an asset of the deceased at box 74. This applies notwithstanding the fact that the deceased would, had he lived, have paid an accountant to prepare a tax return for that period in any event no matter what the outcome.

If loans and overdrafts, or debts due to friends and relatives, are to be included at Question 82, they must also be listed on form IHT419 (see para 4.4.19).

Uncleared cheques can be shown as debts of the deceased but a description must be given of who the cheque was written to, and what it was for. Cheques written as gifts which had not cleared prior to death cannot be shown as debts of the estate, nor are they gifts for the purposes of inheritance tax.

Debts due to persons not based in the United Kingdom should be deducted from foreign assets on Schedule IHT417. The debts on instalment and non-instalment option property are then carried forward to boxes 83 and 84 respectively.

The debts on non-instalment assets shown in box 84 are then deducted from the value of the non-instalment assets in box 77 and the resulting figure is given in box 85. Similarly, the debts on instalment assets shown in box 83 are deducted from the value of instalment assets shown in box 78 and the resulting figure is given in box 86. If the result in either box 85 or box 86 would be a minus figure, instead insert zero and insert that minus figure in box 88 or box 87 respectively. In other words, any 'surplus' debt that cannot be satisfied by instalment option assets is moved into the non-instalment assets column, and *vice versa*. That minus figure is then deducted from either the surplus instalment or non-instalment option assets (as the case may be) and the net value of those assets following this deduction is then shown in box 89 or box 90, depending on what type of assets the surplus fell upon. If, after deducting the debts from all the UK assets, there is still a deficit (i.e. the deceased's debts in the United Kingdom were greater than his assets), the deficit may be deducted from the value of any foreign assets that he owned which will be shown in schedule IHT417. If such a deduction also results in a deficit against the value of foreign property, the net value of assets abroad may be shown as zero in that schedule.

Question 91 asks for a total net value of all the deceased's UK assets.

Questions 92 to 96 are on pages 10 and 11. Question 92 relates to any exemptions or reliefs that are being claimed against non-instalment option assets shown earlier in the form. It does not relate to assets in the deceased's joint name – only those in his sole name. Question 93 similarly relates to exemptions and reliefs that are being claimed against instalment option assets.

For the exemptions and reliefs available, see Chapter 3. Where a specific or pecuniary legacy passes to an exempt beneficiary such as a spouse, the amount of the exemption is easily ascertainable for insertion in box 92 (total exemptions and reliefs). Where the entire residue is exempt, but there are chargeable legacies, care is needed when ascertaining how much property actually qualifies for an exemption. For example, if the deceased left a legacy of £500,000 to his children and the residue of the estate to his spouse, how should the spouse exemption be apportioned between boxes 92 and 93?

Notwithstanding how the legacy is to be funded, HM Revenue and Customs guidance states that the exemption should be apportioned proportionately against instalment and non-instalment option property.

The exemptions and reliefs section in any part of the form can, at lowest, produce a zero, never a negative figure. If a negative would otherwise result, the amount of the exemption or relief is reduced; it cannot be carried to any other section of the form.

If the spouse/civil partner exemption is to be claimed, note that details of the spouse/partner's name, date and country of birth and their country of domicile must be shown. If the charity exemption is being deducted, HM Revenue and Customs wishes to see the full name of the charity, the country in which it was established and its HM Revenue and Customs charities reference if possible.

There are some other less commonly found deductions that can be made at this point:

- Estate duty assets – assets held in trust for the deceased as a result of the death of his spouse before 13 November 1974 and upon which estate duty has been paid may be deducted here providing the deceased did not have the ability to dispose of those assets during his lifetime or under his will or intestacy;
- Excluded property:

  - if the deceased was domiciled outside the United Kingdom and not resident or ordinarily resident in the United Kingdom when he died, cash held in a foreign currency account in a UK high street bank or certain foreign banks (phone the HM Revenue and Customs helpline on 0845 30 20 900 to check whether the bank qualifies for this exclusion) may be excluded property. The sterling value of the cash should be shown at box 52 but then deducted in box 92;
  - if the deceased was not ordinarily resident in the United Kingdom when he died, all UK government securities issued after 29 April 1966 are excluded property. They should be shown in box 62 and their value deducted in box 92;
  - if any trust assets are excluded property, any accrued income shown in box 75 is not excluded property, but any apportioned income shown in the same box will be excluded and should be deducted here.

If business or agricultural property relief is being deducted in either of these boxes, form IHT413 or form IHT414, respectively, must also be completed.

The exemptions and reliefs are then deducted from the non-instalment and instalment option assets at boxes 94 and 95 respectively, and the total net value of the estate is shown on box 96.

Questions 97 to 108 on page 11 ask for details of any other assets not previously shown that need to be taken into account to calculate the overall inheritance tax due. The value of foreign assets shown in boxes 5 and 10 of form IHT417 are entered in boxes 97 and 98 respectively.

The value of assets held in trust and given in boxes 12 and 17 of form IHT418 are entered in boxes 99 and 100 respectively.

Nominated assets are included at box 101. As mentioned in para 1.9.4, assets capable of nomination are largely National Savings products and some building society accounts. These should be detailed in the additional information section on page 15 of the form and any exemptions claimed at the same time, before their value is carried forward to box 101. Their value must not be included when totalling the assets to be copied to form IHT421, as they do not pass under the deceased's will or intestacy.

Boxes 98, 100 and 101 (as non-instalment option assets) are totalled at box 102, and boxes 97 and 99 (as instalment option assets) are totalled at box 103.

Box 104 contains the figure of gifts with reservation of benefit and pre-owned assets that is included in box 17 of form IHT403; box 105 contains the figure for the value of trust assets upon which the trustees are not paying inheritance tax upon delivery of the account which is carried forward from box 18 of form IHT418. If the deceased died in the period 6 April 2006 and 5 April 2007, include the sum of the ASP funds contained in boxes 32 and 42 in box 106. The total value of all these additional assets is then given in box 107. Boxes 96 and 107 are added together to produce the total value of the chargeable estate, which is inserted into box 108. There is a prompt at box 108 to complete Schedules IHT435 and IHT436 if boxes 29a and 29b were ticked on page 5 confirming that a claim for the RNRB and/or a claim for a TRNRB are to be made.

Questions 109 and 110 are on page 11. If there is no tax to pay, page 12 of the form need not be completed and the person filling in the form can move straight to question 121 on page 13 of the form.

If a lay person is completing the form, he does not have to work out the inheritance tax due, but he must tell HM Revenue and Customs whether he wishes to pay the tax due on instalment option property by instalments, or whether he wishes to pay it all straightaway. Page 12 is headed 'Working out the Inheritance tax' and first asks you to tick the appropriate box signifying whether you are calculating the tax yourself or whether you wish HMRC to calculate this. Box 109 asks for confirmation as to whether the reduced rate of inheritance tax is payable and in box 110 you confirm whether or not the estate wishes to utilise the instalment option to pay any tax on instalment option property.

If the personal representatives are unsure, they should respond, 'yes', to allow them maximum flexibility. If instalment option property is later sold, however, the right to pay the inheritance tax by instalments is lost and all the tax on that property becomes payable immediately. In addition, if the personal representatives subsequently assent to a beneficiary any property upon which inheritance tax is payable in instalments, they will no longer control the property but will remain liable for the inheritance tax on it. They should therefore, before they execute the assent, obtain from the beneficiary an indemnity for any outstanding tax payable.

If the election is made to pay by instalments, the value of the assets upon which tax may be paid by instalments should also be entered here.

If the personal representatives decide to calculate the inheritance tax due, depending on the complexity of the calculations, the personal representatives may wish to use the form IHT400 calculation to calculate the liability of the estate to inheritance tax. For personal representatives acting without professional assistance, or practitioners who are less used to completing form IHT400, using the calculation sheet is strongly recommended.

Boxes 111 to 119 are on page 12. If the inheritance tax calculation is 'simple' the inheritance tax due is calculated here. The definition of a 'simple' calculation is one where:

- all the inheritance tax due is being paid within 6 months of the last day of the month in which the deceased died (i.e. no interest is payable);
- all the inheritance tax due is being paid straightaway (i.e. the instalment option is not being taken);
- the total of all lifetime gifts brought into account is below the aggregate nil rate band;
- no double taxation relief is being deducted on any foreign assets; and
- there is no deduction for successive charges relief in relation to property inherited from someone else within the last 5 years where inheritance tax was also paid on those assets within the estate of the previous deceased.

If the calculation does not qualify as 'simple', the form IHT400 calculation must be used to work out the tax due, and the personal representatives should move on to box 120. The calculation form should then be submitted with form IHT400.

At box 111 enter the result of the RNRB calculator or additional threshold calculator found at www.tax.service.gov.uk/calculate-additional-inheritance-tax-threshold. Deduct this sum from the value of the chargeable estate at box 108 to give the value of the chargeable estate after the deduction of the RNRB.

Bring forward the total value of gifts from box 7 of form IHT403 to box 113. Add this to the total value of the chargeable estate that was inserted in box 112 and insert the resulting figure in box 114. The nil rate band in force at the date of the deceased's death can be checked in the form IHT400 Rates and Tables and should then be inserted in box 115. Any nil rate band that can be transferred to the deceased's estate, as calculated on form IHT402, is inserted at box 116, and the total nil rate band is given in box 117. This nil rate band is deducted from the aggregate chargeable transfer figure given in box 114, and the resulting figure (i.e. the amount actually subject to 40 per cent inheritance tax) is shown in box 118. This amount is multiplied by 40 per cent to obtain the inheritance tax payable and this figure is shown in box 119.

Question 120 on page 13 asks whether use of the direct payment scheme is being made. This is a scheme whereby funds can be released from some of the deceased's bank or building society accounts and paid directly by the asset holding institution to HM Revenue and Customs in order to pay the inheritance tax due. It can be used to save the personal representatives from having to take out a loan to pay the inheritance tax due. If the scheme is being used, form IHT423 must be completed. Most high street banks and building societies participate in the scheme but it may be worth checking rather than making an assumption.

Question 121 on page 13 first asks the personal representatives to confirm what type of grant they will be applying for, before going on to tick the boxes relevant to show which schedules have been completed. The box opposite question 121 is extremely important. The personal representatives must insert the numbers of any boxes which give only a provisional valuation. If any provisional valuation is omitted from this box, and it later becomes evident that its value was only an estimate, HM Revenue and Customs may impose penalties upon the personal representatives for failing to disclose it (see para 3.20).

Whilst the personal representatives must sign on page 14 headed 'Declaration continued' the declarations they are making are detailed on page 13 and it is important that the personal representatives are comfortable with these to ensure they are making the declarations properly and honestly.

The Checklist section on page 15 can be used as a checklist for the personal representatives to be certain they have completed everything properly and enclosed any further information that is required.

The Additional Information section on page 16 is for the insertion of additional information as requested in the main form, or for the personal representatives to explain any items in more detail which they feel require clarification. This page of the form also gives details of the HM Revenue and Customs office to where the form should be sent, and contact details should the personal representatives have any further questions or require guidance.

4.4 SCHEDULES

Each of the schedules has space in the top right hand corner for insertion of the deceased's name, date of death and the inheritance tax reference number (if known).

4.4.1 Schedule IHT401 – Domicile outside the United Kingdom

As has already been mentioned, a person cannot be domiciled in the United Kingdom as such, but only in one of the three UK domicile 'jurisdictions' – England and Wales, Scotland or Northern Ireland. The Channel Islands and the Isle of Man do not fall within England and Wales for domicile purposes – they are separate jurisdictions outside the United Kingdom.

If the domicile was outside England and Wales, Scotland or Northern Ireland, form IHT401 must be filled in. 'Domicile' is a nebulous concept. In the United Kingdom, there is a distinction between 'residence', 'ordinary residence' and 'domicile'. In other countries, this distinction is not always made.

Under UK law, a person always has a domicile, but the concept of domicile is not defined anywhere. At birth, a person acquires his father's domicile as his domicile of origin, unless his father and mother were unmarried or do not live together, in which case he takes on his mother's domicile. Once a person is aged over 16, he can lose his domicile of origin and acquire a domicile of choice at any time. Very broadly, this is achieved by displaying a permanent intention to reside in a particular country for the rest of one's days. A person's country of domicile is often understood as the country in which he 'intends to die'. In the case of *Cyganik v Agulian* [2006] EWCA Civ 129, [2006] WTLR 565, the Court of Appeal relied heavily on the decision in *In the Estate of Fuld Deceased (No 3)* [1968] P 675, that the domicile of origin is more enduring than the domicile of choice. The decision to abandon one's domicile of origin should be clear and unequivocal. However, the contrary view was found in *Holliday v Musa* [2010] EWCA Civ 335, [2010] FCR 280, another case involving a Cypriot living in this country; the Court of Appeal held, in an Inheritance Act claim, that where someone had clearly set up his home for a very long time in a country, had had a family there and did not have a home elsewhere, that would provide a strong starting point as to one's domicile. For many years the deceased's permanent home had been in the United Kingdom and that continued after the death of his wife and once he began his relationship with the first claimant. If he had formed an intention to return to Cyprus at some stage it was for many years a vague intention to retire there. By the time of his death, even that intention would seem to have disappeared. The indications were that he had made up his mind, consistent with his permanent home being in the United Kingdom, that it was where he wished to end his days and be buried. There were strong indications that having had a home with his first family in the United Kingdom, he had wished to set up a family home with the first claimant in the United Kingdom. He bought a house for them to live in. He had acquired a domicile of choice in this country.

The decisions in *Cyganik* and *Holliday* were considered in *Morris v Davies and others* [2011] EWHC 1773 (Ch), [2011] WTLR 1643, in which the issue arose as to whether the testator was domiciled in England or in Belgium. In order to show that the testator had acquired a domicile of choice in Belgium, there was a need to prove the combination of residence and an intention to remain permanently or indefinitely in Belgium. On the facts, it appeared that the testator would have moved wherever his job had taken him, but would not have been willing to commit to a future in Belgium. Despite spending considerable time in Belgium, he had retained property in England, as well as a UK passport and driving licence, had regarded himself as British and had stated his intention to return to England.

A woman who married before 1 January 1974 automatically acquired her husband's domicile as her 'domicile of dependence'. For marriages after that date, a wife is permitted to retain her own domicile. However, it is possible for a spouse to elect to be treated as UK domiciled for inheritance tax purposes under sections 267ZA and 267ZB of the Inheritance Tax Act 1984. This might be advantageous if, for example, the individual had a UK domiciled spouse or civil partner and wished to benefit from an unlimited spouse exemption for transfers made to the individual by his UK-domiciled spouse or civil partner.

In addition, statute defines when a person may be deemed to be domiciled in the United Kingdom. Section 267 of the Inheritance Tax Act 1984 provides that a person is deemed to be domiciled in the United Kingdom if he was:

- domiciled in the United Kingdom at any time in the 3 years before his death; or
- resident in the United Kingdom for income tax purposes for at least 17 out of the last 20 tax years before his death, ending with the year of assessment within which he died.

However, from 6 April 2017, the Finance (No 2) Act 2017 has changed the deemed domicile rules, so that any non-UK domiciled person will be treated as UK domiciled for inheritance tax purposes if both of the following conditions are met:

(a) the person is resident in the United Kingdom for income tax purposes for at least 15 out of the last 20 tax years immediately preceding the tax year in which he died; and

(b) the person has been UK resident for at least one of the four tax years ending with the tax year in which he died.

This means that a non-UK-domiciled person will acquire a deemed UK domicile for inheritance tax purposes from the start of his 16th tax year of continuous UK residence. Further, the tax years prior to 6 April 2017 are taken into consideration so that a person who has been UK resident since the tax year 2002–03 will be deemed UK domiciled on 6 April 2017.

The Finance (No 2) Act 2017 has introduced a much stricter regime for non-UK-domiciled persons who were born in the United Kingdom *and* acquired UK domicile of origin at birth. Such persons will be treated as UK domiciled for inheritance tax purposes if the following two conditions are both met:

(a) they are UK resident in the tax year in which they died; and

(b) they have been UK resident for at least one of the two tax years immediately preceding the tax year in which they died.

This means that from 6 April 2017, a formerly UK-domiciled person will acquire a deemed UK domicile for inheritance tax purposes from the start of his second tax year of continuous UK residence.

The concept of domicile is important in UK inheritance tax law, as it governs what assets in a person's estate may be subject to inheritance tax in the United Kingdom. If a person is, or is deemed to be, domiciled in the United Kingdom, his entire worldwide estate may be subject to UK inheritance tax. If he is domiciled abroad, only his assets situated in the United Kingdom may be subject to UK inheritance tax (see *Allen v Revenue and Customs Commissioners* [2005] STC (SCD) 614). There is a possibility that the deceased's assets may be subject to inheritance tax in more than one country. Provisions are in place to relieve the burden of this double taxation. For more detail, see Chapter 3.

If a foreign domicile is to be claimed, the answer 'no' must be given to question 1 on the form. If the answer is 'yes', the deceased will be deemed to be domiciled in the United Kingdom for inheritance tax purposes, and inheritance tax must be paid in the United Kingdom on his worldwide estate.

Question 2 asks whether domicile has been agreed with HM Revenue and Customs for other purposes (e.g. for income tax purposes). If so, details of that agreement should be given in questions 3, 4 and 5.

Question 6 deals with the concept of deemed domicile being imputed from the deceased's residence in the United Kingdom for income tax purposes. Details of when the deceased was resident in the United Kingdom in the 4 tax years prior to his death should be inserted in the table.

Questions 7 to 18 require a brief life history of the deceased, and of her husband if she was a woman who married before 1 January 1974 (because of the domicile of dependence rules outlined above). Information to be included in the answers to these questions includes:

- the deceased's nationality at birth and death;
- where he was born;
- his educational and employment history;
- the date he left the United Kingdom and moved abroad;
- the date upon which he returned to the United Kingdom, how long he stayed in the United Kingdom and the purpose of his stay;
- the reason the deceased did not intend to remain in or return to the United Kingdom at his death.

Question 19 asks 'Who will benefit from the deceased's estate under the law that applies in the country of domicile?', eliciting whether the deceased's will or the rules of intestacy apply to his foreign estate, or whether any rules of forced heirship govern the estate distribution. If the will applies, a copy should be sent to HM Revenue and Customs.

Question 20 asks whether the surviving spouse or civil partnership exemption applies to any part of the deceased's estate, and if so what assets it will apply to. Question 21 asks for general clarification regarding the distribution of the deceased's estate. If advice has been obtained in a foreign jurisdiction regarding the devolution of the estate, it should be attached here.

If the deceased was domiciled abroad, it is almost certain that he will have left assets in another country. The rest of his worldwide estate should be totalled and inserted in answer to question 22 ('Did the deceased leave any assets of any description outside the UK? Give their approximate value').

Question 23 requests clarification as to whether any form of double taxation relief is expected.

If the answer to question 24 ('Is any foreign tax to be paid on assets in the UK as a result of the deceased's death?') is 'yes', evidence of the tax paid should be sent to HM Revenue and Customs as soon as possible in order to claim any relevant reliefs.

4.4.2 Schedule IHT402 – Claim to transfer unused nil rate band

As explained above (see para 4.2.2), it is possible to transfer to the estate of a deceased who died after 9 October 2007 the unused part of any nil rate band of the deceased's spouse/civil partner who had previously passed away (no matter when he died). In order to do so when completing form IHT400, schedule IHT402 must be filled in. Note that this form must be completed within 2 years of the end of the month in which the deceased (for whom form IHT400 is now being completed) died.

Questions 1 to 3 require details of the first deceased's name, date of death and address. Question 4 asks for the date of the marriage or civil partnership, and question 5 asks where it took place. A certified copy of the marriage certificate should be lodged with this application. Question 6 asks whether the first deceased spouse or civil partner left a will, and question 7 asks for confirmation of the value of his chargeable estate passing under his will or intestacy. Question 8 asks whether a grant (or confirmation in Scotland) was obtained in relation to his estate. If so, a copy of it should be attached, and if not his death certificate should instead be enclosed.

Question 9 asks for confirmation of the amount of the nil rate band in force when he died (see IHT400 Rates and Tables on the HM Revenue and Customs website for confirmation if this is not known).

Question 10 asks for details of all gifts made in the 7 years before he died in order to ascertain how much of the nil rate band was eaten into, and therefore how much is left to set against chargeable gifts made upon death (question 11).

Questions 12 to 16 seek to ascertain the assets passing under the estate of the first deceased which ate into his available nil rate band. Question 12 asks for details of the gifts made upon death which were not to his spouse (who has now died), question 13 requires details of assets held as joint tenants and which passed to someone other than the now deceased spouse, and question 14 asks for the value of any trusts of which they were the life tenants and where the assets passed to someone other than the spouse of the first deceased.

Finally, question 15 asks for the value of any gifts with reservation of benefit made by the first deceased (note that by definition a gift to a spouse cannot be a gift with reservation of benefit). The total of all these sums is inserted in box 16 and this utilises the first part of the nil rate band of the first spouse to die.

Exemptions and reliefs can still be set against these gifts (e.g. the charity exemption on a legacy to charity), and these figures should be shown net of their deduction, but the exemptions and reliefs themselves must be listed in box 21 so that HM Revenue and Customs has the opportunity to raise any query it might wish in relation to their application.

Box 17 then shows the nil rate band of the first spouse to die that is available for transfer to the now deceased spouse.

This is not the value that is transferred over to the now deceased spouse – he receives a percentage value of the current nil rate band, not an absolute figure from the estate of the first spouse to die (in order to take account of the fact that the nil rate band increases over time). So the figure in box 17 (the amount of the nil rate band available for transfer) is divided by the figure in box 9 (the total nil rate band in force when the first spouse died) and then multiplied by 100 so that it can be expressed as a percentage to four decimal places in response to question 18. Question 19 asks for confirmation of the value of the nil rate band in force at the point of the current deceased spouse's death. This is then multiplied by the percentage ascertained in box 18, to give the amount of the nil rate band now available to be added to the current deceased spouse's estate at box 20.

Question 22 is only relevant if the first spouse to die died between 6 April 2006 and 5 April 2011. In that situation, it asks whether the first spouse to die was in receipt of an ASP or a pension or annuity from which unauthorised payments were made. If in doubt, ask the company that provided the pension of the first spouse to die. If he was in receipt of either simply tick 'yes'. This will affect the value of the nil rate band to be rolled over, but HM Revenue and Customs will perform the necessary calculations once it has seen form IHT400 now being submitted.

Question 23 is relevant only where the first spouse to die was domiciled in Scotland. It asks whether there was anyone entitled to claim the 'legitim' fund. This is a portion of the first deceased spouse's movable estate which legally can be claimed by his children. If the children claimed their legitim fund, that will eat into the first deceased spouse's available inheritance tax nil rate band (as it is a gift to the children). Incidentally, if the children decide not to claim their legitim fund, that may be treated as a gift by them for inheritance tax purposes. At this point, all HM Revenue and Customs wishes to know is whether there was anyone entitled to claim the legitim fund – any impact upon the nil rate band available for transfer can be calculated later once HM Revenue and Customs has greater detail of the circumstances of the case.

4.4.3 Schedule IHT403 – Gifts and other transfers of value

Form IHT403 deals only with gifts made since 18 March 1986. 'Gift' here is a generic term for an LCT or a PET. Questions 1 to 5 seek to ascertain why the form is being filled in – was it because the deceased made gifts or transfers; created a trust or settlement; added funds to an existing trust or settlement; paid the premiums on any life assurance policy for the benefit of someone other than the deceased himself or his spouse or civil partner; or ceased to benefit from any assets held in a trust or a settlement, within 7 years before the deceased's death. If the 'yes' box is ticked, further information should be given in the table on the form. Question 6 asks whether any gifts are being claimed as exempt because they were made from the deceased's income and if so details should be given later in this form.

PETs that are exempt from the charge to inheritance tax, and which as a result do not need to be declared in the table, are transfers:

- of any asset, made to the deceased's spouse or civil partner, if he was domiciled in the United Kingdom (section 18 of the Inheritance Tax Act 1984);
- outright to any individual, providing that the total value of gifts made in any one year (in aggregate, not per recipient) is less than £3,000 (section 19). In addition, if the deceased did not fully use this £3,000 annual allowance in any year, the unused portion of the allowance can be carried forward to the next year;
- of quoted shares or cash, made outright to any individual, in any one year, totalling less than £250 per recipient (section 20);
- unconditionally, made to an individual, out of the deceased's income, as part of his normal expenditure, and which left the deceased with sufficient income to maintain his usual standard of living (section 21). A good example is the payment by the deceased of the premiums under a life assurance policy which was written into trust for a third party. If the gifts made were in excess of £3,000 per annum, the gifts must be detailed and the exemption claimed. Gifts of less than £3,000 per annum do not need to be shown unless the annual £3,000 allowance mentioned in the second bullet point above was already allocated to a different gift.

For more detail on each of these exemptions, see Chapter 3. The last two are not available to offset against PETs made by virtue of the deceased's ceasing to have any right or interest under a settlement.

If any gifts made do not fall within the above criteria, this does not necessarily mean that inheritance tax is chargeable on them; they should be listed in the table and any exemption claimed. For example, if the deceased gave cash of £2,000 to his granddaughter in year 1, and cash of £4,000 to his daughter in year 2, the gift to the granddaughter would not have to be shown in the table because it was below the annual £3,000 exemption. But the annual exemption would be deducted from the gift, so the total value given away would be reduced to nil. In addition, the gift to the daughter should be shown because it was over £3,000. Initially, the exemption left over from the previous year (£1,000) would be deducted from the value of the gift, then the annual exemption for year 2. Again, the total value gifted in year 2 would be reduced to nil.

The annual small gifts exemption of £250 cannot be combined with the annual exemption, to reduce the value of a gift of £3,250 to nil. It can be utilised only if all the gifts made to a particular person in any one year totalled less than £250.

If the exemption for a regular gift out of income is to be claimed, the personal representatives must also fill in page 6 of the form (see below). If the exemption is being claimed in relation to the premiums that have been paid on a life insurance policy and the policy pays out to someone other than the deceased's spouse or civil partner, a copy of the life insurance document, trust, and any other related documents must be provided. In addition, where the deceased also purchased an annuity at the same time as taking out the life insurance policy – often known as a 'back to back' arrangement – HM Revenue and Customs may seek to limit the exemption for normal gifts out of income. Full documentation in relation to the annuity must be provided at the same time.

If the personal representatives are unsure whether a gift qualifies for a certain exemption, they should declare it on the form, claim the exemption and wait and see what questions are raised by HM Revenue and Customs.

In this context, a 'gift' comprises not only a transfer of an asset from one person to another, but also any transaction that reduces the value of the deceased's estate (section 3 of the Inheritance Tax Act 1984). Thus it includes, for example:

- a sale at an undervalue;
- a grant of a lease at less than a full market rent; and
- the rearrangement of rights attaching to shares in a company which results in a reduction in the value of the deceased's shares.

If the deceased ceased to have a right under a trust before his death, this would also have reduced the value of his estate. The gift must be declared as made by him, even though it may have been the trustees of the trust who decided to remove his rights under it, the deceased having had no control over the decision. If this is the case, the annual exemption and that relating to gifts upon marriage cannot be offset against the value of the gift unless the deceased, within 6 months of the date of it, gave notice to the trustees that the exemption was available.

The value of any gift is always taken at the date upon which it is made and this is the value for inheritance tax purposes. Section 131 of the Inheritance Tax Act 1984 allows the personal representatives to substitute a lower value for the gift than the original value in the following limited circumstances:

- inheritance tax becomes payable on the gift upon the deceased's death (i.e. the gift, when added to previous gifts in the 7 years before death, exceeds the nil rate band); and
- the asset transferred was retained by the donee or his spouse at the date of the deceased's death; or
- the asset transferred was sold in an arm's length transaction by the transferee or his spouse before the deceased's death.

Where the asset transferred was retained by the donee or his spouse at the date of the deceased's death, the value to be substituted is that at the date of death. If the third situation applies – the asset transferred was sold in an arm's length transaction by the transferee or his spouse before the deceased's death – the substituted value is the gross sale proceeds. The new value should be entered in column A at Question 7 and should be used to calculate the value of the gift made. In the description of the assets given away, it should be made clear that a substituted value has been used, and the value at the date of the gift given, in order that HM Revenue and Customs can consider whether the reduction claimed should be allowed.

Once the value of all the PETs and LCTs has been ascertained, that total is the first figure to be set against the nil rate band when calculating the inheritance tax payable in relation to the estate.

Questions 8 to 12 deal with gifts with reservation of benefit. These are gifts made after 18 March 1986 under which:

(a) possession and enjoyment of the property is not *bona fide* assumed by the donee at or before the beginning of the relevant period; or

(b) at any time in the relevant period the property is not enjoyed to the entire exclusion, or virtually to the entire exclusion, of the donor (section 102 of the Finance Act 1986).

For the purposes of this section, 'relevant period' is the period of 7 years ending with the date of death of the deceased, or the period between the date the gift was made and the deceased's death, if shorter. Sections 102A–C provide further clarification of the meaning of a gift with reservation when the asset gifted away is land or an interest in land. Questions 8 to 11 ask, where the deceased transferred any assets during his lifetime:

- whether the person receiving the gift did not take full possession of it;
- where the gift was of land, whether the deceased or the deceased's spouse enjoyed a significant right or interest, or was a party to a significant arrangement, in relation to the land; and
- if the gift was of any other asset, whether the deceased continued to have some right to benefit from all or part of it.

If the answer to any of these questions is 'yes' a gift with reservation of benefit has taken place and the table at question 12 must be completed, giving the details.

If the deceased ceased to take any benefit from the gift with reservation at any time during the 7 years prior to his death, it will have become a PET or LCT at that time (section 102(4) of the Finance Act 1986) and question 7 must be answered in respect of it. However, no exemption can be deducted from the value of the PET or LCT if it is made in this manner.

If the deceased gave land away and ceased to take any benefit from it, but then resumed taking a benefit, that resumption does not turn the original gift into a gift with reservation of benefit, as long as:

- the resumption resulted from a change in his circumstances, which was unforeseen when the gift was first made, and which was not brought about by the deceased to receive the benefit of the exemption; and
- the resumption occurred at a time when the deceased was unable to maintain himself through old age, infirmity or otherwise; and
- the resumption represented reasonable provision by the donee of the land for the care and maintenance of the deceased; and
- the donee was a relative of the deceased or his spouse or civil partner (paragraph 6(b) of Schedule 20 to the Finance Act 1986).

Questions 13 to 16 relate to pre-owned assets tax, which first applied in the tax year 2005–06. The legislation is complex and a complete explanation is beyond the scope of this book. In brief, however, the provisions apply where a person disposed of an asset yet continues to enjoy a benefit from that asset, but the reservation of benefit rules (listed above) do not apply. The deceased may have elected for the assets disposed of to be treated as though they continued to form part of his estate for inheritance tax purposes. The election must have been made before death, on a form IHT500 submitted before 31 January 2007. If such an election was made, the 'yes' box should be ticked in answer to question 14, and full details given in answer to question 16. Question 15 asks whether the deceased contributed to the purchase price of an asset by another person from which he received a benefit (e.g. the deceased paid £100,000 towards the £200,000 purchase price of a holiday property bought in his daughter's name, and then spent 8 weeks of the year holidaying there). Again, if the answer is 'yes', the table at question 16 must be completed.

Question 17 asks for the combined total of all gifts with reservation of benefit and pre-owned assets.

Questions 18 and 19 deal with LCTs made within 7 years of a PET identified by question 1. Those earlier LCTs reduce the value of the nil rate band available to the PET when calculating the inheritance tax payable on it. The earlier LCT is not relevant when calculating the value of the PET that must be aggregated with the deceased's nil rate band. Questions 20 to 22 were introduced as a means of proving the validity of a claim for exemption in respect of gifts made as part of normal expenditure out of income, which is in two parts. Question 20 requires the deceased's income to be broken down and calculated, either for the entire 7 years before death, or, if shorter, for as long as the gifts were given. This should be relatively straightforward, as the information can be extracted from the deceased's tax returns. Question 21 is not complicated, but the figures to be inserted may well be more difficult to calculate. In it, the deceased's expenditure for the 7 years ending with the date of death must be listed. Unless the deceased was aware, prior to death, that this form would have to be completed, he is unlikely to have kept sufficient records to enable the personal representatives to complete this part of the form. The personal representatives may have to order back copies of bank statements to elicit the required information. Question 22 takes the expenditure from the income in order to identify the surplus income in each year, and then underneath it lists, for each year, the value of the gifts for which the expenditure out of income exemption is being claimed, in order to make it simple to check that the exemption claimed is not more than the surplus income. If it is, the claim must be limited to the amount of the surplus income for that year – surplus income from a previous year cannot be carried forward.

The personal representatives must do everything possible to complete the form or they may find the exemption is denied if entitlement cannot be shown.

4.4.4 Schedule IHT404 – Joint owned assets

Form IHT404 deals with assets held in the joint names of the deceased and another person. There is no need to complete separate forms for assets held by the deceased as joint tenant, and for assets held as tenant in common as Question 11 separates them out later. The form is divided between instalment and non-instalment option property, as on form IHT400, with instalment option property being dealt with first, and non-instalment later.

This form should not be used to declare the value of any business assets held by a partnership – these are included at schedule IHT413 instead. Also, jointly owned foreign assets should not be included here but on form IHT417.

Question 1 deals with jointly owned assets upon which the inheritance tax is payable by instalments. The asset, name and relationship of the other joint owner and date upon which the joint ownership started should be described. Columns D and E respectively ask how much each owner provided towards the purchase price and how they shared the income between them. Column F then asks for the value of the entire item, and column G for a value of the deceased's part share. If there is anything to suggest that the proportion belonging to the deceased does not accord with the answers given in columns D and E, an explanation should be provided. For example, if it is claimed that a bank account belonged 50 per cent to the deceased and 50 per cent to a third party, but the deceased took all the income arising on the account, the personal representatives need to explain why the entire account cannot be said to have belonged to the deceased.

If the joint owner was the spouse or civil partner, only columns A, B, F and G need to be completed.

As mentioned at para 2.15, between 10 per cent and 15 per cent may be deducted from the value of the deceased's interest in the asset if the asset was jointly owned. The deduction should be entered in column F of form IHT404.

The amount of any joint mortgage or other loan secured on the instalment option property should be given at question 2, and the proceeds of any joint life assurance policies assigned to pay off that mortgage included at box 1. The net assets upon which inheritance tax is payable by instalments is then given at question 3. Any joint policies that do not provide for a payment on the deceased's death should be detailed on form IHT410 (see para 4.4.10), and also at box 6 on this form – the name of the insurance company, policy number and value of the deceased's interest should all be given.

Question 6 then asks all the same questions as at box 1, but this time for assets upon which the value may not be paid by instalments. Again, debts secured on those assets are detailed at box 7, and the net value of these assets is given in box 8.

Exemptions and reliefs that may be claimed over either type of asset, are claimed at boxes 4 and 9 respectively. The net values of instalment and non-instalment option assets are then given at boxes 5 and 10 respectively and are copied to boxes 49 and 50 of form IHT400.

Questions 11 to 13 aim to separate off the value of any assets passing by survivorship. This does not matter for inheritance tax purposes, but will be relevant to the application for the grant of representation. The net value of assets passing by survivorship is ascertained at question 11. Box 12 clarifies the value of debts secured upon joint assets that pass by survivorship. Box 13 does not specifically relate to assets owned as joint tenants or tenants in common, but confirms the total value of all deductions that can be made from all jointly owned assets, being both debts and reliefs or exemptions.

4.4.5 Schedule IHT405 – Houses, land, buildings and interests in land

This form must be completed for all land and buildings, or interests in land and buildings, held by the deceased in his sole name. If the deceased owned these assets jointly with anyone else, they need not go on this form but are instead only inserted on schedule IHT404. The contact details for the personal representatives or the solicitor acting on their behalf should normally be inserted in boxes 1 to 6. If a professional valuer was employed, and is willing to act on the personal representatives' behalf in negotiating the value of any land or buildings with the district valuer, his details can also be inserted here. In practice, however, it is often easier if negotiations are conducted through the personal representatives or their solicitor, to enable them to control the process.

Question 7 relates to the deceased's main residence. Column B should contain an accurate description of the property so that the district valuer can obtain maps and plans of the area or visit it easily. If the postcode is not known and the land may be difficult to locate, it is generally helpful if the personal representatives can provide a plan to HM Revenue and Customs when the form is sent in. Column D elicits whether the land or property was held freehold or leasehold by the deceased, and any ground rent being paid. If the deceased leased the property to a third party, details of the lease should be included in column E and a copy of the agreement enclosed with the form. The information that must be provided in the lease or given in the form is:

- the date of commencement and expiry;
- the rent payable;
- whether and, if so, when, the rent may be reviewed;
- who pays the outgoings on the property; and
- the name of the tenant.

If any of the reliefs at the head of column F (agricultural, business, woodland or heritage) are being claimed, the value of the relief must be inserted here. The value of the land or buildings without deducting any relief is given in column G.

The total in question 7 must equal the value of the deceased's property carried forward to questions 51 (in most circumstances) or 68 (if it was a farmhouse) of form IHT400 (see para 4.3.1).

Question 8 asks all the same questions, but for any other land, buildings or rights over land held by the deceased.

Question 9 calls for any special factors such as any damage or development potential which may affect its value. HM Revenue and Customs regards development potential as features that may be attractive to a builder or developer such as a large garden or access to land suitable for development. Such features would increase the open market value. Therefore, such features as well as the state of repair of the property should be highlighted to the valuer instructed in preparing the value for inheritance tax purposes. A deduction from the value is permitted only if the damage is substantial; the need for redecoration, for example, does not suffice. If the damage is likely to be covered by insurance, the personal representatives must declare this at questions 10 and 11 and append copies of any correspondence with the insurers.

Question 12 asks whether any property has been sold or whether the intention is to sell within 12 months of the date of death. If the answer is 'yes' it must be confirmed whether the property is on the market, whether a sale has been agreed, or whether contracts have been exchanged. If contracts have been exchanged, the date of exchange must be given. The prospective or agreed selling price is to be shown in column C, and the personal representatives may state in column F whether they wish to use this as the value at the date of death. Column D is used to clarify whether or not the sale is at 'arm's length' and column E seeks to confirm whether there were or will be monies for fixtures and fittings (which do not form part of the property price for these purposes) included in the sale price.

The value submitted in relation to any property is generally the most difficult matter to be agreed with HM Revenue and Customs during the course of the administration. Form IHT405 (and IHT404 for jointly owned property) is automatically forwarded to the district valuer, who considers whether the valuation submitted is appropriate. If he considers it to be incorrect, he opens negotiations with the personal representatives as to what the correct value should be. This is based on the selling prices of other similar properties in the area and any other factors the district valuer decides to take into account. He may also wish to visit the property in person and he will probably research how much the property was purchased for, and when. It is advisable for the personal representatives to co-operate with the district valuer fully in these negotiations. Usually, a compromise can be reached. If not, the district valuer may impose a value upon the personal representatives, although they do have the right to appeal this decision.

4.4.6 Schedule IHT406 – Bank and building society accounts and National Savings & Investments

This form is intended to cover credit balances in the above investments held in the deceased's sole name and which did not form part of the assets of a business or partnership. Overdrawn balances should be shown as liabilities at box 82 of form IHT400 and not included on this form.

Question 1 requires details of bank and building society accounts – who they were held with, what the account number was and what the balance was as at the date of death. Interest accrued but unpaid should also be shown here, although as a separate entry on a line below the credit balance at the date of death. The total figure is carried to box 52 on form IHT400.

The same information is required for National Savings accounts at question 2. Question 3 deals with premium bonds – the bond number, value, uncashed and unclaimed prizes must also be shown. The bond and prize value are then totalled together for the final value of the deceased's premium bonds overall. Similar information is given for any other National Savings investments at question 4. The total values for all the deceased's National Savings investments of any description from questions 2, 3 and 4 are added together and given at question 5, which is carried forward to box 54 of the main form IHT400.

4.4.7 Schedule IHT407 – Household and personal goods

Form IHT407 concerns the deceased's chattels. The current version is much longer than earlier versions. Question 1 relates to jewellery where individual items are valued at £500 or more and requires the description of the item owned, if it has been sold the sale proceeds and date of sale as well as open market value as at the date of death. If the item has been sold and it is argued that the open market value as at the date of death was lower than the sale proceeds, the personal representatives can expect to be questioned as to why the value should have differed.

Question 2 relates to boats, cars, motorcycles and aircraft. For each item, it requires the manufacturer, model, year of registration, registration number, condition (including mileage for cars) and sale proceeds, plus value.

Question 3 deals with antiques, works of art and collections such as coins, books and stamps. Again, the items must be described in full and valued as well as the sale price given.

If a valuation of unsold items has been prepared, it should be appended to the form. If the deceased owned a car, an estimate of its value should be obtained from a professional dealer, or may be taken from a *Glass's* or *Parker's* guide. A private number plate may also have a value, which should be stated separately.

Questions 4 and 5 deal with all other personal items such as jewellery (not included at question 1), furniture, electrical goods and clothing which were not covered in the rest of the form. The personal representatives are asked whether any items were listed specifically on the deceased's home insurance, and if so a copy of the policy must be submitted.

Question 6 then totals the value of all the deceased's personal items shown on the form and this figure is carried forward to box 55 of form IHT400.

4.4.8 Schedule IHT408 – Household and personal goods donated to charity

This form was introduced for use where chattels were left to a specific person and that person has chosen to give the chattels to charity. By completing the form, the charity exemption under section 142 of the Inheritance Tax Act 1984 can be claimed. The intention is to avoid having to prepare and sign a deed of variation in relation to those items which HM Revenue and Customs expects to be of little value. It is not relevant for chattels given directly to charity in the will. The beneficiaries receiving the chattels who have made the donation must all complete the form. They can either state that all the deceased's personal goods were given to charity, or alternatively they can list those items that were donated and their value. The value of the items donated in this manner can then be deducted using the charity exemption at box 92 of form IHT400.

4.4.9 Schedule IHT409 – Pensions

Form IHT409 deals with all pension policies and retirement annuity contracts held by the deceased. For income tax purposes, a pension policy is either 'approved' or 'unapproved' under section 590 of the Income and Corporation Taxes Act 1988. The scheme documentation should confirm whether or not the scheme in question is approved. If a scheme in which the deceased participated was unapproved, details of the benefits payable under it after the deceased's death, and those taken by him during his lifetime, should be included in the additional information section on form IHT400 (see para 4.3.1), and form IHT409 should also be completed.

Some pensions or annuities provide that an income will continue to be paid even after the deceased's death. If that is the case, 'yes' needs to be ticked at question 1 and further information needs to be inserted at questions 2 to 7. The following information should be included:

- the name of the scheme or title of the policy;
- whether the scheme is registered by HM Revenue and Customs for income tax purposes (whether it is 'approved');
- the frequency of payments and the annual gross amount payable;
- the date of the final guaranteed payment; and
- any guaranteed increase in the amount payable. The total value of all future payments can be entered at question 7 and carried forward to box 56 on form IHT400.

If the pension or annuity continues in favour of the deceased's spouse or civil partner it does not need to be listed here, as it will fall within the surviving spouse/civil partner exemption from inheritance tax.

Questions 8 to 16 deal with any lump sum payments to be made to the estate or elsewhere under a pension scheme or policy as a result of the death; and whether the personal representatives receive those payments as of right or at the discretion of the trustees of the scheme. It encompasses details of payments made not to the estate but to a third party, either because of a direction signed by the deceased or at the discretion of the trustees of the scheme. Very broadly, any death benefits payable under a pension scheme only at the discretion of the trustees of the scheme (as under company pension schemes), or which were assigned into trust by the deceased during his lifetime (as can be done in respect of personal pension schemes or retirement annuity contracts) are free from inheritance tax within the deceased's estate. In addition, in an attempt to allow benefits to pass free from inheritance tax, many personal pension providers are now reserving to themselves a discretion to decide who is to receive any lump sum death benefit. The circumstances surrounding the payment of the death benefit are covered in questions 8 to 12. Again, the name or title of the scheme should be given in response to question 13, and whether it was approved at question 14, together with the name of the person who ultimately receives the payment and how much they received at question 16 and 15, respectively.

Questions 17 and 18 are intended to elicit whether the deceased deliberately postponed the taking of benefits from his pension scheme in the knowledge that he was ill, in an attempt to make a lump sum available, free of tax, to his intended beneficiaries. If so, the deceased may have made a PET or LCT at that time. If the personal representatives are aware of this and agree that it was a PET or LCT, the details of the gift must be inserted on form IHT403 (para 4.4.3). Thus, in response to questions 17 and 18 it must be stated whether the deceased, within 2 years of his death:

- disposed of any of the benefits payable under the pension; or
- made any changes to the benefits to which he was entitled under his pension.

If the answer is 'no' to both, move on to question 22. If the answer is 'yes' to either the information required is the name or title of the scheme (question 19); whether it was approved (question 20); and when the benefits were altered (question 21). A description of the change made is needed at page 16 of the main form IHT400, including who benefited from the change. Evidence as to the deceased's health and life expectancy is also needed and a letter from the deceased's doctor will suffice on this point.

Questions 22 to 24 are intended to elicit whether any transfers were made into the deceased's pension at a time when he was ill, as such transfers may well be gifts for inheritance tax purposes.

Questions 25 to 32 concern ASPs. There are specific instructions as to which part of this form should be completed dependent upon the date of death. For instance, this section can be ignored if the date of death is before 6 April 2006 or after 6 April 2011. An ASP is available only where the deceased had reached the age of 75 and had funds remaining in his pension from which an annuity had not been purchased. An ASP would not allow a lump sum to be paid out on the death of the recipient of the pension; instead it may provide a guaranteed income to be paid to the dependants of the recipient. In this way, it is also possible that the deceased may have been a dependant of the pension recipient, and may have been receiving a pension as a result and if so this is covered in the following section.

Full details of the pension scheme are required, and it may be simplest to send the form directly to the pension provider and ask the pension provider to complete the answers to questions 25–32. The figure to be inserted in box 32 is established by deducting the answers given in boxes 29 and 31 from that in box 28.

Questions 33 to 42 deal with a dependant's pension fund and the same criteria regarding the date of death are relevant here as they were at question 25. These should be read carefully to ensure the correct parts of this form are completed. The name of the scheme member must be given (question 34) and the original scheme member's dates of birth (question 35) and death (question 36). The original scheme member's inheritance tax reference should be given if known in box 37. Questions 38 and 39 require details of who administers the scheme, and the scheme reference number. Question 40 asks for the value of the fund at death, and question 41 for the value now passing to charity, together with details of the charity it passes to. Question 42 then covers the net value of the fund after the charity exemption is deducted, and this amount is carried forward to box 106 of the main form IHT400.

In addition to schedule IHT409, if the deceased was a member of an alternatively secured or unsecured pension fund, and following his death the value of the funds chargeable to inheritance tax is nil because all the funds are being used to provide benefits to 'relevant dependants' or a charity, form IHT105 should be completed by the personal representatives and submitted to HM Revenue and Customs. A 'relevant dependant' is someone who, at the date of the deceased's death was:

- a 'dependant' as defined by paragraph 15 of Schedule 28 to the Finance Act 2004, who was the deceased's spouse or civil partner; or
- financially dependent upon the deceased as at the date of death.

The form requires details of the deceased, the relative dependant, the identity and contact details of the scheme administrator and the value of the fund as well as the amount either passing to charity or being used to provide benefits for the relative dependants.

The form may also need to be completed if it is the relevant dependant of the original scheme member who dies and the original scheme member had an ASP fund, or where the relevant dependant dies with an ASP and the original scheme member had an alternatively secured or unsecured pension.

4.4.10 Schedule IHT410 – Life assurance and annuities

Form IHT410 must be completed if the deceased paid any premiums on any life assurance policies, or if he was the life assured under any policy. It also deals with payments made after the deceased's death under purchased life annuities and investment bonds or plans which have a life assurance element to them. If the life assurance policy or annuity was in the joint names of the deceased and someone else, and a payment under it falls due on the deceased's death, it should not be included on this form, but on form IHT404 (see para 4.4.4). If the policy was in joint names and continues after the deceased's death, details of the policy must be given on this form.

Questions 1 and 2 relate to any policy owned by the deceased and not written into trust. The name of the insurance company, policy number and amount payable must be given. Question 3 deals with 'joint life second death' policies which continue after the deceased's death and (as above) confirms that details of these should be included on form IHT404.

Questions 4 and 5 relate to second-hand policies, or policies taken out by the deceased on someone else's life. A copy of the policy document and details of its value at the date of death should be supplied as well as the table at question 5 being completed with the details of the policy, life assured and amount assured. If the deceased paid all the premiums on a policy which was on the joint lives of him and someone else, and the policy was also owned by them jointly, he may have been making a PET and details of the premiums paid should be included on form IHT403 (see para 4.4.3).

The value of the policies shown in questions 2 and 5 are then totalled at question 6 and are carried to box 57 of form IHT400.

If the deceased purchased a life annuity under which regular payments continue to be made after his death, the details to be given in response to question 8 are:

- the name of the annuity company;
- the regularity of the payment;
- the date of the final guaranteed payment and any guaranteed increases in the remaining period; and
- the value of the right to receive the remainder of the payments.

In order to assist in calculating the value of the right to receive the remainder of the payments, HM Revenue and Customs has a calculator on its website into which the relevant information can be inputted and the value calculated online.

Question 9 asks for the gross amount payable annually under the annuity and how that breaks down between capital and income. Note that questions 7 to 9 do not relate to annuities payable under pension schemes – these should be entered on form IHT409 (see para 4.4.9).

Questions 10 and 11 deal with the situation where a lump sum is payable to the estate under a purchased life annuity; the reply must contain the name of the annuity company and the amount payable. If the lump sum does not fall into the estate, an explanation must be given as to whom it passes.

If the answer to question 12, 'Did the deceased, within 7 years of their death, pay any premium on a life insurance policy for the benefit of someone else, other than the deceased's spouse or civil partner?' is 'yes', this would have been a gift by the deceased, and form IHT403 should be completed in respect of it. Question 13 relates to 'back to back' policies, discussed at para 4.4.3.

Question 14 asks whether the deceased had any right to benefit from a life insurance policy taken out on another person's life and held in trust for the benefit of the deceased (and others). If the answer is 'yes', the deceased would have been a beneficiary of a trust, details of which should be given on form IHT418 (see para 4.4.18).

4.4.11 Schedule IHT411 – Listed stocks and shares

Schedule IHT411 consists of two tables in which details are to be inserted of all the deceased's listed stocks, shares and securities. If a stockbroker has been employed to prepare a valuation of the shares this should be included when lodging the account. The information contained within the formal valuation, for instance the amount of stock and the market price per unit as at date of death, should be transposed into the schedule, which then calculates the total value of the stock.

Question 1 requires details of the deceased's treasury bills, exchequer, convertible, consolidated and loan stock, savings and victory bonds, war loans, UK municipal securities and any government stock held on the Bank of England register. The total value should be carried forward to box 62 of form IHT400. The interest due on the assets is shown in the next column and the total is carried forward to box 64 of form IHT400.

Question 2 relates to the deceased's stocks, shares, debentures and other securities listed on the Stock Exchange *Daily Official List*, together with his unit and investment trusts, open ended investment companies (OEICs), Individual Savings Accounts (ISAs), Personal Equity Plans (PEPs) and foreign shares listed on the London Stock Exchange. Shares held on the AIM should not be included in this schedule but rather on schedule IHT412 'Unlisted stocks, shares and control holdings'. Uninvested cash held in a share PEP or ISA should also be shown here unless it is a cash ISA, in which case it should be shown on form IHT406. The total value should be carried forward to box 63 of IHT400. The dividends due on the assets are shown in the next column and the total is carried forward to box 64 of form IHT400.

4.4.12 Schedule IHT412 – Unlisted stocks and shares

Question 1 deals with shares that did not give the deceased control of the company but which were quoted on the AIM, or traded on OFEX, which is a trading facility for unquoted shares. It should also be stipulated whether business property relief is being claimed and if so to what extent (form IHT413 will not then need to be completed in order to claim the relief). The total value of the shares, the dividends due on them at the date of death and the business relief being claimed should be carried forward to boxes 65, 64 and 92 (respectively) of form IHT400.

Question 2 asks for the value of any unlisted shares and securities in private limited companies, business expansion schemes and business start-up schemes. Again there is a facility to claim business property relief, and again the totals should be carried forward to the same boxes of form IHT400.

Question 3 then relates to the same companies as were covered by question 2, but this time only if the shares gave the deceased control of the company. The totals are carried forward to boxes 67, 64 and 93 of form IHT400.

Question 4 requires the same information as question 1, but this time if the shares gave the deceased control of the company. The totals are carried forward again to boxes 67, 64 and 93.

Lastly, question 5 applies to listed stocks, shares and investments that gave the deceased control of the company. For this reason it is likely to be irrelevant for most clients. The totals of the value of the investments, the dividends due on them to the date of death, and the value of the business property relief claimed are again carried forward to boxes 67, 64 and 93 of form IHT400.

Shares traded on NASDAQ (in the USA) or EASDAQ (in Europe) should not be listed on form IHT412, but on form IHT417 (see para 4.4.17) as foreign assets. The method of valuing quoted shares and securities has been discussed above (see para 2.12).

4.4.13 Schedule IHT413 – Business and partnership interests and assets

Schedule IHT413 relates to assets upon which business property relief from inheritance tax is claimed. The availability of this exemption, and the amount of relief available, are dealt with at paras 3.3 *et seq*. A separate form should be completed for each business (or interest in a business) in respect of which the relief is claimed.

Question 1 asks whether the deceased held the business assets throughout the period of 2 years leading to his death. If they did not belong to him throughout the 2 years prior to his death, business property relief may not be available unless the deceased inherited the assets from someone else, or they replaced other business assets that had been disposed of. In that situation, an explanation as to why the personal representatives believe business property relief is due should be given at question 2.

Under section 113 of the Inheritance Tax Act 1984, if the assets were subject to a binding contract for sale at death, they do not qualify for business property relief. But the transaction does qualify for relief if the assets are to be purchased by a company wishing to use the assets in its own business and the consideration for the sale is shares or securities in that company; or the sale is of shares and is taking place solely to facilitate a reconstruction or amalgamation of the company. If either of these situations is relevant, an explanation should be given in reply to questions 3 to 6.

Questions 7 to 17 deal with a business in which the deceased was a sole trader or partner. A useful starting point in valuing such a business is the last set of accounts and the value of the business or the deceased's interest should be inserted at question 7. If the business is simple, combining the value of the capital and current accounts may be sufficient to provide a valuation. Book values of assets should not be used, as they do not necessarily represent the true open market value at the date of death. It is, however, likely that the accountants for the business will have to be approached to prepare a formal valuation. In any event, the accounts for the 3 years prior to the deceased's death should be forwarded to HM Revenue and Customs. A loan account held by the deceased in the business does not qualify for business property relief. A description of how the deceased's value in the business or partnership was calculated should be included at question 9.

The name and principal activity of the business must be shown in reply to question 8. If the business changed its name or activity in the 2 years prior to death, details of its previous name and/or activities should also be supplied.

If the business was a partnership, question 10 should be answered 'yes' and a copy of the partnership agreement supplied. The personal representatives must specify when the partnership began at question 11; the UTR of the partnership at question 12; who provided the partnership capital and in what shares at questions 13 and 14; and how the profits were shared at question 15. Further relevant terms of the partnership should be described at question 25 (Additional information). The personal representatives are expected to confirm at question 16 whether the business or partnership will now be sold. The amount of business property relief being claimed should be inserted at question 17. This figure is transferred to box 93 on form IHT400.

Questions 18 to 21 deal with assets that were owned by the deceased but used by a partnership or company in which he had an interest. The assets should be described and valued at question 18. In response to question 19, the personal representatives should describe the main activities of the business or company. Question 20 confirms whether it was a partnership or a company. The value given in reply to question 21 is transferred to box 93 on form IHT400.

Questions 22 to 24, on claiming business property relief in connection with a lifetime transfer, relate only to gifts made during the deceased's lifetime. Business property relief is generally available only if:

- the recipient of the gift still owned it at the deceased's death (question 22);
- the assets in the hands of the recipient would have qualified for business property relief at the date of death (question 23); and
- the assets were not subject to a binding contract for sale (question 24).

4.4.14 Schedule IHT414 – Agricultural relief

Schedule IHT414 must be completed if agricultural property relief from inheritance tax is being claimed on any of the deceased's assets. For the criteria for qualifying for the relief, and the rates at which it is given, see paras 3.4 *et seq*. A different form should be filled in for each separate property in respect of which agricultural property relief is claimed. It is helpful to include a plan of the land in respect of which the relief is claimed.

Question 1 requires an address and full description of the land over which agricultural property relief is being claimed.

Question 2 deals with how the deceased acquired the property, and the response should make clear whether he bought it or inherited it, or whether it was given to him.

Question 3 asks whether the property, or any part of it, was subject to a binding contract for sale at the date of death. A binding contract for sale is one under which the deceased's personal representatives can be forced to convey the property. If the answer to the question is 'yes', the land subject to the contract does not qualify for agricultural property relief (section 124 of the Inheritance Tax Act 1984), unless the majority of the consideration payable under the sale is shares in a company purchasing the property, and the shares to be made over to the deceased would give him control of the company. The land subject to the contract should be identified on a plan.

Question 4 asks whether any planning consents were in place on any part of the land which have not yet been implemented. This is important because it will affect the value of the land. It is only the agricultural value of the land that may have agricultural property relief claimed – any uplift in value as a result of the planning permission will not qualify for the relief.

Question 5 should be answered to say whether the land was used for arable, pastoral or mixed farming; the type of crop grown or livestock kept; the number and type of livestock; and, if the land was of mixed use, the number of acres used by each.

If the deceased ceased agricultural activities on the land, when and why this happened must also be given in reply to question 5. The land may qualify for agricultural property relief if it was managed under an agro-environmental or habitat scheme arrangement.

Question 6 seeks to determine the deceased's involvement in the activities at question 5 throughout the 2 years before his death in order to ascertain whether agricultural property relief should be awarded as a result of the deceased's endeavours. If the activities were not carried out by him, it will only qualify for agricultural property relief if the activities were carried out throughout the entire 7 years prior to his death (hence question 5). Any further information explaining why the property should nevertheless qualify for agricultural property relief could be given in the final box on page 4 of the form. This is usually because the deceased inherited the property from someone else, or the property replaced other agricultural property.

If the land was let, questions 7 to 11 become relevant. The name of the tenant and their relationship to the deceased should be given at question 8. The date the tenancy commenced should be given at question 9 and the original term of the tenancy at question 10. Question 11 asks for clarification of the rate of relief sought. A copy of the lease is also useful to HM Revenue and Customs.

In response to questions 12 to 15 (which are duplicated in case there are two farmhouses or cottages – further properties will require extra sheets to be completed), on the occupation of any farmhouse, building or cottage, the personal representatives need to give details of:

- the address (question 12);
- whether the property was unoccupied (even for a short period) during the 7 years prior to the deceased's death (question 13);
- who lived in the building and if not the deceased, why they lived there (question 14); and
- the type of tenancy (for example agricultural or assured shorthold) and the rent payable (question 15).

Question 16 relates to farm buildings – HM Revenue and Customs wishes to know the type and nature of the buildings, what they were used for and by whom.

Questions 17 to 20 deal with gifts of agricultural property made by the deceased during his lifetime. For these purposes, the 'relevant period' is the period from the date of the gift to the deceased's date of death (or death of the person who received the gift, if they died first). They ask:

- whether the land qualified as agricultural property during the relevant period (question 17);
- whether the recipient of the gift held the property throughout the relevant period (question 18);
- whether the recipient or someone else occupied the property as agricultural property throughout the relevant period (question 19); and
- whether the property was subject to a binding contract for sale at the end of the relevant period (question 20).

If an asset qualifies for both agricultural property relief and business property relief, agricultural property relief only may be claimed; business property relief may not be claimed in conjunction with agricultural property relief.

4.4.15 Schedule IHT415 – Interest in another estate

Schedule IHT415 relates only to a vested interest the deceased had in another estate, that is, where he was absolutely entitled to the interest at the date of his death, but the assets had not yet been passed to him from the estate. The form does not apply to interests that are contingent or conditional upon the happening of a certain criterion.

Questions 1 to 3 require details of the previous deceased's name, date of death, and inheritance tax reference number or date of grant.

The full nature of the deceased's entitlement should be inserted in reply to question 4, and confirmation of any assets that had already been passed to him should be given in 5 and 6. Question 7 requires information about what the deceased had yet to receive from the estate; whether it was land or buildings, an interest in a business or a controlling shareholding (i.e. assets upon which inheritance tax may be payable by instalments). The value to be given is the value of the assets not passed to the deceased as at the date of his death, and is therefore not the same as the value of those assets for probate purposes in the predecessor's estate. It may be particularly difficult to produce a valuation if the deceased was entitled to the residue of the predecessor's estate. The debts and distributions still to be paid from the other estate must be taken into account and deducted from these assets if they are debts relevant to these assets. If the figure can be provided only as an estimate, this must be clearly marked at question 8. The value of the assets is carried to box 71 of form IHT400.

Any other assets that the deceased was due to receive (and upon which the inheritance tax may not be paid by instalments) should be inserted at question 9. Again, any debts to be set against them should be shown. The total value should be carried forward to box 72 of IHT400. If the values are estimates this should be indicated at question 10.

If inheritance tax was payable on the estate of the predecessor on the passing of the assets to the deceased, those assets may also be taxable in the deceased's estate. 'Double tax' or 'quick succession' relief from inheritance tax may be available. For more detail, see paras 3.8 and 3.9.

4.4.16 Schedule IHT416 – Debts due to the estate

Schedule IHT416 is used to set out details of the debts due to the deceased. A separate form should be completed for each debt. For the purposes of this form, insurance products based on a loan made by the original settlor of a policy of insurance, to the trustees, are a debt that must be included.

If the debt was simply a director's loan account or current account with a company or business, only questions 3 and 9 need be answered. These ask for the amount outstanding at the date of death (both capital and interest), and for any reason why the debt included as part of the deceased's estate should not be the same as its value (at question 3).

The date and original value of the loan are given at questions 1 and 2. Question 4 asks whether the debt was secured by a mortgage. Question 5 requires more details regarding the identity of the borrower and in particular their relationship to the deceased.

If interest is charged on the loan, the amount and rate of interest and the period over which it was charged should be stated in reply to question 6. If capital was repaid to the deceased during his lifetime, the amount and date of the repayment should be given in answer to question 7. If the capital was not repaid, but was released by the deceased during his lifetime, this must have been evidenced in a deed, to be valid. A copy of the deed of release should be attached to the form. The release would also have been a PET or LCT by the deceased if it was made within the 7 years prior to death, and details of it should be included on form IHT403.

In box 8 details of the evidence supporting the loan should be given and the evidence provided to HMRC when lodging the IHT400 Account. If no evidence can be offered, details of the period of the loan prior to death, and when it is to become repayable, should be given.

4.4.17 Schedule IHT417 – Foreign assets

Schedule IHT417 must be completed if the deceased was domiciled (or deemed to be domiciled) in England and Wales, Scotland or Northern Ireland at the date of his death and held assets abroad. For these purposes, if a grant is being applied for in England and Wales, assets situated in Scotland and Northern Ireland, the Channel Islands or the Isle of Man are treated as foreign assets and should be listed on this form. The converse applies if the grant application is being made in Scotland or Northern Ireland.

Questions 1 to 5 and 6 to 10 of the form distinguish between instalment and non-instalment option property, calling for details of the assets outside the United Kingdom. The rules on whether an asset qualifies as instalment option property are the same in relation to foreign assets as in relation to any other asset (see para 3.19.1).

The value of assets should be given both in the relevant foreign currency and in sterling, using the conversion rate in force at the date of death. Conversion rates are dealt with at para 4.3.1. This is in questions 1 and 6. If the asset was a house or land, give also the following information:

- a full description of the property, a copy of any professional valuations, photographs and a plan;
- confirmation of the condition the property is in, whether it is in an urban or rural location, whether it has additional facilities such as a swimming pool;
- whether there was planning permission; and
- whether a sale is imminent.

If the asset is an interest in a business or holding in a company, copies of the latest accounts should be supplied, as well as a description of how the valuation was arrived at.

Questions 2 and 7 ask for details of the debts deductible from the assets in questions 1 and 6. This is basically all debts chargeable against the foreign assets, unless they were charged on UK property owned by the deceased, or they arose in the United Kingdom. In either of those situations it must be shown with all other debts in the main form IHT400. The extra cost of dealing with the asset as a result of its being situated abroad can also be treated as a liability, but only to the extent of the difference between how much the asset costs to be dealt with abroad, compared with how much it would cost to be dealt with in the United Kingdom. In any event, this extra cost is limited to 5 per cent of the gross value of all the deceased's foreign assets.

The net asset position is given at questions 3 and 8. Exemptions or reliefs are given at questions 4 and 9, and the net asset position after deduction of those is shown at questions 5 and 10.

If the net assets in box 5 (net assets, non-instalment property) on schedule IHT417 would be a negative figure, the excess debt may be carried over to box 10 (net assets, instalment property) and *vice versa*. Only if there is a deficit in both boxes may the surplus debt be carried over to form IHT400.

If a share is in a foreign company but listed on the London Stock Exchange it does not qualify as a foreign asset. It should be shown on schedule IHT411 (see para 4.4.11) with the deceased's other shareholdings.

Assets held abroad in joint names should be shown on this form, not on Schedule IHT404. The questions raised on schedule IHT404 (see para 4.4.4) should, however, still be answered on page 16 of the main form IHT400.

The figures from boxes 5 and 10 respectively of schedule IHT417 must be transferred into box 97 (for instalment option property) or box 98 (for non-instalment option property) of form IHT400.

4.4.18 Schedule IHT418 – Assets held in trust

Schedule IHT418 is for listing all the assets held in a trust from which the deceased was entitled to take a benefit at his death. If the deceased was a beneficiary of a trust created by a settlor who was not domiciled in the United Kingdom at the time the trust was set up, and the trust was not UK-based at the time of the deceased's death, only questions 2 to 5 (on the basic details of the trust) need be completed. In these circumstances, the assets in the trust do not form part of the deceased's estate for inheritance tax purposes (section 48(3) of the Inheritance Tax Act 1984).

Assets in a discretionary trust of which the deceased was a beneficiary do not need to be included on schedule IHT418, as a beneficiary of a discretionary trust has no entitlement under that trust. In addition, in certain circumstances, the assets in the trust do not form part of the deceased's estate for inheritance tax purposes and the rest of the form need not be completed. Those circumstances are where the deceased's interest was not:

(a) an interest in possession that commenced before 22 March 2006 and which remained in existence between then and the date of death;
(b) an immediate post-death interest as defined in section 49A of the Inheritance tax Act 1984;

(c) a disabled person's interest as defined in section 89; or
(d) a transitional serial interest as defined in sections 49C to 49E.

Question 1 asks for clarification as to which of these types of interest the deceased's interest was.

Questions 2, 3, 4, 5 and 7 call for basic details regarding the trust, including the name of the settlor, the name of the trust, its UTR, the date of creation of the trust and the names and addresses of the trustees. A copy of the trust deed is also useful for HM Revenue and Customs.

Question 6 asks whether the personal representatives know all the details of the assets contained within the trust. They may not do so – trustees are only obliged to give the overall value of the trust assets, not how these are broken down. Most trustees have no objection to sharing this information in any event. If the details of the trust assets are known, they should be given in questions 8 to 18. If they are not known, only the net value of the trust assets need be given in questions 12 (for instalment option property) and 17 (for non-instalment option property). Questions 8 and 13 ask for the gross value of the assets, and questions 9 and 14 for the debts that may be set against them. Questions 10 and 15 then give the net value of the assets after deduction of debts. Questions 11 and 16 ask for details of any exemptions or reliefs to be applied to the trust assets. Questions 12 and 17 then show the total value of the assets after deduction of debts, reliefs and exemptions. If the trustees are paying the inheritance tax due on the trust assets at the same time as the return is being submitted, the total net value of the instalment option property should be copied from box 12 to box 99 of form IHT400. If not, it should be copied to box 18 of schedule IHT418. Even though the inheritance tax due on non-instalment option property may not be paid by instalments, that does not mean that the trustees have to pay the inheritance tax due on it at the same time as the personal representatives pay the inheritance tax due on the estate. If they are paying the inheritance tax at the same time, the net value shown in box 17 should be copied to box 100 of form IHT400. If not, it should be copied to box 18 of schedule IHT418 and from there on to box 105 of form IHT400.

If the trustees of the trust are willing, the simplest course may be to forward them schedule IHT418 and ask them to complete it and return it to the personal representatives. If they are unwilling to provide even the net figures for questions 2 to 7, 12 and 17, the most practical solution is for the personal representatives to fill in the form to the best of their knowledge and give an explanation in a covering letter when the form is forwarded to HM Revenue and Customs. HM Revenue and Customs is able to bring greater pressure to bear on the trustees to provide the necessary figures.

If a liability is shown in boxes 9 or 14 as income due to the deceased at the date of death, this must be carried forward to box 73 on form IHT400 as an asset of the deceased. If the total of liabilities shown in box 9 is greater than the total assets figure in box 8, the excess liability may be carried over and included in box 14 and *vice versa*. It cannot be carried forward to form IHT400.

If the deceased was a beneficiary of a trust of a life assurance policy, the details should be included on schedule IHT418 and a copy of the policy document forwarded to HM Revenue and Customs.

Questions 19 to 23 relate to any reversionary interest that the deceased may have had in trust assets – i.e. where he would have been entitled to trust assets in the future, but only following someone else's death or in some other circumstance. Question 19 asks if this was relevant. If it was, question 20 asks how the right arose. Question 21 asks for the value of the trust assets as at the date of death, and question 22 asks for details of the settlement, being the date of creation or the date of the settlor's death and who the settlor was. Finally, question 23 asks for details of who is currently receiving the benefit from that settlement, including his name and age.

4.4.19 Schedule IHT419 – Debts owed by the deceased

Schedule IHT419 is used to give more information regarding loans made to the deceased, money spent on the deceased's behalf, liabilities relating to a life assurance policy that are now shown elsewhere in form IHT400 or debts for someone else that the deceased guaranteed, and which the estate must repay. Question 1 asks about money spent on the deceased's behalf. This asks who spent the money, what their relationship to the deceased was, what the money was spent on, why the deceased's own money was not used, why the deceased had not repaid the debt during his lifetime and how much the debt was.

Question 2 deals with loans made to the deceased, including debts due to close friends or relatives. The name of the lender, their relationship to the deceased, together with the date on which the loan was made, and why it was made, (including where it is now represented in the estate), should be explained. Any security taken should be confirmed. The original amount of the loan, together with the amount outstanding at death, should be given.

Question 3 relates to loans made specifically in relation to life insurance policies (such as 'back to back' arrangements). The name of the insurance company, amount owed, and amount insured under the policy should be given.

Question 4 relates to guarantee debts. These arise when one person agrees to repay a loan made to a second person if the second person defaults on the loan. The following details should be given:

- the name of the original debtor and their relationship to the deceased;
- whether the deceased has ever been called upon to fulfil the guarantee and pay part or all of the debt; and
- if not, why a deduction should be allowed.

Section 103 of the Finance Act 1986 deals with loans made to a person after 18 March 1986 where the money lent is gifted back to the person who made the loan; or the money lent is used to purchase a policy of life assurance, the proceeds of which are written into trust. Section 103 may apply even if the loan was repaid before death. If the personal representatives are claiming that such a debt falls within the deceased's estate, and it has not already been detailed in any of the previous boxes, details, similar to those set out above, should be given in reply to question 5. If the money lent was the subject of a later gift made by the deceased, that gift may also have to be declared on Schedule IHT403 (see para 4.4.3). Details of the original debt must be given, if made in these circumstances, even if it was repaid prior to the deceased's death.

4.4.20 Schedule IHT420 – National heritage assets, conditional exemption and maintenance funds

Schedule IHT420 is only relevant:

- where the personal representatives wish to claim the heritage conditional exemption for any of the assets in the estate;
- if the conditional exemption has been allowed on any of the assets in the estate in the past;
- if any of the assets in the estate are maintained from a maintenance fund;
- to claim an exemption from inheritance tax if any of the assets in the estate pass under the deceased's will to the trustees of a maintenance fund.

For these reasons, this schedule will not be used in many estates. For more details on the maintenance fund exemption, see para 3.16; for more details on the heritage fund exemption, see para 3.6. If either the conditional heritage fund exemption or the maintenance fund exemption is being claimed over any assets, those assets should be described (and it should be indicated where else they are shown on form IHT400) and valued at question 1. Question 2 relates to assets in the estate which have previously benefited from either exemption. The asset should be described and cross-referenced to where it appears on form IHT400, the date upon which it was received by the deceased should be given, together with the name of the person to whom it now passes and the current value. Question 3 goes on to ask who gave the asset to the deceased, if they are now dead, their date of death and the reference number from when the exemption was previously agreed.

Question 4 relates to assets in the estate that are maintained by a maintenance fund. The assets should be described and cross-referenced to where they appear in the main form IHT400. The date the maintenance fund was established and the reference for it with HM Revenue and Customs should be given, as well as the name of the person to whom the asset now passes.

4.4.21 Schedule IHT421 – Probate summary

Schedule IHT421 is completed so as to summarise the inheritance tax position. In due course it is endorsed as the receipt for any inheritance tax paid. It relates only to the assets passing under the grant of representation, so must not contain any figures relating to assets held as joint tenants; foreign property passing under a foreign grant; assets held in trust over which the deceased did not have a general power of appointment (or over which he did have such a power but chose not to exercise it in his will); or nominated assets.

4.4.22 Schedule IHT423 – Direct payment scheme

Schedule IHT423 is used where the personal representatives wish to use funds in one or more of the deceased's bank accounts to pay the inheritance tax due. Many banks are now willing to release funds, on receipt of a request signed by all the personal representatives, by means of a cheque made payable to 'HM Revenue and Customs'. Some, however, still decline to do so, and here Schedule IHT423 provides a valuable alternative to taking out a probate loan which is now commonly used in order to pay the inheritance tax due.

Firstly, the personal representatives must telephone HM Revenue and Customs to obtain a reference number for the estate either by going online or using schedule IHT422 (see para 4.5). That reference number must be entered at the head of schedule IHT423 so that it can be quoted on the bank transfer when it is made to HM Revenue and Customs. If the number is not quoted HM Revenue and Customs will have no way of relating the payment to the correct estate. If a reference cannot be obtained over the telephone, the completed form can instead be sent to HM Revenue and Customs, which will insert the reference and return it to the solicitors acting for the personal representatives.

In completing the form, the deceased's name and date of death must also be quoted at the top of the sheet. The bank details are then included in the boxes on the left of the sheet and the amount sought to be released to pay the tax in the boxes on the right. It is helpful to choose an account which has sufficient funds to pay all the tax due, in order to reduce the administration (and possible confusion) that may arise in seeking to transfer funds from several accounts.

The personal representatives must sign the completed form and send it, with the reference number inserted, to the relevant bank of the deceased. At the same time, forms IHT400 and IHT421 are sent to HM Revenue and Customs. For more detail on the submission of form IHT400, see para 4.5.

Alternatively, payment may be made using the deceased's National Savings investments or government stocks. In the case of National Savings, this is done by obtaining a formal valuation from National Savings of the investments held by the deceased and then sending a copy to HM Revenue and Customs together with forms IHT400 and IHT421. The personal representatives should confirm how much tax they wish to pay in this manner. HM Revenue and Customs then liaises directly with National Savings to obtain the required funds. However, it is worth noting that this can be a relatively lengthy process, taking around 4 weeks to complete.

4.4.23 Schedule IHT430 – Reduced rate of inheritance tax

Schedule IHT430 must be completed if the death was on or after 6 April 2012 and the deceased bequeathed at least 10 per cent of his net estate to a qualifying charity. This schedule should also be completed in order to merge components or opt out of the reduced rate of inheritance tax.

The first section deals with the above two elections. The next section 'Working out the inheritance tax' gives all the values required to use the HM Revenue and Customs reduced rate calculator. The overall estate values are required first. The total gross value of all estate components is to be entered at box 1, the value of any nil rate band and transferable nil rate band at box 2 and the value of all gifts subject to inheritance tax (less the value of any gifts with reservation of benefit) at box 3.

The three different components plus gifts with reservation of benefit are then dealt with individually. Boxes 4, 5, 6 and 7 ask for the gross value of each component being general, survivorship, settled property (referred to in the schedule as 'Assets in trust'), and gifts with reservation of benefit, respectively. Boxes 8 to 14 deal with deductions from each component, so that in boxes 8 to 10 the liabilities affecting the three primary components are to be included, and in boxes 11 to 14 the reliefs deductible from each component are to be detailed. Next, the schedule deals with exemptions. In boxes 15 to 17 the charitable exemption applicable to each component should be included and in boxes 18 to 20 any other exemption affecting the components should be included. Following on from this the schedule confirms the net value of each estate component in boxes 21 to 24.

The next section is headed 'Calculation of inheritance tax at the reduced rate' and the schedule confirms that the next step is to apportion the nil rate band and transferable nil rate band less any lifetime gifts (but not gifts with a reservation of benefit) between the estate components. The reduced rate calculator will assist with this and the note at point 4 on page 2 of the schedule gives a worked example of such apportionment. Boxes 25 to 28 are duplicated in order to include information for both the components which qualify for the reduced rate of inheritance tax and those that do not. Therefore at box 25 the net value of the estate components should be included after the charity exemption has been deducted for the components that pay tax at 36 per cent and the components that pay tax at 40 per cent. At box 26 the apportioned nil rate band is to be included between those components that pay tax at 36 per cent and the components that pay tax at 40 per cent. Box 27 asks for the value chargeable to tax for each (and therefore the answer to box 25 less box 26). Lastly, box 28 asks for confirmation of the inheritance tax due at each rate of tax.

The following declaration only needs to be signed if an election to merge components or opt out of the reduced rate of inheritance tax is being made. If so, it must be signed by all of the appropriate persons for each component involved and not by their agents. See para 3.15 for further information on applying for the reduced rate of inheritance tax.

4.4.24 Schedule IHT435 – Claim the residence nil rate band (RNRB)

Schedule IHT435 must be completed in order to claim the RNRB to utilise on a qualifying estate. The following conditions must be met to claim, see however para 3.12 for a detailed analysis of the qualifying criteria:

- the deceased must have died on or after 6 April 2017;
- there must be a qualifying residential interest or former qualifying residential interest within the estate; and
- this qualifying interest must be inherited by the deceased's direct descendants.

The notes to this form are very helpful, and offer a reminder of the qualifying criteria.

Questions 1 to 3 ask for details of the estate in question; if any part of the estate passes to direct descendants, the total value of the estate before deducting reliefs and exemptions (include at 2 the total of box 91 from IHT400, box 12 from

IHT403 and boxes 10 and 15 from IHT418) and the total chargeable estate (include the value at box 108 from IHT400).

Questions 4 to 8 ask for details of the residence on which the RNRB is being claimed. Question 4 asks whether the estate still includes a residential property that the deceased owned and lived in. Only answer 'no' if the down-sizing allowance is being claimed, which is dealt with later in this schedule. Include the address at box 5. If there are more than one such properties within the estate, the personal representatives elect here which property they wish to nominate. Box 6 asks for the value of the property after the deduction of any mortgage or charged debts; this is the value that can be claimed on. At box 7 include the percentage of this property that passes to direct descendants and at box 8 detail their names and their relationship to the deceased. This schedule only allows space to include three direct descendants. If there are others, their details must be included within the Additional Information section on page 16 of the IHT400.

Questions 9 to 11 seek to confirm the chargeable value of the residence. Question 9 queries whether any part of the residence is exempt from inheritance tax or qualifies for any relief. Therefore, if an exempt beneficiary inherits part of the property or if, for instance, agricultural property relief applies to any part of the property, or if the property falls into residue and any part of residue passes to an exempt beneficiary, the answer 'yes' must be given. Question 10 asks whether grossing up or interaction apply to the estate to decipher whether the personal representatives can calculate the RNRB themselves or whether HM Revenue and Customs is required to do so. If either applies, HMRC will step in and calculate the RNRB for the estate; however, it remains necessary to complete the rest of the form. The notes to this form provide guidance at 9 as to when grossing up and interaction will apply. In short, grossing up will apply if there are any gifts in the will that are made free of inheritance tax or if any part of residue passes to an exempt beneficiary; whereas interaction will apply if either business property relief or agricultural property relief is due 'and' any part of the estate is exempt, the will makes specific gifts of assets or the relievable assets are not specifically gifted under the will.

Include the chargeable value of the whole property for inheritance tax purposes (not just the interests that passes to direct descendants) at box 11 and at box 12 include the chargeable value of the interest that passes to direct descendants.

Questions 13 and 14 seek to identify whether the personal representatives are claiming a TRNRB. At box 14 include the value being claimed from either box 15 or box 21 from schedule IHT436. If the TRNRB is being claimed from more than one predeceased spouse or civil partner, the total of these boxes from each completed IHT436 must be added; however, the total TRNRB that can be claimed is limited to the maximum RNRB available for the year the deceased died.

Questions 15 to 18 are to be completed where the personal representatives are claiming a down-sizing allowance. If it is not, tick ‘no’, move to box 25 and enter the value given by the RNRB calculator on the HM Revenue and Customs website at www.gov.uk/guidance/inheritance-tax-residence-nil-rate-band.

In order to claim any down-sizing allowance the deceased must have, on or after 8 July 2015, disposed of a former residence and either replaced this with a less valuable residence, or ceased to own such a property. Further criteria stipulate that the former residence must have qualified for the RNRB if the deceased had retained this until his death and at least some of the estate must pass to the deceased’s direct descendants.

In order to claim a down-sizing allowance tick ‘yes’ at question 15 and include the address of the former residence at box 16. Include the date of disposal of this property at box 17. If there was more than one disposal related to this residence, the personal representatives must choose which disposal to include. The notes to this schedule provide an example of such a scenario being a gift of a half share of the property on one day followed on the next day by a gift of the remaining share. The value of the deceased’s interest in this former residence is to be included at box 18. This is the open market value at the date of disposal less the value of any outstanding mortgage.

Question 19 asks for confirmation as to whether any assets other than the property at box 5 pass to direct descendants. If the answer to this question is ‘no’, move to question 25 and include the value the RNRB calculator provides. If, however, other assets do pass to the deceased’s direct descendants, question 20 asks for confirmation as to whether grossing up or interaction applies, as was asked at box 10. If either applies, move to question 23. If they do not, detail at box 21 the total value of the other assets passing after the deduction of any exemptions, reliefs or liabilities that are taken into account for inheritance tax purposes for these assets. Include in reply to question 22 the name and relationship to the deceased of the direct descendants to inherit these other assets. Again, if there is insufficient space include the other direct descendants on IHT400 on page 16 in the section ‘Additional Information’.

Question 23 seeks to clarify whether, if there were a valid claim for RNRB at the date of disposal of the former residence, any TRNRB would have been available. The answer to this question is ‘no’ if a TRNRB is not being claimed now or if the disposal was made before 6 April 2017. Answer ‘yes’ to this question if a TRNRB is being claimed and the disposal occurred after 5 April 2017, and the date of the deceased's spouse or civil partner's death was before the date of disposal. If the answer is 'yes' to question 23, include the amount of TRNRB that would have been available at the date of disposal.

4.4.25 Schedule IHT436 – Claim to transfer any unused residence nil rate band (TRNRB)

This schedule should be completed where the personal representatives wish to claim a TRNRB against the inheritance tax on the deceased's estate. The TRNRB can therefore only be claimed if a RNRB is also being claimed (using schedule IHT435 – see para 4.4.24) and the deceased's spouse or civil partner predeceased him without utilising all or a part of his available RNRB.

Questions 1 to 6 ask for information about the deceased's spouse or civil partner. Include their title and full name at box 1, the date of their marriage or civil partnership at box 2 and the place they married or formed a civil partnership at box 3 (include a copy of the marriage or civil partnership certificate within the application). Detail the date of death at box 4 and any inheritance tax reference for their estate at box 5. Box 6 asks whether the spouse or civil partner utilised any RNRB. If the estate passed entirely to the deceased or if the property passed to the deceased, tick 'no' and answer questions 7 to 15. If they died on or before 5 April 2017, also tick 'no' at box 6 and answer questions 7 to 15, as the RNRB was not available at the date they died so their estate could not have utilised it. If, however, they died whilst the RNRB was in force and any part of the residential interest passed to direct descendants, tick 'yes' and answer questions 16 to 21 only.

Answer questions 7 to 15 if the RNRB was not utilised on the spouse or civil partner's death. In box 7 include the total value of the spouse or civil partner's estate before the deduction of exemptions or reliefs. At box 8 include the taper threshold in force at the spouse or civil partner's date of death. The taper threshold from 6 April 2017 to 5 April 2020 is £2 million. If the value of box 7 is less than the taper threshold, do not complete boxes 9 to 12 and simply include 100 per cent in box 13. At box 14 include the relevant amount of residential enhancement for the date of the deceased's death:

- £100,000 for deaths on or after 6 April 2017 to 5 April 2018;
- £125,000 for deaths on or after 6 April 2018 to 5 April 2019;
- £150,000 for deaths on or after 6 April 2019 to 5April 2020;
- £175,000 for deaths on or after 6 April 2020 to 5 April 2021.

Multiply the value at box 14 with the percentage at box 13 and include this value at box 15 being the amount of RNRB available to transfer and utilise on the deceased's estate.

If, however, the value at box 7 exceeds the taper threshold at box 8, questions 9 to 12 must also be completed to decipher the level of tapering that applies. At box 9 deduct the value at box 8 from the value at box 7. Divide the value at box 9 by 2 and include the answer at box 10. This is the amount of tapering that applies. Include the applicable value of residential enhancement at box 11 and deduct the value at box 10 from the value at box 11 to determine the value of the unused RNRB from the spouse or civil partner's death. Include this value at box 12. If the value here is negative, there is no valid claim for TRNRB.

Answer questions 16 to 21 if any RNRB was utilised on the spouse's or civil partner's estate. Include either the default allowance or the adjusted allowance at box 16. The default allowance is the total of the residential enhancement together with any TRNRB they were entitled to. If the value of their estate exceeded the taper threshold then the default allowance is reduced or tapered away to give the adjusted allowance. Include the value of the RNRB actually utilised on the spouse or civil partner's estate. Deduct this value from the default or adjusted allowance at box 16 and include the answer at box 18. This is the sum of the unused RNRB from the spouse or civil partner's estate. Box 19 calculates the percentage of RNRB treated as being used on the death of the spouse or civil partner by dividing the unused RNRB at box 18 by the default or adjusted allowance at 16. Include the relevant residential enhancement at box 20 and then at 21 multiply the residential enhancement (box 20) by the percentage of unused RNRB (box 19) to give the amount of TRNRB available.

Once the available TRNRB has been established, the schedule prompts a visit to the RNRB calculator at the HM Revenue and Customs website at www.gov.uk/guidance/inheritance-tax-residence-nil-rate-band to work out the full entitlement to the RNRB on the deceased's death.

4.5 SUBMITTING THE COMPLETED FORMS

Where tax is payable, an inheritance tax reference should be obtained from HM Revenue and Customs at Nottingham, either online at www.hmrc.gov.uk/inheritancetax or by post using form IHT422, giving the details of the person dealing with the estate, what capacity he is acting in, together with the deceased's details including his dates of birth and death, and National Insurance number or income tax reference. HM Revenue and Customs then sends a payslip which must be completed and sent to the collector's office, together with:

- form IHT400 and supporting schedules;
- schedule IHT421;
- supporting documents, such as leases, valuations, accounts or contracts;
- a cheque for the inheritance tax due (or confirmation of the manner in which the tax is to be paid).

HM Revenue and Customs stamps form IHT421 as a receipt for the inheritance tax paid and returns it to the person acting on behalf of the personal representatives. Either it is then forwarded on to the probate registry with the application for the grant or it can simply follow the application for grant which was lodged with the probate registry when the IHT400 was lodged with HMRC. If the personal representatives need the grant particularly urgently, they can ask HMRC to return form IHT421 directly to the probate registry, which may save a day or two.

If there is no inheritance tax to pay, the following items should be sent to HM Revenue and Customs:

- form IHT400 and supporting schedules;
- schedule IHT421; and
- supporting documents.

Schedule IHT421 is stamped and returned by HM Revenue and Customs as soon as it is in agreement that no inheritance tax is payable, or HMRC raises queries. Schedule IHT421 is still stamped as a receipt for form IHT400 and returned to the solicitor for onward transmission to the probate registry.

If the personal representatives are acting in person, they should first submit schedule IHT421, together with the other documents necessary to apply for the grant, to the probate registry and attend for an interview. The documents are examined at the probate registry, and, if everything is correct, schedule IHT421 is returned to the personal representatives. The application for the grant is not processed at the registry until the procedure with HM Revenue and Customs has been completed. HMRC itself calculates the inheritance tax payable, in which case a cheque for the tax need not be sent until it is requested. Only after any inheritance tax has been paid does HMRC complete schedule IHT421 as a receipt and return it to the applicants for lodging in the probate registry, clearing the application for the grant to be processed. Alternatively, a certificate that no inheritance tax is payable allows the application for a grant to be dealt with.

4.6 CHANGES TO THE ESTATE VALUE

If, during the course of the administration, the personal representatives discover further assets, or for any other reason the value of any asset changes, or the initial valuation alters, HM Revenue and Customs must be notified and a corrective account may need to be filed (see para 20.4). HMRC should also be notified if a grant of double probate is applied for (see para 12.6.2).

Allowances against, and relief from, inheritance tax are discussed in Chapter 3. For details on finalising the inheritance tax position and closing matters with HM Revenue and Customs, see Chapter 20.

Chapter 5

Questions Concerning Wills and Codicils

5.1 TRACING THE LAST WILL

A key point to establish at the outset is whether the deceased left a will; and, if so, whether the will in the personal representatives' possession is the most recent. If the practitioner acting in the administration also acted for the deceased in a personal capacity in the period ending with his death, this may be easily done. If not, the deceased's professional advisers and his bankers should be approached to find out what they know.

A solicitor or other professional adviser has no right of lien over a will or codicil in respect of unpaid charges. After the testator's death, his will becomes the possession of his executor(s) and it is a matter for them to decide whether to disclose the content.

The deceased may have deposited his will with the Principal Registry of the Family Division (see para 27.5) so a search should be made. This may be done through any probate registry. Advertisements can also be placed in the *Law Society Gazette*. Wills can be traced by searching the National Will Register, or Certainty National Will Register. These can be used to search for lost wills on payment of the relevant fee. This can be done online by providing some basic information relating to the name of the person whose will is required, his last known address and the contact details of the person making the search. Once this has been completed and payment made, results are emailed within 72 hours. If the search is not successful a record of the search is maintained in the 'Missing Wills Service' at no extra cost. If a will is later found, details will be provided. If the solicitors who prepared the will have ceased to practise, enquiry should be made of the Solicitors Regulation Authority, which will know if there is a successor firm likely to have taken possession of the former firm's wills.

If it is believed that a person has information regarding the existence of a will or codicil, which that person refuses to impart, an order can be obtained under rule 27(6) of the Non-Contentious Probate Rules 1987 (by application under section 122 or section 123 of the Senior Courts Act 1981) for that person to be examined in court or required by subpoena to bring the will or codicil to court (see para 14.4).

Even if the personal representatives are reasonably sure that they have the final will, they must still consider the possibility that the testator may have executed one or more codicil(s), and ensure they are in possession of all such documents, including revoked codicils. If the testator owned property abroad, it may be that he made a will in another country dealing with that property. A copy of any foreign will (court certified if proved by a court abroad or notarial if not so proved) must be obtained. The probate registry will want to see such copy, but the first matter for consideration is the effect of any foreign will on the will to be proved.

5.2 PRE-LODGEMENT ENQUIRIES

Many of the queries which arise in connection with the admission to proof of a will may be resolved by enquiring at a probate registry. A probate practitioner may raise any query or point relating to a non-contentious probate matter, with the registry to which it is intended that the application for a grant will be made, as a 'pre-lodgement enquiry', that is, an enquiry before applying for the grant.

The enquiry may relate not only to some aspect of a will, but to an application for a grant or for a discretionary order; it may seek guidance as to the form of application; by whom it may be made; the documentation required; or the procedure.

The registries prefer enquiries to be made by letter or fax, setting out the relevant facts. Many registries use a pro-forma setting out the problem. See Form C82 in Appendix C. Enquiries may be made by telephone or email.

As a general rule, pre-lodgement enquiries relating to discretionary orders are answered by a registrar, or referred to a registrar before answering. At the Principal Registry of the Family Division the probate manager deals with pre-lodgement enquiries after, where appropriate, referral to a district judge.

5.3 EVIDENCE TO SUPPORT A WILL

If there is a dispute regarding the validity of a will because, for example, there are allegations of undue influence or lack of capacity, then unless the dispute is resolved by agreement, it falls to be determined on application by a probate claim in the Chancery Division under Part 57 of the Civil Procedure Rules 1998 (SI 1998/3132).

Where there is a doubt about due execution, the form of the will when executed, or the validity of alterations to the original text, or where the condition of the will creates doubt about possible revocation in part or in whole, the question falls to be determined by the probate registry, this being non-contentious (common form) work assigned to the Family Division. Enquiry may be made of the probate registry for directions as to whether evidence is necessary and, if so, what form that evidence must take and by whom it must be given.

Where it is clear that evidence is required, however, and that evidence can be readily obtained, there need be no pre-lodgement enquiry. The evidence should be lodged with the application for the grant. Depending on the problem with the will, evidence may be required to be lodged before the grant application if there is need for an order or direction of the or registrar.

5.3.1 Due execution

Rule 12 of the Non-Contentious Probate Rules 1987 deals with providing evidence by affidavit to establish due execution. For specimen forms, see Appendix C.

Where the will lacks an attestation clause, or the attestation clause is defective, or where it appears to the court that there is doubt about due execution, an affidavit establishing due execution, from the attesting witnesses, or one of them, is required. Where the witnesses are unavailable to give evidence, or where tracing a witness would be prohibitively expensive in relation to the value of the estate, or there is other good reason why a witness cannot give evidence, an affidavit may be obtained from any other person present at the execution of the will (see rule 12(1) of the Non-Contentious Probate Rules 1987).

Where evidence to establish due execution cannot be obtained from a person present when the will was executed, the court may accept evidence by affidavit from any other person, showing that the testator's signature is the handwriting of the testator. Evidence may also be given on affidavit by any person who can establish due execution in some other way.

It is a matter of judicial discretion whether such evidence is acceptable. Case law generally inclines towards a presumption in favour of due execution, the courts applying the principle *omnia praesumuntur rite esse acta* ('all things are presumed to have been done correctly'; see *Re Webb (deceased); Smith v*

Johnston [1964] 1 WLR 509). The Court of Appeal considered the question of evidence of execution of a will in *Sherrington v Sherrington* [2005] EWCA Civ 326, [2005] WTLR 587. It was held that a will was not valid unless the witnesses had signed it with the intention of witnessing the testator's signature. Reversing the decision of the court of first instance (which had pronounced against the will's validity on the basis, *inter alia*, that the witnesses did not understand they were witnessing a signature in execution of a will, [2004] WTLR 895) the Court of Appeal said that where a will was *prima facie* duly executed, only the strongest evidence would rebut the presumption of due execution. The decision in *Sherrington* was referred to by the Court of Appeal in *Channon v Perkins* [2005] EWCA Civ 1808, [2006] WTLR 425. In this case, both witnesses accepted that the signatures on the will were their signatures but neither could recall the actual event of witnessing the will. Again reversing the decision of the court of first instance, the Court of Appeal held that the strongest evidence is required to rebut the presumption of due execution of a will which was *prima facie* duly executed. In the particular case the court said that the lapse of 8 years from the date of execution was sufficient to explain the witnesses' loss of recollection of the events.

The guidance given by the Court of Appeal in *Sherrington* and in *Channon v Perkins* on the presumption of due execution was referred to in *Morgan, Griffin v Wood* [2008] WTLR 73. In this case, the witnesses had sworn standard form affidavits of due execution contradicting statements made 2 years earlier in which they had said they could not remember the testatrix signing the will in their presence. As the witnesses had both said they had not sufficiently considered their statements their evidence on affidavit was more credible (the statements did not amount to 'the strongest evidence'); but the real point was that the will, which contained an attestation clause, was signed and witnessed and was therefore *prima facie* valid. In *Salmon v Williams-Reid* [2010] EWHC 1315 (Ch), [2010] All ER (D) 233 (Nov), ChD, which was a contested validity of the will case, the court held the presumption of due execution was fortified by the inclusion of the formal attestation clause and concluded the will had been duly executed and attested in accordance with the requirements of section 9 of the Wills Act 1837.

The decision in *Sherrington* was followed in *Kentfield v Wright* [2010] EWHC 1607 (Ch), [2010] All ER (D) 07 (Jul), ChD. The claimant alleged that the execution of the will had contravened section 9 of the Wills Act 1837 in that the will had not been signed in the presence of the second witness. The claim was dismissed. The court held that on settled law, the strongest evidence was necessary to rebut the presumption of due execution where the will was regular on its face and contained an attestation clause. On the evidence, the deceased's will had been duly and properly executed in accordance with the attestation clause.

More recently, in *Devillebichot (deceased); Brennan v Prior and others* [2013] EWHC 2867 (Ch), the will was challenged, *inter alia*, on the ground of improper execution. The court held that the disputed will was written on a stationer's will form and contained a standard form attestation clause. It had a signature which purported to be that of the testator, and it professed to be witnessed by witnesses. From the evidence, the witnesses were present on the day that the will was executed. On the balance of probabilities, the testator executed the will in accordance with section 9 of the Wills Act 1837. Similarly, In *Paynter and another v Hinch* [2013] EWHC 13 (Ch), [2013] All ER (D) 79 (Feb), the validity of the deceased's will was challenged. The court held that the will was *prima facie* properly executed and there was nothing in the evidence to arouse the court's suspicion to rebut the presumption of due execution and knowledge and approval of the will's content.

In *Ahluwalia v Singh and others* [2011] EWHC 2907 (Ch), the Chancery judge, in allowing a claim contesting the validity of a will, held that the presumption of due execution had, in the circumstances, been rebutted as the witnesses had not been present together at the time the will had been signed by the testator. The decisions in the following cases were considered: *Couwenbergh v Valkova* [2008] EWHC 2451 (Ch), [2008] All ER (D) 264 (Oct) and *Kentfield v Wright* [2010] EWHC 1607 (Ch), [2010] All ER (D) 07 (Jul) were distinguished; *Channon v Perkins (a firm)* [2005] EWCA Civ 1808, [2006] WTLR 425 and *Sherrington v Sherrington* [2005] EWCA Civ 326, [2005] 3 FCR 538 were followed.

The testator's circumstances were that he had six children: three sons and three daughters. By his will he left his estate in unequal shares between his sons and two of his daughters; the third daughter being totally excluded. Probate of the will had been granted in common form to the eldest son, one of the executors.

The cases cited and referred to above all held that where a will contained an attestation clause in the usual form, and was signed and witnessed, there was a presumption of due execution requiring the strongest evidence to rebut the presumption.

Despite what the attestation clause said there was clear evidence in this case from the witnesses that they were not present together when the testator signed. Accordingly, the 'strongest evidence' test had been passed and the will was pronounced against.

A witness may be compelled, under section 122 of the Senior Courts Act 1981, to attend and give evidence about a will (see para 14.4).

5.3.2 Circumstances in which evidence is not required

Where there is doubt about due execution of a will, but the distribution of the estate would be unaffected by proof of the will, the district judge or registrar may dispense with evidence to establish due execution. The distribution of the estate is unaffected if those who would benefit under the will which is in doubt would have received the same benefit under an earlier, valid will or under the intestacy provisions (see rule 12(3) of the Non-Contentious Probate Rules 1987). A statement confirming that rule 12(3) applies may be included in the oath to lead the grant or in a letter accompanying the application. The rule only applies where there is doubtful execution. It cannot be applied if the will is clearly improperly executed, even if the distribution of the estate is unaffected.

5.3.3 Consents

Where it is impossible or impractical to obtain affidavit evidence to establish due execution, the district judge or registrar may admit a will of doubtful execution to proof provided all those prejudiced by the will consent to its admission. The persons prejudiced are those who would receive a benefit, or a greater benefit, under an earlier will or on intestacy. Consent must be given in writing. For a form of consent, see Appendix C30.

5.3.4 Will confirmed by codicil

Where a will has not been properly executed or there is doubt about execution, but it has been confirmed by a properly executed codicil, then the will may be admitted to proof without supporting evidence. Evidence may, however, still be required if there is no confirmation of the will in the codicil, or if the codicil fails to refer to the will and its date at all, or refers to them incorrectly.

5.3.5 Refusal of probate

After considering the evidence, the district judge or registrar may, if satisfied that the will is not properly executed, refuse probate of the will. The original will is endorsed by the district judge or registrar with the refusal and retained in the registry. Usually a will is marked 'probate refused' only when there has been an attempt to prove it.

Thereafter, application may be made in respect of an earlier will, or on an intestacy, as appropriate.

5.4 TESTATOR BLIND OR ILLITERATE: KNOWLEDGE AND APPROVAL OF CONTENTS OF WILL

Where a will has been signed by a testator who was blind or illiterate, or by another person on the direction of and in the presence of the testator, the district judge or registrar, before admitting the will to proof, must be satisfied that the testator had knowledge of the contents of his will at the time of its execution (rule 13 of the Non-Contentious Probate Rules 1987). Other apparent irregularities, such as a particularly frail signature by the testator, may also mean that the district judge or registrar needs to be satisfied that the testator had knowledge of the contents of the will at the time of execution.

No evidence to support the admission to proof of the will is needed if the attestation clause properly records:

- the testator's disability;
- that the will was read or otherwise communicated to him, and by whom, before execution; and
- that the testator had knowledge of the content of the will and approved it.

Nor is evidence required if the attestation clause reflects that the terms of the will were communicated to the testator by sign language, and that the testator appeared to understand and approve the content (see rule 13 of the Non-Contentious Probate Rules 1987).

The frailty of a testator's signature may raise the question of mental capacity to make the will. If there is no challenge to the will on the ground of lack of capacity, there remains the question of the testator's knowledge and approval of the content of the will. The district judge or registrar must be satisfied the testator was aware of and approved the contents of the will before it is admitted to proof. In *Clancy v Clancy* [2003] EWHC 1885, [2003] 3 WTLR 1097 and again more recently in *Perrins v Holland* [2009] EWHC 1945 (Ch), [2009] WTLR 1387, the rule in *Parker v Felgate* (1883) LR 8 PD 171 was revisited and upheld. The rule is that where a testator, when of undoubted capacity, has given instructions for a will and it is prepared in accordance with those instructions, only a slight degree of capacity and ability to understand and approve the content is required at the time of actual execution. The decision in *Perrins* was confirmed by the Court of Appeal [2010] EWCA Civ 840, [2011] 2 All ER 174.

In *Clancy* instructions were given at a time when the testatrix had capacity. She probably did not have capacity at the time of execution as she was in hospital and heavily sedated. In *Perrins* the deceased, who suffered from multiple sclerosis which affected his speech and confined him to a wheelchair, had given instructions for a will in April 2000, but it was not executed until September 2001 by which time the deceased's condition had worsened. It was held in both cases that the lack of testamentary capacity at the time of executing a will does not invalidate it, provided:

- the testator had capacity at the time when giving instructions;
- the preparation of the will was in accordance with those instructions; and
- when executing the will, the testator had awareness that he was signing a will and believed it gave effect to those instructions.

In *Singellos v Singellos* [2010] EWHC 2353 (Ch), [2011] 2 WLR 1111 (a case about the capacity to effect *inter vivos* gifts), the court held a will would be validly executed if: (a) the testator gave settled instructions in respect of it to his solicitor at the time when he had testamentary capacity; and (b) the testator executed the will knowing or believing that it reflected those earlier instructions. That was expressed as the 'third state of mind' referred to in *Parker v Felgate.*

An affidavit dealing with the bulleted points is necessary when there is no, or insufficient, evidence of reading over and the testator's understanding of the contents of the will at the time of execution.

Where the testator is unable to sign his will, it may be signed by another person on his behalf. In *Barrett v Bem (No 2)* [2011] EWHC 1247 (Ch), [2011] WTLR 1117, the court held that the court should not find that a will had been signed by a third party at the direction of the testator unless there was 'positive and discernible communication by the testator that he wished the will to be signed on his behalf by a third party'. In this case, there had been no such communication by the testator, so the signing of the will by the sister (as had been found by the court below) meant the will was not properly executed. The will was pronounced against and the earlier will of the deceased made in 2002 was pronounced for. It follows that unless the attestation clause accurately records the requirement set out above, the will cannot be admitted in common form.

5.5 ESTABLISHING THE DATE OF EXECUTION

There is no requirement in law that a will should be dated and the lack of a date or the inclusion of the wrong date cannot invalidate a will, *per incuriam* in *Corbett v Newey* [1998] Ch 57. However, where there is questionable dating of a will the probate registries will always require evidence to establish the date of execution.

Unless rule 12(3) of the Non-Contentious Probate Rules 1987 applies (see para 5.3.2), evidence is required to establish the date of execution if (see rule 14(4)):

- the date has been omitted from the will or codicil or only partially completed;
- the will contains two different dates (see below);
- the date is in the body of the will or differs from that in the endorsement;
- there are two dates and the applicant's title to the grant depends on the date; or
- the date of execution contained in the will is clearly wrong (e.g. the 31st day of June).

The district judge or registrar has discretion to accept the will to proof without evidence to support the date of execution if the will contains two dates and:

- the difference between those dates is small, for example, up to a month;
- the year has been altered to a new year and execution took place early in the new year;
- the later date appears at the end of the will and there is no reason to doubt that this is the actual date of execution.

It is equally important to establish the date of execution of any codicil; the principles above apply.

5.6 DATE OF WILL MISRECITED IN CODICIL

Where a codicil wrongly gives the date of the will to which it purports to refer, affidavit evidence is required to establish that there is no other will of the date quoted in the codicil. Evidence may be dispensed with if it can be clearly shown there was no will of the other date and that the reference to that date is merely a typographical error. However, if the date is indeed that of an earlier will then, subject to the wording of the codicil (e.g. it may be clear from the references in the codicil to clauses in the will that it could have been intended only as a codicil to the later will), evidence may be required to show there was no intention to revive the earlier will. The evidence would be expected to come from someone (perhaps the draftsman of the codicil) with knowledge of the facts surrounding the making of the codicil.

In *Hoare Trustees v Jaques and others* [2008] EWHC 2022 (Ch), the testatrix had made a will and a first codicil then a second will. Later she made a second codicil to the earlier will reviving it and the first codicil. The solicitor draftsman of the second codicil was unaware of the second will. The court found that it was implicit if not expressed that the testatrix intended to revive her earlier will. The express reference in the second codicil to the 1991 will, coupled with the terms of that codicil, varying clause 3.1 of the 1991 will, constituted a clear expression of the testatrix's intention that the first will, and therefore necessarily the first codicil, were to be revived and the second will revoked.

5.7 CONDITION OF THE WILL

If, on examination of the original will or any codicil, there appears on the document any mark of a pin, staple or clip, leading to a suspicion that another document, perhaps also testamentary, was attached to the will or codicil, evidence to account for the mark may be necessary. The district judge or registrar needs to be satisfied that the documents to be proved contain the full testamentary intentions.

If the explanation of any mark is simple, it may be dealt with in the letter accompanying the application for the grant, for example, the will had been pinned to a letter from the bank which held it in safe custody.

If there is some non-testamentary document attached to the will, it should not be removed. It will avoid questions from the registry if it is clear what is attached. The will should be submitted to proof with the document attached; the document is removed in the registry. The non-testamentary document should not be copied when creating the 'sworn copies' now required to be lodged with the grant application.

If there is no simple explanation, however, an affidavit should be made, dealing with the condition of the will when executed and its condition when found after the testator's death. For a form of affidavit, see Appendix C1.

Where a document is or was attached and contains dispositions, it may be necessary to incorporate that document in the testamentary documents (see para 5.11).

5.8 DAMAGED WILL

When dealing with a will which has been damaged in some way, the court must decide whether the damage was caused by the testator attempting to revoke the will or part of it. Clearly, if the original will was never in the possession of the testator, any damage to it could not have been done by him and there is no question of partial or total revocation.

Where the will has been accidentally damaged, an affidavit explaining the cause of the damage may be made by someone with knowledge of the cause of the damage. The affidavit may be filed with the application for a grant. To avoid delay in the application, however, the affidavit may be submitted to the district judge or registrar as a pre-lodgement matter, to establish whether the evidence is satisfactory. Indeed, it is usually preferable to submit a draft affidavit (see Appendix C1) to the court for approval before it is sworn (see para 5.2). This is still the case, notwithstanding some registries do not settle or approve drafts for which precedents are available from well-known textbooks.

If accidental damage renders the will unsuitable for photocopying the court will usually direct an engrossment be made recreating the will in the form as executed. The original will and the engrossment should be marked with the oath and lodged on application for the grant. It will be the engrossment which is copied to comply with the Practice Direction, issued by the Probate Service Director and effective from 1 January 2009, dealing with the delivery of copies of the will on application for the grant.

5.9 ALTERATIONS TO THE WILL

Section 21 of the Wills Act 1837 provides that no obliteration, interlineation or other alteration made to a will after execution has effect unless executed in the same manner as a will, that is, signed by the testator in the presence of two witnesses who each sign in his presence (see, also, rule 14(1) of the Non-Contentious Probate Rules 1987).

For these purposes, 'alterations' means alterations to the dispositions or the appointment of executors which effects the title to the grant. Where, for example, the address of an executor or beneficiary has been changed, or the testator's wishes as to the disposal of his body have been changed, the district judge or registrar may accept the will to proof without evidence as to the unauthenticated alterations. Such alterations have no effect on the disposition of the estate. If there is any doubt, the will should be referred to a district judge or registrar for pre-lodgement consideration.

Alterations made to a will at the time of execution may be authenticated by the signature or initials of the testator and both witnesses. Alternatively, they may be authenticated by a note or other reference in the attestation clause or at the end of the will, stating that the will was executed containing the alteration.

Alterations made after execution may be acceptable to proof only if the will is re-executed in accordance with section 21 of the Wills Act 1837 (see *In Re White, Barker v Gribble* [1991] Ch 1). If a codicil is executed which confirms the will including the alterations, then the altered will may be proved. If alterations made after execution cannot be validated, they are excluded from probate. The district judge or registrar usually requires an engrossment of the will to be made, restoring it to the form and content when executed. The original will should be marked on swearing the oath and lodged with the engrossment. The latter, when endorsed with the district judge's or registrar's *fiat*, is copied to make the probate and record copies.

5.10 CONDITIONAL WILLS

A conditional will, i.e. a will that only becomes effective as a will on the happening of an event, can only be admitted to proof if the event has occurred. Difficulties can arise when care was not exercised in the expression of the condition when the will was prepared. Any condition contained in a will that cannot be achieved renders the will or that clause inoperative and unacceptable to proof.

The problem on seeking to prove a conditional will is that the district judge or registrar must be satisfied that the condition contained in the will before which it does not operate was a proper condition and that condition has been fulfilled.

In the case of *Corbett v Newey* [1998] Ch 57, on 3 February 1989 the testatrix executed a valid will in which she bequeathed her two farms to her niece and nephew respectively and the residue of her estate to the niece and nephew equally. The testatrix subsequently decided to make *inter vivos* gifts of the farms to the niece and nephew and in July 1989, aware of the effect that would have on her existing will, she instructed her solicitor to change her will, omitting any reference to the two farms and bequeathing her residuary estate to the niece's children. The testatrix's instructions made it clear that she intended that the *inter vivos* gifts and the new will were interrelated transactions and that she did not intend to sign the new will until the gifts were in place. There were delays in completing the conveyancing of the gifts and in September the testatrix executed the new will but left it undated, being under the impression that it was of no effect until dated. It was held that in view of the requirement that every will had to be made with immediate testamentary intent, a testator could not by words or conduct outside the terms of the will impose upon his execution of the document a direction or condition which would postpone or qualify its operation. It followed that, while it was possible to have a will which was on its face conditional, a will which though unconditional on its face purported, through a direction imposed externally by the testator at the time of its execution, to be made conditional in its operation was not a valid will.

In the case of *Govier* [1950] P 237, the court allowed evidence to show that the testators' intention contained in their wills was for the wills to be operative only on the simultaneous deaths of the two testators. The wills contained the phrase 'in the event of our two deaths'.

The most common conditional will is one made in contemplation of marriage and now, perhaps also, the formation of a civil partnership so the oath would need to recite:

> that the marriage [civil registration of the partnership] of the deceased and [*insert name*] took place on the ... day of ... 20... and the will is therefore effective

In *Court and Others v Despallieres* [2009] EWHC 3340 (Ch), [2010] 2 All ER 451, the deceased's will contained a statement that 'my will shall not be revoked by neither subsequent marriage, civil union partnership nor adoption'. The deceased did subsequently form a civil partnership. The court held that the wording of the will was insufficient under section 18B(3) of the Wills Act 1837 to prevent the will's revocation by the formation of the partnership. The will must have been made in contemplation of a marriage/forming a civil partnership with a named person.

5.11 INCORPORATION OF OTHER TESTAMENTARY DOCUMENTS

Where it appears from the condition of the will that there may have been some other document, perhaps testamentary, attached to it, it may be that the other document (if it exists) should be incorporated with the will on proof. The same possibility arises where a will refers to another document which may contain dispositions (see rule 14(3) of the Non-Contentious Probate Rules 1987).

Where a will refers to another document, list or memorandum, that other item must be incorporated and proved with the will. A doubtful case may be referred to the court for a decision before applying for a grant, because if incorporation is directed, the other document must be marked with the will. The preconditions for incorporation are:

- the other document must contain (an) actual disposition(s) of estate (and not simply set out the reason why the estate has been disposed of by the testator in the way it has);

- the other document must have been in existence at the time the will was executed or before a codicil to the will was executed; and
- the will must sufficiently identify the other document by reference to it so that there is no doubt the other document is that mentioned in the will.

If the above criteria are not met in full, the document is not incorporated.

Where incorporation is directed, the oath should refer to the deceased's last will and testament 'as contained in the paper writings marked "A" and "B" (*et seq*) (with a codicil)', the will being marked 'A' and any other documents being lettered in alphabetical sequence.

5.12 MUTUAL WILLS

Mutual wills are usually separate documents executed by two persons in which they mutually agree to the disposition of their property, for example a husband and wife may each execute separate wills in which they each give the other their estate and agree that after the death of the survivor it passes to others. There does not, however, have to be a disposition in favour of the other testator for the doctrine of mutual wills to apply (see *Re Dale (deceased); Proctor v Dale* [1993] 4 All ER 129). More recently, in *Charles v Fraser* [2010] EWHC 2154 (Ch), it was held that for the doctrine of mutual wills to apply there had to be what amounted to a contract between the two testators that both wills would be irrevocable and remain unaltered. A common intention, expectation or desire was not enough. The mere execution of mirror or reciprocal wills did not imply any agreement either to revocation or non-revocation. For the doctrine to apply, it was not necessary that the second testator should have obtained a personal financial benefit under the will of the first testator. The agreement might be incorporated in the will or proved by extraneous evidence. It might be oral or in writing. The agreement had to be established by clear and satisfactory evidence on the balance of probabilities. On the evidence, there had been an agreement between the testatrixes (two sisters) at the time they had made their wills, that each would leave her estate to the other and that the survivor would leave what remained of their conjoined estates to the beneficiaries and in the shares stipulated in clause 5 of their wills. They had made mutual promises to each other and it was either an explicit or an implicit part of those promises that the will of the survivor would not be altered so as to change those gifts. That had been indicated by the way in which the shares of the beneficiaries had been calculated and divided equally between friends and relatives of the testatrixes. The weight of the evidence, that there had been an agreement and that part of it was that the wills were not to be changed, was such that strong grounds were needed for it to be rejected. Accordingly, there had been an agreement between the sisters in 1991, that the respective wills were not to be altered after the death of the first of the sisters.

The final word on establishing whether wills are mutual comes from the Court of Appeal decision in *Fry v Densham-Smith* [2010] EWCA Civ 1410, [2011] WTLR 387, CA. The court held that in order to prove the existence of mutual wills the evidence had to establish: (a) prior agreement by the testators to make mutual wills intending their agreement to become irrevocable on the death of the first to die; and (b) the making of the mutual wills pursuant to the agreement. If the testators failed to execute mutual wills pursuant to their agreement, that agreement did not become irrevocable on the death of the first to die. The evidence required for an express agreement not to revoke the wills had to be certain and unequivocal or clear and satisfactory so as to satisfy the court that, on the balance of probabilities, such an agreement had been made. An agreement would not be implied simply from the fact that the testators made similar wills.

The registries are not concerned that a will is a mutual will. A mutual will will be admitted to proof on application for a grant without question.

5.13 PRIVILEGED WILLS

Any soldier or member of the Air Force on actual military service, or seaman or mariner at sea, may direct the disposal of his estate without the formalities of execution required by section 9 of the Wills Act 1837 (see section 11 of that Act).

A privileged will may be in the form of a letter or statement, including an oral statement made to another person. If the latter, that oral statement must be transcribed into written form. All applications where the privilege is claimed must be referred to a district judge or registrar for directions as to the privilege and, if allowed, the form of the will.

The privilege applies even where the testator dies other than as a result of military service. The privilege accrues at the time of making the will. If no other will is made, then, unless revoked – either informally if the privilege still remains, or formally if the military service to claim privilege no longer applies – the privileged will remains the last will of the testator.

It is often forgotten that the privilege applies to a seaman or mariner being at sea at all times and not only when warlike circumstances exist. In the most recent reported case the court held that 'being at sea' includes the time when making preparation for and travelling to take up a position on board a ship. In *Re Servoz-Gavin deceased* [2009] EWHC 3168 (Ch), [2009] WTLR 1657, the deceased who was a merchant seaman (a radio officer) made an oral statement of his testamentary wishes ('What I told you before still applies. If anything happens to me, if I snuff it, I want everything to go to Auntie Anne') in February1990 to his cousin while in England before setting out on his journey to his ship in Bombay. He had made a previous statement of his wishes in 1985. He died in April 2005. The court held the privilege existed at the time of making the statement and having pronounced for the will in solemn form directed the will should be admitted to proof.

5.14 OMISSION OF OFFENSIVE WORDS FROM A WILL

Section 20 of the Administration of Justice Act 1982 allows the court to direct the insertion of words into a will, or the exclusion of words from it, before admitting the will to proof. Rectification is dealt with below.

Where a will contains words which are offensive, libellous or blasphemous, the court may direct their exclusion from the probate and record copies, and from all other copies supplied after proof. Personal representatives may apply for an order that any such words be omitted.

In *Re Hall's Estate* [1943] 2 All ER 159, it was held that a testator has the right to explain the way he has disposed of his property, but may not use his will 'as a vehicle for slander'.

If a will submitted for proof contains offensive words, the district judge or registrar may refuse to grant probate until application for those words to be omitted is made. Where a disposition is contained within, or surrounded by, offensive words, the form and content of the engrossment is determined by the court.

Unopposed applications may be dealt with by a district probate registrar, but if the application is opposed, application must be made to a district judge of the Principal Registry of the Family Division, on summons. For the procedure, see para 14.7.

5.15 RECTIFICATION

The court has, by virtue of section 20 of the Administration of Justice Act 1982, power to rectify a will by the inclusion and/or exclusion of words. The Family Division's jurisdiction is limited to unopposed applications. 'Unopposed' does not mean 'by consent', but that there is no opposition to the application. If the application is opposed or the proposed modification concerns the construction of a phrase or clause, the matter falls within the jurisdiction of the Chancery Division.

Pre-lodgement enquiry may be made to ascertain whether the district judge or registrar is willing to entertain an application; this is especially important where there is some doubt whether the criteria in section 20 of the Administration of Justice Act 1982 are met. Application may be made without notice or enquiring in advance but the district judge or registrar will require notice to be given to any person whose benefit under the will is adversely affected by the rectification. If rectification is to be permitted, it must be shown that the will as executed failed to carry out the testator's intention by reason of clerical error or failure by the draftsman to understand the testator's instructions. In *Kell v Jones and others* [2013] All ER (D) 153 (Jan), the Chancery Division dismissed the claim for rectification of a will as, although the will as drafted did not correctly reflect the testator's intentions, the error could not have been said to be a clerical error or a failure to understand the testator's instructions. The court can only rectify a will if the error falls with section 20(1) of the Act. For the procedure, see para 10.15; for a form of affidavit, see Appendix C11.

5.16 INTERPRETATION

Section 21 of the Administration of Justice Act 1982 gives the court power to interpret a will in so far as:

- any part of the will is meaningless; or
- the language used in any part of it is ambiguous on the face of it; or
- evidence, other than evidence of the testator's intention, shows that the language used in any part of it is ambiguous in the light of surrounding circumstances.

The probate registry has jurisdiction to interpret a will only to the extent necessary to determine title to the grant. Thus, the district judge or registrar may be asked to interpret the clause appointing executors, or whether there is sufficient evidence to constitute a gift of residue for a beneficiary taking that gift to take letters of administration (with will annexed). The procedure for applying for a direction on interpretation is dealt with at para 10.15.5. A form of affidavit is set out in Appendix C12. Any other clause or phrase used in the will which is ambiguous or meaningless should be dealt with by an application to the Chancery Division under Part 57 of the Civil Procedure Rules 1998.

5.17 LOST WILLS

Where, after the testator's death, the original of his will cannot be found or has been mistakenly destroyed, an application may be made for leave to prove a copy or reconstruction. In *Ferneley v Napier and others* [2010] EWHC 3345 (Ch), [2010] All ER (D) 234 (Dec), a contested lost will case, the court held that it was established law that a will could be proved even if the piece of paper on which it had been written could not be produced. It could be proved if its terms and execution were properly demonstrated by acceptable evidence.

Where the original will was in the testator's possession before his death but cannot be found after it, there is a presumption of revocation by the testator in his lifetime.

Evidence to rebut the presumption of revocation is needed if the will is to be proved. The procedure is dealt with at paras 10.14 *et seq*. For a precedent affidavit, see Appendix C9.

5.18 DECEASED DOMICILED OUTSIDE ENGLAND AND WALES

The probate registry's jurisdiction is largely based on the deceased's domicile. Where the deceased died domiciled outside England and Wales, the normal order of priority to apply for a grant contained in rules 20 and 22 of the Non-Contentious Probate Rules 1987 (see paras 12.1 and 12.3) does not apply. Where the deceased was domiciled outside the United Kingdom, it is advisable to seek the court's directions. Applications for grants in these cases are made under the provisions of rule 30:

Grants where deceased died domiciled outside England and Wales

30.—(1) Subject to paragraph (3) below, where the deceased died domiciled outside England and Wales, a district judge or registrar may order that a grant, limited in such way as the district judge or registrar may direct, do issue to any of the following persons—

(a) to the person entrusted with the administration of the estate by the court having jurisdiction at the place where the deceased died domiciled; or

(b) where there is no person so entrusted, to the person beneficially entitled to the estate by the law of the place where the deceased died domiciled or, if there is more than one person so entitled, to such of them as the district judge or registrar may direct; or

(c) if in the opinion of the district judge or registrar the circumstances so require, to such person as the district judge or registrar may direct.

(2) A grant made under paragraph 1(a) or (b) above may be issued jointly with such person as the district judge or registrar may direct if the grant is required to be made to not less than two administrators.

(3) Without any order made under paragraph (1) above—

(a) probate of any will which is admissible to proof may be granted—

(i) if the will is in the English or Welsh language, to the executor named therein; or

(ii) if the will describes the duties of a named person in terms sufficient to constitute him executor according to the tenor of the will, to that person; and

(b) where the whole or substantially the whole of the estate in England and Wales consists of immovable property, a grant in respect of the whole estate may be made in accordance with the law which would have been applicable if the deceased had died domiciled in England and Wales.

Before considering the procedure for applying for a grant, the deceased's domicile at the time of death must be determined. This is not a matter to be resolved by the probate registry. If necessary, an application to determine domicile may be made to the court under the Domicile and Matrimonial Proceedings Act 1973.

Other important matters may be determined by reference to the deceased's domicile. These include the validity of his will, the estate's liability for inheritance tax or whether the court here would have jurisdiction to entertain an application under the Inheritance (Provision for Family and Dependants) Act 1975 (see *Morgan (as Attorney of Sir Anthony Shaffer) v Diane Cilento and Others* [2004] EWHC 188 (Ch), [2004] WTLR 457 and *Cyganik v Agulian* [2006] EWCA Civ 129, [2006] WTLR 565 and *Holliday v Musa* [2010] EWCA Civ 335, [2010] 3 FCR 280 (para 4.4.1)).

5.18.1 Validity of a will

No will may be admitted to proof unless it meets the requirements of sections 1 and 2 of the Wills Act 1963, set out below:

1. General rule as to formal validity

(1) A will shall be treated as properly executed if its execution conformed to the internal law in force in the territory where it was executed, or in the territory where, at the time of its execution or of the testator's death, he was domiciled or had his habitual residence, or in a state of which, at either of those times, he was a national.

2. Additional rules

(1) Without prejudice to the preceding section, the following shall be treated as properly executed—

(a) a will executed on board a vessel or aircraft of any description, if the execution of the will conformed to the internal law in force in the territory with which, having regard to its registration (if any) and other relevant circumstances, the vessel or aircraft may be taken to have been most closely connected;

(b) a will so far as it disposed of immovable property, if its execution conformed to the internal law in force in the territory where the property was situated;

(c) a will so far as it revokes a will which under this Act would be treated as properly executed or revokes a provision which under this Act would be treated as comprised in a properly executed will, if the execution of the later will conformed to any law by reference to which the revoked will or provision would be so treated;

(d) a will so far as it exercises a power of appointment, if the execution of the will conformed to the law governing the essential validity of the power.

(2) A will so far as it exercises a power of appointment shall not be treated as improperly executed by reason only that its execution was not in accordance with any formal requirements contained in the instrument creating the power.

Where a will was executed in English form, that is, in accordance with section 9 of the Wills Act 1837, in Northern Ireland, the Republic of Ireland, Australia, Canada or New Zealand, and the deceased was domiciled there, that will is acceptable to proof without supporting evidence (Practice Direction, 20 November 1972, unreported).

Where it is clear that validity under the above provisions is established, the will may be submitted for proof applying rule 30 of the Non-Contentious Probate Rules 1987 (see para 5.18). Where any doubt arises, the directions of the district judge or registrar should be sought. Where evidence is required, that evidence may be:

- by production of a decree, order or grant of the court having jurisdiction at the place of domicile which states that the will is valid or has been accepted to proof as valid;
- by notarial statement or act made by a notary practising in the country concerned, establishing validity; or
- by affidavit of law, the deponent being qualified in the law of the place of domicile, which establishes validity (see rule 19).

5.18.2 Scottish wills

A will executed in Scotland in proper Scottish form is acceptable to proof in England and Wales provided the criteria in section 1 of the Wills Act 1963 are met, and provided no confirmation has been obtained in Scotland (see, also, para 13.1).

If the deceased's domicile was Scotland, his will should be proved there to enable the confirmation to be effective to administer the estate throughout the United Kingdom. The same principle applies to someone domiciled in Northern Ireland. Sections 1–3 of the Administration of Estates Act 1971 provide that a grant or confirmation issuing from the court of the country of the place of the deceased's domicile within the United Kingdom is sufficient to administer that deceased's estate wherever situated in the United Kingdom.

If it is unclear where a will made in Scotland or Northern Ireland should be proved, enquiry should be made of the district judge or registrar.

5.18.3 Two or more wills

Where there are two or more wills, both or all should be considered, to determine which is to be proved, or whether both or all need to be proved. For example, if the testator made two wills, neither of which specifically states that it relates to estate in a particular country, it may be necessary to prove both wills, they together comprising the last wishes of the testator for the disposal of his estate.

Even though one of two wills specifically states that it is made in relation to and only disposes of estate in a particular country, its effect on the other will, which purports to be in respect of worldwide estate, must be considered. Similarly, if two or more wills each states that it specifically deals with estate in a particular place, they must all be considered, especially in respect of revocation clauses.

In *Lamothe v Lamothe* [2006] EWHC 1387 (Ch), [2006] WTLR 1431, the question of revocation by a later foreign will was considered. It was argued that the later will, made in Dominica, was intended to dispose only of estate there, but it was worded as disposing of worldwide estate and contained a general revocation clause. The earlier will made in England had been proved here. The court held that the wording of the later will was clear and unequivocal; its effect had been explained to the testatrix by the draftsman in Dominica. The revocation of the earlier will was effective; the English grant was revoked.

It is suggested that where the deceased had executed more than one will, copies of all testamentary dispositions be submitted to the district judge or registrar for directions.

5.19 FORFEITURE OF BENEFIT BY WITNESSES

By virtue of section 15 of the Wills Act 1837, any person who benefits under a will as a specific or residuary legatee and/or devisee loses that benefit if he was a witness to the will. The benefit is also lost if the will was witnessed by the husband, wife or civil partner of the beneficiary. It is only the gift to the beneficiary which is lost; the will remains a validly executed will.

If the will was witnessed by three or more witnesses then the gift to the beneficiary witness may be saved, there being two 'other' (non-beneficiary) witnesses to execution. The gift is also saved if there was a subsequent validly executed codicil which republishes the will.

In *Barrett v Bem (No 2)* [2011] EWHC 1247 (Ch), [2011] WTLR 1117, it was held that the signing of a will by a beneficiary at the direction of and in the presence of the testator did not fall within the ambit of section 15 of the Wills Act 1837. This decision still holds good notwithstanding the decision to admit the will was reversed by the Court of Appeal.

5.20 FORFEITURE OF RIGHT TO BENEFIT

Where a person has been convicted of the murder or manslaughter of the deceased, that person forfeits the right to benefit from the deceased's estate, subject to any relief under the Forfeiture Act 1982 (see *In Re Crippen's Estate* [1911] P 108). The loss of the beneficial right applies whether the entitlement arises from a will or intestacy. In *Re Land Deceased, Land v Land* [2006] EWHC 2069 (Ch), [2007] 1 WLR 1009, it was held that the person convicted of an unlawful killing forfeits his right to benefit under a will or intestacy but is not precluded from seeking benefit from the deceased's estate by application under the Inheritance (Provision for Family and Dependants) Act 1975. In *Henderson v Wilcox* [2015] EWHC 3469 (Ch), [2016] 4 WLR 14, the Chancery Division dismissed an application by the claimant, who had been found guilty of the manslaughter of his mother, to inherit his mother's estate, as justice did not require modification of the forfeiture rule. However, the court held that the forfeiture rule had no application to any interest presently or in future created under two trusts relating to his mother's home.

As to the transfer of the right to benefit, see now the Estates of Deceased Persons (Forfeiture Rule and Law of Succession) Act 2011 and para 6.13.

5.21 EXECUTION OF THE WRONG WILL

Where the testator has mistakenly signed the will of another person, both wills are invalid. In *Re Meyer's Estate* [1908] P 353 the testators each executed the other's codicil; the court found that neither codicil could be admitted to proof as execution was invalid. The decision in *Meyers* was considered more recently in *Marley v Rawlings and another* [2011] EWHC 161 (Ch), [2011] 1 WLR 2146. By mistake the deceased executed the will meant for his wife and his wife executed the will meant for the deceased. No one noticed the error. It was only after the deceased's death that the error came to light. The court held, dismissing the claim, that the effect of signing the wrong document rendered the whole document invalid. Section 9 of the Wills Act 1837 provided a complete answer to the claim, namely that the testator had not intended by his signature to give effect to the will which he had signed. The decision was upheld by the Court of Appeal, that court also finding the provisions of section 9 of the Act had not been complied with: [2012] EWCA Civ 61, [2013] Ch 271. However, since these decisions the Supreme Court has heard an appeal from the Court of Appeal [2014] UKSC 2, [2015] AC 129 and allowed that appeal. The Supreme Court has allowed the will to be rectified by changing the names at the heading to accord with the signatures of the husband and wife. It held the handing of the wife's will to the husband by the solicitor was a clerical error falling within the ambit of section 20 of the Act.

Chapter 6

Intestacy

A full intestacy arises where the deceased failed to leave a valid will. A partial intestacy arises where the will the testator did leave did not dispose of all of the estate. In either of those situations the estate not dealt with by a will must be administered in accordance with the intestacy rules, which are set out in the Administration of Estates Act 1925 and the Intestates' Estates Act 1952.

It is essential to make a thorough search for a will. It is usual to make enquiries of local solicitors or by advertisement through the Law Society, but enquiries should also be made of the probate registry. Under the Wills (Deposit for Safe Custody) Regulations 1978 (SI 1978/1724), a testator may lodge a will for safe keeping in any probate registry, but the will is forwarded and retained in the Principal Registry of the Family Division. The registries' national computer system containing records of grants, etc also contains a record of all wills lodged for safe custody. A search for a will may be made of any registry by letter of application and on payment of the court fee of £10.

Where no will is found, careful enquiries must be made to ascertain whether any will was made but might have been lost. The distribution of the estate may be very different under any will than under the intestacy rules. For the position where there is thought to be a will but no copy can be found, see para 10.14.9.

The order of entitlement to a grant under the intestacy rules is governed by the value of the deceased's estate and the family members he left. The persons entitled to the estate of a person dying intestate since 1 January 1952 are set out below. Title to apply for letters of administration follows the same order of priority (rule 22 of the Non-Contentious Probate Rules 1987, see para 6.2).

Where a life or minority interest arises, there must be at least two administrators, or a trust corporation must take the grant (section 114(2) of the Senior Courts Act 1981). That section also provides that a district judge or registrar may, if the circumstances of the case so warrant, allow a grant to a sole grantee. Where death occurred before 1 October 2014, a life interest arose where there was a surviving spouse or civil partner and issue, but the value of the estate exceeded the statutory legacy payable to the spouse or civil partner so the survivor did not receive the whole estate (see the tables at paras 6.1 and 6.3). For deaths after 1 October 2014, the life interest is replaced by an absolute gift. A minority interest arises where a child aged under 18 is a beneficiary.

6.1 DISTRIBUTION ON INTESTACY

6.1.1 Deceased died leaving spouse or civil partner and issue

Net estate not exceeding the statutory legacy

- £250,000, death on or after 1 February 2009;
- £125,000, death on or after 1 December 1993, but before 1 February 2009;
- £75,000, death on or after 1 June 1987, but before 1 December 1993;
- £40,000, death on or after 1 March 1981, but before 1 June 1987;
- £25,000, death after 14 March 1977, but before 1 March 1981;
- £15,000, death after 30 June 1972, but before 15 March 1977;
- £8,750, death after 31 December 1966, but before 1 July 1972;
- £5,000, death before 1 January 1967.

Distribution of estate:

- All to spouse or civil partner.

Person(s) entitled to letters of administration:

- Spouse or civil partner.

Net estate exceeding the statutory legacy (as above): death before 1 October 2014

Distribution of estate:

- Spouse or civil partner takes:
  - personal chattels;
  - the 'statutory legacy':
  - free of costs and duty, with interest at the appropriate rate and a life interest in one half of the remainder with reversion to issue. The issue receive the other half absolutely.

Person(s) entitled to letters of administration:

- Spouse or civil partner and a child.

Net estate exceeding statutory legacy: death after 1 October 2014

Spouse or civil partner take the statutory legacy as above and half of the remainder absolutely. The issue receive the other half absolutely.

For deaths after 1 October 2014 section 1(1A) of the Inheritance and Trustees' Powers Act 2014 sets the simple interest rate payable on the statutory legacy as the Bank of England rate that had effect at the end of the day on which the intestate died.

6.1.2 Deceased died leaving spouse or civil partner without issue

Net estate not exceeding the statutory legacy

- £450,000, death on or after 1 February 2009;
- £200,000, death on or after 1 December 1993, but before 1 February 2009;
- £125,000, death on or after 1 June 1987, but before 1 December 1993;
- £85,000, death on or after 1 March 1981, but before 1 June 1987;
- £55,000, death after 14 March 1977, but before 1 March 1981;
- £40,000, death after 30 June 1972, but before 15 March 1977;
- £30,000, death after 31 December 1966, but before 1 July 1972;
- £20,000, death before 1 January 1967.

Distribution of estate:

- All to spouse or civil partner.

Person(s) entitled to letters of administration:

- Spouse or civil partner.

Net estate exceeding the statutory legacy (as above): death before 1 October 2014

- the surviving spouse or civil partner receives the statutory legacy (see above) and one half of the remainder absolutely; and
- as to the other half of the remainder:
  - where there are parents, to the parents absolutely in equal shares;

  - where there are no parents, to the brothers and sisters of the whole blood in equal shares, the issue of such brothers and sisters as have predeceased the intestate taking *per stirpes* the share to which their parent would have been entitled.

Person(s) entitled to letters of administration:

- Spouse or civil partner.

Net estate exceeding the statutory legacy (as above): death after 1 October 2014

Spouse or civil partner take the whole estate.

Person entitled to letters of administration:

- Spouse or civil partner.

6.1.3 Deceased died leaving spouse or civil partner without issue, parent, brother or sister of the whole blood or their issue (whatever the value of the estate)

Distribution of estate:

- All to spouse or civil partner.

Person(s) entitled to letters of administration:

- Spouse or civil partner.

6.1.4 Deceased died leaving issue only

Distribution of estate:

- Issue who attain full age or marry under age take equally. Children, including illegitimate children when the intestate died after 4 April 1988, of predeceasing children take their parent's share *per stirpes*.

Person(s) entitled to letters of administration:

- Issue.

6.1.5 Deceased died leaving father or mother only

Distribution of estate:

- Father or mother.

Person(s) entitled to letters of administration:

- Father or mother.

6.1.6 Deceased died leaving father and mother only

Distribution of estate:

- Father and mother in equal shares.

Person(s) entitled to letters of administration:

- Father or mother or both.

6.1.7 Deceased died leaving only brothers and sisters of the whole blood and issue of such brothers and sisters as died in the lifetime of the intestate

Distribution of estate:

- Brothers and sisters of the whole blood in equal shares, the issue of such brothers and sisters as have predeceased the intestate taking their parent's share *per stirpes*.

Person(s) entitled to letters of administration:

- A person or persons entitled to share in the estate.

6.1.8 Deceased died leaving only brothers and sisters of the half blood and issue of such brothers and sisters as died in the lifetime of the intestate

Distribution of estate:

- Brothers and sisters of the half blood in equal shares, the issue of such brothers and sisters as have predeceased the intestate taking their parent's share *per stirpes*.

Person(s) entitled to letters of administration:

- A person or persons entitled to share in the estate.

6.1.9 Deceased died leaving grandparents only

Distribution of estate:

- The grandparents in equal shares.

Person(s) entitled to letters of administration:

- Grandparent (one or more).

6.1.10 Deceased died leaving only uncles and aunts of the whole blood and issue of such uncles and aunts as died in the lifetime of the intestate

Distribution of estate:

- Uncles and aunts of the whole blood in equal shares, the issue of such uncles and aunts as have predeceased the intestate taking their parent's share *per stirpes*.

Person(s) entitled to letters of administration:

- A person or persons entitled to share in the estate.

6.1.11 Deceased died leaving only uncles and aunts of the half blood and issue of such uncles and aunts as died in the lifetime of the intestate

Distribution of estate:

- Uncles and aunts of the half blood in equal shares, the issue of such uncles and aunts as have predeceased the intestate taking their parent's share *per stirpes*.

Person(s) entitled to letters of administration:

- A person or persons entitled to share in the estate.

6.1.12 Deceased died leaving no blood relation taking an interest as above

Distribution of estate:

- the Crown;
- the Duchy of Lancaster;
- the Duchy of Cornwall.

Person(s) entitled to letters of administration:

- the Treasury Solicitor for the use of Her Majesty;
- the Solicitor for the Duchy of Lancaster for the use of Her Majesty;
- the Solicitor for the affairs of the Duchy of Cornwall.

6.1.13 Deceased died leaving a creditor

Person(s) entitled to letters of administration:

- A creditor, but only on clearing all kin and the Crown with a prior entitlement as set out above.

6.2 ENTITLEMENT TO TAKE LETTERS OF ADMINISTRATION

Rule 22 of the Non-Contentious Probate Rules 1987 prescribes the order of entitlement to take letters of administration; it is the same as the order of beneficial entitlement set out above. The rule is set out in full at para 12.3.

6.2.1 Renunciation or disclaimer

A renunciation is a document, executed by a person entitled to take a grant of representation, whereby that person relinquishes his or her title to the grant. It does not confer a right to a grant of representation on any other person; that right remains with the person beneficially entitled. The renunciation may be executed at any time after, but not before, the deceased's death.

A disclaimer is a document executed by a person entitled to benefit in an estate whereby he or she relinquishes that benefit. It cannot direct the beneficial entitlement to any other person; if the beneficiary wishes to achieve that effect, a deed of assignment (see para 12.2.14) or a deed of variation (see para 25.2) is the appropriate course. To qualify as a disclaimer the beneficiary must refuse the gift before taking any benefit from it (see *In Re Hodge, Hodge v Griffiths* [1940] Ch 260). Where a gift under a will or intestacy is disclaimed on or after 1 February 2012, the disclaimant is deemed to have predeceased the deceased. If there is a will then unless the will contains a contrary intention, the property automatically passes to the person next entitled under the will, and similarly if there is an intestacy. The decisions in *Re Scott, Widdows v Friends of the Clergy Corporation* [1975] 1 WLR 1260 and *Re DWS (deceased)* [2001] Ch 568 continue to apply to deaths before 1 February 2012.

For renunciations, see Chapter 9; for disclaimers, see para 25.4.

6.2.2 Accretion

The renunciation of a surviving spouse or civil partner entitled to the whole estate under an intestacy (that is, where the net estate does not exceed the statutory legacy, currently £450,000 where there is no issue, or £250,000 if there is issue (see para 6.1.4 for the effect for deaths after 1 October 2014)) does not convey beneficial entitlement to the assets of the estate. But it does allow an application for a grant to be made by a person who would be entitled to share in the estate in the event of an accretion, that is, if the estate increased in value so that it exceeded the statutory legacy. For example, a husband dies leaving his lawful wife and a son surviving and an estate of £100,000; on the widow's renunciation the son may apply for a grant as a person entitled on accretion. Again, where a wife died before 1 October 2014 leaving her lawful husband, no issue or parent but a brother of the whole blood and an estate of £150,000, on the husband's renunciation, the brother may apply for the grant as a person entitled on accretion. Beneficial entitlement remains with the husband.

6.3 SURVIVING SPOUSE OR CIVIL PARTNER

The rules below apply equally to civil partners as to spouses, and all references to 'spouse' should be treated as references to 'spouse or civil partner' for these purposes.

6.3.1 Life interest arising on intestacy

No life interest arises where death occurred after 1 October 2014. Where death was before that date, consideration needs to be given to the requirement for a second grantee pursuant to section 114(2) of the Senior Courts Act 1981.

6.4 POLYGAMOUS MARRIAGES

The question of polygamous marriages and survivorship by multiple spouses was considered in *Official Solicitor to the Senior Courts v Yemoh* [2010] EWHC 3727 (Ch), [2011] 1 WLR 1450. The facts were that the deceased had died intestate domiciled in Ghana and owning various properties, including property that was at issue, in England. He was party to a number of polygamous marriages under Ghanaian customary law and six of the defendants in the case were his widows. The issue for the court was to decide whether two or more wives could fall within the category of 'surviving spouse' for the purposes of section 46 of the Administration of Estates Act 1925.

The court held that a spouse who had been lawfully married in accordance with the law of the place of an intestate's domicile was entitled to be recognised in England as the surviving spouse for the purposes of section 46 of the Administration of Estates Act 1925. Each of the wives of the deceased was recognised as a wife in the deceased's country of domicile and accordingly section 46 should be interpreted to include multiple spouses in the circumstances of this case.

6.4.1 Redemption of life interest; death before 1 October 2014

A surviving spouse who has a life interest may require the personal representative of the deceased spouse to redeem the life interest by payment of a capital sum (see section 47A of the Administration of Estates Act 1925), so that the whole of the former matrimonial home can belong to the survivor without any trust arising over it. The capital sum is calculated in accordance with the Intestate Succession (Interest and Capitalisation) Order 1977 (SI 1977/1491) as amended with effect from 1 February 2009.

Unless and until a personal representative is constituted, the surviving spouse cannot require redemption. Title to the grant is unaffected by an intention of the surviving spouse to require redemption.

Where the surviving spouse is not also the personal representative, the surviving spouse gives notice to redeem under section 47A of the Administration of Estates Act 1925 to the personal representative. If the surviving spouse is the sole personal representative, notice to redeem is given to the Senior District Judge of the Principal Registry of the Family Division. In either case, notice must be in writing, within 12 months of the date of the issue of the grant. Notice may be given after that time, in special circumstances, with the leave of the court.

The form of notice is prescribed (Form 6 in Schedule 1 to the Non-Contentious Probate Rules 1987; see Appendix C34) and may be lodged in the Principal Registry or (in duplicate) at the district registry from which the grant issued. The original grant should be lodged for notation. Once notice has been given, it cannot be revoked without the consent of the personal representatives.

Under section 145 of the Inheritance Tax Act 1984 any capitalisation is read back to the date of death for the purposes of calculating the inheritance tax payable on the deceased's death. As the value of assets passing to the surviving spouse is inevitably reduced if the life interest is capitalised, careful consideration must be given to the inheritance tax position when deciding whether to capitalise a life interest, as this could result in (more) inheritance tax becoming payable (see, further, para 4.3.1).

6.4.2 Matrimonial home; death before 1 October 2014

A surviving spouse or civil partner has the right to require the matrimonial home to be vested in him in satisfaction of the legacy passing to him under the deceased's estate (section 5 of, and Schedule 2 to, the Intestates' Estates Act 1952). This right is automatic, apart from in the circumstances set out below. Again, notice of the desire to exercise the right must be given in writing to the personal representatives within 12 months of taking out the grant. If the legacy is lower in value than the deceased's share in the matrimonial home, the spouse or civil partner could request that his life interest in the remainder of the deceased's estate is capitalised (as mentioned above) and the home is appropriated to him in satisfaction of that sum together with the legacy. Alternatively, if the legacy and/or the lump sum are still of smaller value than the deceased's share in the home, the spouse or civil partner is permitted to make up the difference himself using his own funds and effectively buy such part of the home as cannot be appropriated to him from the estate.

The value of the home for the purposes of the appropriation is taken as the value at the date upon which the appropriation takes place, and the spouse or civil partner is entitled to request that the personal representatives obtain a new valuation of the home at that time.

If the surviving spouse or civil partner is also a personal representative the normal rules against self-dealing would apply to preclude this transaction. However, paragraph 5 of Schedule 2 to the Intestates' Estates Act 1952 expressly allows an exception to the rule in this circumstance.

As a result of this right being awarded to the surviving spouse or civil partner, the matrimonial home cannot be sold within 12 months of taking out the grant without the consent in writing of the surviving spouse or civil partner, unless the sale proceeds of the home are required for the administration of the estate and no other assets are available to meet those needs, or unless the court so orders (paragraph 4 of Schedule 2 to the Intestates' Estates Act 1952).

As mentioned above, this right is not always automatic. If the house was leased by the deceased under a tenancy which would automatically have determined or could have been determined by notice by the landlord within 2 years of the date of death, the right does not arise. A court order is required before the spouse or civil partner can exercise his right (paragraph 2 of Schedule 2 to the Intestates' Estates Act 1952) if:

- the house was held in conjunction with other land or buildings, such as agricultural land;
- it was also used for non-domestic purposes; or
- it was a hotel or lodging house.

The order is granted only if the court is satisfied that the exercise of the right would not diminish the value of the assets in the residuary estate or make them more difficult to dispose of.

6.4.3 Death of surviving spouse or civil partner before 1 October 2014 and before a grant

Section 1 of the Law Reform (Succession) Act 1995 provides that one spouse or civil partner must survive the other by 28 days to attain a beneficial interest in the deceased spouse's or civil partner's estate. If the surviving spouse or civil partner failed to survive for the requisite period those next entitled in the order of priority prescribed in rule 22 of the Non-Contentious Probate Rules 1987 (see para 6.2) may apply. On application for the grant by the person(s) entitled, the oath to lead the grant should state that the husband, wife or civil partner failed to survive by 28 days and that section 1 therefore applies.

Where the spouse or civil partner survived sufficiently long to acquire a beneficial interest but then dies without taking a grant:

(a) if he was entitled to the whole estate, the grant may be taken by his personal representatives. If application is to be made by someone of lower title under the rule then the personal representative must be cleared off by renunciation or citation (see paras 9.1 and 8.2). If there is no personal representative constituted by a grant then, unless the person(s) entitled to be personal representatives renounce their title, they must be cited to accept or refuse a grant (see para 8.2) or application must be made to pass over their right to the grant by application under section 116 of the Senior Courts Act 1981 (see para 10.13); or

(b) if he was not entitled to the whole estate, the grant may be taken by any of those entitled to share in the estate.

6.4.4 Effect of divorce/nullity decree/final order or judicial separation

A decree of divorce or nullity or final order dissolving or annulling a marriage or civil partnership granted in England and Wales removes the former spouse or civil partner as a person entitled to benefit under the other spouse's or civil partner's intestacy (except where relief is granted on application made under section 1 of the Inheritance (Provision for Family and Dependants) Act 1975 – see para 23.3).

Where the deceased's marriage or civil partnership was dissolved or annulled by decree, order or pronouncement of a foreign court and such decree is recognisable under sections 46–49 of the Family Law Act 1986, the dissolution or annulment has the same effect as an English decree/final order on the right to benefit on a spouse's or civil partner's dying intestate and domiciled in England and Wales. Section 46(2) also provides for the recognition of a dissolution of marriage or civil partnership effected overseas other than by court proceedings.

The oath to lead the grant should recite details of the final order/decree absolute and that the deceased did not thereafter remarry or form a civil partnership.

Under section 18(2) of the Matrimonial Causes Act 1973, where, after a court has pronounced a decree of judicial separation and the separation continues, either party to the marriage or civil partnership dies intestate, the deceased's estate devolves as if the other spouse or civil partner had predeceased.

It follows that where a marriage or civil partnership is dissolved by a legally recognised decree, etc or there is a continuing judicial separation, the surviving spouse or civil partner has no right to benefit under an intestacy, and the estate devolves to children or other issue, including adopted children (see para 6.5.1). For a form of oath, see Appendix C58.

6.5 GRANT TO CHILDREN OR OTHER ISSUE

The benefit of a deceased's estate (and title to the grant) falls to his child(ren) where:

- the deceased never married or formed a civil partnership;
- the deceased married or formed a civil partnership, but the marriage or civil partnership was dissolved or annulled or there was a judicial separation;
- the deceased's spouse or civil partner predeceased him;
- the deceased's spouse or civil partner (deaths after 1 February 2012) disclaims their whole interest in the estate; or
- the surviving spouse or civil partner assigns by deed his whole interest in the estate to the children.

If any child predeceased the deceased leaving issue, such issue take the share to which their parent would have been entitled if that parent had survived. If there is more than one such child, they take in equal shares.

The definition of 'issue of mine' and 'such of my issue' in a will has been held to include children, step-children and their children (see *Reading and another v Reading and others* [2015] EWHC 946 (Ch), [2015] WTLR 1245). However, this definition would not apply on an intestacy.

6.5.1 Effect of adoption order

Under an adoption order, whether made under the Adoption Act 1958 or 1976, or the Adoption and Children Act 2002, or recognisable as valid by those Acts, an adopted child is treated as the lawfully born child of his adoptive parents. The child ceases to be the child of his natural parents (see section 39(2) of the 1976 Act; section 67(2) of the 2002 Act). It follows that an adopted child is entitled to benefit from the estate of his intestate adopted parent(s) equally with a child born of those parents. Similarly, the adoptive parents benefit if their adopted child dies intestate without spouse, civil partner or issue. From the date of the adoption order, the child ceases to benefit from the death intestate of his natural parents. In *Hardy v Hardy* [2013] EWHC 83 (Ch), [2013] All ER (D) 214 (Jan), a testator directed his residuary estate 'be held in trust for such of my children as shall survive me and attain the age of 21 years and if more than one in equal shares absolutely'. The testator was survived by three sons, one of whom was adopted by his mother and step-father (his uncle). Held, on a true construction of the will as the adopted son had been described in the will and included in 'my sons' and had also been appointed an executor and trustee, section 67 was not to apply, in the circumstances of this case, to the adopted son.

An adopted child is entitled to benefit as the child of his adoptive parents from any other estate under the scenarios set out at para 6.1.

6.5.2 Illegitimate children

Since the passing of the Legitimacy Act 1926 an illegitimate child has had the right to inherit under his mother's intestacy.

The Family Law Reform Act 1969 increased an illegitimate child's rights to inherit under an intestacy. In respect of deaths after 1 January 1970, Part IV of the Administration of Estates Act 1925 (from which the tables in para 6.1 are extracted) is construed so that any reference to the issue of an intestate includes a reference to any illegitimate child of his and to the issue of such child, and any reference to a child or children of the intestate includes a reference to any illegitimate child or children.

With effect from 4 April 1988, the Family Law Reform Act 1987 provides that illegitimacy is not relevant in determining an illegitimate person's right to inherit or any right to inherit from an illegitimate person. This means that there is now no difference between legitimate and illegitimate children as regards their rights to inherit.

6.6 GRANT TO PARENTS

Where the deceased died leaving no surviving spouse, civil partner or issue, title to benefit falls to the deceased's parents, in equal shares, or to the survivor of them, absolutely. If both parents survive, either or both may apply for the grant. 'Parents' includes adoptive parents (see para 6.5.1).

6.7 GRANT TO BROTHERS OR SISTERS AND THEIR ISSUE

Where no spouse, civil partner or issue (including adopted children) or parent survives, the deceased's estate passes to brothers and sisters of the whole blood or their issue; failing whom, to the brothers and sisters of the half-blood (that is, with only one parent in common). The child or remoter issue of a brother or sister who predeceased the deceased takes the share to which his parent would have been entitled if alive. Issue of a predeceased sibling of the deceased (nephew or niece) of the whole blood take in preference to a sibling of the half blood.

6.8 GRANT TO GRANDPARENTS

Where no spouse, civil partner, issue (including adopted children), parent or sibling of the whole or half blood, or their issue, survive, title falls to the deceased's grandparents, the benefit being divided equally between those who survive, and any or all survivors may take the grant.

If a grandparent survived but then died without taking a grant, his personal representative may apply, subject to the preference of a live interest (i.e. another surviving grandparent) over that of the personal representative of the now deceased grandparent (see rule 27(5) of the Non-Contentious Probate Rules 1987).

6.9 GRANT TO UNCLES AND AUNTS AND THEIR ISSUE

Where no spouse, civil partner, issue (including adopted children), parent, sibling of the whole or half blood or their issue, or grandparents survive, title falls to uncles and aunts of the whole blood or their issue, failing which to uncles and aunts of the half blood or their issue.

The issue of a predeceased aunt or uncle take the share which their parent would have taken if alive, in equal shares. The children of cousins are second cousins to each other, and are outside the degrees of consanguinity entitling them to benefit on another's death intestate.

6.10 GRANT TO THE CROWN

Where there are no known kin, title to an intestate's estate passes to the Crown. If the Treasury Solicitor claims *bona vacantia* on behalf of the Crown, he has title to take the grant. In any case where there are no known kin, the Treasury Solicitor will take a grant to protect and preserve the estate and then appoint genealogists to search for kin.

6.11 GRANT TO A CREDITOR

On clearing of all kin by predecease, renunciation or citation, a creditor may apply for the grant, although if the Treasury Solicitor claims *bona vacantia* he has preference over a creditor. The procedure in *bona vacantia* cases and creditors' applications is dealt with at para 12.2.5.

6.12 GRANT TO AN ASSIGNEE

Where the only person or all persons entitled to the estate of the deceased under an intestacy assigns his or their interests to another or others, the assignee(s) take the place(s), in the order of priority in rule 22 of the Non-Contentious Probate Rules 1987, of the assignor(s). For the procedure for assignees to apply, see rule 24 and para 12.2.14.

6.13 DISCLAIMER OR FORFEITURE ON INTESTACY

The Estates of Deceased Persons (Forfeiture Rule and Law of Succession) Act 2011, which came into force on 1 February 2012, provides that:

- where any person who is entitled to an interest in the residuary estate of a deceased who died intestate under the provisions of section 46 of the Act set out above, disclaims that entitlement; or
- would have been entitled to benefit had the person not been precluded by the forfeiture rule (see below) from acquiring that benefit,

the person is deemed to have died immediately before the deceased.

The effect of the new provision enables a person with no entitlement to benefit to acquire a benefit if the person entitled before them in the order of priority set out above disclaims their interest or cannot take it because they have forfeited their right. For example, the deceased dies intestate a widower leaving an only child who disclaims his benefit; the benefit passes to any child of his (grandchild of the deceased) or if he has no child to remoter issue. For the wording required in the oath, see para 12.2.14.

The court has power under the Forfeiture Act 1982 to modify the forfeiture rule thus enabling the person whose benefit was forfeit to take the benefit.

A person who unlawfully causes the death of another by murder or manslaughter is prohibited, on grounds of public policy, from benefiting from the estate of the deceased (*Re Crippen* [1911] P 108).

The effect of the decision in *Re DWS (deceased)* [2001] Ch 568 (CA), in which it was held that the rule of public policy disqualifying a murderer did not require the court to treat the murderer as having predeceased his victim for the purposes of the distribution of his estate, and the son of the murderer of the deceased persons (the grandparents) did not therefore inherit his grandparents' estates, is negated by the Estates of Deceased Persons (Forfeiture Rule and Law of Succession) Act 2011.

Where a person had been convicted of manslaughter before the Act came into force his right to the grant to the estate of his victim could be passed over by discretionary order under section 116 of the Senior Courts Act 1981 (see para 10.13). The certificate of conviction should be exhibited to the affidavit (see, also, paras 5.20 and 18.5.4).

6.14 PROPERTY TO WHICH THE INTESTACY RULES APPLY

The rules of intestacy apply only to property that could have been disposed of under the deceased's will had he made one. They do not, therefore, operate in relation to assets held jointly by the deceased and another party, or to assets held in trust for the deceased's benefit and which pass under the terms of the trust after his death. In respect of deaths before 1 January 1996, property received under a trust settlement, or as a gift from the deceased during his lifetime, had to be brought into account when determining the value of assets passing to the children of the deceased under the intestacy rules. However, this requirement, commonly referred to as 'hotchpot', was abolished by section 1(2) of the Law Reform (Succession) Act 1995.

Chapter 7

Caveats

7.1 PURPOSE

A client may give instructions, not to obtain a grant of representation, but to prevent a grant issuing to another person.

Rule 6 of the Non-Contentious Probate Rules 1987, provides that no grant of probate or letters of administration (with will annexed) may issue within 7 days of the deceased's death and no grant of letters of administration within 14 days of the death. These times may be abridged, with leave of a district judge or registrar, but their purpose is to enable a caveat to be entered to prevent a grant issuing. The client who wishes to enter a caveat ('the caveator') may wish to oppose the issue of the grant, or may need further time to make enquiries and obtain information and evidence:

- to oppose the proof of a will;
- to obtain evidence that there is a valid will, or that the purported last will is not valid;
- to satisfy himself that he or the proposed applicant is the nearest kin entitled on intestacy; or
- to oppose a grant issuing to the person entitled because he has doubts the grantee will properly administer the estate.

There may be other reasons to oppose the issue of a grant, but provided the reason can be justified, a caveat should be entered. A caveat must also be entered before citation proceedings are issued (see Chapter 8).

A caveat should be entered only by a person having an interest in the estate who wishes to oppose the issue of a grant to another person. If the purpose is to ascertain when a grant issues, to register a client's interest as a creditor of the estate, to launch proceedings against the estate, or to make a claim under section 1 of the Inheritance (Provision for Family and Dependants) Act 1975 where the deceased died before 1 October 2014, a standing search should be applied for (see para 27.2). Where the death was after 1 October 2014, application may be made under the 1975 Act before or after a grant has been taken to the deceased's estate.

7.2 DEFINITION

A caveat is a notice in writing, lodged in the Principal Registry of the Family Division, a district probate registry or probate sub-registry, to show cause against the issue of a grant to anyone other than the caveator. It requires the court not to allow a grant of representation to issue in the deceased's estate without notice to the caveator. A caveat also prevents the resealing of a colonial grant. The reason for the caveat is not required to be given by the rules.

A caveat does not stop a grant which issues on the day the caveat is entered. All grants are deemed to be sealed (and therefore become operative) immediately before 10 a.m. on the day on which the grant is dated as issuing. Clearly a caveat cannot be entered until after 10 a.m., the time at which all registries are open to the public for the conduct of business.

7.3 ENTERING A CAVEAT

Rule 44 of the Non-Contentious Probate Rules 1987, deals with the procedure for the entry of a caveat and subsequent procedures. The form of a caveat is prescribed by the rules – Form 3 in Schedule 1 (see Appendix C22).

A caveat may not be entered before the death of the person to whose estate the grant would issue.

A caveat is entered by lodging the caveat, in the prescribed form, personally or by post, in any registry or sub-registry, and paying the prescribed fee of £20. The caveat may not be entered until the correct fee is paid. The registry acknowledges the entry of the caveat by notice.

The Practice Direction dated 12 January 1999 [1999] 1 All ER 832 requires the name, address, date of death, etc of the deceased, to be entered on Form 3, as recorded on the death certificate. It is unlikely, and especially because of the time limits imposed by rule 6 of the Non-Contentious Probate Rules 1987 mentioned in para 7.1, that the person wishing to enter a caveat would have that information. Failure to comply with the direction removes from the registry any culpability for issuing a grant notwithstanding an active caveat. To achieve the intended goal of preventing the grant's issue, where the correct spelling of the deceased's names is in doubt or the exact date of death is unknown, Form 3 should contain alternative spellings, or the date of death should be given as a span, for example, 'between the 12th and 31st days of January 2017'. This enables the registry to match the details in the caveat with those of any application for a grant.

The *Probateman* computer system, which links the probate registries into the national index of applications for grants, also deals with caveats. The entry or extension of a caveat is recorded by the entering registry and updating information is automatically sent to any registry at which a grant application is pending. The Leeds District Probate Registry (the nominated registry for the purposes of rule 44(15) of the Non-Contentious Probate Rules 1987) is notified of the entry of all caveats, since all proceedings concerning caveats subsequent to their entry are dealt with at that registry (see para 7.6).

7.4 DURATION AND RENEWAL

Once entered, a caveat remains in force for 6 months from the date of entry. It may be renewed by application on written notice (letter) lodged by post within the last month of the period of 6 months from entry. A caveat may be further extended for periods of 6 months until removed. The caveat remains in force until:

- it is withdrawn by the caveator (before an appearance to a warning is entered; see para 7.7);
- a probate claim under Part 57 of the Civil Procedure Rules 1998 is issued in the Chancery Division; or
- an order to remove it and discontinue proceedings is made after application on summons to a district judge of the Principal Registry of the Family Division or, if the order is consented to, a district probate registrar.

The commencement of a probate claim extends the caveat until the determination of the claim. It prevents any grant issuing, save a grant of administration pending determination of the claim, until the claim is finally determined. The final order pronouncing for or against a testamentary document provides for a grant to issue to the person(s) entitled under the order; that grant issues out of the registry in which the grant application (if any) is pending.

A caveat entered as a prerequisite to citation proceedings remains in force until:

- it is removed by order of a district judge of the Principal Registry of the Family Division on summons;
- it is withdrawn by the caveator; or
- the citation proceedings are determined.

7.5 GRANTS WHICH MAY ISSUE WHILE A CAVEAT IS IN PLACE

A grant *ad colligenda bona*, or a grant pending determination of a probate claim (formerly a 'grant pending suit'), may issue notwithstanding a caveat is in place. A grant *ad colligenda bona* is a limited grant of letters of administration, issued pursuant to an order of a district judge or registrar, for the collection or preservation of a particular part of the deceased's estate where there is an urgent need to administer that part of the estate, or until any dispute is resolved and a full grant may be issued.

A grant pending determination of a probate claim issues pursuant to an order of a district judge, or a Master of the Chancery Division where a claim under Part 57 of the Civil Procedure Rules 1998 has been commenced in that Division. Again, the grant is of letters of administration for a specific purpose pending determination of the dispute. For more details on these grants, see para 12.5.1.

A fee of £20 is payable for the entry or extension of a caveat.

7.6 ISSUING A WARNING TO A CAVEAT

The person(s) applying for the grant or wishing to apply for a grant may issue a 'warning' to the caveator. The form of warning is prescribed by the rules (Form 4, Schedule 1; see Appendix C23). The warning may be entered only at the Leeds District Probate Registry (see Appendix B for the address).

The person warning must state in the warning his interest under a will (giving the date of it), or intestacy, in the deceased's estate. He must also give an address for service in England and Wales.

A warning is a notice to the caveator:

- to enter an appearance within 8 days of service; the warning must set out the interest of the person issuing the warning (that is, why he disputes the will or claim to an intestacy); or
- if the person warning has no contrary interest but wishes to oppose the sealing of a grant, to issue a summons for directions.

There is no fee for issuing a warning to a caveat.

The warning may be served by post, document exchange or fax in accordance with rule 5 of the Rules of the Supreme Court 1965 (SI 1965/1776) (these rules, not the Civil Procedure Rules 1998, continuing to apply to non-contentious probate applications). The warning must be endorsed as to service.

7.7 ENTERING AN APPEARANCE

The caveator has 8 days to enter an appearance to the warning at the Leeds District Probate Registry. The form of appearance is prescribed by the rules (Form 5, Schedule 1; see Appendix C24). When an appearance is entered within that time, no grant may now issue, except to the caveator, without an order of a district judge or registrar removing the caveat.

An appearance may still be entered after the prescribed time (8 days from service of the warning) has expired, provided no affidavit of service has been filed (see below).

No fee is payable on entering an appearance.

Where the caveator does not enter an appearance within the prescribed time, and fails to issue a summons for directions (see para 7.8), the person warning may file an affidavit of service of the warning in the Leeds District Probate Registry. That registry then searches for an appearance or summons, and, if neither has been filed, removes the caveat. The *Probateman* computer system is noted. This will be automatically picked up at the registry at which the grant application is pending so the grant may issue from that registry without further application. If a long time has elapsed between the entry and removal of the caveat the grant issuing registry may check with the extracting solicitors that there have been no changes affecting the grant application, for example change of executor's address or change of estate value.

If no application for a grant has been made, it may now be made in the normal way.

7.8 SUMMONS FOR DIRECTIONS

A caveator having no contrary interest, but objecting to the issue of a grant, may issue a summons for directions. The summons should be issued within the 8 days prescribed by the rules, but may be issued outside that time provided the person seeking removal of the caveat has not filed an affidavit of service of a warning.
A caveator may have no interest in the estate contrary to that of the applicant for the grant. He may accept that the will sought to be proved is the last will of the deceased, or that the applicant for the grant is a person entitled to the share under

the intestacy rules; but the reason for opposing the issue of the grant and the reason for the summons for directions may be that he objects to the particular applicant.

The summons for directions is issued for hearing by the district judge or registrar of the registry in which the application for a grant is pending, or to which it is proposed to apply for a grant. The summons must be supported by an affidavit setting out the facts on which the applicant relies. The issue of a summons is recorded by the issuing registry in the *Probateman* computer system so that the caveat remains in force.

The district judge or registrar hearing the summons may remove the caveat and direct representation be granted to the person warning, or to such other person(s), exercising the court's discretionary powers (see para 10.13) as the court considers appropriate. The court may make such other directions as to further proceedings, and/or the application for a grant, as may be appropriate.

7.9 RESTRICTION ON ENTERING FURTHER CAVEAT

Unless a district judge of the Principal Registry of the Family Division gives leave, no further caveat may be entered by a caveator where:

- the caveat has ceased to have effect by reason of failure to enter an appearance to the warning;
- a district judge or registrar has removed the caveat by order; or
- a decision of the court in a probate claim or citation proceedings has been made.

7.10 WITHDRAWAL OF CAVEAT

The caveator may withdraw his caveat at any time before he enters an appearance to the warning. Where a warning has been entered, then the caveator must give notice of his withdrawal to the person warning. The caveat must be withdrawn at the registry at which it was entered, producing the receipt for the caveat issued by that registry. The *Probateman* computer system is noted by the registry which entered the caveat, the system automatically informing the registry at which the grant application is pending, enabling the grant to issue. Unless there is any reason to doubt that the applicant still wishes to obtain the grant, the grant is issued. Where a lengthy time has elapsed from the entry of the caveat, the registry from which the grant is to issue requests confirmation that the circumstances at the time of the grant application, for example, the estate values, still apply.

No fee is payable on the withdrawal of a caveat.

7.11 DEATH OF CAVEATOR

A caveat which has been properly entered must be removed by order on summons if the caveator dies before other action is taken.

Chapter 8

Citations

8.1 NATURE OF A CITATION

A citation is a direction issued by the court requiring the person cited to take certain prescribed actions, failing which the court will make an order in the terms set out in the citation. A citation may issue requiring the citee:

- to accept or refuse a grant of representation;
- to take a grant of probate; or
- to propound a will.

A citation may issue only at the instance of a person with a direct beneficial interest in the deceased's estate. It must contain an address for service in England and Wales.

The order of priority to take a grant of representation is set out in rules 20 and 22 of the Non-Contentious Probate Rules 1987 (see paras 12.1 and 12.3). Where a person has first title to the grant under the rules, but neglects or refuses to apply for the grant and does not renounce his title, he may be cited to accept or refuse the grant (rule 47(1)). The citation may be issued by a person entitled to the grant in a lower capacity under the rules. For example:

- a residuary legatee or devisee may cite executor(s) to take probate;
- a child with a beneficial interest in the estate of an intestate deceased may cite his surviving parent to take letters of administration;
- a creditor of the deceased may cite the nearest of kin entitled under an intestacy to take letters of administration.

The citor must have a direct beneficial interest in the deceased's estate and be next entitled after the citee.

The citation serves two purposes. Firstly, it directs the person(s) with the higher entitlement to take the grant or renounce entitlement to do so. Secondly, if the citee fails to apply or renounce, it allows the court to direct that a grant issue to the citor. This allows the citor to administer the estate and acquire his benefit.

Where the deceased died testate, all executors who survive must be cited by the beneficiary citor. Similarly, all persons entitled in the same degree, for example, under a will all the other residuary beneficiaries, and on intestacy other siblings of a brother/sister applicant, must be cited. Where there is no known kin entitled under an intestacy, a citation issued at the instance of a creditor must be directed to any kin and to the Treasury Solicitor, or Solicitor for the Duchies of Cornwall and Lancaster, the Crown being entitled to *bona vacantia* in the absence of kin. The 'Treasury Solicitor' means the solicitor for the affairs of Her Majesty's Treasury and includes the solicitor for the affairs of the Duchy of Lancaster and the Duchy of Cornwall (see rule 2 of the Non-Contentious Probate Rules 1987). For the address of the Treasury Solicitor, see Appendix B.

8.2 CITATION TO ACCEPT OR REFUSE A GRANT

The purpose of a citation to accept or refuse a grant is to bring matters to a head, by requiring the person entitled to take the grant to do so, or by the court's directing administration be granted to the citor. This form of citation cannot be issued against an executor who has intermeddled in the estate without taking the grant. An intermeddling executor cannot renounce, that is, refuse to take the grant, but his title may be passed over (see paras 8.3 and 10.13.1), and see *In the Estate of Biggs* [1966] P 118.

For the form of citation, see Appendix C27.

8.3 CITATION TO TAKE PROBATE

Where an executor has intermeddled, that is, begun to collect in and/or distribute the estate, but has not obtained a grant of probate within 6 months of the testator's death, he may be cited to take the grant of probate. If the executor fails to comply with the citation by taking the grant, the citor may:

- apply by summons to the court for an order directing the executor to take probate within a specified time; or
- ask the court to order that a grant issue to himself or to another person named in the summons (see rule 47(5)(c) and (7)(c) of the Non-Contentious Probate Rules 1987).

For the form of citation, see Appendix C25.

Obviously, if the validity of the will is in dispute and proceedings to determine validity are pending, the executor cannot be cited to prove the will.

8.4 CITATION TO PROPOUND A WILL

Where there is thought to be a will, or a later will, the validity of which may be questionable, those persons interested under the alleged will or later will may be cited to propound it, that is, to take the steps necessary for it to be proved.

Any person interested in an intestate estate or under a will, whose interest is or may be adversely affected by, respectively, a will or a later will, may extract the citation. All persons with an interest under the alleged will or later will must be cited. This may be difficult without full knowledge of the alleged will, but rule 48(1) of the Non-Contentious Probate Rules 1987 requires it. Where the difficulty cannot be overcome, an application for the issue of a subpoena for the lodgement of the alleged will in a registry, under section 123 of the Senior Courts Act 1981 (see para 10.4), may be appropriate. Another alternative is to apply under section 122 (see para 14.4) for an order for the attendance of a person with knowledge of the making or whereabouts of the will to be examined before the court about the alleged will.

Where an executor believes there may be a codicil or another codicil to his testator's will, it is for him to seek evidence to support or reject that codicil. The executor is obliged to seek to prove all testamentary documents which together contain his testator's wishes. Thus, citation proceedings by an executor in respect of an alleged codicil are inappropriate.

8.5 PROCEDURE

A citation may issue out of the Principal Registry of the Family Division or a district probate registry. The form of the citation must be settled by a district judge of the Principal Registry or a district registrar (rule 46(1) of the Non-Contentious Probate Rules 1987). A fee of £12 is payable for settling the citation.

The citor (or, with the permission of a district judge or registrar, the citor's solicitor) must depose to and lodge an affidavit verifying all averments made in the citation (rule 46(2) of the Non-Contentious Probate Rules 1987). The affidavit may be submitted in draft for the approval of a district judge or registrar before being sworn. A fee of £12 is payable for the approval.

A caveat (see para 7.1) must be entered by the citor before a citation may issue. This prevents the citee from taking a grant without the citor's being aware of his intentions and able to object. The caveat, unless withdrawn by the caveator, remains in force until the court determines the person who may take the grant and that person makes the application. On application by that person, the caveat ceases to have effect (rule 46(3) of the Non-Contentious Probate Rules 1987).

Every will referred to in a citation should be lodged in the registry before the citation issues. Where, however, the will is not in the citor's possession, and the district judge or registrar is satisfied it is impracticable to require the will to be lodged, lodgement may be dispensed with (rule 46(5) of the Non-Contentious Probate Rules 1987).

Where the will is in the possession of someone other than the citor or citee, an application may be made under rule 50 (applying section 123 of the Senior Courts Act 1981) for the issue of a subpoena for the will to be lodged in the registry. For the procedure for issuing a subpoena, see para 10.4.

No fee is payable on the issue of a citation.

8.5.1 Service

The citation must be served personally, unless a district judge or registrar directs otherwise. Substituted service by special delivery post is possible if the court can be satisfied that the citee cannot be personally served. Alternatively, the court may order substituted service by advertisement. This form of service is not, however, likely to be directed unless there is good reason to suppose the advertisement will come to the notice of the citee. Where the citee's whereabouts are unknown, an application under section 116 of the Senior Courts Act 1981 (see para 10.13) may be more appropriate.

Immediately after service the citation must be endorsed as to service by the server. An affidavit of service should be sworn.

Where there are no known kin, the Treasury Solicitor and the Solicitors for the Duchies of Cornwall or Lancaster are served as agents for the Crown. Service may be effected personally or, with the leave of a district judge or registrar, by post.

8.5.2 Citation to accept or refuse a grant

Any person cited to appear may, within 8 days of service, enter an appearance in the registry from which the citation issued. Even after the 8 days have elapsed, as long as the citor has taken no action, the citee may still enter an appearance. Once the appearance has been entered, a copy, sealed by the registry, is immediately served on the citor (rule 47(6) of the Non-Contentious Probate Rules 1987).

For a form of appearance, see Appendix C29. No fee is payable on the entry of an appearance.

If the citee is willing to take the grant, he files an affidavit requesting the district judge or registrar to make an order for a grant to issue to him. The order usually includes a time limit for making the application, and once the order has been made, the citee then applies for the grant in the usual way (rule 46(4) of the Non-Contentious Probate Rules 1987).

If the citee fails to file an affidavit, or files it but then fails to apply for the grant within the time specified (or, if no time was specified, within a reasonable time), the citor should issue a summons seeking an order for a grant to issue to himself. On the hearing of the summons the district judge or registrar may make such order as he sees fit (rule 47(7)(a) of the Non-Contentious Probate Rules 1987).

Where the citee was an executor who had had power reserved to him on the original grant of probate and he fails to apply for double probate, the citor may issue a summons seeking orders that the appearance be struck out and for the original grant to be endorsed that the citee has been cited, but failed to apply, and therefore all his right and title to act as executor ceases (rule 47(7)(b) of the Non-Contentious Probate Rules 1987). The citor may then apply for letters of administration (with will annexed *de bonis non*; see para 12.6.3) in the usual way.

If the citee fails to enter an appearance within the time limit, the citor may apply by summons for an order for a grant to issue to himself (rule 47(5)(a) of the Non-Contentious Probate Rules 1987). Again, if the citee was an executor who had had power reserved, the citor applies by summons for an endorsement on the original grant that the citee has not entered an appearance and that his rights as executor have ceased. The citor may apply for letters of administration (with will annexed) *de bonis non* in the usual way (rule 47(5)(b)).

All summonses are returnable before the district judge or registrar of the registry from which the citation issued. An affidavit of facts by the citee (or, with permission, his solicitor) must be filed with the summons and a copy served with the summons.

8.5.3 Citation to take probate

If the citee fails to enter an appearance and the time for so doing has expired, the citor may apply by summons for an order that:

- the citee takes the grant within a specified time;
- the grant issues to himself; or
- the grant issues to some other person named in the summons (see rule 47(5)(a) of the Non-Contentious Probate Rules 1987).

A citee who enters an appearance may file an affidavit seeking an order for a grant to issue to him. The district judge or registrar may direct the grant be taken within a specified time.

If the citee fails to file his affidavit or to apply within the time specified (or within a reasonable time, if no time limit was imposed), the citor may apply by summons for an order:

- that the citee takes probate within a specified time;
- that a grant issues to the citor; or
- that a grant issues to some other person named in the summons.

Where an order that a grant issues to some other person named in the summons is sought, the court must be satisfied that the other person named is willing to take the grant and is a fit and proper person to act as administrator (rule 47(7)(c) of the Non-Contentious Probate Rules 1987).

8.5.4 Citation to propound a will

If the citee enters an appearance, he is required to propound the will the subject of the citation with 'reasonable diligence' (rule 48(2)(a) of the Non-Contentious Probate Rules 1987). This may be done by the issue of a probate claim in the Chancery Division for proof of the will in solemn form. But it is now more usual (initially at least) for the will to be lodged in the probate registry and attempts made to resolve matters there without litigation.

If the citee fails to enter an appearance and the time for so doing has expired, or if he enters an appearance but fails to proceed to propound the will, the citor may apply by summons for an order that a grant may issue on the basis that the will the subject of the citation is invalid (rule 48(2)(a) and (b) of the Non-Contentious Probate Rules 1987).

Any summons must be supported by an affidavit of facts (which must also be served on the citee) and the affidavit of service of the citation.

No fee is payable on the issue of a summons.

8.6 ALTERNATIVES TO CITATIONS

8.6.1 Order passing over title

A citation to accept or refuse a grant or a citation to take probate may prove effective in forcing the citee to take the grant to which he is entitled and administer the deceased's estate. The inherent danger in citing a person to take a grant, such a person having already demonstrated reluctance to act, is that that person may indeed take the grant but thereafter not proceed with due diligence to administer the estate.

Where an executor or administrator entitled to apply for a grant shows no inclination to do so within a reasonable time after the deceased's death, an application may be made for a discretionary order under section 116 of the Senior Courts Act 1981 to pass over his title and for representation to be granted to another person. The proposed grantee would be either a person next entitled, or a person whom the court would approve as a fit and proper person to act. For the procedure, see para 10.13.1.

8.6.2 Subpoena to bring in a will

Where the requirement is for a will to be produced, but not to compel any person to prove that will, a subpoena for its production may issue. Section 123 of the Senior Courts Act 1981 provides that where it appears a person has in his possession, custody or power any document which purports to be testamentary, a subpoena may issue requiring him to lodge the document in court. For the procedure, see para 10.4.

8.6.3 Order to attend for examination

Section 122 of the Senior Courts Act 1981 allows the court, on application, to order any person with knowledge of a document which purports to be testamentary to attend before the court to be examined about the will. For the procedure, see para 14.4.

Chapter 9

Renunciations

9.1 INTRODUCTION

An executor entitled to take probate or a person entitled to take letters of administration may abandon that right by signing a renunciation witnessed by a disinterested witness. Renunciation must be absolute, that is, without condition.

The only exception to the general rule is where an executor has intermeddled, that is, commenced the administration by collecting in and dealing with an asset or assets without taking probate of his testator's will. Such an executor cannot renounce but may be cited to take probate (see Chapter 8) or may be passed over by application under section 116 of the Senior Courts Act 1981 (see para 10.13.1).

Renunciation cannot be made before the death of the testator or intestate. A renunciation takes effect from the time it is signed, but may be withdrawn at any time before it is lodged in the probate registry. Once lodged, it may be retracted only with the leave of a district judge or registrar (see para 9.10).

9.2 WHO MAY RENOUNCE

An executor may renounce probate on the death of his testator (but not before).

An executor who is also entitled to a grant in another capacity in the order prescribed by rule 20 of the Non-Contentious Probate Rules 1987 (see para 12.1.1), that is, as a residuary legatee and devisee, may renounce probate but take letters of administration in the lower capacity so that he breaks any chain of representation under section 7 of the Administration of Estates Act 1925 (see para 12.6.1). If the renouncing executor wishes to abandon all his right and title, he must renounce his title in all capacities.

Again, even if there is an effective appointment of an executor who survives, any person next entitled under rule 20 of the Non-Contentious Probate Rules 1987 may renounce letters of administration (with will annexed) and lodge the will and his renunciation in a registry. In effect this applies to a residuary beneficiary or person entitled to the undisposed of estate. The renunciation would, like that of an executor, be recognisable only after the death of the testator and provided that any executor named had predeceased or had also renounced.

9.3 LODGING THE WILL ON RENUNCIATION

A person renounces by filing his renunciation with the original will in the Principal Registry of the Family Division or any district probate registry. The renunciant does not have to wait for the application for the grant to be made by the person(s) entitled.

If the original will is missing, but not revoked, the renunciation of the executor or other person entitled may be lodged with a copy of the will, providing the district judge or registrar accepts the explanation for the absence of the original will.

An original will lodged on renunciation is held in the registry in which it was filed. An entry recording the lodgement is made in the *Probateman* computer system, the national index of probate applications held by the registries. Any future application for a grant thus leads to the discovery of the will. On application for proof of a will so lodged, the will must be marked with the signatures of the deponent to the oath and the commissioner. This requires attendance at the registry in which it is lodged for the oath to be sworn there and the will to be marked in accordance with rule 10(1)(a) of the Non-Contentious Probate Rules 1987, unless a district judge or registrar gives leave to mark a copy under rule 10(2) (see, also, para 12.1.5). The district judge or registrar may be requested to give permission for the original will to be released for marking on swearing the oath, as the will must be copied and the copies lodged with the grant application.

9.4 DECEASED TESTATE

It is usual for the person who is first entitled to be the personal representative but does not wish to be, to lodge a renunciation or, perhaps more accurately, to have it lodged by the person taking the grant, on the application for the grant. Provided the renunciation is effective to clear all title of the renunciant, the person next entitled under rule 20 of the Non-Contentious Probate Rules 1987 may apply for a grant. For a form of renunciation, see Appendix C78.

9.5 DECEASED INTESTATE

A renunciation by the nearest of kin does not pass title to the grant to remoter kin. For example, a spinster dying intestate without issue leaves her parents beneficially entitled to her estate and to the grant. The parents remain the only persons beneficially entitled to the estate even if they renounce. In those circumstances, a sibling of the deceased has no title; there is no one with title to a grant.

If the person beneficially entitled disclaims their interest there is no need to renounce. On disclaiming title the grant passes to the person next entitled under rule 22 of the Non-Contentious Probate Rules 1987, the disclaimant being treated as having predeceased the deceased.

However, there is an exception where the deceased is survived by a spouse or civil partner and issue and the value of the estate is below the statutory legacy (see para 6.1.1) For deaths after 1 October 2014, only issue of the deceased may take the grant on the surviving spouse's or civil partner's renunciation, as persons beneficially entitled to share the estate under an accretion (that is, if the estate increased in value so as to exceed the statutory legacy). Similarly, on the renunciation of the nearest of kin a creditor may take letters of administration (rule 22(3) of the Non-Contentious Probate Rules 1987; para 12.3).

Rule 27(4) of the Non-Contentious Probate Rules 1987 allows letters of administration to be granted to any person entitled without notice to any other person of equal entitlement, for example, a sibling may take without notice to any other sibling. It follows that no renunciation is required from persons of equal entitlement.

A person who has renounced in one capacity cannot then take in a lower capacity (e.g. next of kin and creditor).

9.6 RENUNCIATION BY ATTORNEY

An attorney acting under a registered enduring power of attorney or registered lasting power of attorney where the donor has lost the capacity to manage his own property or affairs within the meaning of the Mental Capacity Act 2005 may renounce administration for the use and benefit of the donor of the power (see rule 35(2)(c) of the Non-Contentious Probate Rules 1987).

An attorney acting under an ordinary power of attorney may effect a renunciation on behalf of the donor – the person entitled to take letters of administration – only if the power of attorney specifically authorises him to do so. The attorney cannot renounce probate if the donor is an executor.

9.7 RENUNCIATION BY A MINOR

In the unlikely event a minor is appointed executor, the minor's right to probate cannot be renounced. Application may be made for a grant of letters of administration (with will annexed) for the use and benefit of the minor by the person entitled under rule 32(1) of the Non-Contentious Probate Rules 1987. Alternatively, the court may be asked to exercise its discretionary power under section 116 of the Senior Courts Act 1981 (see para 10.13) to pass over the minor's title.

Where the minor is entitled to letters of administration his title may be renounced only by the person appointed by order of a district judge or registrar made under rule 32(2) of the Non-Contentious Probate Rules 1987 (see para 10.10). The order specifically authorises the renunciation.

9.8 MENTAL INCAPACITY

Where the person first entitled to a grant lacks capacity to manage his affairs within the meaning of the Mental Capacity Act 2005, probate or administration may be renounced only by a person appointed specifically to do so by order of the Court of Protection. Where there is a registered enduring or registered lasting power of attorney where the donor has lost the capacity to manage his own affairs within the meaning of the Act, the attorney may renounce his right (as attorney) to the grant (see para 9.6).

9.9 RENUNCIATION BY PARTNERS/DIRECTORS IN A FIRM

Where all the partners/directors in a firm were appointed executors (not by their individual names), those partners/directors may renounce their title by any two of them effecting a renunciation on their behalf and with their authority (rule 37(2)(a) of the Non-Contentious Probate Rules 1987). Following the decision in *Re Rogers Deceased* [2006] EWHC 753 (Ch), [2006] 1 WLR 1577, that only equity (that is, profit-sharing) partners/directors may take probate, it follows that only profit-sharing partners/directors need effect the renunciation. However, if the will (also) appoints non-equity partners/directors generically they too must join in the renunciation. For a form, see Appendix C79.

9.10 RETRACTION OF RENUNCIATION

Rule 37(3) of the Non-Contentious Probate Rules 1987 allows a renunciation of probate or administration to be retracted at any time with the leave of a district judge or registrar. Only in exceptional circumstances is an executor who has renounced probate allowed to retract his renunciation if the grant has issued to a person of lesser entitlement under rule 20. For a form of retraction of renunciation, see Appendix C80.

Application for leave to retract is made *ex parte* on affidavit to the district judge or registrar of the registry in which the renunciation is filed. The affidavit must set out why the renunciant wishes to retract and now take a grant.

Chapter 10

Discretionary Orders

10.1 INTRODUCTION

An application for any of a number of discretionary orders under the Non-Contentious Probate Rules 1987 may be made *ex parte* on affidavit. The Rules of the Supreme Court 1965, as in force immediately before 26 April 1999, apply to such applications by virtue of the Non-Contentious Probate (Amendment) Rules 1999 (SI 1999/1015). The Civil Procedure Rules 1998 do not apply save as to the costs of any hearing arising from an application. Although the Non-Contentious Probate Rules 1987 provide for an *ex parte* application, there are many circumstances when the court will require notice to be given to any person whose interest may be prejudiced if the application is granted.

The Non-Contentious Probate Rules 1987 are amended with effect from 20 November 2017 (the Non-Contentious Probate (Amendment) Rules 2017 (SI 2017/1034)) to create a pilot scheme for the delivery of grant applications online. Any such application may only be made at the invitation of the registry. The oath presently required will be replaced by a statement of truth. As this is a pilot scheme by invitation only, and as no Practice Directions have been published to regulate the content of a statement of truth, the text continues to refer to application by oath only.

Both the Principal Registry of the Family Division and the district probate registries have jurisdiction in these matters, but the application should be made to the registry at which it is proposed the application for the grant is to be made.

The affidavit to lead the order should be made by the proposed grantee(s), but may be accepted if made by one of several proposed grantees with the consent of the others. With the permission of the district judge or registrar, the solicitor or probate practitioner, or other person with knowledge of the relevant facts to support the application, may be the deponent. Permission is usually given where the solicitor or probate practitioner has conducted enquiries on behalf of the client, or where the facts relied on are completely within his own knowledge, for example, on an application to allow a copy will to be proved, the original having been lost while in the solicitor's custody.

No separate 'application' for the order is necessary, as the affidavit should conclude with a request for the order sought in precise terms. No court fees are payable for the application.

The procedure for making enquiries before applying for a grant is discussed at para 5.2. Such an enquiry may lead to an application for one of the discretionary orders dealt with in this chapter. It is suggested that, unless it is obvious that the facts relied on to lead the order are sufficiently clear to give the court all the relevant evidence to make its decision on the application, a draft affidavit is submitted for approval in advance; again, the procedure for this is discussed at para 5.2. Prior approval reduces the risk that the court may require further evidence requiring another affidavit, and in the long run, reduces delay and expense.

10.2 DISPENSING WITH NOTICE TO A NON-PROVING EXECUTOR

Rule 27(1) of the Non-Contentious Probate Rules 1987 provides that where, on an application for probate, power is to be reserved to any surviving executor(s) who are not proving and have not renounced, the oath must recite that notice of the application has been given to those executor(s). For the form of notice, see Appendix C35.

Rule 27(3) of the Non-Contentious Probate Rules 1987 allows the district judge or registrar to dispense with the giving of notice where it is impracticable or would cause unreasonable delay or expense to have to give notice. By way of exception to the general rule that applications are made by affidavit, this application may, subject to the district judge's or registrar's requirements, be made by letter. The letter must set out who is applying; who is having power reserved; and the grounds for seeking the dispensation. If satisfied, the court directs no notice be given.

The oath to lead the grant should recite that power is reserved to the non-proving executor(s) and that the giving of notice was dispensed with by direction of the district judge or registrar, quoting the date of the direction. Indeed, now the registries will accept a request to dispense with the giving of notice set out in the oath. If this is done then the recital regarding dispensation referred to in the first sentence will not apply.

10.3 PERSONAL REPRESENTATIVES

10.3.1 Application to join co-administrator

Rule 25(1) of the Non-Contentious Probate Rules 1987 provides that where there is a requirement on granting letters of administration for two grantees (because a life or minority interest arises; see the introduction to para 6), a person entitled to the grant may apply with a person of lower capacity (that is, lower in the order of priority set out in rules 20 and 22; see paras 12.1 and 12.3) where there is no other person of equal title who is ready and willing to apply. There is no need for two executors to take probate when a life or minority interest arises under the will. Section 114 of the Senior Courts Act 1981 requires there to be two grantees on any application for letters of administration, but not for two executors who take probate.

Under rule 25(2) of the Non-Contentious Probate Rules 1987, where there is no such person of a lower capacity willing to be a co-administrator, application may be made for an order for a person with no right to the grant to be joined in the application as proposed co-administrator. The affidavit should be made by the first proposed grantee, setting out the facts relied on. The consent of the proposed second grantee should be exhibited to the affidavit. This form of application is now commonly made where there is a child of age and a minor child; the child of age may apply for a person to be joined as his co-administrator.

The registries will, if requested, now accept the affidavit to lead the appointment of the co-administrator with the sworn oath, the latter being appropriately worded to deal with the contemporaneous application.

No application under this rule is necessary if a minority interest arises and application is made by a person with parental responsibility, such a person being able to nominate his co-administrator under rule 32 of the Non-Contentious Probate Rules 1987.

10.3.2 Application for a grant to a sole grantee

As an alternative to applying for the joinder of a co-administrator, a direction for the grant to issue to a sole grantee may be sought. Where there is good reason, sufficient to satisfy the district judge or registrar that the estate will be properly administered by the person first entitled to the grant acting alone, and/or that there is no one prepared to act as co-administrator, the requirement for a co-administrator may be dispensed with. Section 114(2) of the Senior Courts Act 1981, which provides the requirement for two grantees, also gives the court discretion to dispense with the requirement if the circumstances warrant.

The affidavit should set out the circumstances of the case and why it is considered appropriate for the grant to issue to a sole grantee. If the district judge or registrar permits, application may be made less formally by letter.

10.3.3 Application to add a personal representative

Although any application to add a personal representative would be made after the issue of a grant, the procedure is dealt with here, as the authority to make such an order emanates from section 114 of the Senior Courts Act 1981.

An application under rule 26 of the Non-Contentious Probate Rules 1987, for a personal representative to be added, may be made where:

- after a grant has issued, a minority or life interest is discovered, but there was only one grantee; or
- there was a known minority or life interest, and the grant was issued to two grantees, but one has died.

Although section 114 of the Senior Courts Act 1981 refers to the addition of a personal representative where the grant was of letters of administration there is an implied authority to add a personal representative, where a life or minority interest arises, to a grant of probate. Section 114(5) provides that the addition of a personal representative to act with an executor does not have the effect of creating a chain of representation through the additional personal representative. The district judge or registrar will need to be satisfied there is a special circumstance requiring the addition of a personal representative to act with an executor that cannot be achieved by the executor appointing another trustee (under the provisions of the Trustee Act 2000) to act with him.

Application is made by affidavit by the grantee, with the consent of the proposed additional personal representative. The affidavit should recite the facts relied on and the reason the additional personal representative is needed. The original grant should be lodged with the application. Although there is no statutory requirement for another administrator to be joined if one of the original grantees dies, it is often useful to do so.

The district judge or registrar, if not satisfied with the application, may impound the original grant or revoke it, directing a new application be made. On the other hand, if the district judge or registrar is satisfied that the order is appropriate, the original grant is annotated with the order and the second personal representative added.

Although application under section 50 of the Administration of Justice Act 1985 (which provides the Chancery courts with power to remove and/or substitute a personal representative) would appear, by the nature of the application and the wording of the statute, to be an application entertained following the issue of the grant, the Chancery courts have made orders under this section for the removal or substitution of 'personal representatives' before the grant has issued (see *Goodman and Another v Goodman and Another* [2013] EWHC 758 (Ch), [2014] Ch 186). Practice Direction 57 to the Civil Procedure Rules 1998 has now been amended to provide for application under section 50 pre-grant. It follows that if a second applicant is required, application may be made under section 50 by way of a claim in the Chancery Division pursuant to Part 8 of the Rules. Section 50 may also be invoked to remove or substitute the person first entitled to a grant where there is good reason why that person should not act in the administration. Such application is likely only if there is some other dispute which it is necessary to bring before the court.

10.4 SUBPOENA TO BRING IN A WILL

Section 123 of the Senior Courts Act 1981 provides that:

> Where it appears any person has in his possession, custody or power any document which is or purports to be a testamentary document, the High Court may, whether or not any legal proceedings are pending, issue a subpoena requiring him to bring in the document in such manner as the court may in the subpoena direct.

After a testator's death his will becomes the possession of his executors. It is entirely a matter for them whether any information regarding the will's contents is disclosed. Where, for any good reason, any person requires the original will to be lodged in a registry so they may seek to prove it or have it pronounced against, a subpoena may be requested to issue seeking the will's lodgement.

The procedure is set out in rule 50 of the Non-Contentious Probate Rules 1987, which requires the application to be supported by an affidavit; in fact the application is contained in the affidavit. The affidavit is usually made by the person who requires the will to be lodged so that he may prove it or seek to have it pronounced against. Two copies of the subpoena should be lodged, one of which, sealed, is returned to the solicitors for the applicant for service. For forms of affidavit and subpoena, see Appendices C17 and C81.

The subpoena may direct the testamentary document be lodged in any registry, but it usually directs lodgement at the registry from which the subpoena was issued. The person subpoenaed has 8 days from the date of service within which to lodge the document as directed. The proper officer with whom the testamentary document should be lodged is the probate manager (at either the Principal Registry of the Family Division or a district probate registry).

If the person subpoenaed does not have the testamentary document in his possession, custody or power, he must file an affidavit to that effect in the registry which issued the subpoena (rule 50(2) of the Non-Contentious Probate Rules 1987).

If the person subpoenaed fails to answer the subpoena by lodging the testamentary document or filing an affidavit as described above, proceedings for committal for disobedience may be commenced against him. This application would be to a High Court Judge of the Family Division. The summons seeking committal issues out of the Principal Registry of the Family Division.

Alternatively, the party issuing the subpoena may apply for an order requiring the person subpoenaed to attend before a judge to give evidence regarding the alleged testamentary document under section 122 of the Senior Courts Act 1981 (see para 14.4). If the facts indicate the person subpoenaed is unlikely to comply with the summons to attend and be examined, and a committal application is inappropriate in the circumstances, then it may be preferable to apply for leave to prove a copy of the testamentary document, by application under rule 54 of the Non-Contentious Probate Rules 1987 (see para 10.14).

10.5 LEAVE TO SWEAR DEATH

Death certificates in respect of deaths occurring in the United Kingdom are usually issued by the Registrar of Births, Deaths and Marriages, but the Ministry of Defence (in respect of service personnel) and the Registrar General of Shipping and Seamen (in respect of merchant seamen) also issue certificates which are acceptable as proof of death. A certificate issued by the proper authority of a foreign country registering a death in that country is also acceptable. Where any doubt arises, the direction of a district judge or registrar should be obtained.

Where there is no death certificate or other document acceptable as proof of death, then application may be made for an order giving leave to swear to the death of a presumed deceased person, as having occurred on or since the date he was last seen or known to be alive.

Where the fact of death is known but the date is uncertain, application for the grant may be made without other formality, the oath stating the deceased 'was last known to be alive on [date]'; 'last seen on [date] and his dead body found on [date]'. If the death certificate or other document states the deceased died 'on or about [date]', the oath may simply contain a recital of the statement. Enquiry may be made of the registry for directions as to the form of words to be used, or a draft oath may be submitted for settling.

10.5.1 Making the application

Application for the order is made on affidavit. The affidavit should be deposed to by the person with the best knowledge of the facts – usually the proposed grantee. If the affidavit is not made by a member of the presumed deceased's immediate family, supporting evidence, on affidavit, from a member of the family should also be obtained.

The application should be made to a district judge of the Principal Registry of the Family Division if the application for the grant is to be made there. Otherwise, it should be made to the registrar of the district probate registry where it is proposed the application for the grant will be made.

The affidavit should contain, *inter alia*, details of the following facts:

- the reason the deponent believes the presumed deceased has died;
- when the presumed deceased was last seen or heard from;
- any insurance policies effected on the presumed deceased's life; any reports or enquiries made by the issuing companies; if there is no 'report', then any views expressed in writing by the insurers. The value of any policies should also be given;
- any communication (letter, telephone call, text message) received from the presumed deceased and the date of the communication;
- any advertisement or enquiry for anyone having knowledge of the presumed deceased or his disappearance, and the result (if any) of such advertisement or enquiry;
- whether the deceased had made a will or died intestate and the beneficiaries of his estate;
- any transactions by credit card or through a bank or building society account made after the disappearance, and the date(s) of the last of any such transactions;
- the value of the estate at the date of the presumed death and any increase or decrease since that date.

All letters, reports, replies to enquiries and statements, including bank or building society statements, should be exhibited. If the deceased died testate, a copy of his will should be exhibited.

All reports of official bodies, such as the police or coastguard, must also be exhibited unless their evidence is already contained in a supporting affidavit.

10.5.2 Foreign nationals

If the deceased was a foreign national or not domiciled in England and Wales, details of any enquiry made by any relevant authority (such as the police, the coastguard, or the equivalent) at the place of disappearance should be exhibited. Similarly, if the court having jurisdiction at the place of the disappearance has made a finding, any decree, pronouncement, declaration or order must be exhibited. Such evidence is corroborative but not sufficient alone.

10.5.3 Presumed death in a disaster

Where the death is presumed to have occurred in a disaster involving more than one person, enquiry should be made of the Principal Registry of the Family Division. The Principal Registry maintains a record of the evidence used to support an application for leave to swear death where the presumed deceased was one of many presumed to have died in a disaster. An enquiry may be made of the Principal Registry to see whether any order giving leave to swear death has been made in another estate. If so, the form and content of evidence filed in that application may be disclosed to assist in the later application.

The application, based on the evidence disclosed, may be made to any registry. The discretion of each registrar is, however, unfettered by the outcome of a former application.

10.5.4 Multiple deaths in a disaster

Sometimes a disaster occurs in which numerous people are killed, but, because of the nature of the disaster, bodies are not found and no death certificates issued, with the result that persons are presumed to have died. Where the presumed deaths are as the result of a major disaster the Senior District Judge will issue a circular listing the names of passengers, crew and others who he is satisfied, on the evidence supplied to him, are presumed to have died in the disaster. The circular will provide that no other evidence is required as proof of death of those named and that there is no evidence of who survived whom. In the absence of such circular it will be necessary to apply for leave to swear to the deaths of those presumed to have died. The Principal Registry of the Family Division, through the Senior District Judge, maintains a record of the evidence used to support an application for leave to swear death where the presumed deceased was one of many presumed to have died in a disaster. An enquiry may be made of the Principal Registry to see whether any order giving leave to swear death has been made in another estate. If so, the form and content of evidence filed in that application may be disclosed to assist in the later application.

The application, based on the evidence disclosed, may be made to any registry. The discretion of each registrar is, however, unfettered by the outcome of a former application.

10.5.5 Dissolution of marriage or civil partnership

A spouse or civil partner whose spouse or civil partner is missing and is presumed dead may apply to a divorce county court for a final order dissolving the marriage or partnership (see section 19 of the Matrimonial Causes Act 1973 and section 55 of the Civil Partnership Act 2004).

Even where a decree or final order based on presumption of death has been granted, the decree or final order is insufficient to allow a grant of representation to the presumed deceased's estate to be issued. Application for leave to swear death must still be made but the evidence used to support the decree or final order may be used to support the application for the order.

10.5.6 *Commorientes*

Entitlement to benefit under a will or intestacy may depend on a question of survivorship. But where multiple deaths occurred in a disaster, there may well be uncertainty about who survived whom. The Senior District Judge may issue a circular listing the names of those who died in the disaster, stating that he is satisfied on the evidence before him that there is doubt as to whom, of those known to have died, survived the others (see para 10.5.4).

Section 184 of the Law of Property Act 1925 provides that where two or more persons have died in circumstances rendering it uncertain who survived the other, a younger person is deemed to have survived an older person.

However, this does not apply in respect of a husband or wife dying on or after 1 January 1996 intestate. The surviving spouse must survive by at least 28 days to acquire a beneficial interest in the deceased spouse's estate (section 1 of the Law Reform (Succession) Act 1995). This provision also applies (from 5 December 2005) to a civil partner failing to survive the other by 28 days.

The Principal Registry of the Family Division should be contacted to ascertain whether a *commorientes* circular has been issued in respect of a particular disaster. If not, the application proceeds on evidence put before the district judge or registrar to satisfy him as to survivorship.

10.5.7 Order

The district judge or registrar, if satisfied on the evidence, makes an order giving leave to swear to the death having occurred on or since a specific date. The order is not served, but the registry communicates the details of it to the applicant. The oath to lead the grant recites the details of the order.

10.5.8 Declaration of presumption of death after absence of 7 years

Before 1 October 2014, application could be made to the Chancery Division for a declaration that a person who has been missing for 7 years or more is dead. The evidence to support the application must be strong and subject to extensive enquiries having been made for the missing person. The question of presuming the death of someone who has disappeared and not been heard of for 7 years under the previous provisions was last considered in *Bayes-Walker and another v Bayes-Walker and others* [2011] EWHC 3142 (Ch), [2011] WTLR 1143.

10.6 APPLICATION UNDER THE PRESUMPTION OF DEATH ACT 2013

The Presumption of Death Act 2013 came into force on 1 October 2014. Under section 3(1) of the Act, a declaration of presumed death is conclusive of the presumed death and the date and time of death, and under section 3(2) the declaration is effective against all persons for the purpose of the acquisition of an interest in any property and the ending of the marriage or civil partnership to which the missing person was a party. The above is subject to section 3(3) and (4) (these sub-sections deal with appeals against a declaration) Section 1 of the Act prescribes the qualifications and conditions for any application:

- the person who is missing is thought to have died or has not been known to be alive for a period of at least 7 years;
- any person may apply to the High Court for a declaration that the missing person is presumed to be dead;
- the person was domiciled in England and Wales on the day on which he or she was last known to be alive or the person was habitually resident in England and Wales throughout the period of one year ending with that day; or
- on an application by a spouse or civil partner, the applicant is domiciled in England and Wales on the date of the application or has been habitually resident in England and Wales throughout the period of one year ending with that day;
- the court must refuse the application by someone other than the missing person's spouse, civil partner, parent, child or sibling if the court considers

that the applicant does not have a sufficient interest in the determination of the application.

An application for a declaration of presumed death under the Presumption of Death Act 2013 may be made to either the Family Division or the Chancery Division. The Civil Procedure Rules 1998 apply to these applications but in the Family Division the Family Procedure Rules 2010 apply to the drawing up and service of orders.

10.7 SEVERANCE OF ESTATE

Section 113(1) of the Senior Courts Act 1981 provides that the High Court may grant representation in respect of any part of an estate, limited in any way it thinks fit. An application may be made for a temporary grant (an *ad colligenda bona defuncti* grant), or for a full grant, by order made pursuant to section 116. Both these forms of application are dealt with later in this chapter.

Section 113(2) of the Senior Courts Act 1981 provides that where it is known that the estate is insolvent, it may not be severed except in respect of a trust in which the deceased held no beneficial interest.

Application for the order to sever an insolvent estate in respect of trust property is made to a district judge or registrar of the registry at which the proposed application for the grant is to be made. The application should be made by the person first entitled in priority to the grant. If the person entitled in priority cannot or will not apply, then an application under section 116 of the Senior Courts Act 1981 to pass over his title (see para 10.13) must also be made.

The affidavit must contain details of the insolvent estate and the trust property. If satisfied, the district judge makes the order, setting the limitation to be imposed in the grant. The applicant must then make and file the oath to lead the grant, reciting details of the order.

10.8 REFUSAL OF PROBATE

Where an application to prove a will has been made, and the district judge or registrar has called for evidence to support the execution of the will, but the evidence is unsatisfactory, the district judge or registrar may refuse to grant probate. If the evidence clearly proves the will was not properly executed, the will is endorsed 'probate refused'. But if the evidence is unclear or incomplete, the district judge or registrar may refuse probate at that time, giving the applicant a further opportunity to file evidence to validate the will. If the applicant for the grant wishes he may choose to apply to the Chancery Division for the will to be pronounced for.

Where, before an application for a grant is made, it is clear from the will, or from evidence supplied to the solicitor instructed, that the will is invalid, it should not be submitted for marking that probate is refused. Instead, an application in respect of an earlier valid will, or under the intestacy provisions, as appropriate, should be made in the usual way.

10.9 FOREIGN DOMICILE

Where the deceased died domiciled outside England and Wales, the normal order of priority to take a grant of representation in rules 20 and 22 of the Non-Contentious Probate Rules 1987 (see paras 12.1 and 12.3) does not apply. An application must be made in accordance with rule 30 of the Non-Contentious Probate Rules 1987 (see para 5.18).

The question of domicile is not a matter for the probate court; nor is domicile for tax purposes the same as domicile in respect of application to a probate registry.

10.9.1 Changing domicile

The question of the deceased's domicile, or a change of domicile, may have a bearing on matters arising in the administration of an estate other than the question of the validity of a will. For example, an application for relief under the Inheritance (Provision for Family and Dependants) Act 1975 may be entertained only if the deceased died domiciled in England and Wales.

The question of a change of domicile was considered in *Cyganik v Agulian* [2006] EWCA Civ 129, [2006] WTLR 565, in which an application under the Inheritance (Provision for Family and Dependants) Act 1975 depended on the deceased's domicile. The Court of Appeal reversed the decision of the court of first instance, holding that the deceased had not acquired a domicile of choice in England. The Court of Appeal re-emphasised the principle laid down in *Re Fuld Deceased (No 3)* [1968] P 675, that a domicile of origin is more enduring than a domicile of choice. The intention necessary to abandon a domicile of origin must be clearly and unequivocally proved. However, the view contrary to *Cyganik* was found in *Holliday v Musa* [2010] EWCA Civ 335, [2010] 3 FCR 280, another case involving a Cypriot living in this country; the Court of Appeal held, in an Inheritance Act claim, that where someone had clearly set up their home for a very long time in a country, had had a family there and did not have a home elsewhere, that would provide a strong starting point as to one's domicile. For many years the deceased's permanent home had been in the United Kingdom and that continued after the death of his wife and once he began his relationship with the first claimant. If he had an intention to return to Cyprus at some stage it was for many years a vague intention to retire there. By the time of his death even that intention would appear to have disappeared. The indications were that he had made up his mind, consistent with his permanent home being in the United Kingdom, that that was where he wished to end his days and be buried. There were strong indications that having had a home with his first family in the United Kingdom, he had wished to set up a family home with the first claimant in the United Kingdom. He bought a house for her and himself to live in. He had acquired a domicile of choice in this country.

The decisions in *Cyganik* and *Holliday* were considered in *Morris v Davies and others* [2011] EWHC 1773 (Ch), [2011] WTLR 1643, in which the issue arose as to whether the testator was domiciled in England or in Belgium. In order to show that the testator had acquired a domicile of choice in Belgium, there was a need to prove the combination of residence there and an intention to remain permanently or indefinitely in Belgium. On the facts, it appeared that the testator would have moved wherever his job had taken him, but would not have been willing to commit to a future in Belgium. Despite spending considerable time in Belgium, he had retained property in England, as well as a UK passport and driving licence, had regarded himself as British and had stated his intention to return to England.

The validity of the will of a person domiciled in a foreign country must be established under the provisions of section 1 of the Wills Act 1963 (see para 5.18). If there are different laws for particular states or territories, the evidence must relate to the relevant state or territory.

10.9.2 Application by person entrusted

Rule 30(1)(a) of the Non-Contentious Probate Rules 1987 (see para 5.18 for the text of the rule) allows the person entrusted with the administration of the estate by the court having jurisdiction at the place of the deceased's domicile to apply for an order for a grant to himself. The grant is of letters of administration (with will annexed) if the deceased died testate, or letters of administration if intestate.

If the person entrusted is the executor, or one of the executors, named in the will, then, once validity of the will is established, the executor may apply for a grant of probate without order (rule 30(3)(a) of the Non-Contentious Probate Rules 1987; see para 5.18). If the person entrusted is not the executor named in the will he may apply under this rule without giving notice to the others, by-passing the executor's right to a grant.

Entrusting document

To constitute an entrusting document sufficient for the order, the foreign court must have issued a grant, or made a pronouncement, decree or order which confers upon the administrator the same or substantially the same powers as a full grant of representation issued in England and Wales. An entrusting document conferring the appropriate powers but which is limited to particular assets, for example, personalty, or is for a limited period of time, may be accepted as sufficient. In such a case, the district judge or registrar imposes a similar limitation on the grant in respect of the estate in England and Wales.

If there is any doubt about the sufficiency of the entrusting document or its limitation, it should be referred to a district judge or registrar for directions.

Will proved by foreign court

If the deceased died testate and the entrusting document incorporates or refers to the will, then no separate evidence to validate the will is necessary. The fact that the court of the place of domicile has accepted the will is sufficient to establish validity under section 1 of the Wills Act 1963.

Application for the order

The application for the order may be made by lodging the original grant, decree or order, or a court-certified (official) copy of the relevant document together with (if not incorporated within it) a court-certified (official) copy of the will. These documents are retained by the registry as part of the court record. If the grant, decree or order is not in English, an authenticated translation of it (and of the will, if any) must be lodged. Authentication may be effected by a notarial certificate or by evidence on affidavit by the translator, which sets out his qualifications to effect the translation and exhibits the (copy) entrusting document and the translation. Details of the order must be recited in the oath. For a form of oath, see Appendix C76.

The application may be made either before the application for the grant is submitted, or contemporaneously with it. If the latter, the documents referred to above should be lodged, and a request for the order should be made in the oath to lead the grant. It is far quicker and simpler to apply for the order in the oath to lead the grant.

The lawfully appointed attorney(s) of the person(s) entrusted may make the application. The grant will be for the use and benefit of the persons entrusted and limited until further representation be granted.

10.9.3 Application by person beneficially entitled

Where there is no person entrusted with the administration of the estate by the court of the place of his domicile, or the entrusting document is insufficient, or the person entrusted has since died or become mentally incapable, an application may be made under rule 30(1)(b) of the Non-Contentious Probate Rules 1987 by the person, or one of the persons, beneficially entitled to the estate by the law of the place of domicile.

Although the will names beneficiaries, evidence, not only to validate the will under section 1 of the Wills Act 1963, but also of beneficial entitlement, is necessary. The will cannot speak for itself to establish such entitlement; under the foreign law a gift in a will may not be permissible. Evidence in accordance with rule 19 of the Non-Contentious Probate Rules 1987 (see para 5.18.1) may be given on affidavit by someone qualified in that law, or by notarial statement. If the will has been proved by the court having jurisdiction at the place of domicile then no further evidence is required in respect of the validity of the will. Where the will has not been proved, the evidence to support validity and beneficial entitlement may be included in the same affidavit or notarial statement.

Where the deceased died intestate, evidence of the law of intestacy of the place of domicile is required. This evidence may be given as described above – by court pronouncement, by notarial statement or by affidavit.

Where more than one person is beneficially entitled, the district judge or registrar has discretion to entertain an application by one or some of those persons. The usual rule that no more than four personal representatives may be appointed applies equally to foreign domiciles (see section 114 of the Senior Courts Act 1981).

Application for the order

As in the case of an application under rule 30(1)(a) of the Non-Contentious Probate Rules 1987, an application for an order under rule 30(1)(b) may be made before the grant is issued, either by lodging the evidence, or by a request contained in the oath to lead the grant (supported by the evidence). The evidence, if not in English, must be accompanied by an authenticated translation. If the application is made before the grant is applied for, details of the order must be recited in the oath. For a form of oath, see Appendix C76. No more than four persons beneficially entitled may apply. Similarly to an application by a person entrusted, it is far quicker and simpler to apply for the order in the oath to lead the grant.

The application may be made by the lawfully appointed attorney(s) of the person(s) beneficially entitled. The grant will be for the use and benefit of the persons entitled and limited until further representation be granted.

10.9.4 No person entrusted or evidence of beneficial entitlement

If there is no person entrusted with the administration and no available evidence showing a person is beneficially entitled, or should either such person be unable or unwilling to apply, the court may entertain an application for a discretionary order under rule 30(1)(c) of the Non-Contentious Probate Rules 1987. It is usually wise to seek the views of the district judge or registrar on such an application by way of a pre-lodgement enquiry.

The application must be made before the grant is applied for. The court has absolute and unfettered discretion to appoint any fit and proper person to take the grant.

The application is made on affidavit, usually by the proposed grantee, setting out details of:

- the deceased;
- his domicile;
- whether the deceased died testate or intestate;
- any order which has been made by the court of the place of domicile;
- who benefits from the estate;
- why the person(s) entrusted or beneficially entitled will not, cannot or should not apply;
- the estate values;
- the person seeking the grant and why that person wishes to apply;
- any other relevant factor to assist the court in its decision.

Any evidence of foreign law not contained in a separate affidavit or notarial statement should be exhibited, as should any will. The affidavit should conclude with a request for the order.

The validity of any will must be established.

If satisfied, the district judge or registrar makes the order, details of which must be recited in the oath to be sworn by the person named in the order.

10.9.5 Life or minority interests

In any application made under rule 30(1)(a), (b) or (c) of the Non-Contentious Probate Rules 1987, where a life or minority interest arises, there must be two applicants for the grant unless the district judge or registrar exercises his discretion to allow the grant to issue to a sole grantee (section 114 of the Senior Courts Act 1981 (see para 10.3) applying to foreign domicile cases).

10.9.6 No order required: named executor or executor according to the tenor

Rule 30(3)(a)(i) of the Non-Contentious Probate Rules 1987 provides that probate of any will, the validity of which has been established, may be granted to the executor named in the will without any order. The only proviso is that the will must be in the English or Welsh language, the meaning of 'executor' being regarded as peculiar to English law. Any expression meaning 'executor' in a foreign language, or translated from a foreign language as 'executor', is unacceptable in this context.

If the will is in the Welsh language, a translation into English may be obtained from the Probate Registry of Wales at Cardiff (see Appendix B for the address).

Rule 30(3)(a)(ii) of the Non-Contentious Probate Rules 1987 allows probate of a will, again where validity has been established, to be granted to the person named in it whose duties are described sufficiently to constitute him executor according to the tenor of the will. This applies irrespective of the language in which the original will was written. A verified translation is necessary, on affidavit from a qualified translator, who must set out his qualifications in the affidavit, or by being translated by or the translation certified by a notary. If there is doubt about the sufficiency of the appointment, a pre-lodgement enquiry (with the relevant documents) should be made to the district judge or registrar.

Where rule 30(3)(a)(i) or (ii) of the Non-Contentious Probate Rules 1987, described above, applies, the application may be made by the attorney(s) of the executor or executor according to the tenor.

10.9.7 Immovable estate

Rule 30(3)(b) of the Non-Contentious Probate Rules 1987 provides that where the whole, or substantially the whole, estate in England and Wales consists of immovable property (real estate) the usual rules of entitlement to a grant, had the

deceased died domiciled in England and Wales, apply. This in effect means the order of priority in rules 20 and 22 (see paras 12.1 and 12.3) applies. No distinction is drawn between a testacy or intestacy. If there is a will, however, its validity must be established, but thereafter rule 20 applies.
The rules refer to the whole or substantially the whole estate consisting of immovable property. No definition of 'substantially' exists, but provided the real estate constitutes more than 60 per cent of the total value of the estate it can be argued that it is the substantial part of the estate. The view of the district judge or registrar as to what he regards as 'substantial' should be obtained before application for the grant under this part of the rule.

The oath to lead the grant must contain details of the estate and the values of the real and personal estate; this is particularly important if the 'substantial' test is to be applied.

10.10 MINOR(S) ENTITLED TO A GRANT

Where the person entitled to a grant of letters of administration (with will annexed) or letters of administration under an intestacy is a minor, the grant may be taken for his use and benefit by the person(s) or body having parental responsibility for him, or his guardian, under the Children Act 1989. Rule 32(1) of the Non-Contentious Probate Rules 1987 sets out those to whom a grant may issue without an order of the court.

Rule 32(3) of the Non-Contentious Probate Rules 1987 provides that where there is only one person qualifying under rule 32(1), that person may nominate a fit and proper person to be their co-administrator. Where there is no person or body with parental responsibility, or that person or body cannot, should not or will not apply for the grant, an application must be made under rule 32(2) to a district judge or registrar for an order for a person or persons to be appointed to take the grant for the minor's use and benefit.

10.10.1 Application

The application for a person to be appointed is made on affidavit under rule 32(2) of the Non-Contentious Probate Rules 1987. Although the rule refers to the appointment of 'a person' it is usual for the application to be for the appointment of two persons, rather than one who then has to nominate a co-administrator. The affidavit should recite:

- the details of the deceased;
- whether he died testate or intestate;

- the name of the minor and his age;
- the minor's title to the grant, if necessary clearing others of higher title (executors, for example);
- the person who, or body which, has parental responsibility for him or has been appointed his guardian, and why that person or body cannot or will not take the grant, or that there is no person or body with parental responsibility or guardian;
- where and with whom the minor resides;
- the relationship (if any) of the applicant to the minor;
- whether there are, or are contemplated, any proceedings under the Children Act 1989, and any order made in any such proceedings;
- whether the minor is a ward of court or there are any proceedings pending or contemplated under the court's inherent jurisdiction;
- the value of the estate; and
- any other relevant facts.

The affidavit should conclude with a request for the order.

If the minor has been made a ward of court and the wardship order subsists, the application may be referred to the district judge to whom the wardship is assigned.

The deponents to the affidavit are the proposed grantees, or one of them, provided it is clear on the evidence that the other proposed grantee agrees to act. For a form of affidavit, see Appendix C14.

A draft of the affidavit may be submitted for the district judge or registrar's approval before swearing.

When sworn, the affidavit should be lodged in the registry to which the application for the grant is to be made. If satisfied, the district judge or registrar makes the order, and a copy is sent to those representing the applicants. No fee is payable on the application. No other form of application is required, the request for the order being contained in the affidavit.

The oath to lead the grant must recite the details of the order, and the limitation imposed by it as it is to appear in the grant.

10.11 MENTAL INCAPACITY

Rule 35 of the Non-Contentious Probate Rules 1987 deals with applications on behalf of persons who are entitled to a grant but who lack capacity within the meaning of the Mental Capacity Act 2005.

Rule 35(1) of the Non-Contentious Probate Rules 1987 provides that a capable person entitled to a grant in the same degree as an incapable person must be 'cleared off' (see para 12.2.13) before an application on behalf of the incapable person may be made.

Rule 35(2) of the Non-Contentious Probate Rules 1987 provides the order of priority to apply. For applications under rule 35(2), see para 12.2.13. Where there is no one entitled in the order of priority under rule 35(2) or such a person cannot or will not act, an application for a discretionary order – to appoint someone to take the grant – must be made under rule 35(4).

The affidavit is usually deposed to by the proposed grantee, but may, subject to a district judge's or registrar's discretion, be made by the solicitor instructed if the relevant facts are within his knowledge. The affidavit should contain details of:

- the deceased and whether he died testate or intestate;
- if there is another person of equal title to the grant who is capable, why that person cannot or will not act;
- if testate, whether it is the executor who is incapable of managing his affairs, or, if not the executor, why the executor cannot act (e.g. because he has predeceased, or has renounced probate), and if it is not the executor who is incapable of managing his affairs, details of the residuary beneficiary;
- evidence to support the incapacity should be exhibited to the affidavit. If the incapable person is in an institution, the evidence may comprise a certificate from a responsible medical officer of the institution, in the following form:

> (*Name of Institution*)
>
> (*Name of patient*)
>
> I certify that:
>
> The above-named patient, [who is now residing in this Institution], suffers an impairment of or a disturbance in the functioning of [his] [her] mind or brain as a result of which [he] [she] is unable to make a decision for [himself] [herself] in relation to the application for a grant of representation and subsequent administration of the estate of [name] deceased and in my opinion [he] [she] lacks capacity within the meaning of the Mental Capacity Act 2005 to manage [his] [her] property and affairs
>
> Date:
>
> Signed: ... (*Responsible Medical Officer*)

If the person resides outside an institution, a letter or certificate, in the form above (suitably adapted), from his general practitioner would be appropriate;

- whether any deputy has been appointed by the Court of Protection, or whether any application to that court is pending or contemplated;
- the relationship (if any) of the proposed grantee to the incapable person;
- any other relevant information to support the application.

The affidavit should conclude with a request for the order.

The medical evidence from the responsible medical officer or general practitioner should be exhibited, as should a copy of the will and other testamentary documents.

Notice must be given to the Court of Protection under rule 35(5) of the Non-Contentious Probate Rules 1987 to ensure that no application for authority to act, or the registration of an enduring power of attorney, is pending. Notice may be by letter or pro forma. The acknowledgement of the notice should, if available, be lodged with the affidavit. It often takes some time before the acknowledgment of the notice is sent by the Court of Protection, so it is preferable to say in the affidavit that notice has been given and exhibit a copy of the letter giving notice. If the notice is acknowledged, the acknowledgment should be lodged with the oath.

A draft of the affidavit may be submitted to the district judge or registrar of the registry to which it is proposed to apply for the grant, for his approval before it is sworn (fee £12). For a form of affidavit, see Appendix C13.

The sworn affidavit should be lodged with the exhibits. No fee is payable on the application and no other form of application is required, the request for the order being contained in the affidavit.

A copy of the order, when made (or a notice saying the order has been made), is sent to those instructed. Details of the order giving title to apply for the grant and the limitation imposed must be recited in the oath to lead the grant.

10.12 GRANT *AD COLLIGENDA BONA DEFUNCTI*

When a grant of representation is needed to administer the estate of a deceased person, or a particular part of the estate, as a matter of urgency, but a full grant cannot be extracted in time to deal with the urgency, an application may be made for an order for a grant *ad colligenda bona defuncti*. The purpose of the grant is

to protect or preserve the estate until full representation can be taken. It is now the practice of the registries only to allow such a grant where good reason is shown both for it and why a full grant cannot be taken.
The following are some of the circumstances in which a grant of this type may be appropriate; the list is not exhaustive:

- where contracts for sale of real property have been exchanged and the vendor dies before completion;
- to sell real property where the property is in danger of vandalism or may otherwise deteriorate or become subject to an empty dwelling management order made by a local authority under the Housing Act 2004, or a purchaser has been found at an advantageous price;
- to sell any stocks and shares, or any other particular assets, where to delay sale would cause loss of value to the estate;
- to a creditor, to recover a debt where those entitled to a full grant delay in applying;
- in respect of the deceased's business, to sell, or allow someone to continue to run, the business (but see below).

Application for the order is made on affidavit, usually by the proposed grantee(s), but, with the leave of a district judge or registrar, the affidavit may be deposed to by the solicitor instructed in the application if he has knowledge of the facts.

Where a grant is required to facilitate the continued running of the deceased's business during the pendency of a dispute (e.g. about the validity of the will), it is preferable to apply on notice to a Chancery Master or district judge for an order for a grant pending the determination of a claim. The Chancery Court has greater power under section 117 of the Senior Courts Act 1981 and can direct remuneration of the personal representative appointed to run the business and provide for accounts to be delivered, which is beyond the remit of the probate registrar.

10.12.1 Affidavit

The affidavit must set out details of:

- the deceased and whether he died testate or intestate;
- if the deceased died testate, whether any testamentary document is in dispute;
- if the deceased died intestate, whether there is any dispute about title to the grant;
- why a grant is required as a matter of urgency, and why a full grant cannot be taken in sufficient time;
- the estate to be dealt with by the grant, its value and whether the estate is subject to inheritance tax;

- if there is or may be any person whose interest in the estate may be prejudiced by the grant; and
- any other relevant matter to assist the court in considering the application.

The affidavit concludes with a request for the order, showing the proposed limitation to be included in the grant. Although the grant, when issued, is silent as to the fact of a will or intestacy, a copy of any testamentary document should be exhibited to the affidavit.

The proposed grantee(s) may be the person(s) entitled to a full grant, or any person considered fit and proper to act in the administration who has demonstrated the need for the grant, including the solicitor instructed. It is often preferable for the instructed solicitor to act if urgent conveyancing is required.

Where there is serious contention in the estate, an application by summons should be considered. In *Ghafoor v Cliff* [2006] EWHC 825 (Ch), [2006] 1 WLR 3020, an application for revocation of a grant *ad colligenda bona* was made. It alleged that the affidavit to lead the *ex parte* order contained serious misrepresentations.

The court held that in the majority of cases, applications to the Probate Registry, including those for a grant of administration *ad colligenda bona*, are not contentious and are properly and sensibly made without notice. In a case where there appear to be serious divisions between the executors/beneficiaries and one is accusing the others of dishonesty and misappropriation, the need for an independent appointment on an application for a grant *ad colligenda bona* is clear. Those interested in the estate are entitled to have confidence in the impartiality of the person appointed to represent the estate. The solicitor for one of the parties involved would not reasonably be viewed as independent or impartial.

The court also held that a registrar has power to direct an application be made by summons and to give directions as to the service of that summons (rule 61(1) of the Non-Contentious Probate Rules 1987). Where appropriate, for example, where there is no consensus on issuing a temporary grant, the registrar should direct the matter be brought before him or a district judge, or a judge of the Family Division by summons. The district judge or judge may make appropriate directions as to service, abridging times if there is urgency.

The affidavit to lead an order where no notice is given must be drafted with care, so the district judge or registrar is not misled into the belief that no one is prejudiced by the absence of notice and of the opportunity to object. It follows that application without notice can be entertained only where there is no possibility that the purpose of the temporary grant could be challenged.

10.12.2 Limitation

The usual limitation in a grant *ad colligenda bona defuncti* is 'for the purpose of collecting, getting in and receiving the estate and doing such acts as may be necessary for the preservation of the same until further representation be granted but not further or otherwise'. The court's discretion to issue representation for specific purposes is absolute and unfettered. The limitation may therefore be tailored to suit the requirements of the particular case, for example, 'and to take all steps necessary to effect the sale of the Property ... and to paying the reasonable and proper costs of such sale'.

10.12.3 Approval of draft affidavit

Because of the discretionary nature of the order sought, it is usually wise to seek the view of the district judge or registrar, by way of a pre-lodgement enquiry, as to whether the application will be entertained. Thereafter it is also preferable for a draft affidavit to be submitted for approval (fee: £12). The form of limitation referred to above should be agreed with the district judge or registrar and included in the draft. Experience indicates that this saves time and expense. No fee is payable on the application for the order. The decision in *Ghafoor v Cliff* [2006] EWHC 825 (Ch), [2006] 1 WLR 3020 (para 10.12.1) may, however, prohibit the district judge or registrar from giving approval to the draft evidence if the matter is to come before him or another district registrar or judge on summons.

10.12.4 Grant

For the procedure for applying for the grant after the order has been made, see para 12.5.1.

10.12.5 Estate values and inheritance tax

If the estate qualifies as an excepted estate (see para 4.2), then the current threshold figure for inheritance tax may be inserted in the oath as the value of the gross estate, and the value of the asset being dealt with under the temporary grant is inserted as the net value. If the estate is of such a value that an inheritance tax account (IHT400) must be submitted to HM Revenue and Customs, an account dealing with that part of the estate passing under the *ad colligenda bona defuncti* grant must be delivered. Any tax due on this part of the estate must be paid. Where appropriate, for example, when no monetary value passes under the temporary grant, HM Revenue and Customs may, if requested, dispense with the requirement for an account to be delivered and/or postpone payment of tax. Enquiry should be made of HM Revenue and Customs if dispensation is sought.

The practice is to apply by letter seeking dispensation from delivering an account and enclosing with the letter a draft of the affidavit seeking the order. It is rare for HM Revenue and Customs to refuse permission.

It must be remembered that the registries cannot issue any form of grant until satisfied that no inheritance tax is payable or the tax due has been paid (see section 109 of the Senior Courts Act 1981). If HM Revenue and Customs dispenses with the delivery of an account or postpones payment a copy of the authorising letter must be lodged with the grant application.

10.13 SPECIAL CIRCUMSTANCES

Section 116 of the Senior Courts Act 1981 provides that:

> (1) If by reason of any special circumstances it appears to the High Court to be necessary or expedient to appoint as administrator some person other than the person who, but for this section, would in accordance with probate rules have been entitled to the grant, the court may in its discretion appoint as administrator such person as it thinks expedient.
>
> (2) Any grant of administration under this section may be limited in any way the court thinks fit.

The court's discretion to pass over prior claims to a grant is absolute and unfettered. The court may direct administration be granted to any person who can, on the evidence, satisfy the court that he is a fit and proper person to administer the estate. The grant, when issued pursuant to the order, is a full grant to the whole estate (unlike a grant *ad colligenda bona defuncti* referred to above) although it may, if necessary, be limited under section 116(2) of the Senior Courts Act 1981.

10.13.1 Reasons for an application

The special circumstances where an application may be made are:

- there is an unresolvable conflict between the executors (here, the application would be to pass over them and appoint independent administrators);
- to pass over the right of an executor or administrator who:
  - has failed to apply for a grant within a reasonable time after the death of the deceased;
  - is missing, and enquiries have failed to discover his whereabouts;
  - is considered unsuitable to act in the administration of the estate;

- has been convicted of the murder or manslaughter of the deceased or of any other offence within the provisions of the Forfeiture Act 1982;
- is in dispute with one or more persons equally entitled to the grant as to who should take the grant (again the application would be to appoint independent administrators);
- is an undischarged bankrupt (the application would be to enable the receiver in bankruptcy to take the grant for the benefit of the bankrupt estate);

- the applicant wishes to bring proceedings under the Inheritance (Provision for Family and Dependants) Act 1975 and does not wish also to be the personal representative;
- where there is a dispute over funeral arrangements to pass over the personal representative's authority to make the decision (*Burrows v HM Coroner for Preston* [2008] EWHC 1387 (QB), [2008] 2 FLR 1225, and more recently in *Anstey v Mundle and another* [2016] EWHC 1073 (Ch), [2016] All ER (D) 285 (Feb)).

The above list is not exhaustive. Section 116 of the Senior Courts Act 1981 may also be invoked where an executor or administrator is himself aged, or so ill that he might not survive to complete the administration. In such circumstances, the appointment of an attorney would be inappropriate since the grant would cease to be operative on the donor's death.

The court has power to pass over an executor who has intermeddled in the estate (see para 8.2), but refuses to take probate (see *In the Estate of Biggs* [1966] P 118). This application is preferable to citing a dilatory executor to take probate. If cited to accept or refuse a grant, he may accept, take a grant and be equally dilatory in administering the estate. It is preferable for such an executor to be passed over and not given further opportunity to act.

10.13.2 Affidavit

The affidavit may be made by the proposed grantee or by the solicitor instructed provided the solicitor has knowledge of the relevant facts and obtains the leave of the district judge or registrar. If there is to be more than one grantee, at least one of them should depose to the facts (subject, as has been said, to the solicitor being the deponent).

The affidavit should recite:

- details of the deceased and any will (a copy of which should be exhibited);

- the persons entitled in priority to the grant under rule 20 or rule 22 of the Non-Contentious Probate Rules 1987 (see paras 12.1 and 12.3);
- why the person entitled cannot, will not or should not apply for the grant and why his title to the grant should be passed over;
- details of the enquiries which have been made to find those entitled whose whereabouts remain unknown;
- the gross and net values of the estate;
- any other relevant fact to support the application.

The affidavit should conclude with a request for the order.

Any limitation (which is known) to be imposed in the grant should be included with the request for the order.

10.13.3 Order

If the district judge or registrar is not satisfied, he may refuse the application or give directions for further evidence. He may also direct the matter be brought before the court on summons.

If satisfied on the evidence, the district judge or registrar directs letters of administration to issue (on application) to the persons proposed as grantees.

A copy of the order, or a letter saying the order has been made, is sent by the court to the solicitor for the applicant. The oath to lead the grant recites details of the order as title to take the grant.

10.14 ADMISSION OF A COPY WILL OR NUNCUPATIVE WILL

Where the original of a testamentary document cannot be found after the testator's death, an application may be made for an order to prove a copy, draft or reconstruction. Rule 54 of the Non-Contentious Probate Rules 1987 provides:

> **Grants in respect of nuncupative wills and copies of wills**
>
> 54.—(1) Subject to paragraph (2) below, an application for an order admitting to proof a nuncupative will, or a will contained in a copy or reconstruction thereof where the original is not available, shall be made to a district judge or registrar.
>
> (2) In any case where a will is not available owing to its being retained in the custody of a foreign court or official, a duly authenticated copy of the will may be admitted to proof without the order referred to in paragraph (1) above.
>
> (3) An application under paragraph (1) above shall be supported by an affidavit setting out the grounds of the application, and by such evidence on affidavit as the applicant can adduce as to—

(a) the will's existence after the death of the testator or, where there is no such evidence, the facts on which the applicant relies to rebut the presumption that the will has been revoked by destruction;
(b) in respect of a nuncupative will, the contents of that will; and
(c) in respect of a reconstruction of a will, the accuracy of that reconstruction.

(4) The district judge or registrar may require additional evidence in the circumstances of a particular case as to the execution of the will or as to the accuracy of the copy will, and may direct that notice be given to persons who would be prejudiced by the application.

10.14.1 Executed draft or copy

In *Ferneley v Napier and others* [2010] EWHC 3345 (Ch), [2010] All ER (D) 234 (Dec), a contested lost will case, the court held that it was established law that a will could be proved even if the piece of paper on which it had been written could not be produced. It could be proved if its terms and execution were properly demonstrated by acceptable evidence.

Sometimes the only testamentary document found is an executed draft or copy. If there is evidence to show that no engrossment or other original of the document was executed, the draft or copy may be admitted to proof without application for an order under rule 54 of the Non-Contentious Probate Rules 1987.

It is suggested that, in these circumstances, the matter is referred as a pre-lodgement enquiry for the district judge or registrar to give directions on the procedure to be adopted. If satisfied, the district judge or registrar directs the executed draft or copy be admitted, the oath referring to the will 'as contained in an executed draft'. The district judge or registrar may require notice be given to persons prejudiced by proof of the draft or copy, that is, to those persons who would receive a benefit, or greater benefit, under an earlier valid will (which still exists) or on intestacy.

10.14.2 Original will held by a foreign court or notary

If the original will has been proved by a court in another country, an official copy of the will (i.e. a copy issued by the proving court and certified to be a copy of the will as proved) may be admitted to proof without order under rule 54 of the Non-Contentious Probate Rules 1987, the oath referring to the will 'as contained in an official copy'. Similarly, the original of a notarial will made abroad is retained in the notary's records and cannot be released. A notarially certified copy, that is, a copy certified by the notary to be a true and complete copy, may be admitted, the oath referring to the will 'as contained in a notarially certified copy'.

10.14.3 Lost will

When the original will was in the testator's possession before his death but cannot afterwards be found, there is a rebuttable presumption that the will was revoked by the testator in his lifetime by destruction. Evidence to rebut the presumption must be included in the affidavit, and may comprise evidence indicating that the testator had referred to his will as existing without mentioning revocation; had not consulted his solicitors or other professional advisers with a view to changing or revoking his will; or whatever the facts are to show that the testator did not revoke, or is unlikely to have revoked, his will.

The presumption of revocation was considered in *Rowe v Clarke* [2005] EWHC 3068 (Ch), [2006] WTLR 347. In this case, the original will had been in the testator's possession before his death. The testator and his partner had lived together for a number of years and there was no reason to suppose the testator had deliberately destroyed his will thus disinheriting his partner and creating an intestacy under which his estranged brother inherited the whole estate. There was a presumption of revocation but it was exceptionally weak and therefore the judge pronounced for the copy will.

In *Wren v Wren* [2006] EWHC 2243 (Ch), [2007] WTLR 531, the original will could not be found but the deceased's son, the claimant, alleged he had found the copy will he sought to prove under a floorboard in the house where he had lived with the deceased. The presumption of revocation was rebutted by evidence that the testator had told several of his son's friends and acquaintances he had left his house to his son on his death by his will. There was definitive evidence from the witnesses to the execution of the will that they could remember the testator signing, and their signing, the will on his doorstep. The defendants, two siblings of the claimant, had obtained letters of administration and claimed the will was a forgery. There was also evidence of a handwriting expert indicating the deceased's signature had been simulated, but the evidence against validity of the signature was not conclusive. The court found there was nothing to support the presumption of revocation and the copy will was allowed to proof.

Where there is evidence to show the original will existed after the testator's death, obviously there can be no question of revocation by the testator. The evidence must clearly establish the existence of the original will at the date of death.

10.14.4 Affidavit

The affidavit must be deposed to by someone with knowledge of the facts. Where evidence to rebut the presumption of revocation is necessary, that evidence should come from family, friends or legal adviser. If the will was lost after the death, the solicitor instructed may make the affidavit if he has knowledge of the facts of the loss of the will. Before doing so however, it is best to seek the directions of the district judge or registrar.

The affidavit should contain details of:

- the deceased's address and date of death;
- the making of the will (and any codicils);
- the place of custody of the will;
- the loss of the will (and if lost before the date of death and in the custody of the testator, evidence to rebut the presumption of revocation);
- attempts to find the original will;
- the provenance of the copy;
- any persons prejudiced by proof of the copy will (i.e. persons entitled under an earlier will or an intestacy); and
- who intends to prove the copy will.

The affidavit should exhibit the copy will to be proved and any correspondence relating to the loss of the original will. The court requires to know where the copy was found (it is advisable to take and retain a copy of the exhibited will for marking with the oath (see para 10.14.11)). Details of enquiries made to trace the original will must be recited. The affidavit concludes with a request for the order.

The rule provides that the district judge or registrar may require notice to be given to anyone prejudiced by proof of the copy will. It is generally the case that the court will require notice to be given to anyone who receives a greater benefit under an earlier will or, if there is no earlier will, on intestacy. The district judge or registrar may require the consent of those prejudiced to the copy will being proved.

10.14.5 Copy contained in draft, unexecuted copy or reconstruction

If the copy sought to be proved is not a copy of the original made after execution, then the affidavit must also contain evidence to show the copy document or reconstruction is indeed a copy of the will, or an accurate reconstruction of the will, in both form and content, as when executed. This evidence needs to be especially strong when it is sought to prove a reconstruction of a will. It is always difficult to set up for proof a will contained in a reconstruction because of doubt the original was executed in the reconstructed form. If the reconstructed will is based on a 'mirror image' will made by husband and wife at the same time then there is more chance the reconstruction will be allowed to proof.

Additionally, unless there is evidence from the person seeking the order which shows that the will was duly executed, then evidence on affidavit from one of the attesting witnesses is also required. If the identity of the witnesses cannot be established then there must be evidence from another source to satisfy the court that the will, in the form now sought to be proved, is a true and complete copy of the will as executed.

10.14.6 Incomplete will

There are occasions when the original will, when found after the testator's death, is incomplete; that is, parts or page(s) are missing. Subject to evidence to show the missing parts were not revoked by the testator by destruction, a complete copy may be accepted to proof.

10.14.7 Original will in existence but unobtainable

Where it is known that the original will exists, exhaustive attempts should be made to obtain it for proof.

If the original will is held by an individual abroad, and there is evidence to show that that person refuses to deliver up the will, coupled with the evidence, as above, of the authenticity of the copy, a copy may be admitted to proof.

For the position where the will is held by a notary or foreign court, see para 10.14.2.

If the will is retained in the United Kingdom then a subpoena under rule 50 of the Non-Contentious Probate Rules 1987 should be issued for the will to be lodged in the court (see para 8.6.2). If the subpoena fails, then, subject to the district judge's or registrar's discretion, an application to prove a copy may be made.

10.14.8 Reconstruction

Where there is no original will or copy in any form (that is, carbon copy or photocopy), but there is evidence of the content of the will when executed, an application may be made to prove a reconstruction. Evidence to support the content and form of the will is critical to the success of such an application.

Similarly, evidence to establish the will was executed in that form is required. (see para 10.14.5).

10.14.9 Known will: no copy or evidence of content available

Where it is known that the deceased made a will but there is no evidence to show that it has been destroyed (other than by the deceased), and no copy is available, nor can its content be substantiated, then application must be made as on intestacy.

Application may be made on affidavit of facts to a district judge or registrar for an order for letters of administration to be granted to the person entitled on intestacy, even though there may be a valid will. If the order is made, the oath and the grant are silent as to the deceased's having died testate or intestate and the grant is limited 'until the original will or an authentic copy be proved' (see *In Re Wright's Goods* [1893] P 21).

10.14.10 Nuncupative will

A 'privileged will', that is, a will made, the execution of which does not conform with section 9 of the Wills Act 1837, by a soldier or airman on actual military service or seaman or mariner at sea (see para 5.13), may be accepted to proof. If that will is not written, but by oral statement, then evidence of the substance of the statement or declaration of testamentary wishes must be obtained from the person(s) to whom the declaration was made.

The declaration must be committed to paper, with evidence to support the content, and that the declaration was intended to be testamentary. This declaration must be exhibited to the affidavit.

The affidavit must establish the facts to claim the privilege and establish the content of the oral statement. It is suggested a pre-lodgement enquiry be made of the district judge or registrar as to whether the privilege is to be allowed, and, if so, the form of the will to be submitted.

10.14.11 Order

If satisfied on the evidence, the district judge or registrar orders the copy will to be admitted. The oath should refer to the will 'as being contained in the copy (or executed draft, or as the case may be) exhibited to the affidavit of … sworn on the … and marked …'. The usual limitation is 'until the original will or a more authentic copy be proved', but this limitation may vary depending on the circumstances.

A copy of the order, or notice of the making of the order, is sent to the applicant's solicitors, and the copy will exhibited to the affidavit is returned for marking with the oath. The oath must refer to the copy will and include the limitation. It is now rare for the registries to return the exhibited will, so it is advisable a copy of the exhibit be taken before lodging.

10.14.12 Original will found

If the original will is found after the order has been made but before the application for a grant has been lodged, the original will may be submitted to proof. The application for the grant should be accompanied by a covering letter explaining that the original will has been found.

If the original will is found after the grant has been issued, it may be lodged in the proving registry. No other action need be taken provided the copy will proved was indeed a true and complete copy of the original. The order (and grant) is usually limited 'until the original will or a more authentic copy be proved'. Provided the copy is a copy of the original there is no need to prove the original; the grant, which reflects the order, remains operative to complete the administration of the estate.

10.15 RECTIFICATION

Section 20 of the Administration of Justice Act 1982 is as follows:

> **20 Rectification**
>
> (1) If a court is satisfied that a will is so expressed that it fails to carry out the testator's intentions, in consequence—
>
> (a) of a clerical error; or
>
> (b) of a failure to understand his instructions,
>
> it may order that the will shall be rectified so as to carry out his intentions.
>
> (2) An application for an order under this section shall not, except with the permission of the court, be made after the end of the period of six months from the date on which representation with respect to the estate of the deceased is first taken out.
>
> (3) The provisions of this section shall not render the personal representatives of a deceased person liable for having distributed any part of the estate of the deceased, after the end of the period of six months from the date on which representation with respect to the estate of the deceased is first taken out, on the ground that they ought to have taken into account the possibility that the court might permit the making of an application for an order under this section after

the end of that period but this subsection shall not prejudice any power to recover, by reason of the making of an order under this section, any part of the estate so distributed.

(4) In considering for the purposes of this section when representation with respect to the estate of a deceased person was first taken out, a grant limited to settled land or to trust property shall be left out of account unless a grant limited to the remainder of the estate has previously been made or is made at the same time.

An unopposed application for rectification is governed by rule 55 of the Non-Contentious Probate Rules 1987, which provides:

Application for rectification of a will

55.—(1) An application for an order that a will be rectified by virtue of section 20(1) of the Administration of Justice Act 1982 may be made to a district judge or registrar, unless a probate action has been commenced.

(2) The application shall be supported by an affidavit setting out the grounds of the application, together with such evidence as can be adduced as to the testator's intentions and as to whichever of the following matters are in issue—

(a) in what respects the testator's intentions were not understood; or
(b) the nature of any alleged clerical error.

(3) Unless otherwise directed, notice of the application shall be given to every person having an interest under the will whose interest might be prejudiced, or such other person who might be prejudiced, by the rectification applied for and any comments in writing by any such person shall be exhibited to the affidavit in support of the application.

(4) If the district judge or registrar is satisfied that, subject to any direction to the contrary, notice has been given to every person mentioned in paragraph (3) above, and that the application is unopposed, he may order that the will be rectified accordingly.

The most significant decision on rectification is the Supreme Court's decision, on an appeal from the Court of Appeal, in *Marley and Rawlings* [2014] UKSC 2, [2015] AC 129, in which the court allowed the will of the testator to be rectified. The testator and his wife were visited by their solicitor to enable them to execute the wills which he had drafted on their instructions. The wills were short and, except for the differences required to reflect the identity of the maker, they were in identical terms. The solicitor gave each spouse the other's draft will, and nobody noticed. Accordingly, each signed the other's will and the solicitor and his secretary attested their signature on each document. The court held that the solicitor had made a clerical error when handing out the wills which fell within the ambit of section 20(1)(a) of the Administration of Justice Act 1982.

Marley and Rawlings was applied in *Burnard v Burnard and others Re Estate of Godfrey Harry Burnard* [2014] EWHC 340 (Ch), [2014] All ER (D) 51 (Mar), in which the court considered the true construction of a will and determined what assets formed part of the deceased's estate. There was a clerical error in naming the wrong company in the will.

In *Kell v Jones and others* [2013] All ER (D) 153 (Jan), the Chancery Division dismissed the claim for rectification of a will as, although the will as drafted did not correctly reflect the testator's intentions, the error could not have been said to be a clerical error or a failure to understand the testator's instructions. The distinction between clerical errors and mistakes which were not inadvertent was firmly established and section 20(1)(a) of the Administration of Justice Act 1982 did not extend to errors that were made which had not resulted from the draftsman having failed to advert to the significance of or effect of the words used in his draft.

10.15.1 Affidavit

The affidavit referred to in rule 55(2) of the Non-Contentious Probate Rules 1987 should be made by the draftsman of the will or by someone with knowledge of the facts relating to taking the instructions for and the drafting of the will. The affidavit must set out the error, how it occurred and what the testator's intentions were, that is, the criterion to enable rectification in accordance with section 20(1)(a) and/or (b) of the Administration of Justice Act 1982. The affidavit should exhibit a copy of the will as executed, and a copy of the will in its proposed rectified form.

Rule 55(3) of the Non-Contentious Probate Rules 1987 requires notice to be given to any person who may be prejudiced by the proposed rectification. Notice is by letter to any person who would receive a benefit, or a greater benefit, if the proposed rectification is not effected. The Family Division's jurisdiction is limited to unopposed applications. This does not mean there has to be consent, but that no opposition has been notified. If the application is or becomes opposed, application is made by a probate claim, under Part 57 of the Civil Procedure Rules 1998, in the Chancery Division (see para 10.15.4).

10.15.2 Time for application

Where the error requiring rectification is known about before an application for a grant has been made, the application for rectification should be made before it is sought to prove the will. Section 20(2) of the Administration of Justice Act 1982, however, allows an application to rectify to be made after the grant has been issued, provided it is made within 6 months of the issue of a full grant. An unopposed application outside that time may be made only with the leave of a district judge or registrar. The court will need to be satisfied that the proposed rectification will be effective, and that the part of the estate it concerns has not been administered.

10.15.3 Order

On an application before a grant of representation has been issued, the court, if satisfied on the evidence, orders the will to be proved in its rectified form; the engrossment in that form is endorsed with the district judge's or registrar's *fiat* (order for proof), thereafter to form the probate and record copies. A copy of the order is sent (or notice sent that the order has been made) to the applicant's solicitors but no reference to it need be made in the oath. The original will, not the engrossment, is marked on swearing the oath. The rectified copy, endorsed with the *fiat*, should be copied to be lodged with the grant application.

If the order is made after a grant has been issued, a memorandum of the order is endorsed on the original grant and a copy of the rectified will annexed to it. The record copy grant is annotated in the same way.

No fee is payable on the application.

10.15.4 Opposed applications

If the application is opposed, or becomes opposed after it has been made to the Family Division, the procedure is by way of a Part 57 claim, the application being lodged in Chancery Chambers in the Royal Courts of Justice, or a district registry with Chancery jurisdiction. These registries are at Birmingham, Bristol, Cardiff, Leeds, Liverpool, Manchester, Newcastle-upon-Tyne and Preston. The claim form must be endorsed with, or be served with, particulars of the claim. There is no specific protocol for rectification claims, so the general protocols are applied. Practice Direction 57 of the Civil Procedure Rules 1998 also applies; paragraphs 10.1 and 10.2 of the Direction assume that such an application is made after a grant has been issued, and requires the original grant to be lodged although application may be pre- or post-grant. When the application has been determined, the Chancery Court order must be sent to the probate registry which issued the grant for the records to be notated.

10.15.5 Interpretation

Section 21 of the Administration of Justice Act 1982 provides as follows:

> **21 Interpretation of wills – general rules as to evidence**
>
> (1) This section applies to a will—
>
> (a) in so far as any part of it is meaningless;
> (b) in so far as the language used in any part of it is ambiguous on the face of it;
> (c) in so far as evidence, other than evidence of the testator's intention, shows that the language used in any part of it is ambiguous in the light of surrounding circumstances.
>
> (2) In so far as this section applies to a will extrinsic evidence, including evidence of the testator's intention, may be admitted to assist in its interpretation.

Jurisdiction in respect of the construction of wills does not vest in the Family Division. Construction, that is, establishing the meaning of a gift or the testator's intention regarding any gift, is a matter for the Chancery courts to determine. Application for interpretation/construction is by a claim under Part 8 of the Civil Procedure Rules 1998, using the procedure under Part 57.

Any application for interpretation to a probate registry is limited to determining title to take a grant of representation – invariably because there is a problem in the clause appointing executors. The registries now accept applications for interpretation with the oath to lead the grant, but it is advisable to check with the registry this will be the case.

Application is by affidavit by the will draftsman or someone with knowledge of the testator's intentions regarding the appointment or the naming of a beneficiary when making the will, and of how the wording of the will is ambiguous or meaningless, thus failing to carry out the testator's intentions. A copy of the will should be exhibited.

If satisfied on the evidence, the district judge or registrar directs the will be interpreted so as to carry out the testator's intentions. No order is drawn up.

No fee is payable on the application.

10.15.6 Omission of words from probate and record copy will

Where the original will contains words which are or may be considered offensive, libellous or blasphemous, an application may be made for their omission (see para 5.14). If no application is made the district judge or registrar may refuse to grant probate until application is made.

The application is made on affidavit, usually before the grant has been issued, exhibiting a copy of the will as executed and an engrossment omitting the offending words. The application is made to the district judge or registrar of the registry to which the application for the grant is to be made or where it is pending.

If the offending words contain a gift or are open to other interpretation, an application to the Chancery court, to determine the construction of the phrase or clause in question, or the will as a whole, may be necessary. The directions of the district judge or registrar should be obtained.

The original will must be marked by the deponent and commissioner on swearing the oath, but the engrossment is copied to be lodged with the grant application to form the probate and record copies, and any other copy applied for subsequently.

10.15.7 Submitting draft documents

Any document required by the probate registry in a non-contentious matter may be submitted in draft form for the district judge or registrar to consider and settle or approve. Only those documents which contain incontrovertible facts may be settled. Documents which give evidence or opinion, such as affidavits of due execution or affidavits to lead discretionary orders, may be submitted for approval, the district judge or registrar approving only their form and content as sufficient to enable the court to reach a decision.

Documents which may be submitted for settling include:

- oaths to lead grants;
- renunciations;
- powers of attorney (except enduring or lasting powers of attorney);
- citations;
- nominations of co-administrators; and
- subpoenas.

Documents which may be submitted for approval include:

- affidavits to support execution of a will;
- affidavits to lead the issue of a citation or subpoena;
- affidavits of foreign law; and
- all affidavits to lead discretionary orders.

Specimen forms are contained in Appendix C.

The district judge or registrar does not settle or approve documents to be used in contentious matters even if the matter is coming before the court under the Non-Contentious Probate Rules 1987, for example, an affidavit in support of a summons under rule 27(6) (disputes between persons of equal entitlement).

It is now the policy of the probate registries only to settle oaths where there is a complication; the submission of straightforward oaths is not accepted.

Chapter 11

Trust Corporations

11.1 INTRODUCTION

A trust corporation is defined by section 128 of the Senior Courts Act 1981 as 'the Public Trustee or a corporation either appointed by the court in any particular case to be a trustee or authorised by rules made under section 4(3) of the Public Trustee Act 1906 to act as custodian trustee'. Section 115 of the Act authorises such a corporation to take grants of representation in all forms.

A trust corporation may act alone or with an individual. A grant to a trust corporation issues in the corporation's corporate name.

The procedure for applications by trust corporations is regulated by rule 36 of the Non-Contentious Probate Rules 1987. Rule 36 is amended with effect from 20 November 2017 for the pilot scheme for applications to be made online by invitation of the probate registry. Rule 36 will apply as if:

> (i) in paragraph (1), for 'such officer shall depose in the oath' there were substituted 'the statement of truth must include a statement';
> (ii) in paragraph (2)(b), for 'it shall be deposed in the oath' there were substituted 'the statement of truth must include a statement';
> (iii) in paragraph (4)(c), for 'nominee or attorney shall depose in the oath' there were substituted 'statement of truth must include a statement'.
>
> (3) Where original documents are required by instructions given by the registry to be sent in support of the application, they must be sent separately to the registry in accordance with such instructions.

As no Practice Directions have been issued, the text continues to refer to application on oath.

11.2 RESOLUTION AUTHORISING PERSON(S) TO ACT

Before a trust corporation may apply for a grant, the governing body of that corporation, however constituted, must pass a resolution authorising named officers, or the holders of named positions in the corporation, to swear oaths, affidavits, etc and effect renunciations or other documents required in connection with grants of representation on behalf of the corporation. The resolution may authorise persons other than officers within the corporation, for example, a solicitor, to act on its behalf.

Where the trust corporation acts in numerous estates, a certified copy of the resolution may be lodged with the Senior District Judge of the Principal Registry of the Family Division, each oath to lead a grant thereafter reciting that the resolution is so lodged. Alternatively, a certified copy resolution must be lodged with each application. This also applies to persons holding an official position which acts as a trust corporation, such as the Public Trustee.

11.3 TRUST CORPORATION APPOINTED EXECUTOR

A trust corporation may take probate, with or without any other named executor, renounce probate or have power reserved to it in the same way as an individual who has been appointed executor.

Where a local or branch office of a trust corporation (usually a bank) is appointed executor, the appointment is deemed to be an appointment of the trust corporation, unless there is a clear contrary intention expressed in the will.

A trust corporation which does not wish to act as executor may renounce probate through its authorised officers. If it is not known who is to take a grant, the renunciation and original will may be lodged in a probate registry at any time after the testator's death (see, also, para 9.3). Alternatively, the renunciation may be lodged with the application for the grant.

11.4 TRUST CORPORATION APPOINTED ATTORNEY

Any executor entitled to probate, or other person entitled in priority under rule 20 of the Non-Contentious Probate Rules 1987 to letters of administration (with will annexed), or person entitled in priority under rule 22 where there is an intestacy, may appoint a trust corporation as his attorney to take the grant for his use and benefit as if they were appointing an individual.

11.5 CONSENT TO A TRUST CORPORATION ACTING

11.5.1 Deceased testate

An executor may renounce probate and, where the residuary beneficiaries do not wish to act in the administration (in the order of priority prescribed by rule 20 of the Non-Contentious Probate Rules 1987, see para 12.1), a trust corporation may, with the consent of the residuary beneficiaries, take letters of administration (with will annexed).

If there is no executor or no surviving executor then, again with the consent of the residuary beneficiaries, a trust corporation may act. The residuary beneficiaries do not need to renounce (unless one or more of them is a minor – see para 11.5.3); only an executor, or an executor who is also a residuary beneficiary, must renounce, and, in the latter case, also consent.

11.5.2 Deceased intestate

Similarly, the person(s) entitled under an intestacy to take letters of administration may consent to an application by a trust corporation. All persons of equal first entitlement, for example, issue or siblings, must consent, but do not have to renounce their title except where one or more of them is a minor. Those with no immediate beneficial interest, for example, those entitled on an accretion, are not relevant and their consent is not required.

11.5.3 Persons under a disability

Where all the persons entitled to the estate, whether under a will or on intestacy, are minors, a trust corporation may take the grant with the consent of those entitled under rule 32(1) of the Non-Contentious Probate Rules 1987 (see para 10.10), that is, those, including a local authority, who have parental responsibility for the minors under the Children Act 1989. If there are no persons with parental responsibility a trust corporation may apply to be appointed under rule 32(2) (see para 10.10). The grant is not limited for the use and benefit of the minors, but issues to the trust corporation in its own right.

Where one or more of several persons entitled is a minor, the person with parental responsibility cannot consent to an application by a trust corporation. All those of full age must renounce and consent before the trust corporation may apply and take the grant. In these circumstances, the grant is limited until the minors, or one of them, obtains a grant. The grant does not cease to be effective when the minors, or any one of them, attains 18 years of age.

A trust corporation may be appointed by order under rule 32(2) of the Non-Contentious Probate Rules 1987 to take a grant for the use and benefit of a minor.

A trust corporation may be appointed by order under rule 35(4) of the Non-Contentious Probate Rules 1987 to take a grant for the use and benefit of a person who lacks capacity to manage his affairs within the meaning of the Mental Capacity Act 2005.

11.5.4 Dispensing with renunciation and consent

Rule 36(3) of the Non-Contentious Probate Rules 1987 is the authority for the above requirements relating to renunciation and consent. Where there are special circumstances, a district judge or registrar may, on application, dispense with any renunciation or consent. Application for the dispensation may be made by letter describing the circumstances. The district judge or registrar may require the application to be made on affidavit.

11.6 TRUST CORPORATION A BENEFICIARY

Where a trust corporation is a beneficiary under a will it may apply for a grant, its title to the grant being determined in the normal order of priority under rule 20 of the Non-Contentious Probate Rules 1987; for example, where a trust corporation is a legatee it may apply on the renunciation of the executor and residuary beneficiary. Many charities have now obtained trust corporation status which enables them to take grants in their corporate names.

11.7 NON-TRUST CORPORATIONS

Many smaller, or less well known, charities have not acquired trust corporation status as they have insufficient funds deposited and lack the facilities to undertake trust business. A corporation which is not a trust corporation as defined by rule 2(1) of the Non-Contentious Probate Rules 1987 may take a grant through its nominee or attorney (see rule 36(4)). Thus a non-trust corporation cannot take probate in its corporate name when appointed executor, but may take letters of administration (with will annexed) in the name of the nominee or attorney.

The nominee or attorney must be specifically authorised to act. The resolution appointing the nominee to act, or the power of attorney, must be executed by the governing body of the corporation, however constituted. The original or a copy, certified to be a true and complete copy of the resolution or power, must be lodged with each application for a grant.

The grant issues in the name of the nominee or attorney, for the use and benefit of the corporation, and is limited until further representation be granted.

Where a non-trust corporation is appointed executor with individuals, it may take a grant only if the individuals have predeceased or renounced, their title (to probate) being higher in priority under rule 20 of the Non-Contentious Probate Rules 1987.

A non-trust corporation may renounce its title to a grant through its nominee authorised by the corporation to do so.

Generally, foreign companies, even those within the European Union, do not qualify as trust corporations.

Chapter 12

Applications for Grants

12.1 APPLICATION FOR A GRANT OF PROBATE

12.1.1 Generally

Application for a grant may be made through a solicitor or probate practitioner.

Rule 4 of the Non-Contentious Probate Rules 1987 provides that:

> 4.—(1) A person applying for a grant through a solicitor or probate practitioner may apply at any registry or sub-registry.
>
> (2) Every solicitor or probate practitioner through whom an application for a grant is made shall give the address of his place of business within England and Wales.

Rule 4A of the Non-Contentious Probate Rules 1987 is added as follows with effect from 20 November 2017 for application online made at the invitation of a registry:

> 4A.—(1) An application under this rule must be made by completing and sending an online application form in accordance with instructions given by the registry.
>
> (2) Where an application is made under this rule, rule 8 does not apply, and—
>
> (a) the application must be verified by a statement of truth in the online application form;
>
> (b) rule 10(1)(a) applies as if for 'signatures of the applicant and the person before whom the oath is sworn' there were substituted 'signature of the applicant or of the solicitor or probate practitioner through whom the application is made';
>
> (c) rule 27(1) applies as if at the end there were inserted 'or, where the application is made under rule 4A, the solicitor or probate practitioner through whom the application is made shall confirm in accordance with instructions given by the registry that such notice has been given';
>
> (d) rule 36 applies as if—

(i) in paragraph (1), for 'such officer shall depose in the oath' there were substituted 'the statement of truth must include a statement';

(ii) in paragraph (2)(b), for 'it shall be deposed in the oath' there were substituted 'the statement of truth must include a statement';

(iii) in paragraph (4)(c), for 'nominee or attorney shall depose in the oath' there were substituted 'statement of truth must include a statement'.

(3) Where original documents are required by instructions given by the registry to be sent in support of the application, they must be sent separately to the registry in accordance with such instructions.

There has been no Practice Direction published to deal with what the statement of truth must contain.

Application online is by invitation of the registry only.

12.1.2 Right to a grant

Where the deceased died testate, title to take the grant of representation is governed by rule 20 of the Non-Contentious Probate Rules 1987, which provides as follows:

> 20. Where the deceased died on or after 1 January 1926 the person or persons entitled to a grant in respect of a will shall be determined in accordance with the following order of priority, namely—
>
> (a) the executor;
>
> (b) any residuary legatee or devisee holding in trust for any other person;
>
> (c) any other residuary legatee or devisee (including one for life) or where the residue is not wholly disposed of by the will, any person entitled to share in the undisposed of residue (including the Treasury Solicitor when claiming *bona vacantia* on behalf of the Crown), provided that—
>
> (i) unless a district judge or registrar otherwise directs, a residuary legatee or devisee whose legacy or devise is vested in interest shall be preferred to one entitled on the happening of a contingency, and
>
> (ii) where the residue is not in terms wholly disposed of, the district judge or registrar may, if he is satisfied that the testator has nevertheless disposed of the whole or substantially the whole of the known estate, allow a grant to be made to any legatee or devisee entitled to, or to share in, the estate so disposed of, without regard to the persons entitled to share in any residue not disposed of by the will;
>
> (d) the personal representative of any residuary legatee or devisee (but not one for life, or holding in trust for any other person), or of any other person entitled to share in any residue not disposed of by the will;

(e) any other legatee or devisee (including one for life or holding in trust for any other person) or any creditor of the deceased, provided that, unless a district judge or registrar otherwise directs, a legatee or devisee whose legacy or devise is vested in interest shall be preferred to one entitled on the happening of a contingency;

(f) the personal representative of any other legatee or devisee (but not one for life or one holding in trust for any other person) or of any creditor of the deceased.

Title to the grant falls firstly to the executor, who may take a grant of probate. Executors and only executors take grants of probate. Any other person who proves a will takes a grant of letters of administration (with will annexed). If the executor appoints an attorney to act for him, the attorney is entitled to letters of administration (with will annexed). It follows that all those falling within rule 20(b)–(f) of the Non-Contentious Probate Rules 1987 are entitled to letters of administration (with will annexed).

The Non-Contentious Probate Rules 1987 are amended, with effect from 20 November 2017 (the Non-Contentious Probate (Amendment) Rules 2017) to create a pilot scheme for the delivery of grant applications online. Any such application may only be made at the invitation of the registry. The oath presently required will be replaced by a statement of truth. As this is a pilot scheme by invitation only and, as no Practice Directions have been published to regulate the content of a statement of truth, the text continues to refer to application by oath only.

12.1.3 Executors

The executor's title derives from his testator's will. On the death of the testator all property vests in his executor, even before he has taken probate of the will. The deceased's will becomes the executor's possession and it is a matter for him whether he discloses any information about the contents.

Chain of executorship

Section 7 of the Administration of Estates Act 1925 provides that the executor of a sole or last surviving proving executor (who dies leaving estate unadministered) of a testator becomes the executor of that testator when he obtains probate of his testator's will. Thus the executor, having proved the will of his testator, is entitled to administer any estate of which his testator was the sole or last surviving executor. No further grant is required. So, A dies and B proves his will as sole executor. On B's death (leaving part of A's estate unadministered) C proves B's will and immediately becomes the executor of A's estate. The chain is automatically created and cannot be renounced.

A chain of executorship may continue through several sole or last surviving proving executors and will not be broken by a temporary/limited grant. The chain of executorship is broken when the sole or last surviving proving executor dies intestate; or he fails to appoint an executor in his will; or his appointed executor fails to prove his will.

No further grant is necessary to deal with the unadministered estate of the first to die; both grants being produced together to complete the administration.

When the sole or last surviving executor dies testate but his executor fails to take or renounce probate of his will the chain is in abeyance. The residuary beneficiaries in the will of the first to die may apply for letters of administration (with will annexed) *de bonis non* to the unadministered estate. This grant may be applied for without any order or direction of a district judge or registrar. The grant will, however, be limited until the executor's will is proved by his executor thus creating the chain. The facts relating to the chain being in abeyance must be recited in the oath.

Limitation or condition on appointment

Depending on the wording of the clause appointing the executor, the executor's appointment may be:

- limited to a particular part of the estate, for example, 'literary estate', 'all estate outside Canada';
- contingent upon an event, for example, 'provided he has attained eighteen years of age'; 'but if [name of executor] predeceases me or renounces probate …'; or
- subject to a condition, for example, 'provided he remains a partner in the firm of …'.

Probate in respect of the same part of the estate cannot be granted to more than four executors (section 114(2) of the Senior Courts Act 1981). If there is an appointment of general executors and special executors (e.g. for literary estate), the grant may issue to not more than four general executors and four special executors. In these circumstances it is advisable, for ease of administration, for each set of executors to take separate grants.

Executor according to the tenor of the will

The appointment clause may not expressly appoint a named person executor but, provided the will sufficiently describes the duties of the person named, that person may be the executor 'according to the tenor of the will'. For example, 'I wish X to deal with the collection and distribution of my estate'; or 'I want X to deal with all my requirements in this will'. The oath to lead probate of the will should describe the person as the executor according to the tenor of the will, and this is then reflected in the grant. This is often the case in wills executed abroad where there is an appointment of 'my personal representative' or words of a similar nature.

Void appointment

Uncertainty in the appointment of executors renders a purported appointment void. The appointment of any 'one of' or 'two of' a class of persons is void for uncertainty, for example, 'any one of the partners in the firm of' (see *In Re Baylis' Goods* (1862) 26 JP 599 in which the testator appointed 'any two of my sons'). Similarly, an appointment in the alternative, such as, 'X or Y' without any words qualifying the contingency upon which the alternative appointment is effective, is also void for uncertainty.

If there is evidence to show that the appointment fails to carry out the testator's intentions, an application to rectify the will may be made (under section 20 of the Administration of Justice Act 1982; see para 10.15), or, more usually, for the appointment to be interpreted (under section 21; see para 10.15.5).

Executor a minor

A minor executor's right to probate cannot be renounced on his behalf (see rule 34(1) of the Non-Contentious Probate Rules 1987). A grant for the use and benefit of an executor who is a minor may be taken by the residuary beneficiary, where the minor is not also the residuary beneficiary. If the minor is the residuary beneficiary, administration (with will annexed) may be granted to the person with parental responsibility for him (see rule 32, para 12.2.12). If the minor is a co-executor with a person of full age, the grant may be taken by the executor of age, with power reserved to the minor on attaining his majority.

Executor mentally incapable

Where one of several executors lacks capacity, within the meaning of the Mental Capacity Act 2005, the capable executors may take probate, with power reserved to the incapable executor on regaining his capacity. The giving of notice to him under rule 27(3) of the Non-Contentious Probate Rules 1987 may be dispensed with on application to a district judge or registrar (see para 10.2).

Where the sole or last surviving executor is mentally incapable, letters of administration (with will annexed) may be taken for his use and benefit by those entitled under rule 35(2) of the Non-Contentious Probate Rules 1987 (see para 10.11).

Executor a bankrupt

The fact that an executor is an undischarged bankrupt or is insolvent does not prevent him from acting as an executor. If it is considered inappropriate for an executor to act in such circumstances he may renounce. If the executor refuses to renounce his title, he may be passed over by application under section 116 of the Senior Courts Act 1981 (see para 10.13).

Executor a firm

The appointment of a trading firm – solicitors, accountants or otherwise – is deemed to be an appointment of all the partners in that firm at the date of the will. Unless the will expressly refers to partners in the firm or successor firm at the date of the death, the appointment is of the partners of the firm at the date of execution of the will. Following the decision in *Re Rogers* [2006] EWHC 753 (Ch), [2006] 1 WLR 1577, unless there is a contrary intention expressed in the will, only profit-sharing partners may take probate. If the will appoints partners by name then they may take probate irrespective of their status in the firm.

If the firm is a limited liability partnership or a limited company, the appointment will be deemed to be of the partners, members or directors as appropriate at the appropriate date.

Executor a trust corporation

Where a trust corporation is appointed, the corporation may take probate, the oath to lead the grant being deposed to by an authorised officer of the corporation (see rule 36(1) of the Non-Contentious Probate Rules 1987 and para 11.3).

If a non-trust corporation is appointed, then the appointment as executor fails, but the corporation may take letters of administration (with will annexed) through its authorised nominee or attorney.

Executor an official

Where the appointment is of a person by his official title but not naming him, the executor is the holder of that office at the date of the testator's death, except where the will expressly states otherwise, for example, the appointment of 'the vicar of St Mary's Church, Little Muddicombe' is an appointment of the incumbent of that office at the date of death.

Power reserved

Power reserved means power to take a like grant and only applies to probate. It follows that power may only be reserved to an executor if another executor takes probate. Any executor entitled to take probate who does not want to renounce, but does not wish to take a grant immediately, may have power reserved to him, entitling him to apply for a grant later. The proving executor must give notice of the application for the grant to the executor to whom power is reserved (rule 27 of the Non-Contentious Probate Rules 1987; see para 10.2 on dispensing with notice). A later application by the executor to whom power is reserved would be for double probate (see para 12.6.2).

12.1.4 Time for applying

An application for a grant of probate may be made at any time after the testator's death, but the grant cannot issue within 7 days of the death (see rule 6(2) of the Non-Contentious Probate Rules 1987). Where there is a compelling reason for the grant to issue within the 7-day period, an application may be made to a district judge or registrar for expedition. 'Compelling reasons' may include where the grant is necessary to commence or defend other legal proceedings; or where a part of the deceased's estate requires immediate administration, for example, the completion of a house sale.

12.1.5 Oath to lead the grant

The Non-Contentious Probate Rules 1987 are amended, with effect from 20 November 2017 (the Non-Contentious Probate (Amendment) Rules 2017) to create a pilot scheme for the delivery of grant applications online. Any such application may only be made at the invitation of the registry. The oath presently required will be replaced by a statement of truth. As this is a pilot scheme by invitation only and, as no Practice Directions have been published to regulate the content of a statement of truth, the text continues to refer to application by oath.

The executor(s) deposing to the facts in the oath should be referred to by their true full names, followed by their address(es) and occupations. Rule 1(4) of Order 41 of the Rules of the Supreme Court, as in force immediately before 26 April 1999, remains operative in respect of oaths and affidavits in non-contentious probate proceedings. Where the deponent is applying in a professional capacity, for example, as a profit-sharing partner in a firm of solicitors, his business address may be used. The deponent's occupation should be stated, but if it is omitted, it is not fatal to the application. Indeed, it is not common practice now to include an occupation.

The deceased's full true name, last address (including the postcode), date of death, date of birth and age must be given. The Practice Direction of 12 January 1999, [1999] 1 All ER 832, requires the name and dates to be given as they appear in the death certificate. Any difference in the names should be explained. If the death certificate fails to recite the actual full true name this too must be recited in the oath. Where assets of the deceased are registered in a different name, a statement should be included, in accordance with rule 9 of the Non-Contentious Probate Rules 1987, so that the alternative names may be included in the grant. The fact that the deceased made a will in a name other than his true name is not normally regarded by the registries as sufficient reason to include any name other than the true name in the grant.

Rule 8(2) of the Non-Contentious Probate Rules 1987 requires the oath to state where the deceased was domiciled when he died. The court's jurisdiction is based on domicile so it is crucial this is sworn to. A district judge or registrar may, in exceptional circumstances, direct that domicile need not be stated in the oath or appear in the grant.

Rule 8(3) of the Non-Contentious Probate Rules 1987 requires that the oath contains a statement whether there was or was not settled land vested in the deceased which remained settled after his death.

The oath should conclude with the promise by the deponents to carry out the duties under section 25 of the Administration of Estates Act 1925 ('I will collect, get in and administer according to law *etc*'); a statement of the values of the gross and net estates; and, in 'excepted estate' cases, that there is no requirement to deliver an inheritance tax account.

Rule 10 of the Non-Contentious Probate Rules 1987 provides that the will must be marked by the signature of the deponent(s) and commissioner(s). There is no need for an exhibit clause to be added. Where there is good reason, a district judge or registrar may give leave to mark a copy, for example, when the will has to be sent outside the United Kingdom for a deponent to swear the oath and there is a danger of its being lost.

If the value of the estate is less than £5,000, no fee is payable, but if it exceeds £5,000, a flat fee of £155 is payable. Office copy grants issued at the time the grant is issued are £0.50 each.

The oath may be sworn or affirmed before a practising solicitor, a member of the Chartered Institute of Legal Executives holding a commission, a notary public, justice of the peace, or officer of the court authorised to administer oaths.

For the procedure where an inheritance tax account is required, see Chapter 3. For forms of oath, see Appendices C37–C43.

12.2 APPLICATION FOR LETTERS OF ADMINISTRATION (WITH WILL ANNEXED)

An application for letters of administration (with will annexed) may be made when:

- the appointment of executors is void;
- the executors have predeceased or renounced;
- the sole executor is mentally incapable of managing his affairs;
- the sole executor is a minor; or
- a non-trust corporation is appointed executor.

In other words, the application may be made when all those entitled under rule 20(a) of the Non-Contentious Probate Rules 1987 (see para 12.1) are 'cleared off'.

12.2.1 Attorney of executor

An executor may appoint an attorney who may take the grant for the use and benefit of the executor, but otherwise the order of priority is as set out in rule 20(b)–(f) of the Non-Contentious Probate Rules 1987 (see para 12.1.2). If an attorney applies on behalf of one of several executors, notice must be given to the others. The other executors do not have to consent to the application. Power is not reserved to the other executors, power reserved meaning power to take a like grant (that is, of probate).

12.2.2 Residuary legatee or devisee in trust (rule 20(b))

Those next entitled, after the executor, are the residuary legatee(s) and/or devisee(s) in trust. The will must contain a clear gift of the residue of the estate to named persons to hold the estate on trust. An appointment of a trustee without the gift is insufficient. The trust(s) on which the residue is held must also be declared in the will. If the will contains power to the named trustee to nominate another person to act instead of him, the substituted trustee may apply, lodging the nomination with the oath to lead the grant.

If the wording of the gift to the trustee is such that it imposes a 'secret trust', the actual wording must be considered. Any question arising falls to the Chancery Division to construe, and is not a matter for the probate registry.

12.2.3 Residuary legatee or devisee (rule 20(c))

On clearing the executors and residuary legatees or devisees in trust, the person(s) entitled to the residue are next entitled. This class of person includes a residuary legatee or devisee for life or, where there is no gift (or no effective gift) of all the residue, the person(s) entitled to share in the estate undisposed of by the will. Those entitled to (share) the undisposed of estate are the person(s) being the next of kin entitled under an intestacy in the order of priority prescribed by rule 22 of the Non-Contentious Probate Rules 1987 (see para 12.3). Thus a residuary legatee, a residuary devisee (including those for life) and a person entitled to share in undisposed of estate have equal entitlement to letters of administration (with will annexed) without giving notice to others of equal entitlement.

Preference for vested interest

Rule 20(c)(i) of the Non-Contentious Probate Rules 1987, however, prescribes a preference for a vested interest over a contingent interest. Thus, on a gift of the residuary estate to A and B subject to their attaining the age of 25 years, if A has attained 25 years but B has not then A is preferred to B.

12.2.4 Personal representative of residuary beneficiary (rule 20(d))

After clearing off those entitled under the previous paragraphs, an application may be made by the personal representative of a residuary legatee and/or devisee. The residuary beneficiary must have survived the deceased to take his benefit under the will. Similarly, the personal representative of a person entitled to share in estate undisposed of by the will may take the grant. This paragraph does not apply to residuary legatees and devisees in trust or for life.

12.2.5 Legatee or devisee or creditor (rule 20(e))

On clearing off all those entitled under rule 20(a)–(d) of the Non-Contentious Probate Rules 1987, a specific legatee or devisee or creditor may apply.

Specific legatee or devisee

Where there is no gift of residue, or the residue is only partly disposed of, leaving estate to pass under a partial intestacy, but either: (a) there are no known kin entitled to share in the undisposed of estate; or (b) there are such kin but they have renounced letters of administration (with will annexed), title falls to any person receiving a specific legacy or devise.

If there are no known kin entitled to share in the residual estate undisposed of by the will then notice must be given to the Treasury Solicitor, the Crown being entitled to claim *bona vacantia*. The Treasury Solicitor, acting for the Crown, is entitled to take a grant in priority to a legatee or devisee.

Creditor

When all those entitled to benefit under the will or to the estate undisposed of by the will have been cleared off by their predecease, renunciation or citation, a grant may issue to a creditor. If there is estate which would pass to the Crown as *bona vacantia*, the Treasury Solicitor must renounce or be cited before a creditor may apply. It is suggested that the Treasury Solicitor be notified by letter that there is *bona vacantia*, and that a creditor proposes to apply for a grant. The probate registries usually accept an indication in writing by the Treasury Solicitor that he does not wish to apply, without requiring a formal renunciation.

Where it is not possible to trace kin, or the debt is likely to render the estate otherwise insolvent, an application may be made for a discretionary order for a grant to the creditor under section 116 of the Senior Courts Act 1981, passing over the title, or possible title, of others (see para 10.13).

If the creditor is a trading firm with partners, all the partners must join in the application. Where one or more of the partners applies, the remaining partners must consent to the application. A statement saying they consent should be included in the oath to lead the grant.

Life or minority interest

If a life or minority interest arises, the grant should issue to two or more persons or creditors. Alternatively, application may be made for a discretionary order under section 114 of the Senior Courts Act 1981 to allow the grant to issue to a sole grantee (see para 10.3.2).

12.2.6 Personal representative of legatee, devisee or creditor (rule 20(f))

When all those entitled in priority as shown above have been cleared off, the personal representative of a legatee, devisee or creditor may apply. A legatee or devisee does not include one for life or holding in trust for another person. The personal representative must be so constituted by taking a grant to the estate of the legatee, devisee or creditor; details of that grant must be recited in the oath to establish title. A copy of the grant should be lodged with the application.

12.2.7 Trust and non-trust corporations

The procedure for taking letters of administration (with will annexed) by a corporation is dealt with in Chapter 11.

12.2.8 Preference for persons of age

Subject to a district judge or registrar directing otherwise under rule 27(5) of the Non-Contentious Probate Rules 1987, a residuary legatee or devisee of full age is preferred to the guardian of, or other person with parental responsibility for, a minor who is equally entitled to share the residue with the person of full age.

12.2.9 Determining whether gift is a gift of residue

Not infrequently, especially where the will was not professionally drafted, the wording of a will raises doubt as to whether there is a gift of the residuary estate. If the gift is implied sufficiently or is clear from all the surrounding words used, then the registry accepts an application for a grant by the purported residuary beneficiary. The directions of a district judge or registrar may be obtained, but the Family Division is not the court for construction of wills. If there is a dispute, or if the wording is so unclear that no determination can be made without a trial of the matter, the will may need to be referred to the Chancery Division by probate claim under Part 57 of the Civil Procedure Rules 1998. Where there is consensus, then the distribution may be resolved by all interested parties entering into a deed of variation or a deed of family arrangement as appropriate.

Some words and phrases have been accepted by the courts as sufficient to constitute a gift of residue. These include:

- 'the rest of my money';
- 'all my possessions';
- 'all my belongings';
- 'all my property';
- 'after this the remainder'; and
- 'everything I own'.

12.2.10 Identifying beneficiaries

Similar problems can arise in identifying beneficiaries, especially when indeterminate references to members of the family are included in the will (again these are most likely to be non-professionally drafted wills):

- a gift to 'my relatives' has been held to be a gift to those first entitled under an intestacy;
- a gift to 'my next of kin' has also been held to be a gift to the persons first entitled under an intestacy;
- a gift to 'the issue of our marriage' has been held to be children of the deceased and spouse excluding grandchildren;
- a gift to 'my children' has been held to be a gift to issue living at the date of death.

In respect of the last example, a gift to 'my children', 'children', as a class generally, includes all issue, that is, children, grandchildren, great-grandchildren and so on including illegitimate children and children adopted by the deceased. Children adopted away from the deceased become the children of the adopters from the date of the making of the adoption order and receive no benefit (see section 67 of the Adoption and Children Act 2002). In *Reading and another v Reading and others* [2015] EWHC 946 (Ch), [2015] WTLR 1245, it was held that the words 'issue of mine' in a will should be interpreted to include children, step-children and the children of both the testator's children and step-children rather than descendants of all degrees.

Where title to the grant depends on establishing the identity of the beneficiary, the will should be referred to a district judge or registrar for directions as a pre-grant enquiry.

Where an intended gift of residue is to a surviving spouse with an ensuing gift on death to children, there is a presumption of an absolute gift to the surviving spouse. This applies only where the gift is to a surviving spouse and issue and there are no other words in the will to indicate a contrary intention.

12.2.11 Gift in favour of child or other issue

Section 33 of the Wills Act 1837, as now in force, provides that a gift to a child or remoter descendant of the testator in his will does not lapse if the intended beneficiary predeceases the testator leaving issue. The gift passes to the surviving issue of the intended beneficiary living at the date of death. It follows that a child *en ventre sa mère* is not necessarily excluded, dependent on the wording of the gift.

Section 33 of the Wills Act 1837 also provides for a gift to a class of persons consisting of children or remoter descendants of the testator, where a member of the class predeceases the deceased leaving issue. The gift does not lapse, but passes to the issue of that member living at the date of death.

Section 33 of the Wills Act 1837 operates only provided there is no contrary intention in the will.

12.2.12 Grant on behalf of a minor

Where, under a will or intestacy, a minor is entitled to the grant as a beneficiary, rule 32 of the Non-Contentious Probate Rules 1987 applies. It provides as follows:

> (1) Where a person to whom a grant would otherwise be made is a minor, administration for his use and benefit, limited until he attains the age of eighteen years, shall, unless otherwise directed, and subject to paragraph (2) of this rule, be granted to—
>
> (a) a parent of the minor who has, or is deemed to have, parental responsibility for him in accordance with—
>
> (i) section 2(1), 2(1A), 2(2), 2(2A), 4 or 4ZA of the Children Act 1989,
> (ii) paragraph 4 or 6 of Schedule 14 to that Act, or
> (iii) an adoption order within the meaning of section 12(1) of the Adoption Act 1976 or section 46(1) of the Adoption and Children Act 2002, or
>
> (aa) a person who has, or is deemed to have, parental responsibility for the minor by virtue of section 12(2) of the Children Act 1989 where the court has made a residence order under section 8 of that Act in respect of the minor in favour of that person; or
> (ab) a step-parent of the minor who has parental responsibility for him in accordance with section 4A of the Children Act 1989; or
>
> (b) a guardian of the minor who is appointed, or deemed to have been appointed, in accordance with section 5 of the Children Act 1989 or in accordance with paragraph 12, 13 or 14 of Schedule 14 to that Act, or
>
> (ba) a special guardian of the minor who is appointed in accordance with section 14A of the Children Act 1989; or
> (bb) an adoption agency which has parental responsibility by virtue of section 25(2) of the Adoption and Children Act 2002; or
>
> (c) a local authority which has, or is deemed to have, parental responsibility for the minor by virtue of section 33(3) of the Children Act 1989 where the court has made a care order under section 31(1)(a) of that Act in respect of the minor and that local authority is designated in that order, provided that where the minor is sole executor and has no interest in the residuary estate

of the deceased, administration for the use and benefit of the minor, limited as aforesaid, shall, unless a district judge or registrar otherwise directs, be granted to the person entitled to the residuary estate,

(2) A district judge or registrar may by order appoint a person to obtain administration for the use and benefit of the minor, limited as aforesaid, in default of, or jointly with, or to the exclusion of, any person mentioned in paragraph (1) of this rule; and the person intended shall file an affidavit in support of his application to be appointed.

(3) Where there is only one person competent and willing to take a grant under the foregoing provisions of this rule, such person may, unless a district judge or registrar otherwise directs, nominate any fit and proper person to act jointly with him in taking the grant.

Number of grantees

Where a minority interest exists, the grant should issue to two or more grantees, or to a trust corporation, unless a district judge or registrar (if there are special circumstances), directs otherwise. Examples of 'special circumstances' are where the minority will be of short duration, or where the estate is best administered by a sole grantee because there could be a conflict of interest.

Preference for persons of full age

Where, under a will or intestacy, there is a person of full age equally entitled to benefit and to the grant, the person of full age is preferred as grantee – the person of full age being able to take the grant without limitation – to the persons who would take the grant for the use and benefit of the minor. In special circumstances, a district judge or registrar may allow the persons with parental responsibility for the minor to apply.

Application by person or body having parental responsibility

Rule 32(1)(a)–(c) of the Non-Contentious Probate Rules 1987 prescribe those who, having parental responsibility for the minor child, may take the grant for the minor's use and benefit. For the procedure where a minor is appointed executor, see para 12.1.3.

Those who may apply are:

- a parent (rule 32(1)(a));
- a person who has obtained a residence/child arrangement order (rule 32(1)(aa));
- a step-parent (rule 32(1)(ab));
- a guardian of the minor appointed by the will of the now deceased parent (rule 32(1)(b));

- a special guardian (rule 32(1)(ba));
- an adoption agency (rule 32(1)(bb)); and
- a local authority which has a care order in its favour in respect of the minor (rule 32(1)(c)).

Where the person has acquired parental responsibility under a parental responsibility agreement, a parental responsibility order or other court order, a copy of the order or agreement should be lodged with the application for the grant. However, these documents are now rarely required by the registries; they accept the statement in the oath as sufficient. The oath must recite the authority, for example, 'the lawful adopted father of the said minor by virtue of an adoption order made under the Adoption and Children Act 2002 by the … court and dated …' (see Practice Direction 26 September 1991 [1991] 4 All ER 562).

If there is only one person with parental responsibility able to apply, that person may nominate a co-administrator under rule 32(3) of the Non-Contentious Probate Rules 1987. The nomination must be in writing. Any fit and proper person may be nominated. For a form of oath and nomination, see Appendices C69 and C32.

Application to be appointed to take a grant

If there is no person with parental responsibility, or the person(s) with parental responsibility cannot or will not act, then an application may be made to a district judge or registrar under rule 32(2) of the Non-Contentious Probate Rules 1987 for a person to be appointed to take the grant for the minor's use and benefit. Although the rule refers to 'a person' it is the usual practice of the district judges and registrars to appoint two or more persons to act, to avoid the need for the person appointed to nominate a co-administrator. For the procedure on such an application, see para 10.10.

12.2.13 Beneficiary mentally incapable

Where the residuary beneficiary, or indeed any person entitled to a grant, lacks capacity within the meaning of the Mental Capacity Act 2005 to manage his affairs, rule 35 of the Non-Contentious Probate Rules 1987 applies. Rule 35 provides:

> **Grants in case of mental incapacity**
>
> 35.—(1) Unless a district judge or registrar otherwise directs, no grant shall be made under this rule unless all persons entitled in the same degree as the person who lacks capacity within the meaning of the Mental Capacity Act 2005 referred to in paragraph (2) below have been cleared off.
>
> (2) Where a district judge or registrar is satisfied that a person entitled to a grant lacks capacity within the meaning of the Mental Capacity Act 2005 to manage

his affairs, administration for his use and benefit, limited until further representation be granted or in such other way as the district judge or registrar may direct, may be granted in the following order of priority—

(a) to the person authorised by the Court of Protection to apply for a grant;
(b) where there is no person so authorised, to the lawful attorney of the person who lacks capacity within the meaning of the Mental Capacity Act 2005 acting under a registered enduring power of attorney or lasting power of attorney;
(c) where there is no such attorney entitled to act, or if the attorney shall renounce administration for the use and benefit of the person who lacks capacity within the meaning of the Mental Capacity Act 2005, to the person entitled to the residuary estate of the deceased.

(3) Where a grant is required to be made to not less than two administrators, and there is only one person competent and willing to take a grant under the foregoing provisions of this rule, administration may, unless a district judge or registrar otherwise directs, be granted to such person jointly with any other person nominated by him.
(4) Notwithstanding the foregoing provisions of this rule, administration for the use and benefit of the person who lacks capacity within the meaning of the Mental Capacity Act 2005 may be granted to such other person as the district judge or registrar may by order direct.
(5) Unless the applicant is the person authorised in paragraph 2(a) above, notice of an intended application under this rule shall be given to the Court of Protection.

As provided by rule 35(2)(c) of the Non-Contentious Probate Rules 1987 above, where there is a capable person equally entitled to the grant, that person is preferred and no grant is made under the provisions of this rule unless a district judge or registrar so directs.

Person authorised

To constitute a person entitled under rule 35(2)(a) of the Non-Contentious Probate Rules 1987 there must be an order of the Court of Protection specifically authorising the person named in the order to take the grant for the patient's use and benefit. The fact that someone has been appointed deputy for the patient does not itself provide authority to apply. If an application is to be made for the appointment of a deputy, and it is known that authority is required, an application for authority may be included in the application for that appointment. A copy of the authorising order must be lodged with the application for the grant and the applicant appropriately described as the person authorised in the oath. It is probably easier and quicker to apply to the district judge or registrar under rule 35(4) (see para 10.11) for someone to be appointed to take the grant rather than to include it in a deputyship application.

Attorney under a registered enduring power of attorney or lasting power of attorney

In the absence of a person authorised by order of the Court of Protection, an attorney acting under a registered enduring power of attorney or lasting power of attorney is next entitled. Notice of the proposed application must be given to the Court of Protection in accordance with rule 35(5) of the Non-Contentious Probate Rules 1987 and the court's acknowledgement of the notice must be lodged with the application for the grant.

The original power of attorney, or a copy certified (by the solicitors acting) to be a true and complete copy of the power, must be lodged with the application for the grant.

The oath must recite that no one has been authorised by the Court of Protection and that the applicant is acting under the registered enduring power of attorney or lasting power of attorney.

The Enduring Powers of Attorney Act 1985 was repealed and replaced by the Mental Capacity Act 2005, with effect from 1 October 2007. Part 2 of Schedule 5 to the 2005 Act provides that any enduring power of attorney executed or registered before the coming into force of the 2005 Act continues to have effect as if the 1985 Act had not been repealed. An attorney acting under a power of attorney registered before the 2005 Act came into force may apply for a grant as above.

An enduring power of attorney executed before 30 September 2007 also remains effective for use as an 'ordinary' power unless revoked by the donor or until either the donor or the attorney is adjudged bankrupt. The power is not revoked by the donor lacking mental capacity but suspended. To become effective again it must be registered with the Office of the Public Guardian.

On an application for a grant by the attorney of a donor who lacks capacity, the original enduring power of attorney endorsed with the seal of the Office of the Public Guardian confirming it has been registered must be lodged together with a copy for retention by the registry.

An attorney who has obtained a grant for the use and benefit of his donor who subsequently loses his capacity may (if the donor retains title) apply for a grant *de bonis non* to continue to administer the estate under the power once it has been registered. Until registration the power is suspended and so the original grant cannot be used to administer the estate.

Similarly, an attorney acting under a registered lasting power of attorney may apply as above. There are two forms of lasting power of attorney; for probate purposes, only a power to deal with property and financial affairs is effective. The lasting power of attorney must be registered at the Office of the Public Guardian to be effective.

On an application for a grant by the attorney of a donor who lacks capacity:

- the original lasting power of attorney endorsed with the seal of the Office of the Public Guardian confirming it has been registered; or
- a certified copy (certified by the solicitors acting in accordance with section 3 of the Powers of Attorney Act 1971); or
- an office copy issued by the Office of the Public Guardian;

must be lodged together with a copy for retention by the registry. As registration can be effected before capacity is lost the application must be accompanied by a medical certificate confirming that the donor is now suffering from an impairment of, or a disturbance in, the functioning of the mind or brain as a result of which he lacks capacity within the meaning of the Act and is unable to make a decision for himself in relation to the application for the grant or the administration of the estate.

Residuary beneficiary where there is a will

If there is no one authorised and no one appointed under a registered enduring or lasting power of attorney then, where the incapable person is a sole executor or residuary legatee and devisee in trust, the residuary beneficiary may apply for the grant. In practice, however, it is usually the case that the residuary beneficiary is also the person who is mentally incapable.

Medical evidence

No evidence to substantiate the incapacity is required by the probate registry if application is made by the person authorised by the Court of Protection or the attorney under a registered enduring power of attorney. On registering an enduring power of attorney the Office of the Public Guardian now simply gives notice to other interested persons leaving it to them to object if they do not think the donor lacks capacity. The district judge or registrar accepts this as sufficient and does not require evidence of capacity.

When application is made under a lasting power of attorney the oath must confirm the lasting power of attorney remains in full force and effect and whether or not the donor lacks mental capacity within the meaning of the Mental Capacity Act 2005.

Medical evidence, by certificate or letter from the patient's general practitioner or a responsible medical officer, is required by the district judge or registrar where the application is made by a residuary legatee or devisee, or where the application is made under rule 35(4) of the Non-Contentious Probate Rules 1987 for a person to be appointed to take the grant. For the procedure for an application under rule 35(4), see para 10.11.

12.2.14 Assignment, disclaimer and forfeiture

Assignee

Rule 24 of the Non-Contentious Probate Rules 1987 provides that:

> **Right of assignee to a grant**
>
> 24.—(1) Where all the persons entitled to the estate of the deceased (whether under a will or on intestacy) have assigned their whole interest in the estate to one or more persons, the assignee or assignees shall replace, in the order of priority for a grant of administration, the assignor or, if there are two or more assignors, the assignor with the highest priority.
>
> (2) Where there are two or more assignees, administration may be granted with the consent of the others to any one or more (not exceeding four) of them.
>
> (3) In any case where administration is applied for by an assignee the original instrument of assignment shall be produced and a copy of the same lodged in the registry.

Any person beneficially entitled to the estate, or to share in the estate, may assign by deed his whole benefit to another or others; those to whom the benefit is assigned then take the place, in the order of priority prescribed by rule 20 of the Non-Contentious Probate Rules 1987, which the assignor held. Title to take the grant depends upon those with a higher priority under the rule, for example, the executor, being cleared off by renunciation. Subject to their clearing off the assignee may take the grant.

The whole interest must be transferred by the assignment. The deed may be a deed of assignment, variation or family arrangement; provided the effect of the deed is to assign a whole interest, the deed in any of these forms is acceptable to the probate registries. The original deed, or a copy certified to be a true and complete copy, must be lodged with the application for a grant. The deed must be stamped under the Stamp Act 1891 unless it bears a certificate in proper form that it falls within the scope of the Stamp Duty (Exempt Instruments) Regulations 1987 (SI 1987/516).

Where there is more than one assignee any one (or more) of them may apply for the grant with the consent of those not applying. The consent in writing must be lodged with the application for the grant, and details recited in the oath.

Disclaimer

The Estates of Deceased Persons (Forfeiture Rule and Law of Succession) Act 2011, which came into force on 1 February 2012, added section 46A to the Administration of Estates Act 1925 to vary the intestacy rules, and amended the Wills Act 1837 by adding a new section 33A. The new sections deal with the effect of a person entitled under an intestacy or a will who disclaims their benefit.

The disclaimant must disclaim their entire benefit, which then has the effect of passing that benefit as though the disclaimant had predeceased the deceased. Where the beneficiary disclaims his benefit under an intestacy, the oath should recite the following wording:

> That AB died intestate (state any relevant clearing) leaving CD his/her (state relationship to deceased) and only person entitled to his/her estate who, by virtue of a deed of disclaimer dated ... is deemed to have died immediately before the deceased. I am the ... and only/one of the persons entitled to the estate.

If the disclaimer is of a gift in a will then the wording above should be adapted to fit the circumstances and how title to the grant is acquired.

Forfeiture

The effect of the Act for unlawful killings for dates of death on or after 1 February 2012 is that it is no longer necessary to apply for an order under section 116 of the Senior Courts Act 1981 in cases where the applicant seeks to pass over a person who has been convicted of unlawfully killing the deceased, and to whom the forfeiture rule does not apply.

The oath should recite the following wording:

> That AB died (state marital status if intestate) leaving CD his/her ... (state relationship to deceased) and only person entitled to his/her estate who was on the ... day of ... convicted of his/her murder/manslaughter by ... Court in England and Wales and that the said CD has therefore forfeited his/her right to inherit the estate of the said deceased under the terms of the Estates of Deceased Persons (Forfeiture Rule and Law of Succession) Act 2011 and is deemed to have died immediately before the deceased. That at the date of this application no appeal has been made against the conviction. That I understand that a successful appeal against the conviction in the future may affect the entitlement to a grant and the distribution of the estate.

The oath should then go on to state the title of the applicant, for example, child and one of the persons entitled to the estate.

An official copy of the conviction certificate should be filed and the extracting solicitors should confirm that the 3-month forfeiture rule does not apply in the matter or, if it does, that 3 months have elapsed since the conviction and that no proceedings to modify the rule have been commenced within that time.

12.2.15 Application for the grant

An application for letters of administration (with will annexed) may be made at any time after the testator's death but the grant may not issue within 14 days of the death (see rule 6(2) of the Non-Contentious Probate Rules 1987).

An application may be made to a district judge or registrar for leave to abridge the time and expedite the issue of the grant. There must be good reason for the district judge or registrar to exercise his discretion under the rule, such as to commence litigation in another court, or to complete the urgent sale of property where the deceased had signed a contract for sale before his death.

12.2.16 Oath to lead the grant

The proposed administrators must depose to the relevant facts, giving proper clearings and title to the grant. The details to be included in the oath are described in the procedure for an application for probate, as are the requirements of rules 8, 9 and 10 of the Non-Contentious Probate Rules 1987 (see para 12.1.5). For the procedure where an inheritance tax account is required to be delivered, see Chapter 3. For forms of oath, see Appendices C45–C53.

12.3 APPLICATION FOR LETTERS OF ADMINISTRATION

Letters of administration are granted when the deceased died wholly intestate. If there was a will but it was not properly executed, or has been pronounced against in a claim in the Chancery Division, then, in the absence of any earlier will, an intestacy ensues. Title to the grant follows the order of beneficial entitlement to (share) the estate and is prescribed by rule 22 of the Non-Contentious Probate Rules 1987 as follows:

> (1) Where the deceased died on or after 1 January 1926, wholly intestate, the person or persons having a beneficial interest in the estate shall be entitled to a grant of administration in the following classes in order of priority, namely—
>
> (a) the surviving spouse or civil partner;
> (b) the children of the deceased and the issue of any deceased child who died before the deceased;

(c) the father and mother of the deceased;
(d) brothers and sisters of the whole blood and the issue of any deceased brother or sister of the whole blood who died before the deceased;
(e) brothers and sisters of the half blood and the issue of any deceased brother or sister of the half blood who died before the deceased;
(f) grandparents;
(g) uncles and aunts of the whole blood and the issue of any deceased uncle or aunt of the whole blood who died before the deceased;
(h) uncles and aunts of the half blood and the issue of any deceased uncle or aunt of the half-blood who died before the deceased.

(2) In default of any person having a beneficial interest in the estate, the Treasury Solicitor shall be entitled to a grant if he claims *bona vacantia* on behalf of the Crown.
(3) If all persons entitled to a grant under the foregoing provisions of this rule have been cleared off, a grant may be made to a creditor of the deceased or to any person who, notwithstanding that he has no immediately beneficial interest in the estate, may have a beneficial interest in the event of an accretion thereto.
(4) Subject to paragraph (5) of Rule 27, the personal representative of a person in any of the classes mentioned in paragraph (1) of this rule or the personal representative of a creditor of the deceased shall have the same right to a grant as the person whom he represents provided that the persons mentioned in sub-paragraph (b) to (h) of paragraph (1) above shall be preferred to the personal representative of a spouse or civil partner who has died without taking a beneficial interest in the whole estate of the deceased as ascertained at the time of the application for the grant.

Rule 27(5) of the Non-Contentious Probate Rules 1987, referred to above, sets out the preference for a 'live' interest over a 'dead' interest. A living person entitled to benefit in the order of priority under this rule is preferred as grantee to the personal representative of a person of equal entitlement who, if living, would be entitled to the grant. For example, where the deceased died a widow without issue or parent or any other person entitled to share in the estate by virtue of any enactment (e.g. an adopted child), leaving two brothers of the whole blood one of whom has since died, the living brother is preferred to the personal representatives of the now deceased brother.

For the distribution of an intestate's estate and title to the grant, see Chapter 6.

12.3.1 Oath to lead the grant

For specimen forms of oath, see Appendices C54–C70. The correct wording to establish title and clearing must be set out in the oath. The requirement will also apply to a statement of truth to support an online application made under the pilot scheme (see para 12.1.1). The following descriptions are used:

To clear	*Status of deceased*
Spouse or civil partner	widow or civil partner widower or civil partner bachelor (never married or formed civil partnership) spinster (never married or formed civil partnership) single man (marriage or civil partnership dissolved) single woman (marriage or civil partnership dissolved)
Children or remoter issue	without issue
Parents	(or) parent
Brothers/sisters, nephews/ nieces or their issue	(or) brother or sister of the whole blood [and/or half-blood] or issue thereof
Grandparents	(or) grandparent
Uncles/aunts, cousins or their issue	(or) uncle or aunt of the whole blood [and/or half - blood] or issue thereof

Where the grant is applied for by those entitled after children or remoter issue in the table above, illegitimate and adopted children must be cleared off by the addition of the words, 'or any other person entitled in priority to share in the estate by virtue of any enactment'.

For example, if the deceased died intestate a single man, leaving as his nearest relative a child of a cousin, the title and clearing to appear in the oath should be:

> ... died intestate a single man, whose marriage with [name of former spouse] was dissolved by final [decree] [order] dated the [date] of the [name of court] in England and Wales and that the deceased did not thereafter remarry or form a civil partnership, without issue or parent or brother or sister of the whole or half blood or their issue or grandparent or uncle or aunt of the whole blood or any other person entitled in priority to share in the estate by virtue of any enactment. I am the cousin german of the whole blood once removed being the son of (*name of cousin*) who was the daughter of (*name of uncle or aunt*) both of whom predeceased the deceased and the only person entitled to the estate of the deceased.

Rules 8 and 9 of the Non-Contentious Probate Rules 1987, described in para 12.2.5 in the context of applications for probate, apply to any oath or application and are therefore relevant to an application in an intestacy.

12.4 APPLICATION BY AN ATTORNEY

Rule 31 of the Non-Contentious Probate Rules 1987 provides:

> (1) Subject to paragraphs (2) and (3) below, the lawfully constituted attorney of a person entitled to a grant may apply for administration for the use and benefit of the donor, and such grant shall be limited until further representation be granted, or in such other way as the district judge or registrar may direct.
>
> (2) Where the donor referred to in paragraph (1) above is an executor, notice of the application shall be given to any other executor unless such notice is dispensed with by the district judge or registrar.
>
> (3) Where the donor referred to in paragraph (1) above lacks capacity within the meaning of the Mental Capacity Act 2005 and the attorney is acting under an enduring power of attorney or lasting power of attorney, the application shall be made in accordance with rule 35.

By virtue of rule 31(1) of the Non-Contentious Probate Rules 1987 any person entitled to take a grant in the order of priority contained in rules 20 and 22 may appoint an attorney to apply on his behalf. The attorney may apply without leave. For application by the attorney of an executor, see para 12.2.1.

12.4.1 Form of power of attorney

The power of attorney may be general in form under section 10 of the Powers of Attorney Act 1971, as contained in Schedule 1 to the Act. Alternatively, the power may be specific in that it authorises the donee to take the grant and administer the estate. An enduring power of attorney which has not been registered may be used as an ordinary power of attorney, even after the coming into force of the Mental Capacity Act 2005 on 1 October 2007. Once registered, rule 31(3) of the Non-Contentious Probate Rules 1987 applies. A lasting power of attorney becomes effective only when registered, but can be used as an ordinary power of attorney, i.e. when the donor remains capable, provided the oath confirms the donor retains capacity within the meaning of the 2005 Act. If the power appoints more than one attorney jointly they must both apply, but if the appointment is joint and several, either or both may apply.

12.4.2 Execution of power

A power of attorney in general form or one limited to obtaining the grant must be signed by the donor before a disinterested witness who also signs the power. The date of execution must be inserted.

If the power was executed abroad in a non-English speaking country, then, provided it is in English and witnessed by a notary or consular officer, it is acceptable. If the power is not so witnessed, there must be evidence that the donor understood English. If the power is in a foreign language, there must be lodged an authenticated translation certified by a competent translator.

Where there is doubt as to the sufficiency of the power of attorney, it should be referred to a district judge or registrar for directions.

12.4.3 Retention of power

If the power of attorney is limited to extracting the grant it is retained in the registry. A general power, or power for other purposes, will be returned if a copy certified to be a true and complete copy is also lodged.

12.4.4 Limitation in grant

The grant is usually 'for the use and benefit of [donor] and limited until further representation be granted', that is, it ceases to operate on the issue of another grant but need not be revoked before the second grant may issue. So, if the donor or donee dies, or the power is revoked, the authority of the attorney ends and the grant ceases to be effective from the date on which a further grant issues.

A district judge or registrar may impose any other limitation if necessary.

12.5 LIMITED GRANTS

12.5.1 Grant following discretionary order

For applications for discretionary orders, see Chapter 10. Following such an order, the application for the grant is made in the usual way, the oath to lead the grant reciting details of the order and any limitation in the grant imposed by the order. Generally these grants are full grants to the whole estate.

These grant applications, although not necessarily unusual, require special consideration and are dealt with below.

Letters of administration ad colligenda bona defuncti

An application for this form of grant may be made in respect of a part of the estate requiring immediate administration before a full grant is taken or, perhaps, because a full grant cannot now be taken.

Initially it is preferable to make a pre-lodgement enquiry (see para 5.2) of the district judge or registrar, to ascertain whether the application will be entertained; if so, an application for the order should then be made (see para 10.12).

The oath: When an order has been made for an *ad colligenda bona* grant, the oath to lead the grant should recite details of the order and the limitation imposed by it. The oath should not mention any will or recite an intestacy. It must, however, contain the statements required by rule 8 of the Non-Contentious Probate Rules 1987 – on domicile, whether a life or minority interest arises, and as to settled land.

Inheritance tax account: Where the whole estate qualifies as an excepted estate (see para 4.2), no inheritance tax account need be submitted to HM Revenue and Customs. The oath to lead the limited grant should recite the appropriate gross and net figures which the estate does not exceed, and that no account is required to be delivered. Form IHT205 (see para 4.2.1) is submitted to the probate registry with the application for the grant.

Where the whole estate attracts payment of inheritance tax, the tax on that part of the estate passing under the grant *ad colligenda bona* must be paid before the grant may issue. It is suggested that, before applying for the grant, HM Revenue and Customs be contacted for their requirements. In some circumstances (usually where no monetary value passes under the temporary grant), and subject to HM Revenue and Customs' agreement, the delivery of an account at this stage may be dispensed with. But before issuing the grant, the probate registry would need to see the written agreement of HM Revenue and Customs that no account is required at this stage.

Section 109 of the Senior Courts Act 1981 prohibits the issue of any grant until the district judge or registrar is satisfied that all tax currently payable has been paid (or other arrangements are in place).

Because the grant is required urgently (and its issue is usually expedited), arrangements with HM Revenue and Customs must be entered into with equivalent urgency.

Limitation: The grant is always limited, *inter alia*, until further representation be granted. On the issue of the full grant, the *ad colligenda bona defuncti* grant ceases to be effective.

Grant under section 113 of the Senior Courts Act 1981

A grant limited to trust property where the deceased life tenant's estate is insolvent may be issued solely for the purpose of dealing with the trust property.

The procedure for applying for an order to sever the estate under section 113 of the Senior Courts Act 1981 is dealt with at para 10.7. Once the order has been made, an application for the grant is made in the usual way; details of the order and limitation should be recited in the oath.

Grant pending determination of a probate claim

Where a claim has been lodged in the Chancery Division under Part 57 of the Civil Procedure Rules 1998, an application may be made, to a Chancery Master or district judge, under section 117 of the Senior Courts Act 1981, for an order for a grant of letters of administration to deal with a part of the estate requiring urgent administration. This application has, in effect, much the same result as an application for a grant *ad colligenda bona* in a non-contentious matter except that, in appropriate cases, the Chancery Master or district judge has power to direct the remuneration of the administrator. Application for the order is made on application or notice in accordance with Part 57.

An application for the grant pursuant to the order must be made to the Principal Registry of the Family Division, as no grant may issue out of a district registry where there is unresolved contention (see rule 7(1) of the Non-Contentious Probate Rules 1987).

The oath to lead the grant must be accompanied by a copy of the order appointing the administrator and recite details of that order. If an inheritance tax account needs to be delivered, then form IHT400 must be lodged with HM Revenue and Customs, and form IHT421 lodged with the application for the grant.

Grant to prosecute or defend claim

An application for a grant limited to a specific purpose may be made where:

- it is necessary to constitute a personal representative to prosecute a claim on behalf of the estate, or defend a claim against the estate; or
- to constitute a defendant for a claim under the Inheritance (Provision for Family and Dependants) Act 1975 (death before 1 October 2014).

Such an application is required only where there is no personal representative, or the person entitled to become the personal representative refuses to apply.

An application by a person with no title to a grant is made under the court's discretionary power under section 116 of the Senior Courts Act 1981 (see para 10.13). Once the order is made an application for the grant proceeds in the usual way, the oath to lead the grant reciting the details of the order.

Where the grant is required so that a person may launch proceedings under the Inheritance (Provision for Family and Dependants) Act 1975 (death before 1 October 2014), there is nothing to prevent the person wishing to make the claim also being the personal representative if so entitled under the usual order of priority. For example, where the deceased dies intestate a single man leaving minor children, his former spouse, if she has parental responsibility for the minors, may take the grant for their use and benefit and then commence her application by a claim in the county court. Once the proceedings have been issued, an application should be made to the district judge for directions as to who will represent the minors' interest.

Where the grant is required to prosecute or defend a claim there is often little or no estate to pass under the grant. Even if the value of the estate is nil, the excepted estate provisions (see para 4.2) may be used to avoid the need to deliver an inheritance tax account. Any damages or other monies recovered as a result of the action do not pass under a grant limited to prosecuting a claim unless the limitation imposed so provides. A full grant should be taken by the person entitled in the normal order of priority.

Grant limited to settled land

Under rule 29 of the Non-Contentious Probate Rules 1987, no grant of probate or administration in respect of the general estate can issue including settled land. Since the Non-Contentious Probate Rules 1987 came into force a separate grant is required to administer settled land. A grant of administration, limited to dealing with settled land, issues pursuant to the rule, which provides:

> (1) In this rule 'settled land' means land vested in the deceased which was settled prior to his death and not by his will, and which remained settled land notwithstanding his death.
>
> (2) The person or persons entitled to a grant of administration limited to settled land shall be determined in accordance with the following order of priority:
>
> > (i) the special executors in regard to settled land constituted by section 22 of the Administration of Estates Act 1925;
> >
> > (ii) the trustees of the settlement at the time of the application for the grant; and
> >
> > (iii) the personal representatives of the deceased.
>
> (3) Where there is settled land and a grant is made in respect of the free estate only, the grant shall expressly exclude the settled land.

Where the land is vested in more than one life tenant, a settled land grant issues only on the death of the last surviving tenant.

Definition: Settled land is defined by section 1 of the Settled Land Act 1925. To require a grant in respect of settled land the land must have been settled by vesting assent on a person or persons (the life tenant(s)), and remain settled land after the death of that person or of the last surviving such person. Settlements of assets other than land do not fall within the ambit of the Act and are dealt with not under rule 29 of the Non-Contentious Probate Rules 1987, but under rules 20 and 22 (see paras 12.1 and 12.3) as appropriate.

The first and obvious matter to be determined before making an application for a grant is whether there was indeed settled land which remains settled land, that is, that the deceased was not a life tenant such that the settlement ceases on death. Capital sums arising from the sale of settled land during the tenant's life qualify only if reinvested in land and resettled. This and, indeed, settled land grants in general are becoming less common since the Trusts of Land and Appointment of Trustees Act 1996 came into force on 1 July 1997. Any settlement created after the commencement of the 1996 Act cannot be a settlement for the purposes of the Settled Land Act 1925. It follows there will be a diminishing need for settled land grants.

12.5.2 Special executors

The first entitled to a grant are the special executors for settled land created by section 22 of the Administration of Estates Act 1925. Obviously, 'special executors' can be appointed only under the will of the tenant for life, but even though executors, they may take only letters of administration limited to the settled land. There is no grant of 'probate' of settled land. The life tenant's will is not proved on application for a grant limited to settled land. The special executors are those appointed by the tenant for life as an express appointment in his will, but in default of an express appointment of others, the trustees of the settlement at the date of death of the tenant for life are deemed to have been appointed special executors.

12.5.3 Trustees of the settlement

Thus, only the trustees at the date of death may qualify as special executors. If there is no express appointment of executors and there were no trustees at the date of death (or the trustees have themselves subsequently died), the current trustees of the settlement may take the grant, such trustees being constituted under section 30 of the Settled Land Act 1925.

12.5.4 Life tenant's personal representatives

Where there are no special executors or trustees of the settlement, the grant limited to settled land may be taken by the life tenant's personal representatives, i.e. those who have taken a grant of representation to the life tenant's free estate.

12.5.5 Oath

The oath to lead the grant must set out the applicants' title to the grant, that is, the capacity in which they apply, clearing those with prior entitlement. The oath should also recite details of any other grant taken in respect of the life tenant's free estate. The values to be inserted are those contained in the inheritance tax account. An account must be delivered to HM Revenue and Customs.

The oath must be accompanied by a true and complete copy of the will or other document creating the settlement and the assent vesting the land in the life tenant.

If the estate value exceeds £5,000, the usual grant fee (£155) is payable.

12.6 SECOND AND SUBSEQUENT GRANTS

12.6.1 Chain of executorship

An executor who proves his testator's will also becomes the executor of any estate of which his testator was the last surviving or sole proving executor. This is by way of a chain of representation under section 7 of the Administration of Estates Act 1925. Although it may appear that a second grant may be necessary where a chain of executorship exists, no further grant is required. The chain is broken in the circumstances set out at para 12.1.3.

Where there would be a chain if the executor proved his testator's will, but he does not do so, the chain is in abeyance. A grant of letters of administration (with will annexed) may be made to any person next entitled under rule 20 of the Non-Contentious Probate Rules 1987 (see para 12.1), limited until the executor proves the will.

The chain of representation passes only through the last surviving or sole proving executor; it is a chain of *executorship*; no chain is created through letters of administration.

12.6.2 Grant of double probate

When probate has been granted to one or more of several named executors with power reserved to others, the others, or any of them, may apply for a grant of double probate at any time, provided the number of executors acting under the original grant and those under the double probate grant does not exceed four (section 114(1) of the Senior Courts Act 1981).

An application for double probate may be made to any registry, not necessarily that which issued the original grant.

The oath gives details of the former grant; to whom power was reserved; and to whom (if any) power remains reserved. The estate values may be those used originally if the estate is an excepted estate; or, if it is not, the values of the unadministered estate. If an account was originally delivered, then an account in form A5C must be delivered *to the probate registry* on application for the grant.

If the oath is sworn in the registry from which the original grant issued, the original will may be marked; otherwise an official copy should be requested and marked.

The fee for the grant is £20. The fee for the copy will is £10.

12.6.3 Letters of administration (with will annexed) *de bonis non*

Where a grant of probate or letters of administration (with will annexed) has issued, but the grantee dies or becomes incapable within the meaning of the Mental Capacity Act 2005 of managing his affairs, a new grant is required to deal with any estate remaining unadministered.

Death of grantee

Where probate has been granted and the proving executor dies but there survives an executor to whom power had been reserved, that executor may take double probate (see para 12.6.2), unless a chain of executorship is created by an executor proving the will of the now deceased proving executor (see, also, para 12.6.1).

The non-proving executor to whom power had been reserved may be cited to accept or refuse probate of the will if he is unwilling to renounce his title. If he fails properly to deal with the citation, his rights to probate are extinguished and an application for letters of administration (with will annexed) *de bonis non* may be made. For the procedure on citations, see Chapter 8.

If the original grant was of letters of administration (with will annexed) and the administrator dies, then the new grant in respect of the unadministered estate is also letters of administration (with will annexed), taken by a person of equal or next entitlement under rule 20 of the Non-Contentious Probate Rules 1987 (see para 12.1).

Incapacity of grantee

Where the grant is of probate to two or more executors, and one becomes incapable after the grant has been issued, the original grant must be revoked and a new grant of probate taken by the capable executor(s), with power reserved to the incapable executor on regaining his capacity. For the procedure for revocation, see para 26.3.2.

Similarly, where letters of administration (with or without will annexed) have been granted to two or more grantees and one becomes incapable, the original grant is revoked and a new grant issued to the capable administrator(s).

Where the grant issued to a *sole* executor or administrator and the grantee becomes incapable of managing his affairs, the grant is not revoked or impounded. Instead, a new grant may be taken by a person of equal or next entitlement for the use and benefit of the now incapable grantee. Title to the grant, when all executors have been cleared, follows the order of priority for an original grant prescribed by rule 20 of the Non-Contentious Probate Rules 1987. The preference in rule 20(d) – for a 'live' interest over a 'dead' interest – also applies.

Oath to lead the grant

The oath should recite details of the original grant and clear off executors and those entitled in priority in the usual way. The oath must also, where appropriate, show how the chain of executorship is broken or is in abeyance.

The estate values for the original grant, if that was an excepted estate, may be used again, although the grant is in respect of unadministered estate only. If an inheritance tax account was originally delivered, then an account in form A5C must be delivered to the registry with the oath and other documents.

The original will may be marked on swearing the oath in the registry in which it is lodged (the issuing registry); otherwise the probate copy (the copy inside the original grant) may be marked, but the grant is then retained by the registry. It is usually simpler to request an official copy of the will for marking from the registry which issued the original grant (the fee for the office copy is £10). The oath should refer to whichever form of will is being produced and marked. For a precedent oath, see Appendix C39.

The fee for the grant is £20; official copies cost £0.50 each.

12.6.4 *Cessate* grant

A *cessate* grant may issue to deal with estate remaining unadministered, where an original grant was issued subject to a limitation, but the limitation no longer applies, for example, where:

- the grant issued for the use and benefit of a minor child until he attains 18 years of age and he has attained 18;
- the grant issued for the use and benefit of an incapable person within the meaning of the Mental Capacity Act 2005 and the person has regained capacity;
- the grant was limited for a period of time and the time has expired; or
- the grant had issued for the use and benefit of the donor of a power of attorney who now wishes to take the grant himself or through another attorney.

A *cessate* grant is a grant in respect of the whole estate, although it recites the values of the unadministered estate, and is required only if there remains unadministered estate when the limitation expires.

Original grant for the use of minor(s)

Letters of administration (with or without will) issued for the use and benefit of minor(s) are limited until the minor, or one of them, attains the age of 18. The grant ceases to be operative when the minor, or the eldest, attains his majority, at which time a *cessate* grant should be taken if the estate remains unadministered. The minor now of age or, if a minority interest still exists, the minor now of age and the person with parental responsibility for the child who remains a minor, are entitled to apply. If there is no one willing or able to join with the child now of age in the grant application, application may be made under rule 25 of the Non-Contentious Probate Rules 1987, on affidavit by the child now of age, for the joinder of a co-administrator. The registries now prefer application under rule 25 to join the person with parental responsibility.

The *cessate* grant is 'limited until further representation be granted' if there remains a minority interest. The grant taken by a person now absolutely entitled remains operative even after the youngest minor attains the age of 18.

Original grant for use of mentally incapable person

Letters of administration (with or without will) issued for the use and benefit of a person incapable of managing his affairs within the meaning of the Mental Capacity Act 2005 are usually limited until further representation be granted, but may, where the grant issues to a person authorised by the Court of Protection, be limited during the patient's incapacity.

Where the grant was limited until further representation be granted, on the death of the grantee, a further grant may be made under rule 35 of the Non-Contentious Probate Rules 1987 (see para 12.2.13) for the patient's use. If the patient dies, a grant *de bonis non* may be taken by a person entitled thereto under rule 20 or rule 22 (see paras 12.1 and 12.3). If the patient recovers his capacity he may apply for a grant to himself but he need not do so: the original grant remains effective and continues until a further grant is taken. On an application by the former patient, he must prove his capacity.

Where the grant was limited during the patient's incapacity, and the patient recovers, he may take a grant to himself, but must provide evidence of his recovery on application for the grant. If a patient dies before the estate is fully administered, a grant *de bonis non* may be taken by the person(s) next entitled under rule 20 or rule 22 of the Non-Contentious Probate Rules 1987. If the administrator dies before completing the administration, a *cessate* grant may be taken by the person authorised to do so by further order of the Court of Protection, or by a person appointed by a district judge or registrar on application made under rule 35(4) (see para 10.11).

Procedure

The procedure for applying for a *cessate* grant is the same as for a grant *de bonis non*. Details of the former grant must be recited in the oath and, where the deceased died testate, an office copy of the will, marked by the commissioner and deponent, must be lodged. The deponent swears to administer the whole estate, but, as in a grant *de bonis non*, the value of the unadministered estate is given. Where an inheritance tax account was delivered on application for the original grant, an account in form A5C is delivered to the registry with the oath. As the grant is a second grant to the same estate a fee of £20 is payable. For a precedent oath, see Appendix C74.

12.6.5 Representative or 'leading' grants

Sometimes it is necessary to obtain a representative grant, often referred to as a 'leading' grant, to establish title to take a grant where the executor or administrator has died leaving estate unadministered. For example, where probate has been taken by a sole executor who was also the sole beneficiary under the will, and he dies intestate before completing the administration, a grant must be taken to his estate to constitute a personal representative to take the grant *de bonis non* to complete the administration. Similarly, on an intestacy, where a grant is taken by the only person entitled to the deceased's estate, and the administrator dies without completing the administration, a representative grant must be taken.

If the executor/administrator dies without any estate of his own requiring a grant, an application for a discretionary order under section 116 of the Senior Courts Act 1981 (see para 10.13) may be made, instead of an application for a representative grant.

Where a representative grant is required, application for both grants may be made together. If the representative grant has already been issued, the oath to lead the *de bonis non* grant recites the type and date of the representative grant, for example, 'I am the personal representative of [name of first administrator] letters of administration having issued out of the ... Registry on ...'. If the applications are made together the oath should recite, 'I am the proposed personal representative of ... letters of administration to his estate being applied for contemporaneously with this application'.

The registry issues the representative grant first.

12.6.6 Testamentary documents found after a grant has been issued

Where a copy, draft or reconstructed will has been proved with leave under rule 54 of the Non-Contentious Probate Rules 1987 (see para 10.14) and the original will is later found, then, provided the copy will proved was a true and complete copy of the original, no action need be taken. The grant would have been limited until the original will or a more authentic copy is proved, so it remains effective until the original is proved. The original will may be lodged in the registry where the copy was proved.

Where, however, the original will differs from the copy proved, the grant must be revoked and the original proved.

Where a codicil is in dispute, probate of the will alone may be granted, except where the disputed codicil alters the appointment of executors. When the dispute is resolved, the codicil, if accepted as valid, may be proved alone.

Where a codicil is discovered after probate of the will had been granted then, again, the codicil may be proved alone provided the appointment of executors is unaltered.

The oath to lead the grant must recite details of the original grant.

12.7 ISSUE OF THE GRANT

All grants are deemed to issue (that is, to pass under the seal of the court) at the earliest time the registry is open for business on the day on which they are dated; this is 10 a.m. in all the registries.

The grant, of whatever kind, should issue within 7–14 working days of the receipt of the application in the registry. This may vary from registry to registry and is, of course, subject to the provisos that all the necessary documents are submitted and are properly completed; there is no defect in the will and/or codicil; all fees have been paid; inheritance tax (if due) has been paid and there is no official impediment (such as a caveat) to the issue of the grant.

The grant is sent to the address or document exchange box number which appears on the oath to lead the grant, unless prior arrangements have been made for collection from the registry.

Although the registries endeavour to avoid errors, unfortunately they do occasionally occur. The form and content of the grant should therefore be checked. If there is an error, the grant should be returned to the registry for correction (see para 26.2.1).

Chapter 13

Scottish, Northern Irish and Colonial Grants

13.1 SCOTTISH CONFIRMATIONS AND NORTHERN IRISH GRANTS

By virtue of section 1(1) of the Administration of Estates Act 1971, where a person dies domiciled in Scotland and a confirmation or certificate of confirmation issues from the Scottish courts, the confirmation or certificate is sufficient to administer estate throughout the United Kingdom. The confirmation or certificate must carry a notation that the deceased's domicile is in Scotland. The confirmation or certificate is not 'resealed' to give it effect in England and Wales.

Similarly, under section 1(4) of the Administration of Estates Act 1971, a grant of representation issued in Northern Ireland, bearing a notation of the deceased's domicile there, is sufficient to administer estate throughout the United Kingdom without being 'resealed'.

Sections 2 and 3 of the Administration of Estates Act 1971 provide, *inter alia*, for the recognition of a grant issued in England and Wales bearing a notation of the deceased's domicile, as sufficient to administer estate throughout the United Kingdom, without its being resealed by the court in Scotland or Northern Ireland.

Where a confirmation or grant issues, but the deceased is not domiciled in the part of the United Kingdom whose court issued the confirmation or grant, the confirmation or grant is limited to the administration of estate in that part of the United Kingdom. So, a grant of representation issued in England and Wales to the estate of a person domiciled in Scotland would be 'limited to estate in England and Wales and until representation is granted in Scotland'. This is to avoid duplication of representation.

It is therefore preferable to take a confirmation or grant from the court of the place of domicile so that all estate in the United Kingdom may be administered in its entirety.

13.2 COLONIAL GRANTS

The Colonial Probates Acts of 1892 and 1927 provide for the resealing of grants issued by the courts of specified countries, with the result that the grant becomes effective to administer estate in England and Wales. The reciprocating countries, provinces and territories are specified by Order in Council and currently are:

Alberta	Antigua
Australian Capital Territory	Bahamas
Barbados	Belize
Bermuda	Botswana
British Antarctic Territory	British Columbia
British Sovereign Base Areas in Cyprus	Brunei
Cayman Islands	Christmas Island
Cocos (Keeling) Islands	Cyprus (only grants issued by the recognised government of Cyprus; grants issued by the courts of the Turkish Republic of North Cyprus cannot be resealed)
Dominica	Falkland Islands
Falkland Island Dependencies	Fiji
Gambia	Ghana
Gibraltar	Grenada
Guyana	Hong Kong (the Act remains in force for Hong Kong notwithstanding the change in the status of Hong Kong on 1 July 1997)
Jamaica	Kenya
Kiribati	Lesotho
Malawi	Malaysia
Manitoba	Montserrat

New Brunswick	New Guinea Territory
New South Wales	New Zealand
Newfoundland	Nigeria
Norfolk Island	Northern Territory of Australia
North-West Territories of Canada	Nova Scotia
Ontario	Papua New Guinea
Prince Edward Island	Queensland
St Christopher (Kitts)	Nevis and Anguilla
St Helena	St Lucia
St Vincent	Saskatchewan
Seychelles (Republic)	Sierra Leone
Singapore	Solomon Islands
South Africa	South Australia
Sri Lanka	Swaziland
Tasmania	Tortola
Trinidad and Tobago (Republic)	Turks and Caicos Islands
Tuvalu	Uganda
Victoria	Western Australia
Zambia	Zimbabwe

The procedure for resealing is governed by rule 39 of the Non-Contentious Probate Rules 1987, as follows:

(1) An application under the Colonial Probates Acts 1892 and 1927 for the resealing of probate or administration granted by the court of a country to which those Acts apply may be made by the person to whom the grant was made or by any person authorised in writing to apply on his behalf.
(2) On any such application an Inland Revenue affidavit or account shall be lodged.
(3) Except by leave of a district judge or registrar, no grant shall be resealed unless it was made to such a person as is mentioned in sub-paragraph (a) or (b) of paragraph (1) of Rule 30 or to a person to whom a grant could be made under sub-paragraph (a) of paragraph (3) of that rule.
(4) No limited or temporary grant shall be resealed except by leave of a district judge or registrar.
(5) Every grant lodged for resealing shall include a copy of any will to which the grant relates or shall be accompanied by a copy thereof certified as correct by or

under the authority of the court by which the grant was made, and where the copy of the grant required to be deposited under subsection (1) of section 2 of the Colonial Probates Act 1892 does not include a copy of the will, a copy thereof shall be deposited in the registry before the grant is resealed.

(6) The district judge or registrar shall send notice of the resealing to the court which made the grant.

(7) Where notice is received in the Principal Registry of the resealing of a grant issued in England and Wales, notice of any amendment or revocation of the grant shall be sent to the court by which it was resealed.

13.2.1 Who may apply?

By virtue of rule 39(3) of the Non-Contentious Probate Rules 1987 a grant may be resealed only if the grantee was a person qualifying under:

- rule 30(1)(a) – a person entrusted with the administration by the court of the place of domicile;
- rule 30(1)(b) – a person beneficially entitled to (share in) the estate by the law of the place of domicile; or
- rule 30(3)(a) – the executor named in, or according to the tenor of, the will.

A person not so qualifying may apply for resealing only with the leave of a district judge or registrar. Application for leave is made to the district judge or registrar by letter.

Thus, to qualify as above the grant must have been issued by the courts of the country of the place of domicile, and the grantee must be the person entrusted and/or beneficially entitled. The only exceptions are where the grantee is the executor, or there is separate evidence to establish beneficial entitlement. For example, the deceased died domiciled in Zimbabwe and the grant issued from the court in South Africa; the grantee is not entrusted by the court of the place of domicile so rule 30(1)(a) of the Non-Contentious Probate Rules 1987 does not apply; if there is evidence of beneficial entitlement under the law of the place of domicile, rule 30(1)(b) may apply; or the grantee is the executor and rule 30(3)(a) applies. In the example, only a person beneficially entitled or the executor may apply to reseal.

13.2.2 Form of grant which may be resealed

The following may be resealed:

- the original grant;
- a duplicate sealed by the court of issue with its seal;

- a copy certified by the proper officer of the court of issue; or
- an exemplification of the original grant.

It is the practice to reseal only grants which are in English, or in a foreign language and English, for example, grants from South Africa. Only with the leave of a district judge or registrar may a temporary or limited grant be resealed.

Documents not on the face of them appearing to be grants may be accepted for resealing. Elections to Administer sealed by the courts of Australia and New Zealand may be accepted, as may Appointments of Estate Trustees issued by the courts in Canada. Where doubt arises, the document should be submitted to the district judge or registrar for directions as to admissibility.

13.2.3 Will to be lodged

Whatever the form of grant, if the deceased was testate but a copy of the will or other testamentary document is not included in the grant, a copy will must be lodged with the grant on the application to reseal. If the testamentary document is not included in the copy grant, that is, where they are separate documents, there must be sufficient evidence to establish that the documents are inter-related. This is usually clear from the documents themselves and the court certificates endorsed on them.

13.2.4 Authority to apply

Where the application to reseal is being made by someone other than the grantee, the person applying must have the grantee's written authorisation to apply. The authorisation may be in the form of a power of attorney or letter. The crucial point is that the authorisation must be in writing.

Where the grant issued to two or more grantees they must all join in the application to reseal or authorise one of them to apply. Thus, where the grantee has died after the issue of the grant, it cannot be resealed. Where one of two or more grantees has died the grant may be resealed on application by the survivor(s). The district judge or registrar will require sufficient evidence of the death of the other grantee.

Where the grant was extracted by lawyers acting for the grantee, the district judge or registrar may accept a letter from the lawyers as sufficient authority to apply on the grantee's behalf.

13.2.5 Inheritance tax accounts

Even if the deceased died domiciled outside the United Kingdom, an inheritance tax account must usually be delivered to HM Revenue and Customs. The 'excepted estate' provisions apply only if:

- the deceased died on or after 6 April 2002;
- the deceased was never domiciled in the United Kingdom for tax purposes;
- for deaths on or after 1 September 2006, the deceased was not a person by reason of whose death one of the ASP fund provisions applies; and
- the estate in England and Wales does not exceed £100,000 or £150,000 for deaths on or after 1 September 2006.

Where these conditions are met, the letter accompanying the application to reseal must confirm that that is the case.

Where the estate qualifies as an excepted estate, form IHT207 must be delivered to the registry with the other documents. Where the estate does not so qualify, form IHT400, together with form IHT421, must be delivered to HM Revenue and Customs. IHT421 will be returned stamped (and, if necessary receipted) to show the account has been controlled and any tax due paid. The IHT421 must be lodged with the grant on application to reseal.

13.2.6 Making the application

Application may be made to any registry or sub-registry by lodging the following documents:

- the original grant, court-certified copy, duplicate or exemplification;
- a court-certified copy of all testamentary documents;
- copies of each of the above documents for retention by the court;
- the power of attorney or other written authority of the grantee;
- form IHT421 (stamped and, where appropriate, receipted).

Where the value of the net estate exceeds £5,000, a fee of £155 is payable for resealing. No fee is payable where the net estate is less than £5,000. Office copies are £0.50 each. These are the same fees as for a full 'English' grant.

Chapter 14

Applications on Summons

14.1 INTRODUCTION

Under the Non-Contentious Probate Rules 1987, certain matters which are contentious may be brought before a district judge or registrar on summons, supported by an affidavit of facts. The Civil Procedure Rules 1998 do not apply to proceedings (save in respect of costs) brought under the Non-Contentious Probate Rules 1987. The Rules of the Supreme Court 1965, as in force as at 26 April 1999, continue to apply.

14.2 DISPUTES BETWEEN PERSONS OF EQUAL ENTITLEMENT

14.2.1 Rule 27

Rule 27(4) of the Non-Contentious Probate Rules 1987 allows a grant of administration (with or without will annexed) to be granted without notice to any other person entitled in the same degree. One of several residuary beneficiaries under a will, or one of several of a class of person entitled under an intestacy, may simply apply for the grant. The giving of notice is restricted to executors capable of proving, that is, taking probate, who will have power reserved (rule 27(3)).

Rule 27(6) of the Non-Contentious Probate Rules 1987 allows for a dispute between persons entitled to a grant in the same degree to be brought before a district judge or registrar for determination. Either party to the dispute may issue a summons, supported by an affidavit of facts. Each party to the dispute must have equal entitlement under rule 20 or rule 22 (see paras 12.1 and 12.3).

The affidavit must set out:

- details of the applicant's title to the grant;
- the reason the applicant should be preferred; and
- details of any others also entitled, and their views or preferences. For example, three siblings, A, B and C, are entitled to administer their mother's estate; A applies for a grant; B opposes it and C supports A.

The court has unfettered discretion to override several supportive interests if it considers the administration would be better achieved by another interested party.

The application may be made whether or not either of the disputing parties has applied for the grant. To avoid a grant issuing as of right to another person entitled, it may be prudent to enter a caveat (see Chapter 7). The issue of the summons is entered into the registry's computer system (and so into the national records) so no grant should issue.

14.2.2 Between administrators

Applications to resolve disputes between administrators are the most common applications under the rule. They are made where one party considers the other unfit to act because of:

- an incompatible interest;
- ill-health;
- financial instability;
- distance of place of residence; and
- the ease of or cost to the estate of administration.

Where no real ground for preference is established, the court may favour the earliest application, or the application supported by the majority of those entitled, but these are only factors to be weighed in the balance; the court's discretion is absolute and unfettered.

14.2.3 Between executors

It was held in *Smethurst v Tomlin and Bankes* (1861) 2 SW & Tr 143 that the court should not intervene in a dispute between executors as to which should take probate, the testator's choice of those named to be his executors being sacrosanct. The courts do, however, entertain disputes between executors if they are based on the issues listed above in respect of administrators.

14.2.4 Appointment of independent administrators

When dealing with disputes between persons of equal entitlement, the court may exercise its discretion under section 116 of the Senior Courts Act 1981 to appoint 'independent' administrators – persons with no title to a grant but who are prepared to take on the administration.

Before issuing a summons under the rule, consideration should be given to a consent application under section 116 of the Senior Courts Act 1981 (perhaps appointing a solicitor to represent each of the disputing parties). The application is made on affidavit (see para 10.13) which should recite the details of the dispute, the proposed applicants and the latter's consent to act.

14.2.5 Passing over

For the procedure for applying for an order to pass over a person entitled to a grant, see also para 10.13. Where the district judge or registrar directs that notice be given to a person whose right is to be passed over, and that person opposes the application, the matter should be brought before the court on summons. The affidavit to lead the *ex parte* order may be used as the affidavit to support the summons.

The court is now more likely to require notice to be given, because of the right of the respondent, under the Human Rights Act 1998, to be heard on any matter affecting him, and following the decision in *Ghafoor v Cliff* [2006] EWHC 825 (Ch), [2006] 1 WLR 3020.

14.3 APPLICATION TO REMOVE A CAVEAT

For the procedure on caveats, see Chapter 7.

Rule 44(6) of the Non-Contentious Probate Rules 1987 provides for a caveator who has no interest contrary to that of the applicant for the grant, but who nevertheless opposes the issue of the grant to the applicant, to issue a summons seeking an order preventing the grant from issuing to the applicant. A contrary interest means, *inter alia*, a question over the will or a dispute as to a relationship.

It may be that the caveator has no interest contrary to that of the applicant for the grant; there may be no dispute about the will or codicil or about the relationship of the applicant to the deceased giving title to the grant. But the caveator may object to the applicant as grantee on grounds such as, that the applicant is financially unsound, is of bad character, is a drunk or drug addict, or has otherwise given cause to suspect he will not administer the estate properly and that is the reason for the caveat.

The summons must be supported by an affidavit of facts. The summons is usually issued out of the registry at which the application for a grant is pending. If no application for a grant is pending, the summons may issue out of any registry but may, under rule 62A of the Non-Contentious Probate Rules 1987, be transferred for hearing to a more convenient registry.

The summons should issue within 8 days of the service on the caveator of the warning to the caveat, but may issue at any time provided the applicant has not filed his affidavit in the Leeds District Probate Registry (see para 7.8) and no appearance to the warning has been entered.

It is for the caveator to show cause (that is, good reason) why the applicant should not have the grant; for example, that the proposed applicant is of bad character, or there is real concern that he would not administer the estate properly.

After an appearance has been entered the caveat remains in force until the determination of the probate claim in the Chancery Division or order made on summons. Where no probate claim has been issued, either the applicant or the caveator may seek the removal of the caveat and discontinuance of the proceedings by issuing a summons returnable before a district judge of the Principal Registry of the Family Division. Where the application is by consent it may be dealt with by a registrar. The summons, if not by consent, must be supported with an affidavit of facts.

14.4 APPLICATION FOR AN ORDER FOR A PERSON TO ATTEND FOR EXAMINATION

Section 122 of the Senior Courts Act 1981 provides for application to be made by summons, supported by an affidavit of facts, for an order that a person with knowledge of a will attend to be examined regarding that will. The application is not restricted to witnesses giving evidence of execution, but may be directed to a person with knowledge of the whereabouts of a will or other testamentary document. The summons and affidavit must be served personally.

Application for the order to attend is made to a district judge or registrar and may issue out of any registry. The initial hearing may be before a district judge or registrar, but the order may, if the district judge or registrar is satisfied that it should be heard by a judge, direct attendance before a High Court judge of the Family Division.

The court may make an order for the production of the testamentary document. Where it is known a person holds a testamentary document but refuses or neglects to release it for proof, a subpoena may be issued for its lodgement in court (see para 8.6.2).

If a probate claim has been issued, application for an order to attend must be made to the Chancery Division under Part 57 of the Civil Procedure Rules 1998 and Practice Direction 57.

14.5 SUMMONS FOR DELIVERY OF AN INVENTORY AND ACCOUNT

Rule 8 of the Non-Contentious Probate Rules 1987 requires every application for a grant to be made on oath. Every oath must contain the statement of the duties of, and undertakings by, a personal representative prescribed by section 25 of the Administration of Estates Act 1925, which are to:

(a) collect, get in and administer according to law the real and personal estate of the deceased;
(b) when required to do so by the court, exhibit in the court a full inventory of the said estate and render an account thereof to the court; and
(c) when required to do so by the High Court exhibit on oath in the court a full inventory of the estate and when so required render an account of the administration of the estate to the court.

Any person having a beneficial interest in the estate or a creditor of the estate, may issue a summons, supported by an affidavit of facts, out of the registry which issued the grant of representation, calling on the personal representative to deliver an inventory of the estate and an account of his administration (see rule 61 of the Non-Contentious Probate Rules 1987). This is usually done when there has been a failure by the personal representative to administer the estate or there is thought to be some maladministration.

There is no requirement for any particular period of time to elapse between the issue of the grant and the application by summons. The summons may issue before the 'executor's year' (see para 16.4) has expired. Obviously, the personal representative must be given a reasonable period of time after the issue of the grant to administer the estate.

On hearing, the court may make an order for the delivery of an inventory and account. On receiving the documents, the applicant is in a position to consider further action in another court if there appears to have been fraud or maladministration.

If there has been maladministration then application may be made to the Chancery Division under section 50 of the Administration of Justice Act 1985 for the removal and/or substitution of the personal representative. Application is by way of a probate claim under Part 57 of the Civil Procedure Rules 1998. In *Heyman and another v Dobson and another* [2007] EWHC 3503 (Ch), [2010] WTLR 1151, it was held that there were sufficient grounds for an application to remove a personal representative if the personal representative had produced an account of his administration of the estate which the beneficiaries did not accept. In this case an order had been made summarily by a Master in the Chancery Division and that order was appealed. The judge, in refusing the appeal, said there were sufficient grounds for removing the personal representative. The representative's conduct in dealing with the estate was improper.

14.6 SUMMONS AFTER CITATION PROCEEDINGS

Where the person cited to accept or refuse a grant, to take probate, or to propound a testamentary document, enters an appearance but thereafter fails to prosecute his application for (or refuse) the grant with due diligence, a summons may be issued by the citor for an order to strike out the appearance and for a grant to issue to the citor. The summons should be entered at the registry where the citation proceedings are pending, returnable before the district judge or registrar of that registry. The summons must be supported by an affidavit of the facts setting out the chronology of events to show the lack of proceeding with reasonable diligence.

The court may order a grant to issue (where the citation is related to taking a grant) to the citor; or direct that the will sought to be propounded is valid and for a grant to issue accordingly.

14.7 PROCEDURE

14.7.1 Venue

The district judge or registrar may direct any matter be brought before the court on summons (rule 61(1) of the Non-Contentious Probate Rules 1987). Unless the matter is one which must be heard by a district judge of the Principal Registry of the Family Division, the summons should issue out of the registry in which the application for a grant is pending, or to which it is intended to apply. Any summons for hearing before a High Court judge must issue out of the Principal Registry of the Family Division. The summons must set out clearly and concisely the order sought and whether costs are to be asked for.

14.7.2 Fees

There is no fee payable to the registry on any application made by summons under the Non-Contentious Probate Rules 1987.

14.7.3 Service

All summonses must be supported by an affidavit, usually deposed to by the applicant. The summons must be lodged in duplicate in the registry. One copy is returned, sealed and endorsed with the date of hearing. The copy summons and copy affidavit must be served on the person(s) named as respondent(s) not less than 2 clear days before the hearing date. Summonses should be served in accordance with rule 5 of Order 65 of the Rules of the Supreme Court – personally, by post, email or fax (if service is so accepted). The district judge or registrar must be satisfied at the hearing that service was properly effected.

14.7.4 Transfer

Rule 62 of the Non-Contentious Probate Rules 1987 allows a registrar to transfer any application to another registry. Rule 62A allows any registrar to hear and dispose of any matter which would normally fall to be heard by another registrar. Rule 62A applies on application by either party or by the court of its own motion.

14.7.5 Orders

All orders are drawn up by the court and copies sent by post. Any order requiring a penal notice must be endorsed appropriately by the person in whose favour the order was made and must be served personally. It appears to be the practice of the registries now not to send copies of the order made, but to notify the applicant by letter of the date of it and its effect.

14.7.6 Appeal

Any order, direction or requirement of a district judge or registrar is subject to appeal to a High Court judge of the Family Division.

Rule 65 of the Non-Contentious Probate Rules 1987 deals with appeals and provides that any appeal is made by summons issued within 7 days of the making of the order. The summons is issued by the Clerk of the Rules to the Family Division in the Royal Courts of Justice.

14.7.7 Costs

Parts 43–48 of the Civil Procedure Rules 1998 apply to a bill of costs, and proceedings relating thereto. A registrar may deal with costs and has full power to determine by whom, and to what extent, costs are to be paid.

The provisions for summary assessment of costs apply to applications made by summons to a district judge or registrar. A breakdown of the costs of the application, including the costs of the hearing, must be served on the opposing party and produced at the hearing. Generally, costs are summarily assessed to avoid the need for detailed assessment.

Costs orders for detailed assessment made by a registrar may be assessed by him. Rule 60 of the Non-Contentious Probate Rules 1987, introduced by the Non-Contentious Probate (Amendment) Rules 2003 (SI 2003/185), means that the same procedure relating to costs and the assessment of costs applies in non-contentious probate matters as in any other proceedings in the Family Division. The guideline rates of remuneration published by the Senior Courts Costs Office apply.

Chapter 15

Collecting in the Assets

15.1 TIME FOR COLLECTING IN ASSETS

Once the grant of representation has been obtained, the personal representatives should proceed to collect in all of the deceased's outstanding assets that could not be accessed without production of a grant. In *In Re Tankard* [1942] Ch 69, it was held that once the personal representatives have obtained the grant they should collect in the deceased's assets as quickly as reasonably practicable given the nature of the assets, and pay the deceased's debts with due diligence, having regard to the circumstances of the case. This is particularly important in respect of assets that are vulnerable to fluctuations in value, such as shares in public limited companies. If the personal representatives delay in collecting in such assets, they must have a good reason for doing so, or they may be liable to the beneficiaries for any resulting loss to the estate.

15.2 CONSULTATION WITH THE BENEFICIARIES

As a matter of good practice, the personal representatives should consult the beneficiaries of the estate as to which assets are to be liquidated and which transferred *in specie*, although they are not bound to comply with the beneficiaries' wishes. It is generally advisable to start this consultation process early on in the administration of the estate so that by the time the grant has been issued, the personal representatives already know how they are to dispose of each asset.

The capital gains tax effects of a sale of assets by the personal representatives and beneficiaries are discussed at para 21.4. Before deciding to sell an asset and collect in the cash, the personal representatives should consider whether the capital gains tax consequences could be more favourable if the assets are appropriated to the beneficiaries themselves and sold by them in their personal capacities.

15.3 AUTHORITY OF THE PERSONAL REPRESENTATIVES

Where there is more than one personal representative, technically any one of them has the authority to bind all the personal representatives in relation to personalty, but not real property. Good communication between the personal representatives is vital to ensure that they do not commit themselves to dealing with the same asset in different ways, and any solicitor acting on behalf of the personal representatives should encourage them to act only upon unanimous decisions. In any event, most institutions require the signature of all the personal representatives before they will deal with any asset.

The formalities for collecting in each asset vary depending on the type of asset. Some useful examples are given below.

15.4 BANK ACCOUNTS

A bank account can generally be closed using a written authority signed by all the personal representatives. If, though, the account is one into which dividends on the deceased's shares are paid, the account should not be closed, but cleared out and left open, so that dividends can continue to be collected until the deceased's shares are sold. Even after that, dividends can continue to be paid on shares until 2 or 3 months after their sale so it may be wise to keep the account open until the personal representatives are sure it is dormant.

When closing a bank account, the personal representatives should ask for a certificate of the interest paid on the account for the period from the date of death onwards, together with the income tax deducted from that interest. This will be useful to them when completing the income tax returns for the period of administration.

15.5 BUILDING SOCIETY ACCOUNTS

Building society accounts are usually closed using the society's standard forms, or a written authority signed by all the personal representatives. Any restrictions on the account regarding the notice period that must be given before a withdrawal can be made cease to apply once the account holder has died. The points made above in relation to keeping the account open to collect dividends, and about the provision of a tax certificate, apply.

The personal representatives should consider whether the closure of a building society account would jeopardise any benefits available upon any proposed demutualisation of the building society.

15.6 PREMIUM BONDS

Premium bonds cannot be transferred directly to a beneficiary but must instead be encashed. They may, however, remain in the prize draw for a period of one year from the date of death and the personal representatives must decide whether this would delay the administration of the estate. In any event, a direction for the bonds to remain in the draw can be revoked at any time and the bonds encashed. Prizes won form part of the estate, but no income tax is payable on them.

15.7 NATIONAL SAVINGS CERTIFICATES

National Savings certificates can be transferred *in specie*, or encashed using the prescribed forms.

15.8 ISAs AND PEPs

At present, ISAs and PEPs lose their special tax status on the death of the holder and are treated in the same manner as any other savings or shareholding account. However, in February 2017 draft regulations were published which, if approved and enacted, will amend the Individual Savings Account Regulations 1998 (SI 1998/1870) to extend ISA tax advantages to investments held within an account after the death of the account holder. Practically, this will mean that personal representatives and beneficiaries or legatees should not face income tax or capital gains tax on investments retained in an ISA during the administration of the deceased's estate. This draft legislation also seeks to modify the additional ISA allowance (discussed below) available to surviving spouses and civil partners of the deceased to take this change into account.

ISAs and PEPs can be liquidated using a written authority from the personal representatives. The rules of the provider may permit any shares to be transferred *in specie*.

A surviving spouse or civil partner may be able to utilise the additional ISA allowance that was introduced on 6 April 2015. Only a surviving spouse or civil partner of an ISA holder who died on or after 3 December 2014 may utilise this allowance. The value of this additional allowance is equal to the value of the deceased's ISAs (other than junior ISAs) at the date of death.

A statement, showing the income accruing on the account from the date of death onwards, should be requested. If the account comprises shares, dividends should be shown on this statement. The statement may show entries marked 'income tax rebate'. This is the rebate of income tax already paid on income payments made during the deceased's lifetime. These rebates are in fact assets to which the deceased was entitled during his lifetime and should be included as part of his capital estate for inheritance tax purposes.

15.9 LIFE ASSURANCE POLICIES AND PENSION SCHEME DEATH BENEFITS

Any benefit due under a life assurance policy or pension scheme is paid to the personal representatives, or trustees if the death benefit was written into trust. If the deceased was the sole trustee of any trust, the death benefit cannot be obtained until a grant has been issued, as it is the personal representatives who are entitled to claim it. The paying company usually provides forms for claiming death benefit.

Interest should be payable on any policy proceeds not paid out immediately upon death; a tax deduction certificate, showing the interest credited and income tax paid, should be requested.

15.10 INTERESTS IN TRUSTS AND OTHER ESTATES

Interests in trusts and other estates are paid directly from the trust or estate, on production of the grant of representation, to the trustees/personal representatives of the estate. A set of trust or estate accounts, showing how the payment is made up as to income and capital, should be requested; this is relevant to the income tax position of the personal representatives. If the deceased was using any trust property, it should have been returned to the trustees upon his death.

15.11 LAND

If the personal representatives are unsure what is to be done about land that was in the deceased's sole name, they can register it in their own names as legal owners. To do this, the following must be sent to the Land Registry:

- a completed form AP1 (application to change the register);
- the grant of representation;
- the land or charge certificate (if either exists and can be located); and
- the appropriate fee.

Often, however, it is more convenient to leave the title in the name of the deceased until it is sold or assented to a beneficiary. Rule 162 of the Land Registration Rules 2003 (SI 2003/1417) as amended by the Land Registration (Amendment) Rules 2008 (SI 2008/1919) provides that the personal representatives need not transfer legal title into their names before a sale takes place.

If the land is to be assented to a beneficiary, a land registry form AS1 (assent of whole of registered title(s)) is used.

If the land was in the deceased's name jointly with a third party, legal title is transferred into the name of that party automatically upon the deceased's death. If the land was held as joint tenants, no further action need be taken – the co-owner can apply to be registered as sole owner of the land immediately; or a death certificate can be placed with the title deeds for production on later sale.

If the beneficial interest was held as tenants in common, there must be at least two owners of the legal title before the legal interest can be dealt with. Thus, if the deceased was co-owner with one other person, a new trustee must be appointed. The two legal owners may then execute, in relation to the legal title to the land, a form TR1 (transfer of whole of registered title(s)) if the deceased's interest is to be sold; or form AS1 if it is to be assented to a beneficiary. The personal representatives should deal with the beneficial interest by executing a separate form of assent.

If the land (whether held in the deceased's sole name or in joint names) was unregistered, an assent leads to an automatic first registration (section 4 of the Land Registration Act 2002), in the same way as does a transfer on sale. In addition, the personal representatives must demonstrate the validity of their action in assenting the land by providing a copy of the will to the land registry; or, in the case of an intestacy, swearing a statutory declaration explaining how the estate devolves under the intestacy rules.

15.12 LEASEHOLD PROPERTY

Obligations in respect of any leasehold property bind the personal representatives, although the lease itself may be an asset within the estate. If the personal representatives enter into possession of leasehold property (e.g. by allowing a business to continue to be run from the property), they may become personally liable for the breach of any covenants in the lease during the administration of the estate. If they do not enter into possession, they are liable only in their capacity as personal representatives and thus any penalty for a breach would be borne by the estate. Personal representatives must carefully consider their actions in relation to the property, and whether those actions could be construed as 'entering into possession'.

The most favourable manner of dealing with leasehold property may be to surrender the lease, as all obligations of the personal representatives and the estate would cease at that point. Alternatively, the personal representatives might consider assigning the lease, but, should the assignee default under its terms, the landlord may seek damages from the personal representatives in their personal capacity if there are insufficient funds in the estate to meet the claim. On the other hand, section 26 of the Trustee Act 1925 gives some protection to personal representatives, providing that they are not personally liable in relation to any claim under a lease that has been assigned if they first set aside a fund sufficient to meet any future claim.

15.13 BUSINESS INTERESTS OF A SOLE TRADER

The business interests of a sole trader may be more difficult to deal with because the deceased was himself the business. If the business is to be sold, the personal representatives must decide whether the business assets are to be sold off piecemeal, in which case they simply need to be maintained until sold; or whether the business is to be sold as a going concern. In the latter case, an agent should be appointed to manage the business until it is ready to be sold. If the sale proceeds are to pass to a single beneficiary, it may be wise for that beneficiary to act as manager, or participate in the choice of manager, to avoid any suggestion of negligence on the part of the personal representatives. If the business is to be assented to a beneficiary, this should take place as soon as possible to reduce any risk that the business may diminish in value.

If the personal representatives carry on the deceased's business otherwise than with a view to its sale, they are liable for all the trade debts incurred, unless the will gives them specific authority to carry on the business (*Dowse v Gorton* [1891] AC 190), or to postpone a sale (*Re Crowther* [1895] 2 Ch 56). Further, they may not use, for the purposes of the business, any of the deceased's assets which he did not himself use for those purposes unless the will permits it (*McNeillie v Acton* (1853) 4 DGM & G 744). If the deceased's creditors have not authorised the continuation of the business, debts owed to them take precedence over the personal representatives' right of indemnity against the deceased's estate for liabilities incurred in the business (*In Re Oxley* [1914] 1 Ch 604 (CA)).

The personal representatives are in an invidious position – if they do nothing, the value of the business will diminish and they may find themselves under attack by the estate beneficiaries, but if they allow the business to continue trading they may become liable to existing and future creditors. Bearing all the above points in mind, the personal representatives would be wise to obtain the consent of the beneficiaries of the estate and the creditors of the deceased's business before they arrange for it to continue after the deceased's death.

If the business is to continue trading, the personal representatives must:

- inform HM Revenue and Customs and any insurers;
- make the position clear on all trading documents seen by creditors and customers;
- notify banks and employees, and anyone with whom the deceased held a contract; and
- review health and safety issues affecting staff and customers.

On the sale of the business, the personal representatives must consider the warranties and indemnities they are both willing and able to give to prospective purchasers, and ensure that all relevant contracts are transferred to the purchaser.

15.14 PARTNERSHIP ASSETS

Partnership assets are distributed according to the partnership deed. The deed may set out the criteria for valuing a partner's share in the business on his death. It may also stipulate that the partnership must purchase the deceased partner's share from his estate according to that valuation.

Partnership deeds relating to professional firms, such as accountancy or the law, commonly state that the personal representatives of a deceased partner are not permitted to make any enquiries as to how the share was valued, but that, in effect, they must take the amount passed over to them with no knowledge of whether or not it has been calculated on a fair basis. The only reassurance in this situation is that each partner must have agreed to this basis for valuing the shares, and therefore the personal representatives are simply abiding by the agreement the deceased partner made.

In *Re White (deceased)* [2001] Ch 393, it was held that the amount required to buy out a deceased partner's share need be based only on the historic value of the land belonging to the partnership, as this had always been the basis on which the partnership accounts were prepared.

15.15 ASSETS AT LLOYD'S

Lloyd's assets can be collected in and distributed, subject to the retention at Lloyd's of a fund sufficient to meet the excess on any estate protection plan (see para 2.14), and subject to obtaining a *Re Yorke* order (see para 24.8) if necessary.

There may be questions of how profits should be distributed and losses paid. Many wills specifically deal with the bequest of Lloyd's assets; even if this is not the case, providing the relevant definition in the will is sufficiently wide to cover assets held at Lloyd's as well as all profits and losses, there may be no issue. But if the capital of the Lloyd's assets passes in one manner and the income in another (e.g. if the assets pass into a life interest trust), there may be a problem. Most wills contain anti-apportionment clauses so that the profits derived from participation in Lloyd's are treated as income arising in the year in which they are paid, and thus pass to the life tenant of the trust. But anti-apportionment clauses generally extend only to income, not to liabilities, so that losses arising in relation to a deceased's Lloyd's participation during his lifetime are treated as capital liabilities and thus paid from the capital of the trust fund. The impact of those losses will be felt by the remaindermen rather than the life tenant (although this does mean that his income reduces as the amount in the trust fund reduces). This can cause conflict between remaindermen and the life tenant, unless profits are paid net after deduction of losses, which may rectify the situation.

15.16 STOCKS AND SHARES

Many estates contain stocks and shares. It is worth considering these in some detail, since they are often the assets that the beneficiaries of the estate are least likely to wish to sell.

The principle behind dealing with stocks and shares is the same whether they are a portfolio of quoted shares or a holding of shares in a private family company. The principle is that all the beneficiaries must be treated equally. Clearly, there is little risk of any difficulty where there is a single, residuary beneficiary of the shares – the beneficiary asks the personal representatives either to appropriate the shares to him *in specie*, or to sell the shares and remit the proceeds. Likewise, where the shares are specifically bequeathed to one or more persons, problems should not arise because those persons have the right to have the shares appropriated to them directly.

Where, however, the shares are bequeathed to more than one person, or where they fall into residue, the personal representatives may be faced with the difficult choice between selling or appropriating the shares, and, if the latter, how the appropriation should be made. In the commentary below, a distinction is drawn between quoted shares and unquoted shares in a private company, because their likely treatment is different.

15.16.1 Quoted shares

As mentioned elsewhere, the personal representatives should liaise with the beneficiaries of the estate to ascertain their wishes. The personal representatives cannot be compelled to appropriate shares to beneficiaries in satisfaction of a residuary interest, but it is good practice at least to seek their opinions and to meet their wishes where possible.

All in favour of sale

If all the beneficiaries wish the shares to be sold the decision is simple and it would be unusual for the personal representatives to disagree. The only real consideration is whether the shares should be sold by the personal representatives, or whether the beneficial interest in them ought to be appropriated to the beneficiaries so that the sale is made by them. The choice depends on the capital gains tax position of the personal representatives and beneficiaries, and the personal representatives should consider this carefully.

All in favour of appropriation

On the other hand, the beneficiaries may wish the shares to be appropriated to them *in specie*. If the shares are the subject of a specific bequest the personal representatives cannot deny this wish unless the shares need to be sold to pay the debts of the estate, but they do have discretion if the shares fall into residue. Each shareholding should be split between the beneficiaries, in the proportions to which they are entitled to them or to the residuary estate. There may be holdings that cannot be split exactly equally, but the personal representatives must undertake the division as fairly as possible. If the shares fall into residue, they should be appropriated at their market value on the date on which the appropriation takes place, not the probate value. This allows the personal representatives to ascertain how much each beneficiary has received, and then any beneficiary who has received slightly less can receive a balancing payment from the residue of the estate.

If the shares are the subject of a specific bequest but cannot be divided equally between the beneficiaries entitled (e.g. 100 shares between three people), the personal representatives must decide what to do, in consultation with them. They may agree to an unequal division, or one beneficiary may decide to 'buy' the extra shares he receives from the other beneficiaries (the transaction would be subject to stamp duty). A third alternative is for the extra shares that cannot be divided equally to be sold and the sale proceeds split between the beneficiaries, although this is unlikely to be cost-efficient if the number and value of shares is small.

Mixed wishes

If any residuary beneficiary does not wish to receive the shares *in specie*, the personal representatives can either sell the shares that would have been appropriated to him on the open market and remit the sale proceeds to him; or, if all the beneficiaries are agreeable, his shares can be appropriated to the other beneficiaries and he will receive a greater cash sum from the residue. If shares are being sold on behalf of one beneficiary and being appropriated to others, the appropriation date should generally be taken as the date upon which the shares are sold, to preserve equality between all the beneficiaries.

Very small holdings

The share portfolio may comprise a number of small holdings that are not worth subdividing between the beneficiaries. It may be logical for each beneficiary to take all the shares in one or more of the individual holdings, so that the holdings are not fragmented. But the effect may be that a particular beneficiary perceives that he is receiving an asset of less value than another beneficiary, so it is strongly recommended that personal representatives attempt an appropriation of this kind only if all the beneficiaries are in complete agreement over which holding(s) each of them is to receive.

Complicated appropriation calculations can be time-consuming and this should be explained to the beneficiaries. It may be more cost- and time-effective for the entire portfolio to be sold and the cash proceeds distributed. The registrars of some companies offer a cheap dealing facility for particularly small holdings and it may be worthwhile checking whether this is available before stockbrokers' dealing fees are incurred.

Cost-ineffective holdings

Some holdings may not be cost-effective to deal with at all. A good example is holdings in small African mining companies that occasionally come to light. The fees for, and paperwork involved in, dealing with holdings such as these can be out of proportion to their value. If these holdings are not producing any dividend (and frequently they are not), it is not financially viable to deal with them. They should be left in the name of the deceased, providing all the beneficiaries agree that this is the most sensible course of action. Alternatively, it may be possible to donate these shareholdings to a charity if the charity is willing to take them on.

ShareGift (Registered Charity no. 1052686) is one such charity that accepts transfers of cost-ineffective holdings at no cost to the estate.

Settlement date

If shares are to be sold, the personal representatives may need to think about what the settlement date of the sale should be. Most sales are undertaken on a 'T plus 3' or 'T plus 5' basis. This means that the settlement date for the delivery of the signed stock transfer form and the remittance of the monies by the purchaser is 3 or 5 working days after the transaction is undertaken. But where the number of personal representatives is such that it may take some time for a stock transfer form to be circulated for signature, and the personal representatives particularly wish to agree the sale as soon as possible (e.g. because of fears that the share price will fall), stockbrokers can agree a sale on a 'T plus 15' basis. This effectively gives the personal representatives 3 weeks before the signed stock transfer forms must be produced, although it does of course delay receipt of the sale proceeds.

Loan stock

If the deceased owned loan stock that requires encashment rather than sale, there may be only two dates in the year upon which encashment may take place. The personal representatives should ascertain these dates as early as possible in the administration, to ensure that encashment is not delayed by missing a date.

15.16.2 Unquoted shares

Unquoted shares are often shares in 'family companies' and more often than not are specifically dealt with in the will, if one exists. They should be dealt with carefully to avoid pitfalls. Consider the situation where a father owns all the shares in a family business that he runs with his son. Upon the father's death, his entire estate is to be divided equally between his son and daughter. The daughter would like one half of the family company shares, but the son wants them all to be appropriated to him and the daughter to take a balancing payment from the estate.

In the first place, the articles of association of the company should be checked for any restrictions on the transfer of the deceased's shares. The directors of the company may have power to refuse to register a new shareholder in the company's statutory books. This can lead to deadlock between the beneficiaries of the deceased's estate and the directors of the company, if they are different people. In this situation, unless the deadlock can be broken, the personal representatives have no option but to apply to court for guidance.

The articles may provide that on the deceased's death the remaining shareholders have rights of pre-emption over his shares. If so, the beneficiaries cannot require the shares to be transferred into their names until those rights have been properly dealt with.

The points raised above regarding the sale or appropriation of shares apply to private as to public company shares.

Chapter 16

Powers and Duties of the Personal Representatives

16.1 INTRODUCTION

The personal representatives derive their powers from two sources – statute, and, if the deceased died testate, the will. For many years, most of the personal representatives' powers were set out in the Trustee Act 1925, which was highly restrictive. Since the commencement of the Trustee Act 2000, on 1 February 2001, personal representatives have greater powers under statute and are much less reliant on the provisions of the deceased's will for the powers they need to administer the estate effectively. Similarly, from 1 October 2014 the Inheritance and Trustees' Powers Act 2014 has also extended their powers by amending those given in sections 31 and 32 in the 1925 Act.

The Trustee Act 2000 applies to all deaths, whether they occurred before or after the commencement of the Act, apart from the sections on the remuneration of personal representatives, which apply in respect of deaths after 1 February 2001 only. The application of each of these sections is subject to any contrary intention in the will, if any, although a will would have to specifically state that a section is not to apply, rather than simply being more narrowly drafted than the section. Examples of common alterations of the statutory provisions are given in this chapter. However, many of the changes brought in by the Inheritance and Trustees' Powers Act 2014 in respect of a personal representative's or trustee's power apply only to wills and trusts created on or after 1 October 2014.

The more important powers conferred by the Trustee Act 2000 and the Inheritance and Trustees' Powers Act 2014 are discussed below.

16.2 POWERS TO DEAL WITH PROPERTY

Section 39 of the Administration of Estates Act 1925 stated that personal representatives have the power to sell, mortgage or charge any property comprised in the estate. This was altered in relation to real property by the Trusts of Land and Appointment of Trustees Act 1996, so that personal representatives have all the powers of an absolute owner when deciding how to deal with land.

Section 33 of the Administration of Estates Act 1925 provided that where a person died intestate, a trust for sale over his property was created. Section 5 of the Trusts of Land and Appointment of Trustees Act 1996, in force from 1 January 1997, provides that if an estate contains real property, a trust of land with a power to postpone sale, rather than a trust for sale, arises in respect of that land.

In addition, section 212 of the Inheritance Tax Act 1984 states that, to fund the inheritance tax due in relation to an estate, the personal representatives may sell, mortgage or charge the property upon which the tax is payable.

Section 3 of the Trustee Act 2000 allows trustees a general power of investment as though they were the absolute beneficial owner of monies held by them. It is arguable whether this should apply to personal representatives, as their duty is to distribute the estate, rather than invest monies held in it, unless they are actually holding those monies as trustee.

16.3 POWER TO INSURE

Section 19 of the Trustee Act 1925 allowed personal representatives to insure against fire and for only three-quarters of the value of an asset. Section 34 of the Trustee Act 2000 replaced this to allow personal representatives to insure against any risk, and for the full value of the property. The only restriction on the personal representatives now is that if an asset is held as bare trustee for a beneficiary, and that beneficiary directs the personal representatives not to insure the asset, they are obliged not to do so.

16.4 POWER TO POSTPONE DISTRIBUTION

Section 44 of the Administration of Estates Act 1925 established the 'executor's year'. It allows the personal representatives one year from the date of the deceased's death within which they should realise the estate and pay out any legacies. If they postpone distribution beyond that year, interest becomes payable on the legacies.

A testator cannot alter this in his will by requiring the personal representatives to make payments earlier, although he could, for example, provide that interest is to be paid on a legacy from the date of death.

16.5 POWER TO APPROPRIATE

Under section 41 of the Administration of Estates Act 1925, the personal representatives may appropriate any asset towards the satisfaction of a legacy or interest in residue, whether the legacy or interest is absolute or settled in trust. They may make such an appropriation only with the consent of the beneficiary entitled. Where the beneficiary is under the age of 18 or is mentally incapacitated and therefore unable to give consent, consent may be given by a parent or guardian, or by the beneficiary's receiver, respectively.

If the asset is to pass into a life interest trust, consent needs to be given by the life tenant only, not the remaindermen. A difficulty may arise if the beneficiary is a discretionary trust, as the class of beneficiaries is wide and not all the potential beneficiaries of the trust may be alive at that time to give consent. Often the will dispenses with the need for such consent.

Lastly, if the personal representative is also the beneficiary to whom the asset is being appropriated, there may be a concern about self-dealing. The will may specifically allow the appropriation to take place in these circumstances.

16.6 POWER TO DISTRIBUTE TO A MINOR

Under section 21 of the Law of Property Act 1925, an unmarried minor cannot give a good receipt for either income or capital; a married minor can give a valid receipt for income only. In such a situation the personal representatives would have to hold a legacy or share of residue due to a minor until the minor is 18. To avoid this, section 42 of the Administration of Estates Act 1925 allows the personal representatives to appoint trustees to hold a legacy or share of residue to which a minor beneficiary is absolutely entitled, and to obtain a proper discharge from the trustees. The will may extend the power in section 42 to allow the personal representatives to accept the receipt of the minor's parent or guardian for any capital or income paid over to him, to which the minor is absolutely entitled.

If the entitlement of the minor is contingent, for example until he attains 25 years of age, section 42 of the Administration of Estates Act 1925 does not avail the personal representatives, as it does not apply to contingent interests. The personal representatives must continue to hold the legacy or share in residue for the minor until he satisfies the contingency.

16.7 POWER TO MAINTAIN

Where a beneficiary has a vested interest in an estate, the personal representatives or trustees holding the interest in trust for him may use the income generated by it for the maintenance, education or benefit of the beneficiary, at their discretion, while he is under the age of 18 (section 31(1)(i) of the Trustee Act 1925). However, section 8 of the Inheritance and Trustees' Powers Act 2014 amends section 31 so the personal representatives or trustees have the power to apply the amount of income that they see fit. For wills and trusts created before 1 October 2014, section 31 still applies and requires the trustees to take into account various factors when deciding whether or not to make the distribution, and provides that the payment of income must '… in all the circumstances, be reasonable …'. The will often modifies this, so that the trustees need not take the listed items into account, but may pay out income at their unfettered discretion.

Once the beneficiary reaches the age of 18, he is entitled to the income generated by that interest (section 31 of the Trustee Act 1925).

Section 42 also applies where the beneficiary has only a contingent interest in the legacy if the legacy itself carries a right to intermediate income. This is the case if:

- the legacy is not pecuniary;
- the legacy is a pecuniary legacy but the deceased was the parent of, or someone standing *in loco parentis* to, the beneficiary;
- the will specifies that the right to intermediate income applies or demonstrates a general intention to maintain the beneficiary.

If income is not paid out it must be accumulated and the accumulations paid out once the beneficiary becomes entitled to the capital or to a life interest in it, whether that entitlement is at age 18 or later. The accumulated income may, however, be paid in a later year than the year in which it was generated as though it was income arising in the year of payment (section 31(2) of the Trustee Act 1925).

16.8 POWER TO ADVANCE CAPITAL

Section 32 of the Trustee Act 1925 allows trustees to pay over capital to which a beneficiary is entitled, whether the interest is vested or contingent, to that beneficiary. The payment must be for the advancement or benefit of the beneficiary to whom it is paid, and for wills and trusts created before 1 October 2014, it may not exceed one half of the monies to which he would be entitled in total. However, section 9 of the Inheritance and Trustees' Powers Act 2014 extends this power for wills and trusts created on or after 1 October 2014, allowing personal representatives or trustees to apply the whole of a beneficiary's interest in capital to them.

Any monies paid to him must be brought into account at the time at which he would become absolutely entitled to any remaining monies within the trust. This section is often modified in wills created before 1 October 2014 to state that the personal representatives may pay over the whole interest to which a beneficiary would become entitled, not just half.

The Inheritance and Trustees' Powers Act 2014 further amends the application of section 32 in all wills and trusts regardless of their date of creation, to allow the trustees to treat any advance made to a beneficiary as a proportionate part of their entitlement rather than the advancement being treated as a set sum when bringing it into hotchpot. Further, this Act also confirms the position set out in *Re Collard's Will Trusts* [1961] Ch 293, that any such advancement may apply to any trust asset and not merely cash.

16.9 POWER TO CHARGE

Until the Trustee Act 2000, professional personal representatives did not have a statutory power to charge for their professional services. This is altered by sections 28 and 29 for deaths since the commencement of the Act. Section 28 provides that where a will allows a personal representative to be paid, that charging clause does not take effect as a gift for the purposes of section 15 of the Wills Act 1837 (which states that gifts to beneficiaries who witness the will are invalid) or section 34(3) of the Administration of Estates Act 1925 (which refers to Part II of Schedule 1, stating the order in which debts are to be paid from an insolvent estate). This means that the fees of a professional personal representative are treated as an administration expense of the estate for insolvency purposes, and that a professional executor may now act as witness to a will without invalidating his charging clause.

Section 29 of the Trustee Act 2000 allows a trust corporation or personal representative acting in a professional capacity other than a sole personal representative to charge for his services even if this is not permitted in the will. The other personal representatives must agree to such remuneration for it to be permissible.

Both these sections take effect subject to any contrary intention expressed in the will, and do not apply to sole personal representatives. In any event the Client Care Practice Note (SRA Handbook 2011) – 19 September 2011 and the Client Care Letters Practice Note (SRA Code of Conduct 2007) – 10 March 2010 oblige the solicitor acting on behalf of an estate to write to the client (in this case the personal representatives) setting out the terms of his engagement and his charging structure. This rule should always be followed, to prevent any argument later as to the appropriate level of the solicitor's fees. If the solicitor is also the personal representative, it would be wise to address this letter to the beneficiaries of the estate, again to reduce the risk of conflict.

In *Barrett v Rutt-Field, Matthews and Marshall Sutton Jones* [2006] WTLR 1505 the claimant was the sole beneficiary. One of the executors was a partner in the third defendant firm. The beneficiary applied to have the solicitor's costs for the administration of the estate assessed. Bills had been delivered to and approved by the executors. The court held that the beneficiary was not the 'client' and therefore not a person entitled to challenge the costs. The court also held that as a matter of best practice solicitors acting for personal representatives who are not the beneficiaries should obtain prior agreement to their basis for charging from both executors and beneficiaries, and keep both fully informed as costs are incurred by the delivery of interim bills.

The question of the way in which a solicitor's remuneration is calculated was considered by the Court of Appeal in *Jemma Trust v Liptrott* [2003] EWCA Civ 1476, [2004] 1 WLR 646. The costs judge had decided it was wrong to add an 'estate value element' when calculating charging rates, but the Court of Appeal reversed this decision, holding that solicitors can charge on an exclusive hourly basis or with a value added element provided the end result is fair to the client and the solicitors. Whatever the system for calculating charges, the basis must be explained to and approved by the client.

16.10 POWER TO RECOUP EXPENSES

Section 31 of the Trustee Act 2000 specifies that any personal representative is entitled to be reimbursed for any expenses properly incurred by him when acting on behalf of the estate.

16.11 POWER TO DELEGATE

Section 11 of the Trustee Act 2000 allows personal representatives to appoint agents to exercise any 'delegable function'. The section goes on to clarify what is not a 'delegable function', broadly:

- any decision regarding the distribution of the estate;
- any decision as to whether fees should be paid from income or capital;
- any power to appoint trustees (e.g. as trustee of a legacy holding for a minor);
- the delegation of any 'delegable function' or the appointment of a nominee or custodian. This simply means that once a function has been delegated by the personal representatives, they cannot allow the delegatee to delegate his powers.

Section 22 of the Trustee Act 2000 states that the appointment must be kept under review and section 23 sets out the circumstances in which the personal representatives are not liable for the actions of the agent.

16.12 POWER TO APPOINT AN ATTORNEY

The Trustee Delegation Act 1999 (section 5) amended section 25 of the Trustee Act 1925 to allow a personal representative to appoint an attorney to act in his stead. Such an appointment must be renewed every 12 months. A sample form of appointment is given in the section. The attorney is permitted to be a sole or co-personal representative. If an attorney is appointed, the co-personal representatives must be notified of the appointment within 7 days of its being made, although failure to give this notice does not render the actions of the attorney invalid. In any event, the will may contain a power for an executor to appoint an attorney.

16.13 POWERS CONFERRED BY A WILL

Other powers not provided for by statute, but often found specifically within a will, are discussed below.

16.13.1 Power to permit self-dealing

A personal representative is not permitted to make a profit from his office. However, a personal representative may appropriate or sell assets to himself provided this is done at a proper value. If power to do so is not given in the will the transaction may be voidable at the instance of the beneficiary, or the personal representative may have to account for any profit made resulting from the transaction (see, also, *Kane v Radley-Kane* [1998] 3 All ER 753).

16.13.2 Power to carry on the deceased's business

The personal representatives should carry on the deceased's business only with a view to its sale, generally within the 'executor's year'. If the business is continued for longer than that, the personal representatives may become personally liable for the debts of the business. On the other hand, the will may permit the personal representatives to carry on any business in which the deceased participated for such period of time as they deem necessary or expedient.

16.13.3 Power to lend and borrow

The will may specifically authorise the personal representatives to lend money, generally to a beneficiary of the estate, or to borrow money on any terms they think fit. This power can be especially useful in confirming the personal representatives' ability to take out a loan to pay any inheritance tax due.

16.13.4 Power to permit enjoyment of land and chattels

The personal representatives may be specifically authorised to allow any beneficiary to occupy land or use chattels comprised in the estate for as long as they think fit and on any terms. This may be relevant where a person who is a beneficiary under the will was living in a property with the deceased. The personal representatives will be able to allow that person to live in the property and use all the chattels that are kept there without payment of rent, at least until the person finds a new home (providing the person is also a beneficiary under the will).

16.14 DUTIES OF PERSONAL REPRESENTATIVES

The duty of the personal representatives is to the beneficiaries and it is an overriding duty to administer the estate properly and with all due expediency. Every oath to lead a grant of representation must contain, *inter alia*, an undertaking to the court to perform the duties of personal representatives and administer the estate according to law (see section 25 of the Administration of Estates Act 1925). The exact nature of the duty varies according to the stage the administration of the estate has reached. For example, at the beginning of the administration the personal representatives must ensure they locate the deceased's last will and any codicil(s). Once the grant has been received, they have the duty to collect in the assets and pay the debts as quickly as possible. The duties of the personal representatives at all the various stages are discussed in detail throughout this book.

Section 1(1) of the Trustee Act 2000 imposes an overriding duty on all personal representatives:

> Whenever the duty under this subsection applies to a trustee, he must exercise such care and skill as is reasonable in the circumstances, having regard in particular—
>
> (a) to any special knowledge or experience that he has or holds himself out as having, and
> (b) if he acts as trustee in the course of a business or profession, to any special knowledge or experience that it is reasonable to expect of a person acting in the course of that kind of business or profession.

Chapter 17

Paying the Debts of the Estate

17.1 INTRODUCTION

Personal representatives should pay the debts of the estate as soon as possible after obtaining the grant. *In Re Tankard* [1942] Ch 69 requires them to pay the debts with 'due diligence', having regard to the assets in their hands properly applicable for that purpose. As a practical measure, debts should always be paid quickly to stop interest accruing on them.

All debts of the estate must be paid in full before any distribution of legacies or residue can be made. There are two main considerations regarding the payment of debts, firstly the order in which they are paid, which is particularly relevant for insolvent estates, and, secondly, the property that may be used to pay them.

17.2 IDENTIFYING THE DEBTS

Identifying the creditors of the deceased and the enquiries that should be made of them have been discussed in Chapter 2. The personal representatives must take steps to ensure that all debts claimed against the estate were genuinely incurred by the deceased. For example, a false claim may be submitted in response to a newspaper advertisement for creditors, a bogus invoice being sent to the personal representatives with a claim that the deceased incurred the debt during his lifetime. The amount claimed is often not significant, so as to excite little interest by the personal representatives. If the personal representatives receive a claim of this nature, they should check with the family of the deceased and write to the creditor asking for further details. If the personal representatives pay a debt such as this without making proper enquiries, and it later becomes apparent that the claim was fraudulent, they may become personally liable to the beneficiaries for the loss to the estate.

It is suggested that if the personal representatives are not entirely satisfied that a debt is genuine, but decide to pay it, they should take an indemnity from the residuary beneficiaries that they will not make a claim against the personal representatives if the debt later turns out to be false.

Another difficulty arises where the personal representatives suspect a debt exists, but have received no claim from the creditor. If the debt has not become statute barred, they cannot distribute the funds required to pay the debt in case it is claimed later, but they ought not to pay a liability that has not been claimed since again this would cause a loss to the estate. The most practical course is to retain sufficient funds to meet the debt until the time limit passes for it to become statute barred, or distribute the funds to the estate beneficiaries but take an indemnity from them against the debt being claimed at a later date.

17.3 ORDER OF PRIORITY FOR PAYMENT

There is a specific statutory order in which debts of the estate must be paid. This ranks creditors by class and requires that all the debts in the highest class must be paid in full before debts in the next highest class are paid, and so on.

The order is not strictly relevant if the estate is solvent, as the assets are sufficient to meet all the deceased's debts. The Administration of Insolvent Estates of Deceased Persons Order 1986 (SI 1986/1999) sets out the order of priority which cannot be varied. It is:

(a) secured creditors;
(b) funeral, testamentary and administration expenses. Funeral expenses having priority as per *Sharp v Lush* (1879) 10 Ch D 468;
(c) debts preferred by statute;
(d) preferential debts (listed in Schedule 6 to the Insolvency Act 1986, although section 251 of the Enterprise Act 2002 removed the Crown Preference categories as of 15 September 2003). This means there are two categories of preferential debts being arrears of state and occupational pension contributions and monies owed to employees in respect of salaries and accrued holidays (although there are limits set);
(e) ordinary debts;
(f) interest on debts;
(g) deferred debts.

The amount of funeral expenses, properly allowable as a debt for these purposes, may be different from the amount which is deductible for inheritance tax purposes. Section 172 of the Inheritance Tax Act 1984 states that 'reasonable' expenses are allowable for inheritance tax purposes. Both provisions generally include mourning expenses, newspaper advertisements and tombstones.

If the personal representatives have placed their advertisements under section 27 of the Trustee Act 1925 (see para 24.6) and undertaken any other action required to ascertain the debts of the estate, and are sure that the estate is solvent, the statutory order of priority need not be followed, as the estate is sufficient to pay all the debts in full. But if the personal representatives are at all unsure whether the estate will cover all the liabilities, they should pay the deceased's debts in accordance with the order of priority above. If they do not, and find that they have paid an 'inferior' debt leaving insufficient funds to pay a 'superior' debt, they become personally liable to pay the 'superior' debt.

The personal representatives should also be careful to establish whether they have sufficient funds to pay all the debts in each class. If they pay one debt in a class in full, and then discover that they do not have enough to pay all the debts in that class in full, they may be personally liable for the rest of the debts in that class. On the other hand, section 10(2) of the Administration of Estates Act 1971 may provide a defence if the personal representatives had no reason to believe that the estate was insolvent, and payment was made in good faith. The section does not, however, provide a defence to a claim by creditors in a superior class who have not been paid in full.

17.4 ORDER OF PRIORITY OF PROPERTY

The order in which property is to be used to pay the debts of a deceased whose estate is solvent is set out in Part II of Schedule 1 to the Administration of Estates Act 1925. The order of property is:

(a) property undisposed of by the will, subject to the retention of a fund to meet the pecuniary legacies;
(b) property included in a residuary gift, subject to the retention of a fund to meet pecuniary legacies to the extent that they have not already been provided for above;
(c) property specifically appropriated, devised or bequeathed by the deceased for the payment of debts;
(d) property charged with, or devised or bequeathed subject to, the payment of debts;
(e) the fund retained to meet pecuniary legacies;
(f) property specifically devised or bequeathed, rateably according to value;
(g) property appointed by will under a general power.

Personal representatives taking out a loan to pay inheritance tax (see para 3.22.3) usually give an undertaking that the loan is to be treated as a first charge on the deceased's assets. This does not fit completely with the statutory order given above. But given that inheritance tax is payable on the value of the deceased's net estate, it is difficult to envisage a situation in which inheritance tax would be payable and yet the estate would not be sufficient to meet the debts chargeable on it. In practice, therefore, there would appear to be no irregularity in the personal representatives' giving such an undertaking.

17.4.1 Contrary intention in the will

The statutory order in which the deceased's property should be used to pay the debts of the estate is subject to any contrary intention in the deceased's will, so the personal representatives should always read the will carefully before deciding how the liabilities are to be paid.

Section 35 of the Administration of Estates Act 1925 goes on to state that if a debt was charged on a specific asset, that asset must be used to discharge the debt, unless the will expresses a contrary intention. The best example is a house owned by the deceased, upon which a mortgage is secured. If the deceased left the house to his wife in his will 'subject to mortgage' (or without making any reference to the mortgage at all), the wife could either take the house from the personal representatives, sell it to pay off the mortgage and retain the excess proceeds; or she could take the house and continue to pay the mortgage herself. If the house is left to the wife 'free of mortgage', the mortgage would first be discharged from the residue of the deceased's estate and the house transferred to the wife, debt-free. If the deceased's will directs a specific fund from which the debt is to be paid, and that fund is insufficient, the burden of the undischarged debt falls back onto the charged asset.

The usual direction in a will that the deceased's assets should be collected in and used to pay off his debts before the residue is paid out is not enough to constitute a 'contrary intention' for the purposes of section 35 of the Administration of Estates Act 1925. The will must directly contemplate that the debt secured on a specific asset should not be discharged by that asset.

Taking the example a step further, a problem may arise where the deceased left his house to his wife, and left the residue of his estate to his son. If he took out a life assurance policy to pay off the mortgage on his death, but failed to assign the policy to the mortgagee or his wife, the life assurance policy would fall into the residue of the estate and thus to the son, and would not be available to pay off the mortgage. In that situation the personal representatives may suggest that the son and mother execute a deed of variation (see para 25.2) to pass the proceeds of the life assurance to the mother.

17.4.2 Assets falling outside the statutory categories

Certain assets in the deceased's estate may not fall into any of the statutory categories set out above. For example, the deceased may, in his will, have left someone an option to purchase an asset. If the asset is sold under the option, the proceeds of sale fall into one of the classes above. But if the will provided for the sale to be at an undervalue, the asset may instead, if the personal representatives so choose, be sold for its full value free of the option and the proceeds of sale used to discharge the debt. Indeed, the personal representatives would be bound to make that choice if, without the proceeds of sale at full market value, the estate would be insufficient to meet its debts. Any other action would be a breach of the personal representatives' duty to the creditors of the estate. Assets gifted by way of *donatio mortis causa* (see para 1.9.9) or nominated assets may also be used. In each case, the assets should be used as a last resort only, if all the assets listed are insufficient to discharge the deceased's debts.

17.4.3 Marshalling

A creditor is not concerned to establish whether he has been paid from the correct fund; his main concern is to obtain satisfaction of his invoice. If the deceased's funds are used in the wrong order, any adverse effect on the interests of the beneficiaries must be rectified. This is a process known as 'marshalling' and is achieved by compensating each beneficiary for what he would have received at the time he should have received it from the fund that should have been used to pay the debt.

17.5 INSOLVENT ESTATE

Where the deceased was insolvent at the time of his death and an individual voluntary arrangement had been approved by the court, the estate is administered in accordance with that arrangement. But if the arrangement had not been approved by the court, even if it had been agreed by the deceased's creditors, it cannot be enforced after death.

If a bankruptcy petition had been presented before death, but no order had been made, the bankruptcy proceedings may continue as though the deceased were alive.

If a petition had not been presented but the deceased's estate is insolvent, the personal representatives have three options:

- they can administer the estate themselves according to the rules (the Administration of Insolvent Estates of Deceased Persons Order 1986, and section 421 of the Insolvency Act 1986);
- they can obtain an insolvency administration order from the court and administer the estate under the court's direction (under Part 64 of the Civil Procedure Rules 1998); or
- they (or a creditor of the deceased) can present a bankruptcy petition to the court and obtain an insolvency administration order. The estate would then vest in the official receiver until a trustee in bankruptcy takes over and administers the estate.

If an insolvency administration order is granted, it takes effect as though the order were made on the date of death (rule 12 of Schedule 1 to the Administration of Insolvent Estates of Deceased Persons Order 1986). Section 284 of the Insolvency Act 1986 confirms that, following the granting of the order, all payments out of the estate are void unless they are made by the trustee in bankruptcy. In *Re Vos, Dick v Kendall Freeman* [2005] WTLR 1619 an insolvency administration order was made some 8 years after the death of the deceased but backdated to the date of death. The solicitors acting for the personal representative sought to recover their costs (having delivered and been paid interim bills) but the court held that payments made by the personal representative to the solicitors between death and vesting in the trustee in bankruptcy were void and would not stand unless ratified by the court; the court refused to ratify the payments. The salutary warning is to proceed with caution if the estate is or could become insolvent. Indeed, it is best to proceed as if the estate was insolvent.

17.5.1 Applicant for the grant

In practical terms, the administration of an insolvent estate can be difficult, notably in ensuring that the right debts are paid in the right amount at the right time. A personal representative who has no personal interest in the administration of the estate would do well to consider renouncing the right to probate or letters of administration and leaving the estate to be administered by someone who does have such an interest, such as a creditor of the deceased. If a creditor does not wish to take out a grant, he can present a bankruptcy petition so that a trustee in bankruptcy can be appointed to administer the estate, as mentioned at para 17.5.

If the personal representatives have already taken out the grant of representation and it then becomes apparent that the estate is insolvent, they can apply to be removed or replaced, under section 50 of the Administration of Justice Act 1985 (see *Re Vos*, para 17.5). The court cannot, however, remove all the personal representatives without appointing others in their place. Any application by the personal representatives must deal with their substitutes; the court will not allow personal representatives to relinquish their responsibilities and leave the estate unrepresented (see section 50(1)(b)).

17.5.2 Onerous property

If the deceased was insolvent, some of the assets in the estate may cause problems for the personal representatives. For example, a lease under which the deceased was the tenant may in fact be a burden on the estate, rather than of benefit to it. The personal representatives should try to surrender or assign the lease, although any assignment may render the estate liable for any acts of default of the assignee (see para 15.12). If the estate is subject to an insolvency administration order the trustee in bankruptcy may disclaim any onerous property such as a lease, which is often the most practical course.

17.5.3 Joint property

An insolvency administration order serves to sever any joint tenancies held by the deceased with another person, so that his share in the joint property is available to meet his liabilities. In *Re Palmer (Deceased) (a debtor)* [1994] Ch 316 (CA), however, it was held that such an order, granted after death, is treated as made immediately after the deceased's death, by which time the property held by the deceased as joint tenant has already passed by survivorship and is therefore not available to meet the deceased's liabilities.

This principle was amended by section 12 of the Insolvency Act 2000, which inserts a new section 421A into the Insolvency Act 1986. This means that where an insolvency administration order has been made, the petition for which was presented within 5 years of the date of death, the court may (upon application) make an order that the surviving joint tenant must pay an amount to the estate equal to the value of the property that has been lost to the estate.

17.5.4 Property gifted or sold for less than market value

Section 339 of the Insolvency Act 1986 provides that, if the deceased made any gifts or transactions at an undervalue in the 2 years prior to the presentation of a successful bankruptcy petition, those gifts or transactions may be set aside during his lifetime. If the gift or transaction was made within 5 years of the presentation of the petition and the deceased became insolvent as a result of it, that gift or transaction may also be set aside. Section 423 goes even further, providing that if the deceased undertook any transaction, the purpose of which was to put his assets beyond the reach of his creditors, the transaction may be set aside no matter when it was undertaken.

Section 341 of the Insolvency Act 1986 (as amended by the Administration of Insolvent Estates of Deceased Persons Order 1986, above) confirms that each of the above sections applies to a deceased's estate, but that the relevant time period does not end with the presentation of a bankruptcy petition, but on the date of death. Any application to set aside a transaction cannot be made by the personal representatives of a deceased, but must be made by a trustee in bankruptcy.

Chapter 18

Paying the Legacies

18.1 INTRODUCTION

There are three main matters to be established before making payments of legacies and of residue under the deceased's estate:

- identifying the beneficiary entitled;
- establishing what each beneficiary is entitled to receive; and
- the time at which each legacy should be paid.

18.2 IDENTIFYING THE BENEFICIARIES ENTITLED

Identifying the beneficiaries is straightforward when they are named in a will. It may be more difficult where they are referred to in the will or under the intestacy rules as members of a certain class; here, all the members of the class must be located. Unless it is specifically excluded by the will, the Family Law Reform Act 1987 provides that illegitimate and legitimated children are all treated as children of their biological parents. The Adoption and Children Act 2002 (section 67) provides that adopted children are treated as the natural children of their adoptive parents. Step-children are not treated as children of their step-parents unless they have been adopted. Personal representatives should therefore be careful, in particular, to establish whether the deceased had any illegitimate children, although if they have made the proper advertisements for claimants under section 27 of the Trustee Act 1925 (see para 24.6), this will provide protection against a later claim by any illegitimate children of whom they were unaware.

Problems have arisen in recent years in connection with claims in estates by children born by artificial insemination, where the identity of a parent has not been established. An order specifying parentage may have been made after the birth of the child. If such an order has not been made or cannot be located, the personal representatives may need to apply to the court for further information and directions.

If the gift is to a class of persons, the point at which entry to the class closes must be established. This may be specified in a will, but if not, the gift is subject to the 'class closing rules' which derive from common law. If the gift is made to a class and at least one person is already absolutely entitled to his share of the gift (e.g. a gift to 'my grandchildren as shall attain the age of twenty-five' and one grandchild is aged 25 at the date of death), the class closes at the date of death. If there are potential beneficiaries alive at the date of death but no one in the class has become absolutely entitled at that time, the class closes when the first beneficiary to do so attains an absolute entitlement, such as when the first grandchild reaches the age of 25. If there are no potential beneficiaries living at the date of death, for example, if the deceased had no living grandchildren, the class remains open indefinitely. This is also the case if the class takes only the income generated by a pool of capital; here the income is distributed between those falling into the class each year.

If a life interest was created and the gift of capital is to a class, the class closing rules do not come into operation until the life interest ceases.

Any reference to a living person includes an unborn child *en ventre sa mère*.

If a beneficiary is described by reference to his status or relationship to the deceased, subject to any contrary intention in the will, the person who occupied that status or relationship at the time the will was executed is the person entitled. So a gift to 'my housekeeper' would be a gift to the deceased's housekeeper at the date of the will, but a gift to 'my housekeeper at the date of my death' takes effect to benefit the person occupying that position when the testator died. The intestacy rules also describe a person by reference to relationship to the deceased, again meaning the person having that relationship at the date of death.

If a beneficiary cannot immediately be located at the date of the deceased's death, any expenses incurred in finding him are payable out of his legacy. But if the difficulties arise from ambiguity in the will (in which case they are likely to relate to establishing the identity of the beneficiary rather than to finding a beneficiary who is thought to exist), the costs of resolving the ambiguity must be met from the deceased's estate.

18.3 ESTABLISHING WHAT EACH BENEFICIARY IS ENTITLED TO RECEIVE

18.3.1 Specific legacies

A specific legacy is a gift of a particular asset, not cash. A specific gift of personal property is referred to as a legacy, and a specific gift of real property, a devise. If a specific gift is of a physical asset, a beneficiary who is absolutely entitled must bear the cost of insuring the asset from the date of death, and the costs of maintenance, storage and of transporting it to him. Personal representatives should carefully check the scope of the legacy. For example, if a house is devised, does the gift include any land adjacent to the house but which was not purchased at the same time? Or is a gift of shares a gift of all the deceased's shares in a company, or of the ordinary shares only?

18.3.2 Pecuniary legacies

A pecuniary legacy is a legacy of an amount of money. A legacy does not become pecuniary simply because it consists of money, but rather because it is a stated sum. So for example, a gift of 'the contents of my HSBC account' would be specific not pecuniary, because it is of a specific asset, even though the account comprises cash. Expenses incurred by the personal representatives in the payment of these legacies are payable out of residue.

18.3.3 Residuary gifts

A residuary gift is a gift of the remainder of the deceased's assets after the other legacies and debts have been paid (see Chapter 19).

These distinctions are not particularly significant in many estates, but they become important if the residue is insufficient to pay the deceased's debts, as they govern the order of property used to meet the remaining liabilities (see para 17.4).

18.3.4 General legacies

Specific and pecuniary legacies can be subdivided into two categories – general and demonstrative. A general legacy is paid out of the deceased's general estate. It can be pecuniary in nature, in that it is simply of cash, or it can be of an asset that is not within the deceased's estate at the time of his death, and therefore must be purchased by the personal representatives for a beneficiary. For example, a gift of 'a Rolex watch' is not dependent upon the deceased's having owned a Rolex watch at his death. If he did not, the personal representatives must buy a Rolex watch for the beneficiary named.

18.3.5 Demonstrative legacies

A demonstrative legacy is one directed to be paid out of a specific fund. If that fund is insufficient to meet the legacy, it is paid out of the deceased's other assets. To the extent that it can be paid out of the intended fund, it is classed as a specific legacy. Any amount that cannot be met out of the fund and is paid from the deceased's general estate falls into the category of pecuniary legacy.

18.3.6 Cumulative and substitutional legacies

If a beneficiary has been left two legacies in the deceased's will and codicils, it must be established whether or not the legacy is cumulative. If legacies of a different asset or amount are made in the same document, or if legacies of the same amount are made in two different documents, the legacies are presumed to be cumulative and both are permitted, unless the later gift is interpreted as in substitution for the earlier gift. If the same amount is gifted more than once to the same person in a single document, only one legacy of that amount may take effect.

If a will makes a gift to a beneficiary, and a codicil makes a further gift to the same person, the documents must be read together to discover whether there is any evidence that the testator intended the second gift to replace the first gift, or whether the gifts should be treated as cumulative.

The will may impose requirements on a legacy before it becomes vested, that is, before the beneficiary is absolutely entitled to the asset as against the personal representatives. Examples of the different categories of such requirement are given below.

18.3.7 Contingent gifts

The beneficiary becomes entitled to a contingent gift only on satisfying a specified requirement. The most common requirement is that the beneficiary should attain a particular age.

18.3.8 Conditional gifts

The beneficiary becomes entitled to the conditional gift only if a certain event, such as marriage, takes place.

It is sometimes difficult to distinguish between a contingent legacy and a conditional legacy. Generally, contingencies are events which will be fulfilled over the passage of time, providing the beneficiary lives long enough to do so (e.g. 'attaining twenty-five years'), whereas conditions require action on the part of the beneficiary or a third party (e.g. 'he is still in my employ at my death').

18.3.9 Gifts in trust

While contingent and conditional gifts are simple forms of trust, in that the legacy is held in trust for the beneficiary until the contingency or condition is satisfied, legacies may also be held upon more complex forms of trust (see para 19.2).

18.3.10 Gifts to executors

A legacy to an executor in a will is presumed to be conditional upon that person's acting as executor, unless the will identifies the executor as a relative or friend of the testator. This does not, however, apply in relation to gifts of residue to an executor (*Griffiths v Pruen* (1840) 11 Sim 202) subject to any contrary intention in the will.

18.3.11 Gifts to debtors

If a general legacy or share in residue is given to a debtor of the deceased, the debt must be set off against the legacy, unless the will releases the debt.

18.3.12 Annuities

An annuity is general if the will does not specify the fund from which it is to be paid, or demonstrative if it does. If only a certain amount is to be paid under the annuity, and the fund retained to meet it produces excess income in any year, that excess income can be paid to the residuary beneficiaries of the estate or retained to meet any income shortfall in the future. If the personal representatives are directed in the will to purchase an annuity, rather than simply pay the income of a particular fund to the annuitant, the gift is treated as a pecuniary legacy of the amount required to buy the annuity at the date of the deceased's death. In that situation the annuitant can elect to take the capital sum required to buy the annuity if he wishes to do so, rather than having the annuity bought for him.

The way a clause gifting an annuity is worded can greatly affect the exact amount to which the annuitant is entitled. If the beneficiary is bequeathed '£100 per annum', this is the gross amount due to him, but the personal representatives must deduct basic rate income tax before paying the annuity, and provide the annuitant with a tax deduction certificate. If the gift is of 'such sum as after the deduction of income tax amounts to £100 per annum', the personal representatives must pay over an annuity, net of basic rate income tax, of £100 per annum. Finally, if the will gifts '£100 per annum free of all income tax', again the beneficiary can demand £100 after the payment of basic rate income tax; if he is a higher rate taxpayer, he can recover the higher rate tax from the personal representatives.

18.3.13 Precatory trusts

A will may deal with the testator's chattels in three different ways:

- it can gift them specifically to someone;
- it can make no reference to them and allow them to fall into residue; or
- it can pass them to a precatory trust.

The intestacy rules provide for the first two of these options only, depending on whether or not the deceased left a surviving spouse or civil partner. A precatory trust is a trust whereby one or more people (often the personal representatives) are given the deceased's chattels beneficially. As they receive them as legatees, not as trustees, they can choose to keep the chattels or do with them as they wish. But in a precatory trust, the will goes on to request that the beneficiaries dispose of the deceased's chattels in accordance with any letter of wishes written by him during his lifetime. These wishes are not binding, but they do impose a moral obligation on the 'trustees'.

Precatory trusts are often useful because they allow the deceased much more flexibility when dealing with his chattels. The letter of wishes can be as long or short as he desires, and can be changed at any time without changing the will. There are usually fewer problems of misdescription in a letter of wishes because legal terminology need not be used. The transfer of a chattel by the 'trustee' to the intended recipient is read back into the deceased's will for inheritance tax purposes providing it is made within 2 years after death (section 144 of the Inheritance Tax Act 1984). But it is a disposal by the 'trustee' for capital gains tax purposes, although a marked increase in the value of a chattel over so short a period of time is unlikely.

18.3.14 Secret trusts

A will may provide for the creation of a secret trust. This can be one of two types – fully secret or half secret.

A fully secret trust arises where a gift is expressed to be made to one beneficiary absolutely, but that beneficiary was made aware, before the date of death, that he is to hold the asset on trust for a third party and he agrees to this. In this situation the personal representatives must treat the gift like any other; they are not necessarily aware of the existence of the trust. Therefore, if the secret trustee witnesses the will or predeceases the deceased, the gift and the trust fail.

Under a half secret trust, the gift is made in the will but is expressed to be made to a person 'upon trust'. The terms of the trust are not specified in the will. As the trustee is not stated to be a beneficiary, the gift does not fail if the trustee witnesses the will or predeceases the deceased if the terms of the trust are known. However, to qualify as a half secret trust, the terms of the trust must be communicated to the trustee before or at the same time of the making of the will, and the trustee must have accepted these terms before or simultaneously with the making of the will.

18.4 TIME FOR PAYMENT OF LEGACIES

Section 44 of the Administration of Estates Act 1925 created the 'executor's year'. The section provides that no personal representative is obliged to pay any legacy within one year of the deceased's death but that interest is due on unpaid pecuniary legacies once the year has elapsed. Paragraph 15 of Practice Direction 40A to the Civil Procedure Rules 1998, which replaced Order 44 of the Rules of the Supreme Court with effect from 2 December 2002, provides for interest to be payable at such rate as the court shall determine. In 2003, Lord Justice May held that the rate of interest payable on pecuniary legacies after the first anniversary of the death is at the basic rate payable on funds held in court, then 4 per cent. Although not specifically determined, that rate applied from 2 December 2002. The rate changed to 2 per cent from 1 February 2009, then to 1 per cent from 1 June 2009, then to 0.3 per cent from 1 July 2009, then to 0.1 per cent from 6 June 2016. The latter rate remains the current rate at the time of going to press. This is subject to any contrary intention expressed in the deceased's will. A pecuniary legacy charged on an interest in land carries interest from the date of death.

A legacy given in satisfaction of a debt owed by the deceased carries interest from the date of death if the debt itself bore interest.

The first instalment of an annuity is due on the first anniversary of the death.
A specific legatee with a vested interest is entitled to all the income generated by the asset until it is passed to him.

If a specific gift is contingent or conditional, the wording of the will and statute govern whether the beneficiary is entitled to the income of the asset from the date of death onwards. Under section 31(3) of the Trustee Act 1925 a legacy from parent to child (or to someone to whom he stands *in loco parentis*) carries a right to the intermediate income from the asset if the gift is to vest when the beneficiary reaches the age of 18 or marries under that age, and if the will makes no other provision for the maintenance of that child (*Re Pollock* [1943] Ch 338 (ChD)). In any event, a contingent legacy to an infant not falling within the criteria above carries a right to intermediate income if the will showed an intention for the child to be maintained out of the legacy and the will provided no other fund for his maintenance (*Re Churchill* [1909] 2 Ch 431).

Personal representatives must be careful about the inter-relationship between these provisions and those under the Apportionment Act 1870, where that statute is not excluded by the will. The Act states that for the purposes of deciding the beneficiary to whom it must be paid, any income paid in relation to an asset after the date of the deceased's death must be allocated between capital and income beneficiaries depending on the date upon which the income arose. For example, the deceased died on 30 June and a dividend on his shareholding in ABC plc was paid on 31 July for the period 1 June to 31 July. If the Apportionment Act 1870 was not excluded by the will, the beneficiary to whom the shares were gifted would be entitled to 31/61sts of the income, being the proportion of the income arising from the date of death to 31 July. The other 30/61sts of the income would be allocated to the capital of the estate. If the will excludes the Act, the entire dividend would be payable to the recipient of the shares. The income tax rules do not, however, follow the Apportionment Act, and so for income tax purposes the personal representatives would be taxed as having received the entire dividend. This should have no impact, as the personal representatives are liable to income tax only at the basic rate, which should have already been satisfied by the 10 per cent tax credit given with most dividends.

The rules under the Apportionment Act 1870 are not excluded on an intestacy, although it would be open to the beneficiaries of the estate to agree that they are not to apply.

18.5 FAILURE OF LEGACIES

There are several ways in which a legacy may fail, in whole or in part.

18.5.1 Ademption

Section 24 of the Wills Act 1837 provides that, on a gift of property under a will, the property is ascertained at the deceased's death unless a contrary intention is shown. In *Re Sikes* [1927] 1 Ch 364 (ChD), it was confirmed that the use of the word 'my' when describing an asset showed such a contrary intention, because the testator must have been thinking of the property he owned at the time he made the will. Therefore a specific legacy of an asset referred to in the will as belonging to the deceased adeems if that exact asset does not form part of the deceased's estate upon his death. For example, a gift of 'my Rolls-Royce' will take effect as a gift of the Rolls-Royce the deceased owned at the date he signed his will. If he does not own that Rolls-Royce on the day he dies, the gift adeems, even if he owns a different Rolls-Royce at that time. On the other hand, if the gift had been of 'such Rolls-Royce as I shall own at the date of my death', the gift would not fail. The final possibility is that the will could have made a gift of 'a Rolls-Royce'. In that situation it would be of no consequence whether the deceased owned a Rolls-Royce at the date he signed the will or the date he died. If there was not one in his estate at his death, the personal representatives would have to purchase a Rolls-Royce for the beneficiary from the deceased's estate.

In this context, it is important to distinguish a change in the substance of the gift from a change in its form. If an asset changes in form, such as on the re-organisation of a company, so that the 50 x £1 shares held by the deceased become 100 x 50p shares, the asset can be seen to be substantially the same, so that the gift does not fail. But if the asset changes in substance, as where the deceased elected to redeem the shares on the re-organisation and take cash in exchange, the gift would not take effect.

If a contract had been made for the sale of an asset gifted in the will, and that contract had not been completed prior to death, the gift does not take effect as though it were of the proceeds of sale unless the will specifically allows this.

If the testator later granted an option over property already specifically bequeathed in his will, the proceeds of sale under the option fall into the residue of the deceased's estate. But if the option was granted before the execution of the will, or if a codicil was executed, republishing the will after the option was signed, the gift takes effect subject to the option and the proceeds of sale pass to the beneficiary receiving the asset under the will.

18.5.2 Abatement

If the deceased's residuary estate is insufficient to discharge its liabilities, the legacies under the will must abate. The order in which gifts abate is the same as the order of priority to pay debts (see para 17.4). If there is more than one gift in the class that abates, the abatement is calculated proportionately.

18.5.3 Lapse

If an intended beneficiary predeceases the testator, the gift to him lapses and does not take effect, although it may take effect as a gift to a substitutional beneficiary. A will may extend this doctrine so that the beneficiary has to outlive the deceased for a specified period of time, such as a calendar month, before the gift becomes effective. The intestacy rules make a similar provision in that a spouse or civil partner must survive the deceased by 28 days to attain a vested interest in the estate (section 46(2A) of the Administration of Estates Act 1925).

Section 33(1) of the Wills Act 1837 may apply to rescue a gift to the children or remoter issue of the deceased who predecease him. It states that if a gift is made to a child or remoter issue of the testator in his will, and that beneficiary predeceases the testator, the gift takes effect as a gift to the beneficiary's children or issue *per stirpes*. This section has effect subject to any contrary intention in the deceased's will. Often such an intention is expressed because the will does not provide for the situation in which the beneficiary survives the testator but does not live to a specified age or fulfil any other contingency imposed.

The intestacy rules also provide for the issue of any class of relative who would be entitled to a share in the deceased's estate, but who predeceases the deceased, to take the parent's share in the estate (section 47 of the Administration of Estates Act 1925).

18.5.4 Forfeiture

It is a rule of common law (the forfeiture rule), embodied in the Forfeiture Act 1982, that a person may not profit from his own wrongdoing. Therefore, if the deceased died as the result of murder or manslaughter by a beneficiary under his will or intestacy, the gift to that beneficiary lapses (*In the Estate of Crippen* [1911] P 108; see, also, paras 5.20 and 6.13).

A beneficiary disentitled under the Forfeiture Act can make an application for provision from the deceased's estate under the Inheritance (Provision for Family and Dependants) Act 1975, providing he has not become disentitled because he has been convicted of the murder or manslaughter of the deceased. Such an application should be made within 3 months of the applicant's conviction for the offence in question (see *Re Land Deceased, Land v Land* [2006] EWHC 2069 (Ch), [2007] 1 WLR 1009; see, also, now *Chadwick v Collinson* [2014] EWHC 3055 (Ch) and *Henderson v Wilcox* [2015] EWHC 3469 (Ch), [2016] 4 WLR 14).

The Estates of Deceased Persons (Forfeiture Rule and Law of Succession) Act 2011, in force as from 1 February 2012, provides that where a person would have been entitled to benefit under the deceased's will or intestacy but is prevented from acquiring that benefit because of the forfeiture rule, that person is to treated as having predeceased the deceased. Thus the benefit lost passes to the person(s) equally or next entitled or will fall into residue as appropriate.

18.5.5 Witnessing the will

Any person, and the spouse or civil partner of that person, taking a beneficial interest under a will is barred from taking the interest if he also acted as witness to the will (section 15 of the Wills Act 1837). This does not apply if the trustee of a trust created in the will acts as a witness, as the witness has no beneficial interest in the bequest. In *Barrett v Bem (No 2)* [2011] EWHC 1247 (Ch), [2011] WTLR 1117 it was held that the signing of a will by a beneficiary at the direction of and in the presence of the testator did not fall within the ambit of section 15. This decision still holds good notwithstanding the decision to admit the will was reversed by the Court of Appeal [2012] EWCA Civ 52, [2012] Ch 573.

If the trust was secret in nature (whether fully or half secret, see para 18.3.14) the beneficiary of the trust may witness the will because on the face of it he is not a beneficiary (*Re Young, Young v Young* [1951] Ch 185). Likewise, the trustee of a half-secret trust may act as a witness because the will states that he is merely a trustee and not a beneficiary. However, if a trustee of a fully secret trust witnesses the will, the gift is invalid, as on the face of the will that person is the intended beneficiary.

A will is republished on the execution of a codicil to it, so that if a beneficiary under the original will witnessed the signature of the will, the gift to him is reinstated after the execution of the codicil, providing he does not also act as witness to that.

18.5.6 Dissolution or annulment of marriage or civil partnership

Sections 18A and 18C of the Wills Act 1837 (as amended by section 3 of the Law Reform (Succession) Act 1995 and substituted by the Civil Partnership Act 2004, respectively) state that when a marriage or civil partnership ended in dissolution or annulment, the following do not take effect, unless there is a contrary intention in the will:

- any appointment of the former spouse or civil partner as executor;
- any power of appointment conferred on the former spouse or civil partner; and
- any gift to the former spouse or civil partner in the will.

The former spouse or civil partner is treated as having died on the date the decree of dissolution or annulment was made absolute or final. These sections of the 1837 Act do not apply to a judicially separated spouse or separated civil partner, who is still treated as a 'full' spouse or civil partner for the purposes of the legislation.

The intestacy provisions in the Administration of Estates Act 1925 do not mention a former spouse or civil partner, who are therefore not entitled to anything on the deceased spouse's or civil partner's intestacy.

18.5.7 Ademption of legacy by portion

Where a legacy or share of residue has been left to a child of the deceased (or someone to whom the deceased stood *in loco parentis*), but the deceased had made provision for the child during his lifetime (such provision being known as a 'portion'), the beneficiary's entitlement under the estate may be deemed to be satisfied to the extent of the portion. This may be the case even if the donee does not know about the *inter vivos* gift or the provision made for him under the will or intestacy, and even if the gift is not made directly to the donee but is instead made for his benefit (*Re Cameron* [1999] Ch 383 (ChD)).

A gift of 'pure bounty' does not amount to a portion; a portion is a substantial sum the donee receives to establish him in life or similar.

If a gift may constitute a portion, the question of whether it adeems a gift made under the deceased's will or intestacy depends on the donor's intention.

18.5.8 Uncertainty

If a beneficiary, or the gift a beneficiary is to receive, cannot be identified with certainty, the gift may be declared invalid for uncertainty. If the personal representatives are at all unsure about the nature of a legacy or the identity of an intended beneficiary they must consider their situation carefully as they may be personally liable for any incorrect payment made. If the uncertainty is not substantial, the personal representatives may choose to deal with the matter by paying out what they consider to be the correct legacy to the correct beneficiary and taking an indemnity from that beneficiary against any later claim against the estate.

If the problem cannot be resolved in this manner, the personal representatives may apply to the court for directions under Part 64 of the Civil Procedure Rules 1998 if the matter is opposed. Application is by way of a Part 8 claim. Where the matter is unopposed, it may be referred to counsel, of at least 10 years' call, for an opinion and then by making a without notice application under section 48 of the Administration of Justice Act 1985. The application should be made to the Chancery Division, and the resulting order authorises the personal representatives to act on the written opinion of counsel on the construction of the will. If any person objects to the proposed construction of the will, the case proceeds as though an application had been made to the High Court regarding the construction of the will as above.

If a gift is exclusively charitable but the personal representatives cannot properly ascertain the identity of the charitable beneficiary intended, the gift may be 'rescued' by the doctrine of *cy-près*. A detailed discussion of the doctrine is outside the scope of this book, but if *cy-près* applies, the personal representatives make an application to the court for the approval of a scheme for the administration of the legacy. Under section 16 of the Charities Act 1993 the Charity Commission has power to establish such a scheme, but it cannot decide that a gift is charitable to the detriment of others. It must wait until the court orders that a gift is charitable and asks the Commission to establish a scheme for the application of the monies bequeathed.

Alternatively, the personal representatives can approach the Treasury Solicitor for a 'sign manual direction' by the Attorney General as to who is to receive the legacy. This procedure is available only if the deceased made a gift (not upon trust) in his will for charitable purposes, but no specific charitable object has been named, or where a charity has been named but it does not actually exist. The Treasury Solicitor investigates and makes a recommendation to the Attorney General as to the charity that would be a suitable recipient of the legacy. If the Attorney General agrees, the direction is given to the personal representatives, who must pay the legacy in accordance with it. Such a direction does not, however, protect the personal representatives from a claim by a beneficiary that a legacy should not be paid out, and so should be sought only where all the beneficiaries are in agreement.

18.5.9 Election

The doctrine of election is important when the deceased, in his will, bequeathed to a beneficiary an asset that did not belong to him, and then left another asset that did belong to him, to the owner of the first asset, as compensation. The beneficiary whose asset has been given away in the will takes the asset bequeathed to him only if he either agrees to give his own asset to the other beneficiary named in the will or, if he wishes to keep his own asset, pays compensation to the then disappointed beneficiary for his loss. The value for compensation purposes is the value at the date of death. For example, Thomas dies and leaves 'Bluefield' to Roger. His will also states that he leaves 'Greenfield' to Peter. Thomas owns

Bluefield, but does not own Greenfield, and never has done. Roger owns Greenfield. The doctrine of election would apply here so that Roger is permitted to take the gift of Bluefield only if he agrees to give Greenfield or suitable compensation to Peter.

18.5.10 Bankruptcy of the beneficiary

If a beneficiary under a will or intestacy has been declared bankrupt at the date of death, or between death and receipt of the legacy, this does not affect the validity of the gift. The gift may, though, be claimed by his trustee in bankruptcy, by serving written notice on the personal representatives under section 307 of the Insolvency Act 1986. If such a written notice has not been served on the personal representatives and they do not know (and have no reason to suspect) the beneficiary is a bankrupt, they should not be held liable for the payment of any legacy directly to the beneficiary. It is, however, recommended that a bankruptcy search is carried out against every beneficiary in order fully to protect the personal representatives (see *Re Bennett* [1907] 1 KB 149, in which it was held that a payment made in good faith by the personal representatives to a bankrupt beneficiary did not render the personal representatives liable).

18.5.11 Mental incapacity

The lack of capacity of a beneficiary does not affect his entitlement to benefit under a will or intestacy, although he is unable to provide a proper receipt for the legacy or share of residue when it is paid over to him. It should instead be paid over to his receiver, deputy or attorney.

18.6 ASSETS FROM WHICH THE LEGACIES ARE PAID

Once it has been established that the gift may actually take effect, the practicalities of transferring the legacy must be examined.

If a legacy is of a specific asset that the deceased held at the date of his death, the asset itself must be transferred to the beneficiary. But where the legacy is pecuniary in nature, the personal representatives must consider the fund from which the legacy is to be paid. Most wills contain a direction that the deceased's estate must be sold and the cash proceeds used to pay any debts and taxes, as well as any legacies, before the residue is transferred to the residuary beneficiary. A partial intestacy in relation to the residue is of no consequence because the legacies have been directed to be paid before the amount of the residue is established.

If the will contains no direction as to the sale of the deceased's assets and payment of his debts and legacies, and there is a partial intestacy in the estate, the personal representatives will not know whether to pay the debts and legacies from the disposed of, or from the undisposed of, residue. Section 33 of the Administration of Estates Act 1925 (as amended by the Trusts of Land and Appointment of Trustees Act 1996) states that property undisposed of by the deceased's will is held on trust by the personal representatives with a power for them to sell it. The proceeds of that sale are to be used to discharge the deceased's debts and legacies, and only to the extent that they are insufficient to do so, is the disposed of residue used.

Section 33 of the Administration of Estates Act 1925 does not, however, apply if a contrary intention has been expressed, such as an express direction in the will for the personal representatives to sell the deceased's assets, but no direction regarding the payment of legacies. In this situation, the personal representatives have no guidance on paying the legacies (how the debts are to be paid is explained at para 17.3). The rules are unclear as to whether the legacies should still be paid from the undisposed of residue, or whether the rules in force before 1926 should be applied. These stated that legacies could be paid from residuary personalty only, not from real property, unless a contrary intention was expressed in the will, and that legacies would abate to the extent that personal property was insufficient to meet them. A contrary intention could, however, be inferred from the deceased's leaving the entire residue to one beneficiary (*Greville v Browne* [1859] 7 HLC 689) or by directing in his will that the pecuniary legacies were to be paid from a mixture of real property and personalty (*Roberts v Walker* [1830] 1 R & M 752).

There is an argument that, rather than applying the pre-1925 rules, the personal representatives should apply the rules in section 34(3) of the Administration of Estates Act 1925, on the payment of debts, to paying the legacies. These rules are outlined at para 17.4.

If the personal representatives find themselves in this position of uncertainty, and cannot resolve it by agreement with the beneficiaries, they would be well advised to seek direction from the court.

18.7 INHERITANCE TAX ON GIFTS

The personal representatives should ascertain whether each gift is 'free of' or 'subject to' any inheritance tax payable on it. If the will does not specify, the gift is deemed to be free of inheritance tax. Whether or not a gift bears its own tax is important, as it determines whether the inheritance tax payable on the legacy is deducted from the legacy itself or from the residue. This also affects the total amount of inheritance tax payable. The rules regarding the calculation and grossing up of legacies are complex and a detailed consideration of them is outside the scope of this book; a brief summary of the more usual situations is given below.

18.7.1 Legacies within the nil rate band; residue exempt

Here no grossing-up calculations are required as there is no inheritance tax to pay.

18.7.2 Legacies exceed nil rate band, subject to tax; residue exempt

Here the inheritance tax payable on the legacies is deducted from them before they are paid to the beneficiaries. For example, Bob leaves an estate worth £900,000 in total, with £400,000 to his daughter Claire subject to tax and the residue to his wife Sarah. The nil rate band of £325,000 is deducted from the legacy to Claire, leaving a taxable legacy of £75,000, upon which Claire must pay inheritance tax at 40 per cent, which equals £30,000. Claire receives £370,000 after tax. Sarah receives £500,000.

18.7.3 Legacies exceed nil rate band, free of tax; residue exempt

In these circumstances the legacy must be grossed up and the inheritance tax payable is deducted from the residue before it is paid out. Using the example above, the gift to Claire must be grossed up, so that after paying the inheritance tax on it, Claire is left with £400,000. The taxable part of the legacy is grossed up (multiplied by 100/60) and added back to the value of the legacy before this is deducted from the residue of his estate. So £75,000 x 100/60 + £325,000 = £450,000. Inheritance tax of £50,000 is payable. Claire receives £400,000 and Sarah receives £450,000.

18.7.4 Legacies within or exceeding the nil rate band, subject to tax; residue taxable

Here no grossing up of the legacies is required because the entire estate is taxable.

18.7.5 Legacies within or exceeding the nil rate band, free of tax; residue taxable

Again, no grossing up of the legacies is required because the entire estate is taxable.

The will may provide for combinations of the situations mentioned above, where the legacies are a mixture of those bearing their own tax and those free of tax, or where the residue is partially taxable and partially exempt.

18.8 RECEIPTS

The personal representatives should always be careful to obtain a receipt from any beneficiary following the payment of a legacy to him, to avoid any question of whether or not the legacy has been paid in full.

Chapter 19

Distribution of the Residue

19.1 INTRODUCTION

Before distributing the residue of the deceased's estate the personal representatives should take careful steps to ascertain the nature of each residuary beneficiary's interest. Like legacies (see para 18.3), interests in residue can be vested, contingent or conditional. They can fail in the same ways as have been described above (see paras 18.5 *et seq*). If a gift of any part of residue under a will fails in its entirety, that part of residue passes according to the rules of intestacy.

19.2 CREATION OF A WILL TRUST OR TRUST ON INTESTACY

Legacies and shares in residue can be held in trust. A detailed discussion of the different types of trust is beyond the scope of this book, but a short summary of the main types of trust is given below.

19.2.1 Interest in possession (or life interest) trusts

This arrangement gives a named person, or class of persons, the right to take the trust income for a set period of time, such as the person's lifetime, or until a certain event happens, such as marriage. On the expiration of that period of time or the happening of the event, the life interest terminates and the assets in the trust pass to the remaindermen outright, or into a further trust for them.

This type of trust is generally used where the deceased wished a named person to benefit from his estate for the rest of that person's life, but wanted to ensure that the capital would finally pass elsewhere. A common example of the circumstances in which a life interest trust is established is where a husband and wife have both been previously married and wish to protect the capital in their estates for the children of their first marriages. They may choose to leave the residue of their estates on a life interest trust for the survivor of them, with the capital passing to their respective children from their first marriages upon the death of the survivor.

The intestacy rules also create a life interest trust in one half of the residuary estate for the benefit of the surviving spouse or civil partner when the deceased died intestate before 1 October 2014 with a free estate of over £250,000, and was survived by a spouse or civil partner and issue. Section 3 of the Inheritance and Trustees' Powers Act 2014 amended the intestacy rules so that for deaths on or after this date the surviving spouse, where there are also surviving children, will take this half share of residue absolutely.

19.2.2 Discretionary trusts

A discretionary trust can have a wide class of beneficiaries, none of whom has a right to take anything from the trust. The decision as to who is allocated income or capital from the trust and when they receive it, is left to the trustees, who are often guided by a letter of wishes written by the deceased during his lifetime. Such a letter is not binding, but provides assistance to the trustees in understanding why the trust was created.

This type of trust is often found in the context of inheritance tax planning for a husband and wife. Their wills may provide for the creation of a discretionary trust on the death of the first of them to die, to hold assets to the value of the nil rate band. In this manner, the survivor can be a beneficiary of the discretionary trust and thus take a benefit from the assets in the trust during his lifetime, without the trust assets falling into that person's estate for inheritance tax purposes upon that person's death.

Further, section 144 of the Inheritance Tax Act 1984 provides that where property is settled by the deceased's will on a discretionary trust, distributions from that trust after 3 months but within 2 years of the deceased's death are 'read back' for inheritance tax purposes into the will as though they were distributions made under it. In this manner, the deceased can leave his entire estate into such a trust and allow the trustees of the trust flexibility to distribute his estate as they see fit, depending on the circumstances at his death, without losing the possibility of invoking the surviving spouse or charity exemptions. This type of trust can be more useful than relying on a deed of variation or disclaimer to alter the distribution of the estate after the testator's death, because any minor or incapacitated beneficiaries would not be able to give their consent to such documents.

19.2.3 Accumulation and maintenance trusts

Accumulation and maintenance trusts have many of the characteristics of a discretionary trust, but more favourable tax consequences, although the rules on their use and operation are restrictive and complex, particularly following implementation of the Finance Act 2006. They are often used by a grandparent wishing to benefit grandchildren. They provide for a class of beneficiaries of the trust, the constitution of which is restricted by section 71 of the Inheritance Tax Act 1984. While each beneficiary is under the age of 18, the trustees can choose how to allocate income and capital between the class of beneficiaries. Once a beneficiary has attained 18, he must become absolutely entitled to his share of the trust assets.

19.2.4 Protective trusts

A protective trust may be created pursuant to section 33 of the Trustee Act 1925. This provides that a specified person may have a life interest in the trust until an event occurs that would deprive the beneficiary of the right to the income from the trust, for example, he becomes bankrupt or attempts to sell his life interest. In that situation, the life interest trust automatically terminates and the trust becomes discretionary in nature. The class of discretionary beneficiaries is listed in the section, and comprises the beneficiary, his spouse, children and remoter issue.

This type of trust is generally used where the deceased doubted the intended beneficiary's financial wisdom, and wished to protect the beneficiary's interest in the trust fund no matter what the beneficiary's own financial position might be in the future.

19.3 WHAT TO DISTRIBUTE

The deceased's estate usually comprises all types of asset, including cash, shares and land. Some of these assets must be liquidated to pay the debts, the tax due on the estate, and any legacies. The remaining assets are the residue. It is rare that the residue consists solely of a sum of money. The personal representatives must decide whether to sell the deceased's assets and make a cash transfer of the residue, or appropriate assets *in specie*. The decision is governed in part by their powers. Section 41 of the Administration of Estates Act 1925 gives the personal representatives power to appropriate assets to a beneficiary only with that beneficiary's consent (see para 16.5). Most modern wills, however, extend this power to allow personal representatives to appropriate assets to a beneficiary at their discretion.

No beneficiary has a right to any asset in the residue of the deceased's estate – they have only a chose in action to ensure that the estate is properly administered. It is, though, good practice to consult the residuary beneficiaries and find out what their preferences are; indeed, section 11 of the Trusts of Land and Appointment of Trustees Act 1996 imposes a duty on personal representatives, where the estate comprises land, to consult beneficiaries of an estate as to their wishes regarding the administration of the estate, and to give effect to those wishes so far as possible. This can be unduly onerous, and is often excluded by a will.

The fact that the personal representatives can or do consult the residuary beneficiaries does not oblige them to comply with the beneficiaries' wishes. In *Lloyds Bank v Duker* [1987] 1 WLR 1324, the deceased held 999 shares in a private limited company. One of the residuary beneficiaries had been bequeathed 46/80ths of the estate, the remainder being split between a number of other beneficiaries. It was held that the beneficiary taking the largest proportion of the estate could not compel the personal representatives to transfer 574 of those shares to him, where the personal representatives were of the opinion that to appropriate that number of shares to him would be to confer a much greater benefit than the transfer of the sale proceeds of 574 shares would do.

19.4 VALUE FOR APPROPRIATION

If an asset is to be appropriated *in specie*, the value for administration purposes is the value of the asset at the date on which the appropriation takes place, not the probate value. This is less important where assets are being appropriated to all the residuary beneficiaries as the position should be roughly equal between them. Where, however, the personal representatives are selling assets on behalf of one beneficiary but appropriating similar assets to a different beneficiary, the value is crucial. In this situation, to ensure equality, the date of appropriation should generally be taken to be the same as the date of sale.

For example, the deceased's residuary estate comprises £10,000 and 500 shares in ABC plc. At the date of death, the shares are worth £20 each, giving a total value of £10,000. The residue is split equally between Bob and Jim. Bob would like his proportion of the shares in ABC plc *in specie*, but Jim would like the cash proceeds of sale and instructs the personal representatives to sell 250 shares on his behalf. They are sold for £10 per share. If the appropriation value were taken to be the same as the probate value, Bob would receive 250 shares worth £5,000 (at probate prices), and Jim would receive the sale proceeds – £2,500. Jim would then be 'compensated' by giving him £2,500 in cash, and the remaining £7,500 would be split between them – £3,750 each. The value of assets in Bob's possession would actually be shares worth £2,500 and cash of £3,750, giving him

£6,250 in total. However, Jim would have £8,750 in cash. Had the shares been appropriated to Bob at the same value as Jim's shares were sold, Jim would not have received any 'compensation' and thus their positions would have been equal.

The will should be studied carefully – it may allow personal representatives to appropriate assets at probate value, at the value at the date of appropriation, or at any other value they deem suitable, although this does not detract from the personal representatives' obligation to treat the residuary beneficiaries equally, which cannot be achieved if unfair appropriation values are used.

19.5 TREATING THE BENEFICIARIES EQUALLY

The above point demonstrates the importance of treating the residuary beneficiaries equally. There may be a problem where one beneficiary wishes to receive one entire asset held by the deceased and another beneficiary wishes to receive an entirely different asset. For example, the deceased held two plots of land, Bluefield and Redfield. Both were valued at £10,000 for the purposes of probate. The residue of the deceased's estate is to be divided equally between Mary and Susan. Technically, each piece of land ought to be assented to them jointly. However, if Mary wishes to receive Bluefield and Susan wishes to receive Redfield, the personal representatives can choose to appropriate one piece of land to each of them.

If Bluefield had instead been worth £12,000, Mary would be receiving more than her fair share of the estate. If there is no cash in the estate with which to compensate Susan, Mary can still receive Bluefield but she must purchase part of it from the estate for £2,000. That £2,000 is then divided equally between herself and Susan as residuary beneficiaries. This operates as a partial disposal by the personal representatives for capital gains tax and stamp duty land tax purposes.

19.6 TIME FOR DISTRIBUTION

When dealing with the residue of an estate, the personal representatives should not wait until they have ascertained the exact quantum that each beneficiary will receive, before making a distribution. Administering an estate can be a lengthy affair and it is good practice to make interim distributions to the residuary beneficiaries as soon as possible. On the other hand, the personal representatives should not allow themselves to be pressured into transferring too much or too early. It is preferable to distribute on a small scale as and when possible, than to make a large distribution and then have to ask the residuary beneficiaries to return some money because an unexpected debt has been discovered. The personal representatives should be concerned to distribute to each residuary beneficiary the same amount at the same time, unless all the beneficiaries agree otherwise. A fair balance must be kept between all beneficiaries at all times.

Before any interim distribution is made it is good practice to prepare a first set of estate accounts. This gives the personal representatives a good picture of the financial situation of the estate and highlights any outstanding issues.

If the residuary beneficiary is not yet entitled to his interest in residue absolutely as against the personal representatives, no distribution should be made unless the personal representatives are certain they have the power to do so; the asset may instead need to be held by trustees (see below).

19.7 TO WHOM THE RESIDUE IS DISTRIBUTED

If the residuary beneficiary is absolutely entitled, the distribution can be made to him directly. If the residue passes into trust, the personal representatives must pass the assets to the trustees named in the will or arising under the intestacy. If no trustees were specifically appointed (and if in the case of a minor, the parent or guardian is not permitted to give a valid receipt), section 42 of the Administration of Estates Act 1925 allows a trust corporation or two individuals to be appointed as trustees of residue and for the personal representatives to receive a full discharge from their responsibilities relating to the assets held in trust.

19.8 MAKING THE DISTRIBUTION

Making the distribution requires the personal representatives to decide how title to each asset is to pass. There are two types of interest to be transferred, beneficial and legal. A beneficial interest in any asset can be transferred by the execution of a simple assent of beneficial interest by the personal representatives. For assets other than land, an assent is a resolution signed by the personal representatives evidencing their intention to transfer the beneficial ownership in the stated asset to the relevant beneficiary. To convey a beneficial interest in land, the personal representatives must execute a deed.

Following an assent, the personal representatives hold the legal title as bare trustees for the beneficiary entitled. If an asset is to be sold, but it has been decided, for capital gains tax purposes, that the sale is to be made by the beneficiary rather than by the personal representatives, the personal representatives need only assent the beneficial interest in the asset to the beneficiary and then sell as bare trustees for him; they do not need to transfer the legal title to him as well.

If the personal representatives are to act as trustees of an interest in residue, they must evidence this change in the nature of their ownership by completing some form of document, so that the date upon which the asset concerned became held in trust can easily be identified. In the case of land, the document required is an assent; in the case of other assets, the personal representatives may make a simple resolution listing the assets passing to them as trustees.

The method of transferring legal title in an asset depends on the nature of the asset, and takes effect as a transfer of the beneficial interest if that has not already been dealt with, unless a contrary intention appears in the document effecting the transfer. For capital gains tax purposes, a transfer is read back as though it occurred at the date of death (section 62(1) of the Taxation of Chargeable Gains Act 1992).

19.9 TRANSFERRING LEGAL TITLE

19.9.1 Land

Land is transferred using a land registry form AS1 (assent of whole of registered title(s)). Section 36(4) of the Administration of Estates Act 1925 provides that the transfer of title to land must be in writing, signed by the personal representatives, and must name the person in whose favour it is given. A notice of the assent should be endorsed on the grant of representation; the assentee is entitled to insist on this (section 36(5)). If no notice of assent is endorsed on the grant, a *bona fide* purchaser for value of the land takes the land free of any assentee's interest. A purchaser buying land from an assentee is likewise permitted to rely on the assent as proper evidence of the assentee's entitlement to the land.

19.9.2 Shares

Shares are transferred using a stock transfer form (or 'Crest' transfer form if the legal title to them is in the name of a nominee).

19.9.3 Bank and building society accounts

Cash held in bank and building society accounts is transferred by the completion of the appropriate form supplied by the bank or building society, or by the personal representatives submitting their own written authorisation.

19.9.4 National Savings investments

Prescribed forms for transferring National Savings products are simple to use, and should be obtained from National Savings.

19.9.5 Chattels

Chattels can generally be transferred by simple delivery, although some chattels, such as cars, have registration documents that should be completed. If chattels are particularly valuable it is suggested that an assent is completed as formal evidence of the transfer.

It is good practice for all the personal representatives to sign any transfer, and this is generally required by the transferring institutions in any event.

19.10 TAXATION OF RESIDUE

If the residue of the deceased's estate passes entirely to exempt, or entirely to non-exempt, beneficiaries, calculating the inheritance tax payable should be simple. If, on the other hand, the residue is divided between exempt and non-exempt beneficiaries, such as the spouse and children of the deceased, careful attention must be paid to the inheritance tax calculation. Section 41 of the Inheritance Tax Act 1984 provides that none of the tax payable on a non-exempt share of residue may be borne by the exempt residue.

A will normally specifies whether the distribution of residue between exempt and non-exempt beneficiaries is to take place before or after the payment of inheritance tax. Where the residue is divided between the beneficiaries and then the tax payable is calculated, the position is relatively simple. But in *Re Benham's Will Trusts* [1995] STC 210 (ChD) the deceased's will specified that the exempt and non-exempt beneficiaries should receive the same after the inheritance tax due had been paid. This leads to a circular problem – the amount to be divided cannot be ascertained until the tax has been calculated, but the tax payable cannot be calculated until it is known how much the beneficiaries will receive. The solution is to 'gross up' the non-exempt beneficiary's share in residue. This can be a highly complicated calculation, outside the scope of this book. HM Revenue and Customs' website offers practical guidance, and a formula for the grossing up calculation (see para 18.7). Very basically, if grossing up takes place, the exempt beneficiary receives less, and the non-exempt beneficiary receives more, than if the residue were divided and then the tax paid.

Often a will does not state whether the share of each beneficiary is to be calculated by reference to the estate before or after inheritance tax, and the personal representatives do not know what the deceased intended. This was considered in *Re Ratcliffe* [1999] STC 262. The result of the case is that if the will is of a standard form, directing the payment of debts, taxes, etc. and then the distribution of residue, the residue of the estate is calculated and divided between the beneficiaries in the appropriate shares; and then the inheritance tax payable is ascertained. This means that no grossing up calculations are necessary.

If the will specifically refers to the *Re Benham* situation or directs that the shares should be calculated only after the inheritance tax has been paid, the residue passing to the non-exempt beneficiary must be grossed up.

If the will is unclear, the most practical solution is for the personal representatives to ask the beneficiaries to agree the interpretation of the will. If this is not possible, the *Re Benham* calculation should be prepared. The exempt beneficiary should receive his share of residue on this basis, and the non-exempt beneficiary should be given what he would receive if grossing up were not undertaken (that is, each beneficiary receives that which would be payable to him under the least favourable scenario). Inheritance tax should be paid as though *Re Benham* does not apply (which gives the lesser of the two amounts of inheritance tax payable), and the rest of the money in the estate should be retained until the court has decided how the will should be interpreted, and thus how much inheritance tax is payable and how much each residuary beneficiary should receive.

19.11 PRACTICAL POINTS

19.11.1 Receipts

As in the case of legacies, a residuary beneficiary should always be asked to provide a receipt for all distributions made to him.

19.11.2 Accounts

As mentioned in para 19.6, the personal representatives should prepare a set of interim accounts before the first interim distribution is made. Ideally, copies should be given to the residuary beneficiaries so they can see how the administration of the estate is progressing. They will also be able to raise any queries regarding assets during the course of the administration rather than at the end, which should help avoid delay. Once the administration of the estate has been finalised and the final distribution is made to the residuary beneficiaries, they should each be asked to sign a set of estate accounts (see para 22.1) and return them to the personal representatives as evidence that they fully understand and approve of how the estate has been administered.

19.11.3 Capital gains tax

If assets in the estate are to be sold, the simplest course is usually for the personal representatives to sell them and divide the proceeds. This may not, however, have the most advantageous capital gains tax consequences. Capital gains tax in the context of the administration of the estate is discussed in Chapter 21. The personal representatives need to consider whether better use could be made of the beneficiaries' annual capital gains tax exemptions if assets were to be appropriated to beneficiaries and sold by them, rather than being sold by the personal representatives. This is particularly important if the residuary beneficiary is a charity. Charities do not pay capital gains tax on gains realised on assets sold by them, but personal representatives do. Likewise, a beneficiary may intend to move into property which comprises part of the estate, in which case it may be possible for the 'principal private residence' exemption to apply on any gain made on any future sale of the property by the beneficiary in residence.

Chapter 20

Finalising Liability to Inheritance Tax

20.1 INTRODUCTION

The inheritance tax calculated as due when form IHT400 is originally submitted (see para 4.5) is unlikely to be the same as the amount finally payable. There can be many reasons for this – the value of an asset as originally submitted may transpire to be higher or lower than first thought; assets may be discovered that were not known about at the outset of the administration; or assets may be sold for less than their original valuation.

20.2 DISCOVERY OF FURTHER ASSETS

As mentioned elsewhere, if, during the course of the estate administration, an asset is discovered to have belonged to the deceased of which the personal representatives were previously unaware, they should take steps to notify HM Revenue and Customs as soon as possible, to avoid any penalty being imposed. A valuation of the asset as at the date of death should be produced quickly, and it is recommended that any extra inheritance tax payable is forwarded to HM Revenue and Customs at the same time as they are notified of the asset, to avoid any criticism of the personal representatives. Notification can be by way of letter; a new account or corrective account need not always be filed.

20.3 UPDATING THE VALUES OF ASSETS

Occasionally it becomes apparent that the value of an asset as originally submitted on form IHT400 was incorrect, or a provisional valuation may need to be updated. If so, the personal representatives should again notify HM Revenue and Customs by way of letter as soon as possible and pay any additional inheritance tax.

Where new assets are discovered, or their values are updated, with the result that extra inheritance tax is payable, interest is also due if the time for paying the tax has passed.

20.4 FILING A CORRECTIVE ACCOUNT

As an alternative to notifying HM Revenue and Customs of changes in the value of assets or the discovery of further assets by letter, the personal representatives may complete a corrective account, form C4, and forward it to HM Revenue and Customs. This may be useful if the changes are discovered towards the end of the administration and the personal representatives believe that once HM Revenue and Customs has been notified of the changes, the inheritance tax position will be finalised.

On the other hand, it may be inappropriate to file several corrective accounts. Therefore, if alterations are discovered some time before the administration of the estate has been finalised, it is simpler to keep HM Revenue and Customs appraised of those changes by letter. This minimises the interest on the additional inheritance tax due, by paying the tax as quickly as possible, and reduces the likelihood that HM Revenue and Customs will seek to impose a penalty for failing to declare the alteration as early as possible.

In addition, for a solicitor appointed to act on behalf of the personal representatives it is administratively more convenient to send a letter to HM Revenue and Customs than to prepare a corrective account, circulate it to the personal representatives for signature and then forward it to HM Revenue and Customs.

20.5 LOSS ON SALE OF SHARES

Section 179 of the Inheritance Tax Act 1984 allows for relief from inheritance tax where 'qualifying investments' are sold within 12 months of the date of death for a price lower than the probate value. If the relief is allowed, the price for which the investments were sold becomes the value upon which inheritance tax payable is calculated. This means that the personal representatives may reclaim any excess inheritance tax paid. In addition, the sale price becomes the base cost of the shares for capital gains tax purposes.

'Qualifying investments' are defined in section 178(1) of the Inheritance Tax Act 1984 as quoted shares or securities, holdings in an authorised unit trust, and shares in a common investment fund.

The relevant date of sale is the date on which the sale is agreed, not the date on which the purchase monies are paid over. If the sale is pursuant to an option, the sale date is the date the option was granted (section 189 of the Inheritance Tax Act 1984).

However, the relief is available only if all the qualifying investments sold within the 12-month period have produced an overall loss – the personal representatives cannot pick and choose the investments in respect of which they wish to claim the relief.

The expenses of sale and other items, such as stamp duty, cannot be taken into account – the prices compared must be the gross probate value as against the gross selling price. Interest on loan stock is taken into account as part of the sale price or probate value, but the value of a dividend if the share was 'ex-dividend' at the date of death or sale is not.

If a holding is cancelled within 12 months of the date of death, the personal representatives are treated as though they made a sale of the holding for the nominal consideration of £1 per share (section 186A of the Inheritance Tax Act 1984).

If the holding, when sold, is not the same as it was at the date of death, for example, because of a re-organisation, sales are dealt with as provided in sections 181–184 of the Inheritance Tax Act 1984. Obviously, if all the new holdings have been sold, the position is broadly the same as if the shares held at the date of death were sold. It becomes more complicated if not all the new shareholdings are disposed of.

The relief is limited if the personal representatives purchase shares in the same company any time before the expiry of 2 months after the last sale has taken place (section 180 of the Inheritance Tax Act 1984).

To claim the relief, the 'appropriate person' must complete form IHT35 (claim for relief – loss on sale of shares). The 'appropriate person' is the person paying the inheritance tax – usually the personal representatives. The form must be signed by that person, not someone acting on his behalf.

The personal representatives must be careful about when to complete the form. It should not be filed within 12 months of the date of death unless all the deceased's investments have been sold and the personal representatives are certain they are in a position to make the claim. If the form is submitted within the 12-month period and not all the qualifying investments have been sold, the relief granted is provisional until that 12-month date has passed. The personal representatives have a 4-year period in which to lodge this claim starting from the first anniversary of the date of death.

If the personal representatives have suffered a loss within the 12 months from the date of death and they want to claim relief, they should defer the crystallisation of any other sales that will produce a gain until after the 12 months have expired.

Even if a relievable loss has arisen, the personal representatives should consider whether they would prefer to set it against gains on the sale of other assets, such as the deceased's house, to mitigate the capital gains tax due. It is suggested that the personal representatives consider all the possible tax permutations and calculate the tax payable and repayable in the different scenarios before taking a final decision.

20.6 LOSS RELIEF ON THE SALE OF A PROPERTY

Relief from liability to inheritance tax in respect of a loss incurred on selling property operates in a manner similar to that in relation to the sale of qualifying investments, discussed above. It is granted by section 191 of the Inheritance Tax Act 1984 and applies to the sale of an 'interest in land' owned by the deceased. An 'interest in land' does not extend to interests in land arising by way of mortgage or other security (section 190).

For the purposes of the relief, a sale is made once contracts are exchanged, unless the sale is made pursuant to an option that was granted within 6 months of the exchange. In that case, the date of sale is the date the option was granted (section 198 of the Inheritance Tax Act 1984).

To qualify for the relief, the sale must be made within 4 years of the date of death and cannot be to someone with an existing interest in the land sold, the spouse, children or remoter issue of such a person, or the trustees of any trust under which any of the persons listed above has an interest in possession (section 191(3) of the Inheritance Tax Act 1984). If the land was sold pursuant to a compulsory purchase order, the time period is extended indefinitely, providing the notice to treat in relation to the order was served within 4 years from the date of death (section 197).

The values taken into account are the probate value compared with the gross sale price. The expenses of sale are not deductible.

If the person making the claim also buys any interest in the land sold at any time between the date of death and 4 months from the date of the last sale, that is taken into account for the purposes of the relief, which is then restricted (section 192 of the Inheritance Tax Act 1984).

If the difference between the sale price and the probate value is smaller than the lesser of £1,000 or 5 per cent of the probate value, the relief cannot be claimed.

If the property sold is a lease with less than 50 years to run, section 194 of the Inheritance Tax Act 1984 operates to adjust the sale price by reference to the amount of time left to run on the lease.

Again the person who makes the claim and signs the claim form (form IHT38, Claim for relief – loss on sale of land) must be the 'appropriate person' responsible for the payment of inheritance tax on the land. The claim must be made within 7 years of the date of death, although this can be extended where the sale is to an authority with compulsory purchase powers. Relief is available on all sales made within the relevant time period, so the personal representatives should not make the claim within the 4-year period unless all the deceased's land has been sold already, particularly as the claim cannot be withdrawn once it has been made. Section 191 of the Inheritance Tax Act 1984 does not specifically state that the sale must produce a loss. Therefore, on the face of it, a sale producing a gain but in an estate where inheritance tax is not payable could be suitable for a section 191 election. In practice, however, the relief would be denied by HM Revenue and Customs in this situation.

20.7 OVERPAYMENT OR UNDERPAYMENT

Once any revised values have been submitted and agreed by HM Revenue and Customs, the personal representatives may reclaim any overpaid inheritance tax. If form IHT35 (Claim for relief – loss on sales of shares) or form IHT38 (Claim for relief – loss on sales of land), or form C4 (corrective account), have been submitted, these are automatically treated as applications for repayment of tax, but if HM Revenue and Customs has simply been notified of alterations in value by letter, the personal representatives must formally ask for any overpaid inheritance tax to be returned to them. Alternatively, they can wait until they make the application for clearance (see para 20.9), which should act as a trigger for HM Revenue and Customs to return any outstanding inheritance tax.

In any event, any repayment due that is less than £25 must be specifically applied for within 6 years of becoming due, or it will not be paid.

When HM Revenue and Customs makes a repayment, it is paid with interest, at the same rate as that payable on an underpayment of inheritance tax. For income tax purposes, however, the repayment is not income in the hands of the personal representatives and so is not liable to income tax.

If the personal representatives have not paid enough inheritance tax, but they have received a clearance certificate, or the amount underpaid is small (a decision made by HM Revenue and Customs case by case), or more than 6 years have passed since the later of the date for payment or the date upon which payment was made, HM Revenue and Customs cannot claim any further payment of inheritance tax (section 240 of the Inheritance Tax Act 1984). But if underpayment is a result of fraud, wilful default or neglect by the person liable to pay the tax, the period of 6 years does not begin to run until that fraud, wilful default or neglect came to the attention of HM Revenue and Customs.

20.8 DOUBLE TAX TREATIES

A detailed consideration of double taxation treaties is outside the scope of this book. But if the estate qualifies for relief under a double taxation treaty, or the unilateral relief given by the Inheritance Tax Act 1984 in relation to foreign property (see para 3.9), it may be possible to reclaim UK inheritance tax which has been paid. Such a claim is usually made by letter to HM Revenue and Customs. Double tax treaties exist with many countries now. The full list is set out alphabetically on the HM Revenue and Customs website, www.gov.uk/government/collections/tax-treaties.

20.9 CLEARANCE CERTIFICATE

Once the personal representatives are satisfied that they have paid all the inheritance tax due in relation to the estate, they can make an application for clearance under section 239 of the Inheritance Tax Act 1984. The application is made on form IHT30 (application for a clearance certificate), which must be signed by each of the personal representatives and sent in duplicate to HM Revenue and Customs. If HM Revenue and Customs agrees that all the inheritance tax due has been paid, HMRC used to stamp copies of the certificate and return one to the personal representatives. However, HMRC will now confirm by way of letter that all the inheritance tax has been paid on the estate as declared to it.

If tax on instalment option property is outstanding, an application for clearance can be made only in relation to non-instalment option property.

Once the certificate is given, the personal representatives cannot be held liable for any further inheritance tax in relation to the property comprised in the application for clearance, and nor can anyone else, unless:

- there was fraud or failure to disclose material facts;
- any further property comes to light; or
- any extra inheritance tax becomes payable as a result of a deed of variation or other variation of the estate under section 142 of the Inheritance Tax Act 1984 (see para 25.2).

It is always advisable to obtain a clearance certificate on behalf of the personal representatives; they can then proceed to make the final distributions from the estate in the knowledge that there will be no further inheritance tax demands made of them.

20.9.1 Life tenancies

Problems can arise if the deceased was the life tenant of an interest in possession trust. The assets in the trust may form part of the deceased's estate for inheritance tax purposes, and, if so, the nil rate band is apportioned between the free estate and the trust. This means that as the value of the estate alters, so the proportion of the nil rate band allocated to the estate changes. An application by the personal representatives for clearance of the free estate cannot be examined until an application by the trustees has been made, as the two tax situations are linked. The consequence is that one party may be delayed in the distribution of the trust or estate, if the other party is slower in making its application. There is very little that can be done about this and the beneficiaries may simply have to be patient.

If clearance has been given to both the trust and the estate, and then a further asset is discovered – say in relation to the trust – the overall inheritance tax payable by the trust is increased, but so is the nil rate band allocated to the trust, and so the inheritance tax due by the estate is greater. HM Revenue and Customs deals with matters such as these case by case. It may be persuaded to write off the additional inheritance tax payable by the estate if it is small, or the personal representatives may be willing to pay the tax due if they still hold estate funds. Alternatively, the trustees may be persuaded to pay the entire additional inheritance tax since they are at fault. The trust beneficiaries might be dissatisfied and might seek to raise a claim against the trustees if this is the case. Thus, any party applying for a clearance certificate must be as certain as possible that all the outstanding assets have been declared at their correct values before the application is made.

Chapter 21

Taxation During the Administration

21.1 INTRODUCTION

There are two elements of income tax and capital gains tax to be paid during the estate administration. The first is the tax due for the period up to the date of death, the second is the tax arising during the period of the administration.

21.2 INCOME AND CAPITAL GAINS TAX TO THE DATE OF DEATH

As part of the administration process the personal representatives must ascertain whether it is necessary to complete a tax return for the deceased to the date of his death, or to reclaim any overpaid income tax. The deceased's accountant (if he had one) should be able to help. If the deceased did not normally complete a tax return, it is unlikely that the personal representatives need to complete one for the period from 5 April last to the date of death, but they should nevertheless check the income and gains arising during that time. If income or capital gains tax does need to be claimed or repaid, this is a capital liability or asset and must be shown as such on form IHT400 (see Chapter 4).

If a tax return for the period is submitted, and any liability to tax has been established and the amount due paid, the personal representatives should ask HM Revenue and Customs for written confirmation that their files in relation to the deceased during his lifetime have been closed. This provides the personal representatives with some assurance that there should be no additional liability, unless any income or gains not previously declared to HM Revenue and Customs come to light.

21.3 INCOME TAX DURING THE ADMINISTRATION

Personal representatives need to keep track of the estate income and gains passing through their hands. If they receive income or realise gains that are taxable, they may be required to submit a return for the estate. Whether or not they are required to do so depends upon the size of the estate and the income or gain during the administration period.

HM Revenue and Customs confirms that a trust and estate tax return must be submitted and the estate registered under HM Revenue and Customs Trust Registration Service (see para 3.19 for further details) if:

- the total income tax and capital gains tax due for the administration period was more than £10,000;
- in any tax year that ended before 6 April 2016, more than £250,000 came from the sale of the estate's assets by administrators or executors;
- in the current tax year, more than £500,000 came from the sale of the estate's assets by administrators or executors; or
- the estate was worth more than £2.5 million at the date of death.

If a return is not required, the personal representatives can use 'informal arrangements' to settle the tax due by writing to HM Revenue and Customs confirming:

- the income tax and capital gains tax due for the administration period;
- the name, address, National Insurance number, and UTR of the deceased; and
- the name and contact details of the personal representatives.

HM Revenue and Customs will then send a payment slip for the tax to be paid.

Personal representatives pay income tax at the basic rate, no matter how much income they receive. On the other hand, they receive no allowances; there is no personal allowance – all income is taxable.

21.3.1 Interest on a loan to pay inheritance tax

If the personal representatives took out a loan to pay the inheritance tax due, any interest payable on that loan during the 12 months from the date on which it was taken out can be deducted from the gross income of the estate for income tax purposes (section 364 of the Income and Corporation Taxes Act 1988). In the first instance, the interest is deducted from the income arising in the estate in the same tax year. If this is insufficient, it can be set against previous years' income, and if it exceeds that, it can be set against later years' income. This provision applies only to loans taken out to pay inheritance tax; it does not apply to an overdraft used to pay inheritance tax or to interest at a rate greater than a normal commercial rate (section 353). Further, it applies only to personal representatives, and to the deceased's personal property alone – not to trustees or trust property. It applies to a loan taken out to pay the inheritance tax due on the initial delivery of the account, but not to any loans taken out to pay any inheritance tax due later, such as on instalment option property (section 364(1)). Further, it does not apply to interest arising on inheritance tax itself, such as where the inheritance tax is paid late (section 233 of the Inheritance Tax Act 1984).

21.3.2 Apportioned income

If the Apportionment Act 1870 applies to the estate, the income arising within it must be apportioned between capital and income, depending on the period to which it relates. This is discussed in more detail at para 18.4. The Apportionment Act 1870 does not, however, apply for income tax purposes. This means that the personal representatives may have to pay income tax on that which is actually classed as capital for estate administration purposes.

21.3.3 Bonds

Detailed rules apply to the transfer of bonds, as the income on these assets is treated as accruing from day to day. Interest on a bond is paid to the person in whose name the bond is registered a certain number of days before the interest payment date. This means that if a bond is sold close to the interest payment date, the seller may still receive the entire interest payment, even though he does not own the bond for the final part of that period. Accordingly he should rebate to the purchaser an amount equal to the income arising during the period for which the purchaser owned the bond. Alternatively, if the bond is sold in sufficient time for the purchaser to be registered as the new owner before the next interest payment date, the purchaser would receive some interest that relates to the period during which the seller owned the bond. He may have to pay the seller an amount equal to this accrued income.

The provisions on the sale of bonds are in sections 710–738 of the Income and Corporation Taxes Act 1988. Very briefly, they require that if a bond is sold and the seller has to rebate interest to the purchaser, the seller is entitled to deduct that rebate from the net interest on the bond declared as received by him, and the purchaser must declare this as his own income. Similarly, if the purchaser has to pay accrued income to the seller, the purchaser can deduct this accrued income from the interest on the bond shown on his tax return, but the seller must show it as interest received on his tax return. These provisions apply to personal representatives as to individuals.

21.3.4 Income tax effects for beneficiaries

Situations in which a beneficiary is entitled to income from an estate or from a particular asset are discussed at paras 18.4 *et seq*. Income arising to the estate that is paid to a legatee should always be paid net of basic rate tax, even if the beneficiary is not resident in the United Kingdom. In that situation, the beneficiary may reclaim any income tax credited as paid by him. The only circumstance in which payment is made gross is when it is statutory interest on a pecuniary legacy that is being paid more than a year after the deceased's death. Interest is then paid at the gross rate, which is the same as the basic rate paid on funds in court (currently 0.1 per cent, from 6 June 2016) unless the beneficiary is not resident in the United Kingdom, when it should be paid net of basic rate tax.

Whenever income is paid to a beneficiary, the personal representatives should also supply the beneficiary with a completed form R185 (estate income). This is a statement, signed by the personal representatives or someone on their behalf, showing how much income tax has been paid in the estate on the income passed to the beneficiary, and the nature of the income. The beneficiary will need the form when completing his own tax return for the year in which he receives the income from the estate. There is no requirement to for the personal representatives to provide this form to the beneficiaries where the only income is untaxed bank interest of less than £100. Rather, the personal representatives should provide the beneficiaries with a breakdown of any untaxed bank interest on a separate sheet for the beneficiaries to declare. Moreover, there is no absolute obligation for personal representatives to provide this form at all; however, it is best practice to do so as it assists in fulfilling their obligations to account to the beneficiaries.

Income paid to beneficiaries is usually treated as received by them in the tax year in which it is actually paid. This may not correspond with the tax year when it is received by the estate. The only circumstance in which this principle does not apply is in relation to life interest trusts created within the estate. Where the income is paid to the life tenant, the income is treated as received by him in the same year as it is received by the personal representatives. This is because the life tenant is absolutely entitled under the terms of the trust to receive all the income, even though the assets generating the income may not have been formally appropriated to the trust at that point.

Where a distribution is made to a beneficiary entitled to both income and capital, for example, where the beneficiary is absolutely entitled to residue, it is necessary to distinguish between the amount distributed as income and the amount distributed as capital. If income has accrued to the residue and a distribution is made to the residuary beneficiary, that beneficiary is treated as though he received income to the extent of the accrued income within the estate. Any excess of the amount distributed over the amount of the income accrued is treated as a capital distribution. For this reason the personal representatives should, where there is accrued income in the estate, ask the residuary beneficiaries if they have any preference as to the tax year in which a distribution is made.

21.3.5 Tax relief for accrued income

If there was accrued income in the estate at the date of death, for example, a dividend on a share that was quoted as 'ex-dividend' at the date of death, that accrued income is subject to inheritance tax in the estate. When the income is paid to a beneficiary, if the beneficiary is a higher rate taxpayer, he then pays 40 per cent income tax on the dividend as well. This leads to a double charge to 40 per cent tax. Section 699 of the Income and Corporation Taxes Act 1988 contains provisions to avoid this double charge arising. To declare this potential double charge to tax, the personal representatives should complete a form 922A (statement of residuary income). The relief may be claimed only if one of the residuary beneficiaries is a higher rate income tax payer. The relief is given to the personal representatives by a deduction from the residuary income of the estate.

21.4 CAPITAL GAINS TAX

The personal representatives must pay capital gains tax on any gains accruing on the sale of an asset which forms part of the estate. Their base cost of such an asset is its value at the date of the deceased's death, as agreed with HM Revenue and Customs.

21.4.1 Reduction in gain

HM Revenue and Customs Statement of Practice 2/04 (for deaths after 6 April 2004) sets out an allowance under which the personal representatives may, for capital gains tax purposes, reduce the gain made on the sale of an asset to allow for their administration costs of establishing title to the asset concerned. The amount of reduction allowable depends on the entire value of the estate, as follows:

Gross value of estate	*Reduction allowable*
Less than £50,000	1.8 per cent of the probate value of the assets sold
£50,001–£90,000	£900 divided between all the assets sold in proportion to their probate value
£90,001–£400,000	1 per cent of the probate value of the assets sold
£400,001–£500,000	£4,000 divided between all the assets sold in proportion to their probate value
£500,001–£1 million	0.8 per cent of the probate value of the assets sold
£1 million–£5 million	£8,000 divided between all the assets sold in proportion to their probate value
Over £5 million	0.16 per cent of the probate value of the assets sold, subject to a maximum of £10,000

For deaths from 5 April 1993 to 5 April 2004, see the schedule published in Statement of Practice 8/94.

In addition, the costs of ascertaining the market value of the asset at the date of death are deductible from the gain made before the taxable gain is calculated (section 38 of the Taxation of Chargeable Gains Act 1992). This does not extend to the cost of any negotiation with HM Revenue and Customs about the value of the asset.

21.4.2 Rates and allowances

Personal representatives pay capital gains tax on residential property at the rate of 28 per cent and 20 per cent on all other chargeable assets. They have an annual allowance, the same as any individual, for the remainder of the tax year in which the deceased died, and the following two tax years. After that they have no annual allowance. If possible, therefore, disposals by the estate should be made in the tax year of death and the following two tax years, to ensure that the allowances are fully utilised.

21.4.3 Allowances and exemptions

The sale of an asset by the personal representatives is always a disposal by them, but a transfer to a beneficiary is not. In the latter situation, the base cost at which the beneficiary takes the asset is the market value at the date of the deceased's death. If an asset is appropriated to the beneficiary by reference to a different value, for example, as a proportion of residue, the appropriation value has no effect for capital gains tax purposes.

If a gain is to be realised on a sale, the personal representatives should consider whether the gain would be better realised by the beneficiary directly rather than by them. This may be advantageous if the beneficiary is a lower rate taxpayer; or is a charity that does not have to pay capital gains tax; or is non-resident; or if the expected gain would fall within the beneficiary's annual allowance.

If the sale of an asset is expected to realise a loss, the personal representatives cannot transfer the loss to the beneficiary; they may set it off only against gains made during the course of the administration of the estate. They may therefore be better off appropriating the asset to a beneficiary and allowing the beneficiary to realise the loss in his personal capacity so that he can set it off against his personal gains.

Personal representatives are entitled to taper relief on an asset in the same manner as an individual, the amount of the gain subject to capital gains tax reducing the longer the asset has been held. The period of ownership commences with the date of death. If the asset is transferred to an individual, the transferee is also entitled to taper relief, and again the qualifying period commences with the date of death. The personal representatives should, though, consider whether the asset would qualify as a business asset either in their hands or the beneficiary's – it may be more or less advantageous for them, rather than the beneficiary, to dispose of the asset, as business assets accrue relief more quickly than non-business assets.

21.4.4 Agreeing a valuation

If the personal representatives need to fill in a capital gains tax return, they should complete form SA905 (trust and estate capital gains), in addition to completing the estate income tax return. They should tick the relevant box in response to the question of whether an estimate or valuation has been used, as the probate value will have been used as the base cost of the asset. HM Revenue and Customs should accept this as the base cost if it accepted it as an accurate value of the asset at the date of death. But a query may arise in relation to an asset that was relieved from tax, either because it qualified for relief (as a business asset, for example) or because the beneficiary (the spouse of the deceased, say) receiving the asset was exempt from inheritance tax. In such a situation HM Revenue and Customs may not have enquired in any detail into the market value of the asset at the date of death, and the personal representatives may be concerned that HM Revenue and Customs will query whether the valuation of the asset at the date of death is correct. To forestall such queries and resolve the issue as soon as possible, the personal representatives may complete a form CG34 (application for post-transaction valuation check) with details of the asset and the base cost they wish to submit. Although this form may not be completed and submitted until after the disposal of the asset, it does facilitate agreeing the market value of the asset at the date of death as soon as possible, helping to avoid delays in the administration.

21.4.5 Deceased's home

The deceased's home is often of particular concern. It may appreciate in value between the time of the deceased's death and the time of sale. Any gain made on a sale by the personal representatives is subject to capital gains tax and is not exempt from tax simply because it was the deceased's main residence. Further, if the sale price is substantially higher than the probate value, HM Revenue and Customs is likely to seek to increase the market value at the date of death. Additional inheritance tax then becomes payable on the increase in probate value, and capital gains tax is calculated by reference to the revised probate value.

If the deceased lived in the property with another person as their joint residence, and the deceased's share in the property passes to that person under the will, then the beneficiary should qualify for the principal private residence exemption on the property in relation to the deceased's share from the date of death. Any disposal should therefore be made by the beneficiary to ensure that all exemptions are fully utilised. If the co-owner was married to the deceased, the co-owner is in any event treated as though he had owned the property throughout the entire period of the marriage.

If the long-term plan is to sell the home, but one of the beneficiaries of the estate is willing and does not have a home of his own, it may be possible for the beneficiary to move into the deceased's home and treat it as his main residence, providing there is nothing in the will to prevent this. As long as the beneficiary lives there for a reasonable period of time, and treats the property as his principal residence, either he or the personal representatives may then sell the home and claim relief from capital gains tax on the basis of the principal private residence exemption.

21.4.6 Joint ownership deduction

As noted at para 1.9.3, if the deceased owned a property in conjunction with a third party, it may be possible for the personal representatives to claim a deduction in the value of the property in the estate for inheritance tax purposes. If such a deduction has been claimed, it is the reduced value that operates as the base cost of the home for the purposes of capital gains tax. The personal representatives should bear in mind the long term capital gains tax consequences when deciding how much to claim by way of such a deduction.

21.4.7 Deceased's chattels

Section 262 of the Taxation of Chargeable Gains Act 1992 provides that if a chattel is sold for less than £6,000, no capital gains tax is payable on any gain made in relation to that sale. This applies equally to individuals and personal representatives.

Chapter 22

Completing the Administration

22.1 ESTATE ACCOUNTS

Section 25 of the Administration of Estates Act 1925 imposes an obligation on personal representatives, when required to do so by the High Court, to exhibit a full inventory of the estate and render an account of the administration to the court. This obligation is recited in the wording used in the oath sworn by the personal representatives on the application for a grant (see para 14.5). The effect is that accounts in relation to the deceased's estate must be prepared.

The accounts should be supplied to the residuary beneficiaries as a matter of good practice, so that they can examine how their entitlement has been calculated. The case of *In Re Tillott, Lee v Wilson* [1892] 1 Ch 86 (ChD) confirms that all beneficiaries and creditors are entitled to inspect the accounts free of charge upon request. It is not necessary to supply a copy of the accounts to any creditor or non-residuary beneficiary unless they specifically ask for it.

If the personal representatives are unco-operative in supplying a copy of the accounts to those entitled, a beneficiary can issue a summons supported by an affidavit of facts under rule 61(2) of the Non-Contentious Probate Rules 1987, for an order that the accounts be prepared by the personal representatives and submitted to court for examination. The summons, which carries no court fee, issues out of the registry which issued the grant. It is heard and determined by the district judge (Principal Registry of the Family Division) or registrar of that registry.

Personal representatives often seem daunted by the prospect of creating a set of accounts. The key is to keep full records of all transactions throughout the estate administration. It is advisable to start drafting the accounts as soon as possible, and not to wait until towards the end of the administration. Firstly, it is much easier to add to the accounts as time goes on, and, secondly, the residuary beneficiaries are often keen to see interim accounts, to give them a rough idea of what their final entitlement will be. For an example of a set of accounts relating to a straightforward estate, see para 22.3.

Accounts can be an extremely valuable tool in the swift and accurate administration of an estate if they are prepared and used correctly. The first four main sections in an accurate set of accounts are listed below.

22.1.1 Capital account

The capital account should show the original market value of each asset at the date of death, together with any increase or decrease in this value when sold or appropriated. For the sake of simplicity, shares (or properties, if there are several) should be shown on a separate schedule and the total carried forward to the capital account.

The deceased's liabilities at the date of death should be shown, together with any liabilities charged against capital arising during the estate administration, including inheritance tax and capital gains tax. The net total of the capital assets must be sub-totalled and carried forward to the distribution account.

22.1.2 Income account

The income account should show all the income due to the estate during the administration. It may also be helpful to confirm the income tax paid on each element of the income, as this can be useful when completing form R185 (see para 22.2.7). It is helpful to separate the income between the various tax years in which it arose, to assist when filling in the estate tax return. Again, different types of income, such as dividend income or rents, should be shown on supporting schedules and carried forward to the income account. Whether or not the Apportionment Act 1870 has been excluded (see para 18.4) affects the division of notional income between the capital and income accounts of the estate.

Expenses charged against income and income tax payable should be deducted from income, to give the net amount of income carried forward to the distribution account. Examples of the charges that may be raised against income are:

- interest on inheritance tax;
- interest on loans taken out to pay inheritance tax and legacies;
- the cost of running repairs to, and insurance premiums on, real property; and
- rents and utility bills arising after the deceased's death.

22.1.3 Distribution account

The distribution account shows how all the assets in the estate have been distributed. The first entry should be the total of the capital and income accounts – the overall value of the estate.

From this total are deducted the legacies, so that the amount falling into residue can be established. Finally, the residue is shown as apportioned between the residuary beneficiaries, with the value of interim payments, together with their nature (cash, land appropriated, etc.) and the date of each distribution.

22.1.4 Balance sheet

It is not vital to include a balance sheet but it can be useful for checking the accuracy of the accounts as the administration progresses. One half of the balance sheet comprises the sub-total of the capital and income accounts combined, to show the net value of the estate. The other half shows the value of the estate that has already been distributed, together with the value of the assets remaining in the personal representatives' hands awaiting distribution or liquidation. The two halves should equal each other.

22.1.5 Items to be included in the accounts

It is a matter of preference for the personal representatives whether the accounts include all the estate assets, or only those that actually pass through their hands. Incorporating in the accounts joint assets passing by survivorship can give a fuller picture of the estate, but since the personal representatives have no access to such assets nor any real control over them, it may be simpler to leave them out.

Again, it is a matter for the personal representatives to decide whether they wish simply to provide a basic set of accounts or whether they prefer a fuller document, perhaps including the deceased's full name, address, dates of birth and death, together with a summary of the provisions of the will.

22.2 FINAL DISTRIBUTION

The final distribution should not be made until the administration of the estate has been completely finished. This is the time at which the personal representatives divest themselves of the last of the monies in the estate and therefore they must be certain they have no further obligations to meet. There are various checks that the personal representatives should make before they make the final distribution.

22.2.1 Inheritance tax clearance certificate

If inheritance tax was payable in relation to the estate, HM Revenue and Customs should be asked to supply a clearance certificate to confirm that all outstanding inheritance tax has been paid. If inheritance tax is still due in relation to instalment option property, a certificate can still be applied for in relation to the non-instalment option assets.

If an inheritance tax account was submitted but no inheritance tax was due on the estate, the personal representatives should send a form IHT30 to HM Revenue and Customs for stamping and return unless they have already received a signed and stamped letter from HMRC confirming that the inheritance tax position is settled as this has the same effect as a clearance certificate – confirmation that no inheritance tax was payable.

22.2.2 Indemnity from beneficiaries

If, as mentioned above, there remains instalment option property on which inheritance tax is being paid by instalments, and the assets are being transferred to the beneficiaries, the personal representatives need to ensure that the beneficiaries will meet the future inheritance tax due. They should do this by obtaining the signatures of the relevant beneficiaries to an agreement that binds them to pay all future inheritance tax due on the instalment option property and confirms that they indemnify the personal representatives against any claims in respect of that inheritance tax.

22.2.3 Closure of HM Revenue and Customs records

HM Revenue and Customs should be asked for written confirmation that it has closed its records in relation to the deceased's income and capital gains tax affairs, and also those of the estate. This is again to protect the personal representatives against future tax claims in relation to the deceased or his estate.

22.2.4 Discharge of debts

The personal representatives should double check that they have discharged all outstanding debts of the deceased or the estate. They should ensure that the final distribution is not made within the 2 months that must elapse to obtain protection under section 27 of the Trustee Act 1925 (see para 24.6) and that any claims made pursuant to the advertisement have been investigated and paid where due. If there are 'stale' debts, that is, debts in respect of which no attempt to secure repayment has been made for some time, but they are not statute-barred by the Limitation Act 1980 (see para 23.4), consideration should be given to obtaining directions from the court (see *Re K (Deceased)* [2007] EWHC 622 (Ch), [2007] WTLR 1007).

22.2.5 Inheritance Act claims

Under the Inheritance (Provision for Family and Dependants) Act 1975, anyone wishing to make a claim for financial provision from the deceased's estate must bring the claim within 6 months of the date the full grant is issued (a limited or temporary grant is insufficient to start time running for application under the Act). If the personal representatives anticipate such a claim, they would be wise not to make any distributions from the estate within that 6-month timescale. In any event, it may be unwise for the estate to be fully distributed within such a period. The Act also makes provision for a claim to be made after the 6-month period has elapsed but this requires application to the court for leave to bring the proceedings.

22.2.6 Expenses and fees

The personal representatives must ensure they have recouped all out-of-pocket expenses and professional fees before the final distribution is made. The fees of a solicitor or other professional person acting on their behalf should also be reserved from the final amount to be distributed.

22.2.7 Documents to accompany the final distribution

As mentioned above, any beneficiary receiving income from an estate should be supplied with a form R185, confirming the gross income paid to him, together with the income tax deducted therefrom during the final tax year of the administration.

Each residuary beneficiary should be supplied with a set of final estate accounts. The residuary beneficiaries should each be asked to sign a form confirming that they accept the accounts as correct and have received the entirety of their entitlements from the estate. Some beneficiaries are conscientious and sign and return these forms upon receipt; others may be less diligent. This should not trouble the personal representatives too greatly; if a beneficiary cashes the final cheque sent to him and does not contact the personal representatives with any query in relation to it, he is estopped from raising any issues regarding that distribution. On the other hand, the personal representatives may be concerned about not hearing from a beneficiary, particularly if the beneficiary has been troublesome or unco-operative during the administration. In such a situation the personal representatives may prefer to send the form to the beneficiary for signature, along with the final accounts, explaining that as soon as they receive back the signed documents, they will send a cheque in settlement of the outstanding sum due. This can slightly prolong the administration of the estate, and does lead to a little more work for the personal representatives, but may be wise in the long run.

22.3 SAMPLE ESTATE ACCOUNTS

Donald Smith died on 20 December 2011 leaving various assets, including his house at 2 Moss Street, valued at £200,000. This is sold for £208,900. He left his shares in HSBC to his nephew Derek Smith, and the residue of his estate equally between his daughter Susie and his son Neville.

CAPITAL ACCOUNT

		£	£
Assets			
	2 Moss Street	200,000	
	Plus gain on sale	8,900	
	Abbey National account	150,000	
	National Savings certificates	20,000	
	HSBC plc shares	5,000	
			383,900
Liabilities			
Pre-death			
	Credit card	444	
	Electricity bill	56	
Post-death			
	Council tax	100	
	Funeral	2,000	
	Inheritance tax	35,800	
	Capital gains tax	40	
			38,440
	Carried forward to Distribution Account		345,460

INCOME ACCOUNT

	£	£
Interest on Abbey National account	500	
Dividend on HSBC shares	30	
		530
Less interest on loan to pay inheritance tax	1,400	
Carried forward to Distribution Account		(870)

DISTRIBUTION ACCOUNT

	£	£
Carried forward from Capital Account		345,460
Carried forward from Income Account		(870)
Total		344,590
Distributed as to:		
Derek Smith		
HSBC plc shares	5,000	
Plus dividend	30	
		5,030
Residue:		
Susie Smith (one half)		
Interim payment (21 February 2012)	75,000	
		75,000
Neville Smith (one half)		
Interim payment (21 February 2012)	75,000	
		75,000
Amount remaining to be distributed		189,560

BALANCE SHEET

	£
Amount remaining to be distributed	189,560
Made up as to:	
Solicitors' Client Account	189,560

Chapter 23

Claims By and Against the Estate

23.1 INTRODUCTION

Various types of claim may be made by and against a deceased's estate. Some of the more common claims are considered in this chapter.

If a claim is brought by or against the estate, the personal representatives have the power, under section 15(c) of the Trustee Act 1925, to 'pay or allow any debt or claim on any evidence that he or they think sufficient'. In addition, under section 15(f), the personal representatives may 'compromise, compound, abandon, submit to arbitration, or otherwise settle any debt, account, claim, or thing whatever relating to the testator's or intestate's estate'. A compromise made by one personal representative binds all of them. The section goes on to provide that no personal representative is responsible for any loss occasioned in relation to any act or thing done by him (which includes compromising a claim), providing that he has complied with the duty of care set out in section 1(1) of the Trustee Act 2000 (see para 16.14). That duty of care calls for a conscious decision by the personal representatives; it is not sufficient for the personal representatives to say they decided not to pursue a matter if in fact they simply failed to consider it properly.

Having said this, personal representatives should, to avoid any complaint against them, liaise with the residuary beneficiaries wherever possible regarding the most appropriate form of defence to a claim, or whether to continue to prosecute an action. Litigation can be extremely expensive and personal representatives are well advised to weigh up the potential cost against the likely benefits. They can also be required to act as a 'cool head of reason', where one or more beneficiaries expresses a wish to pursue a claim to obtain 'justice', particularly if this may be at the expense of the residuary estate.

If the personal representatives reach a compromise of any claim by or against the estate, they would be wise to obtain an indemnity from the beneficiaries of full age and capacity that no personal representative will be pursued in respect of that compromise at any later time. In any event, personal representatives should take professional legal advice when bringing or defending an action, to ensure that their actions are reasonable.

If the personal representatives are at all uncertain whether to continue an action, and either do not wish to, or cannot, obtain the required authority from the residuary beneficiaries, they can instead make an application under Part 8 of the Civil Procedure Rules 1998 for directions as to how to proceed.

23.2 CLAIMS IN RELATION TO THE VALIDITY OF THE WILL

A third party may bring a claim against the estate on the basis that the will (or a codicil) was invalid. This could be for several reasons.

23.2.1 Will improperly executed

A will may be invalid if it was not duly executed (see para 5.3.5).

23.2.2 Undue influence

A third party may claim that the deceased was unduly influenced in making his will. This does not apply where the beneficiary became friends with the deceased in the hope that the deceased would remember him in his will, but rather where the deceased was forced into making the will by the actions or persuasion of the beneficiary. The burden of proof in such a claim is on the claimant.

23.2.3 Lack of testamentary capacity

The test for capacity to make a will was set down in *Banks v Goodfellow* (1870) LR 5 QB 549. The testator must:

- understand the nature and effects of the will he is making;
- understand the extent of the property that he has to dispose of; and
- appreciate the moral claims that may be made on his estate (i.e. the people he ought to provide for).

A will may be valid if the testator had capacity at the time of giving instructions for the will to be made, but had lost that capacity by the time he executed the will (*Parker v Felgate* (1883) 8 PD 171 as considered in *Clancy v Clancy* [2003]

EWHC 1885 (Ch), [2003] 3 WTLR 1097). The question of testamentary capacity has been considered more recently in *Key and others v Key and others* [2010] EWHC 408 (Ch) where the testator's decision-making powers and powers of comprehension were considered. In this case, it was held the testator lacked capacity as his decision-making powers had been affected by the recent death of his wife. The decision in *Key* was further considered in *Cowderoy v Cranfield* [2011] EWHC 1616 (Ch), [2011] WTLR 1699. The rule in *Parker v Felgate* was considered and upheld in *Perrins v Holland* [2009] EWHC 1945 (Ch), [2009] WTLR 1387. The decision in *Perrins* confirmed by the Court of Appeal [2010] EWCA Civ 840, [2011] 2 All ER 174 was a case where the testator suffered from multiple sclerosis which it was unsuccessfully claimed impaired his capacity.

Providing that, on the face of it, the will appears to have been properly executed, by a testator of full capacity acting of his own free will, it is for the third party to raise a real doubt about capacity. If this is achieved, the evidential burden is shifted back to the propounder to establish capacity.

23.3 INHERITANCE ACT CLAIMS

In England and Wales, everybody has complete freedom of testamentary disposition. This means that the law does not stipulate any class of persons who must benefit from the estate of a deceased. The Inheritance (Provision for Family and Dependants) Act 1975 was introduced to allow a person who believes he ought to have been named as a beneficiary of the estate of a deceased (who died domiciled in England and Wales), either under the will or the intestacy rules, to make a claim for financial provision from that estate. This Act has since been amended by the Law Reform (Succession) Act 1995, the Civil Partnership Act 2004 and the Inheritance and Trustees' Powers Act 2014. The class of potential claimants under the Act is limited by section 1 to:

- the spouse or civil partner of the deceased;
- a former spouse or former civil partner who has not remarried or formed another civil partnership;
- a person who was cohabiting with the deceased as his spouse or civil partner in the 2 years before his death;
- a child of the deceased including those illegitimate, legitimated and adopted;
- for death on or after 1 October 2014, a person (not being a child of the deceased) who was treated as a child of the deceased's marriage or civil partnership; the relationship between the deceased and the claimant must have been akin to parent and child;
- any person other than those mentioned above who was being maintained either wholly or partly by the deceased immediately before his death; for deaths on

or after 1 October 2014, a substantial contribution to the claimant's reasonable needs other than for full, valuable consideration under an arrangement of a commercial nature equates to the claimant being maintained.

The right to make an application under this Act is personal to the claimant so that the personal representatives of a claimant who has died before an order has been made cannot carry on the action.

A successful claimant receives only such sum as would make reasonable financial provision for his needs, except that the deceased's spouse or civil partner may receive such sum as is reasonable in all the circumstances, whether or not that is the sum required for his maintenance (section 1(2) of the Inheritance (Provision for Family and Dependants) Act 1975). This is an objective test based on the facts known at the time of the hearing and not at the time of death. Facts unknown to the deceased can therefore be considered by the court including any change in circumstances of a beneficiary or claimant.

A claim under the Inheritance (Provision for Family and Dependants) Act 1975 must be brought within 6 months of the full grant of representation being issued, although the court has discretion to extend this time limit. Time does not run from the issue of a limited or temporary grant. Claims can now be brought before the grant is given as paragraph 6 of Schedule 2 to the Inheritance and Trustees' Powers Act 2014 amends section 4 of the Inheritance (Provision for Family and Dependants) Act 1975 to expressly permit such an application. In any event, a potential claimant would be well advised to notify the personal representatives of his intention to bring an action. Negotiations can then be started to compromise the claim quickly, if at all possible.

To ascertain when a grant of representation has issued, the potential claimant should lodge a standing search in any probate registry or sub-registry (see para 27.2). Under a standing search, probate records are checked for the previous 12 months and, if no grant is identified, the search remains effective for 6 months from the date of entry of the search (see rule 43(1) of the Non-Contentious Probate Rules 1987). The person lodging the search is notified, by whichever registry issues the grant, when the grant is issued. A caveat (see Chapter 7) should not be lodged, as this will only delay the issue of the grant.

Orders made under this Act vary widely, and include orders for the payment of a lump sum or regular income, or that assets should be transferred into a trust for the claimant, or the variation of existing trusts. The Order is made against the net estate and for these purposes includes all property disposable by will or passing on intestacy, less liabilities and tax, any property the subject of an *inter vivos* general power of appointment which has not been exercised, assets that qualify as *donatio mortis causa* and nominations. Section 9 of the Inheritance (Provision for Family and Dependants) Act 1975 permits the court to treat the deceased's share of a property held as joint tenants as part of the net estate if it considers it to be just in all of the circumstances.

The effect of any order (including a consent order) under the Inheritance (Provision for Family and Dependants) Act 1975 is that the transfer of assets to the claimant takes effect as though, for inheritance tax purposes, the deceased's estate had devolved in accordance with the order (section 146 of the Inheritance Tax Act 1984). In addition, if the outcome of the claim is determined by the court (rather than by a compromise agreed between the parties), the effect of the order is that, for income tax and capital gains tax purposes, the disposition takes effect as though made by the deceased's will (section 19(1) of the Inheritance (Provision for Family and Dependants) Act 1975). Even if the claim is settled by compromise, section 19 may still apply, but careful consideration is to be given to the drafting of the order to ensure it complies with section 19.

23.4 LIMITATION PERIODS

An action against an estate cannot accrue indefinitely. Limitation periods are set out in the Limitation Act 1980. A creditor wishing to bring a claim must do so within 6 years of the date on which the loss occurred. The loss arises only when sufficient of the estate has been distributed that the creditor can no longer be paid. But if the will charges a particular asset with the repayment of a debt, that debt does not become statute-barred until 12 years after the date of death.

If a beneficiary wishes to make a claim against an estate, he has 12 years from the date of accrual of his right (the date of death) in which to bring it, although interest can be claimed for only 6 years from the date of accrual of the right (see section 22(a) of the Limitation Act 1980).

If a beneficiary wishes to bring an action for fraud against a personal representative, or make a claim that a personal representative has received estate property and converted it for his own use (not as a beneficiary), there is no limit. If, though, the beneficiary knew of the potential claim for some time and did nothing about it, the personal representatives may be able to raise a defence of acquiescence to their actions.

Personal representatives have 12 years to claim the assets of an estate that are in the hands of a third party; the period starts when the existence of the assets comes to their attention.

Chapter 24

Liabilities of the Personal Representatives

24.1 PERSONAL LIABILITY

A personal representative is personally liable for any tort he commits as a personal representative during the administration of the estate. He is likewise personally liable for a contract he enters into as a personal representative to the extent that it cannot be met by the estate, or is found to have been entered into improperly.

If the personal representative causes loss to a third party by an act or omission during the administration of the estate, and that act or omission was reasonable, the personal representative is entitled to an indemnity from the estate for any action brought against him in relation to that loss.

If a personal representative acts in breach of duty as a personal representative and causes loss to the estate, he is personally liable for that loss. But the position is different where a loss arises without any breach of duty by the personal representative, or where the loss arises from his negligence but not his wrongdoing.

Some of the mechanisms delimiting the liabilities and obligations of personal representatives are examined below.

24.2 EXPRESS CLAUSE IN THE WILL

Many modern wills expressly limit the personal liability of personal representatives to actions that are fraudulent or which comprise wrongdoing. Such a provision often stipulates that a personal representative is not liable for loss to the estate resulting from mere negligence.

24.3 ACQUIESCENCE OR AGREEMENT OF CREDITOR OR BENEFICIARY

If the personal representatives act in breach of their duty to the estate and thereby cause loss to the estate, or, as a result, a creditor cannot be paid in full, the personal representatives may still be protected from liability. This is so if the beneficiary of the estate or the unpaid creditor can be shown to have been fully aware of the breach of duty and to have acquiesced in it. The rule applies to breaches resulting from both acts or omissions of the personal representatives.

If the beneficiary or creditor went even further and agreed to the personal representatives' breach, section 62 of the Trustee Act 1925 operates to impound the interest of that creditor or beneficiary to provide protection to the personal representatives.

24.4 AGENTS, NOMINEES AND CUSTODIANS

Under section 23 of the Trustee Act 2000, a personal representative is not liable for the action or default of any agent, nominee or custodian appointed by him, providing he complied with the duty of care imposed on him when appointing that agent, nominee or custodian and when reviewing its activities. The scope of the duty of care is laid out in section 1.

24.5 LIMITATION OF LIABILITY

Under section 30 of the Trustee Act 1925, each personal representative was responsible for the correct application only of the estate assets that passed through his hands, and not of those assets that passed through the hands of a co-personal representative. This section was repealed by the Trustee Act 2000, although it is possible that the courts would still apply the rule, for example, by invoking section 61 of the Trustee Act 1925 to produce the same result.

24.6 ADVERTISING

It is entirely possible that if the personal representatives of an estate distribute the estate and are then unable to meet debts of the estate of which they later become aware, they are personally liable to pay those debts without recourse against the beneficiaries. Section 27 of the Trustee Act 1925 provides that if the personal representatives place a notice of their intention to distribute the estate in the

London Gazette, and in a newspaper local to the place where any land in the estate is situated, together with any other notices that a court might order, the personal representatives may distribute the estate free from any claims of which they have not been notified. The notice should specify:

- the name of the deceased;
- the personal representatives' intention to distribute the estate;
- the time period (at least 2 months) within which any claim must be made; and
- the address to which notice of the claim must be made.

It is advisable also to specify the deceased's address and date of death.

Advertisements can be placed via the internet at www.legalads.co.uk.

Whilst an executor may place advertisements under section 27 of the Trustee Act 1925 immediately as his power stems from the will, an administrator must wait for the grant to be issued before placing these advertisements, as his power derives from the grant.

The personal representatives should also make such other searches as a prudent purchaser would make, for example, bankruptcy searches, local land charges searches and searches of the land registry and land charges register.

If these searches are made, the personal representatives are then not liable for any claims by creditors or beneficiaries of which they have received no notification. Those creditors or beneficiaries may still, however, follow the assets into the hands of the beneficiaries receiving them on distribution, and claim against them. Knowledge that a debt exists (even if it has not been claimed), or that a beneficiary exists (but not how to trace him), means that the personal representatives have no protection under this section (see *Re K (Deceased)*, para 22.2.4).

24.7 RELIEF FROM PERSONAL LIABILITY

If a personal representative is found to be personally liable for an action in breach of trust, but the court feels that he acted honestly and reasonably, and ought fairly to be excused for the breach, the court can relieve the personal representative from the personal liability, either wholly or in part. The fact that the personal representative acted in accordance with legal advice is not necessarily sufficient to qualify for relief under this section (*Marsden v Regan* [1954] 1 WLR 423 (CA)).

24.8 LLOYD'S ESTATES

The personal representatives of a Lloyd's name must be aware that the estate may have a future liability to Lloyd's, but they have no means to quantify the liability. Most Lloyd's names purchase estate protection plans that will meet all Lloyd's liabilities, subject to an excess. But there is still a remote possibility that the company providing the estate protection plan may become insolvent and unable to meet the liability. In that case, the responsibility to discharge the debt would fall back on the personal representatives. To administer the estate properly, the personal representatives ought not to make any distributions until the final Lloyd's liability has been quantified and paid. But in practice, this would delay the administration by a number of years.

The case of *Re Yorke deceased* [1997] 4 All ER 907 (ChD) provides a solution. It allows the personal representatives to make an application to the court to seek directions as to the distribution of the estate. Pursuant to the application, the court may sanction the distribution of the deceased's estate without taking an indemnity from the beneficiaries or making a retention pending future Lloyd's liabilities. If the personal representatives comply with the directions given, they are protected from personal liability should any future Lloyd's debts arise which they cannot meet. This would not, however, absolve the beneficiaries from liability to pay the Lloyd's debt.

A Practice Note of 25 May 2001, [2001] 3 All ER 765, governs the process for applying for *Re Yorke* directions. The decision in *Re Yorke* has been applied in a more recent case, *Re K (Deceased)* [2007] EWHC 622 (Ch), [2007] WTLR 1007, which dealt with the responsibility of personal representatives regarding 'stale claims' by creditors. Again, the court held that the only way for the personal representative to obtain complete protection was by court directions.

24.9 GENERAL ADMINISTRATION ORDER

Part 64 of the Civil Procedure Rules 1998 allows the personal representatives (or a beneficiary or creditor) to apply to the court for a general administration order. If the estate is below £30,000, the application would be to the county court (this would be the county court of any places with district registries that have Chancery Division jurisdiction). Such an order governs the manner in which the estate must be administered; and the personal representatives cannot carry out any action without the prior approval of the court. This provides them with full protection in relation to any action they undertake. But because of its onerous nature, such an order is not given readily and the personal representatives should normally try to find an alternative manner of administering the estate. If they are in sufficient doubt about a specific issue, they should instead apply to the court for directions on that issue. In the light of the decision in *Re Vos, Dick v Kendall Freeman* [2005] WTLR 1619, solicitors acting for personal representatives need to exercise great care if the estate is or could become insolvent.

24.10 HM REVENUE AND CUSTOMS

As mentioned elsewhere, it is the responsibility of the persons liable to pay the inheritance tax in relation to an estate to make full disclosure. In the first instance, these duties fall to the personal representatives. If full disclosure is not made, or the inheritance tax due is not paid in full, interest and penalties accrue. There may be substantial problems in relation to transfers made by the deceased during his lifetime, which are not always easily discoverable, the personal representatives having to rely largely on information from third parties.

HM Revenue and Customs in its guidance at IHTM 30044 confirms its earlier press release of 13 March 1991 that personal representatives are not usually pressed for payment from their personal reserves if the personal representatives:

- made the fullest enquiries reasonably practicable in the circumstances to discover lifetime transfers;
- did everything in their power to make a full disclosure of those transfers;
- obtained a certificate of discharge and divided the estate between the beneficiaries before the transfer came to light.

24.11 DEALING WITH THE INTERESTS OF BENEFICIARIES

Many problems can arise when dealing with beneficiaries' interests, for example, in tracing beneficiaries who are known to exist, dealing with incapacitated beneficiaries and establishing the exact interests of different beneficiaries.

24.11.1 Payment into court

Under section 63 of the Trustee Act 1925, personal representatives may pay assets held by them into court (the Court Funds Office at the Royal Courts of Justice), and the receipt of the court officer provides them with a proper and full discharge in relation to those assets. This can be useful, for example, if a beneficiary is a minor and the personal representatives do not want to continue to hold assets for him until he reaches the age of 18, or if assets are due to a beneficiary who is mentally incapable but no receiver, deputy or attorney has been appointed.

If an issue arises as to the person actually entitled to the estate, or if a beneficiary cannot be traced, one of the other options discussed below may be more practical.

24.11.2 *Benjamin* order

If a beneficiary of the estate cannot be traced, the personal representatives can apply to court for a *Benjamin* order. This arises from the case of *Re Benjamin* [1902] 1 Ch 723, but the order is now applied for, under Part 64 of the Civil Procedure Rules 1998, to the Chancery Division (either to the central office in the Royal Courts of Justice in London or to any of the Chancery district registries). The personal representatives must show the court the steps they have taken, including instructing title research agents or private investigators, to establish whether the beneficiary is still alive, and any evidence they have regarding his whereabouts or last known actions. The intended beneficiaries should be joined as parties to the proceedings as defendants. The court may order that certain steps or investigations are undertaken at a preliminary hearing. The application will not be remitted for an order until these have been completed.

Providing the court agrees that the personal representatives have done all they can to trace the beneficiary, it can make an order allowing them to distribute the estate on the basis that the beneficiary predeceased the deceased, leaving no issue.

Seeking a *Benjamin* order can be a costly exercise, and in most instances is not the most practical solution.

24.11.3 Indemnity

An indemnity can be used to resolve a number of issues – for example, where the personal representatives are not completely sure of the correct interpretation of the will, or where a beneficiary cannot be traced. In situations such as these the personal representatives can agree to distribute the estate on a particular basis, taking an indemnity from each recipient, to the effect that if any third party challenges the basis upon which the distribution was made, that recipient will fund the costs of answering that challenge and any amount payable to the third party as a result.

This may be an appropriate course where the amounts in question are relatively low, or where the basis for the distribution is unlikely to be challenged. An indemnity is only useful, however, if the party giving it is solvent and able to meet the required costs if and when the indemnity is called in. If the beneficiary no longer has the monies to fund the indemnity, the personal representatives could find themselves personally liable. Further, a minor beneficiary cannot give an indemnity.

24.11.4 Indemnity insurance

Indemnity insurance is most commonly used to deal with a missing beneficiary. If the personal representatives do not wish to apply for a *Benjamin* order, but the sums involved are too great to be satisfied by taking an indemnity, the personal representatives may take out insurance to cover the possibility of the missing beneficiary claiming his share of the estate in the future. The premium is payable out of the estate. The known beneficiaries usually prefer this course to setting aside funds with which to meet any claim by the disappointed beneficiary. The courts have often referred to insurance as a sensible, practical solution (*Evans v Westcombe* [1999] 2 All ER 777 (ChD)); although the personal representatives must be careful to ensure that the policy covers the amount that the disappointed beneficiary would have received, together with any interest payable on it.

Chapter 25

Variations, Disclaimers and Other Opportunities

25.1 INTRODUCTION

A deed of variation or a disclaimer may be executed to alter the distribution of the deceased's estate. This may be because the intended beneficiaries wish to modify the provisions of the will or intestacy, or because they wish to make them more tax efficient.

25.2 DEED OF VARIATION

25.2.1 Purpose

A deed of variation is an instrument by which the intended recipient of an asset ('beneficiary 1') can direct that the asset passes to a different person ('beneficiary 2'). Beneficiary 1 stipulates in the deed that the asset will pass to beneficiary 2 in his stead. Beneficiary 1 could of course simply give the asset to beneficiary 2 after he has received it from the estate. The advantage of a deed of variation is that, if it is signed within 2 years of the deceased's death, and contains an election (that is, a statement) that the personal representatives wish it to do so, the estate is treated for inheritance tax and/or capital gains tax purposes as though the deceased had executed a will containing the gift made in the deed. This means that the gift by beneficiary 1 to beneficiary 2 is not a PET or LCT by him for inheritance tax purposes (see para 2.21), nor is it a disposal by him for capital gains tax. The statutory provisions allowing this are section 142(1) of the Inheritance Tax Act 1984 and section 62(6) of the Taxation of Chargeable Gains Act 1992.

25.2.2 Signatories

The deed must be signed by every beneficiary who thereby gives up something. For example, if an asset was directed in the will to be held on trust for A for life, remainder to B, and it is decided that the asset should instead pass to C outright, both A and B would have to sign the deed of variation.

A deed of variation cannot be executed by a minor beneficiary, nor can it be signed by his parent, but must be approved by the court on behalf of the minor.

Further, if the execution of the deed leads to a greater amount of inheritance tax becoming payable, it must also be signed by the personal representatives. They may not refuse to execute the deed unless they hold insufficient assets to pay the additional tax. Other persons who may be adversely affected by the deed, such as trustees of an interest in possession trust under which the deceased had a life interest, do not need to join in the election, even though the result may be that the trust has to pay more inheritance tax.

25.2.3 Conditions

More than one deed of variation can be executed in relation to an estate, but each asset can be subject to only one variation. Thus, if the deceased's will passed his house to A, and A used a deed of variation to pass the house to B, B could not execute a deed of variation to pass the house on to C. For this reason it is important to give full consideration to the effects of a proposed deed of variation, and to whether the beneficiary under the deed actually wishes to receive the asset.

A deed of variation can be used even if beneficiary 1 has accepted and received the asset left to him under the will or intestacy. It can also be executed in relation to part only of the asset gifted. In these respects it differs from a deed of disclaimer (see para 25.4).

A deed of variation can be used only in relation to assets in the deceased's free estate at his death. This means that it cannot be used in relation to gifts with reservation of benefit, or to alter the terms of any trust under which he was a beneficiary (section 142(5) of the Inheritance Tax Act 1984), unless the trust assets were subject to a general power of appointment exercisable by the deceased under his will, as the assets could then be disposed of by the deceased's will.

It can, however, be used to bring into the estate assets that the deceased could dispose of by will, by severing the joint tenancy of any asset held by the deceased with a third party. The third party must sign the deed of variation to signify his consent. It is commonly used to sever the joint tenancy of the matrimonial home retrospectively, where one spouse has died and the half share in the home is required in order fully to constitute a nil rate band discretionary trust.

A variation must be made in writing. In practice, it is usually made by deed; however, there is no requirement for it to be so unless the variation is in respect of a trust of land.

A variation must be made within 2 years of the anniversary of the deceased's death to be retrospective for both inheritance tax and capital gains tax purposes.

25.2.4 Taxation

As already mentioned, the Inheritance Tax Act 1984 and the Taxation of Chargeable Gains Act 1992 operate to 're-write' the dispositions effected by the deed back into the deceased's will, if the appropriate election is made in the deed. This is particularly important as, once an election has been made, it cannot be revoked. The election is a statement made within the deed (and therefore deemed to be made by the parties executing the deed) that the provisions of section 142(1) of the Inheritance Tax Act 1984 and/or section 62(6) of the Taxation of Chargeable Gains Act 1992 should apply, and therefore that the gift should be treated as though it were made by the deceased in his will.

Deeds of variation call for careful planning to ensure they achieve the desired result. For example, if the deceased left his shares in ABC plc (valued at £100,000 at the date of his death) to his wife in his will, they would qualify for the surviving spouse exemption from inheritance tax. If the wife wishes to pass the shares on to their child, she would have to decide whether to make the inheritance tax election in the deed. If the deceased had used his entire inheritance tax nil rate band before his death and the election were made, the gift would be treated as passing to his child under his will and inheritance tax would be payable accordingly. In that situation, it would probably be advisable not to make the election. The gift would then be treated as a PET by the wife and, providing she survives for 7 years from the date of that gift, its value should fall out of her estate for inheritance tax purposes upon her death.

On the other hand if the deceased's inheritance tax nil rate band were available on his death, the election should be made so that the gift of the shares is treated as having been made by the deceased's will. No inheritance tax would be payable as the gift would fall within the nil rate band, and the wife would not have to survive 7 years for it to become non-chargeable.

Whether or not the inheritance tax election is made has no bearing on whether a capital gains tax election should be made, and *vice versa*. These are independent decisions. In the example above, if the shares were valued at £105,000 when they were to be passed to the child, and the wife has her full capital gains tax allowance available for the year, it would probably be inappropriate to make the capital gains tax election. The gift would be treated as a disposal by the wife for capital gains tax purposes, but if the gain fell within her allowance, no capital gains tax would be payable. On the other hand, if the gain on the shares were £20,000, it would probably be advisable to make the election. The child's base cost of the shares for capital gains tax purposes would then be the probate value of £100,000.

If the deed is used to create a trust, the beneficiary disposing of the asset under the deed is not the settlor of the trust for inheritance tax purposes (the settlor is the deceased), but he is the settlor for income tax and capital gains tax purposes. This means that if he is also a beneficiary of that trust, all its income and capital gains are taxed in his hands.

25.2.5 Consideration

Sections 142(3) of the Inheritance Tax Act 1984 and 62(8) of the Taxation of Chargeable Gains Act 1992 specifically state that if the beneficiary making the gift under the deed receives any form of consideration, whether in money or money's worth, for the execution of the deed, the deed has no effect for the purposes of inheritance tax or capital gains tax.

The only form of consideration that is permitted is the 'exchange' of assets received under the will by two or more beneficiaries. So if Blueacre is left in a will to A and Whiteacre to B, A and B may execute a deed of variation to exchange gifts. If, however, Whiteacre is valued at £50,000 less than Blueacre, B cannot give A £50,000 in addition, as this would be a consideration.

25.2.6 Income arising before the variation

A deed of variation is effective only for inheritance tax and capital gains tax purposes, not for income tax purposes. This means that any income paid to the original beneficiary before the variation was signed is still his and must be declared by him for income tax purposes. That income could specifically be redirected to the new beneficiary under the deed, but nevertheless remains subject to income tax in the hands of the original beneficiary. Once the deed of variation has been signed, the future income must be distributed in accordance with it.

25.2.7 Notice of election

For many years, notices of elections under the Inheritance Tax Act 1984 or the Taxation of Chargeable Gains Act 1992 had to be given to the tax authorities in order to be valid. Since 1 August 2002, the election need only be contained in the deed itself to be valid, but HM Revenue and Customs requires written notice if additional inheritance tax or capital gains tax will become payable.

25.2.8 The 'real world'

A relatively recent development concerning deeds of variation relates to so-called 'real world' situations. Suppose A dies and leaves his entire estate on a life interest trust to B, remainder to C. Within 2 years, B dies and the assets in the trust pass to C. If inheritance tax were payable on the assets in A's estate, and then also on the trust assets in B's estate, C may ask B's personal representatives to execute a deed of variation in relation to A's estate, whereby the estate is left outright to C, thereby avoiding the double charge to inheritance tax. This is similar to the situation that arose in *Soutter v IRC* [2002] STC (SCD) 385. The Inland Revenue (as it was) argued that the variation had no 'real world' effect, as, by the time the deed was executed, C was beneficially entitled to the trust assets. In that case, the Special Commissioners agreed with the Inland Revenue – that there were no assets upon which the deed of variation could 'bite', because the deed sought to bring into effect that which would have happened anyway. The case is specific to life interest trusts, and does not apply to absolute gifts. This is because, under a life interest trust, there is nothing that could be 'given back' to A's estate following B's death – his life tenancy is over. In the case of an absolute gift, B's estate could still return the asset that is the subject of the variation to A's estate, for onward transmission to C under the deed. There is some argument as to whether a disclaimer by B's personal representatives might have been effective as an alternative, providing he had not received any income from the life interest trust. Personal representatives should consider current case law carefully if they are contemplating a deed of variation in a situation such as this.

25.2.9 Stamp duty and stamp duty land tax

A deed of variation is exempt from stamp duty under category M of the Schedule to the Stamp Duty (Exempt Instruments) Regulations 1987, but the deed must contain a certificate to that effect. It is also exempt from stamp duty land tax under paragraph 4 of Schedule 3 to the Finance Act 2003, providing the only consideration is the making of a variation of another disposition under the will or the intestacy rules.

25.2.10 Tax planning

Some examples of when a deed of variation may be used for tax planning purposes are:

- to create a discretionary trust of the deceased's inheritance tax nil rate band or to make an outright gift of it where the deceased left a surviving spouse or civil partner;
- to give assets qualifying for relief from inheritance tax to non-exempt beneficiaries, such as the deceased's children;
- to give additional assets to the deceased's spouse so that they qualify for the exemption from inheritance tax;
- to gift 10 per cent of the net estate to a qualifying charity to qualify for the reduced rate of inheritance tax.

25.2.11 Charitable giving and the reduced rate of inheritance tax

Details of the requirements for the reduced rate of inheritance tax to apply to an estate are set out in para 3.17, which also provides guidance as to how to calculate the charitable giving condition. It is also possible for a variation to be executed so that the lower rate of inheritance tax of 36 per cent applies to the estate whether this is to increase an existing legacy in a will to ensure qualification for the lower rate of tax or to include a new gift to charity. A gift by way of variation, however, will only qualify providing the charity in question is notified of the variation. An exchange of correspondence with the charity in relation to the gift in the variation is sufficient evidence of the notification.

The HM Revenue and Customs *Inheritance Tax Manual* sets out at IHTM 45008 an approved example of a legacy that will always meet the 10 per cent test, and this guidance also refers to a model clause developed by the Society of Trust and Estate Practitioners.

It is worth highlighting that where a variation is made to sever a joint tenancy, the assets affected remain within the survivorship component rather than being transferred to the general component. This is because paragraph 3(2) of Schedule 1A defines the survivorship component as all the property comprised in the deceased's estate that, immediately before death, was liable to pass by survivorship.

25.3 ORDER PURSUANT TO AN INHERITANCE ACT CLAIM

Section 146 of the Inheritance Tax Act 1984 states that where an order is made under section 2 of the Inheritance (Provision for Family and Dependants) Act 1975, for the purposes of inheritance tax, the deceased's estate is treated as though it had devolved in accordance with the provisions of the order. Interest is therefore not payable on any tax underpaid or overpaid from any date earlier than the date of the court order.

25.4 DISCLAIMER

A disclaimer is made where a person entitled to assets from the deceased's estate, under either a will or an intestacy, does not wish to accept them. It differs from a deed of variation in both the requirements relating to it, and the effects.

25.4.1 Requirements

Although section 142 of the Inheritance Tax Act 1984 provides that a disclaimer must be made in writing, in *Cook (Watkins Executors) v IRC* [2002] WTLR 1003, there was the suggestion that it could be inferred from the conduct of the disclaimant. The HM Revenue and Customs *Inheritance Tax Manual* at IHTM 35161 confirms that a disclaimer can be made in writing or by conduct, but it will not be effective for the purposes of section 142 if it is not made in writing. For practical purposes, however, it is recommended that a disclaimer is always evidenced by deed. A disclaimer is not effective once the asset has been accepted by the intended beneficiary – he cannot choose to reject it later. The asset in question must be accepted or rejected in its entirety. This is why some wills break down each gift into a number of gifts of £1 each, so that a gift of an asset can be partially disclaimed, by accepting or rejecting individual gifts of £1.

25.4.2 Effects

A disclaimant has no control over the destination of the gift he disclaims. The estate is administered as though the disclaimant had predeceased the deceased, so that any substitutional gift takes effect (see, now, the Estates of Deceased Persons (Forfeiture and Law of Succession) Act 2011).

A disclaimer by a beneficiary with a prospective entitlement under a testator's estate which is executed during the testator's lifetime has no effect (see *Smith v Smith* [2001] 1 WLR 1937 (ChD)).

A disclaimer must be made in writing within 2 years of the deceased's death, and must not be made for consideration in money or money's worth from a source outside the estate. If any of these conditions is not met, the disclaimer will not be effective for the purposes of section 142 of the Inheritance Tax Act 1984 and section 62 of the Taxation of Chargeable Gains Act 1992.

A disclaimant can subsequently retract his disclaimer as long as no person has altered his position by reliance on it.

25.4.3 Taxation implications

The taxation implications of a disclaimer are also different from those of a variation. If the disclaimer is made within 2 years of the deceased's death and the other conditions above are met, section 142 of the Inheritance Tax Act 1984 and section 62 of the Taxation of Chargeable Gains Act 1992 take effect automatically. There is no need for any written election to be made.

The personal representatives do not need to join in any disclaimer, even if extra inheritance tax becomes payable – they can do nothing about this.

If the assets subject to the disclaimer pass into a trust when the disclaimer becomes effective, the disclaimant is not the settlor of that trust for income tax or capital gains tax purposes. This may be advantageous if the disclaimant or his minor children are to be beneficiaries of that trust, as the income and capital gains of it are not assessable on him.

25.4.4 Income arising before the disclaimer

Any income that arose on the asset before the disclaimer becomes effective should not be paid to the disclaimant. If it is, and the disclaimant accepts the income, he receives a benefit from the asset and is unable to disclaim it. All the income arising on the asset must therefore pass to the new beneficiary.

25.4.5 Joint property, trust assets and gifts with reservation of benefit

It is not possible to use a disclaimer to redirect an interest which passes by survivorship.

Like a deed of variation, a disclaimer cannot be used in relation to assets subject to a gift with reservation of benefit. It can be used in relation to trust property under section 93 of the Inheritance Tax Act 1984, but only by the life tenant of an interest in possession trust, to accelerate the interest of the remaindermen. It cannot be used by the remaindermen, as, at the point they become entitled, the property is no longer held in a life interest trust, but belongs to them absolutely or contingently.

25.4.6 Stamp duty

A disclaimer is not subject to stamp duty.

25.5 TWO-YEAR DISCRETIONARY TRUSTS

To preserve flexibility in his estate, a testator may, in his will, create a discretionary trust, into which certain assets, or his entire estate, may pass. If a distribution is made from this trust within 2 years of the deceased's death and before an interest in possession subsists in the asset distributed, that disposition is treated as though it had been made by the deceased in his will for inheritance tax purposes (section 144 of the Inheritance Tax Act 1984). This means that assets can be appointed out of the trust to exempt beneficiaries, such as the deceased's spouse or civil partner, and any inheritance tax paid on those assets is refunded, because they qualify for the surviving spouse or civil partner exemption from inheritance tax.

The disadvantage is that the inheritance tax must be paid in the first instance, until the appointment is made. Before the Finance (No 2) Act 2015 was given Royal Assent, the personal representatives had to wait at least 3 months from the date of death before they made such a distribution or the desired inheritance tax consequences would not have been achieved (*Frankland v IRC* [1996] STC 735 (ChD)). However, for deaths on or after 10 December 2014, the so-called '*Frankland* trap' has been removed so that the trustees of a relevant property trust created by a will can make such an appointment within 3 months of the testator's death, and this appointment will be treated as being made by the testator for inheritance tax purposes under section 144.

The final disadvantage is that there is no reciprocal provision in the Taxation of Chargeable Gains Act 1992. This means that any appointment from the trust is a disposal for capital gains tax purposes by the personal representatives. It does not automatically qualify for holdover relief from this tax under section 260 of the Taxation of Chargeable Gains Act 1992 as the appointment does not give rise to an event for inheritance tax purposes.

25.6 PRECATORY TRUSTS

It is common for a testator to leave his chattels to certain specified persons, with a direction that those persons distribute the chattels in accordance with a letter of wishes written by him during his lifetime. Under section 143 of the Inheritance Tax Act 1984, inheritance tax is payable on those chattels as though they were gifted absolutely to the specified persons. But if those persons dispose of the chattels within 2 years of the death, the estate is taxed as though the will made the same distribution.

Section 143 of the Inheritance Tax Act 1984 does not apply to chattels alone, but to any asset that can be bequeathed (other than land, which must be devised).

Thus, a testator could leave, say, £20,000 to a specified person, and ask that person to make gifts to charities that he notifies to him by letter. If the gifts to charity are made within 2 years of the deceased's death, they qualify for the charities exemption from inheritance tax.

25.7 OTHER OPPORTUNITIES

Once the administration of an estate has been finalised, the beneficiaries may need further professional advice. For example, they may be advised to make their own wills, perhaps with some inheritance tax planning advice. Alternatively, they may wish to consider executing lasting powers of attorney to ensure that their affairs can be properly dealt with, should they lose capacity. These are all matters which a solicitor acting for the personal representatives may be able to deal with.

Finally, beneficiaries taking substantial sums of money under an estate may need investment advice; the solicitor for the personal representatives may be able to give advice or recommend an adviser.

Chapter 26

Notation, Amendment and Revocation of Grants

26.1 NOTATION

In certain circumstances an original grant must be notated with an event or order which affects the use of the grant in the administration of the estate. Notation is effected by the registry.

26.1.1 Domicile

Rule 8(2) of the Non-Contentious Probate Rules 1987 provides that the oath to lead a grant shall, unless otherwise directed by a district judge or registrar, contain a statement of the deceased's domicile at death. The domicile is recited in the grant. A grant issued in England and Wales, referring to domicile in England and Wales, is effective to administer estate throughout the United Kingdom.

If an oath was, with leave, silent as to the place of the deceased's domicile, the grant is likewise silent, but the grant may later be notated with the domicile. Entitlement to benefit from an estate may vary depending on the deceased's domicile, for example, if the deceased died domiciled in France, the French law requiring that statutory legacies (reserved portions) be paid to members of kin, even if there is a will, applies. In such a case, the executor, or, if more than one, any one of them, or all the administrators, must first make an affidavit deposing to the place of the deceased's domicile at death. The affidavit must be lodged in the registry with the original grant. If satisfied, the district judge or registrar directs notation of the domicile to be made on the grant, together with a note of his direction and the date of it.

26.1.2 Election to redeem life interest

The surviving spouse or civil partner of an intestate, who died before 1 October 2014, and whose estate exceeded the value of the statutory legacy (see paras 6.1 *et seq*), may elect to redeem the life interest to which he is entitled, being property then in possession. Redemption is effected by paying the appropriate amount determined by reference to the Intestate Succession (Interest and Capitalisation) Order 1977 (SI 1977/1491), as amended.

Notice of the election to redeem is served on the personal representatives or, where the surviving spouse or civil partner is the sole personal representative, on the Senior District Judge. Notice in Form 6 of Schedule 1 to the Non-Contentious Probate Rules 1987 (see Appendix C34) is lodged in the Principal Registry of the Family Division, or, in duplicate, in the district registry from which the grant issued. The original grant must be lodged. The notice must be lodged within one year of the issue of the grant unless, in special circumstances, the court extends the time for lodging.

If satisfied, the registry notates the original grant and the record copy (the copy retained in the Probate Records Centre, by sending notice to the Birmingham District Probate Registry) of the filing of the election and returns the grant to the grantee.

26.1.3 Further personal representative

When an order has been made following an application under rule 26 of the Non-Contentious Probate Rules 1987 for the appointment of an additional personal representative (see para 10.3.3), the original grant must be notated with the additional personal representative's name and address. The original grant and the record copy are notated in red ink, and details of the order added as a marginal note. The registry notifies the Birmingham District Probate Registry, which effects the annotation of the record copy held at the Probate Records Centre (see para 27.1) and thereafter returns the original grant to the extracting solicitors.

26.1.4 Substituted personal representative

Application may be made under section 50 of the Administration of Justice Act 1985 for the removal and/or substitution of an executor or administrator. The application is made under Part 57 of the Civil Procedure Rules 1998, to the Chancery Division.

When an order has been made for the removal and/or substitution of a personal representative, the original grant (which will have been lodged in the Chancery Registry with the application under section 50 of the Administration of Justice Act 1985) is forwarded to the issuing probate registry for notation. The original grant and record copy are notated in red ink with the effect of and details of the Chancery order. Thereafter the original grant is returned, as appropriate, to the extracting solicitors or those representing the substituted personal representative. The registry notifies the Birmingham District Probate Registry, which effects the annotation of the record copy held at the Probate Records Centre.

Application under section 50 of the Administration of Justice Act 1985 may also be made as a pre-grant application (see *Goodman and another v Goodman and another* [2013] EWHC 758 (Ch), [2014] Ch 186). Practice Direction 57 to the Civil Procedure Rules 1998 now contains the instruction to the Chancery Court making such an order to notify the Leeds District Probate Registry of the order, so the registries do not issue a grant to someone removed by the order.

26.1.5 Bankruptcy administration order

Where the deceased died bankrupt, the bankruptcy court may order the powers of the personal representative be transferred, usually to the receiver in bankruptcy, by order under the Insolvency Act 1986. The effect of such order, called an administration order, is notated on the original grant and record copy by the registry from which it issued. The registry notifies the Birmingham District Probate Registry, which effects the annotation of the record copy held at the Probate Records Centre.

26.1.6 Rectification of will

The procedure to apply to rectify a will is dealt with at paras 10.15 *et seq*. Where an order is made to rectify after the grant has issued, the original grant must be notated with the effect of the order. If the order is made by a district judge or registrar the original grant should have been lodged with the application. Where the application was opposed, but an order to rectify was made by the Chancery Division, the original grant is sent to the issuing registry. The original grant is notated with a marginal note of the order, and a memorandum of its effect on the will, or a copy of the will as rectified, is annexed. The registry notifies the Birmingham District Probate Registry, which effects the annotation of the record copy held at the Probate Records Centre.

26.1.7 Orders made under the Inheritance (Provision for Family and Dependants) Act 1975

A copy of every final order made under the Inheritance (Provision for Family and Dependants) Act 1975 (other than an order made under section 15(1)) must be sent to the Principal Registry of the Family Division for entry and filing. A memorandum of the order must be endorsed on, or permanently annexed to, the probate or letters of administration under which the estate is being administered.

The original grant of representation and a copy of the order are sent to the Principal Registry by the court which made the order. If the grant was made in the Principal Registry a memorandum of the order is prepared by the probate department and photocopied. A copy of the memorandum is attached to the grant, and a further copy is sent to HM Revenue and Customs Inheritance Tax Department. The order and another copy of the memorandum are sent to the Birmingham Probate Registry for filing at the Probate Records Centre with the original will, or if there is no will, with the oath to lead the grant of administration.

Where the grant issued from a district probate registry the grant and copy order are sent to that registry and the same procedure is followed.

26.1.8 Second or subsequent grant

There is no notation on the original grant of the issue of a grant of double probate, a grant *de bonis non*, or a *cessate* grant.

26.2 AMENDMENT

Rule 41 of the Non-Contentious Probate Rules 1987 deals with the procedure for applications to amend grants. Where the grant contains an error, that is, a clerical error arising from a mistake in the application or by the registry in preparing the grant, it may be amended. Where the defect in the application affects title to the grant then the grant must be revoked (see para 26.3).

26.2.1 Error by registry

The personal representatives (or their solicitors) should, immediately on receiving the grant from the registry, check it to ensure it is in proper form and contains the correct names and addresses of the deceased and the personal representatives. If an error has been made by the registry, the grant and all office copies should be returned within 28 days of issue. Provided it is returned within this time a new grant is issued, but if after that time, the original grant is manually amended in red ink and notated with the district judge or registrar's order to amend. Where the probate copy will in the grant is incomplete, the original grant should be returned for the full testamentary document to be annexed.

26.2.2 Error by applicant

Where the oath to lead the grant was defective in that it failed to give full correct names or addresses, an application for amendment may be made by the applicant or the extracting solicitors. The application should be made on affidavit, deposed to by the person with best knowledge of the error. The district judge or registrar has discretion to accept a less formal method of application, by letter, depending on the circumstances.

Provided the application is made within 28 days of the date of the original grant, a new grant is issued in proper form. Where application is made after 28 days have elapsed the original grant is manually annotated with the amendment and order to amend.

26.2.3 Error in limitation

Where there is an error in a limitation on a grant, whether the error was made in the probate registry or arose from a defect in the application, the limitation is amended. This may be done without affidavit evidence in support if the grant fails to follow the limitation imposed in a discretionary order.

26.2.4 Codicil found after will proved

Where a codicil to a will is found after probate of the will has been granted, the original grant is not amended, nor is the original grant notated. Instead, an application for a grant in respect of the codicil alone is made. Only where the codicil changes the appointment of executors, or affects the title of the person who took the grant, is the original grant recalled and revoked. Where the original grant is not revoked both grants are used together in the administration of the estate. Where the grant is revoked, probate of both the will and codicil must be applied for.

26.2.5 Changes in estate value

Where, after the issue of a grant, it is discovered that the estate values quoted in the oath or inheritance tax account were wrong, the grant may be amended to show the correct figures.

As a general rule, it is not the practice of the probate registries to amend the values of the gross and/or net estate appearing in the grant. Where correction is necessary, an application should be made to HM Revenue and Customs with an explanation or corrective account (see para 20.4). The original grant should be lodged with HM Revenue and Customs for that office to control the estate value figures.

26.2.6 Addition of alias name

Where, after the grant has issued, it is found that assets are registered in an alternative name of the deceased, the grant may be amended to include such name. The procedure for amendment set out above applies. Similarly, with good reason, an alternative address may be added.

26.3 REVOCATION

Section 121(1) of the Senior Courts Act 1981 gives the court authority, of its own motion, to call in and, if necessary, revoke a grant which ought not to have issued. Rule 41 of the Non-Contentious Probate Rules 1987 provides the procedure for application for revocation of a grant to a district judge or registrar. Other than in exceptional circumstances a grant is revoked only with the consent of the grantee or all grantees.

No fee is payable to the probate registry on application to revoke.

26.3.1 Grant issued on false premise

A grant of probate is revoked where:

- the will proved was not the last valid will of the deceased;
- a codicil, or further codicil, is found which affects the appointment of executors;
- evidence is produced which clearly shows the will was not duly executed;
- there is evidence to show that the testator revoked the original will, a copy having been accepted to proof;
- a will is proved in common form even though there is a pending probate claim concerning the validity of the will.

A grant of letters of administration is revoked where:

- a valid will is found after letters of administration had been taken on an intestacy;
- the grantee is found not to be the nearest of kin to the deceased and therefore not beneficially entitled to the estate.

In addition, there are cases common to testacy and intestacy where a grant issued on a false basis must be revoked:

- where a grant has issued in respect of the estate of a living person;
- where leave to swear to the death of the deceased was given by order under rule 53 of the Non-Contentious Probate Rules 1987 but the 'deceased' is subsequently found to be alive;
- where the applicant for the grant himself dies before the grant is issued.

A grant is deemed to be issued when 'passed under seal of the court' at the earliest time the registry is open to the public on the day of issue, that is, 10 a.m. in all the registries. Thus, if there is evidence to show the grantee died at 2 p.m. on the date the grant was issued, it was properly issued and a grant *de bonis non* may be taken. But, if the grantee died at 8 a.m. on the day of issue, the grant must be revoked and a new original grant taken by a person of equal or next entitlement.

26.3.2 Grantee lacking mental capacity within the meaning of the Mental Capacity Act 2005

Where a sole grantee, in whatever capacity he was entitled to the grant, becomes incapable of managing his affairs through lack of mental capacity within the meaning of the Mental Capacity Act 2005, the grant is not revoked. Instead, a new grant may be applied for by a person of equal entitlement under rule 20(b)–(f) or rule 22 of the Non-Contentious Probate Rules 1987, in the order of priority provided by rule 35(2), or by discretionary order under rule 35(4) (see para 12.2.13). The grant is a grant *de bonis non* for the use and benefit of the former grantee. The only exception to this general rule is where the grant issued to one of several appointed executors, the others having power reserved. These others may take a grant of double probate (see para 12.6.2).

26.3.3 Several grantees

Where one of two or more proving executors becomes mentally incapable of managing his affairs the grant must be revoked and a new grant of probate issued to the capable executors. Power is reserved to the incapable executor on regaining his mental capacity.

Similarly, where letters of administration with or without will annexed have been taken out and one of the grantees becomes incapable, the grant must be revoked. A new grant may be taken by those persons with the same entitlement under rule 20 or rule 22 of the Non-Contentious Probate Rules 1987. The application for revocation and for the new grant may be combined in one affidavit if the grant issued to one or more executors, one of whom is now incapable of managing his affairs.

26.3.4 Relief from duties

Where there is a conflict in the administration of the estate between the grantees, or between the grantee(s) and the beneficiaries, the grantee may apply for revocation of the grant. Similarly, where the grantee becomes ill or incapacitated (other than through lack of mental incapacity) in some way he may apply to be relieved of his duties by having the grant to him revoked. Any person who takes on the mantle of personal representative is relieved of those duties only in exceptional circumstances, even if all interested parties agree to the revocation of the grant. An order for revocation in these circumstances is in the discretion of the district judge or registrar and orders are not lightly made. It is recommended the view of the district judge or registrar is taken before any papers are drafted to lead the application.

26.3.5 Grant issued too soon

Rule 6(2) of the Non-Contentious Probate Rules 1987 provides that no grant of probate or letters of administration (with will annexed) may issue within 7 days of the deceased's death, and no grant of letters of administration may issue within 14 days of the deceased's death. A district judge or registrar has power to abridge these times in extenuating circumstances.

If a grant has issued without leave before the expiry of the necessary times it is not usually revoked. The court does, however, of its own motion, revoke a grant if any person can show that he was prevented from objecting to the grant being issued and/or from entering a caveat because of the registry's error in issuing the grant before time without leave. A grant should not now issue without leave within the prescribed times because the registries' computer system has been programmed not to allow the issue of the grant before the appropriate time has elapsed.

26.3.6 Grantee's disappearance or failure to administer

Where representation has been granted but the grantee disappears, leaving part of the estate unadministered, or fails to administer it fully, an application to revoke the grant may be made.

This situation usually falls into the 'exceptional circumstance' criterion for revocation without the grantee's consent. The application may, by way of exception to the usual rule, be made without lodging the original grant. It is suggested that an enquiry be made of the district judge or registrar before applying to revoke. If the district judge or registrar agrees to entertain the application, an affidavit of facts to lead the order should be drafted and lodged. In the present situation for the registries, and with fewer registrars in post, it is unlikely, save in the most exceptional circumstances, that this form of application will be considered.

The alternative, in this situation, is to apply to the Chancery Division under section 50 of the Administration of Justice Act 1985 (see para 26.3.9).

26.3.7 Revocation opposed

Where it is said that the grant should not have issued because there is a dispute about the validity of the will or the grantee's title to the grant, and the application to revoke is opposed, the application must be made to the Chancery Division (see Parts 7 and 57 of the Civil Procedure Rules 1998).

26.3.8 Application for new grant

Whether the order to revoke is made by the Family Division or the Chancery Division, any consequent application for a new grant may be made to any probate registry. The oath to lead the new grant must recite details of, and the order revoking, the former grant.

The new grant is a full grant to the whole estate, although the estate values referred to in the oath relate only to the estate remaining unadministered.

26.3.9 Removal or substitution of grantee

Where the problem lies not with the grant, but with the grantee, an application may be made to the Chancery Division under section 50 of the Administration of Justice Act 1985 for the removal and/or substitution of the grantee.

If the grantees (or one of them) fail(s) to participate in the administration of the estate or maladministers the estate, grantee(s) concerned may be removed, and, if appropriate, another substituted. Clearly, if the offending grantee is a sole grantee, then there must be substitution. Indeed the Act provides a sole grantee will not be removed without substitution.

In *Heyman and another v Dobson and another* [2007] EWHC 3503 (Ch), [2010] WTLR 1151, it was held that there were sufficient grounds for an application to remove a personal representative if the personal representative had produced an account of his administration of the estate which the beneficiaries did not accept. In this case an order had been made summarily by a Master and that order was appealed. The judge, in refusing the appeal, said there were sufficient grounds for removing the personal representative. The representative's conduct in dealing with the estate was improper.

Application under section 50 of the Administration of Justice Act 1985 is a probate claim, the procedure for which is governed by Part 57 of the Civil Procedure Rules 1998. The procedure for issue follows Part 7. The application may be made to Chancery Chambers at the Royal Courts of Justice in London, or to any of the designated district registries with Chancery jurisdiction.

Chapter 27

Searches and Copies

27.1 RECORDS OF GRANTS OF REPRESENTATION

A record of every grant of representation issued between 1858 and 1998 is maintained in indexes (called 'calendars') available for search and inspection in the probate registries. Generally, district probate registries hold calendars for the last 50 years only; searches for earlier documents may be made in the Principal Registry of the Family Division. Some of these records (those since 1972) are on microfiche, but otherwise are in book form. Records of grants issued since November 1998 are held in the *Probateman* computer system. Records since January 2000 are held at the Probate Records Centre (which is privately run but is under the control of the Birmingham District Probate Registry).

Registries usually hold the files on grants which have issued for 2 years from the date of issue. Older files are archived in the Probate Records Centre and may be retrieved for inspection at a registry. These files comprise original wills and any other documents required before the grant could issue. The Probate Records Centre is in the process of transferring all records (from 1858) formerly held in paper or microfiche form to electronic storage. Copies of those records already transferred can be obtained by the registries from the Centre, usually by the next day.

Facilities are now in place to search and order probate records online at https://probatesearch.service.gov.uk/#wills. In order to search for and order a copy of a grant and any will, the site requires the surname and year of death of the deceased. A successful search displays the name of the deceased, the date of the grant, the probate number, the date of death, the record available to order, the grant and will, if any, and the probate registry which issued the grant. The fee is £10, payable by credit or debit card, following which the site informs the applicant when the probate record will be available to download and print (about 10 days).

27.2 STANDING SEARCH FOR A GRANT

Rule 43 of the Non-Contentious Probate Rules 1987 provides that any person who wishes to be notified of the issue of a grant may enter a standing search for the grant in any registry or sub-registry. The application is made by lodging form 2 of the forms prescribed by the Non-Contentious Probate Rules 1987 (see Appendix C36). The full information required by the form must be given or the search will not be entered.

Thus, if an application under section 1 of the Inheritance (Provision for Family and Dependants) Act 1975 (in the estate of a deceased dying before 1 October 2014), or any other litigation against the estate, is contemplated, a standing search should be entered. Similarly, a creditor of the deceased may wish to know when representation is granted so that he may make his claim to the personal representatives.

A copy of any grant issued in the 12 months before the entry of the search, or which issues within the 6 months after the entry of the search, is sent to the person who entered the search by the issuing registry.

A standing search remains effective for 6 months after entry, but may be extended on application in writing made within the last month of the 6-month period, and so on *ad infinitum*.

A fee of £10 is payable for the entry of a standing search and for each extension.

27.3 SEARCH FOR A CAVEAT

Any solicitor or probate practitioner may request a search of the records to ascertain whether an effective caveat has been entered against the issue of a grant in any particular estate. Application may be made by personal attendance at, or by post to, the Principal Registry of the Family Division or any district registry.

No fee is payable for the search, but if an effective caveat is found a fee of £10 is payable for a copy of the caveat.

27.4 COPIES OF WILLS AND GRANTS

From the time a will is proved it becomes a 'public' document and copies of it, and of any grant of representation, may be obtained by any person on request and on payment of the requisite fee.

Rules 58 and 59 of the Non-Contentious Probate Rules 1987, which deal with copies of documents held by probate registries, also provide for wills to be open to inspection or refused inspection, at the discretion of a district judge or registrar.

Copies of grants and wills may be requested from the registry which issued the grant or from the Principal Registry of the Family Division. Where it is known from which registry the grant issued, the application should be made to that registry. See para 27.1 for obtaining copies by online search.

27.4.1 Types of copy supplied

Plain copies (i.e. neither sealed nor certified) of:

- wills which have been refused admission to probate;
- wills which are inoperative and not proved;
- wills which have been proved in part;
- wills which were proved in the form of an engrossment endorsed with the court's *fiat*;
- grants of probate or letters of administration (with will annexed) which have been revoked (and the will has not been proved again);
- powers of attorney (where the original is not held by the registry),

may be obtained from the registry in which they are held.

Sealed, but not certified, copies of:

- oaths;
- affidavits;
- orders (except for orders giving leave to swear death);
- powers of attorney (where the original is held); and
- renunciations,

may be obtained from the registry holding the records of the issue of the grant. Office copies of grants and oaths may be obtained at the time of application for the grant.

Once a grant of representation has issued, sealed and certified copies of the grant and proved testamentary documents may be obtained. Each document is sealed with the seal of the High Court, Family Division and certified by a district judge or registrar as a true copy of the grant and proved will and/or codicil. Sealed and certified copies may be obtained on the issue of the grant.

27.4.2 Copies for use abroad

Apostilles

Usually, a sealed and certified copy of a grant or will endorsed with the 'apostille' is sufficient evidence for use in countries which are signatories to the Hague Convention on Recognition of Documents dated 5 October 1961.

The endorsement of the apostille is made on application to the Legalisation Department of the Foreign and Commonwealth Office (see Appendix B for the address). A sealed and certified copy of the relevant document(s) to be enclosed should be sent with the fee. The fees per apostille have increased to £30 for standard applications (4-day service) submitted to the Milton Keynes office and £75 for the Premium Business Service (same-day service). These fees exclude return postal charges.

Exemplification

An exemplification is sometimes required as evidence in the courts of other countries. An exemplification is a statement of the details of the grant of representation. It contains a résumé of the grant and an exact copy of all testamentary documents proved. A certificate verifying authenticity of the documents is signed by a district judge or registrar.

An application for an exemplification must be made to the registry from which the grant issued on payment of the requisite fee.

Exemplifications are usually required for applications to reseal abroad under the Colonial Probates Acts.

Special copies

A 'special copy' or 'special certificate' is again sometimes required by courts of foreign countries. A special copy is an exemplification signed by a district judge or registrar and countersigned by the President of the Family Division. This form of copy is often required where the foreign authority needs confirmation the grant is still in full force and effect.

27.4.3 Duplicate grants

Where the original grant had been lost or inadvertently destroyed and an original grant is required for administrative purposes, a duplicate may be issued.

An application may be made only by the original grantee. It is made by letter setting out how (if known) the original has been lost or destroyed and the reasons why a duplicate grant (and not a plain or certified copy) is required.

A duplicate grant is an exact replica of the original and bears the original date of issue, but it is notated in the margin that it is a duplicate of the original, and with the date of issue of the duplicate.

27.4.4 Fees

The following fees are payable for copies and are prescribed by Schedule 1, Fee 8 of the Non-Contentious Probate Fees Order 2004 (SI 2004/3120) as amended.

On a request for a copy of any document whether or not provided as a certified copy:

- for the first copy, £10;
- for every copy of the same document if supplied at the same time, £0.50. In practice, the registries charge £0.50 for each copy applied for at the time the grant is issued;
- where copies of any document are made available on a computer disk or in other electronic form, for each copy, £10;
- where a search of the index is required, in addition to the fees above as appropriate, for each period of 4 years searched after the first 4 years, £6.

The fee for a duplicate grant, prescribed by Schedule 1, Fee 2 of the Order, is £20.

27.5 DEPOSIT OF WILLS FOR SAFE KEEPING

It is strongly recommended that a will is executed in the offices of the solicitors who drafted it and retained by those solicitors. But if the testator cannot be persuaded to leave his will, it may be lodged for safe custody in the Principal Registry of the Family Division. The Wills (Deposit for Safe Custody) Regulations 1978 (SI 1978/1724) apply.

A will may be lodged for deposit personally by the testator or his authorised agent at any district registry or the Principal Registry of the Family Division, but may be lodged by post only at the Principal Registry. The will must be sealed up in the envelope provided by the registry. A certificate of deposit is provided. Wills lodged in a district probate registry are forwarded to the Principal Registry.

The registry immediately records the deposit on the *Probateman* computer system.

A fee of £20 is payable for the deposit of a will.

27.5.1 Withdrawal

After deposit, a testator may withdraw his will on written request, supported by the certificate of deposit, to the Principal Registry of the Family Division. A district judge must be satisfied before the original will is released (a copy is retained). Except on the written request of the testator the original is not released during his lifetime.

27.5.2 Death of the testator

After the testator's death the original will may be released by a district judge on production of the certificate of deposit and proof of death. No fee is payable for the withdrawal of a will.

Appendix A

Checklist of Information and Documents

The following may be used as a checklist when taking instructions and when gathering the information and documents needed before applying for a grant.

- Deceased's personal details:
  - name;
  - address including postcode;
  - dates of birth and death (obtain death certificate);
  - National Insurance number, tax self-assessment number and HM Revenue and Customs office;
  - brief summary of family situation;
  - on intestacy, details of next of kin and family tree.
- Will and codicils:
  - dates of will and codicils;
  - current location (if not handed over);
  - check whether funeral wishes mentioned;
  - full names and addresses of executors.
- Assets – details and approximate values of all property owned by the deceased (ascertain whether property owned in deceased's sole name or jointly with another person or held by deceased in an alternative name):
  - deceased's home:
    - location of title deeds;
    - if the deceased sold his home on or after 8 July 2015, a copy of the signed TR1/contract in this sale;
  - other properties owned by the deceased:
    - location of title deeds;

- business/partnership in trading company;
- bank/building society accounts (obtain up to date statements);
- National Savings certificates (obtain certificates);
- premium bonds (obtain holder's card);
- other National Savings investments;
- stocks and shares (obtain certificates or confirm identity of nominee name);
- life assurance policies (obtain original policy documents);
- cash (e.g. cash found at home);
- furniture and personal possessions;
- other assets and location of title documents.

• Liabilities – all money owed by the deceased together with any relevant documents, for example:

- mortgages (obtain last statement);
- outstanding bills (e.g. gas, electricity, council tax);
- funeral director's invoice;
- other debts.

• Trusts:

- details of any trusts made by the deceased;
- details of any trusts in which the deceased had an interest.

• Gifts and receipts:

- details of gifts made by the deceased in the 7 years before death;
- details of money and property inherited by the deceased in the last 5 years.

• Miscellaneous:

- copy of last tax return and name of accountant (if any);
- pension book (obtain);
- social security benefits received;
- insurance policies relating to house, contents and car.

Appendix B

Useful Addresses

Association of British Insurers	One America Square 17 Crosswall London EC3N 2LB 0207 600 3333 info@abi.org.uk
Attendance Allowance	Attendance Allowance Unit Mail Handling Site A Wolverhampton WV98 2AD Attendance Allowance helpline 0800 731 0122 0800 731 0317 (textphone)
A K Biggs, Probate Consultant	Willow Lodge Newton Lane Newton Valence Alton GU34 3NA keithbiggs63@googlemail.com
Cardiff Probate Registry of Wales	3rd Floor Cardiff Magistrates' Court Fitzalan Place Cardiff CF24 0RZ 029 2047 4373

Department for Work and Pensions Debt Management contact centre	Contact Centre Bradford (RFE) PO Box 175 Micheldean GL17 0XH 0800 916 0647 0800 916 0651 (textphone)
Disability Living Allowance	Contact details available at www.gov.uk/disability-benefits-helpline
Experian	The Sir John Peace Building Experian Way NG2 Business Park Nottingham NG80 1ZZ 0115 941 0888
Foreign and Commonwealth Office Legalisation Office	PO Box 6255 Milton Keynes MK10 1XX DX 310701 Milton Keynes 03700 00 22 44 legalisationenquiries@fco.gov.uk
General Register Office Certificate Services Section	PO Box 2 Southport PR8 2JD 0300 123 1837 certificate.services@gro.gsi.gov.uk
Government Legal Department Bona Vacantia Division	PO Box 2119 Croydon CR90 9QU 020 7210 4700
HM Revenue and Customs Capital Taxes Office	HM Revenue and Customs BX9 1BJ 0300 123 1072

HM Revenue and Customs Inheritance Tax and Probate	HM Revenue and Customs BX9 1BJ 0300 123 1072
HM Revenue and Customs Northern Ireland Corporate Tax Office Custom House	Custom House Square Belfast BT1 3ET 03000 599 000 or 03000 599 001
Leeds District Probate Registry	York House 31 York Place Leeds LS1 2BA DX 26451 Leeds Park Square 0113 389 6133
London Stock Exchange Historic Price Service	Interactive data Fitzroy House 13–17 Epworth Street London EC2A 4DL 020 7825 8300 NB This address should only be used by people who cannot use the online service at www.londonstock.exchange.com or who need dates pre-June 1999.
National Savings & Investments	Glasgow G58 1SB 08000 560585
Office of the Public Guardian	PO Box 16185 Birmingham B2 2WH 0300 456 0300
Pensions and Overseas Benefits Directorate	Tyneview Park Newcastle Upon Tyne NE98 1BA 0845 301 3011

Personal Independence Payment	Contact details available at www.gov.uk/disability-benefits-helpline
Principal Registry of the Family Division London Probate Department	7th Floor 42–49 High Holborn First Avenue House Holborn London WC1V 6NP DX 160011 Kingsway 7 0300 123 1072
Shares and Assets Valuation	HM Revenue and Customs BX9 1BJ 0300 123 1082
Treasury Solicitor	1 Kemble Street London WC2B 4TS

Appendix C

Specimen Forms

Affidavits

C1 AFFIDAVIT OF CONDITION OF WILL OR OF ALTERATIONS TO WILL

In the High Court of Justice

Family Division

[Principal/(*place*) District Probate] Registry

In the Estate of (*name of deceased*), Deceased

I, (*insert the full name, address and occupation or description of the deponent*) make oath and say that:

(1) I am (*insert title to grant, e.g. 'the sole executor'; 'one of the residuary legatees and devisees'*) named in the last Will and Testament of (*insert the deceased's full name and last permanent address*) deceased the said Will being dated the ... day of ... 20... and now produced to me marked ... and having perused the said Will and in particular observed (*describe the circumstances of the finding of the Will and its then condition together with (if known) an explanation for its condition. If the Will has been damaged since being found, set out details of how the damage occurred. If the Will contains unauthenticated alterations this affidavit may need supplementing by evidence from a witness to the Will with knowledge of the alteration at execution*).

(2) The said Will is now, in all respects, in the same condition as when found by me as aforesaid.

(*If another document was attached but subsequently removed, add a further paragraph dealing with the attachment, the nature of it and its removal.*)

Sworn by the above-named deponent ...

at (*place*) on (*date*)

Before me, (*name*) A Commissioner for Oaths/Solicitor.

C2 AFFIDAVIT OF SEARCH FOR WILL

In the High Court of Justice *(etc. as in Form C1)*

I, (*insert the full name, address and occupation or description of the deponent*) make oath and say that:

(1) I am (*insert title to grant, e.g. 'the sole executor'; 'one of the residuary legatees and devisees'*) named in the last Will and Testament of (*insert the deceased's full name and last permanent address*) deceased, the said Will [being undated/being incompletely dated/dated the ... day of ... 20...] being now produced to me and marked ...

(2) I have made all possible searches and enquiries for any other Will including a search of the home of the deceased and of all places where it is likely that he kept his important papers or valuable personal belongings.

(3) I have been unable to discover any testamentary document other than the said Will.

(4) I have made enquiries of (*insert details of the enquiries made, e.g. of solicitors, bankers, accountants, relatives or friends who might have been entrusted with the original Will*).

(5) I believe the deceased died without having left any Will or testamentary document other than the said Will referred to above.

Sworn *(etc. as in Form C1)*

C3 AFFIDAVIT OF HANDWRITING

In the High Court of Justice *(etc. as in Form C1)*

I, (*insert the full name, address and occupation or description of the deponent)* make oath and say that:

(1) I am (*insert the relationship of the deponent to the deceased, e.g. 'the brother', 'a friend', 'a work colleague'*) of ... deceased. I [worked with the deceased for many years (*or as may be*)] and frequently received correspondence from him and saw him sign his name to documents so that I am well acquainted with his handwriting and signature.

(2) I have examined the paper writing now produced to me and marked ... which purports to contain the last Will and Testament of the deceased dated the ... day of ... 20... and being subscribed thus (*insert details of the signature, e.g. 'I M A Forgery'*).

(3) I believe [the whole of the said Will together with] the signature of (*insert the deceased's name*) to be in the true and proper handwriting of the deceased.

Sworn *(etc. as in Form C1)*

C4 AFFIDAVIT OF DUE EXECUTION

In the High Court of Justice *(etc. as in Form C1)*

I, *(insert the full name, address and occupation or description of the deponent)* make oath and say that:

(1) I am one of the subscribing witnesses to the last Will and Testament of (*insert the deceased's full name and last permanent address*) deceased. *Where the deponent is not a subscribing witness this paragraph should state* 'I was present at the execution of …' *or whatever the situation is enabling the deponent to give evidence of execution. An explanation of why a subscribing witness is not making the affidavit (e.g. his death) must be included*).

(2) [The said Will] [A copy of the said Will] is now produced to me and marked … and dated the … day of … 20… The deceased executed the said Will on (*insert the date the Will was executed. If it is wrongly dated or undated, insert the true date of execution or an estimated date*) by signing his name [at the foot or end thereof as the same now appears] thereon [in the presence of me (*insert the names of the witnesses; if the deponent was a witness, insert the deponent's name first*) and … the other subscribing witness thereto] [both] [all] of us being present at the same time and we then [both] [all] attested the said Will [in the presence of the deceased] [in the presence of … [who have predeceased the deceased] [whose whereabouts are unknown]].

(3) [Before the execution of the said Will by the deceased the same was read over to him by (*insert the name of the witness or other person who read over the Will*) and at the time he seemed perfectly to understand the same and its contents.]

(4) [The deceased died a (*insert status, e.g. widower without issue, parent, brother, sister of the whole blood or any other person entitled in priority to share in the estate by virtue of any enactment*) and that I am (*insert relationship to the deceased*) being one of the persons entitled to the deceased's estate if he had died intestate and that (*insert the names of the other persons entitled to share; if none, delete 'one of the persons' and insert 'the only person'*) are all *sui juris* and have consented to the admission of the said Will to proof without further proof of execution as appears from the consents now produced to and marked by me …].

(5) [The deceased executed the said Will on the date stated thereon by signing his name at the foot or end thereof as the same now appears in the presence of me and … [both] [all] of us being present at the same time and that after the deceased had signed we attested and subscribed the said Will in the presence of the deceased but that (*insert the name(s) of the other subscribing witness(es)*) and I signed our names above that of the deceased because there was insufficient space for us to sign below the deceased's signature.]

(6) [The deceased executed his last Will on the date stated thereon by acknowledging his signature as the same now appears thereon to be his signature in the presence of me and (*insert the name(s) of the other subscribing witness(es)*) both of us being present at the same time by indicating his signature on the said Will and asking us to witness his signature and we then attested and subscribed the said Will in the presence of the deceased.]

Sworn *(etc. as in Form C1)*

C5 AFFIDAVIT OF EXECUTOR'S IDENTITY

In the High Court of Justice *(etc. as in Form C1)*

I, (*insert the full name, address and occupation or description of the deponent*) make oath and say that:

(1) (*Insert the deceased's full name and last permanent address*) deceased, died on the ... day of ... 20... having made and duly executed his last Will and Testament dated the ... day of ... 20..., wherein he appointed (*insert the name of the executor as it appears in the Will*) as [his sole executor] [one of his executors].

(2) I was at the date of execution of the said Will living at (*insert the address*) [and was the only person of that name living at that address at the time (*or as may be*)].

(3) The deceased told me he had appointed me as his executor.

(4) [I am sometimes known] [The deceased always referred to me] as (*insert the name appearing in the Will*).

Sworn *(etc. as in Form C1)*

C6 AFFIDAVIT OF ALIAS

In the High Court of Justice *(etc. as in Form C1)*

I, (*insert the full name, address and occupation or description of the deponent*) make oath and say that:

(1) [(*insert the deceased's true name*) otherwise (*insert the alias name(s)*) of (*insert the deceased's last permanent address*)] died on the ... day of ... 20... [having made and duly executed his last Will and Testament dated the ... day of ... 20... and thereof appointed me (*insert the deponent's name and capacity, e.g. 'one of the executors', or the deponent's relationship to the deceased*).

(2) [I am the lawful son (*or as may be*) of [(*insert the deceased's true name*) otherwise (*insert the alias name(s)*) of (*insert the deceased's last permanent address*)] deceased who died on the ... day of ... 20... intestate].

(3) [The true name of the deceased was (*insert the deceased's true name*).]

(4) [The deceased made and executed his said Will in the name of (*insert the alias name(s)*)].

(5) [The deceased held (*identify the asset(s) held in the alias name*) in the name of (*insert the alias name(s)*)].

In the circumstances it is desired that the grant should issue in the name of (*insert the deceased's true name*) otherwise (*insert the alias name(s)*).

Sworn *(etc. as in Form C1)*

C7 AFFIDAVIT IN SUPPORT OF APPLICATION FOR LEAVE TO SWEAR DEATH

In the High Court of Justice *(etc. as in Form C1)*

I, (*insert the full name, address and occupation or description of the deponent*) make oath and say that:

(1) (*insert the full name, address, occupation or description, and age or date of birth, of the presumed deceased*)

(2) The presumed deceased was last seen alive on the ... day of ... 20... (*Where death is alleged to have occurred in a common disaster, e.g. in an air accident, details of the presumed deceased's being aboard and the view taken by the airline's insurers should be included; reports of rescue services (if any) should be exhibited or put on separate affidavit, as should any supporting evidence by other persons. Insert details of the time and place at which the presumed deceased was last seen and by whom; if known, include the deceased's reason for being in that place. Describe inquiries made by the police or any other official body, and of advertisements inserted in newspapers with a view to tracing the presumed deceased and the results. Insert details of any letters and/or telephone calls received from the presumed deceased since his disappearance. Exhibit any relevant correspondence, reports, newspapers or other documents.*)

(3) The presumed deceased died [testate] [intestate]. (*If the presumed deceased died testate the Will should be lodged with this affidavit. If he died intestate, or the residue of the estate is not fully disposed of by the Will, insert the names of persons entitled to share in the estate, or in the undisposed of residue, and their relationship to the presumed deceased.*)

(4) The presumed deceased had (*insert details of all insurance policies on the presumed deceased's life and recite the views of the insurers, exhibiting relevant correspondence*).

(5) The presumed deceased had accounts with (*insert the names of the bank(s) and/or building society(ies) with which the presumed deceased held accounts*) and that these accounts have not been used since the presumed deceased disappeared. (*Insert the amounts in the accounts, and details of all assets which comprise the estate.*)

(6) I believe the presumed deceased died on or since (*insert the date of the presumed death*).

Sworn *(etc. as in Form C1)*

C8 AFFIDAVIT IN SUPPORT OF APPLICATION UNDER SECTION 116 OF THE SENIOR COURTS ACT 1981 TO PASS OVER RIGHT TO GRANT

In the High Court of Justice *(etc. as in Form C1)*

I, (*insert the full name, address and occupation or description of the deponent*) make oath and say that:

(1) (*insert the deceased's full name and last permanent address*) deceased, died on the ... day of ... 20... [having made and duly executed his last Will and Testament dated the ... day of ... 20... [wherein he appointed (*insert the name of the executor*) his sole executor]] [[intestate] a bachelor without issue or parent leaving ... his brother of the whole blood (*or as may be*).]

(2) The said (*insert the name of the executor or person entitled on intestacy, or as may be*) cannot now be traced. Despite extensive enquiries, his whereabouts cannot now be determined (*or as may be, giving the reason for passing over the right of the person entitled to the grant*).

(3) I am the (*insert the relationship of the applicant to the deceased, if any, and all other relevant information to enable the court to determine whether the applicant is a proper person to be granted administration*).

(4) The gross value of the estate amounts to £ ...

(5) No life or minority interest arises in the estate.

I apply for an order under section 116 of the Senior Courts Act 1981 directing that letters of administration be granted to me.

Sworn *(etc. as in Form C1)*

C9 AFFIDAVIT IN SUPPORT OF APPLICATION TO PROVE A COPY WILL

In the High Court of Justice *(etc. as in Form C1)*

I, (*insert the full name, address and occupation or description of the deponent*) make oath and say that:

(1) (*insert the deceased's full name and last permanent address*) deceased, died on the ... day of ... 20..., domiciled in England and Wales having made and duly executed his last Will and Testament dated the ... day of ... 20... [with ... codicil[s] thereto].

(2) Following execution the Will was [retained by his solicitors and there is an entry in their wills register of this fact] [deposited with ... Bank] [handed to the deceased].

(3) Following the death of the deceased the original of the said [Will] [and/or codicil] cannot be found.

(4) (*Insert details of the loss of the original document. Where the Will had been in the testator's possession immediately before death, include evidence to rebut the presumption that the testator revoked it by destruction.*)

I produce herewith marked ... a [carbon copy] [copy draft] [photocopy] [reconstruction] (*where no copy of the Will is available and the application is to prove a reconstruction, set out the evidence to establish that the proposed reconstruction is an accurate reflection of the original Will as executed*).

I request the court to make an order under and pursuant to rule 54 of the Non-Contentious Probate Rules 1987 admitting the said copy Will to proof; the grant to be limited until the original Will or a more authentic copy be proved. (*This is the usual limitation, but the court may impose a further or different limitation if the circumstances so warrant.*)

Sworn *(etc. as in Form C1)*

C10 AFFIDAVIT IN SUPPORT OF APPLICATION FOR GRANT OF ADMINISTRATION LIMITED UNTIL WILL PROVED

In the High Court of Justice *(etc. as in Form C1)*

I, (*insert the full name, address and occupation or description of the deponent*) make oath and say:

(1) That (*insert the deceased's full name and last permanent address*) died on the ... day of ... 20... domiciled in England and Wales.

(2) That the deceased is [known] [believed] to have made and executed a Will on [or about] the ... day of ... 20... (*insert the reason for the belief that there was a Will and the date, or approximate date, of its execution*) but following his death neither the original nor any copy can be found. There is no, or insufficient, evidence of the content or tenor of the Will to create a reconstruction. (*Insert details of the enquiries made to find the Will and/or a copy.*)

I request the court to order that letters of administration be granted to [me] [...] the said grant to be limited until the original Will or an authentic copy be proved.

Sworn *(etc. as in Form C1)*

C11 AFFIDAVIT IN SUPPORT OF APPLICATION TO RECTIFY A WILL

In the High Court of Justice *(etc. as in Form C1)*

I, (*insert the full name, address and occupation or description of the deponent*) make oath and say that:

(1) (*insert the deceased's full name and last permanent address*) deceased, died on the ... day of ... 20... having made and duly executed his last Will and Testament dated the ... day of ... 20... [with a codicil thereto dated the ... day of ... 20...] a copy of which is exhibited hereto marked ... [and therein named me sole executor] [and that I am one of the partners in the firm of ..., Solicitors which firm drew up the said Will [and codicil]] and that I am the draftsman of the said Will [and codicil]].

(2) [[In the said Will the appointment of executors [has been omitted] [is defective (*insert details of the defect*)] [Clause ... has been omitted from the said Will] [Clause ... of the said Will was not intended by the testator to be revoked by the said codicil.]]

[Since the sealing of the grant of probate on the ... day of ... 20... it has been discovered that the original last Will and Testament of the deceased dated the ... day of ... 20... is defective in that (*insert details of the defect; this paragraph is to be completed where rectification is sought after the Will has been proved*).]

(3) It is clear from the [[draft] [Will] [codicil]] [exhibited hereto and marked ... [instructions taken from the deceased] that the words ... should be [inserted] [excluded] [amended to read ....]

(4) The error arose because (*insert how the error occurred, e.g. clerical error or failure to understand instructions*).

(5) [No one is prejudiced by the rectification sought.] [[The consent[s]] [The reply/ies to notice] of ..., being the persons prejudiced by the rectification, are exhibited hereto and marked ...].] (*Rule 55 requires notice to be given to persons prejudiced by the rectification, unless the court directs otherwise.*)

I request an order be made to rectify the said [Will] [codicil] accordingly pursuant to section 20 of the Administration of Justice Act 1982.

Sworn *(etc. as in Form C1)*

C12 AFFIDAVIT IN SUPPORT OF APPLICATION FOR INTERPRETATION OF A WILL

In the High Court of Justice *(etc. as in Form C1)*

I, (*insert the full name, address and occupation or description of the deponent*) make oath and say that:

(1) (*insert the deceased's full name and last permanent address*) deceased, died on the ... day of ... 20... having made and duly executed his last Will and Testament dated the ... day of ... 20... [with a codicil thereto dated the ... day of ... 20...] [and therein named me sole executor] [and that I am one of the partners in the firm of ..., Solicitors] [which firm drew up the said Will [and codicil] and that I am the draftsman of the said Will [and codicil]].

(2) [In the said Will the appointment of executors is defective because (*describe the defect in the appointment clause; the testator's intention must be clear and unequivocal and the clause must fail to give effect to that intention*).] [The gift of ... is meaningless or ambiguous because (*describe how the gift fails to carry out the testator's intention. The jurisdiction of a district judge or registrar to construe a gift is limited to establishing title to the grant through that gift*).]

I request the court to interpret the Will under section 21 of the Administration of Justice Act 1982 accordingly to give effect to the testator's intention.

Sworn *(etc. as in Form C1)*

C13 AFFIDAVIT IN SUPPORT OF APPLICATION FOR THE APPOINTMENT OF A PERSON TO TAKE ADMINISTRATION FOR THE USE AND BENEFIT OF A PERSON WHO LACKS CAPACITY WITHIN THE MEANING OF THE MENTAL CAPACITY ACT 2005

In the High Court of Justice *(etc. as in Form C1)*

I, (*insert the full name, address and occupation or description of the deponent*) make oath and say that:

(insert the deceased's full name and last permanent address) deceased, died on the ... day of ... 20... domiciled in England and Wales [having made and duly executed his last Will and Testament dated the ... day of ... 20... [and therein appointed ... his sole executor and residuary legatee and devisee]] [intestate leaving ..., the only person entitled to his estate (*insert the title and clearing of the order of priority under rule 22 down to the incapable person*)] who suffers an impairment of or a disturbance in the functioning of [his] [her] mind or brain as a result of which [he] [she] is unable to make a decision for [himself] [herself] in relation to the application for a grant of representation and subsequent administration of the estate of the deceased and lacks capacity to manage [his] [her] property and affairs within the meaning of the Mental Capacity Act 2005.

(1) No one has been authorised by the Court of Protection to apply for letters of administration [(with Will annexed)] of the estate of the deceased and there is no one acting under a registered [enduring] [lasting] power of attorney.

(2) I am the (*insert the relationship of the deponent to the deceased and/or whether the applicant is, or intends to become, the receiver for the patient*).

(3) I have given notice of the proposed application to the Office of the Public Guardian pursuant to rule 35(5). (*Notice of the application (by letter) must be given to the Office of the Public Guardian; its acknowledgement of the notice must be exhibited to the affidavit or lodged with the application for a grant.*)

I exhibit hereto (*exhibit medical evidence to establish the incapacity. A letter or report from the patient's GP is usually sufficient, or, if the patient is in an institution, a certificate by a responsible medical officer of the institution*).

I apply to the court for an order directing that letters of administration [(with Will annexed)] be granted to me under and pursuant to rule 35(4) of the Non-Contentious Probate Rules 1987 for the use and benefit of the said ... and until further representation be granted.

Sworn *(etc. as in Form C1)*

C14 AFFIDAVIT IN SUPPORT OF APPLICATION FOR THE APPOINTMENT OF PERSONS TO TAKE ADMINISTRATION FOR THE USE AND BENEFIT OF A MINOR

In the High Court of Justice *(etc. as in Form C1)*

We, (*insert the full names, addresses and occupations or description of the deponents*) make oath and say that:

(1) (*insert the deceased's full name and last permanent address*) deceased, died on the ... day of ... 20... domiciled in England and Wales,[[having made his last Will and Testament in which he appointed ... the executor] [and/or residuary beneficiary]] [intestate] (*insert status, e.g. 'a single man*) leaving ... his daughter and only person entitled to his estate (*or as may be*) who is now a minor aged ... years. [We exhibit hereto marked 'A' a copy of the said will]

(2) [The marriage of the deceased with ... was dissolved by final decree of the ... Court in England and Wales and the deceased did not thereafter remarry or form a civil partnership (*if the decree or order was made by a court outside England and Wales, insert evidence to show that it is capable of recognition under section 46 of the Family Law Act 1986.*)]

(3) [(*Insert the name of the former spouse or other person with parental responsibility*), the person with parental responsibility for the said minor [has renounced administration for the use and benefit of the said minor] [refuses or neglects to apply for letters of administration for the use and benefit of the said minor] [(*or as may be*)] [has consented to this application and we exhibit hereto marked ['A'] *or* ['B'] [*as appropriate*] the consent].]

(4) There is no person [save ...] having parental responsibility for the said minor under section 2(1), 2(1A) (2) (2A) or 4 or 4(ZA) of or paragraph 4 or 6 of Schedule 14 to the Children Act 1989 or by virtue of an adoption order made under the Adoption and Children Act 2002 and there is no person appointed or deemed to be appointed guardian of the said minor under section 5 or paragraph 12, 13 or 14 of Schedule 14 to the Children Act 1989.

(5) The said minor has not been made a ward of court and there are no proceedings pending under the Court's inherent jurisdiction nor have there been or are there pending any proceedings in any court to which the Children Act 1989 applies. (*If there have been proceedings, insert details of them and of any order(s) made.*)

(6) We are (*set out the relationship, if any, to the minor child and/or the deceased and any other evidence relevant to the application*).

(7) The said minor resides at (*insert the minor's current address and who presently cares for him*).

(8) The gross value of the estate is £ … and the net value, £ …

We apply for an order under rule 32(2) of the Non-Contentious Probate Rules 1987 directing that letters of administration be granted to us for the use and benefit of the said minor and until [he] [she] shall attain the age of eighteen years.

Sworn *(etc. as in Form C1)*

C15 AFFIDAVIT TO ESTABLISH VALIDITY OF WILL: FOREIGN DOMICILE

In the High Court of Justice *(etc. as in Form C1)*

I, (*insert the full name, address and occupation or description of the deponent*) make oath and say that:

(1) I am [the sole executor] [one of the executors] [(*or as may be*)] named in the [last Will and Testament] [Codicil] bearing date the ... day of ... 20... of (*insert the deceased's full name and last permanent address*) who died on the ... day of ... 20..., the said [Will] [Codicil] being now produced to and marked by me ...

(2) [The said [Will] [Codicil] was executed in (*insert the country, or where the state or territories of that country have separate systems of law, the state or territory*)].

[At the time of execution of the said [Will] [Codicil] the deceased was domiciled in or had his habitual residence in (*insert the country, or where the state or territories of that country have separate systems of law, the state or territory*)].

[At [the time of execution of the said [Will] [Codicil]] [the date of his death] the deceased was a national of (*insert the country, or where the state or territories of that country have separate systems of law, the state or territory*)].

(3) Of the systems of internal law in force in (*insert the country, or where the state or territories of that country have separate systems of law, the state or territory*) relating to the formal validity of Wills at the time of execution of the said [Will] [Codicil] or at the time of the deceased's death the deceased was most closely associated with the ... internal system of law by reason of (*insert the basis for the connection, e.g. residence, religion, place of birth, ownership of property. To validate a Will in 'English form' where the deceased was a British national, it must be shown that he was most closely connected with the system of law in England and Wales*).

(4) The said [Will] [Codicil] is therefore valid under section 1 of the Wills Act 1963 and admissible to proof in England and Wales.

Sworn *(etc. as in Form C1)*

C16 AFFIDAVIT TO ESTABLISH VALIDITY OF WILL AND BENEFICIAL ENTITLEMENT: FOREIGN LAW

In the High Court of Justice *(etc. as in Form C1)*

I, [an advocate (*or as may be*)] make oath and say that:

(1) I am fully conversant with the laws and constitutions of (*insert the country, or where the state or territories of that country have separate systems of law, the state or territory*) and [practised] as an [advocate (*or as may be*)] in that [country] [state] [province] for ... years. (*Insert any other qualifications to establish the deponent's knowledge of the law concerned.*)

(2) I am informed and verily believe that (*insert the deceased's full name and last permanent address*) deceased died on the ... day of ... 20..., domiciled in (*insert the country, or where the state or territories of that country have separate systems of law, the state or territory*) [having made his last Will and Testament dated the ... day of ... 19...] [intestate].

(3) I have referred to the [official] [notarial] [certified] copy of the last Will and Testament of the deceased, which is now produced to and marked by me ... and I say that the said Will was made in conformity with and is valid by the said laws and constitutions. (*Where the Wills Act 1963 is relied on, recite the law which validated the Will in the place where the deceased died domiciled.*)

(4) [In accordance with the said laws and constitutions the original of the said Will is deposited [at] [with] ... and cannot be removed from such custody. The said copy produced to and marked ... by me is acceptable as evidence of the contents of the original Will in the Courts of (*insert the country, or where the state or territories of that country have separate systems of law, the state or territory*).]

(5) [(*Name of place of domicile*) is not a country which requires court intervention before the estate of a deceased person can be administered.] [No one has been entrusted with the administration of the estate of the deceased by the court having jurisdiction at the place where he died domiciled.]

(6) In the circumstances, I say that (*insert the name(s) of the person(s) beneficially entitled to share the estate*) [is] [are] beneficially entitled to [share in] the said estate by the said laws and constitutions of (*insert the country, or where the state or territories of that country have separate systems of law, the state or territory*).

Sworn *(etc. as in Form C1)*

C17 AFFIDAVIT IN SUPPORT OF APPLICATION FOR A SUBPOENA FOR THE PRODUCTION OF A TESTAMENTARY DOCUMENT

In the High Court of Justice *(etc. as in Form C1)*

I, (*insert the full name, address and occupation or description of the deponent*) make oath and say that:

(1) (*insert the deceased's full name and last permanent address*) deceased, died on the ... day of ... 20... domiciled in England and Wales having made and duly executed his last Will and Testament dated the ... day of ... 20..., and therein appointed ... his executor[s] and appointed me [one of] the residuary legatee[s] and devisee[s].

(2) The said Will is now in the possession, custody or power of (*insert the name(s) of the person(s) having custody of the Will*) and that [he] [she] [they] [has] [have] neglected or declined to prove the said Will or renounce probate thereof [(*or as may be*)].

(3) The said (*insert the name(s) of the person(s) having custody of the Will*) reside[s] at ... [respectively].

I request that the said Will be brought in to the [Principal] [... District Probate] Registry in order that I may prove the same or otherwise act as I may be advised.

Sworn *(etc. as in Form C1)*

C18 AFFIDAVIT OF SERVICE OF WARNING

In the High Court of Justice *(etc. as in Form C1)*

I, (*insert the full name, address and occupation or description of the deponent*) make oath and say that:

On the ... day of ... 20... I duly served (*insert the full name of the caveator or his solicitors*) with a true copy of the warning now produced to and marked by me ... [by delivering to and leaving the same with (*insert name of person served*) [a clerk in the firm of ...]] [before the hour of 4 in the afternoon] [before the hour of 12 noon on a Saturday] [by sending the same by [prepaid] [registered] [recorded delivery] post to the address for service given in the caveat] [by leaving the same at the ... Document Exchange for box number ... at ... Exchange] [by leaving the same at the ... Document Exchange for transmission to the ... Document Exchange, box number ...] included in the address for service given in the caveat.

Sworn *(etc. as in Form C1)*

C19 AFFIDAVIT OF SERVICE OF CITATION

In the High Court of Justice *(etc. as in Form C1)*

I, (*insert the full name, address and occupation or description of the deponent*) make oath and say that:

(1) I served *(insert the full name, address and occupation or description of the citee*) with a true copy of the citation issued out of the (*insert the name of the registry which issued the citation*) by delivering to and leaving the same with him. A sealed copy of the citation is exhibited hereto marked ...

(2) I established the identity of the person served by (*recite how identity was established, e.g. the citee identified himself by producing his driving licence*).

Sworn *(etc. as in Form C1)*

C20 AFFIDAVIT IN SUPPORT OF APPLICATION FOR AN ORDER AMENDING A GRANT OF REPRESENTATION

In the High Court of Justice *(etc. as in Form C1)*

I, (*insert the full name, address and occupation or description of the deponent*) make oath and say that:

(1) On the ... day of ... 20... a grant of [probate] [letters of administration [(with Will annexed)]] of the estate of (*insert the deceased's full name and last permanent address*) deceased [was] granted at the [Principal] [... District Probate] Registry to me this deponent [the sole executor named in the Will of the deceased] [the residuary legatee and devisee named in the Will of the deceased] [the lawful widow and the only person entitled to share in the estate of the deceased (*or insert the grantee's title to the grant*)].

(2) In the said grant of [probate] [letters of administration [(with Will annexed)]] (*recite the error or omission appearing in the grant*) is stated whereas (*insert what should have appeared in the grant*) should have appeared.

(3) The error arose (*explain how the error or omission arose*).

I apply for an order that the said grant of [probate] [letters of administration [(with Will annexed)]] be amended by (*insert the correction sought*).

Sworn *(etc. as in Form C1)*

C21 AFFIDAVIT IN SUPPORT OF APPLICATION FOR AN ORDER REVOKING A GRANT OF REPRESENTATION

In the High Court of Justice *(etc. as in Form C1)*

I, (*insert the full name, address and occupation or description of the deponent*) make oath and say that:

(1) On the ... day of ... 20... a grant of [probate] [letters of administration [(with Will annexed)]] of the estate of (*insert the deceased's full name and last permanent address*) deceased [was] granted at the [Principal] [... District Probate] Registry to me this deponent [the sole executor named in the Will of the deceased] [the residuary legatee and devisee named in the Will of the deceased] [the sister of the whole blood and the only person entitled to share in the estate of the deceased (*or insert the grantee's title to the grant*)].

(2) The said grant of [probate] [letters of administration [(with Will annexed)]] issued on the basis that [the Will dated ... was the last Will of the deceased] [the deceased died intestate a bachelor without issue] (*or as may be*) whereas [the deceased had in fact made a later Will dated ...] [was married to ... who remained his lawful wife] [the grantee died before the grant of ... issued] (*or as may be*).

I hereby apply for an order that the said grant of [probate] [letters of administration [(with Will annexed)]] issued on the ... day of ... 20... be revoked and declared null and void.

Sworn *(etc. as in Form C1)*

C22 CAVEAT

The Non-Contentious Probate Rules 1987, Schedule 1, Form 3

In the High Court of Justice *(etc. as in Form C1)*

Let no grant be sealed in the estate of (*insert the full name and address of the deceased. The deceased's names as they appear in the death certificate should be given; see Practice Direction 22 March 2002 [2002] 1 WLR 1303. Failure to give the full true name may mean that an application for a grant will not be matched to the caveat. Where there is doubt about the full true name, give alternative names or spellings, e.g. 'Frederick' or 'Frederic', 'William' or 'Bill'. Similarly, if the date of death is not known, insert a span, e.g. 'between the 1st and 31st July 2006'*) deceased, who died on the ... day of ... 20... without notice to (*insert the name of the party by whom or on whose behalf the caveat is entered*).

Dated the ... day of ... 20...

Signed ... (*to be signed by the caveator's solicitor or by the caveator if acting in person.*)

whose address for service is ...

[Solicitor for the said ...]

C23 WARNING TO CAVEATOR

The Non-Contentious Probate Rules 1987, Schedule 1, Form 4

In the High Court of Justice

Family Division

The Leeds District Probate Registry

In the Estate of …, Deceased

To ... of ... a party who has entered a caveat in the estate of ... deceased.

You have eight days (starting with the day on which this warning was served on you):

(i) to enter an appearance either in person or by your solicitor or probate practitioner at the Leeds District Probate Registry, York House, 31 York Place, Leeds LS1 2BA setting out what interest you have in the estate of the above-named ... of ... deceased contrary to that of the party at whose instance this warning is issued; or

(ii) if you have no contrary interest but wish to show cause against the sealing of a grant to such party, to issue and serve a summons for directions by a District Judge of the Principal Registry or a Registrar of a District Probate Registry.

If you fail to do either of these the court may proceed to issue a grant of probate or administration in the said estate notwithstanding your caveat.

Dated the … day of … 20…

Issued at the instance of (*set out the name and interest (including the date of the Will, if any, under which the interest arises) of the party warning, the name of his solicitor and the address for service. If the party warning is acting in person, this must be stated*).

C24 APPEARANCE TO WARNING

The Non-Contentious Probate Rules 1987, Schedule 1, Form 5

In the High Court of Justice

Family Division

The Leeds District Probate Registry

In the Estate of ..., Deceased

Caveat number ... dated the ... day of ... 20...

Full name and address of deceased: ...

Full name and address of person warning: ...

(set out the interest of the person warning as shown in the warning).

Full name and address of caveator: ...

(set out the interest of the caveator, stating the date of the Will (if any) under which such interest arises).

Enter an appearance for the above-named caveator in this matter.

Dated the ... day of ... 20...

Signed ... [Solicitor for the said ...][... in person]

whose address for service is ...

C25 CITATION TO TAKE PROBATE AGAINST AN EXECUTOR WHO HAS INTERMEDDLED

In the High Court of Justice *(etc. as in Form C1)*

ELIZABETH THE SECOND by the Grace of God, of the United Kingdom of Great Britain and Northern Ireland and of the Other Realms and Territories, Queen, Head of the Commonwealth, Defender of the Faith.

To (*insert the name of the intermeddling executor – the citee*).

TAKE NOTICE that (*insert the name of the beneficiary – the citor*) has stated in an affidavit sworn on the ... day of ... 20... that (*insert the name and address of the deceased*) died on the ... day of ... 20... domiciled in England and Wales, having made and duly executed his last Will and Testament dated the ... day of ... 20... now remaining in [the Principal Registry of the Family Division of the High Court of Justice] [the ... District Probate Registry], that you the said (*insert the name of the citee*) are appointed sole executor in that Will, that the said (*insert the name of the citor*) is interested in the estate of the said deceased under the said Will and that you the said (*insert the name of the citee*) have intermeddled in the estate of the said deceased.

NOW THIS IS TO COMMAND YOU the said (*insert the name of the citee*) that within eight days after service hereof on you, inclusive of the day of such service, you do cause an appearance to be entered in the [Principal Registry of the Family Division, First Avenue House, 42–49 High Holborn, London WC1V 6NP] [the ... District Probate Registry at ...] and show cause why you should not be ordered to take probate of the said Will.

Dated the ... day of ... 20...

Extracted by ... of ..., Solicitor

Signed ... District Judge/Registrar

C26 CITATION AGAINST EXECUTOR TO WHOM POWER WAS RESERVED, TO ACCEPT OR REFUSE PROBATE

In the High Court of Justice *(etc. as in Form C1)*

ELIZABETH THE SECOND *(etc. as in Form C25)*

To (*insert the full name and address of the executor cited – the citee*).

TAKE NOTICE that (*insert the name and address of the citor*) has stated in an affidavit sworn on the ... day of ... 20... that probate of the Will of (*insert the name and address of the deceased*) was on the ... day of ... 20... granted by our High Court of Justice at [the Principal Registry of the Family Division of the High Court of Justice] [the ... District Probate Registry] thereof to (*insert the name of the proving executor*) one of the executors named therein, power of making a like grant being reserved to (*insert the name of the citee*) the other executor named therein, that the said (*insert the name of the proving executor*) died on the ... day of ... 20... leaving part of the estate of the said deceased unadministered and that on the ... day of ... 20... probate of the Will of the said (*insert the name of the proving executor*) was granted by this court at the said Registry to (*insert the name of the sole executor*) the sole executor thereof.

NOW THIS IS TO COMMAND YOU the said (*insert the name of the citee*) that within eight days after service hereof on you, inclusive of the day of such service, you do cause an appearance to be entered in [The Principal Registry of the Family Division, First Avenue House, 42–49 High Holborn, London WC1V 6NP] [the ... District Probate Registry at ...] and accept or refuse probate of the said Will of the said ... deceased.

AND TAKE FURTHER TAKE NOTICE that, in default of your so appearing and accepting or extracting probate of the said Will, your rights as such executor will wholly cease, and the representation to the said ... deceased will devolve as if you had not been appointed executor.

Dated the ... day of ... 20...

Extracted by ... of ..., Solicitor

Signed ... District Judge/Registrar

C27 CITATION TO ACCEPT OR REFUSE A GRANT

In the High Court of Justice *(etc. as in Form C1)*

ELIZABETH THE SECOND *(etc. as in Form C25)*

To (*insert the full name and address of the person cited*)

Whereas it appears by the affidavit of (*insert the name and address of the citor*) sworn on the ... day of ... 20... that (*insert the name and address of the deceased*) died on the ... day of ... 20...

[having made and duly executed his last Will and Testament dated the ... day of ... 20... [now remaining in [the Principal Registry of the Family Division of the High Court of Justice] [the ... District Probate Registry]] and (*insert the title to the grant*) [thereof appointed you the sole executor] [wherein he named you the residuary legatee and devisee.]] *or*

[intestate a [widow] [widower] (*insert any further clearings*) or [any other person entitled in priority to share in the estate by virtue of any enactment] leaving (*insert the name of the citee*) the lawful (*insert the relationship to the deceased*) and [one of] (*or as may be*) the person[s] entitled to share in the estate of the said deceased.]

NOW THIS IS TO COMMAND YOU the said (*insert the name of the citee*) that within eight days after service hereof on you, inclusive of the day of such service, you do cause an appearance to be entered in the [Principal Registry of the Family Division, First Avenue House, 42–49 High Holborn, London WC1V 6NP] [the ... District Probate Registry at ...] and accept or refuse [a grant of probate of the said Will] [letters of administration [(with Will annexed)]] of all the estate which by law devolves to and vests in the personal representatives of the said deceased or show cause why a grant should not be granted to (*insert the name of the citor*).

AND TAKE NOTICE that in default of your appearing and accepting and extracting [a grant of probate of the said Will] [letters of administration [(with Will annexed)]] our said Court will proceed to grant letters of administration [(with Will annexed)] to the said (*insert the name of the citor*) notwithstanding your absence.

Dated the ... day of ... 20...

Extracted by ... of ..., Solicitor

Signed ... District Judge/Registrar

C28 CITATION TO PROPOUND PAPER WRITING

In the High Court of Justice *(etc. as in Form C1)*

ELIZABETH THE SECOND *(etc. as in Form C25)*

To (*insert the full name and address of the person cited*).

Whereas it appears by the affidavit of (*insert the name of the citor*) sworn on the … day of … 20… that (*insert the name and address of the deceased*) died on the … day of … 20… domiciled in England and Wales a [widow] [widower] leaving the said (*insert the name of the citor*) his (*insert the relationship to the deceased*) and the only person entitled to his estate and that the said deceased left a certain paper writing dated the … day of … 20… purporting to be a Will now remaining in [the Principal Registry of the Family Division of the High Court of Justice] [the ... District Probate Registry], whereby he appointed you the said (*insert the name of the citee*) sole executor and residuary legatee and devisee.

NOW THIS IS TO COMMAND YOU the said (*insert the name of the citee*) that within eight days after service hereof on you, inclusive of the day of such service, you do cause an appearance to be entered in the [Principal Registry of the Family Division, First Avenue House, 42–49 High Holborn, London WC1V 6NP] [the ... District Probate Registry at ...] and propound the said paper writing should you think it in your interest to do so, or to show cause why letters of administration of all the estate which by law devolves to and vests in the personal representative of the said deceased should not be granted to the said (*insert the name of the citor*).

AND TAKE NOTICE that in default of your appearing and doing as aforesaid our said Court will proceed to issue a grant of representation of the said estate as if the said purported Will were invalid, notwithstanding your absence.

Dated the … day of … 20…

Extracted by ... of ..., Solicitor

Signed ... District Judge/Registrar

C29 APPEARANCE TO CITATION

The Non-Contentious Probate Rules 1987, Schedule 1, Form 5

In the High Court of Justice *(etc. as in Form C1)*

Caveat number ... dated the ... day of ... 20...

Citation dated the ... day of ... 20...

Full name and address of deceased: ...

Full name and address of citor: ... (*set out the interest of the citor, as shown in the citation*).

Full name and address of person cited: ... (*set out the interest of the person cited, stating the date of the Will (if any) under which such interest arises*).

ENTER AN APPEARANCE for the above-named person cited in this matter.

Dated the ... day of ... 20...

Signed ... [Solicitor for the said ...] [... in person]

whose address for service is ...

C30 CONSENT TO WILL BEING PROVED

In the High Court of Justice *(etc. as in Form C1)*

(1) WHEREAS (*insert the full name and address of the deceased*) died on the … day of … 20… having made and duly executed his last Will and Testament dated the … day of … 20… and in the said Will appointed ... [the sole executor] [the residuary legatee and devisee] thereof.

(2) The following [alterations (*or as may be*)] appear in the said Will namely (*describe the alteration or other apparent irregularity giving rise to the need for consent by those who could be prejudiced*).

(3) (*insert the names of the witnesses*) [are dead] [cannot be found] (*or as may be*).

(4) The said deceased died a (*insert deceased's status, e.g. a widower, clearing kin down to the person(s) entitled to share if the deceased had died intestate)* [or any other person entitled in priority to share in his estate by virtue of any enactment] *(include words in [ ] where no issue survive)* leaving *(insert the names of all persons, and their interests, who would be prejudiced if the Will were to be accepted to proof in its correct form)*. I, (*insert the name of the person consenting*), as a person whose interest is prejudiced by proof of the said Will do hereby give my consent to [probate of the Will] [letters of administration (with Will annexed)] being granted to (*insert the name of the applicant*).

Signed by the said ...

in the presence of ... of ...

the … day of … 20…

C31 CONSENT TO TRUST CORPORATION APPLYING

In the High Court of Justice *(etc. as in Form C1)*

Whereas (*insert the full name and address of the deceased*) died on the … day of … 20… domiciled in England and Wales [intestate (*insert the deceased's status, e.g. a widow*) leaving *(insert the names of the next of kin entitled to share in the estate*) the only person entitled to his estate] [having made and duly executed his last Will and Testament dated the … day of … 20… wherein he named ... sole executor and residuary legatee and devisee].

Now [I] [we], the said (*insert the name(s) of the beneficiary/ies consenting*) hereby consent to letters of administration [with the said Will annexed] of the estate of the said deceased being granted to (*insert the name of the trust corporation*).

Signed by the said ...

in the presence of ... of ...

the … day of … 20…

C32 NOMINATION OF SECOND ADMINISTRATOR, MINORITY INTEREST ARISING

In the High Court of Justice *(etc. as in Form C1)*

Whereas (*insert the full name and address of the deceased*) deceased died on the ... day of ... 20... domiciled in England and Wales intestate (*insert the deceased's status, e.g. 'a widow'*) leaving (*insert the names of the minor(s) entitled to share and their relationship to the deceased, e.g. 'his sons'*) the only person[s] entitled to [share in] his estate.

And whereas the said (*insert the names of the minor(s)*) [is] [are] [a] [minor[s]] aged ... [and ... respectively].

And whereas there is no step-parent, guardian, special guardian, adoption agency or local authority or any other person with parental responsibility for the said minor[s].

Now I, the said (*insert the name of the applicant*) do hereby nominate and appoint (*insert the name and address of the proposed second co-administrator, his relationship to the children and the capacity in which parental responsibility was obtained*) to be my co-administrator in the estate of the said intestate, he being a fit and proper person to act in that capacity.

Signed by the said ...

in the presence of ... of ...

the ... day of ... 20...

C33 NOMINATION OF PERSON BY RESOLUTION TO ACT ON BEHALF OF NON-TRUST CORPORATION

At the meeting of the (*insert the title of the governing body, e.g. 'board of directors'*) of (*insert the name of the charity, or as may be, the non-trust corporation*) on the … day of … 20… it was resolved that (*insert* either *the name(s) of the person(s) appointed* or *the positions of officers entitled to act by virtue of holding those positions, e.g. secretary, chief executive, legacy officer*) be nominated to act on behalf of … [in all matters relating to the estate of persons in which (*insert the name of the charity, or as may be*) has an interest] [in the estate of … deceased] (*delete as appropriate for general authorisation or for authorisation limited to a specific estate*).

Signed … (*signature of authorising officer, e.g. the company secretary*)

the … day of … 20…

C34 NOTICE OF ELECTION TO REDEEM LIFE INTEREST

(For a life interest to be created, the deceased must have died before 1 October 2014.)

The Non-Contentious Probate Rules 1987, Schedule 1, Form 6

In the High Court of Justice *(etc. as in Form C1)*

Whereas ... of ... died on the ... day of ... 20... [wholly] [partially] intestate leaving [his] [her] lawful [wife] [husband] [civil partner] [and ... lawful issue of the said deceased].

And whereas [probate] [letters of administration] of the estate of the said ... were granted to me the said ...[and to ... of ...] at the ... Probate Registry on the ... day of ... 20...

And whereas [the said ... has ceased to be a personal representative because ...] and I am [now] the sole personal representative.

Now I, the said ... hereby give notice in accordance with section 47A of the Administration of Estates Act 1925 that I elect to redeem the life interest to which I am entitled in the estate of the late ... by retaining £ ..., its capital value, and £ ..., the costs of the transaction.

Dated the ... day of ... 20...

Signed ...

To the Senior District Judge of the Family Division.

C35 NOTICE TO EXECUTOR HAVING POWER RESERVED

In the Estate of ..., Deceased

TAKE NOTICE that (*insert the full name and address of the deceased*) died on the ... day of ... 20... having appointed (*insert the names of all the executors appointed, except where the appointment is of partners in a firm, when 'the partners in the firm of ...' should be inserted*) as executors of his Will, and that (*insert the name(s) of the proving executor(s)*) being [one] [two] [(*or as may be*)] of the executors intend to apply for probate with power reserved to you (*insert the name(s) of the executor(s) to whom power is reserved*).

Signed ...

the ... day of ... 20...

C36 NOTICE OF APPLICATION FOR A STANDING SEARCH

The Non-Contentious Probate Rules 1987, Schedule 1, Form 2

In the High Court of Justice *(etc. as in Form C1)*

[I] [We] apply for the entry of a standing search so that there shall be sent to [me] [us] an office copy of every grant of representation in England and Wales in the estate of (*insert the full name and address of the deceased*).

[Alternative or alias name: (*if the deceased was known by an alternative forename or surname, insert the alternative name(s)*).]

Exact date of death: (*insert the date of death as it appears in the death certificate, or, if not known, a span of dates, e.g. '1st to 7th March 2006'*)

which either has issued not more than twelve months before the entry of this application or issues within six months thereafter.

Signed: ... Name in block letters: ...

Address: ... Reference (if any): ...

The Non-Contentious Probate Rules 1987 are amended with effect from 20 November 2017 (the Non-Contentious Probate (Amendment) Rules 2017) to create a pilot scheme for the delivery of grant applications online. Any such application may only be made at the invitation of the registry. The forms presently required will be replaced by a statement of truth. As this is a pilot scheme by invitation only and, as no Practice Directions have been published to regulate the content of a statement of truth, the text continues to refer to application by oath only.

C37 GENERAL FORM OF OATH FOR EXECUTORS

The Non-Contentious Probate Rules 1987 are amended with effect from 20 November 2017 (the Non-Contentious Probate (Amendment) Rules 2017) to create a pilot scheme for the delivery of grant applications online. Any such application may only be made at the invitation of the registry. The forms presently required will be replaced by a statement of truth. As this is a pilot scheme by invitation only and, as no Practice Directions have been published to regulate the content of a statement of truth, the text continues to refer to application by oath only. The following oath forms continue to apply for applications for grants.

In the High Court of Justice *(etc. as in Form C1)*

[I] [We] (*insert the full and correct names of each executor applying. If any name is different from that given in the Will, an explanation must be given; e.g. following a change of name on marriage, 'formerly ... having married ... since the date of the Will'. Further evidence may be required if any difference is not properly explained*) of (*insert the full, permanent postal address (including postcode) of each executor. An executor acting in a professional capacity may give his business address. Following the address of each executor, insert his occupation or description, e.g. 'journalist', 'retired'*) make oath and say:

(1) That [I] [we] believe the paper writing now produced to and marked by [me] [us] to be the true and original last Will and Testament (*where the Will to be proved comprises more than one document, insert the words 'as contained in the paper writings marked ...'. Add, if appropriate, 'together with [a] [two] [three] codicil[s]'. Each executor and the commissioner must mark the documents with their signatures)* of *(insert the full true name and address (including postcode) of the deceased; see Practice Direction 22 March 2002 [2002] 1 WLR 1303. If the deceased held property in a former name or alias, insert 'formerly or otherwise known as ...'. Any substantial discrepancy in the name must be explained in the oath, as must the reason for including the alternative or alias name in the grant. The last residential address of the deceased should be given*) deceased, who was born on the ... day of ... 19... and died on the ... day of ... 20... (*insert the dates of birth and death as they appear in the death certificate; see Practice Direction 12 January 1999. The death certificate need not be lodged*) aged ... domiciled in England and Wales.

(2) That to the best of [my] [our] knowledge and belief there was [no] land vested in the said deceased immediately before his death which was settled previously to his death (and not by his Will [and codicil[s]) and which remained settled land notwithstanding his death. (*Where there is such settled land and the grant sought is to be in respect of free estate only, the word 'no'*

should be omitted and the words 'save and except settled land' added to para. 5 after the word 'deceased'.)

(3) That [I am the [sole] [surviving] executor] [We are the [surviving] executors] (*or as may be*) named in the said Will. (*The deponent(s) must swear that they are the executor(s) named in the Will in accordance with their appointment. Following the decision in* Re Rogers deceased *[2006] EWHC 753 (Ch), only profit-sharing partners in a firm (unless appointed by name) may act as executors. They must be described as such in the oath. Where one or more executor(s) has renounced probate, add '[name] having renounced probate'. The form(s) of renunciation must be lodged with the other documents.*)

(4) [That notice of the application has been given to ... the executor[s] to whom power is to be reserved (*where power is to be reserved to executors who are partners in a firm, notice need not be given, nor need their names be recited*) [save ...]] (*Where a district judge or registrar has dispensed with giving such notice, add 'after the giving of notice to whom was dispensed with by direction dated ...'. If the appointment is limited in any way, e.g. to literary estate, the limitation should be set out.*)

(5) That [I] [we] will collect, get in and administer according to law the real and personal estate of the said deceased; when required to do so by the Court, exhibit in the Court a full inventory of the said estate and render an account thereof to the Court; and when required to do so by the High Court, deliver up to that Court the grant of probate.

(6) That to the best of [my] [our] knowledge, information and belief the gross value of the estate passing under the grant [amounts to] [does not exceed] £ ... and the net value [amounts to] [does not exceed] £ ... [and that this is not a case in which an Inheritance Tax Account is required to be delivered]. (*When an inheritance tax account is required, insert the actual gross and net values of the estate; where an account is not required, insert the approximate gross value. The net estate figure should be the actual value rounded up to the nearest £1,000; see Practice Direction 22 March 2002 [2002] 1 WLR 1303.*)

(7) That [I] [we] further make oath and say that the deceased's name and dates of birth and death as recited above are as they appear in the death certificate *(or set out any variation and the reason for it)*.

Sworn by the above-named deponent[s] ...

at ... on [date]

Before me, ... A Commissioner for Oaths/Solicitor.

C38 OATH FOR EXECUTORS WHO ARE PROFIT-SHARING PARTNERS IN A FIRM

In the High Court of Justice *(etc. as in Form C1)*

[I] [We] (*insert the full and correct names of each executor applying. If any name is different from that given in the Will, an explanation must be given; e.g. following a change of name on marriage, 'formerly ... having married ... since the date of the Will'. Further evidence may be required if any difference is not properly explained*) of (*insert the full, permanent postal address (including postcode) of each executor. An executor acting in a professional capacity may give his business address. Following the address of each executor, insert his occupation or description, e.g. 'journalist', 'retired'*) make oath and say:

(1) That [I] [we] believe the paper writing now produced to and marked by [me] [us] to be the true and original last Will and Testament (*where the Will to be proved comprises more than one document, insert the words 'as contained in the paper writings marked ...'. Add, if appropriate, 'together with [a] [two] [three] codicil[s]'. Each executor and the commissioner must mark the documents with their signatures*) of (*insert the full true name and address (including postcode) of the deceased; see Practice Direction 22 March 2002 [2002] 1 WLR 1303. If the deceased held property in a former name or alias, insert 'formerly or otherwise known as ...'. Any substantial discrepancy in the name must be explained in the oath, as must the reason for including the alternative or alias name in the grant. The last residential address of the deceased should be given)* deceased, who was born on the ... day of ... 19... and died on the ... day of ... 20... *(insert the dates of birth and death as they appear in the death certificate; see Practice Direction 12 January 1999*) aged ... domiciled in England and Wales.

(2) That to the best of [my] [our] knowledge and belief there was [no] land vested in the said deceased immediately before his death which was settled previously to his death (and not by his Will [and codicil[s]]) and which remained settled land notwithstanding his death. (*Where there is such settled land and the grant sought is to be in respect of free estate only, the word 'no' should be omitted and the words 'save and except settled land' added to para. 6 after the word 'deceased'.*)

(3) That the said deceased appointed in the said Will [and codicil[s]] the profit-sharing partners at the date of his death in [the firm of ...] [the firm which at the date of his death had succeeded to and carried on the practice of the firm of ...] to be the executors [and trustees] of the said Will.

(4) That [I am] [we are] [one] [two] of the profit-sharing partners in the firm of ... [being the successor firm to ...] at the date of death of the said deceased and as such [one] [two] of the executors named in the said Will.

(5) [That power is reserved to all the other profit-sharing partners in the said firm of ... at the said date of death and as such the other executors.]

(6) That [I] [we] will collect, get in and administer according to law the real and personal estate of the said deceased; when required to do so by the Court, exhibit in the Court a full inventory of the said estate and render an account thereof to the Court; and when required to do so by the High Court, deliver up to that Court the grant of probate.

(7) That to the best of [my] [our] knowledge, information and belief the gross value of the estate passing under the grant [amounts to] [does not exceed] £ ... and the net value [amounts to] [does not exceed] £ ... [and that this is not a case in which an Inheritance Tax Account is required to be delivered.] (*When an inheritance tax account is required, insert the actual gross and net values of the estate; where an account is not required, insert the appropriate gross value. The net estate figure should be the actual value rounded up to the nearest £1,000; see Practice Direction 22 March 2002 [2002] 1 WLR 1303.*)

(8) That [I] [we] further make oath and say that the deceased's name and dates of birth and death as recited above are as they appear in the death certificate *(or set out any variation and the reason for it)*.

Sworn *(etc. as in Form C37)*

C39 OATH FOR DOUBLE PROBATE

In the High Court of Justice *(etc. as in Form C1)*

[I] [We] (*insert the full and correct names of each executor applying. If any name is different from that given in the Will, an explanation must be given; e.g. following a change of name on marriage, 'formerly ... having married ... since the date of the Will'. Further evidence may be required if any difference is not properly explained*) of *(insert the full, permanent postal address (including postcode) of each executor. An executor acting in a professional capacity may give his business address. Following the address of each executor, insert his occupation or description, e.g. 'journalist', 'retired'*) make oath and say:

(1) That [I] [we] believe the paper writing now produced to and marked by [me] [us] to be [an official copy of] the true and original last Will and Testament [and codicil[s]] of (*insert the full true name and address (including postcode) of the deceased; see Practice Direction 22 March 2002 [2002] 1 WLR 1303. If the deceased held property in a former name or alias, insert 'formerly or otherwise known as ...'. Any substantial discrepancy in the name must be explained in the oath, as must the reason for including the alternative or alias name in the grant. The last residential address of the deceased should be given*) deceased, who was born on the ... day of ... 19... and died on the ... day of ... 20... (*insert the dates of birth and death as they appear in the death certificate; see Practice Direction 12 January 1999*) aged ... domiciled in England and Wales.

(2) That to the best of [my] [our] knowledge and belief there was [no] land vested in the said deceased immediately before his death which was settled previously to his death (and not by his Will [and codicil[s]]) and which remained settled land notwithstanding his death. (*Where there is such settled land and the grant sought is to be in respect of free estate only, the word 'no' should be omitted and the words 'save and except settled land' added to para. 6 after the word 'deceased'.*)

(3) That on the ... day of ... 20... probate of the said Will was granted to (*insert the names of the proving executor(s)*) at the [Principal Registry] [... District Probate Registry] [one] [two] of the executors named in the said Will [power being reserved of making the like grant to (*insert the names of the executor(s) to whom power was reserved*) the other executor[s] named in the said Will.

(4) That [I am] [we are] [one of] [two of] the other executor[s] named in the said Will.

(5) [That notice of the application has been given to ... the executor[s] to whom power is to be reserved. (*Where power is to be further reserved to another executor, this should be recited and a statement that notice has been given*

should be added (see clause 4 of form 37, above). Delete this clause if there is no further reservation of power.)]

(6) That [I] [we] will collect, get in and administer according to law the real and personal estate of the said deceased; when required to do so by the Court, exhibit in the Court a full inventory of the said estate and render an account thereof to the Court; and when required to do so by the High Court, deliver up to that Court the grant of probate.

(7) That to the best of [my] [our] knowledge, information and belief the gross value of the estate now unadministered passing under the grant [amounts to] [does not exceed] £ ... and the net value [amounts to] [does not exceed] £ ... [and that this is not a case in which an Inheritance Tax Account is required to be delivered.] (*When an inheritance tax account is required, insert the actual gross and net values of the estate; where an account is not required, insert the appropriate gross value. The net estate figure should be the actual value rounded up to the nearest £1,000; see Practice Direction 22 March 2002 [2002] 1 WLR 1303.*)

(8) That [I] [we] further make oath and say that the deceased's name and dates of birth and death as they are recited above are as they appear in the death certificate *(or set out any variation and the reason for it)*.

Sworn *(etc. as in Form C37)*

C40 OATH FOR TRUST CORPORATION APPOINTED EXECUTOR

In the High Court of Justice *(etc. as in Form C1)*

I (*insert the deponent's full name and address, which may be the business address. Insert also the deponent's occupation if necessary as authority to swear the oath*) in the employ of (*insert the name and address of the trust corporation*) whose registered office is at ... make oath and say:

(1) That I believe the paper writing now produced to and marked by me to be the true and original last Will and Testament [and codicil[s]] of (*insert the full true name and address (including postcode) of the deceased; see Practice Direction 22 March 2002 [2002] 1 WLR 1303. If the deceased held property in a former name or alias, insert 'formerly or otherwise known as ...'. Any substantial discrepancy in the name must be explained in the oath, as must the reason for including the alternative or alias name in the grant. The last residential address of the deceased should be given*) deceased, who was born on the ... day of ... 19... and died on the ... day of ... 20... (*insert the dates of birth and death as they appear in the death certificate; see Practice Direction 12 January 1999)* aged ... domiciled in England and Wales.

(2) That to the best of my knowledge and belief there was [no] land vested in the said deceased immediately before his death which was settled previously to his death (and not by his Will [and codicil[s]]) and which remained settled land notwithstanding his death. (*Where there is such settled land and the grant sought is to be in respect of free estate only, the word 'no' should be omitted and the words 'save and except settled land' added to para 5 after the word 'deceased'.*)

(3) That the said deceased appointed in the said Will [and codicil[s]] the said corporation ('the company') [and (*insert the full names of any other executor(s) appointed)*] to be the [sole] executor[s] of the said Will.

(4) That the said company by a resolution dated the ... day of ... 20... [a certified copy of which is lodged herewith appointed me for the purpose of applying for a grant] [a certified copy of which has been lodged with the Senior District Judge and is still in force authorised persons holding my position to apply for grants of representation] and that the said company is a trust corporation as defined by rule 2(1) of the Non-Contentious Probate Rules 1987 and has power to accept the grant now applied for.

(5) That the said company will collect, get in and administer according to law the real and personal estate of the said deceased; when required to do so by the Court, exhibit in the Court a full inventory of the said estate and render

an account thereof to the Court; and when required to do so by the High Court, deliver up to that Court the grant of probate.

(6) That to the best of my knowledge, information and belief the gross value of the estate passing under the grant [amounts to] [does not exceed] £ ... [and that this is not a case in which an Inheritance Tax Account is required to be delivered.] *(When an inheritance tax account is required, insert the actual gross and net values of the estate; where an account is not required, insert the appropriate gross value. The net estate figure should be the actual value rounded up to the nearest £1,000; see Practice Direction 22 March 2002 [2002] 1 WLR 1303.)*

(7) That I further make oath and say that the deceased's name and dates of birth and death as they are recited above are as they appear in the death certificate *(or set out any variation and the reason for it).*

Sworn *(etc. as in Form C37)*

C41 OATH FOR EXECUTORS: LOST OR RECONSTRUCTED WILL

In the High Court of Justice *(etc. as in Form C1)*

[I] [We] (*insert the full and correct names of each executor applying. If any name is different from that given in the Will, an explanation must be given; e.g. following a change of name on marriage, 'formerly ... having married ... since the date of the Will'. Further evidence may be required if any difference is not properly explained*) of (*insert the full, permanent postal address (including postcode) of each executor. An executor acting in a professional capacity may give his business address. Following the address of each executor, insert his occupation or description, e.g. 'journalist', 'retired'*) make oath and say:

(1) That [I] [we] believe the paper writing now produced to and marked by [me] [us] to contain the last Will and Testament as contained in the [carbon copy] [draft] [photocopy] [reconstruction] exhibited to the affidavit of (*insert the name of the deponent to the affidavit pursuant to which the order to admit the copy was made*) sworn on the ... day of ... 20... and marked '...' of (*insert the full true name and address (including postcode) of the deceased; see Practice Direction 22 March 2002 [2002] 1 WLR 1303. If the deceased held property in a former name or alias, insert 'formerly or otherwise known as ...'. Any substantial discrepancy in the name must be explained in the oath, as must the reason for including the alternative or alias name in the grant. The last residential address of the deceased should be given)* deceased, who was born on the ... day of ... 19... and died on the ... day of ... 20... *(insert the dates of birth and death as they appear in the death certificate; see Practice Direction 12 January 1999*) aged ... domiciled in England and Wales.

(2) That to the best of [my] [our] knowledge and belief there was [no] land vested in the said deceased immediately before his death which was settled previously to his death (and not by his Will [and codicil[s]]) and which remained settled land notwithstanding his death. (*Where there is such settled land and the grant sought is to be in respect of free estate only, the word 'no' should be omitted and the words 'save and except settled land' added to para. 6 after the word 'deceased'.*)

(3) That by order of [Mr/Mrs/Miss Registrar] [District Judge] ... of this Division dated the ... day of ... 20... it was ordered that the last Will and Testament of the said deceased be admitted to proof as contained in the said [carbon copy] [draft] [photocopy] [reconstruction].

(4) That [I am the [sole] [surviving] executor] [we are the [surviving] executors] (*or as may be*) named in the said Will. (*The deponent(s) must swear that they are the executor(s) named in the Will in accordance with their appointment. Following the decision in* Re Rogers deceased *[2006] EWHC 753 (Ch), only profit-sharing partners in a firm (unless appointed by name) may act as*

executors. They must be described as such in the oath. Where one or more executor(s) has renounced probate, add '[name] having renounced probate'. The form(s) of renunciation must be lodged with the other documents.)

(5) That notice of the application has been given to ... the executor[s] to whom power is to be reserved. (*Where power is to be reserved to executors who are partners in a firm, notice need not be given, nor need their names be recited.*) [save ...]] (*Where a district judge or registrar has dispensed with giving such notice, add 'after the giving of notice to whom was dispensed with by direction dated ...'. If the appointment is limited in any way, e.g. to literary estate, the limitation should be set out.*)

(6) That [I] [we] will collect, get in and administer according to law the real and personal estate of the said deceased limited until the original Will or a more authentic copy be proved; when required to do so by the Court, exhibit in the Court a full inventory of the said estate and render an account thereof to the Court; and when required to do so by the High Court, deliver up to that Court the grant of probate.

(7) That to the best of [my] [our] knowledge, information and belief the gross value of the estate passing under the grant [amounts to] [does not exceed] £ ... and the net estate [amounts to] [does not exceed] £ ... [and that this is not a case in which an Inheritance Tax Account is required to be delivered.] (*When an inheritance tax account is required, insert the actual gross and net values of the estate; where an account is not required, insert the appropriate gross value. The net estate figure should be the actual value rounded up to the nearest £1,000; see Practice Direction 22 March 2002 [2002] 1 WLR 1303.*)

(8) That [I] [we] further make oath and say that the deceased's name and dates of birth and death as they are recited above are as they appear in the death certificate *(or set out any variation and the reason for it)*.

Sworn *(etc. as in Form C37)*

C42 OATH FOR SPECIAL EXECUTORS

In the High Court of Justice *(etc. as in Form C1)*

[I] [We] (*insert the full and correct names of each executor applying. If any name is different from that given in the Will, an explanation must be given; e.g. following a change of name on marriage, 'formerly ... having married ... since the date of the Will'. Further evidence may be required if any difference is not properly explained*) of (*insert the full, permanent postal address (including postcode) of each executor. An executor acting in a professional capacity may give his business address. Following the address of each executor, insert his occupation or description, e.g. 'journalist', 'retired'*) make oath and say:

(1) That [I] [we] believe the paper writing now produced to and marked by [me] [us] to be the true and original last Will and Testament *(where the Will to be proved comprises more than one document, insert the words 'as contained in the paper writings marked ...'. Add, if appropriate, 'together with [a] [two] [three] codicil[s]'. Each executor and the commissioner must mark the documents with their signatures*) of (*insert the full true name and address (including postcode) of the deceased; see Practice Direction 22 March 2002 [2002] 1 WLR 1303. If the deceased held property in a former name or alias, insert 'formerly or otherwise known as ...'. Any substantial discrepancy in the name must be explained in the oath, as must the reason for including the alternative or alias name in the grant. The last residential address of the deceased should be given*) deceased, who was born on the ... day of ... 19... and died on the ... day of ... 20... (*insert the dates of birth and death as they appear in the death certificate; see Practice Direction 12 January 1999*) aged ... domiciled in England and Wales.

(2) [That on the ... day of ... 20... probate of the said Will in respect of all the estate save and except [his publishing business (*or as may be*)] was granted at the ... District Probate Registry to (*insert the names of the general executors*), his general executors.] (*Include this paragraph only if a grant in respect of the general estate has already been issued.*)

(3) That [I am] [we are] [one] [two] [of] the special executor[s] named in the said Will in respect of the deceased's [publishing business].

(4) That notice of the application has been given to ... the other special executor[s] to whom power is to be reserved (*where power is to be reserved to executors who are partners in a firm, notice need not be given, nor need their names be recited*) [save ...]]. (*Where a district judge or registrar has dispensed with giving such notice, add 'after the giving of notice to whom was dispensed with by direction dated ...'. If the appointment is limited in any way, e.g. to literary estate, the limitation should be set out.*)

(5) That to the best of [my] [our] knowledge and belief there was [no] land vested in the said deceased immediately before his death which was settled previously to his death [and not by his Will] and which remained settled land notwithstanding his death.

(6) That [I] [we] will collect, get in and administer according to law the real and personal estate of the said deceased limited to the deceased's [publishing business]; when required to do so by the Court, exhibit in the Court a full inventory of the said estate and render an account thereof to the Court; and when required to do so by the High Court, deliver up to that Court the grant of probate.

(7) That to the best of [my] [our] knowledge, information and belief the gross value of the estate passing under the grant limited as aforesaid [amounts to] [does not exceed] £ ... and the net estate [amounts to] [does not exceed] £ ... [and that this is not a case in which an Inheritance Tax Account is required to be delivered.] (*When an inheritance tax account is required, insert the actual gross and net values of the estate; where an account is not required, insert the appropriate gross value. The net estate figure should be the actual value rounded up to the nearest £1,000; see Practice Direction 22 March 2002 [2002] 1 WLR 1303.*)

(8) That [I] [we] further make oath and say that the deceased's name and dates of birth and death as they are recited above are as they appear in the death certificate *(or set out any variation and the reason for it)*.

Sworn *(etc. as in Form C37)*

C43 OATH FOR EXECUTORS: WILL PRONOUNCED FOR IN A PROBATE CLAIM

In the High Court of Justice *(etc. as in Form C1)*

[I] [We] (*insert the full and correct names of each executor applying. If any name is different from that given in the Will, an explanation must be given; e.g. following a change of name on marriage, 'formerly ... having married ... since the date of the Will'. Further evidence may be required if any difference is not properly explained*) of (*insert the full, permanent postal address (including postcode) of each executor. An executor acting in a professional capacity may give his business address. Following the address of each executor, insert his occupation or description, e.g. 'journalist', 'retired'*) make oath and say:

(1) That [I] [we] believe the paper writing now produced to and marked by [me] [us] to be the true and original last Will and Testament (*where the Will to be proved comprises more than one document, insert the words 'as contained in the paper writings marked ...'. Add, if appropriate, 'together with [a] [two] [three] codicil[s]'. Each executor and the commissioner must mark the documents with their signatures*) of (*insert the full true name and address (including postcode) of the deceased; see Practice Direction 22 March 2002 [2002] 1 WLR 1303. If the deceased held property in a former name or alias, insert 'formerly or otherwise known as ...'. Any substantial discrepancy in the name must be explained in the oath, as must the reason for including the alternative or alias name in the grant. The last residential address of the deceased should be given*) deceased, who was born on the ... day of ... 19... and died on the ... day of ... 20... (*insert the dates of birth and death as they appear in the death certificate; see Practice Direction 12 January 1999*) aged ... domiciled in England and Wales.

(2) That to the best of [my] [our] knowledge and belief there was [no] land vested in the said deceased immediately before his death which was settled previously to his death (and not by his Will [and codicil[s]]) and which remained settled land notwithstanding his death. (*Where there is such settled land and the grant sought is to be in respect of free estate only, the word 'no' should be omitted and the words 'save and except settled land' added to para 6 after the word 'deceased'.*)

(3) That on the ... day of ... 20... the Honourable [Mr] [Mrs] Justice ..., one of the Justices of the Chancery Division of the High Court of Justice, in a claim entitled (*insert the title and number of the claim*) pronounced for the force and validity of the said Will [and codicil[s]] dated ... [respectively] and ordered that the said Will [and codicil[s]] be admitted to proof and probate thereof be granted to ...] [and against the validity of the Will [and codicil[s]] dated ... [and the ... day of ... [19] [20]...] respectively].

(4) That [I am] [we are] [the sole] [surviving] executor[s] named in the said Will.

(5) [That notice of this application has been given to ... the other executor[s] named in the said Will.]

(6) That [I] [we] will collect, get in and administer according to law the real and personal estate of the said deceased; when required to do so by the Court, exhibit in the Court a full inventory of the said estate and render an account thereof to the Court; and when required to do so by the High Court, deliver up to that Court the grant of probate.

(7) That to the best of [my] [our] knowledge, information and belief the gross value of the estate passing under the grant [amounts to] [does not exceed] £ ... and the net estate [amounts to] [does not exceed] £ ... [and that this is not a case in which an Inheritance Tax Account is required to be delivered.] *(When an inheritance tax account is required, insert the actual gross and net values of the estate; where an account is not required, insert the appropriate gross value. The net estate figure should be the actual value rounded up to the nearest £1,000; see Practice Direction 22 March 2002 [2002] 1 WLR 1303.)*

(8) That [I] [we] further make oath and say that the deceased's name and dates of birth and death as they are recited above are as they appear in the death certificate *(or set out any variation and the reason for it)*.

Sworn *(etc. as in Form C37)*

C44 OATH FOR ATTORNEY OF AN EXECUTOR

In the High Court of Justice *(etc. as in Form C1)*

I (*insert the full names and permanent address of the applicant*) make oath and say:

(1) That I believe the paper writing now produced to and marked by me to contain the true and original last Will and Testament [and [one] [two] codicil[s]] of (*insert the full true name and address (including postcode) of the deceased; see Practice Direction 22 March 2002 [2002] 1 WLR 1303. If the deceased held property in a former name or alias, insert 'formerly or otherwise known as ...'. Any substantial discrepancy in the name must be explained in the oath, as must the reason for including the alternative or alias name in the grant. The last residential address of the deceased should be given*) deceased, who was born on the ... day of ... 19... and died on the ... day of ... 20... (*insert the dates of birth and death as they appear in the death certificate; see Practice Direction 12 January 1999*) aged ... domiciled in England and Wales wherein he appointed (*insert the name of the executor*) his sole executor (*or as may be*). *(If an executor other than the donor of the power of attorney survives and does not renounce, notice of the application must be given to him; rule 31(2) of the Non-Contentious Probate Rules 1987).*

(2) That no minority or life interest arises in the estate. (*Where a minority or life interest arises, the grant must issue to at least two grantees, that is, two attorneys or a trust corporation must be appointed. The district judge or registrar may, in special circumstances, allow the grant to issue to a sole grantee under s. 114, Senior Courts Act 1981.*)

(3) That to the best of my knowledge and belief there was no land vested in the said deceased immediately before his death which was settled previously to his death (and not by his Will [and codicil[s]]) and which remained settled land notwithstanding his death.

(4) That I am the lawful attorney of the said (*insert the name of the executor; clear off any other executor(s)*).

(5) That I will collect, get in and administer according to law the real and personal estate of the said deceased for the use and benefit of the said (*insert the name of the executor)* and until further representation be granted; when required to do so by the Court, exhibit in the Court a full inventory of the said estate and render an account thereof to the Court; and when required to do so by the High Court, deliver up to that Court the grant of letters of administration (with Will annexed).

(6) That to the best of my knowledge, information and belief the gross value of the estate passing under the grant [amounts to] [does not exceed] £ ... and

the net value [amounts to] [does not exceed] £ ... [and that this is not a case in which an Inheritance Tax Account is required to be delivered.] (*When an inheritance tax account is required, insert the actual gross and net values of the estate; where an account is not required, insert the appropriate gross value. The net estate figure should be the actual value rounded up to the nearest £1,000; see Practice Direction 22 March 2002 [2002] 1 WLR 1303.*)

(7) That I further make oath and say that the deceased's name and dates of birth and death as they are recited above are as they appear in the death certificate *(or set out any variation and the reason for it).*

Sworn *(etc. as in Form C37)*

C45 OATH FOR ADMINISTRATION (WITH WILL ANNEXED)

In the High Court of Justice *(etc. as in Form C1)*

[I] [We] (*insert the full and correct names and addresses of each applicant*) of make oath and say:

(1) That [I] [we] believe the paper writing now produced to and marked by [me] [us] to be the true and original last Will and Testament (*where the Will to be proved comprises more than one document, insert the words 'as contained in the paper writings marked ...'. Add, if appropriate, 'together with [a] [two] [three] codicil[s]'. Each deponent and the commissioner must mark the documents with their signatures*) of (*insert the full true name and address (including postcode) of the deceased; see Practice Direction 22 March 2002 [2002] 1 WLR 1303. If the deceased held property in a former name or alias, insert 'formerly or otherwise known as ...'. Any substantial discrepancy in the name must be explained in the oath, as must the reason for including the alternative or alias name in the grant. The last residential address of the deceased should be given*) deceased, who was born on the ... day of ... 19... and died on the ... day of ... 20... (*insert the dates of birth and death as they appear in the death certificate; see Practice Direction 12 January 1999*) aged ... domiciled in England and Wales.

(2) That no minority or life interest arises in the estate. (*Where a minority or life interest arises, the grant must issue to at least two grantees, that is, two attorneys or a trust corporation must be appointed. The district judge or registrar may, in special circumstances, allow the grant to issue to a sole grantee under s. 114, Senior Courts Act 1981.*)

(3) That to the best of [my] [our] knowledge and belief there was [no] land vested in the said deceased immediately before his death which was settled previously to his death (and not by his Will [and codicil[s]]) and which remained settled land notwithstanding his death. (*Where there is such settled land and the grant sought is to be in respect of free estate only, the word 'no' should be omitted and the words 'save and except settled land' added to para. 7 after the word 'deceased'.*)

(4) [That the said deceased did not in his Will name any executor.]

[That the purported appointment of an executor in the said Will is void for uncertainty.]

[That ... the sole executor named in the said Will survived the said deceased but has since died without having proved the said Will.]

[That ... one of the executors named in the said Will died during the lifetime of the deceased and ... the other executor named in the said Will has renounced probate thereof.]

[That ... the [sole] [surviving] executor named in the said Will has renounced probate thereof.]

(5) That I am the [residuary legatee and devisee in trust in the said Will] [[residuary] [legatee] [and] [devisee]] [substituted [residuary legatee and devisee] [residuary legatee] [devisee]]. (*Insert the deponent's capacity, clearing off those with a prior entitlement to the grant. Where the deponent is one of two or more persons entitled to apply, add the words 'one of the persons entitled'.*)

(6) That [I] [we] will collect, get in and administer according to law the real and personal estate of the said deceased; when required to do so by the Court, exhibit in the Court a full inventory of the said estate and render an account thereof to the Court; and when required to do so by the High Court, deliver up to that Court the grant of letters of administration (with Will annexed).

(7) That to the best of [my] [our] knowledge, information and belief the gross value of the estate passing under the grant [amounts to] [does not exceed] £ ... and the net value [amounts to] [does not exceed] £ ... [and that this is not a case in which an Inheritance Tax Account is required to be delivered.] (*When an inheritance tax account is required, insert the actual gross and net values of the estate; where an account is not required, insert the appropriate gross value. The net estate figure should be the actual value rounded up to the nearest £1,000; see Practice Direction 22 March 2002 [2002] 1 WLR 1303.*)

(8) That [I] [we] further make oath and say that the deceased's name and dates of birth and death as they are recited above are as they appear in the death certificate *(or set out any variation and the reason for it)*.

Sworn *(etc. as in Form C37)*

C46 OATH FOR ADMINISTRATION (WITH WILL ANNEXED) BY LEGATEE WHERE (SUBSTANTIALLY) THE WHOLE ESTATE IS DISPOSED OF BY THE WILL

In the High Court of Justice *(etc. as in Form C1)*

I (*insert the full names and permanent address of the applicant*) make oath and say:

(1) That I believe the paper writing now produced to and marked by me to be the true and original last Will and Testament (*where the Will to be proved comprises more than one document, insert the words 'as contained in the paper writings marked ...'. Add, if appropriate, 'together with [a] [two] [three] codicil[s]'. Each deponent and the commissioner must mark the documents with their signatures*) of (*insert the full true name and address (including postcode) of the deceased; see Practice Direction 22 March 2002 [2002] 1 WLR 1303. If the deceased held property in a former name or alias, insert 'formerly or otherwise known as ...'. Any substantial discrepancy in the name must be explained in the oath, as must the reason for including the alternative or alias name in the grant. The last residential address of the deceased should be given*) deceased, who was born on the ... day of ... 19... and died on the ... day of ... 20... (*insert the dates of birth and death as they appear in the death certificate; see Practice Direction 12 January 1999*) aged ... domiciled in England and Wales.

(2) That no minority or life interest arises in the estate. (*Where a minority or life interest arises, the grant must issue to at least two grantees, that is, two attorneys or a trust corporation must be appointed. The district judge or registrar may, in special circumstances, allow the grant to issue to a sole grantee under s. 114, Senior Courts Act 1981.*)

(3) That to the best of my knowledge and belief there was [no] land vested in the said deceased immediately before his death which was settled previously to his death [and not by his Will] and which remained settled land notwithstanding his death. (*Where there is such settled land and the grant sought is to be in respect of free estate only, the word 'no' should be omitted and the words 'save and except settled land' added to para. 7 after the word 'deceased'.*)

(4) [That the said deceased did not in his Will name any executor.]

[That the purported appointment of an executor in the said Will is void for uncertainty.]

[That ... the sole executor named in the said Will survived the said deceased but has since died without having proved the said Will.]

[That ... one of the executors named in the said Will died during the lifetime of the deceased and ... the other executor named in the said Will has renounced probate thereof.]

[That ... the [sole] [surviving] executor named in the said Will has renounced probate thereof.]

(5) That (*insert names*) the residuary legatee(s) and devisee(s) named in the said Will [[has] [have] renounced letters of administration with Will annexed] [died in the lifetime of the said deceased] (*insert the manner by which the residuary legatee(s) and devisee(s) has/have been cleared off*).

(6) That I am a [legatee] [devisee] named in the said Will. The said Will disposes of [substantially] the whole known estate. [£ ... of the total value of the known estate of £ ... is disposed of by the said Will.] (*Insert the capacity in which the grant is applied for, and the manner in which all others with a prior entitlement to a grant are cleared off.*)

(7) That I will collect, get in and administer according to law the real and personal estate of the said deceased; when required to do so by the Court, exhibit in the Court a full inventory of the said estate and render an account thereof to the Court; and when required to do so by the High Court, deliver up to that Court the grant of letters of administration (with Will annexed).

(8) That to the best of my knowledge, information and belief the gross value of the estate passing under the grant [amounts to] [does not exceed] £ ... and the net value [amounts to] [does not exceed] £ ... [and that this is not a case in which an Inheritance Tax Account is required to be delivered.] (*When an inheritance tax account is required, insert the actual gross and net values of the estate; where an account is not required, insert the appropriate gross value. The net estate figure should be the actual value rounded up to the nearest £1,000; see Practice Direction 22 March 2002 [2002] 1 WLR 1303.*)

(9) That I further make oath and say that the deceased's name and dates of birth and death as they are recited above are as they appear in the death certificate *(or set out any variation and the reason for it).*

Sworn *(etc. as in Form C37)*

C47 OATH FOR ADMINISTRATION (WITH WILL ANNEXED) BY PERSON ENTITLED TO THE ESTATE NOT DISPOSED OF BY THE WILL

In the High Court of Justice *(etc. as in Form C1)*

I (*insert the full names and permanent address of the applicant*) make oath and say:

(1) That I believe the paper writing now produced to and marked by me to be the true and original last Will and Testament (*where the Will to be proved comprises more than one document, insert the words 'as contained in the paper writings marked ...'. Add, if appropriate, 'together with [a] [two] [three] codicil[s]'. Each deponent and the commissioner must mark the documents with their signatures*) of (*insert the full true name and address (including postcode) of the deceased; see Practice Direction 22 March 2002 [2002] 1 WLR 1303. If the deceased held property in a former name or alias, insert 'formerly or otherwise known as ...'. Any substantial discrepancy in the name must be explained in the oath, as must the reason for including the alternative or alias name in the grant. The last residential address of the deceased should be given*) deceased, who was born on the ... day of ... 19... and died on the ... day of ... 20... (*insert the dates of birth and death as they appear in the death certificate; see Practice Direction 12 January 1999*) aged ... domiciled in England and Wales).

(2) That no minority or life interest arises in the estate. (*Where a minority or life interest arises, the grant must issue to at least two grantees, that is, two attorneys or a trust corporation must be appointed. The district judge or registrar may, in special circumstances, allow the grant to issue to a sole grantee under s. 114, Senior Courts Act 1981.*)

(3) That to the best of my knowledge and belief there was [no] land vested in the said deceased immediately before his death which was settled previously to his death (and not by his Will [and codicil[s]]) and which remained settled land notwithstanding his death. (*Where there is such settled land and the grant sought is to be in respect of free estate only, the word 'no' should be omitted and the words 'save and except settled land' added to para. 7 after the word 'deceased'.*)

(4) [That (*insert the name of the executor and residuary legatee and devisee*) died in the lifetime of the said deceased.] [That (*insert the name of the executor*) renounced probate of the said Will and (*insert the name of the residuary legatee and devisee*) died in the lifetime of the said deceased.] (*Or as may be, to establish the applicant's title to a grant.*)

(5) That the said deceased died a (*insert the status of the deceased at death and clearings down to the applicant's relationship*) [or any other person entitled in priority by virtue of any enactment.]

(6) That I am (*insert the relationship to the deceased*) and [one of] [the only] person[s] entitled to share in the estate now undisposed of by the said Will.

(7) That I will collect, get in and administer according to law the real and personal estate of the said deceased; when required to do so by the Court, exhibit in the Court a full inventory of the said estate and render an account thereof to the Court; and when required to do so by the High Court, deliver up to that Court the grant of letters of administration (with Will annexed).

(8) That to the best of my knowledge, information and belief the gross value of the estate passing under the grant [amounts to] [does not exceed] £ ... and the net value [amounts to] [does not exceed] £ ... [and that this is not a case in which an Inheritance Tax Account is required to be delivered.] (*When an inheritance tax account is required, insert the actual gross and net values of the estate; where an account is not required, insert the appropriate gross value. The net estate figure should be the actual value rounded up to the nearest £1,000; see Practice Direction 22 March 2002 [2002] 1 WLR 1303.*)

(9) That I further make oath and say that the deceased's name and dates of birth and death as they are recited above are as they appear in the death certificate *(or set out any variation and the reason for it)*.

Sworn *(etc. as in Form C37)*

C48 OATH FOR ADMINISTRATION (WITH WILL ANNEXED): FIRST NAMED RESIDUARY LEGATEE AND DEVISEE DISCLAIMING BENEFIT

In the High Court of Justice *(etc. as in Form C1)*

[I] [We] (*insert the full and correct names and address(es) of each applicant*) of make oath and say:

(1) That [I] [we] believe the paper writing now produced to and marked by [me] [us] to be the true and original last Will and Testament (*where the Will to be proved comprises more than one document, insert the words 'as contained in the paper writings marked ...'. Add, if appropriate, 'together with [a] [two] [three] codicil[s]'. Each deponent and the commissioner must mark the documents with their signatures*) of (*insert the full true name and address (including postcode) of the deceased; see Practice Direction 22 March 2002 [2002] 1 WLR 1303. If the deceased held property in a former name or alias, insert 'formerly or otherwise known as ...'. Any substantial discrepancy in the name must be explained in the oath, as must the reason for including the alternative or alias name in the grant. The last residential address of the deceased should be given*) deceased, who was born on the ... day of ... 19... and died on the ... day of ... 20... (*insert the dates of birth and death as they appear in the death certificate; see Practice Direction 12 January 1999*) aged ... domiciled in England and Wales.

(2) That no minority or life interest arises in the estate. (*Where a minority or life interest arises, the grant must issue to at least two grantees, that is, two attorneys or a trust corporation must be appointed. The district judge or registrar may, in special circumstances, allow the grant to issue to a sole grantee under s. 114, Senior Courts Act 1981.*)

(3) That to the best of [my] [our] knowledge and belief there was [no] land vested in the said deceased immediately before his death which was settled previously to his death (and not by his Will [and codicil[s]]) and which remained settled land notwithstanding his death. (*Where there is such settled land and the grant sought is to be in respect of free estate only, the word 'no' should be omitted and the words 'save and except settled land' added to para. 7 after the word 'deceased'.*)

(4) [That the said deceased did not in his Will name any executor.]

[That the purported appointment of an executor in the said Will is void for uncertainty.]

[That ... the sole executor named in the said Will survived the said deceased but has since died without having proved the said Will.]

[That ... one of the executors named in the said Will died during the lifetime of the deceased and ... the other executor named in the said Will has renounced probate thereof.]

[That ... the [sole] [surviving] executor named in the said Will has renounced probate thereof.]

(5) That *(insert name)* the lawful [widow][husband] of the deceased and the first named residuary legatee and devisee in the said Will has by deed of disclaimer dated ... *(insert date disclaimer executed)* disclaimed all [his][her] right and title to and interest in the estate of the deceased and is therefore by virtue of Section 46A of the Administration of Estates Act 1925 as amended by the Estates of Deceased Persons) Forfeiture Rule and Law of Succession) Act 2011 deemed to have died immediately before the deceased.

(6) That [I am][We are] the [substituted [residuary legatee[s] and devisee[s]] [residuary legatee[s]] [devisee[s]]].

(7) That [I] [we] will collect, get in and administer according to law the real and personal estate of the said deceased; when required to do so by the Court, exhibit in the Court a full inventory of the said estate and render an account thereof to the Court; and when required to do so by the High Court, deliver up to that Court the grant of letters of administration (with Will annexed).

(8) That to the best of [my] [our] knowledge, information and belief the gross value of the estate passing under the grant [amounts to] [does not exceed] £ ... and the net value [amounts to] [does not exceed] £ ... [and that this is not a case in which an Inheritance Tax Account is required to be delivered.] *(When an inheritance tax account is required, insert the actual gross and net values of the estate; where an account is not required, insert the appropriate gross value. The net estate figure should be the actual value rounded up to the nearest £1,000; see Practice Direction 22 March 2002 [2002] 1 WLR 1303.)*

(9) That [I] [we] further make oath and say that the deceased's name and dates of birth and death as they are recited above are as they appear in the death certificate *(or set out any variation and the reason for it).*

Sworn *(etc. as in Form C37)*

C49 OATH FOR PERSONAL REPRESENTATIVE OF RESIDUARY LEGATEE AND DEVISEE

In the High Court of Justice *(etc. as in Form C1)*

I (*insert the full names and permanent address of the applicant*) make oath and say:

(1) That I believe the paper writing now produced to and marked by me to be the true and original last Will and Testament (*where the Will to be proved comprises more than one document, insert the words 'as contained in the paper writings marked ...'. Add, if appropriate, 'together with [a] [two] [three] codicil[s]'. Each deponent and the commissioner must mark the documents with their signatures*) of (*insert the full true name and address (including postcode) of the deceased; see Practice Direction 22 March 2002 [2002] 1 WLR 1303. If the deceased held property in a former name or alias, insert 'formerly or otherwise known as ...'. Any substantial discrepancy in the name must be explained in the oath, as must the reason for including the alternative or alias name in the grant. The last residential address of the deceased should be given*) deceased, who was born on the ... day of ... 19... and died on the ... day of ... 20... (*insert the dates of birth and death as they appear in the death certificate; see Practice Direction 12 January 1999*) aged ... domiciled in England and Wales.

(2) That no minority or life interest arises in the estate. (*Where a minority or life interest arises, the grant must issue to at least two grantees, that is, two attorneys or a trust corporation must be appointed. The district judge or registrar may, in special circumstances, allow the grant to issue to a sole grantee under s. 114, Senior Courts Act 1981.*)

(3) That to the best of my knowledge and belief there was [no] land vested in the said deceased immediately before his death which was settled previously to his death (and not by his Will [and codicil[s]]) and which remained settled land notwithstanding his death. (*Where there is such settled land and the grant sought is to be in respect of free estate only, the word 'no' should be omitted and the words 'save and except settled land' added to para. 7 after the word 'deceased'.*)

(4) [That the said deceased did not in his Will name any executor.]

[That the purported appointment of an executor in the said Will is void for uncertainty.]

[That (*insert the name and manner of clearing*) the sole executor named in the said Will survived the said deceased but has since died without having proved the said Will.]

[That (*insert the name and manner of clearing*) one of the executors named in the said Will died during the lifetime of the deceased and (*insert the name and manner of clearing*) the other executor named in the said Will has renounced probate thereof.]

[That (*insert the name and manner of clearing*) the [sole] [surviving] executor named in the said Will has renounced probate thereof.]

(5) That (*insert the name and manner of clearing*) the residuary legatee[s] and devisee[s] predeceased the deceased.

(6) That I am the [executor of the Will of (*insert the name and manner of clearing*)] [the administrator of the estate of (*insert the name and manner of clearing*)], one of the residuary legatee(s) and devisee(s), [probate of his Will] [letters of administration of his estate] [having been granted to me out of the ... Registry on the ... day of ... 20...][being applied for contemporaneously with this application].

(7) That I will collect, get in and administer according to law the real and personal estate of the said deceased; when required to do so by the Court, exhibit in the Court a full inventory of the said estate and render an account thereof to the Court; and when required to do so by the High Court, deliver up to that Court the grant of letters of administration (with Will annexed).

(8) That to the best of [my] [our] knowledge, information and belief the gross value of the estate passing under the grant [amounts to] [does not exceed] £ ... and the net estate [amounts to] [does not exceed] £ ... [and that this is not a case in which an Inheritance Tax Account is required to be delivered.] (*When an inheritance tax account is required, insert the actual gross and net values of the estate; where an account is not required, insert the appropriate gross value. The net estate figure should be the actual value rounded up to the nearest £1,000; see Practice Direction 22 March 2002 [2002] 1 WLR 1303.*)

(9) That [I] [we] further make oath and say that the deceased's name and dates of birth and death as they are recited above are as they appear in the death certificate *(or set out any variation and the reason for it)*.

Sworn *(etc. as in Form C37)*

C50 OATH FOR LEGATEE, DEVISEE OR CREDITOR

In the High Court of Justice *(etc. as in Form C1)*

I (*insert the full names and permanent address of the applicant*) make oath and say:

(1) That I believe the paper writing now produced to and marked by me to be the true and original last Will and Testament (*where the Will to be proved comprises more than one document, insert the words 'as contained in the paper writings marked ...'. Add, if appropriate, 'together with [a] [two] [three] codicil[s]'. Each deponent and the commissioner must mark the documents with their signatures*) of (*insert the full true name and address (including postcode) of the deceased; see Practice Direction 22 March 2002 [2002] 1 WLR 1303. If the deceased held property in a former name or alias, insert 'formerly or otherwise known as ...'. Any substantial discrepancy in the name must be explained in the oath, as must the reason for including the alternative or alias name in the grant. The last residential address of the deceased should be given*) deceased, who was born on the ... day of ... 19... and died on the ... day of ... 20... (*insert the dates of birth and death as they appear in the death certificate; see Practice Direction 12 January 1999*) aged ... domiciled in England and Wales.

(2) That no minority or life interest arises in the estate. (*Where a minority or life interest arises, the grant must issue to at least two grantees, that is, two attorneys or a trust corporation must be appointed. The district judge or registrar may, in special circumstances, allow the grant to issue to a sole grantee under s. 114, Senior Courts Act 1981.*)

(3) That to the best of my knowledge and belief there was [no] land vested in the said deceased immediately before his death which was settled previously to his death (and not by his Will [and codicil[s]]) and which remained settled land notwithstanding his death. (*Where there is such settled land and the grant sought is to be in respect of free estate only, the word 'no' should be omitted and the words 'save and except settled land' added to para. 7 after the word 'deceased'.*)

(4) [That the said deceased did not in his Will name any executor.]

[That the purported appointment of an executor in the said Will is void for uncertainty.]

[That (*insert the name and manner of clearing*) the sole executor named in the said Will survived the said deceased but has since died without having proved the said Will.]

[That (*insert the name and manner of clearing*) one of the executors named in the said Will died during the lifetime of the deceased and (*insert the name and manner of clearing*) the other executor named in the said Will has renounced probate thereof.]

[That (*insert the name and manner of clearing*) the [sole] [surviving] executor named in the said Will has renounced probate thereof.]

(5) That (*insert the name and manner of clearing*) the residuary legatee[s] and devisee[s] named in the said Will [has] [have] renounced letters of administration [with Will annexed] [That (*insert the name and manner of clearing*) the residuary legatee(s) and devisee(s) named in the said Will died in the lifetime of the said deceased.] (*Insert the manner in which the residuary beneficiaries are cleared off.*)

(6) That I am a [[legatee] [devisee] named in the said Will] [creditor of the said deceased.] (*Insert the capacity in which the grant is applied for, clearing off those with a prior entitlement.*)

(7) That I will collect, get in and administer according to law the real and personal estate of the said deceased; when required to do so by the Court, exhibit in the Court a full inventory of the said estate and render an account thereof to the Court; and when required to do so by the High Court, deliver up to that Court the grant of letters of administration (with Will annexed).

(8) That to the best of my knowledge, information and belief the gross value of the estate passing under the grant [amounts to] [does not exceed] £ ... and the net value [amounts to] [does not exceed] £ ... [and that this is not a case in which an Inheritance Tax Account is required to be delivered.] (*When an inheritance tax account is required, insert the actual gross and net values of the estate; where an account is not required, insert the appropriate gross value. The net estate figure should be the actual value rounded up to the nearest £1,000; see Practice Direction 22 March 2002 [2002] 1 WLR 1303.*)

(9) That I further make oath and say that the deceased's name and dates of birth and death as they are recited above are as they appear in the death certificate *(or set out any variation and the reason for it).*

Sworn *(etc. as in Form C37)*

C51 OATH FOR ADMINISTRATION FOR THE USE AND BENEFIT OF AN EXECUTOR OR RESIDUARY LEGATEE WHO LACKS CAPACITY WITHIN THE MEANING OF THE MENTAL CAPACITY ACT 2005

In the High Court of Justice *(etc. as in Form C1)*

[I] [We] (*insert the full names and addresses of the applicant(s)*) make oath and say:

(1) That [I] [we] believe the paper writing now produced to and marked by [me] [us] to be the true and original last Will and Testament (*where the Will to be proved comprises more than one document, insert the words 'as contained in the paper writings marked ...'. Add, if appropriate, 'together with [a] [two] [three] codicil[s]'. Each deponent and the commissioner must mark the documents with their signatures)* of *(insert the full true name and address (including postcode) of the deceased; see Practice Direction 22 March 2002 [2002] 1 WLR 1303. If the deceased held property in a former name or alias, insert 'formerly or otherwise known as ...'. Any substantial discrepancy in the name must be explained in the oath, as must the reason for including the alternative or alias name in the grant. The last residential address of the deceased should be given*) deceased, who was born on the ... day of ... 19... and died on the ... day of ... 20... (*insert the dates of birth and death as they appear in the death certificate; see Practice Direction 12 January 1999*) aged ... domiciled in England and Wales.

(2) That no minority or life interest arises in the estate. (*Where a minority or life interest arises, the grant must issue to at least two grantees, that is, two attorneys or a trust corporation must be appointed. The district judge or registrar may, in special circumstances, allow the grant to issue to a sole grantee under s. 114, Senior Courts Act 1981.*)

(3) That to the best of [my] [our] knowledge and belief there was [no] land vested in the said deceased immediately before his death which was settled previously to his death (and not by his Will [and codicil[s]]) and which remained settled land notwithstanding his death. (*Where there is such settled land and the grant sought is to be in respect of free estate only, the word 'no' should be omitted and the words 'save and except settled land' added to para. 6 after the word 'deceased'.*)

(4) That in his said Will the said deceased appointed (*insert the name(s) of the executor(s) and the manner of clearing*) leaving (*insert the name of the residuary beneficiary*) the residuary legatee and devisee who suffers an impairment of or a disturbance in the functioning of [his] [her] mind or brain as a result of which [he] [she] is unable to make a decision for [himself] [herself] in relation to the application for a grant of representation and subsequent administration of the estate of the deceased.

(5) [That by order dated the … day of … 20… of the Court of Protection I was authorised to apply for letters of administration (with Will annexed) either alone or with a co-administrator for the use and benefit of (*insert the name of the residuary beneficiary*).]

[That [I am] [we are] the lawful attorney[s] of the said (*insert the name of the residuary beneficiary*), acting under an [enduring] [lasting] power of attorney which has been registered with the Office of the Public Guardian.]

[By order of [Mr] [Mrs] [District Judge] [Registrar] ... dated the … day of … 20… made under and by virtue of rule 35(4) of the Non-Contentious Probate Rules 1987, [I was] [we were] appointed to apply for letters of administration (with Will annexed).]

(6) That [I] [we] will collect, get in and administer according to law the real and personal estate of the said deceased for the use and benefit of the said (*insert the name of the residuary beneficiary*) [during his incapacity] [until further representation be granted]; when required to do so by the Court, exhibit in the Court a full inventory of the said estate and render an account thereof to the Court; and when required to do so by the High Court, deliver up to that Court the grant of letters of administration (with Will annexed).

(7) That to the best of [my] [our] knowledge, information and belief the gross value of the estate passing under the grant [amounts to] [does not exceed] £ ... and the net value [amounts to] [does not exceed] £ ... [and that this is not a case in which an Inheritance Tax Account is required to be delivered.] (*When an inheritance tax account is required, insert the actual gross and net values of the estate; where an account is not required, insert the appropriate gross value. The net estate figure should be the actual value rounded up to the nearest £1,000; see Practice Direction 22 March 2002 [2002] 1 WLR 1303.*)

(8) That [I] [we] further make oath and say that the deceased's name and dates of birth and death as they are recited above are as they appear in the death certificate *(or set out any variation and the reason for it)*.

Sworn *(etc. as in Form C37)*

C52 OATH FOR NOMINEE OF RESIDUARY LEGATEE AND DEVISEE WHICH IS A NON-TRUST CORPORATION

In the High Court of Justice *(etc. as in Form C1)*

I (*insert the full names and permanent address of the applicant*) make oath and say:

(1) That I believe the paper writing now produced to and marked by me to be the true and original last Will and Testament (*where the Will to be proved comprises more than one document, insert the words 'as contained in the paper writings marked ...'. Add, if appropriate, 'together with [a] [two] [three] codicil[s]'. Each deponent and the commissioner must mark the documents with their signatures*) of (*insert the full true name and address (including postcode) of the deceased; see Practice Direction 22 March 2002 [2002] 1 WLR 1303. If the deceased held property in a former name or alias, insert 'formerly or otherwise known as ...'. Any substantial discrepancy in the name must be explained in the oath, as must the reason for including the alternative or alias name in the grant. The last residential address of the deceased should be given*) deceased, who was born on the ... day of ... 19... and died on the ... day of ... 20... (*insert the dates of birth and death as they appear in the death certificate; see Practice Direction 12 January 1999*) aged ... domiciled in England and Wales.

(2) That no minority or life interest arises in the estate. (*Where a minority or life interest arises, the grant must issue to at least two grantees, that is, two attorneys or a trust corporation must be appointed. The district judge or registrar may, in special circumstances, allow the grant to issue to a sole grantee under s. 114, Senior Courts Act 1981.*)

(3) That to the best of my knowledge and belief there was [no] land vested in the said deceased immediately before his death which was settled previously to his death (and not by his Will [and codicil[s]]) and which remained settled land notwithstanding his death. (*Where there is such settled land and the grant sought is to be in respect of free estate only, the word 'no' should be omitted and the words 'save and except settled land' added to para. 7 after the word 'deceased'.*)

(4) [That the said deceased did not in his Will name any executor.]

[That the purported appointment of an executor in the said Will is void for uncertainty.]

[That (*insert the name and manner of clearing*) the sole executor named in the said Will survived the said deceased but has since died without having proved the said Will.]

[That (*insert the name and manner of clearing*) one of the executors named in the said Will died during the lifetime of the deceased and (*insert the name and manner of clearing*) the other executor named in the said Will has renounced probate thereof.]

[That (*insert the name and manner of clearing*) the [sole] [surviving] executor named in the said Will has renounced probate thereof.]

(5) [That (*insert the name of the non-trust corporation*) the residuary legatee and devisee named in the said Will is not a trust corporation as defined by rule 2(1) of the Non-Contentious Probate Rules 1987.]

(6) That by a resolution dated the ... day of ... 20... I was duly appointed by the said (*insert the name of the non-trust corporation*) as its nominee for the purpose of applying for letters of administration (with Will annexed) to the estate of the said deceased. (*Amend this paragraph as appropriate if the authority is a general authority applying also to estates other than the estate in question.*)

(7) That I will collect, get in and administer according to law the real and personal estate of the said deceased for the use and benefit of the said (*insert the name of the non-trust corporation*) and until further representation be granted; when required to do so by the Court, exhibit in the Court a full inventory of the said estate and render an account thereof to the Court; and when required to do so by the High Court, deliver up to that Court the letters of administration (with Will annexed).

(8) That to the best of my knowledge, information and belief the gross value of the estate passing under the grant [amounts to] [does not exceed] £ ... and the net value [amounts to] [does not exceed] £ ... [and that this is not a case in which an Inheritance Tax Account is required to be delivered]. (*When an inheritance tax account is required, insert the actual gross and net values of the estate; where an account is not required, insert the appropriate gross value. The net estate figure should be the actual value rounded up to the nearest £1,000; see Practice Direction 22 March 2002 [2002] 1 WLR 1303.*)

(9) That I further make oath and say that the deceased's name and dates of birth and death as they are recited above are as they appear in the death certificate *(or set out any variation and the reason for it)*.

Sworn *(etc. as in Form C37)*

C53 OATH FOR ADMINISTRATION (WITH WILL ANNEXED): GIFT SAVED UNDER SECTION 33 OF THE WILLS ACT 1837

In the High Court of Justice *(etc. as in Form C1)*

I (*insert the full names and permanent address of the applicant*) make oath and say:

(1) That I believe the paper writing now produced to and marked by me to be the true and original last Will and Testament (*where the Will to be proved comprises more than one document, insert the words 'as contained in the paper writings marked ...'. Add, if appropriate, 'together with [a] [two] [three] codicil[s]'. Each deponent and the commissioner must mark the documents with their signatures*) of (*insert the full true name and address (including postcode) of the deceased; see Practice Direction 22 March 2002 [2002] 1 WLR 1303. If the deceased held property in a former name or alias, insert 'formerly or otherwise known as ...'. Any substantial discrepancy in the name must be explained in the oath, as must the reason for including the alternative or alias name in the grant. The last residential address of the deceased should be given*) deceased, who was born on the ... day of ... 19... and died on the ... day of ... 20... (*insert the dates of birth and death as they appear in the death certificate; see Practice Direction 12 January 1999*) aged ... domiciled in England and Wales.

(2) That no minority or life interest arises in the estate. (*Where a minority or life interest arises, the grant must issue to at least two grantees, that is, two attorneys or a trust corporation must be appointed. The district judge or registrar may, in special circumstances, allow the grant to issue to a sole grantee under s. 114, Senior Courts Act 1981.*)

(3) That to the best of my knowledge and belief there was [no] land vested in the said deceased immediately before his death which was settled previously to his death (and not by his Will [and codicil[s]]) and which remained settled land notwithstanding his death. (*Where there is such settled land and the grant sought is to be in respect of free estate only, the word 'no' should be omitted and the words 'save and except settled land' added to para. 7 after the word 'deceased'.*)

(4) [That the said deceased did not in his Will name any executor.]

[That the purported appointment of an executor in the said Will is void for uncertainty.]

[That (*insert the name and manner of clearing*) the sole executor named in the said Will survived the said deceased but has since died without having proved the said Will.]

[That (*insert the name and manner of clearing*) one of the executors named in the said Will died during the lifetime of the deceased and (*insert the name and manner of clearing*) the other executor named in the said Will has renounced probate thereof.]

[That (*insert the name and manner of clearing*) the [sole] [surviving] executor named in the said Will has renounced probate thereof.]

(5) That (*insert the name of the residuary legatee and devisee*) the son of the said deceased and the residuary legatee and devisee named in the said Will predeceased the deceased leaving issue who survived the said deceased.

(6) That I am [one of] the issue of the said (*insert the name of the residuary legatee and devisee*), being his daughter and [one of the persons] [the person] now entitled to [share in] the residue under the said Will by virtue of section 33 of the Wills Act 1837.

(7) That I will collect, get in and administer according to law the real and personal estate of the said deceased; when required to do so by the Court, exhibit in the Court a full inventory of the said estate and render an account thereof to the Court; and when required to do so by the High Court, deliver up to that Court the letters of administration (with Will annexed).

(8) That to the best of my knowledge, information and belief the gross value of the estate passing under the grant [amounts to] [does not exceed] £ ... and the net value [amounts to] [does not exceed] £ ... [and that this is not a case in which an Inheritance Tax Account is required to be delivered]. (*When an inheritance tax account is required, insert the actual gross and net values of the estate; where an account is not required, insert the appropriate gross value. The net estate figure should be the actual value rounded up to the nearest £1,000; see Practice Direction 22 March 2002 [2002] 1 WLR 1303.*)

(9) That I further make oath and say that the deceased's name and dates of birth and death as they are recited above are as they appear in the death certificate *(or set out any variation and the reason for it).*

Sworn *(etc. as in Form C37)*

C54 OATH FOR ADMINISTRATION: SURVIVING SPOUSE OR CIVIL PARTNER

In the High Court of Justice *(etc. as in Form C1)*

I (*insert the full names and permanent address of the applicant*) make oath and say:

(1) That (*insert the full true name and address (including postcode) of the deceased; see Practice Direction 22 March 2002 [2002] 1 WLR 1303. If the deceased held property in a former name or alias, insert 'formerly or otherwise known as ...'. Any substantial discrepancy in the name must be explained in the oath, as must the reason for including the alternative or alias name in the grant. The last residential address of the deceased should be given*) was born on the ... day of ... 19... and died on the ... day of ... 20... (*insert the dates of birth and death as they appear in the death certificate; see Practice Direction 12 January 1999*) aged ... domiciled in England and Wales intestate.

(2) That no minority or life interest arises in the estate.

(3) That to the best of my knowledge and belief there was [no] land vested in the said deceased immediately before his death which was settled previously to his death and which remained settled land notwithstanding his death. (*Where there is such settled land and the grant sought is to be in respect of free estate only, the word 'no' should be omitted and the words 'save and except settled land' added to para. 5 after the word 'deceased'.*)

(4) That I am the lawful [widow] [husband] [civil partner] of the deceased and the only person [now] entitled to [his] [her] estate.

(5) That I will collect, get in and administer according to law the real and personal estate of the said deceased; when required to do so by the Court, exhibit in the Court a full inventory of the said estate and render an account thereof to the Court; and when required to do so by the High Court, deliver up to that Court the letters of administration.

(6) That to the best of [my] [our] knowledge, information and belief the gross value of the estate passing under the grant [amounts to] [does not exceed] £ ... and the net value [amounts to] [does not exceed] £ ... [and that this is not a case in which an Inheritance Tax Account is required to be delivered]. (*When an inheritance tax account is required, insert the actual gross and net values of the estate; where an account is not required, insert the appropriate gross value. The net estate figure should be the actual value rounded up to the nearest £1,000; see Practice Direction 22 March 2002 [2002] 1 WLR 1303.*)

(7) That I further make oath and say that the deceased's name and dates of birth and death as they are recited above are as they appear in the death certificate *(or set out any variation and the reason for it).*

Sworn *(etc. as in Form C37)*

C55 OATH FOR ADMINISTRATION: CHILD, SURVIVING SPOUSE OR CIVIL PARTNER HAVING DISCLAIMED BENEFIT

In the High Court of Justice *(etc. as in Form C1)*

I (*insert the full names and permanent address of the applicant*) make oath and say:

(1) That (*insert the full true name and address (including postcode) of the deceased; see Practice Direction 22 March 2002 [2002] 1 WLR 1303. If the deceased held property in a former name or alias, insert 'formerly or otherwise known as ...'. Any substantial discrepancy in the name must be explained in the oath, as must the reason for including the alternative or alias name in the grant. The last residential address of the deceased should be given*) was born on the ... day of ... 19... and died on the ... day of ... 20... (*insert the dates of birth and death as they appear in the death certificate; see Practice Direction 12 January 1999*) aged ... domiciled in England and Wales intestate.

(2) That no minority or life interest arises in the estate.

(3) That to the best of my knowledge and belief there was [no] land vested in the said deceased immediately before his death which was settled previously to his death and which remained settled land notwithstanding his death. (*Where there is such settled land and the grant sought is to be in respect of free estate only, the word 'no' should be omitted and the words 'save and except settled land' added to para. 6 after the word 'deceased'.*)

(4) That (*insert name*) the lawful [widow] [husband] [civil partner] of the deceased and the only person entitled to [his] [her] estate having disclaimed [his][her]interest by deed of disclaimer dated the (*insert date disclaimer executed*) is by virtue of Section 46A of the Administration of Estates Act 1925 as amended by the Estates of Deceased Persons) Forfeiture Rule and Law of Succession) Act 2011 deemed thereby to have died immediately before the deceased.

(5) I am the [son][daughter] of the deceased and the only person now entitled to [his][her] estate.

(6) That I will collect, get in and administer according to law the real and personal estate of the said deceased; when required to do so by the Court, exhibit in the Court a full inventory of the said estate and render an account thereof to the Court; and when required to do so by the High Court, deliver up to that Court the letters of administration.

(7) That to the best of my knowledge, information and belief the gross value of the estate passing under the grant [amounts to] [does not exceed] £ ... and the net value [amounts to] [does not exceed] £ ... [and that this is not a case in which an Inheritance Tax Account is required to be delivered]. (*When an inheritance tax account is required, insert the actual gross and net values of the estate; where an account is not required, insert the appropriate gross value. The net estate figure should be the actual value rounded up to the nearest £1,000; see Practice Direction 22 March 2002 [2002] 1 WLR 1303.*)

(8) That I further make oath and say that the deceased's name and dates of birth and death as they are recited above are as they appear in the death certificate *(or set out any variation and the reason for it).*

Sworn *(etc. as in Form C37)*

C56 OATH FOR ADMINISTRATION: CHILD OR OTHER ISSUE WITH BENEFICIAL INTEREST, SPOUSE HAVING SURVIVED BUT SINCE DIED

In the High Court of Justice *(etc. as in Form C1)*

[I] [We] (*insert the full names and address of the applicant(s)*) make oath and say:

(1) That (*insert the full true name and address (including postcode) of the deceased; see Practice Direction 22 March 2002 [2002] 1 WLR 1303. If the deceased held property in a former name or alias, insert 'formerly or otherwise known as ...'. Any substantial discrepancy in the name must be explained in the oath, as must the reason for including the alternative or alias name in the grant. The last residential address of the deceased should be given*) was born on the ... day of ... 19... and died on the ... day of ... 20... (*insert the dates of birth and death as they appear in the death certificate; see Practice Direction 12 January 1999*) aged ... domiciled in England and Wales intestate, leaving [his lawful widow] [her lawful husband] [one of the] person[s] entitled to share [his] [her] estate who has since died without obtaining letters of administration of [his] [her] estate.

(2) That no minority or life interest arises in the estate. (*Where a minority or life interest arises, the grant must issue to at least two grantees, that is, two attorneys or a trust corporation must be appointed. The district judge or registrar may, in special circumstances, allow the grant to issue to a sole grantee under s. 114, Senior Courts Act 1981.*)

(3) That to the best of [my] [our] knowledge and belief there was [no] land vested in the said deceased immediately before [his] [her] death which was settled previously to [his] [her] death and which remained settled land notwithstanding [his] [her] death. (*Where there is such settled land and the grant sought is to be in respect of free estate only, the word 'no' should be omitted and the words 'save and except settled land' added to para. 5 after the word 'deceased'.*)

(4) That I am the [grandson (or as may be)] of the said deceased and one of the persons beneficially entitled to share the estate, being the [son (or as may be)] of ... the only [daughter (or as may be)] of the said deceased who predeceased the said deceased (*insert the title and clearing according to the circumstances*).

(5) That [I] [we] will collect, get in and administer according to law the real and personal estate of the said deceased; when required to do so by the Court, exhibit in the Court a full inventory of the said estate and render an account thereof to the Court; and when required to do so by the High Court, deliver up to that Court the letters of administration.

(6) That to the best of [my] [our] knowledge, information and belief the gross value of the estate passing under the grant [amounts to] [does not exceed] £ ... and the net value [amounts to] [does not exceed] £ ... [and that this is not a case in which an Inheritance Tax Account is required to be delivered]. *(When an inheritance tax account is required, insert the actual gross and net values of the estate; where an account is not required, insert the appropriate gross value. The net estate figure should be the actual value rounded up to the nearest £1,000; see Practice Direction 22 March 2002 [2002] 1 WLR 1303.)*

(7) That [I] [we] further make oath and say that the deceased's name and dates of birth and death as they are recited above are as they appear in the death certificate *(or set out any variation and the reason for it).*

Sworn *(etc. as in Form C37)*

C57 OATH FOR ADMINISTRATION: SPOUSE OR CIVIL PARTNER ENTITLED TO WHOLE ESTATE HAVING SURVIVED BUT SINCE DIED

In the High Court of Justice *(etc. as in Form C1)*

I (*insert the full names and permanent address of the applicant*) make oath and say:

(1) That (*insert the full true name and address (including postcode) of the deceased; see Practice Direction 22 March 2002 [2002] 1 WLR 1303. If the deceased held property in a former name or alias, insert 'formerly or otherwise known as ...'. Any substantial discrepancy in the name must be explained in the oath, as must the reason for including the alternative or alias name in the grant. The last residential address of the deceased should be given*) was born on the ... day of ... 19... and died on the ... day of ... 20... (*insert the dates of birth and death as they appear in the death certificate; see Practice Direction 12 January 1999*) aged ... domiciled in England and Wales intestate, leaving (*insert the name of the surviving spouse or civil partner*) [his lawful widow] [her lawful husband] [his lawful civil partner] the only person entitled to [his] [her] estate who has since died without obtaining letters of administration of [his] [her] estate.

(2) That no minority or life interest arises in the estate.

(3) That to the best of my knowledge and belief there was [no] land vested in the said deceased immediately before [his] [her] death which was settled previously to [his] [her] death and which remained settled land notwithstanding [his] [her] death. (*Where there is such settled land and the grant sought is to be in respect of free estate only, the word 'no' should be omitted and the words 'save and except settled land' added to para. 5 after the word 'deceased'.*)

(4) That I am the [proposed] [executor] [administrator] of the estate of (*insert the name of the surviving spouse or civil partner*), [probate of [his] [her] Will] [letters of administration of [his] [her] [estate] [having been granted to me out of the ... [Probate] Registry on the ... day of ... 20...] [being applied for contemporaneously with the application for the grant.] (*An application for the 'representative' or 'leading' grant may be made before or together with this application for the grant.*)

(5) That I will collect, get in and administer according to law the real and personal estate of the said deceased; when required to do so by the Court, exhibit in the Court a full inventory of the said estate and render an account thereof to the Court; and when required to do so by the High Court, deliver up to that Court the letters of administration.

(6) That to the best of my knowledge, information and belief the gross value of the estate passing under the grant [amounts to] [does not exceed] £ ... and the net value [amounts to] [does not exceed] £ ... [and that this is not a case in which an Inheritance Tax Account is required to be delivered]. (*When an inheritance tax account is required, insert the actual gross and net values of the estate; where an account is not required, insert the appropriate gross value. The net estate figure should be the actual value rounded up to the nearest £1,000; see Practice Direction 22 March 2002 [2002] 1 WLR 1303.*)

(7) That I further make oath and say that the deceased's name and dates of birth and death as they are recited above are as they appear in the death certificate *(or set out any variation and the reason for it)*.

Sworn *(etc. as in Form C37)*

C58 OATH FOR ADMINISTRATION: SURVIVING CHILD

In the High Court of Justice *(etc. as in Form C1)*

I (*insert the full names and permanent address of the applicant*) make oath and say:

(1) That (*insert the full true name and address (including postcode) of the deceased; see Practice Direction 22 March 2002 [2002] 1 WLR 1303. If the deceased held property in a former name or alias, insert 'formerly or otherwise known as ...'. Any substantial discrepancy in the name must be explained in the oath, as must the reason for including the alternative or alias name in the grant. The last residential address of the deceased should be given*) deceased was born on the ... day of ... 19... and died on the ... day of ... 20... (*insert the dates of birth and death as they appear in the death certificate; see Practice Direction 12 January 1999*) aged ... domiciled in England and Wales intestate a widow[er].

(2) That no minority or life interest arises in the estate. (*Where a minority or life interest arises, the grant must issue to at least two grantees, that is, two attorneys or a trust corporation must be appointed. The district judge or registrar may, in special circumstances, allow the grant to issue to a sole grantee under s. 114, Senior Courts Act 1981.*)

(3) That to the best of my knowledge and belief there was [no] land vested in the said deceased immediately before [his] [her] death which was settled previously to [his] [her] death and which remained settled land notwithstanding [his] [her] death. (*Where there is such settled land and the grant sought is to be in respect of free estate only, the word 'no' should be omitted and the words 'save and except settled land' added to para. 5 after the word 'deceased'.*)

(4) That I am the [son] [daughter] of the said deceased and [one of the persons] [the only person] entitled to [share] [his] [her] estate.

(5) That I will collect, get in and administer according to law the real and personal estate of the said deceased; when required to do so by the Court, exhibit in the Court a full inventory of the said estate and render an account thereof to the Court; and when required to do so by the High Court, deliver up to that Court the letters of administration.

(6) That to the best of my knowledge, information and belief the gross value of the estate passing under the grant [amounts to] [does not exceed] £ ... and the net value [amounts to] [does not exceed] £ ... [and that this is not a case in which an Inheritance Tax Account is required to be delivered]. (*When an inheritance tax account is required, insert the actual gross and net values of the estate; where an account is not required, insert the appropriate gross*

value. The net estate figure should be the actual value rounded up to the nearest £1,000; see Practice Direction 22 March 2002 [2002] 1 WLR 1303.)

(7) That I further make oath and say that the deceased's name and dates of birth and death as they are recited above are as they appear in the death certificate *(or set out any variation and the reason for it)*.

Sworn *(etc. as in Form C37)*

C59 OATH FOR ADMINISTRATION: PARENTS

In the High Court of Justice *(etc. as in Form C1)*

[I] [We] of (*insert the full names and permanent address of the applicant*) make oath and say:

(1) That (*insert the full true name and address (including postcode) of the deceased; see Practice Direction 22 March 2002 [2002] 1 WLR 1303. If the deceased held property in a former name or alias, insert 'formerly or otherwise known as ...'. Any substantial discrepancy in the name must be explained in the oath, as must the reason for including the alternative or alias name in the grant. The last residential address of the deceased should be given*) deceased was born on the ... day of ... 19... and died on the ... day of ... 20... (*insert the dates of birth and death as they appear in the death certificate; see Practice Direction 12 January 1999*) aged ... domiciled in England and Wales intestate a [widower] [widow] [bachelor] [spinster] [single man] [single woman] (*if the deceased died a single person, that is, the marriage or civil partnership was dissolved, insert details of the decree absolute or final order*) without issue or any other person entitled in priority to share [his] [her] estate by virtue of any enactment.

(2) That no minority or life interest arises in the estate.

(3) That to the best of [my] [our] knowledge and belief there was [no] land vested in the said deceased immediately before [his] [her] death which was settled previously to [his] [her] death and which remained settled land notwithstanding [his] [her] death. (*Where there is such settled land and the grant sought is to be in respect of free estate only, the word 'no' should be omitted and the words 'save and except settled land' added to para. 5 after the word 'deceased'.*)

(4) That [I am] [we are] the [mother] [father] [parents] of the said deceased and the only person[s] entitled to [his] [her] estate.

(5) That [I] [we] will collect, get in and administer according to law the real and personal estate of the said deceased; when required to do so by the Court, exhibit in the Court a full inventory of the said estate and render an account thereof to the Court; and when required to do so by the High Court, deliver up to that Court the letters of administration.

(6) That to the best of [my] [our] knowledge, information and belief the gross value of the estate passing under the grant [amounts to] [does not exceed] £ ... and the net value [amounts to] [does not exceed] £ ... [and that this is not a case in which an Inheritance Tax Account is required to be delivered]. (*When an inheritance tax account is required, insert the actual gross and net values of the estate; where an account is not required, insert the appropriate*

gross value. The net estate figure should be the actual value rounded up to the nearest £1,000; see Practice Direction 22 March 2002 [2002] 1 WLR 1303.)

(7) That [I] [we] further make oath and say that the deceased's name and dates of birth and death as they are recited above are as they appear in the death certificate *(or set out any variation and the reason for it)*.

Sworn *(etc. as in Form C37)*

C60 OATH FOR ADMINISTRATION: BROTHER AND SISTER

In the High Court of Justice *(etc. as in Form C1)*

[I] [We] of (*insert the full names and permanent address of the applicant(s)*) make oath and say:

(1) That (*insert the full true name and address (including postcode) of the deceased; see Practice Direction 22 March 2002 [2002] 1 WLR 1303. If the deceased held property in a former name or alias, insert 'formerly or otherwise known as ...'. Any substantial discrepancy in the name must be explained in the oath, as must the reason for including the alternative or alias name in the grant. The last residential address of the deceased should be given*) deceased was born on the ... day of ... 19... and died on the ... day of ... 20... (*insert the dates of birth and death as they appear in the death certificate; see Practice Direction 12 January 1999*) aged ... domiciled in England and Wales intestate a [widower] [widow] without issue or parent or any other person entitled in priority to share [his] [her] estate by virtue of any enactment.

(2) That no minority or life interest arises in the estate. (*Where a minority interest arises, the grant must issue to at least two grantees, that is, two attorneys or a trust corporation must be appointed. The district judge or registrar may, in special circumstances, allow the grant to issue to a sole grantee under s. 114, Senior Courts Act 1981.*)

(3) That to the best of [my] [our] knowledge and belief there was [no] land vested in the said deceased immediately before [his] [her] death which was settled previously to [his] [her] death and which remained settled land notwithstanding [his] [her] death. (*Where there is such settled land and the grant sought is to be in respect of free estate only, the word 'no' should be omitted and the words 'save and except settled land' added to para. 5 after the word 'deceased'.*)

(4) That [I am] [we are] the [brother] [sister] [brother and sister] of the whole blood of the said deceased and [two of the persons] [the only person[s]] entitled to [his] [her] estate. (*Where there are no surviving brothers, sisters, nieces or nephews of the whole blood, a brother, sister, niece or nephew of the half blood may apply; the form should be reworded appropriately.*)

(5) That [I] [we] will collect, get in and administer according to law the real and personal estate of the said deceased; when required to do so by the Court, exhibit in the Court a full inventory of the said estate and render an account thereof to the Court; and when required to do so by the High Court, deliver up to that Court the letters of administration.

(6) That to the best of [my] [our] knowledge, information and belief the gross value of the estate passing under the grant [amounts to] [does not exceed] £ ... and the net value [amounts to] [does not exceed] £ ... [and that this is not a case in which an Inheritance Tax Account is required to be delivered]. (*When an inheritance tax account is required, insert the actual gross and net values of the estate; where an account is not required, insert the appropriate gross value. The net estate figure should be the actual value rounded up to the nearest £1,000; see Practice Direction 22 March 2002 [2002] 1 WLR 1303.*)

(7) That [I] [we] further make oath and say that the deceased's name and dates of birth and death as they are recited above are as they appear in the death certificate *(or set out any variation and the reason for it).*

Sworn *(etc. as in Form C37)*

C61 OATH FOR ADMINISTRATION: NEPHEW OR NIECE

In the High Court of Justice *(etc. as in Form C1)*

I (*insert the full names and permanent address of the applicant*) make oath and say:

(1) That (*insert the full true name and address (including postcode) of the deceased; see Practice Direction 22 March 2002 [2002] 1 WLR 1303. If the deceased held property in a former name or alias, insert 'formerly or otherwise known as ...'. Any substantial discrepancy in the name must be explained in the oath, as must the reason for including the alternative or alias name in the grant. The last residential address of the deceased should be given*) deceased was born on the ... day of ... 19... and died on the ... day of ... 20... (*insert the dates of birth and death as they appear in the death certificate; see Practice Direction 12 January 1999*) aged ... domiciled in England and Wales intestate a [widower] [widow] without issue or parent or brother or sister of the whole blood or any other person entitled in priority to share [his] [her] estate by virtue of any enactment.

(2) That no minority or life interest arises in the estate. (*Where a minority interest arises, the grant must issue to at least two grantees, that is, two attorneys or a trust corporation must be appointed. The district judge or registrar may, in special circumstances, allow the grant to issue to a sole grantee under s. 114, Senior Courts Act 1981.*)

(3) That to the best of my knowledge and belief there was [no] land vested in the said deceased immediately before his death which was settled previously to his death and which remained settled land notwithstanding his death. (*Where there is such settled land and the grant sought is to be in respect of free estate only, the word 'no' should be omitted and the words 'save and except settled land' added to para. 5 after the word 'deceased'.*)

(4) That I am the [nephew] [niece] of the whole blood of the said deceased and [one of the persons] [the only person] entitled to [share] [his] [her] estate.

(5) That I will collect, get in and administer according to law the real and personal estate of the said deceased; when required to do so by the Court, exhibit in the Court a full inventory of the said estate and render an account thereof to the Court; and when required to do so by the High Court, deliver up to that Court the letters of administration.

(6) That to the best of my knowledge, information and belief the gross value of the estate passing under the grant [amounts to] [does not exceed] £ ... and the net value [amounts to] [does not exceed] £ ... [and that this is not a case in which an Inheritance Tax Account is required to be delivered]. (*When an inheritance tax account is required, insert the actual gross and net values of the estate; where an account is not required, insert the appropriate gross*

value. The net estate figure should be the actual value rounded up to the nearest £1,000; see Practice Direction 22 March 2002 [2002] 1 WLR 1303.)

(7) That I further make oath and say that the deceased's name and dates of birth and death as they are recited above are as they appear in the death certificate *(or set out any variation and the reason for it)*.

Sworn *(etc. as in Form C37)*

C62 OATH FOR ADMINISTRATION: COUSIN GERMAN

In the High Court of Justice *(etc. as in Form C1)*

I (*insert the full names and permanent address of the applicant*) make oath and say:

(1) That (*insert the full true name and address (including postcode) of the deceased; see Practice Direction 22 March 2002 [2002] 1 WLR 1303. If the deceased held property in a former name or alias, insert 'formerly or otherwise known as ...'. Any substantial discrepancy in the name must be explained in the oath, as must the reason for including the alternative or alias name in the grant. The last residential address of the deceased should be given*) deceased was born on the ... day of ... 19... and died on the ... day of ... 20... (*insert the dates of birth and death as they appear in the death certificate; see Practice Direction 12 January 1999*) aged ... domiciled in England and Wales intestate a [spinster (or as the case may be)] without issue or parent or brother or sister of the whole or half blood or their issue or grandparent or uncle or aunt of the whole blood or any other person entitled in priority to share [his] [her] estate by virtue of any enactment.

(2) That no minority or life interest arises in the estate. (*Where a minority interest arises, the grant must issue to at least two grantees, that is, two attorneys or a trust corporation must be appointed. The district judge or registrar may, in special circumstances, allow the grant to issue to a sole grantee under s. 114, Senior Courts Act 1981.*)

(3) That to the best of my knowledge and belief there was [no] land vested in the said deceased immediately before her death which was settled previously to her death and which remained settled land notwithstanding [his] [her] death. (*Where there is such settled land and the grant sought is to be in respect of free estate only, the word 'no' should be omitted and the words 'save and except settled land' added to para. 5 after the word 'deceased'.*)

(4) That I am the cousin german of the whole blood of the said deceased and [one of the persons] [the only person] entitled to [share] [his] [her] estate.

(5) That I will collect, get in and administer according to law the real and personal estate of the said deceased; when required to do so by the Court, exhibit in the Court a full inventory of the said estate and render an account thereof to the Court; and when required to do so by the High Court, deliver up to that Court the letters of administration.

(6) That to the best of my knowledge, information and belief the gross value of the estate passing under the grant [amounts to] [does not exceed] £ ... and the net value [amounts to] [does not exceed] £ ... [and that this is not a case in which an Inheritance Tax Account is required to be delivered]. (*When an inheritance tax account is required, insert the actual gross and net values of*

the estate; where an account is not required, insert the appropriate gross value. The net estate figure should be the actual value rounded up to the nearest £1,000; see Practice Direction 22 March 2002 [2002] 1 WLR 1303.)

(7) That I further make oath and say that the deceased's name and dates of birth and death as they are recited above are as they appear in the death certificate *(or set out any variation and the reason for it).*

Sworn *(etc. as in Form C37)*

C63 OATH FOR ADMINISTRATION: ASSIGNEE(S)

In the High Court of Justice *(etc. as in Form C1)*

[I] [We] (*insert the full names and address of the applicant(s)*) make oath and say:

(1) That (*insert the full true name and address (including postcode) of the deceased; see Practice Direction 22 March 2002 [2002] 1 WLR 1303. If the deceased held property in a former name or alias, insert 'formerly or otherwise known as ...'. Any substantial discrepancy in the name must be explained in the oath, as must the reason for including the alternative or alias name in the grant. The last residential address of the deceased should be given*) deceased was born on the ... day of ... 19... and died on the ... day of ... 20... (*insert the dates of birth and death as they appear in the death certificate; see Practice Direction 12 January 1999*) aged ... domiciled in England and Wales intestate leaving (*insert the name of the surviving spouse*) [his] [her] lawful [widow] [husband] and the only person now entitled to [his] [her] estate. (*Insert any other status of the deceased, the title of the deponents, and any clearings.*)

(2) That no minority or life interest arises in the estate.

(3) That to the best of [my] [our] knowledge and belief there was [no] land vested in the said deceased immediately before [his] [her] death which was settled previously to [his] [her] death and which remained settled land notwithstanding [his] [her] death. (*Where there is such settled land and the grant sought is to be in respect of free estate only, the word 'no' should be omitted and the words 'save and except settled land' added to para. 5 after the word 'deceased'.*)

(4) By a Deed of Assignment (*the deed of assignment, or a certified true and complete copy, must be lodged*) dated the ... day of ... 20... the said (*insert the name of the surviving spouse*) assigned to [me] [us] [and to ...] all [his] [her] right and title to and interest in the estate of the said deceased.

(5) That [I] [we] will collect, get in and administer according to law the real and personal estate of the said deceased; when required to do so by the Court, exhibit in the Court a full inventory of the said estate and render an account thereof to the Court; and when required to do so by the High Court, deliver up to that Court the letters of administration.

(6) That to the best of [my] [our] knowledge, information and belief the gross value of the estate passing under the grant [amounts to] [does not exceed] £ ... and the net value [amounts to] [does not exceed] £ ... [and that this is not a case in which an Inheritance Tax Account is required to be delivered]. (*When an inheritance tax account is required, insert the actual gross and net values of the estate; where an account is not required, insert the appropriate*

gross value. The net estate figure should be the actual value rounded up to the nearest £1,000; see Practice Direction 22 March 2002 [2002] 1 WLR 1303.)

(7) That [I] [we] further make oath and say that the deceased's name and dates of birth and death as they are recited above are as they appear in the death certificate *(or set out any variation and the reason for it)*.

Sworn *(etc. as in Form C37)*

C64 OATH FOR ADMINISTRATION: PERSON ENTITLED ON ACCRETION

For use only where the net estate does not, at the date of death, exceed the spouse's statutory legacy.

In the High Court of Justice *(etc. as in Form C1)*

I (*insert the full names and permanent address of the applicant*) make oath and say:

(1) That (*insert the full true name and address (including postcode) of the deceased; see Practice Direction 22 March 2002 [2002] 1 WLR 1303. If the deceased held property in a former name or alias, insert 'formerly or otherwise known as ...'. Any substantial discrepancy in the name must be explained in the oath, as must the reason for including the alternative or alias name in the grant. The last residential address of the deceased should be given*) deceased was born on the ... day of ... 19... and died on the ... day of ... 20... (*insert the dates of birth and death as they appear in the death certificate; see Practice Direction 12 January 1999)* aged ... domiciled in England and Wales intestate leaving (*insert the name of the surviving spouse*) [his] [her] lawful [widow] [husband] and the only person now entitled to [his] [her] estate who has renounced letters of administration of the estate.

(2) That no minority or life interest arises in the estate.

(3) That to the best of my knowledge and belief there was [no] land vested in the said deceased immediately before [his] [her] death which was settled previously to [his] [her] death and which remained settled land notwithstanding [his] [her] death. (*Where there is such settled land and the grant sought is to be in respect of free estate only, the word 'no' should be omitted and the words 'save and except settled land' added to para. 5 after the word 'deceased'.*)

(4) That I am the [son] [daughter] of the said deceased and a person who may have a beneficial interest in [his] [her] estate in the event of an accretion thereto.

(5) That I will collect, get in and administer according to law the real and personal estate of the said deceased; when required to do so by the Court, exhibit in the Court a full inventory of the said estate and render an account thereof to the Court; and when required to do so by the High Court, deliver up to that Court the letters of administration.

(6) That to the best of my knowledge, information and belief the gross value of the estate passing under the grant [amounts to] [does not exceed] £ ... and the net value [amounts to] [does not exceed] £ ... [and that this is not a case

in which an Inheritance Tax Account is required to be delivered]. (*When an inheritance tax account is required, insert the actual gross and net values of the estate; where an account is not required, insert the appropriate gross value. The net estate figure should be the actual value rounded up to the nearest £1,000; see Practice Direction 22 March 2002 [2002] 1 WLR 1303.*)

(7) That I further make oath and say that the deceased's name and dates of birth and death as they are recited above are as they appear in the death certificate *(or set out any variation and the reason for it)*.

Sworn *(etc. as in Form C37)*

C65 OATH FOR ADMINISTRATION: CREDITOR

In the High Court of Justice *(etc. as in Form C1)*

I (*insert the full names and permanent address of the applicant*) make oath and say:

(1) That (*insert the full true name and address (including postcode) of the deceased; see Practice Direction 22 March 2002 [2002] 1 WLR 1303. If the deceased held property in a former name or alias, insert 'formerly or otherwise known as ...'. Any substantial discrepancy in the name must be explained in the oath, as must the reason for including the alternative or alias name in the grant. The last residential address of the deceased should be given*) deceased was born on the ... day of ... 19... and died on the ... day of ... 20... (*insert the dates of birth and death as they appear in the death certificate; see Practice Direction 12 January 1999*) aged ... domiciled in England and Wales intestate leaving [his] [her] lawful [widow] [husband] and the only person now entitled to [his] [her] estate who has renounced letters of administration of the estate. (*Insert any other status of the deceased and the appropriate clearings.*)

(2) That no minority or life interest arises in the estate.

(3) That to the best of my knowledge and belief there was [no] land vested in the said deceased immediately before [his] [her] death which was settled previously to [his] [her] death and which remained settled land notwithstanding [his] [her] death. (*Where there is such settled land and the grant sought is to be in respect of free estate only, the word 'no' should be omitted and the words 'save and except settled land' added to para. 5 after the word 'deceased'.*)

(4) That I am a creditor of the said deceased.

(5) That I will collect, get in and administer according to law the real and personal estate of the said deceased; when required to do so by the Court, exhibit in the Court a full inventory of the said estate and render an account thereof to the Court; and when required to do so by the High Court, deliver up to that Court the letters of administration.

(6) That to the best of my knowledge, information and belief the gross value of the estate passing under the grant [amounts to] [does not exceed] £ ... and the net value [amounts to] [does not exceed] £ ... [and that this is not a case in which an Inheritance Tax Account is required to be delivered]. (*When an inheritance tax account is required, insert the actual gross and net values of the estate; where an account is not required, insert the appropriate gross value. The net estate figure should be the actual value rounded up to the nearest £1,000; see Practice Direction 22 March 2002 [2002] 1 WLR 1303.*)

(7) That I further make oath and say that the deceased's name and dates of birth and death as they are recited above are as they appear in the death certificate *(or set out any variation and the reason for it).*

Sworn *(etc. as in Form C37)*

C66 OATH FOR ADMINISTRATION: ATTORNEY

In the High Court of Justice *(etc. as in Form C1)*

I (*insert the full names and permanent address of the applicant*) make oath and say:

(1) That (*insert the full true name and address (including postcode) of the deceased; see Practice Direction 22 March 2002 [2002] 1 WLR 1303. If the deceased held property in a former name or alias, insert 'formerly or otherwise known as ...'. Any substantial discrepancy in the name must be explained in the oath, as must the reason for including the alternative or alias name in the grant. The last residential address of the deceased should be given*) deceased was born on the ... day of ... 19... and died on the ... day of ... 20... (*insert the dates of birth and death as they appear in the death certificate; see Practice Direction 12 January 1999*) aged ... domiciled in England and Wales intestate (*insert the deceased's status, e.g. 'a widow'*) and without any person entitled in priority to share in [his] [her] estate leaving (*insert the name and relationship of the person beneficially entitled*) [one of the persons] [the person] entitled to share in [his] [her] estate.

(2) That no minority or life interest arises in the estate. (*Where a minority or life interest arises, the grant must issue to at least two grantees, that is, two attorneys or a trust corporation must be appointed. The district judge or registrar may, in special circumstances, allow the grant to issue to a sole grantee under s. 114, Senior Courts Act 1981.*)

(3) That to the best of my knowledge and belief there was [no] land vested in the said deceased immediately before [his] [her] death which was settled previously to [his] [her] death and which remained settled land notwithstanding [his] [her] death. (*Where there is such settled land and the grant sought is to be in respect of free estate only, the word 'no' should be omitted and the words 'save and except settled land' added to para. 5 after the word 'deceased'.*)

(4) That I am the lawful attorney of the said (*insert the name of the person entitled who has executed the power of attorney*).

(5) That I will collect, get in and administer according to law the real and personal estate of the said deceased for the use and benefit of the said (*insert the name of the person entitled who has executed the power of attorney*) limited until further representation be granted; when required to do so by the Court, exhibit in the Court a full inventory of the said estate and render an account thereof to the Court; and when required to do so by the High Court, deliver up to that Court the letters of administration.

(6) That to the best of my knowledge, information and belief the gross value of the estate passing under the grant [amounts to] [does not exceed] £ ... and

the net value [amounts to] [does not exceed] £ ... [and that this is not a case in which an Inheritance Tax Account is required to be delivered]. (*When an inheritance tax account is required, insert the actual gross and net values of the estate; where an account is not required, insert the appropriate gross value. The net estate figure should be the actual value rounded up to the nearest £1,000; see Practice Direction 22 March 2002 [2002] 1 WLR 1303.*)

(7) That I further make oath and say that the deceased's name and dates of birth and death as they are recited above are as they appear in the death certificate *(or set out any variation and the reason for it).*

Sworn *(etc. as in Form C37)*

C67 OATH FOR ADMINISTRATION: CHILD AND ATTORNEY OF ANOTHER CHILD

In the High Court of Justice *(etc. as in Form C1)*

We (*insert the full names and address of the applicant(s)*) make oath and say:

(1) That (*insert the full true name and address (including postcode) of the deceased; see Practice Direction 22 March 2002 [2002] 1 WLR 1303. If the deceased held property in a former name or alias, insert 'formerly or otherwise known as ...'. Any substantial discrepancy in the name must be explained in the oath, as must the reason for including the alternative or alias name in the grant. The last residential address of the deceased should be given*) deceased was born on the ... day of ... 19... and died on the ... day of ... 20... (*insert the dates of birth and death as they appear in the death certificate; see Practice Direction 12 January 1999*) aged ... domiciled in England and Wales intestate a [widower] [widow] leaving ... and ... [his] [her] [son] [and] [daughter] the only persons entitled to share [his] [her] estate.

(2) That no minority or life interest arises in the estate.

(3) That to the best of our knowledge and belief there was [no] land vested in the said deceased immediately before her death which was settled previously to her death and which remained settled land notwithstanding her death. (*Where there is such settled land and the grant sought is to be in respect of free estate only, the word 'no' should be omitted and the words 'save and except settled land' added to para. 5 after the word 'deceased'.*)

(4) That I the said (*insert the name of the first deponent*) am the [daughter] of the said deceased and I, (*insert the name of the second deponent*) am the lawful attorney of ..., the [son] of the deceased.

(5) That we will collect, get in and administer according to law the real and personal estate of the said deceased limited until further representation be granted; when required to do so by the Court, exhibit in the Court a full inventory of the said estate and render an account thereof to the Court; and when required to do so by the High Court, deliver up to that Court the letters of administration.

(6) That to the best of our knowledge, information and belief the gross value of the estate passing under the grant [amounts to] [does not exceed] £ ... and the net value [amounts to] [does not exceed] £ ... [and that this is not a case in which an Inheritance Tax Account is required to be delivered]. (*When an inheritance tax account is required, insert the actual gross and net values of the estate; where an account is not required, insert the appropriate gross*

value. The net estate figure should be the actual value rounded up to the nearest £1,000; see Practice Direction 22 March 2002 [2002] 1 WLR 1303.)

(7) That [I] [we] further make oath and say that the deceased's name and dates of birth and death as they are recited above are as they appear in the death certificate *(or set out any variation and the reason for it)*.

(8) I, *(insert the name of the child)* consent to the grant being limited as aforesaid.

Sworn *(etc. as in Form C37)*

C68 OATH FOR ADMINISTRATION FOR THE USE AND BENEFIT OF A PERSON WHO LACKS CAPACITY WITHIN THE MEANING OF THE MENTAL CAPACITY ACT 2005

In the High Court of Justice *(etc. as in Form C1)*

I (*insert the full names and permanent address of the applicant*) make oath and say:

(1) That (*insert the full true name and address (including postcode) of the deceased; see Practice Direction 22 March 2002 [2002] 1 WLR 1303. If the deceased held property in a former name or alias, insert 'formerly or otherwise known as ...'. Any substantial discrepancy in the name must be explained in the oath, as must the reason for including the alternative or alias name in the grant. The last residential address of the deceased should be given*) deceased was born on the ... day of ... 19... and died on the ... day of ... 20... (*insert the dates of birth and death as they appear in the death certificate; see Practice Direction 12 January 1999*) aged ... domiciled in England and Wales intestate (*insert the status of the deceased, e.g. 'widow without issue'*) [or any other person entitled in priority to share in [his] [her] estate by virtue of any enactment] leaving (*insert the name of the incapable person and the relationship to the deceased, e.g. 'brother of the whole blood'*) who now suffers an impairment of or a disturbance in the functioning of [his] [her] mind or brain as a result of which [he] [she] is unable to make a decision for [himself] [herself] in relation to the application for a grant of representation and subsequent administration of the estate of the deceased within the meaning of the Mental Capacity Act 2005.

(2) [That by an order of the Court of Protection dated the ... day of ... 20... I was authorised to apply for letters of administration for the use and benefit of (*insert the name of the incapable person*) and during [his] [her] incapacity.]

[That no one has been authorised by the Court of Protection to apply for letters of administration. I am the lawful attorney of the said *(insert the name of the incapable person*) acting under [an enduring] [a lasting] power of attorney which was registered in the Office of the Public Guardian on the ... day of ... 20....]

[That no one has been authorised by the Court of Protection to apply for letters of administration for the use and benefit of the said (*insert the name of the incapable person*) and there is no one acting under a registered [enduring] [lasting] power of attorney.]

[That by order dated the the ... day of ... 20... made by [District Judge] [District Probate Registrar] ... of this Division it was ordered under and pursuant to rule 35(4) of the Non-Contentious Probate Rules 1987 that letters of administration be granted to me for the use and benefit of the said (*insert the name of the incapable person*) and until further representation be granted.]

(3) That no minority or life interest arises in the estate (*or as may be*).

(4) That to the best of my knowledge and belief there was no land vested in the said deceased immediately before his death which was settled previously to his death and which remained settled land notwithstanding his death. (*Where there is such settled land and the grant sought is to be in respect of free estate only, the word 'no' should be omitted and the words 'save and except settled land' added to para 6 after the word 'deceased'.*)

(5) That I will collect, get in and administer according to law the real and personal estate of the said deceased for the use and benefit of the said (*insert the name of the incapable person*) [during [his] [her] incapacity] [limited until further representation be granted]; when required to do so by the Court, exhibit in the Court a full inventory of the said estate and render an account thereof to the Court; and when required to do so by the High Court, deliver up to that Court the letters of administration.

(6) That to the best of my knowledge, information and belief the gross value of the estate passing under the grant [amounts to] [does not exceed] £ ... and the net value [amounts to] [does not exceed] £ ... [and that this is not a case in which an Inheritance Tax Account is required to be delivered]. (*When an inheritance tax account is required, insert the actual gross and net values of the estate; where an account is not required, insert the appropriate gross value. The net estate figure should be the actual value rounded up to the nearest £1,000; see Practice Direction 22 March 2002 [2002] 1 WLR 1303.*)

(7) That I further make oath and say that the deceased's name and dates of birth and death as they are recited above are as they appear in the death certificate *(or set out any variation and the reason for it).*

Sworn *(etc. as in Form C37)*

C69 OATH FOR ADMINISTRATION: PERSON WITH PARENTAL RESPONSIBILITY AND NOMINATED CO-ADMINISTRATOR FOR THE USE AND BENEFIT OF MINOR(S)

In the High Court of Justice *(etc. as in Form C1)*

We (*insert the full and correct names of the person with parental responsibility applying, and his/her full, permanent postal address (including postcode)*) and (*insert the full names and address of the nominated co-administrator*) make oath and say:

(1) That (*insert the full true name and address (including postcode) of the deceased; see Practice Direction 22 March 2002 [2002] 1 WLR 1303. If the deceased held property in a former name or alias, insert 'formerly or otherwise known as ...'. Any substantial discrepancy in the name must be explained in the oath, as must the reason for including the alternative or alias name in the grant. The last residential address of the deceased should be given*) deceased was born on the ... day of ... 19... and died on the ... day of ... 20... (*insert the dates of birth and death as they appear in the death certificate; see Practice Direction 12 January 1999*) aged ... domiciled in England and Wales intestate a single [man] [woman] (*or as may be*) leaving (*insert the names of the deceased's surviving child(ren)*) [his] [her] [son[s]] [daughter[s]] and the only person[s] entitled to [his] [her] estate who [is] [are] now [a] minor[s] aged ... [and ... respectively].

(2) [That the marriage of the said deceased with (*insert the name of the surviving parent*) was dissolved by final [decree] [order] of the ... Court dated the ... day of ... 20... and the said deceased did not thereafter remarry or form a civil partnership.]

(3) That the said (*insert the name of the applicant with parental responsibility*) is the (*insert the relationship to the minor(s) and title under rule 32(1)(a)–(c) of the Non-Contentious Probate Rules 1987, e.g. 'the parent of the minor having parental responsibility pursuant to section 2(1) or (2) of the Children Act 1989*) of the said minor[s] and that there is no other person [having parental responsibility for] [appointed guardian of] the said minor[s].

(4) That the said (*insert the name of the applicant with parental responsibility*) has nominated by a nomination dated the ... day of ... 20... the said (*insert the name of the co-administrator*) to be [his] [her] co-administrator, [he] [she] being a fit and proper person to act in that capacity.

(5) That a minority but no life interest arises under the intestacy.

(6) That to the best of our knowledge and belief there was [no] land vested in the said deceased immediately before [his] [her] death which was settled

previously to [his] [her] death and which remained settled land notwithstanding [his] [her] death. (*Where there is such settled land and the grant sought is to be in respect of free estate only, the word 'no' should be omitted and the words 'save and except settled land' added to para 7 after the word 'deceased'.*)

(7) That we will collect, get in and administer according to law the real and personal estate of the said deceased for the use and benefit of the said minor[s] until [he] [she] [one of them] shall attain the age of eighteen years; when required to do so by the Court, exhibit in the Court a full inventory of the said estate and render an account thereof to the Court; and when required to do so by the High Court, deliver up to that Court the letters of administration.

(8) That to the best of our knowledge, information and belief the gross value of the estate passing under the grant [amounts to] [does not exceed] £ ... and the net value [amounts to] [does not exceed] £ ... [and that this is not a case in which an Inheritance Tax Account is required to be delivered]. (*When an inheritance tax account is required, insert the actual gross and net values of the estate; where an account is not required, insert the appropriate gross value. The net estate figure should be the actual value rounded up to the nearest £1,000; see Practice Direction 22 March 2002 [2002] 1 WLR 1303.*)

(9) That we further make oath and say that the deceased's name and dates of birth and death as they are recited above are as they appear in the death certificate *(or set out any variation and the reason for it).*

Sworn *(etc. as in Form C37)*

C70 OATH FOR ADMINISTRATION: PERSON(S) APPOINTED TO TAKE LETTERS OF ADMINISTRATION FOR THE USE AND BENEFIT OF MINORS

In the High Court of Justice *(etc. as in Form C1)*

[I] [We] (*insert the full names and address of the applicant(s)*) make oath and say:

(1) That (*insert the full true name and address (including postcode) of the deceased; see Practice Direction 22 March 2002 [2002] 1 WLR 1303. If the deceased held property in a former name or alias, insert 'formerly or otherwise known as ...'. Any substantial discrepancy in the name must be explained in the oath, as must the reason for including the alternative or alias name in the grant. The last residential address of the deceased should be given*) deceased was born on the ... day of ... 19... and died on the ... day of ... 20... (*insert the dates of birth and death as they appear in the death certificate; see Practice Direction 12 January 1999*) aged ... domiciled in England and Wales intestate a widow[er] [single man] [single woman] leaving (*insert the full names of the surviving minor child(ren)*) [his] [her] child[ren] and the only person[s] entitled in priority to [share in] [his] [her] estate who [is a minor aged ...] [are minors aged ... and ... respectively].

(2) [That there is no person or body with or deemed to have parental responsibility and that there is no person or body appointed or deemed to be appointed guardian of the said minor[s].]

(3) That (*insert the full names and address of the applicant(s)*) [was] [were] appointed by order of [District Judge] [Registrar] ... dated the ... day of ... 20... for the purpose of taking letters of administration of the estate of the said deceased for [his] [her] [their] use and benefit until [he] [she] [one of them] shall attain the age of eighteen years.

(4) That a minority but no life interest arises under the intestacy.

(5) That to the best of [my] [our] knowledge and belief there was [no] land vested in the said deceased immediately before [his] [her] death which was settled previously to [his] [her] death and which remained settled land notwithstanding [his] [her] death. (*Where there is such settled land and the grant sought is to be in respect of free estate only, the word 'no' should be omitted and the words 'save and except settled land' added to para 6 after the word 'deceased'.*)

(6) That [I] [we] will collect, get in and administer according to law the real and personal estate of the said deceased for the use and benefit of the said minor[s] limited until [he] [she] [one of them] shall attain the age of eighteen years; when required to do so by the Court, exhibit in the Court a full

inventory of the said estate and render an account thereof to the Court; and when required to do so by the High Court, deliver up to that Court the letters of administration.

(7) That to the best of [my] [our] knowledge, information and belief the gross value of the estate passing under the grant [amounts to] [does not exceed] £ ... and the net value [amounts to] [does not exceed] £ ... [and that this is not a case in which an Inheritance Tax Account is required to be delivered]. *(When an inheritance tax account is required, insert the actual gross and net values of the estate; where an account is not required, insert the appropriate gross value. The net estate figure should be the actual value rounded up to the nearest £1,000; see Practice Direction 22 March 2002 [2002] 1 WLR 1303.)*

(8) That [I] [we] further make oath and say that the deceased's name and dates of birth and death as they are recited above are as they appear in the death certificate *(or set out any variation and the reason for it).*

Sworn *(etc. as in Form C37)*

C71 OATH FOR ADMINISTRATION *AD COLLIGENDA BONA DEFUNCTI*

In the High Court of Justice *(etc. as in Form C1)*

I (*the applicant is the person named in and authorised by the order*) make oath and say:

(1) That (*insert the full true name and address (including postcode) of the deceased; see Practice Direction 22 March 2002 [2002] 1 WLR 1303. If the deceased held property in a former name or alias, insert 'formerly or otherwise known as ...'. Any substantial discrepancy in the name must be explained in the oath, as must the reason for including the alternative or alias name in the grant. The last residential address of the deceased should be given*) deceased was born on the ... day of ... 19... and died on the ... day of ... 20... (*insert the dates of birth and death as they appear in the death certificate; see Practice Direction 12 January 1999*) aged ... domiciled in England and Wales. (*This form of grant is always of letters of administration. The oath and the grant are silent as to the deceased's having been testate or intestate.*)

(2) That [no] [a] minority [and a] [but no] life interest arises in the estate.

(3) That by order of [District Judge] [Registrar] ... dated the ... day of ... 20... it was ordered that letters of administration of the estate of the said deceased be granted to me limited to (*recite the limitation imposed in the order*).

(4) That to the best of my knowledge and belief there was [no] land vested in the said deceased immediately before his death which was settled previously to his death and which remained settled land notwithstanding his death. (*Where there is such settled land and the grant sought is to be in respect of free estate only, the word 'no' should be omitted and the words 'save and except settled land' added to para 5 after the word 'deceased'.*)

(5) That I will collect, get in and administer according to law the real and personal estate of the said deceased limited to collecting, getting in and receiving the estate and doing such acts as may be necessary for the preservation of the estate and until further representation be granted but no further or otherwise (*or as may be, according to the order*); when required to do so by the Court, exhibit in the Court a full inventory of the said estate and render an account thereof to the Court; and when required to do so by the High Court, deliver up to that Court the grant of letters of administration.

(6) That to the best of my knowledge, information and belief the gross value of the estate passing under the grant [amounts to] [does not exceed] £ ... and the net value [amounts to] [does not exceed] £ ... [and that this is not a case

in which an Inheritance Tax Account is required to be delivered]. (*When an inheritance tax account is required, insert the actual gross and net values of the estate; where an account is not required, insert the appropriate gross value. The net estate figure should be the actual value rounded up to the nearest £1,000; see Practice Direction 22 March 2002 [2002] 1 WLR 1303.*)

(7) That I further make oath and say that the deceased's name and dates of birth and death as they are recited above are as they appear in the death certificate *(or set out any variation and the reason for it).*

Sworn *(etc. as in Form C37)*

C72 OATH FOR ADMINISTRATION PURSUANT TO ORDER UNDER SECTION 116 OF THE SENIOR COURTS ACT 1981

In the High Court of Justice *(etc. as in Form C1)*

[I] [We] (*insert the full names and address of the applicant(s)*) make oath and say:

(1) That [[I] [we] believe the paper writing now produced to and marked by [me] [us] to be the true and original last Will and Testament] (*Where the Will to be proved comprises more than one document, insert the words 'as contained in the paper writings marked ...'. Add, if appropriate, 'together with [a] [two] [three] codicil[s]'. Each deponent and the commissioner must mark the documents with their signatures*) of (*insert the full true name and address (including postcode) of the deceased (see Practice Direction 22 March 2002 [2002] 1 WLR 1303). If the deceased held property in a former name or alias, insert 'formerly or otherwise known as ...'. Any substantial discrepancy in the name must be explained in the oath, as must the reason for including the alternative or alias name in the grant. The last residential address of the deceased should be given*) deceased, who was born on the ... day of ... 19.., and died on the ... day of ... 20... (*insert the dates of birth and death as they appear in the death certificate; see Practice Direction 12 January 1999*) aged ... domiciled in England and Wales [intestate].

(2) That no minority or life interest arises in the estate. (*Where a minority or life interest arises, the grant must issue to at least two grantees; this should be dealt with in the affidavit to lead the order). The district judge or registrar may, in special circumstances, allow the grant to issue to a sole grantee under s. 114, Senior Courts Act 1981.*)

(3) That to the best of [my] [our] knowledge and belief there was [no] land vested in the said deceased immediately before his death which was settled previously to his death [and not by his Will] and which remained settled land notwithstanding his death. (*Where there is such settled land and the grant sought is to be in respect of free estate only, the word 'no' should be omitted and the words 'save and except settled land' added to para. 5 after the word 'deceased'.*)

(4) That by order of [District Judge] [Registrar] ... dated the ... day of ... 20... it was ordered that letters of administration of the estate of the said deceased be granted to [me] [us] pursuant to s. 116, Senior Courts Act 1981.

(5) That [I] [we] will collect, get in and administer according to law the real and personal estate of the said deceased (*recite any limitation imposed by the order)*; when required to do so by the Court, exhibit in the Court a full inventory of the said estate and render an account thereof to the Court; and

when required to do so by the High Court, deliver up to that Court the grant of letters of administration.

(6) That to the best of [my] [our] knowledge, information and belief the gross value of the estate passing under the grant [amounts to] [does not exceed] £ ... and the net value [amounts to] [does not exceed] £ ... [and that this is not a case in which an Inheritance Tax Account is required to be delivered]. (*When an inheritance tax account is required, insert the actual gross and net values of the estate; where an account is not required, insert the appropriate gross value. The net estate figure should be the actual value rounded up to the nearest £1,000; see Practice Direction 22 March 2002 [2002] 1 WLR 1303.*)

(7) That [I] [we] further make oath and say that the deceased's name and dates of birth and death as they are recited above are as they appear in the death certificate *(or set out any variation and the reason for it)*.

Sworn *(etc. as in Form C37)*

C73 OATH FOR ADMINISTRATION *DE BONIS NON*

In the High Court of Justice *(etc. as in Form C1)*

[I] [We] (*insert the full names and address of the applicant(s)*) make oath and say:

(1) That [[I] [we] believe the paper writing now produced to and marked by [me] [us] to be [the true and original] [an office copy of the] last Will and Testament] (*Where the Will to be proved comprises more than one document, insert the words 'as contained in the paper writings marked ...'. Add, if appropriate, 'together with [a] [two] [three] codicil[s]'. Each deponent and the commissioner must mark the documents with their signatures*) of (*insert the full true name and address (including postcode) of the deceased (see Practice Direction 22 March 2002 [2002] 1 WLR 1303). If the deceased held property in a former name or alias, insert 'formerly or otherwise known as ...'. Any substantial discrepancy in the name must be explained in the oath, as must the reason for including the alternative or alias name in the grant. The last residential address of the deceased should be given*) deceased, who was born on the ... day of ... 19.., and died on the ... day of ... 20... (*insert the dates of birth and death as they appear in the death certificate; see Practice Direction 12 January 1999*) aged ... domiciled in England and Wales [wherein [he] [she] did not name any executor] [wherein [he] [she] named ... the sole executor who died on the ... day of ... 20....] [intestate.]

(2) That on the ... day of ... 20... letters of administration [(with Will annexed)] were granted to (*insert the name of the grantee*) [the residuary legatee and devisee in trust (*or as may be*)] named therein and that the said (*insert the name of the grantee*) died on the ... day of ... 20... leaving part of the estate of the said deceased unadministered (*insert details of the previous grant; the grantee(s); the title to the previous grant; and the reason the original grant has ceased to be effective. Where the application is made to a registry other than the registry which issued the original grant, the original grant or an office copy must be lodged with this oath.*)

(3) That no minority or life interest arises in the estate. (*Where a minority or life interest arises, the grant must issue to at least two grantees, that is, two attorneys or a trust corporation must be appointed. The district judge or registrar may, in special circumstances, allow the grant to issue to a sole grantee under s. 114, Senior Courts Act 1981.*)

(4) That to the best of [my] [our] knowledge and belief there was [no] land vested in the said deceased immediately before his death which was settled previously to his death [(and not by his Will)] and which remained settled land notwithstanding his death. (*Where there is such settled land and the grant sought is to be in respect of free estate only, the word 'no' should be omitted and the words 'save and except settled land' added to para 6 after the word 'deceased'.*)

(5) That [I am] [we are] the residuary legatee[s] (*or as may be*) named in the said Will. (*Insert the applicant's title to the grant and any other clearings of persons with prior entitlement other than those already mentioned.*)

(6) That [I] [we] will collect, get in and administer according to law the unadministered real and personal estate of the said deceased; when required to do so by the Court, exhibit in the Court a full inventory of the said estate and render an account thereof to the Court; and when required to do so by the High Court, deliver up to that Court the grant of letters of administration.

(7) That to the best of [my] [our] knowledge, information and belief the gross value of the estate passing under the grant [amounts to] [does not exceed] £ ... and the net value [amounts to] [does not exceed] £ ... [and that this is not a case in which an Inheritance Tax Account is required to be delivered]. (*When an inheritance tax account is required, insert the actual gross value of the unadministered estate; where an account is not required, insert the appropriate gross value. The net estate figure should be the actual value rounded up to the nearest £1,000; see Practice Direction 22 March 2002 [2002] 1 WLR 1303.*) Theses figures can be the same as used on the original grant application.

(8) That [I] [we] further make oath and say that the deceased's name and dates of birth and death as they are recited above are as they appear in the death certificate *(or set out any variation and the reason for it).*

Sworn *(etc. as in Form C37)*

C74 OATH FOR *CESSATE* GRANT OF ADMINISTRATION

In the High Court of Justice *(etc. as in Form C1)*

I (*insert the full names and permanent address of the applicant*) make oath and say:

(1) That I believe the paper writing now produced to and marked by me to be the true and original last Will and Testament (*Where the Will to be proved comprises more than one document, insert the words 'as contained in the paper writings marked ...'. Add, if appropriate, 'together with [a] [two] [three] codicil[s]'. Each deponent and the commissioner must mark the documents with their signatures*) of (*insert the full true name and address (including postcode) of the deceased (see Practice Direction 22 March 2002 [2002] 1 WLR 1303). If the deceased held property in a former name or alias, insert 'formerly or otherwise known as ...'. Any substantial discrepancy in the name must be explained in the oath, as must the reason for including the alternative or alias name in the grant. The last residential address of the deceased should be given*) deceased, who was born on the ... day of ... 19.., and died on the ... day of ... 20... (*insert the dates of birth and death as they appear in the death certificate; see Practice Direction 12 January 1999*) aged ... domiciled in England and Wales [wherein [he] [she] did not name any executor] [wherein [he] [she] named (*insert the full name of the executor*) the sole executor] [who predeceased the said deceased] [who survived the deceased but died without proving the said Will] [who has renounced probate of the said Will] and wherein [he] [she] named me (*insert the name of the beneficiary*) [the residuary legatee and devisee (*or as may be*)] (*Insert the relationship of the applicant to the deceased and the capacity in which the grant is applied for; persons with a prior entitlement must be cleared off*) [intestate].

(2) That on the ... day of ... 20... letters of administration [(with Will annexed)] (*or as may be*) of the estate of the said deceased were granted out of the [Principal] [District Probate] Registry to (*insert the name of the previous grantee and his relationship to the applicant*) for my use and benefit (*insert the appropriate eventuality, e.g. 'during my incapacity'; 'until I attained the age of eighteen years'*).

(3) [That I have regained my mental capacity.] [That on the ... day of ... 20... I attained the age of eighteen years] (*or as may be*) by reason of which the said grant has ceased and expired.

(4) That no minority or life interest [now] arises in the estate.

(5) That to the best of my knowledge and belief there was [no] land vested in the said deceased immediately before his death which was settled previously to his death [and not by his Will] and which remained settled land notwithstanding his death. (*Where there is such settled land and the grant*

sought is to be in respect of free estate only, the word 'no' should be omitted and the words 'save and except settled land' added to para 7 after the word 'deceased'.)

(6) That I am [the lawful widow] [the residuary legatee and devisee] (*or as may be*) [named in the said Will].

(7) That I will collect, get in and administer according to law the real and personal estate of the said deceased (*recite any limitation imposed by the order*); when required to do so by the Court, exhibit in the Court a full inventory of the said estate and render an account thereof to the Court; and when required to do so by the High Court, deliver up to that Court the grant of letters of administration [(with Will annexed)].

(8) That to the best of my knowledge, information and belief the gross value of the estate passing under the grant [amounts to] [does not exceed] £ ... and the net value [amounts to] [does not exceed] £ ... [and that this is not a case in which an Inheritance Tax Account is required to be delivered]. (*When an inheritance tax account is required, insert the actual gross and net values of the estate; where an account is not required, insert the appropriate gross value. The net estate figure should be the actual value rounded up to the nearest £1,000; see Practice Direction 22 March 2002 [2002] 1 WLR 1303.*)

(9) That I further make oath and say that the deceased's name and dates of birth and death as they are recited above are as they appear in the death certificate *(or set out any variation and the reason for it).*

Sworn *(etc. as in Form C37)*

C75 OATH FOR ADMINISTRATION (WITH OR WITHOUT WILL ANNEXED): TRUST CORPORATION

In the High Court of Justice *(etc. as in Form C1)*

I, (*insert the full name and address of the deponent; the business address or registered office of the trust corporation; and the deponent's position in the trust corporation, by virtue of which he is authorised to act, e.g. 'manager'*) make oath and say:

(1) That [I believe the paper writing now produced to and marked by me to be the true and original last Will and Testament of] (*Where the Will to be proved comprises more than one document, insert the words 'as contained in the paper writings marked ...'. Add, if appropriate, 'together with [a] [two] [three] codicil[s]'. Each deponent and the commissioner must mark the documents with their signatures*) of (*insert the full true name and address (including postcode) of the deceased (see Practice Direction 22 March 2002 [2002] 1 WLR 1303). If the deceased held property in a former name or alias, insert 'formerly or otherwise known as ...'. Any substantial discrepancy in the name must be explained in the oath, as must the reason for including the alternative or alias name in the grant. The last residential address of the deceased should be given*) deceased [who] was born on the ... day of ... 19... and died on the ... day of ... 20... (*insert the dates of birth and death as they appear in the death certificate; see Practice Direction 12 January 1999*) aged ... domiciled in England and Wales [intestate] leaving (*set out the title of those with a prior right to a grant and the manner of clearing them off; e.g. 'spinster without issue leaving ... her mother and only person entitled to her estate'*) who has/have consented to a grant of letters of administration [with Will annexed] to (*insert the name of the trust corporation*).

(2) That the said (*insert the name of the trust corporation*) is a Trust Corporation as defined by rule 2(1) of the Non-Contentious Probate Rules 1987 and has power to accept the grant now applied for and that the said (*insert the name of the trust corporation*) by a resolution dated the ... day of ... 20... [a certified copy of which is lodged herewith] [which has been lodged with the Senior District Judge of the Family Division in which I am identified by the position I hold and which resolution is still in force] appointed me for the purpose of applying for letters of administration [(with Will annexed)] of the said deceased's estate.

(3) That no minority or life interest [now] arises in the estate.

(4) That to the best of my knowledge and belief there was [no] land vested in the said deceased immediately before his death which was settled previously to his death [and not by his Will [and codicil[s]] and which remained settled land notwithstanding his death. (*Where there is such settled land and the grant sought is to be in respect of free estate only, the word 'no' should be*

omitted and the words 'save and except settled land' added to para 5 after the word 'deceased'.)

(5) That the said (*insert the name of the trust corporation*) will collect, get in and administer according to law the real and personal estate of the said deceased; when required to do so by the Court, exhibit in the Court a full inventory of the said estate and render an account thereof to the Court; and when required to do so by the High Court, deliver up to that Court the letters of administration [(with Will annexed)].

(6) That to the best of my knowledge, information and belief the gross value of the estate passing under the grant [amounts to] [does not exceed] £ ... and the net value [amounts to] [does not exceed] £ ... [and that this is not a case in which an Inheritance Tax Account is required to be delivered]. (*When an inheritance tax account is required, insert the actual gross and net values of the estate; where an account is not required, insert the appropriate gross value. The net estate figure should be the actual value rounded up to the nearest £1,000; see Practice Direction 22 March 2002 [2002] 1 WLR 1303.*)

(7) That I further make oath and say that the deceased's name and dates of birth and death as they are recited above are as they appear in the death certificate *(or set out any variation and the reason for it).*

Sworn *(etc. as in Form C37)*

C76 OATH FOR ADMINISTRATION: FOREIGN DOMICILE

In the High Court of Justice *(etc. as in Form C1)*

I, (*insert the full names and permanent address of the applicant*) make oath and say:

(1) That I believe the paper writing now produced to and marked by me to contain [an official copy of] [a notarially certified copy of] (*or as may be*) the true and original last Will and Testament [and codicil[s]] of] (*Where the Will to be proved comprises more than one document, insert the words 'as contained in the paper writings marked ...'. Add, if appropriate, 'together with [a] [two] [three] codicil[s]'. Each deponent and the commissioner must mark the documents with their signatures*) of *(insert the full true name and address (including postcode) of the deceased (see Practice Direction 22 March 2002 [2002] 1 WLR 1303). If the deceased held property in a former name or alias, insert 'formerly or otherwise known as ...'. Any substantial discrepancy in the name must be explained in the oath, as must the reason for including the alternative or alias name in the grant. The last residential address of the deceased should be given*) deceased, who was born on the ... day of ... 19... and died on the ... day of ... 20... (*insert the dates of birth and death as they appear in the death certificate; see Practice Direction 12 January 1999*) aged ... domiciled in (*insert the country or, if appropriate, the state or territory, of domicile*).

(2) That (*insert the name of the person entrusted or beneficially entitled*) is [the person] [one of the persons] [entrusted with the administration of the estate of the said deceased by the Court having jurisdiction at the place where the deceased died domiciled] [beneficially entitled to [share] in the estate of the deceased by the law of the place where the deceased died domiciled]. [That by order of Mr [District Judge] [Registrar] ... dated the ... day of ... 20... it was ordered that letters of administration [(with Will annexed)] of the estate of the said deceased be granted to me under and by virtue of rule 30(1)[(a)] [(b)] [(c)] of the Non-Contentious Probate Rules 1987.] (*Where an attorney applies for the grant, this should be stated; and the words 'for the use and benefit of the said ... and until further representation be granted' added after the word 'deceased'. Where an order under rule 30(1)(a) or (b) has not been made, a request for such an order may be made in the oath by adding the appropriate words, e.g. 'that I am the person entrusted with administration by the court of the place having jurisdiction where the deceased died domiciled as evidenced by the affidavit made by ... and I hereby apply for an order under rule 30(1)[(a)] [(b)]'.*)

(3) That no minority or life interest [now] arises in the estate. (*If such an interest does arise, at least two applicants will be required.*)

(4) That to the best of my knowledge and belief there was [no] land vested in the said deceased immediately before his death which was settled previously to

his death [and not by his Will] and which remained settled land notwithstanding his death. (*Where there is such settled land and the grant sought is to be in respect of free estate only, the word 'no' should be omitted and the words 'save and except settled land' added to para 5 after the word 'deceased'.*)

(5) That I will collect, get in and administer according to law the real and personal estate of the said deceased (*recite any limitation imposed by the order*); when required to do so by the Court, exhibit in the Court a full inventory of the said estate and render an account thereof to the Court; and when required to do so by the High Court, deliver up to that Court the letters of administration [(with Will annexed)].

(6) That to the best of my knowledge, information and belief the gross value of the estate in England and Wales passing under the grant amounts to £ ... and the net value of the estate [amounts to] [does not exceed] £ ... [and that this is not a case in which an Inheritance Tax Account is required to be delivered]. (*Where the deceased died domiciled outside England and Wales, an inheritance tax account must be delivered before a grant may issue. The gross and net values in the oath must be as in the Account and form IHT421. Where the deceased died on or after 6 April 2002, was never domiciled in the United Kingdom for tax purposes, and the estate in England and Wales was less than £100,000 (£150,000 for deaths on or after 1 September 2006), no account need be delivered, the excepted estate provisions applying.*)

(7) That I further make oath and say that the deceased's name and dates of birth and death as they are recited above are as they appear in the death certificate *(or set out any variation and the reason for it)*.

Sworn *(etc. as in Form C37)*

C77 POWER OF ATTORNEY TO TAKE LETTERS OF ADMINISTRATION (WITH WILL ANNEXED)

In the High Court of Justice *(etc. as in Form C1)*

(1) (*Insert the full name and address of the deceased*) was born on the ... day of ... 19... and died on the ... day of ... 20... domiciled in England and Wales [having made and duly executed [his] [her] last Will and Testament dated the ... day of ... 20... and in the said Will appointed (*insert the name of the donor)* [the sole executor] [one of the executors] thereof [residuary legatee and devisee] (*or as may be*) [intestate a [widow[er]] [spinster without issue] *(or as may be)* (*insert the full name and address of the attorney*) leaving (*insert the name of the donor*).

(2) I (*insert the name of the donor*) of ... do hereby nominate constitute and appoint (*insert the full name and address of the attorney*) to be my lawful attorney for the purpose of obtaining letters of administration [(with Will annexed)] of the estate of the said deceased to be granted to [him] [her] for my use and benefit until further representation be granted and I hereby promise to ratify and confirm whatever my said attorney shall lawfully do or cause to be done in the premises.

Signed by the said ...

the ... day of ... 20...

in the presence of ...

C78 GENERAL FORM OF RENUNCIATION

In the High Court of Justice *(etc. as in Form C1)*

(*Insert the full name and address of the deceased)* deceased died on the ... day of ... 20... [having made and duly executed [his] her] last Will and Testament dated the ... day of ... 20...] [intestate] [wherein [he] [she] appointed (*insert the name of the renunciant*) [the sole executor] [and residuary legatee and devisee] [one of the executors] [who has since died without proving the said Will] [wherein [he] [she] did not appoint any executor but named me (*insert the name of the renunciant*) [as residuary legatee and devisee]. (*or*)

[wherein [he] [she] named me residuary legatee and devisee.] (*or*)

[leaving me (*insert the name of the renunciant*), (*insert the name and relationship to the deceased, reciting the title to the grant and any clearings*).]

I, the said (*insert the name of the renunciant*) declare that I have not intermeddled in the said deceased's estate and will not hereinafter intermeddle therein with the intent of defrauding creditors and do hereby renounce all my right and title to [probate and execution of the said Will] [and to letters of administration [(with Will annexed)]] of the estate of the said deceased.

Signed by the said ...

the ... day of ... 20...

in the presence of (*to be signed by a witness who has no interest in the estate*)

C79 RENUNCIATION OF PROBATE BY PROFIT-SHARING PARTNERS FOR THEMSELVES AND OTHER PROFIT-SHARING PARTNERS IN A FIRM

In the High Court of Justice *(etc. as in Form C1)*

Whereas (*insert the full name and address of the deceased*) deceased died on the ... day of ... 20... [having made and duly executed [his] her] last Will and Testament dated the ... day of ... 20... wherein [he] [she] appointed the profit-sharing partners in the firm of ... [or the firm which at the date of death had succeeded to and carried on the practice] to be the executors of [his] her] Will.

And whereas at the date of death of the deceased ... (*insert the names of all the profit-sharing partners)* were the profit-sharing partners.

Now we (*insert the names of the renunciants)* with the authority of the other said partners do hereby on our own behalf and that of all the other profit-sharing partners in the said firm renounce all our and their right and title to probate and execution of the said Will [and to letters of administration (with Will annexed) as residuary legatees and devisees in trust] and we declare that we and the other profit-sharing partners have not intermeddled in the deceased's estate and will not hereinafter intermeddle therein with the intent of defrauding creditors.

Signed *(etc. as in Form C77)*

C80 RETRACTION OF RENUNCIATION

In the High Court of Justice *(etc. as in Form C1)*

(*Insert the full name and address of the deceased*) deceased died on the ... day of ... 20... [having made and duly executed [his] her] last Will and Testament dated the ... day of ... 20... and therein appointed me (*insert the name of the renunciant*) [[his] her] sole executor (*or as may be*)] [leaving me (*insert the name of the renunciant*)] [the residuary legatee and devisee in trust] (*or as may be*) [intestate leaving me (*insert the name of the renunciant*)].

And whereas I renounced [probate and execution] [letters of administration [(with Will annexed)]] of the estate of the said deceased and whereas a grant of [probate] [letters of administration [(with Will annexed)]] was made at the ... Registry to (*insert the name of the grantee*) and whereas the said (*insert the name of the grantee*) died on the ... day of ... 20... leaving part of the said estate unadministered.

Now I the said (*insert the name of the renunciant*) do hereby declare that I retract my said renunciation of [probate] [letters of administration [(with Will annexed)]] of the estate of the said deceased.

Signed *(etc. as in Form C77)*

C81 SUBPOENA TO BRING IN TESTAMENTARY DOCUMENT

In the High Court of Justice *(etc. as in Form C1)*

ELIZABETH THE SECOND by the Grace of God, of the United Kingdom of Great Britain and Northern Ireland and of the Other Realms and Territories, Queen, Head of the Commonwealth, Defender of the Faith.

To (*insert the name of the person alleged to hold the Will*).

TAKE NOTICE that (*insert the name of the applicant*) has stated in an affidavit sworn on the ... day of ... 20... and filed in [the Principal Registry of the Family Division of the High Court of Justice] [the ... District Probate Registry] that a certain document, being or purporting to be testamentary, namely a [Will] [codicil] (*or as may be*) dated the ... day of ... 20... of (*insert the name of the deceased*) deceased late of ... who died on the ... day of ... 20... is now in your possession, custody or power.

NOW THIS IS TO COMMAND YOU the said (*insert the name of the person alleged to hold the Will*) that within eight days after service hereof on you, inclusive of the day of such service, you do bring into and leave with the proper officer of the [Principal Registry of the Family Division, First Avenue House, 42–49 High Holborn, London WC1V 6NP] [the ... District Probate Registry at ...] aforesaid the said ...

Witness the Right Honourable (*insert name of current Lord Chancellor*), Lord High Chancellor of Great Britain.

Signed ... District Judge/Registrar

Subpoena issued by ... of ...

(*To be endorsed prominently on the front of the copy to be served:*)

You the within-named ... are warned that disobedience to this subpoena by the time therein limited would be a contempt of court punishable by imprisonment.

[The Principal Registry of the Family Division of the High Court of Justice is at First Avenue House, 42–49 High Holborn, London WC1V 6NP] [The District Probate Registry is at ...] and the proper officer is the Probate Manager.

C82 PRE-LODGEMENT ENQUIRY FORM

Name of deceased ____________________

Date of death ____________________

Domicile of deceased at date of death ____________________

CASE HISTORY (please state all relevant facts):

What direction/order are you applying for and why?

The following documents are enclosed (please tick):

- ☐ original or copy will/codicil;
- ☐ copies of foreign wills/codicils (and translations if necessary);
- ☐ copies of former and or leading grants, entrusting documents (and translations if necessary);
- ☐ certificate of inheritance;
- ☐ court orders (e.g. Court of Protection order, parental responsibility/residence order);
- ☐ medical evidence (mental capacity cases);
- ☐ decree absolute/judicial separation;
- ☐ draft affidavit;
- ☐ other – please state.

N.B. Further information or documents may be required before any directions can be given.

Index

References are to page numbers